THE SOCIOLOGY OF CITIES

WILLIAM A. SCHWAB
University of Arkansas

PRENTICE HALL
Englewood Cliffs, New Jersey 07632

Library of Congress Cataloging-in-Publication Data

Schwab, William A.
    The sociology of cities / William A. Schwab.
        p.   cm.
    Includes bibliographical references and index.
    ISBN 0-13-817610-8
    1. Sociology, Urban.   I. Title.
HT151.S322   1992
307.26 —dc20
                                                            91-16942
                                                            CIP

Production Editor: KERRY REARDON
Acquisitions Editor: NANCY ROBERTS
Copy Editor: PAT JOHNSON
Cover Designer: SUZANNE BEHNKE
Prepress Buyer: KELLY BEHR
Manufacturing Buyer: MARY ANN GLORIANDE

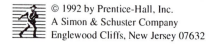 © 1992 by Prentice-Hall, Inc.
A Simon & Schuster Company
Englewood Cliffs, New Jersey 07632

Previously published as *Urban Sociology:
A Human Ecological Perspective.*

Printed in the United States of America

10 9 8 7 6 5 4 3 2 1

ISBN 0-13-817610-8

PRENTICE-HALL INTERNATIONAL (UK) LIMITED, *LONDON*
PRENTICE-HALL OF AUSTRALIA PTY. LIMITED, *SYDNEY*
PRENTICE-HALL CANADA INC., *TORONTO*
PRENTICE-HALL HISPANOAMERICANA, S.A., *MEXICO*
PRENTICE-HALL OF INDIA PRIVATE LIMITED, *NEW DELHI*
PRENTICE-HALL OF JAPAN, INC., *TOKYO*
SIMON & SCHUSTER ASIA PTE. LTD., *SINGAPORE*
EDITORA PRENTICE-HALL DO BRASIL, LTDA., *RIO DE JANEIRO*

To

Judy

In Memory

of my father, Frank A. Schwab
whose passion for books, love of knowledge
and intellectual curiosity enriched and shaped my life.

CONTENTS

PART II: THE GROWTH AND CHANGE OF URBAN REGIONS

PART IV: SOCIAL CONSEQUENCES AND SOCIAL RESPONSES TO URBANIZATION

$\mathcal{P}$REFACE

The idea for this book arose from my experiences in teaching undergraduate courses in urban sociology. Urban sociology is an eclectic field drawing not only from the works of sociology but also from psychology, anthropology, history, and other disciplines. Urban sociology is also a dynamic and exciting discipline and during the past decade new theoretical approaches and analytical techniques have been brought to bear on the study of the city. There are three dominant theoretical approaches in the discipline—human ecology, critical/Neo-Marxian Theory, and social psychology—and I have attempted to weave these different perspectives throughout the text. Much of what urban sociologists do is invisible to the general public. In the introductions of many of the chapters, the special topic inserts, and the examples used throughout the text, I have tried to show the reader the importance of urban sociology to day-to-day life. AIDS, urban crime, and homelessness are all too familiar to us, but what most Americans do not realize is that city classification schemes developed by urban sociologists determine how federal funds are distributed, and the research by urban sociologists on the spatial distribution of AIDS across the neighborhoods in our cities has helped the medical community chart the spread of the epidemic. Thus, the chapters of this book systematically examine central issues and topics in urban sociology. Chapter 1, "Theories of the City," provides an overview of the historical development of the three dominant theoretical perspectives in contemporary urban sociology—human ecology, Neo-Marxian, and social psychological. The background, theory, terminology, and present state of each of these perspectives is presented. The other chapters are organized under four broad headings—The Urbanization Process, The Growth and Change of Urban Regions, The Internal Structure of the Metropolis, and Social Consequences and Social Responses to Urbanization.

PART 1: THE URBANIZATION PROCESS

Many Americans assume that the rest of the world lives at a level of urbanization similar to our own. This is a mistaken impression; present United Nations figures show that only about 25 percent of the world's population lives in cities of 100,000 persons or more. Urban growth in the developing world, however, is occurring at an unprecedented rate, and rapid growth poses serious adjustment problems for these nations. Therefore, one of the major foci of urban sociology is the study of the urbanization process from a cross-cultural perspective.

Although urban sociologists have studied the city for most of this century, problems in the conceptualization and measurement of the urbanization process have still not been solved. Questions raised in the second chapter, "Urbanization, Modernization, and Economic Development," are: What criteria are used to define a population concentration as urban? Does one set a minimum population size—25,000 persons or more—or include such criteria as density, population composition, and technological sophistication? Moreover, are the concepts and theories developed to describe and explain the urbanization experience of the West relevant in the study of the Third World? This discussion is continued in Chapter 3, "Urbanization in the Less Developed World." Questions asked include: What is the relationship between the processes of urbanization and modernization? Is the process of urbanization linked to demographic processes and, if so, how? What are spontaneous settlements and how do they fit into the development process? What are the major theories that describe economic and urban development? Answers to these questions provide policy makers in the developed and developing worlds with the basic knowledge necessary for the creation of population and development policy.

The emergence and rise of cities have long been of interest to the ecologist, historian, archeologist, and geographer. Chapter 4, "The Origins of Cities," is concerned with the why, where, how, and when of the emergence of man's earliest settlements. In addition, this chapter examines the characteristics and forms of the ancient, preindustrial, and industrial cities of the eighteenth, nineteenth, and twentieth centuries, and the forces that brought about their evolution from one urban form to another. A special section deals with the history of urbanization in the United States.

PART II: THE GROWTH AND CHANGE OF URBAN REGIONS

From looking at a map of the United States, one might conclude that cities are distributed in a patterned way across the landscape. What factors determine this pattern? Why will a city spring up at one location and not another? Chapter 5, "Theories of Location," explores these and other questions and presents three theories commonly used to explain the location of cities.

In the United States and other nations of the world, one finds an enormous variation in the size, economic function, and character of cities. In Chapter 6, "The Classification and Rating of Cities," the urban sociologist's attempt to uncover the underlying dimension of cities through the construction of city typologies is discussed.

These typologies permit the systematic examination of the differences between the various forms of urban settlement. The use of these classification schemes by the federal government is also discussed. In addition, the rating of cities by magazines like *Money* is discussed and the implications of these ratings for poorly rated communites are explored. A question asked in this chapter is: "Can city ratings guide a person's selection of a new community?"

Cities do not exist in isolation but in a complex network of political, economic, and social relationships with other cities. Chapter 7, "The System of Cities," explores the historical development of the nation's system of cities from Revolutionary times to the present. The second half of this chapter describes the growth of the sunbelt and the decline of the snowbelt. Special emphasis is given to the role of the federal government in shaping the growth and decline of both regions.

PART III: THE INTERNAL STRUCTURE OF THE METROPOLIS

Driving into any large metropolitan area on the interstate highway system, one can view a cross section of the city. At the periphery, one sees the new low-density suburban housing. Next, the older, well-established suburbs come into view. Closer in, one passes working-class neighborhoods, slums, industrial areas, and finally the high-rise office buildings of the central business district. Clearly, the city is not uniform and undifferentiated but is divided into functionally identifiable subareas. Each of these subareas is distinguished by groups of people and physical structures that are more or less homogeneous.

Part III of this work explores the forces and processes that bring about the sorting of people and institutions into generally homogeneous subareas of cities to form a mosaic of social worlds. Chapter 8, "Social Area Analysis and Factorial Ecology," introduces a model central to the ecological approach, which is based on the close relationship between the social forms in the modern city and the character of the larger containing society. The major emphasis of social area analysis is on the social rather than the physical character of the city. The importance of this approach to target marketing, health care research, and AIDS is presented.

In Chapter 9, "The Use of Space Within Urban Areas," the physical manifestations of the underlying social organization of society are explored by examining general models of urban geometry including those of Burgess, Hoyt, Harris and Ullman, and White. David Harvey's Neo-Marxian perspective is provided as an alternative to the human ecological perspective.

In the final chapter of this section, "The Suburbanization Process," the overall suburbanization process is considered. Are suburbs a new post-World War II phenomenon or does their emergence represent the normal development of the city's fringe? What is the popular image of the suburbs—the people who live there and the homes they build—and is this image correct? Do suburbs pay their fair share of central city services or are central city residents subsidizing the suburban way of life? These and other questions central to the study of suburbanization are addressed in this chapter.

PART IV: SOCIAL CONSEQUENCES AND SOCIAL RESPONSES TO URBANIZATION

The focus of the final section of the text is shifted from the ecological forces and patterns that shape the metropolis to the social aspects of urban life. For example, the "community" has been a central theme in sociology for more than 150 years, and this concept is examined in Chapter 11. This chapter first describes the evolution of the concept community through the works of three influential nineteenth-century theorists—Maine, Tonnies, and Durkheim. Second, the influence of these theorists on the works of Robert Park and the Chicago School is assessed. Third, the community units operating in contemporary urban settings are described along with the participation of urbanites in local community affairs. Finally, the exciting research on social networks is presented with special emphasis on Claude Fischer's book, *To Dwell Among Friends*.

Chapter 12, "The Segregation and Location of Groups in U.S. Cities," provides an overview of the most important topic in contemporary ecological research—the segregation of status, ethnic, and racial groups in U.S. cities. Why does segregation occur? The ecological, voluntary, and involuntary factors that operate to concentrate groups in certain parts of the city are systematically analyzed. Special attention is given to the social consequences of these segregation patterns for all of American society.

Chapter 13, "Urban Problems," explores some of the most intractable problems facing American society—homelessness, AIDS, and crime. All of these problems are societal problems, but are concentrated in their most pernicious and visible forms in our cities. The history, scope, and possible solutions for each of the problems are discussed.

The purpose of the final chapter, "The Structure and Role of Government in the Metropolis," is to examine the role of government in addressing the problems of cities. First, the past and present structure of city government, and its position in the nation's federal system are explained. Second, the changing relationships between and within the levels of government are explored. The changing role of the federal government in urban affairs is surveyed. Changes in the relationship between the federal government and the cities during the Reagan era are described, and the impact of this "new federalism" on cities is assessed. Third, the channels through which funds and services flow between governmental units are described. Fourth, the relationship between the structure of metropolitan government and its fiscal affairs is examined with special emphasis on the problems of taxation, spillover of services, and the fragmentation of local government. Finally, the policy alternatives available to the nation's urban areas are explored. Should the administration of cities be centralized in Washington and in regionalized programs, or should control be returned to local governments (decentralization)? The final section of the book pulls together what we know about the structure of the city and applies it to current urban policy.

Together, the fourteen chapters of this text should give the reader an understanding of the structure and character of the modern city.

$\mathcal{A}$CKNOWLEDGMENTS

I began this project in 1989 thinking I could complete it in eighteen months. Like so many things in life, eighteen months somehow stretched into three years. Now that my work is at a close, I would like to acknowledge those people who aided me along the way.

First, I would like to thank Nancy Roberts, my editor at Prentice Hall. Nancy had faith in my project, gracefully accepted the delays, and gave the project leadership and direction. Thank you, Nancy, I will always be grateful.

On the production side, I would like to thank Kerry Reardon and her staff at Prentice Hall for their fine job of producing the book. My copy editor, Pat Johnson, deserves special recognition for her thorough and sensitive editing of the manuscript.

Closer to home, I would like to thank my colleagues Frank Farmer, Pat Koski, Bill Mangold, and Don Sieger for their encouragement, support, and willingness to listen these past three years. My researcher, John Kammin, deserves special thanks for running down all those obscure citations I always needed immediately. I would also like to thank Dolores Porter for her help in typing manuscripts, and cheerfully doing all those other tasks that are necessary in writing a book.

Finally, I would like to thank my wife Judy, who with a gentle hand helped me along the path to becoming a writer. Judy, you are a gifted writer and teacher, and I will always be your most grateful student. Voice, unity and coherence, and all the other words of your craft now have meaning to me. Thank you for your passion for the written word, your understanding of the writing process, and your support of my work over the years. There is much of you in this book because there is so much of you in my life.

William Schwab
Fayetteville
April 10, 1991

xiv

THEORIES OF THE CITY

INTRODUCTION

Cities have always fascinated me. I remember as a young boy driving through the neighborhoods of Cincinnati on family outings wondering to myself why the people and buildings were located where they were. I pursued a degree in urban planning before choosing urban sociology for my doctoral work. I believe it was the depth and scope of urban sociology that eventually attracted me to it. Where else can one study the historical development of cities, compare urban patterns across cultures, explore the behaviors associated with urban life, describe the contribution cities make to the national economy, examine the internal structure of cities, and study neighborhoods with the same techniques used by anthropologists to study preliterate tribes? The sheer scope of the field is one of its great strengths, but it also has raised some disturbing questions for me: What is urban sociology? Is urban sociology simply the study of any social structure, process, or behavior that happens to occur in an urban setting, or are these things unique to the city? Does the field of urban sociology have a unique theoretical perspective, or has it borrowed selectively from other fields within sociology? Is even the concept "urban" relevant in a mass society where people living in urban and rural settings share similar lifestyles and culture?

These are questions which have troubled many in my discipline, and over the past two decades scholars have debated the question, "What is urban sociology?" In my opinion, the most fruitful answers to the question have come from the theorists. Theory is at the core of any discipline, and Kuhn (1970) and other historians of science have argued that the development of all disciplines is written in the shifts in

1

their paradigms. This chapter, therefore, presents three major theoretical approaches in the discipline of urban sociology. The first, the Chicago School, was founded by Robert Park at the University of Chicago in the early decades of this century. The Chicago School introduced the ecological perspective to the study of urban phenomena; many have called it the first comprehensive theory of the city. The second evolves from the work of Georg Simmel and his interest in the conditions found in the metropolis that influence an urban culture. The works of Simmel profoundly influenced the work of Louis Wirth, and Wirth's famous essay, "Urbanism as a Way of Life," is reviewed and critiqued in this section. The chapter ends with a discussion of the works of Karl Marx and the attempts by neo-Marxists to apply this approach to the city. At present, the work of the Neo-Marxists is the most dynamic and exciting of the three schools. Although these theories bring different perspectives to the city, they share a common effort—an attempt to fuse a theory of specific social processes with an analysis of spatial forms.[1]

THE PROBLEMS WITH FOLK SOCIOLOGY

One of the problems facing the discipline of sociology is that everyone is a sociologist. Each of us knows a great deal about the society in which we live because we have grown up in it. Many people feel that they are just as qualified as those trained in sociology to analyze the events around them. We are rational animals and we need to make sense of the world around us, so we all explain events like a divorce, the needless death of a child, or academic success or failure with common-sense explanations like: "The marriage was doomed from the beginning." "Look at how much taller she was." "It was God's will that you lost your baby." "I flunked because they were out to get jocks." Sociologists refer to these common-sense explanations and beliefs we all use to give meaning to everyday events as *folk sociology*. The problem with folk sociology is that its explanations tend to be simplistic and often based in myths and distortions. A more serious problem is that one's perspective is tied to one's unique position in the social structure. For example, we are all aware that there is prejudice and discrimination against blacks in this society. Few of us in the course of our everyday lives learn what is behind these feelings. We have no way of knowing how widespread these feelings are, how prejudice (attitudes) is manifested into discrimination (behavior), how the intensity of prejudice is distributed across our population, or how recent events have affected the rise and fall of prejudice and discrimination in this society. There is an alternative, an approach that can answer these questions; it is called *science*.

SCIENCE

Science is a method of inquiry. Science is a method of collecting and organizing knowledge and a set of rules on how this knowledge is to be acquired. Science, moreover, is the most efficient way humankind has developed for gathering and verifying knowledge, and our modern way of life, in large part, is due to advances made possible through this method. Therefore, the scientific method as applied by the discipline of urban sociology has the simple purpose of allowing researchers to learn more about cities than they might otherwise in the course of day-to-day living. As we will see in the chapter on segregation (Chapter 12), the scientific method has been used to describe the distribution of prejudicial feelings in the population, and to describe the consequence of these feelings in the residential segregation of whites and blacks in our cities.

Science consists of two primary activities: constructing theories and testing theories. A *theory* is a statement that states how and why several concepts are related. *Concepts* are abstractions, a term used to represent classes of phenomena. Three concepts have already been used in this chapter—prejudice, discrimination, and segregation—and these concepts can be woven together in such a way as to predict some outcome. This is precisely what the Chicago School and the other theorists have attempted to do with their theories of the city. Without theory, there could be no science, and if sociologists did not construct and test theories, sociology would not be a social science; it would be philosophy or religion.

THE ECOLOGICAL APPROACH TO THE CITY

The field of human ecology was founded in this country by Robert Park more than seventy years ago. For many years, American urban sociology was human ecology. The enormous output of empirical research and theoretical essays by human ecologists has led some sociologists to call human ecology the closest thing to a systematic theory of the city that we have ever developed. There have been three major shifts in the paradigm of this theoretical perspective. From 1914 to the early 1940s, Robert Park and his colleagues and students at the University of Chicago formed the so-called Chicago School; in the 1940s, Walter Firey and other critics of the Chicago School became known as the Sociocultural School; and the publication of Amos Hawley's work, *Human Ecology*, in 1950 formed the underpinnings of the Neoorthodox School. The three schools share a common interest: the city as the dominant adaptation of our species to the problems of survival. In the following, we trace the historical development of the field of human ecology.

ROBERT PARK AND THE CHICAGO SCHOOL

The field of ecology has its roots in the works of the nineteenth-century English naturalist Charles Darwin. Darwin is best known for his theory of evolution introduced in 1859 in his book *Origin of Species*. Darwin's theory of evolution is based on his observations of the interrelation and coordination of the numerous and divergent species found in nature. Darwin called this interdependence of organisms in the environment "the web of life," and Darwin and other natural scientists discovered many complex food chains. They found that nature exists in delicate balance and that a minor alteration in one link of a food chain can have repercussions for others. For example, the destruction of an animal of prey, such as the fox, at the top of a food chain may enable mouse and rabbit populations to grow unchecked; this growth in turn may have consequences for other plant and animal species.

These early natural scientists established ecology as a separate field with a basic terminology, theory, and method (Park, 1961, pp. 22–28). These scientists' systematic study of natural interrelationships led to the development of an ecological model that accounted for much of the natural world: the impersonal and unexplained forces operating in nature were shown to lead to an ordering of the natural world.

Darwin's idea of the web of life and the ecological perspective in general greatly stimulated the imagination of sociologist Robert Park at the University of Chicago. Upon joining the faculty of the Department of Sociology and Anthropology at the University of Chicago in 1914, Park began to formulate a program to study the city of Chicago from an ecological perspective. Park believed the general approach of the plant and animal ecologists could be used to study human societies but that the biological model should be used with caution.

AREAS OF AGREEMENT

There were certain broad areas of agreement between Park and the nineteenth-century ecologists. First, both saw underlying ecological processes in nature and society, patterns that are recurrent and therefore discoverable through the scientific method. Second, both saw a unity in the natural world, an interdependence among members of the same system as well as a dependence on climate and terrain. Third, both agreed on the "iron law of nature"—a species either adapts to its environment or it becomes extinct. Finally, Park held that nature and society have no ultimate purpose. This notion was in sharp contrast to the ideas of other sociologists who saw society moving to some higher and more complex form.

AREAS OF DISAGREEMENT

Park noted important differences between biological ecology and human ecology. The source of these differences is the nature of human beings and their societies. First, in human society a division of labor and a complex system for the exchange of goods and services lessen the members' dependence on a local environment. A population can trade with people hundreds of miles away for food and other resources, and thus can fundamentally modify its relationship to the environment.

Second, humans through their inventions have the capacity to modify their environments dramatically. The beaver and other animals have this ability, but it is very limited in comparison with that of humans.

Finally, humans have developed language and culture that make possible forms of social organization much more complex than those of any other animal species. Ants, termites, and other species survive because of their social structure, but their systems have a simple division of labor and a rigidity not found in human societies (Park, 1961, p. 28).

social structure/mode of subsistence
Discussion

THE BIOTIC AND CULTURAL SPHERES

To make ecological principles relevant to the study of human society, Park formulated a complicated theory of society as composed of two elements—the biotic and the cultural. According to Park, the biotic level is the foundation of society: it is where humans either adapt to the environment or become extinct. The biotic sphere consists of the basic necessities of life such as available water, a particular soil type, and other resources. These factors determine the size of a population in a particular area; they are the resources that the population will be able to use in adapting to the environment. It is on the biotic level that the ecological principles of competition and symbiosis operate. In the struggle for existence, humans compete for the environment's scarce resources, but they also live in a society with a division of labor. Thus competition among humans must always involve an automatic and unplanned degree of cooperation among groups with different functions in society, that is, symbiosis. *compete*

In cities, these unplanned adjustments during the struggle for existence lead to the spatial distribution of people into different areas. Park and his colleagues applied the term *natural areas* to slums, rooming-house districts, wealthy suburbs, and other homogeneous areas of the city because they resulted from unplanned biotic forces. That is, each natural area came into existence through the competition of individuals and groups for space. Once established, these areas provided homes and services for their inhabitants and carried out other functions that contributed to the survival of the entire community. *institutions*

According to Park and his colleagues, the cultural level of society is built upon the biotic level. The cultural level is a structure based on customs, norms, laws, and institutions. It involves the unique aspects of the human species—reason, morality, and psychological makeup.

A working-class neighborhood demonstrates the relationship between the two levels of society. This natural area comes into existence because it is the location in the city where members of the working class can afford to buy housing and still pay the transportation costs to their place of employment—biotic factors. Once established, this natural area develops norms and values as well as institutions such as schools, churches, and fraternal organizations—the cultural level of society.

PARK'S RESEARCH PROGRAM

Though Park was aware that the cultural level could affect the biotic (for example, new technology could permit greater exploitation of the environment), much of the research that he directed was focused on the basic forces within the biotic sphere.

There was good reason for Park's insistence that human ecology should be concerned with the collection of basic knowledge about the city. American cities in the early twentieth century faced a multitude of problems, including massive levels of poverty and social disorganization, deplorable housing and sanitation conditions, and inadequate transportation. Yet little data had ever been collected concerning this nation's cities. As a sociologist, Park believed that meaningful social reform was impossible unless it was based on verifiable facts. Moreover, he felt that the collection of this information could best be achieved by judiciously applying the rigorous scientific methods of the biological sciences—the ecological perspective.

Park was also aware that social relationships were often reflected in the spatial relationships among areas within the city. Thus, from the beginning, Park emphasized the location and spatial relationships of institutions, groups, and subareas within the city and the processes that modify these patterns over time. As we see in subsequent chapters, this emphasis continues to shape our study of human ecology.

Park put his beliefs into action in 1916 with the publication of his benchmark work, "The City: Suggestions for the Investigation of Human Behavior in the Urban Environment." In this article, Park outlined a research program that was to occupy the Chicago ecologists for the next two decades. Park listed basic questions whose answers are essential to the understanding of how cities function. A few examples follow (Park, 1969, pp. 91–130).

1. What are the sources of a city's population? How is city growth a combination of natural increase and net migration?

2. What are the city's natural areas? How is the distribution of the city's population among the neighborhoods affected by economic interests such as land values and by noneconomic factors as well?

3. What are the social rituals of various neighborhoods—what things must one do in the area to be fully socially integrated and to avoid being looked upon with suspicion or thought peculiar?

4. Who are the local leaders? How do they embody local interests? How do they attain and maintain social influence and power? How do they exercise control?

5. Do social classes in fact become cultural groups? Do they acquire an exclusiveness independent of race and nationality?

6. Do children in the city follow in the occupational footsteps of their fathers?

7. How is social unrest generated and manifested? Are strikes and mob violence produced by the same conditions that generate financial panics, real estate booms, and mass movements of the general population?

8. What changes have taken place in the family? In what areas of family life has change been the greatest? How has such change been induced by the urban environment?

9. How have educational and religious institutions been modified by the process of urbanization?

10. Does property ownership affect school truancy, divorce, or crime? In what areas of the city and among which groups is crime endemic?

Most of these questions appear to be fairly simple. However, in 1916 little was systematically known about population and housing characteristics or the ethnic and racial groups and the institutions of the city, and even less was known about how a city actually operated. Therefore, Park's emphasis on basic research as the focus of human ecology was well founded.

Park made yet another contribution to the field of sociology in the early years of his career. The field of sociology as it is known today really did not exist in 1916. Sociologists were involved in either philosophizing about what society was or should be, or were concerned with social problems and deviant forms of social behavior. Park's contribution to the field was in placing the emphasis of his work on the study of "normal" behavior and in conducting this research empirically. In other words, theories on how society operated were to be tested in the real world. The character of Park's research approach is clearly reflected in a quotation from a work published after his death. Park states:

> I expect that I have actually covered more ground tramping about in cities in different parts of the world than any other living man. Out of all this, I gained among other things, a conception of the city, the community, and the region, not as a geographical phenomenon but as a kind of social organism (1952, p. 5).

PUBLICATIONS

Park's research program was very successful. By the 1930s a wealth of research had already been completed that directly addressed many of the questions raised 15 years earlier. The first of the studies to reach book form was *The Hobo,* by Nels Anderson, published in 1923. Anderson had experienced hobo life firsthand before beginning his graduate studies at the University of Chicago in 1921. Park and his colleagues encouraged Anderson to capitalize on his unique experiences while pursuing his graduate studies. They saw in Anderson's research an opportunity to combine the study of a natural area common to most large cities, the hobo area, with the more general ecological and sociological topics of mobility, isolation, and disorganization. Anderson used no formal research technique in *The Hobo,* but rather provided informal descriptions of the hobos' lifestyle and the employment agencies, flophouses, and pawnshops that made up their world. Anderson's work was later augmented with more formal studies such as Harvey Zorbaugh's *The Gold Coast and the Slum,* published in 1929, and Edwin H. Sutherland and Harvey J. Locke's *10,000 Homeless Men,* published in 1936 (Faris, 1967, pp. 64–67).

The Hobo was the first volume in a series of books on urban ecology published by the University of Chicago Press. Books that followed included Fredrick Thrasher's *The Gang* (1927), Louis Wirth's *The Ghetto* (1928), Clifford Shaw's *Delinquency Areas* (1929), Cressey's *The Taxi Dance Hall* (1932), Clifford Shaw's *The Jackroller* (1930), and Faris and Dunham's *Mental Disorders in Urban Areas* (1939). These works taken as a whole give an important insight into the character and functioning of the early twentieth-century city.

ZORBAUGH'S *THE GOLD COAST AND THE SLUM*

A good example of the kind of research carried out by the Chicago ecologists is found in one of the better-known works in the series, Harvey Zorbaugh's *The Gold Coast and the Slum,* published in 1929. The title of the book refers to the Near North Side, a one-square-mile area just north of what was at that time Chicago's central business district. Park and his colleagues were deeply interested in the real world, and the Near North Side was a perfect natural laboratory. For example, Zorbaugh found along the Gold Coast area adjacent to Lake Michigan the wealthiest and most influential families in Chicago and a few blocks to the west a concentration of the city's poorest—"Hobohemia." In addition, the Near North Side had a rooming-house district, a Greenwich Village-type bohemian area, ethnic enclaves of Sicilians and Italians, and a rialto or "bright lights district." Zorbaugh describes the diversity of the area:

> (At this time in the Near North Side) live ninety thousand people, a population representing all types and contrasts that lend to a great city its glamour and romance.....(The area) has the highest residential land values in the city and among the lowest, it has more professional men, more politicians, more suicides, more persons in *Who's Who* than any other community in Chicago (Zorbaugh, 1929, pp. 507).

Here in one small area was the diversity of a city in an exaggerated form that made it relatively easy to study.

Zorbaugh's approach in studying the area was twofold. First, he conducted a careful census of the number and types of people and institutions in the area to obtain a general picture of its "natural areas" or social worlds. Second, Zorbaugh carried out a form of sociological research known as *participant observation*—living, visiting, and observing in the various natural areas to gain an understanding of their functioning. As a result, Zorbaugh gives not only a picture of who lived in the Near North Side, but also an insight into the social processes and networks that had emerged there (see Figure 1.1).

Zorbaugh devotes one chapter of his book to each of the six natural areas of the Near North Side (see Fig. 1.1). One of the more interesting is the Gold Coast, the area with the greatest concentration of wealth in Chicago.

The Gold Coast was Lake Shore Boulevard and two adjoining streets where 2000 of the 6000 families listed in Chicago's *Social Register* lived. The *Social Register* was a thin blue book containing a "complete list of Chicago's socially acceptable." How did a person become a member of the Social Register and therefore of high society? One member suggested that "one must not be employed, one must make application, and one must be above reproach." However, most of the members of high society had no idea how one's name was included in the Register; they accepted the "list of the chosen" without question.

Zorbaugh in his research uncovered the "social game" or social process of becoming a member of this exclusive list. It was actually very simple; all one had to do was be invited to a dinner party of one of the "well-established" society families. Having accomplished this feat, one would be included on other lists of social functions, asked to join certain clubs and, at the end of this process, perhaps included in the *Social Register*.

The crucial step in breaking into society was getting the first invitation. Ambitious nonmembers, Zorbaugh found, had developed a number of techniques for doing so. One of the most common techniques was using children as a means of social climbing. Climbers would send their children to the same schools or move into the

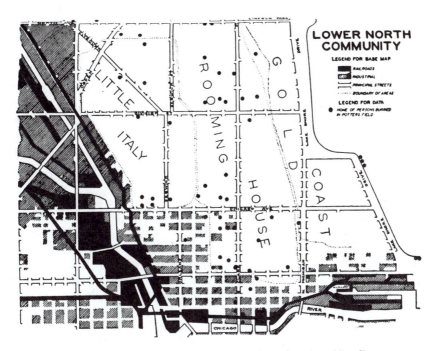

FIGURE 1.1 Near North Side, the Setting for *The Gold Coast and the Slum*.

Source: Reprinted from "Near North Side" from *The Gold Coast and the Slum* by H. Zorbaugh by permission of The University of Chicago Press © 1929.

same apartment complex as established families with children of the same age, hoping a friendship would develop between the children and win an invitation for the parents. Another proven technique was to discover the pet charity of an upper-class woman and devote energy and money to the charity's projects; then, out of gratitude, one might be invited to a social engagement.

This "social game" and the upper-class's idleness; exorbitant expenditures on clothing, automobiles, and homes; and endless rounds of social engagements seem on the surface to be frivolous. Zorbaugh, however, found a more serious side of the Gold Coast inhabitants. In many respects, they were the only people in Chicago with sufficient wealth and leisure to support the arts and charities and to provide unremunerated civic leadership. Gold Coast people were led to such efforts in part by their strong conviction that people of means owed these works to "the less fortunate." Their benevolence, however, was tempered by the need to play the "social game" to retain their social positions.

There was a more disturbing side to this bastion of wealth. Zorbaugh found that the Gold Coast was by no means a true community. There was less group consciousness among members of the Register than one would expect. The general pattern was that families would socialize on a regular basis with ten to twelve other families and had little interest in other members of society. One informant, for example, prided herself on having lived next to the same upper-class family for more than twenty-five years without ever having met them. If one views this behavior in combination with the upper class's continuous travels to Europe, summer retreats to Michigan, and winter vacations in the South, one can easily understand why many of the Gold Coast families suffered—like many of the less fortunate inhabitants of the Near North Side—from the loneliness and anonymity of the city.

Zorbaugh draws a much bleaker picture of the rest of the Near North Side. He describes the rooming-house district with its transient, childless, lonely, and suicide-prone population. On the west were the slums of Little Italy and Little Hell with their newly arrived immigrants eking out a bare existence. The "bright light" district along Clark Street featured open prostitution and tawdry cabarets. To the south on Clark Street were the used-clothing stores, pawnshops, and diners frequented by the derelicts of Hobohemia. The bohemians of the Village, by definition individuals living on the fringes of society, completed the picture.

The only features common to the diverse elements of the Near North Side were an absence of a sense of community and inability of the area to solve its own problems. A recurring problem of all societies is the maintenance of order; order was imposed on the Near North Side by the police and other formal institutions of the city of Chicago. Zorbaugh sums up his view of the Near North Side in the following statement:

> The isolation of the populations crowded together within these few hundred blocks, the superficiality and externality of their contacts, the social distances that separate them, their absorption in the affairs of their own little worlds—these, and not mere size and numbers, constitute the social problem of the inner city. The community, represented by the town or peasant village where everyone knows everyone else clear down to the ground, is gone. Over large areas of the city "community" is little more than a geographical expression. Yet the old tradition of control persists despite changed conditions of life. The inevitable result is cultural disorganization. (Zorbaugh, 1929, p. 16)

THEORIES AND RESEARCH OF THE CHICAGO SCHOOL

Titles of the major works of the Chicago School are indicative of the real-world interests of the researchers. For example, Shaw's *The Jackroller* (1930) is about the subculture of the mugger. Cressey's *The Taxi Dance Hall* (1932) explores the operation of the dime-a-dance halls that provided cover for prostitution then, much as some massage parlors do today. *The Hobo, The Gang,* and *The Ghetto* also examine problems still found today.

Taken as a whole, these works give the impression that the Chicago ecologists were interested only in the seamier side of urban life, and to a degree the impression is correct. The small towns and rural areas in which Park and other major figures in the Chicago School were raised shaped their value systems and impressions of what a community should be (Hinkle, 1954). Their own background clashed with the value systems and conditions in the city they chose to study throughout their professional careers. Chicago in the 1920s was a new city and one of the fastest-growing centers in the world. The problems Chicago faced in coping with rapid growth, an ethnically diverse population, and the negative by-products of industrialization led to an interest in the social disorganization and deviancy associated with urbanization. The Chicago ecologists also had strong ties to the reform movements of the day and felt that the knowledge gained in their area could contribute to the solution of problems. The limited scope of the area studies eventually led them to shift the emphasis of their work to developing general theories to explain social disorganization and models designed to explain urban growth and change. This work was fundamental to the understanding of processes operating in the urban sphere.

CRITICS OF THE CHICAGO SCHOOL

The Chicago School made significant contributions not only to the understanding of the early twentieth-century city, but also to the entire field of sociology. Inevitably, the free exchange of ideas led to differences of opinion. During the 1930s and the decades that followed, books and articles were published questioning the concepts and theoretical underpinnings of the classical Chicago School. By far the most devastating criticism of the classical position is found in a work by Milla Alihan (1964), *Social Ecology,* first published in 1938. Alihan scrutinized the works of the Chicago School and noted in her book that these ecologists could not demonstrate empirically which aspects of human behavior were purely biotic and which were purely cultural. In other words, she could not find the two levels of society hypothesized by Park. Other critics, August Hollingshead (1947) and W. E. Gettys (1940), made the same point and thus weakened the theoretical underpinnings of the classical school.

During the same period Gehlke and Biehl (1934) and Robinson (1950) attacked the research of the Chicago School on statistical grounds. Hatt in 1946 showed that the concept of natural area—such as the Gold Coast and the slum—did not apply to the city of Seattle.

By 1950 the Chicago School had weathered more than two decades of criticism and had been dramatically modified. Some of the theories and concepts had been found to be invalid. The members of this classical school, however, were pioneers. Their work is as readable today as it was 50 years ago and gives a personal insight into the structures and people of a city of the past. The ethnographic studies of this school are also of great value to historians. And more important, the pioneering work of the classical ecologists formed the foundation on which the modern field of ecology is built.

HUMAN ECOLOGY TODAY

During the 1930s and early 1940s interest in human ecology generally declined in the United States. This decline is explained, in part, by the national preoccupation with the events of the Great Depression and World War II. In addition, in the field of sociology itself, other theoretical approaches were coming into vogue. The underlying soundness of the ecological approach, however, is shown by the reemergence of interest in the field in the late 1940s and early 1950s. By 1950 few researchers agreed with the Chicago, or classical, ecologists that society is composed of two elements, the cultural and the biotic, but this dichotomy continues to influence contemporary ecology. Those researchers who place primary emphasis on cultural variables are referred to as *sociocultural ecologists*. A second group known as *neoorthodox ecologists* are closer to the classical ecologists in emphasizing ecological rather than cultural factors in their theories (Theodorson, 1961, p. 129).

SOCIOCULTURAL APPROACH

The sociocultural approach emphasizes the role of culture and values in explaining the location of groups and institutions within cities. The application of this approach to the analysis of land use patterns is shown in a book by Walter Firey (1947), *Land Use in Central Boston.* Firey argues that the classical ecologists placed too much emphasis on impersonal ecological forces and too little on the role of sentiment and symbolism in human affairs. Specifically, Firey shows how "sentiments" significantly influence the ecological processes in Boston. In a series of case studies, Firey illustrates that the land uses in many areas of Boston differ significantly from predictions made by the classical ecologists. Boston's Beacon Hill, for example, is a residential area only a few minutes' walking distance from the city's central business district. According to the "classical models" this residential area should be declining physically while commercial activities gradually take over. In reality, it is one of the most prestigious residential areas in Boston, inhabited by many of Boston's old, established families. Similarly, both the Boston Common and the King's Chapel Burying Ground areas are centrally located and of great commercial value, but sentiment based on their historic character has prevented more profitable uses being made of the land.

Support for the sociocultural approach has also come from a large number of studies on the spatial patterning of various ethnic groups within the city. Jonassen (1949), Gans (1962), and others have shown that both the initial selection of a residential location and the continued existence of ethnic enclaves are related to a host of cultural factors including preferred family forms, religious and political affiliation, and their degrees of acceptance by the urban community. Therefore, members of the sociocultural school maintain that an understanding of the spatial patterning of groups and institutions within cities is possible only if culture and values are made central to ecological theory (Timms, 1971, pp. 91–93).

NEOORTHODOX APPROACH

The neoorthodox approach is more important than the sociocultural in contemporary ecology. This approach had its beginning in 1950 with the publication of Amos Hawley's *Human Ecology,* a restatement of the classical or Chicago School's position. In *Human Ecology,* Hawley clarifies concepts and works out the theoretical weaknesses that had been identified by Alihan, Hollingshead, and others some years earlier.

One major weakness of the classical position was Park's insistence that there are two levels of society—biotic and cultural—and that the biotic is the proper focus of human ecology. Hawley agreed that there are forces and processes over which humans have little control, but disagreed with Park on the notion that cultural phenomena are outside the scope of human ecology. Hawley argued that the human being, like any other animal, must adapt to the environment or face extinction. Ants, for example, have adapted to their environments by developing an elaborate social structure based on a division of labor—as has humankind. People, in addition, have developed sophisticated technologies and other cultural elements in adapting to the environment. Therefore, Hawley viewed human social organization, technology, and culture as nothing more than one of the many types of adaptive mechanisms found in nature.

Hawley's ecological approach differed from Park's in other respects. It focused primarily on the present form and evolution of the community. Hawley saw community as the one unit of analysis where all the key elements of society are present in a relatively small geographic area that can be easily studied. Moreover, he defined "community" as the complex system of interdependence that develops as a population collectively adapts to an environment. The key word in this definition is *interdependence*. The Chicago School was concerned with social disorganization and conflict. Hawley, in contrast, was impressed with the community's ability to remain in a stable state until disrupted by an outside influence. Hawley therefore provided numerous hypotheses on the structure, functioning, and changes of the community system and in so doing provided the theoretical framework for much of present-day ecological research.

GEORG SIMMEL AND LOUIS WIRTH: THE CITY AS A CULTURAL FORM

The industrial revolution and the growth of large cities are inseparable processes. These intertwined forces transformed the social and physical landscape of nineteenth-century Europe and North America and swept away a communal way of life that had lasted a millennium. Comparing the rural and the emerging urban way of life—what had been and what was becoming—is a second theoretical approach to the study of the city. Robert Nisbet (1966) in *The Sociological Tradition* feels it is one of the discipline's major contributions to social thought. He states, "Nowhere has sociology's contribution to modern social thought been more fertile, more often borrowed from by other social sciences, especially with reference to the contemporary study of undeveloped nations, than in the topological use of the idea of community." All of the major figures in nineteenth- and twentieth-century sociology used some form of this urban/rural dichotomy to describe the momentous changes that had occurred in the evolution of urban/industrial societies. Max Weber writes of rationalization; Durkheim, of mechanical and organic solidarity; Tönnies, of Gemeinschaft and Gesellschaft; and Becker, of the sacred and the secular. The topological approach used by these and other theorists is discussed in depth in Chapter 11, "The Community." In this chapter, our interest lies in urban phenomena and in a conceptual framework for urban sociology. In this section, we explore the works of two theorists, Georg Simmel and Louis Wirth, who were interested in describing the conditions responsible for the emergence of a culture and way of life unique to the city.

GEORG SIMMEL: THE METROPOLIS AND MENTAL LIFE

I have always found the work of Georg Simmel one of the most readable of the early sociologists. He was a brilliant lecturer and teacher, wrote extensively for the popular and scholarly press, and became one of the best-known sociologists of his day. He can best be described as a social psychologist, and he brought his rich insight to the study of phenomena as diverse as the dyad and triad, dinner parties, and urban life. The eclectic nature of his interests, the mixed audience that he served, the often incomplete development of his ideas in his work, along with the rampant anti-Semitism in the Germany of his day contributed to his marginal position in the academic community (Coser, 1971, pp. 177–215). All the early European theorists—Weber, Durkheim, Tönnies, and Marx—wrote about the city, but none are as interesting or as insightful as Simmel.

Simmel's theory of the city was presented in a lecture given in the winter of 1902–1903. His lecture, "The Metropolis and Mental Life," has been reprinted many times; it explores the relationship between the urban environment and the behaviors, attitudes, and experiences found there. Employing his social psychological perspective, he shows how behaviors ranging from individuality, a blasé attitude, and emphasis on precise time schedules are shaped by the conditions found in the city.

Simmel's discussion of cities might best be called the study of the urban personality type. Simmel's major interest was discovering how an individual living in a city copes with diversity. Simmel's main point was that because of the concentration of large numbers of people at high densities in cities, an individual is constantly bombarded by physical and social stimuli. These stimuli are so numerous and diverse that an individual exposed to them simply cannot respond to them all. Therefore, the urbanite must have some sort of screening device that enables her or him to respond appropriately to the most important stimuli. One major screening device is the money economy, an invention of cities. In day-to-day life, an urbanite is constantly involved in the exchange of dollars and cents. To survive in a world where the common denominator is money, an individual must respond to the world not with the heart but with the mind. To Simmel, a heightened awareness of the world, cynicism, and rationality are the most obvious personality manifestations of the urban way of life.

Simmel noted another personality change wrought by the urban setting, the blasé attitude, promoted by the intense stimulation of the metropolis and the predominance of its money economy. The incessant bombardment of incompatible stimuli upon individuals ultimately exhausts their mental energies, making it impossible for them to respond to new situations. This process, he believed, is reinforced by a money economy. In the day-to-day process of economic exchange a person is constantly reminded of the purchasability of things. "Things" include not only material goods but also the services of people. This evaluation process influences all other aspects of life; individuals are evaluated for what they have, not for what they are. Outward signs of one's status—dress, grooming, and the like—become the basis on which a person is evaluated by others. Therefore, the essence of the blasé attitude consists of the "blunting of discrimination... and...money with all its colorlessness and indifference becomes the common

veblen

denominator of all values; irreparably it hollows the core of things, their individuality, their specific value, and their incomparability" (Simmel, 1950, p. 414).

The blasé attitude that comes from the dehumanizing aspects of a money economy as well as the concentration of large populations in the limited space of the city may help to explain the inability of urbanites to respond to new situations. This may help explain the bizarre and often tragic personal events that occur in the largest cities. A good example is the case of Catherine Genovese, who was brutally murdered in full view of 38 residents of a respectable New York City neighborhood. Not one person helped her or even bothered to call the police until after she was dead. This absence of a response by bystanders might be attributed to conditions of the city that Simmel so richly describes.

According to Simmel, the ability of an urban individual to absorb and process stimuli decreases as the size of the city increases. Moreover, as the size and density of a city increase, each individual is less able to comprehend and control situations and thus develops feelings of powerlessness, isolation, social withdrawal, and alienation—characteristics that have been the concern of sociologists through most of this century and that are thought to be at the root of many urban problems.

Georg Simmel is one of the founders of sociology, and he was one of the few of his contemporaries interested in local phenomena. The work of Simmel had a profound affect on American sociology, but nowhere is it more apparent than in the work of Louis Wirth.

LOUIS WIRTH: URBANISM AS A WAY OF LIFE

Louis Wirth was a student of Robert Park in the department of sociology and anthropology at the University of Chicago. Wirth's classic essay, "Urbanism as a Way of Life," is often attributed to the Chicago School, but it is treated separately here because it is viewed as the definitive statement on the culture of urbanism.

Louis Wirth's essay was published in 1938. In it, Wirth analyzes the ecological and demographic structure of the city and then considers the psychological and behavioral consequences of living there. These consequences formed a new way of life that Wirth called *urbanism*.

Urbanism is an ideal type. An ideal type is a concept that summarizes the general characteristics of an entire category of phenomena. Ideal types do not attempt to describe each member of a group perfectly; rather, they summarize the "essential" characteristics of the group. Researchers use a form of ideal type when they conduct market surveys to determine who the "typical" buyer of a product is. Similarly, in day-to-day life we often make up stereotypes of people and things in our environment to try to make things more understandable. Sociologists do essentially the same thing when they construct ideal types, carefully analyzing the characteristics of a category of social things (in Wirth's case, large cities) and then identifying those qualities that best describe the entire group.

To Wirth, the three most distinguishing characteristics of cities were (1) their large size, (2) their great density, and (3) their heterogeneous population. These qualities stand in sharp contrast to the traditional rural-folk societies that Wirth used for comparison. These variables that we term "ecological" in turn explain the unique social forms and psychological patterns found in the city. We should note that although Wirth analyzed the effects of size, density, and heterogeneity as distinct and independent ecological variables, he recognized that the three were interdependent in the real world.

CONSEQUENCES OF SIZE

In Wirth's view, as the size of a city's population increases, there is also an increase in the variety of people living there. Because these diverse types of people are involved in the ecological processes of competition and cooperation, individuals will, over time, come together to form groups similar in their racial, ethnic, occupational, and social-status characteristics. These groups are highly differentiated, yet if the community is to survive they must also be interdependent. The result is that, over time, a complex set of commensal and symbiotic relationships develops among these groups.

Nowhere is this social complexity seen more clearly than in the spatial complexity of the city. Social differentiation leads to increased spatial segregation among the wide variety of racial, ethnic, social-status, and occupational groups found in the city. The city becomes a "mosaic of social worlds" but with a major consequence—this increased social complexity weakens the traditional bonds of kinship, neighborhood, and family. In their place develops a new set of techniques for maintaining order—formal social controls. Therefore, according to Wirth, our laws, courts and police departments, bureaucracies, professional codes of conduct, mass media, and modern corporations are inevitable by-products of urbanism because they serve essential functions. They order and clarify roles, simplify economic and personal relationships, and structure the complex ecological system called the city.

Accompanying this movement toward increased dependency on formal social controls is a second set of relationships stemming directly from increased population size. Any human grouping, whether it be a city or a college campus, that grows beyond several hundred persons limits the possibility that each member can know all others personally. Although urban dwellers daily come in contact with far more people than their rural counterparts, they have less knowledge of these people and their contacts are often impersonal and superficial. In short, urbanites have many acquaintances, but few friends. Secondary relationships replace primary ones. Most important, people no longer interact with their entire personalities, but rather interaction is limited to those elements associated with a specific role. Consequently, in these relationships people often are considered "things" to be used for some personal end. Gone in these relationships are the pleasures of spontaneous, open self-expression normally found in primary groups. Gone too are the obligations and the controls on behavior that primary groups afford—the way traditional societies maintained order. It is the disappearance of this control function of the primary groups, along with the disintegration of a common moral order, that Wirth viewed as a major source of the social disorganization that the Chicago ecologists felt characterized the urban milieu.

How did Wirth come to his conclusions?

CONSEQUENCES OF DENSITY

Density reinforces the effects of size. For example, a person moving from a small town to a city would experience a shift from mostly primary to a mixture of primary and secondary relationships, informal to formal means of control, as well as an increase in the number of strangers encountered in day-to-day living. Moreover, in the city, strangers are in closer physical proximity because of high density, and according to Wirth this has major consequences.

First, the large number of people living at high density in the city means that the individual is under a constant barrage of stimuli. In order to function in this environment the individual must filter or screen out all but the most important stimuli. The urbanite becomes insensitive to personal differences and becomes increasingly dependent on visual clues to direct behavior. A policeman's uniform, someone's dress and grooming, and other visual symbols of status are used to determine the appropriate behavior in a given social situation. The so-called blasé attitude that characterizes the personalities of many urbanites is both a response to this "stimulus overload" and a manifestation of the desire of urbanites to protect themselves from the personal demands of strangers.

Second, Wirth's work suggests that repeated physical proximity with strangers, combined with the predominance of secondary relationships and the urbanite's blasé attitude, fosters a pervasive spirit of competition and exploitation. Constant crowding among socially distant people gives rise to elevated levels of anxiety that often are expressed as conflicts between individuals (assaults, murders) and violence within and between groups (race riots, gang wars).

Third, the nervous tension and anxiety that often accompany the urban way of life are accentuated by the rapid pace and complicated technology of the city. The tempo and technology are necessary so that predictable routines can be followed by the city's mass of unrelated individuals. Without these devices, there would be unchecked competition, and exploitation and chaos would prevail. The clock and the traffic signal are symbolic of the formal technological controls that impose order on an otherwise chaotic situation.

CONSEQUENCES OF HETEROGENEITY

The chief consequence of urban heterogeneity is its impact on the class structure. In folk-rural societies the class structure is rigid; the social class of the family of one's birth determines one's class standing for life. This is not to say vertical social mobility is absent in traditional societies, but it is rare.

In sharp contrast are urban societies, where increased heterogeneity leads to increased social interaction among the rich variety of personality types found in the city. The social interaction among these diverse individuals breaks down rigid class distinctions and greatly complicates the social stratification system. Moreover, social mobility is common within the urban milieu. As a result of these changes, traditional ties to family and neighborhood are weaker, and a different pattern of group affiliations emerges.

In traditional societies, membership in one group automatically entails membership in larger, more encompassing groups. Membership in a family in such societies would automatically confer membership in the clan, village community, and tribe. These memberships, moreover, are compatible and encompass all the roles the individual is expected to play in life. These roles are therefore fixed and compatible and provide the individual with both a stable place in the social order and a stable personality stemming from an absence of role conflict.

In contrast, group affiliations in urban societies are often unrelated and transitory and are based on the interests of the individual. More often than not, membership in one group is totally unrelated to membership in another. For example, a student could be a member of a fraternity or sorority, an honorary society, and a sports team and not share the same group affiliations with any other person on campus. More important is the fact that turnover in these groups is high, and since people define who they are—their "selves"—through these intersecting group memberships, urbanites are in a continual process of defining and redefining who they are. In addition, the urbanite often defines himself or herself with contradictory or conflicting roles.

As a result of both a highly mobile social structure and fluctuating group memberships, the urban personality structure becomes fluid, detached, and disintegrated. The term *anomie* has been developed to describe the state of society in which the normative standards of conduct and belief are weak and individuals suffer from disorientation, anxiety, and isolation.

How does urban society composed of people who have highly fragmented and diverse personality types maintain order? The answer is that a successful society structures itself using the lowest common denominator—institutions and facilities adjust to the needs of the average person. Mass media, mass production, and mass education have all adjusted to mass requirements. This "leveling" tendency of urban society and the accompanying fluid nature of the urban personality were viewed by Wirth as a direct consequence of the increased heterogeneity of the urban population.

In summary, Louis Wirth hypothesized that the growing size, density, and heterogeneity of the urban environment led directly to a variety of changes in the social structure of the city and the urban personality. Most important of these changes were the growing importance of secondary relationships over primary ones and the role of formal social controls in maintaining order within the city. Consequently, the social disorganization that had been a major theme in the early works of the Chicago School was seen as a predictable outcome of the shifts in the three ecological variables—size, density, and heterogeneity.[2]

CRITICS OF WIRTH

Wirth's theory contends that ecological factors—the concentration of large, heterogeneous populations—lead to the weakening of primary relationships, psychological stress, and dependence on formal means of social control. The ultimate consequences of these processes are alienation, disorganization, and deviant behavior. Yet in the 1940s and later decades a number of urban researchers discovered close-knit primary groups thriving in the centers of the largest cities (Gans, 1962; Jonassen, 1949; Whyte, 1955). Moreover, the "urban villages" appear to have been shaped not by the size, density, and heterogeneity of the city, but by factors like ethnicity, life cycle, and social class. In general, these researchers took exception to Wirth's theory and argued that no particular social effects could be attributed to the factors he had identified. There were serious flaws in the critics' arguments as well: cultural factors like lifestyle, ethnicity, and social status could not account for the diversity of behavioral and cultural patterns found in the city.

In 1975, Claude Fischer combined Wirth's position with those of his critics into a single theory. Fischer suggests that the factors—size, density and heterogeneity—contribute to social disorganization, alienation, and deviancy but not in the way hypothesized by Wirth. Fischer posits that these factors, instead of having a direct effect on social disorganization and deviancy, are mediated by class, ethnicity, race, and the like. Urbanism, in other words, brings about a large enough concentration of persons "to maintain viable unconventional subcultures. It is the behavioral expression of those subcultures which come to be called 'deviant'" (Fischer, 1975, p. 1332).

The foregoing point is important and needs elaboration. An increase in the size of a city's population results in an increase in the number and types of groups within its population. Groups similar in occupation, class, stage in the life cycle, and so on, through time develop distinguishable subcultures. More important, the social differences that emerge are reflected in the differential use of space within the city. This usage can take the form of an ethnic neighborhood or the exclusive patronage of a bar or restaurant by a subculture, for example, "gay bars," "singles bars," and the like. The urban landscape, therefore, is a mosaic of social worlds, and within each are subcultures with their own beliefs, values, norms, and customs. Subcultures with large populations may even build their own churches, schools, banks, fraternal organizations, and newspapers and thus reinforce the exclusionary character of the group. In this sense the city, rather than being normless, is a complex aggregation of divergent normative systems.

An individual faced with a problem or decision normally would select a solution from her or his immediate social surroundings or subculture. If the solution is the same as the one prescribed by the larger society, there is no problem, but if the solution conflicts, the individual's behavior and the subculture that supports it would be labeled deviant. A good example is the juvenile gang. Within the context of this subculture, mugging, purse snatching, and breaking-and-entering would be considered acceptable behavior. From the perspective of the larger society, such behavior is considered deviant.

Therefore, social disorganization and deviancy are explained largely by nonecological factors, whereas ecological factors (size, density, heterogeneity) are important in explaining subcultures. For example, a small town may have a few delinquent youths, but only in a larger city will there be sufficient numbers to establish a delinquent subculture. In general, the more urban a place, the larger the number of subcultures and the higher the probability of unconventional deviant subcultures.

NEO-MARXIAN THEORY AND THE CITY

Karl Marx was a socialist theoretician and organizer, a major figure in the history of economic thought, and a social theorist. He was the first to use the concept of class and to explore the role of conflict in the process of social change. His writings influenced the terminology and content of the nascent discipline of sociology. His writings on scientific socialism provide the ideological underpinnings of governments that govern half the world's population. His theories provide an alternative to the study of all social phenomena, and his work has not only influenced sociology but all the social sciences and humanities as well (Coser, 1971, pp. 43–44).

Karl Marx presented no theory of the city. To him, the city had ceased to be an important unit of analysis because, by the mid-nineteenth century, economic, political, and social processes were carried out on the level of nation states (Saunders, 1986, pp. 240–242). He recognized the city as an important element in the emergence of a class consciousness and revolutionary action, but considered the city itself to be a product of general social processes. This view has changed in the past 20 years. In the 1960s, a number of European socialists began to apply Marxian theory to the city. These theorists argued that the structure, and, more importantly, the problems of cities in capitalist societies were the product of their underlying economic order. They said urban problems mirrored the contradictions built into the capitalistic system and in the minds of many the only solution was changing the system.[3]

MARX'S DOCTRINE OF SOCIETY

To understand the neo-Marxian approach to the city, one needs to know something of Marx's overall doctrine of society.[4] The means by which society wrests its livelihood from nature is at the center of Marx's analysis of society. All societies, past and present, simple and complex, must provide for the necessities of life—food, clothing, shelter, and so on. But Marx argued that humans are a perpetually dissatisfied lot and once the means are found to meet these basic needs, a new set of needs arises which creates new demands, and the process is repeated through time. According to Marx, the crucial event in history occurred when society created a division of labor, and in turn, classes in their quest to fulfill needs. Classes were defined by the relationship of groups to the means of production. The means of production is everything besides human labor that goes into producing wealth—land, factories, machines, and capital. One class, the bourgeoisie, owns these means of production. The other class, the proletariat, is everyone who does not own the means and therefore must sell her or his labor.[5] In Marx's paradigm, therefore, the emergence of classes and the tension, conflict, and struggle that ensue are a normal and necessary part of society. Class conflict from this perspective is the engine of change, propelling society from one evolutionary stage to another (Coser, 1971, pp. 43–57; Saunders, 1986, pp. 13–28).

ECONOMIC DETERMINISM

Marx was an economic determinist. He believed that no phenomenon could be studied in isolation; rather, it could be understood only by placing it in a fully developed social, political, economic, and historical context. But, as an economic determinist, Marx felt that ultimately all phenomena were related to the means of production and the relationship of groups to these means. In other words, the character, form, and structure of society was determined by the underlying economic order.

Karl Marx's paradigm of society is presented in Figure 1.2. Marx envisioned society as composed of two elements—a substructure and a superstructure. The substructure had two elements, the means of production and the relationship of groups to the means of production (class relationships). The means of production refers to the general pattern of technology and social organization used by society to wrest a livelihood from nature. Historically there have been only a few basic patterns—hunting and gathering, agricultural, and industrial. Relationships to the means of production are class relationships—who owns and who controls the means of production.

To Marx, the substructure was reality. The superstructure, which contains everything else in society—political, religious, educational institutions, the form of the family, and even values, norms, tastes, the arts, and music—were a reflection of this underlying economic order. Change in the substructure—the way society organizes itself to wrest its livelihood from nature—is revolutionary because it fundamentally reshapes every other institution and every aspect of life found in the superstructure. This is why we refer to the agricultural revolution, the industrial revolution, and the postindustrial revolution as revolutions.

	Institutions
	Politics the Arts
	Religion taste
	Education etc.
SUPERSTRUCTURE	
	Culture
	Values
	Norms
	Roles
SUBSTRUCTURE	1. Means of Production
	2. Relationship to means of production = class

FIGURE 1.2 Marx's Paradigm of Society.

*Cites important localism
Ku government.
Never found in Komunal
areas*

EXAMPLES OF CHANGE IN CHINA, THE SOVIET UNION, AND THE UNITED STATES

Not very long ago, students in China were camped in Tiananmen Square in Beijing in front of the Great Hall of the People—the seat of China's government. They were calling for the resignation of Communist Party leader Deng Xiaoping, the senior leader who during his career survived purges, house arrest, and political humiliation to lead the restructuring of the Chinese economy. Premier Deng introduced free market elements to a few sections of China's socialist economy. Deng, however, is now viewed as one of the hard liners resisting democratic reforms in the nation's political system. Party theorists in the Soviet Union stated publicly that the modernization program which liberalized elements of the centrally controlled economy of China would also modify the relationships of groups to the means of production and would bring about change in the political order (Quinn-Judge, 1989, p. 3). The killing and wounding of thousands in Beijing by the People's Army may suggest that the hard liners have won and the students have lost their fight for democracy, but Marxian theory predicts that the hard liners have won the battle and lost the war—economic liberalization must be accompanied by political liberalization—either now or in the future.

Contrast the experiences of China to the other great Communist nation in the world, the Soviet Union. The thrust of Mikhail Gorbchev's modernization program, glasnost (openness) and perestroika (restructuring), is consistent with the dualism in Marx's conceptualization of society. He realized that economic reforms would have to be accompanied by political reforms: restructuring the economy (substructure) would require a change in political relationships (superstructure). In a Marxian sense, the Soviet Union is in the midst of its second revolution of this century.

Closer to home, a number of sociologists argue that a quiet revolution is underway in the United States. By the mid-1990s, pension funds will hold more than half the stock in publicly owned companies in the U.S. economy. In theory, a socialist state will have been created through capitalist means. Accordingly, Marxian theorists would argue that this shift in ownership should have repercussions in other spheres of our society.

APPLYING THE DIALECTIC

From this perspective, history is a record of the struggle of identifiable groups for the scarce resources of society.[6] In applying the dialectic, one finds in China students and sympathetic workers against the entrenched leadership, the People's Army, and the bureaucracy; in the Soviet Union, the entrenched bureaucracy and to a degree the military, against democratic reformers. (If we broaden the analysis, we could say the ethnic republics—the Baltic States, Georgia, and so on—against the Soviets.) As one can see, regardless of how complex the social situation or the period in history, the thrust of Marx's approach is elegant in its simplicity. One cuts through the layers of detail to the essence of the situation—the groups and their relationships to the means of production—that is at the root of the conflict. There are always winners and losers with any social change and few people willingly give up wealth and privilege. The wrenching changes in the two largest Communist nations attest to the problems inherent in any social change. Closer to home, the difficult economic changes in American society over the past two decades reflect a restructuring of our economy and the concomitant institutional changes that must accompany it.

CAPITALISM AS A STAGE IN HISTORY

To this point we have shown that Marx's aim was to explain social change and produce a theory of history. Moreover, he believed that the engine of change was the conflict between social classes. These conflicts are the mechanisms that drive societies to a new form, and history is a record of one ruling class being overthrown by another. Capitalism is one stage in this historical development.

Capitalism, as defined by Webster, is an economic system based on private ownership of the means of production and a system by which people compete to gain profits in a free market. The most distinguishing characteristic of the capitalist is the reliance on free market. Prices and wages are not set by the state but by supply and demand. The essence of the system is that individuals operating out of their own narrow self-interest (remember that Ivan Bosky proselytized that greed was good) seek to maximize their personal gain, and their gains can be accumulated in the form of private property, secure from arbitrary seizure by government. If you are smarter, a risk taker, or willing to work harder, theoretically, you should do better than your competitor. In this way, capitalism motivates everyone to try to become wealthier, their collective efforts increase production, and the standards of living rise.

CONTRADICTION IN CAPITALISM

Marx saw capitalism as unleashing the productive forces of society, but this increase in productivity was done at a cost—the exploitation and alienation of humans. By pursuing self-interest humans ruthlessly exploit one another. The irony in Marx's view was that capitalist societies were the first with the productive capacity to overcome the misery of poverty, but the contradiction in capitalism was that it was incapable of doing so. One reason is a problem overlooked by Adam Smith, Ricardo, and the other early theorists of capitalism: in the competition between capitalists there is always a winner. Once a business has won, in effect destroying its competition, there are no market forces to dampen prices. The deregulation of the airline industry in this country in 1981 is an example. The airline industry was one of the most heavily regulated in this nation. With deregulation, dozens of carriers competed for the expanding passenger market and ticket prices fell dramatically. By the end of the decade, however, 85 percent of the passenger traffic was carried on the planes of six companies, and two of the oldest airlines, TWA and Pan Am, were on the brink of extinction. Eastern had gone out of business. A number of airlines—Frontier, Republic, Peoples, Ozark Airlines—were gobbled up through merger or acquisition by the larger carriers. This is not a new pattern but a perennial problem in capitalism—in Marxian terms, a contradiction. The antitrust legislation of the late nineteenth century and the creation of federal regulatory agencies in the early twentieth century were a recognition of this flaw in the logic of capitalism.

There are other contradictions in capitalism. For instance, once a stratification system comes into existence, the ruling class develops a variety of techniques to perpetuate inequality from generation to generation. The bourgeoisie not only control the means of production but also the reins of state. They write laws and create a system of income and estate taxes that are, in a sense, rigged and permit the perpetuation of inequality from generation to generation. Because of these contradictions in the logic of capitalism, Marx believed that capitalist societies would increasingly become more unequal, and would eventually consist of a small ruling elite (the bourgeoisie), possessing enormous wealth and power and a huge mass of wage slaves (the proletariat) sweating out their lives in dismal factories. Thus Marx proposed revolutions, in which the masses could seize collective ownership of the means of production and turn the immense capacities of modern industrial societies to the benefit of all. The experiences of the major communist nations in the world suggest that theory does not always work in practice.

THE RISE OF A NEO-MARXIAN THEORY OF THE CITY

Traditionally neo-Marxists have paid little attention to the problems of the city. While cities were considered vital for the creation of class consciousness and the site of class struggles, they were regarded as products of larger processes being played out on the level of the nation state. This changed in the 1960s and the early 1970s, when cities became a crucible of change. The antiwar, civil rights, feminist, and gay social movements played themselves out in an urban milieu. White flight from the central city to the suburbs, the riots in Hough, Watts, and Newark, the emergence of community groups to fight for their neighborhoods against urban renewal and highway construction all had a class dimension. In the 1970s the oil crisis, stagflation, a housing crisis, and a decline in the nation's standard of living were most visible in our cities. Many came to see these intense conflicts as a form of class struggle, and Marx emerged as a viable alternative to other theories of the city.[7] Although, in many respects, the United States had the most serious urban problems in the West, it was Europeans with their long tradition in Marxian methods that brought Marx to bear on the city (Tabb and Sawers, 1978).[8]

MANUEL CASTELLS: A NEO-MARXIAN URBAN SOCIOLOGY

The Spanish sociologist, Manuel Castells, has had the greatest impact on American urban sociology. Castells's neo-Marxian approach to the city was initially developed in his book *The Urban Question* (1977).

As a neo-Marxian, Castells views the function of the city as economic.[9] He narrows this view even more by arguing that its economic function is one of consumption rather than production because it is in cities where capitalist societies reproduce their labor forces. It is here where workers consume food, clothing, shelter, and the other goods and services necessary to replenish their capacity to do labor. It is also here where one of the major contradictions in the capitalist system manifests itself. Capitalism is a system where individuals pursue their self-interest in order to accumulate private property. In an attempt to maximize their profit, they need to minimize costs—costs of material, rent, and most importantly labor. A fundamental conflict arises between the need to produce the highest possible profit and the need to invest in the needs of labor. Further, since labor is sold like any other commodity and capitalists operate out of their own self-interest, they have little motivation to invest in the housing, education, medical, and other services necessary to maintain a viable labor force. The result is that the quality of life of workers deteriorates. The contradiction is that private capitalists operating out of their own self-interest, doing what our system says they should be doing, exploit and impoverish the labor force and unintentionally sow the seeds for urban disorder and, if left unchecked, the destruction of the system itself. To prevent this from happening, Castells states, requires the intervention of the state. He writes, "The state apparatus not only exercises class domination, but also strives, as far as possible, to regulate the crises of the system, in order to preserve it" (Castells, 1977, p. 208). Thus, the state maintains the capitalist system by investing in low-cost housing, subsidizing food costs, providing public education and basic medical services, and a whole spectrum of services necessary to keep the urban system in working order. Castells argues that only through the creation of a welfare state has capitalism been saved from destruction by its own excesses.

There is a rub. According to Castells, the state reduces class conflict by providing the goods and services necessary to replenish the labor supply, but by doing so it creates a new set of contradictions—massive urban and national debt. Why? Because the state pays the cost of these services while private capitalists reap the profits created by labor. Castells's point may be well taken when you look to the fiscal problems faced by the central city governments of our largest and oldest metropolitan areas. In the 1970s, two city governments, New York and Cleveland, came to the brink of financial collapse and were saved only through massive state and federal loans. In the 1990s, New York, Philadelphia, and 15 other cities are in the same plight. Recently, Bridgeport, Connecticut declared bankruptcy; the first city to do so in 50 years. This condition was created because the capitalist system demands the concentration of banking, finance, legal, marketing, advertising, and other services in a central downtown location, often at a high cost to city government. At the same time, in order to minimize class conflict the state must absorb "the surplus population and provide welfare and public services to the larger unemployed and underemployed population concentrated in the inner cities" (Castells 1977, pp. 415–420).

As the level of debt increases (the national debt now exceeds $3 trillion), there eventually must be a reduction in services. During the Reagan years, the growth of the military budget was accomplished, in part, by cuts in social programs. The millions of homeless in our central cities can be directly attributed to an 80 percent reduction in low-income housing programs between 1981 and 1988. On the local level, New York and other cities, through years of neglect, have brought the water, sewerage, streets, bridges, and other parts of the infrastructure to the verge of collapse. Public housing and neighborhood development and preservation programs have also been permitted to wither. These problems have to be solved somehow. The money has to come from somewhere. It usually comes from the social service budget. The result has been a decline in the quality of life of labor. The decline in the quality of life of labor may lead to urban social movements against the capitalist state, but according to Castells, there is a problem in the United States because there is no socialist organization to organize this unrest. Since there is little organized resistance to these cuts, unrest will be manifested in other ways—drug addiction, child and spouse abuse, crime, wilding by youth gangs, and civil disorders. Although many of Castells's worst predictions have not come to pass (he would argue because of massive police repression by the state), he does give us an alternative theoretical approach for understanding urban problems by linking them theoretically to the contradictions inherent in the capitalist system.

In his more recent work, *Grassroots* (1983), Castells modifies his analysis of the relationship between the community and society. Although there are many similarities with his earlier work, he now argues that community organizations, whether they be black, ethnic, or gay, are responding to the social conditions and political realities of the local communities in which they live. More importantly, Castells sees the Marxian paradigm of little use in exploring these movements. Marx still forms the backdrop. Although these groups are responding to local conditions, they occur within the context of the larger capitalist society.

Both works contribute to an understanding of the complex interrelationship between societal forces and their manifestation on the local level, and how the form that these conditions take on the local level influences the response of community groups.

DAVID HARVEY: A NEO-MARXIAN URBAN GEOGRAPHY

To Castells, the city is the container in which the state supplies the items of consumption necessary for the reproduction of labor. The use of space within the city is the product of struggles between dominant and exploited groups pursuing their own goals. Castells, however, is interested in the issue of consumption within the urban context, not in the use of space per se. (To a degree, it is an aspatial urban sociology.) In other words, the city is the backdrop in which larger social processes are played out. To find scholars interested in the link between spatial patterns and social processes, we turn to urban geography.

David Harvey is to urban geography what Manuel Castells is to urban sociology. Harvey (1973, 1982, 1985a, 1985b), in a series of books and articles spanning nearly two decades, brings the perspective of Marx to geography, a discipline concerned with the spatial features of social processes and forms. A theme that runs throughout all of his works is the injustice of the capitalist system and how these injustices are manifest in the urban environment. The role of class struggle, the inherent contradictions in capitalism, and the incessant striving of capitalists for profits are at the heart of his analysis.

According to Harvey, cities mirror the logic of capitalism, and understanding the city requires an understanding of rules that guide the process of investment in the built environment. Harvey states this well in his own words:

> The system of production which capital established was founded on a physical separation between a place of work and a place of residence. The growth of the factory system, which created this separation, rested on the organization of cooperation, division of labor, and economies of scale in the work process as well as on the application of machinery. The system also promoted an increasing division of labor between enterprises and collective economies of scale through the agglomeration of activities in large urban centers. All of this meant the creation of a built environment to serve as a physical infrastructure for production, including an appropriate system for the transport of commodities. There are abundant opportunities for the productive employment of capital through the creation of a built environment for production. The same conclusion applies to investment in the built environment for consumption. The problem is, then, to discover how capital flows into the construction of this built environment and to establish the contradictions inherent in this process. (Harvey, 1985, p. 15)

Harvey's thesis is that the spatial patterns in capitalist cities reflect the inherent injustices and contradictions of capitalism. The primary contradiction in capitalism is the need for profits and the fact that competition leads to overproduction, glutted markets, falling prices, rising unemployment, and a falling rate of profit. In order to maintain profits, individual capitalists develop short-term strategies that may in the long run be harmful to them as a class. One strategy is to adopt new technology that will allow more goods to be produced at lower prices so as to beat out the competition. The problem is that the competition will likely adopt the same technology and an even larger glut of goods will flood the market. A second strategy is to relocate the operations to another site closer to raw materials, labor, and markets. The problem with this strategy is that it affects the value of the investment at the old site and the morphology of the entire city—the web of communication, economic, and transportation patterns that make production possible. A third strategy is to shift investments away from production to other spheres of the economy—office towers, shopping centers, apartment complexes, and the like—in order to maintain the level of profit. By investing in these nonproduction activities, capitalists reduce the glut of goods by lowering production, but in the process they restructure the urban environment and create a glut of offices, retail establishments, and apartments. The collapse of the real estate markets in Dallas and Houston, the historically high vacancy rates in office buildings in most U.S. cities, and the crisis in the savings and loan industry attest to the tendency of capitalism to overproduction. The irony is that the rebuilding and restructuring of the metropolis eventually leads to a more efficient use of urban space, a more efficient use of space means more efficient production, and more efficient production leads to an even larger glut of commodities on the market. Thus, according to Harvey the growth and development of our cities is a history of the incessant pursuit of profit by capitalists. In their pursuit of property, accumulation is pursued for accumulation's sake, and production for production's sake. Through this process, the structure of the city is incessantly changed to accommodate new forms of production, but these changes must be accommodated by the existing urban structure. Vast tracts of the city become obsolete, and block after block of offices and shops remain vacant because of the inherent contradiction in capitalism towards overproduction.

As in all other spheres of life, those in a position of dominance are in a position to maximize the benefits and minimize the costs of change. The wealthy can move to the suburbs and avoid the crime, pollution, transportation snarls, and poor schools and other public services of the central city—the backwash of this process. Labor typically reaps few of its benefits but absorbs most of the cost of urban growth and change. Therefore, the wealth of the suburbs as contrasted to the poverty in the central cities, the concentration of business and commerce in the central business district and manufacturing at the periphery, and the separation of racial, ethnic, and income groups into their own neighborhoods, in Harvey's view, do not occur by chance but through the pursuit of the capitalist class of its own ends. The injustice of poverty and its many ills are, therefore, a predictable outcome of the unjust and exploitative character of the capitalist system. In his words, "A genuinely humanizing urbanism has yet to be brought into being. It remains for revolutionary theory to chart the path from an urbanism based in exploitation to an urbanism appropriate for the human species. And it remains for revolutionary practice to accomplish such a transformation" (Harvey 1973, p. 314).

David Harvey's books have had a profound effect on American urban sociology, but probably nowhere has the influence been more fruitful than in the work of Logan and Molotch. Their book, *Urban Fortunes: A Political Economy of Place,* was inspired by Harvey's work and combines their traditional work in ecology with the neo-Marxian perspective developed by Harvey and others. We now turn to their approach, which fuses the perspectives of ecology with the concerns of Marx by exploring the role of place in the urban environment.

JOHN LOGAN AND HARVEY MOLOTCH: THE CITY AS A GROWTH MACHINE

John R. Logan and Harvey L. Molotch are American sociologists, and they bring the unique perspectives of this nation's sociology to the study of the city. My students find their book the most palatable of the neo-Marxian approaches because they don't cloak their argument in socialist jargon. Their book, *Urban Fortunes: The Political Economy of Place,* published in 1987, is a synthesis of elements of the ecological perspective with elements of Harvey and Castells's neo-Marxian approach. The work has as its central theme the notion that local conflicts over growth are central to the organization of cities. They reject the classical economic and ecological approaches as too deterministic; they are also out of the mainstream of neo-Marxian approaches, because they do not see urban structure and problems flowing out of the logic and contradictions of capitalism. Instead, they have investigated how various kinds of people and institutions struggle to achieve their opposing goals in the creation of the metropolis (Logan and Molotch, 1987, p. vii). Their theory is critical, but grounded in their utilitarian research in segregation, stratification, neighborhoods, and urban growth and change.

The point of departure for their theory is the concept of place and the opposing and incompatible demands associated with place. A place is a parcel of land with clearly defined boundaries, which may or may not hold a structure. Places are not only sites where we live but also commodities that can be bought and sold. Title or legal ownership can be transferred from one party to another.

Within the urban field, every place is unique. Even if identical homes are built on lots across the street from each other, each place (the land and the structure, which sell as a unit) differs in subtle ways in their access to parks, schools, shopping, and other services. Place also can have a potent psychological component. Most people have intense attachments to their homes and neighborhoods, and the place where you live locks you into a complex web of social and economic relationships—neighbors, family, schools, shopping, employment, and so on. When you move, then, you are not simply exchanging one place for another, you are modifying the social/spatial web in which you live.

Every place (every piece of real estate) has both a use value and an exchange value. If you rent, your residence provides a "home" (use value), and at the same time rent (exchange value) for the landlord. Therefore, built into the very character of place is the potential for conflict between those who are interested in maintaining its present use value (a home in which to live) and those who want to buy, sell, or rent it for a profit. In capitalist societies, the market is the arena where the value of real estate is determined, but Logan and Molotch are quick to point out that value is not simply a matter of supply and demand. The value of place is determined by the social context in which it occurs. A complex of individuals, groups, and institutions come to bear on each place, determining acceptable uses and the potential for its exchange. For example, I live in a single-family dwelling in a neighborhood zoned residential. I could probably sell my home at a much higher profit if the new owner could divide it into flats. However, such conversion is prevented by zoning laws, the threats of lawsuits from neighbors, the unwillingness of banks to lend money to a potential buyer who might threaten the collateralized loans of other homes in the neighborhood, and the refusal of the city to issue a building permit for the conversions. Therefore, market transactions do not take place in a vacuum but within a well-defined structure.

As the neo-Marxists note, we live in a class-stratified society, and class differences are manifested in social relationships within society and in the spatial relationships between neighborhoods within cities. Just as your life chances are determined by the social class into which you are born, life chances—the quality of your education, your chances of being victimized by crime, and so on—are tied to the place where you live. Therefore, when you buy or rent in a neighborhood you and those around you are sharing similar services, and thus you have a common stake in the future. Moreover, your collective interests in maintaining the use value of the neighborhood may collide with those who wish to profit from its exchange value. Social differences between groups are reflected in the spatial differences between them. Just as social stratification systems do not occur by chance, the use of space within cities is determined by groups who have special access to the structure that determines land use. Therefore, the ability of a group to win in the conflict over space is determined by its location in the stratification system.

Who are these actors? How are they tied to the social market? First of all there is government, which constructs the regulatory framework within which the use and exchange value are determined. The capitalist system in which we live defines place as a commodity that can be bought and sold. The state, also, determines the rights and privileges among market participants. Property owners have free reign to exact rent from their real estate. Renters and boarders with the lowest housing status in our society have few rights other than the right to move. Government also builds and maintains the infrastructure—roads, water and sewerage systems, schools, hospitals, and the like—which profoundly affects the present and future exchange value of place. If you can manipulate government decisions, then you may increase the exchange value of your real estate.

It is within this general land use system erected by government that others with interests in the use and exchange value of place operate. Entrepreneurs and speculators attempt to profit from the future change in the use value of real estate. They may do this by anticipating future growth of a city and buy undeveloped land wisely, or they may attempt to rig the system by influencing key government officials on decisions which influence growth. Logan and Molotch argue that entrepreneurs, speculators, contractors, builders, real estate firms, banks and savings and loans, utilities, and commercial retailers do not operate alone but form what they call a *growth machine*. The growth machine operates on a scale ranging in size from a neighborhood to an entire city, but which collectively creates conditions favorable for growth (p. 32). Growth machine activists are not concerned with the consequences of their actions, only profits. Their practices are justified by the ideology of capitalism and the belief in the sanctity of a free market. In truth, key actors, because of key position in the growth machine, are able to reap the profits of growth, but they pay for few of its costs. The costs of growth—higher taxes and user charges, traffic congestion, pollution, and the like—are borne by all the citizens of the region. Just as there is inherent conflict between the use and exchange value of place, there is inherent conflict between those who promote and benefit from growth and those who pay the bills.

SUMMARY

Science is a method of collecting and organizing knowledge and a set of rules on how this knowledge is to be acquired. The scientific method as used by the discipline of urban sociology has the simple purpose of allowing researchers to learn more about cities than they would otherwise in the course of day-to-day living. Urban sociology is the scientific study of the behaviors, structures, and processes that occur within the city. As with all scientific disciplines, urban sociology has two primary activities: constructing theories and testing theories. The shift in the theories or paradigms of a discipline sketches its history. This chapter describes the development of the dominant theoretical schools of the field of urban sociology. The conceptual frameworks of Robert E. Park and the Chicago School, Georg Simmel and Louis Wirth and their theories on the city and culture, and the neo-Marxian school are presented.

The father of human ecology in the United States is Robert Park, a member of the Department of Sociology and Anthropology at the University of Chicago from 1914 to 1933. In his article "The City: Suggestions for the Investigation of Human Behavior in the Urban Environment," published in 1916, Park launched a research program that was to occupy the Chicago School for the next two decades. This research program led to the publication of dozens of books on the city, indirectly addressing many of Park's research questions. The majority of these works were written about groups *(The Hobo)*, subareas *(The Ghetto, The Gold Coast and the Slum)*, or urban institutions *(The Taxi Dance Hall)*.

Today, there are two schools of human ecology. Sociocultural ecologists place primary emphasis on cultural factors in their research, but neoorthodox ecologists are closer to the classical school in emphasizing the role of ecological factors in their analysis of urban structure and change.

The work of Georg Simmel and Louis Wirth explores the relationship between the structure of the city and the unique behavior that occurs there: it might be called the first social psychological theory of the city. Simmel in his famous lecture, *The Metropolis and Mental Life,* presented a theory that attempts to explain how people cope with the stimuli and the stress created by the high density of the metropolis. Simmel argues that the incessant bombardment of incompatible stimuli upon individuals exhausts them, and in order to cope they have devised a number of screening devices. In Simmel's conceptual framework, these screening devices lead to behaviors ranging from individuality, a blasé attitude, to bystander apathy. These same conditions make individuals less able to comprehend and control situations and thus they develop feelings of powerlessness, isolation, social withdrawal, and alienation—characteristics that have been the concern of sociologists through most of this century. Wirth (1938) restated Simmel's ideas in demographic terms. He argued that city growth with the concomitant increases in size, density, and heterogeneity of population leads to a substitution of secondary relationships for primary ones and a greater dependency on formal means of social control. With respect to population density, Wirth notes that as a city grows a person increasingly lives among strangers (heterogeneity) and at the same time is forced to live close to other people (density). Heterogeneity combined with increased physical proximity, according to Wirth, is a source of tension and a contributing factor to interpersonal and group conflict, that is, a factor contributing to social disorganization.

In the 1940s, a number of researchers found ethnic groups living in large cities who did not have the characteristics described by Wirth. They suggested nondemographic factors such as ethnicity, social status, and stage in the family life cycle were more important than size, density, and heterogeneity in describing an urban way of life. Claude Fischer combined the work of Wirth and his critics in a single theory that describes the emergence of subcultures in the urban environment. Size, density, and heterogeneity are hypothesized as important in creating the critical mass of people capable of creating a subculture. Once an ethnic, racial, or occupational subculture emerges, it develops norms, roles, and institutions that may or may not be in agreement with the encompassing culture.

Although Karl Marx and all of the early European theorists had an interest in cities, Marx never developed a theory of the city. Marx felt that social and economic forces, by his time, had transcended the city and operated on the level of nation states. Cities were appreciated for their role in developing a class consciousness and as a stage for revolutionary change, but in Marx's work they were seen as a product of societal forces. The upheavals in Western societies in the 1960s and 1970s rekindled theorists' interest in the city. Many of the problems faced by European and North American nations were found to have deep class undertones. As a result, European scholars began to develop a distinct neo-Marxian theory of the city.

Manuel Castells's contributions to the development of neo-Marxian urban sociology were discussed. As a neo-Marxian theorist, Castells views the function of the city as one of economic consumption. Specifically, the city is viewed as the environment in which workers replenish their working capacity by consuming housing, food, clothing, and other services. It is in this environment where the major contradictions in the capitalist system manifest themselves. Individual capitalists in the pursuit of profit and the accumulation of wealth have little incentive to invest in the goods and services necessary to maintain the labor force. This exploitation leads to a drop in the quality of life of labor and sows the seeds for disorder and the eventual destruction of the system itself. To maintain the system, and to address this contradiction of capitalism, Castells argues, requires the intervention of the state. The state provides public housing, subsidized food, and other services but in so doing goes deeply in debt. The mounting debt requires a cut in services and once again the quality of life of workers declines, creating conditions ripe for a host of social ills.

The urban geographer David Harvey uses Marx to describe the physical structure of the city. According to Harvey, cities mirror the logic of capitalism, and understanding the city requires an understanding of the rules that guide the process of investment in the built environment. To Harvey, the major contradiction of capitalism is the need for profits and the fact that competition leads to overproduction, glutted markets, falling prices, rising unemployment, and a falling rate of profit. A number of strategies to cope with a declining rate of profit are described, but the one most important to Harvey's analysis is the shift of capital from production (the primary circuit) to offices, warehouses, shopping centers, and the like (the secondary circuit). In the short run, this reduces the overproduction of goods, but it creates a glut of commercial, retail, and wholesale establishments. Therefore, the history of the city in capitalist societies is the incessant restructuring of the city to accommodate new forms of production. Tracts of the old city must be destroyed to accommodate the new, and as in all things in life, labor bears the brunt of this change. High-status individuals insulate themselves from urban problems by moving to the suburbs or exurbs. Harvey suggests that the only way to create a truly humanizing urban way of life is through revolutionary change.

Logan and Molotch are American sociologists who combine elements of human ecology with a modified neo-Marxian approach to the city. Their theory revolves around the opposing and incompatible demands associated with place. Built into the character of every place is the potential for conflict between those who want to use the place and those who want to profit from it.

Logan and Molotch argue that entrepreneurs, speculators, realtors, contractors, developers, bankers, utilities, and others form a loose coalition to promote the growth and development of the city. They call them the *growth machine*. The strategic position of these people in the system allows them to affect decisions, which permits them to profit from the exchange value of place. Much of the conflict found in any urban area is between members of the growth machine and those groups interested in maintaining the use value of their neighborhoods and homes. These theorists also show the linkage between the processes that maintain the inequality of our social stratification system and those that maintain spatial inequality. Once a social stratification system and its manifestation in a class-stratified housing market come into existence, potent forces work to maintain this pattern through time.

It is the nature of the scientific method that one can never prove a theory true—one can only prove it false. As we have shown, each of the three theoretical schools have their critics, as they should, because only through the free exchange of ideas can any discipline develop. Therefore, where relevant, these theoretical perspectives are used in the remaining chapters of the text to illuminate urban structures and processes as well as the changes in the larger encompassing society which affect the city and its urban way of life.

NOTES

1. This chapter provides a brief overview of three dominant theoretical approaches to the city. An extensive analysis of these theories is beyond the scope of this text. For those interested in pursuing these theoretical schools in greater depth, I would suggest the following books: Lewis Coser, *Masters of Sociological Thought,* Robert Nisbet, *The Sociological Tradition,* Michael P. Smith, *The City and Social Theory,* and Larry Lyon, *The Community in Urban Society,* and of course the original works of the theorists themselves. In my opinion, the best summary and critical analysis of these theories is found in Peter Saunders's book, *Social Theory and the Urban Question.* A complete citation for each of these works can be found in the bibliography.

2. Wirth's negative view of the city was not original. His work was deeply influenced by Simmel and other European social philosophers. Moreover, his writing was in tune with a general antiurban bias that pervaded the American culture in the nineteenth and early twentieth centuries. This antiurban tradition started with Thomas Jefferson and continued through the nineteenth century in the writings of such men as Thoreau, Emerson, and Melville. In the late nineteenth century the antiurban tradition was apparent in the efforts of American city planners to provide open space in place of physical structures and environments that deconcentrate populations. The parks and parkway programs undertaken by many American cities in the nineteenth and early twentieth centuries are a product of this tradition (Hawley, 1972, pp. 521–523).

3. My students are required to read the works of neo-Marxists, and they are often bothered by the tone of writers like Castells and Harvey, and so would many of you be. The point that I make to them is that there are a whole series of interrelated urban problems associated with the private ownership of the means of production and a free market. This is not to say that in socialist nations, where the means of production are owned by the state, there are no urban problems. Anyone who has traveled in the Soviet Union and the Eastern Bloc nations can attest to the problems in their cities. The problems are no less severe, just different.

In addition, it is important to realize that there are no pure capitalist or socialist nations. Capitalist nations do not provide all their goods and services through a free market; mass transit, defense, medical care, and social security are all socialist elements in our capitalist economy. Socialist nations also have capitalist elements. Recent events in the Soviet Union, Poland, and Hungary suggest that these societies are moving toward free market elements in spheres of their centrally controlled economies—capitalistic elements in their socialist economies.

4. The most complete statement of Marx's ideas are found in his classic treatise *Capital,* first published in 1868. For an outline of his views, see the *Communist Manifesto,* first published in 1848.

5. Marx realized that in capitalist societies there were many people who did not fit into the two categories, bourgeoisie and proletariat. In this society, the middle class, which includes merchants, and self-employed professions do not fit into either category. This, however, does not distract from the analysis of the economic forces that are at the root of his historical analysis.

6. The dialectic approach explores the conflicts, contradictions, and tensions in social life. Contradictions are treated as normal, not an abnormal part of social life. Simmel, Marx, and other theorists used the dialectic, but most of you are familiar with Marx's use of it. The thesis, the phenomena, problem, or proposition under examination is examined in terms of its antithetical opposite—the antithesis. The outcome is the synthesis, which becomes the thesis in the next iteration of the analysis. In Marx's hands the dialectic becomes the tool for examining history. At each stage of history, contradictions in the existing system create groups (in capitalism, the bourgeoise and the proliterate) with different relationships to the means of production. Their conflict framed in terms of the thesis/antithesis leads to a synthesis—a resolution of the conflict.

7. If one applies his paradigm of society (the substructure and superstructure), then, cities must reflect the underlying economic reality. Further, the size, form, and location of cities, and their internal structure—the location of homes, factories, businesses—as well as the transportation system that ties them all together must reflect the underlying substructure of society. The cities in capitalist societies should have one form, the cities in socialist societies another. If this is true, then the urban problems we face as a society in housing, transportation, crime, and drug abuse reflect the underlying contradictions of a capitalist economic system. This is the logic used by neo-Marxian theorists in Europe and North America to bring the works of Marx to bear on the city.

8. Ironically, Europeans from Tocqueville to Castells and Harvey seem to bring special insights to the problems faced by American society. To balance this discussion, you may want to look at the work, *Without Marx or Jesus?* written by the influential French socialist, Jean Paul Revel. Revel shocked many European socialists when he argued that a new form of revolution had been introduced to the twentieth century, not in Russia, Cuba, or any of the other socialist nations, but in the United States. What was unique about America's revolution against itself was that this society, according to Revel, had redefined the role of men and women, blacks and whites, and modified many of its institutions in a unique way—through already existing social institutions.

9. Castells's work is based in the epistemology (the study or theory of how we know, i.e., the grounds for knowledge) of the French theorist Louis Althusser (1967, 1971). In his work Althusser modifies Marx's notion of the substructure to include cultural, political, as well as economic elements. Castells argues that the city system cannot be political because city governments are subservient to national governments, and they cannot be cultural because cities share a culture with the rest of society. Therefore, it must be economic. There are two elements of the economic system—processes of production and consumption. Castells argues that since production includes the extraction of raw materials, their transportation, and modification before consumption in a system that transcends urban systems, cities must be viewed as consumption, not production, units.

CHAPTER 2

URBANIZATION, MODERNIZATION, AND ECONOMIC DEVELOPMENT

INTRODUCTION

Paging through any major work on cities exposes the reader to many new terms—megalopolis, metropolis, Metropolitan Statistical Area, urban, urbanism, and urbanization. The use of these terms in the literature is often confusing because different authors use different terms to mean the same things. More than one student of the city has suggested that our inability to cope with urban problems may derive from our inability to define the problems clearly in the first place (Eldridge, 1956; Anderson, 1959; Downs, 1973). This chapter explores the conceptual and measurement problems associated with the urbanization process. In addition, patterns of urbanization in the more developed nations of the world are explored, as well as the relationship of urbanization to the processes of modernization and economic development. This chapter is followed by one that examines the special problems faced by the nations of the less developed world as they urbanize and strive to develop.

MEASURING URBANIZATION

Just as urban sociologists lack consensus about the definition or urbanization, they fail to agree how it should be measured. Essentially, two problems emerge when we attempt to measure urbanization. First, how great a population concentration is necessary to constitute an urban place—2000, 10,000, or 100,000 people? Second, once a population figure has been agreed upon, how does one go about delimiting the city's boundaries? In short, what is urban?

For the past 40 years, the United Nations has been attempting to formulate a set of standard measures for urbanization as a basis for international comparisons. This attempt has been frustrated by the dozens of definitions of "urban" now in use in the world. An analysis of these definitions, however, shows that they fit into three broad categories.

The most widely used definition of "urban" is based on population size: approximately thirty-five percent of the countries providing data to the United Nations use a definition based solely on size. The minimum population size considered urban varies considerably, from as low as 250 inhabitants to as high as 40,000.

The second type of definition is based on legal or government criteria. In some nations a population concentration is considered urban regardless of size if it is an administrative center—a county seat, for example. Similarly, incorporation—the recognition by the state of a population concentration as a legal entity—also is used as a criterion for defining a place as urban.

The third type of urban definition combines several criteria, usually size and legal or administrative standards. Most state governments in the United States, for example, require a population concentration to reach a predetermined size before it can be incorporated. In other nations, these criteria are combined with other requirements, such as number of inhabitants employed in nonagricultural jobs.

DIFFERENT COUNTRIES' CRITERIA OF URBANIZATION[1]

In international comparisons, the degree of urbanization frequently is considered simply the percentage of the total population of a country living in urban areas, according to each country's own definition of urban. This approach presents numerous problems, some of which can be seen in Table 2.1. For instance, the wide variation in the definitions used in several European and North American countries suggests that Denmark is more urban than the United States and that Iceland is as urban as the Netherlands. This impression is misleading. A method preferred by Kingsley Davis (1969, 1972a) and other sociologists when making comparisons between countries is to find the percentage of each country's population in cities of 100,000 or more inhabitants. This method reveals that Iceland has no cities with population of over 100,000, whereas the Netherlands has 45.1 percent of its population in cities of 100,000 or more inhabitants.

This approach is not without problems, however. A country with a small population and therefore small cities may have the same degree of urbanization as a country with a large population and large cities. Note in Table 2.1 that although Denmark and the United States have similar urban populations, nearly 30 percent of Denmark's population is in one large city (Copenhagen), whereas the United States has 32 cities with more than one-half million inhabitants holding 77 percent of its urban population.

Another problem is related to how the cities are distributed. Hypothetically, two countries of the same size, with the same percentage of their populations in cities of 100,000 or more, could have entirely different settlement patterns. Country A might

TABLE 2.1 Urban Definition, Percent Urban by Definition, and Percent of Total Population in Cities of 100,000 or More and 500,000 or More.

COUNTRY	URBAN DEFINITION	PERCENT URBAN BY COUNTRY'S DEFINITION	PERCENT OF POPULATION IN CITIES OF 100,000 OR MORE	PERCENT OF URBAN POPULATION IN CITIES OF 500,000 OR MORE
Australia	Population size 1500 or more	86%	64.7%	68%
Denmark	Population size 250 or more	84%	38.3%	29.8%
United States	Population size 2500 or more	74%	58.4%	77%
Netherlands	Population size 6000 or more	88%	45.1%	23.9%
Iceland	Legal-administrative	90%	0	0
New Zealand	Legal-administrative	84%	45.9%	22.1%
Canada	Population size 2000 or more	77%	49.3%	62%
Spain	Population size 10,000 or more	91%	33.4%	44%
Italy	Legal-administrative	72%	29.4%	52%

The influence of the legal definition of a nation's urban population is apparent in this table. In most nations a single criterion—size—is used, but in this table the minimum population size of an urban place ranges from 250 persons in Denmark to 10,000 persons in Spain. In contrast, Iceland and New Zealand consider a place to be urban regardless of size as long as certain legal or administrative functions are carried out within its borders. The problems these conflicting definitions create may be seen by comparing the first column of figures with the last two columns. The resulting discrepancies show that a standard measure must be employed in making international comparisons or urbanization.

Source: Adapted from Population Reference Bureau, 1989. *World Population Data Sheet.* Washington, D.C.: Population Reference Bureau, Inc.

have many cities of the same size, evenly dispersed, and Country B might have one large city that dominates the entire country—a settlement pattern called *primacy.*

Over the past two decades, ecologists, demographers, and urban sociologists have attempted to come to grips with these measurement problems by developing indices of urbanization (Arriage, 1970; Gibbs, 1961; Mehta, 1963; Subramanian, 1971). These indices have been sensitive to both the size of a nation's urban population and the spatial distribution of cities, yet none of the indices is widely used. The reasons are that in general they are cumbersome and difficult to calculate and, more important, the necessary data are simply not available for many nations. Therefore, when making international comparisons, most researchers use the degree-of-urbanization measure (percentage of total population in cities of 100,000 or more) despite its major problems.

DELINEATING BOUNDARIES

Another concern in measuring a country's urbanization is establishing the boundaries of the cities to be measured. Should one use political boundaries or boundaries based on population density and employment? In the United States, for example, the larger urban places have a central city defined by politically established boundaries, but these central cities are surrounded by densely populated suburban areas whose inhabitants are employed in nonagricultural jobs. A case in point is Cincinnati, Ohio, where 356,000 people resided within the political limits of the city in 1986. This figure, however, represents only 24 percent of the population living in the Cincinnati metropolitan area.

The problems in delineating city boundaries have been addressed by many countries, including the United States. The definitions used by the United States Census Bureau in delineating urban places show the lengths to which one must go to define urban boundaries accurately.

UNITED STATES CENSUS DEFINITIONS[2]

Until 1950, the official definition of urban used by the United States Census was an incorporated place of 2500 or larger.[3] This definition was thought to be too narrow, and since 1950 the urban definition has included both incorporated and unincorporated places.

The current definition of urban includes the population living in the following types of population concentrations:

1. Places of 2500 inhabitants or more incorporated as cities, villages, boroughs, and towns, but excluding those persons living in the rural portions of extended cities.

2. Unincorporated places of 2500 inhabitants or more.

3. Other territory, incorporated or unincorporated, on the fringes of large cities with a population of 50,000 or more.

Additional detailed rules cover both incorporated and unincorporated areas in New England, Pennsylvania, New Jersey, and elsewhere.

To provide a better distinction between urban and rural population in the vicinity of large cities, the Census Bureau uses four other terms—urbanized area, metropolitan statistical area, primary metropolitan statistical area, and consolidated metropolitan statistical area.

URBANIZED AREA

An urbanized area is defined by population density. Each urbanized area includes a central city and the surrounding closely settled urban fringe (suburbs) that together have a population of 50,000 or more. The urbanized area criteria define a boundary based primarily on a population density of at least 1000 persons per square mile, but the boundary may include some less densely settled areas within corporate limits and areas like industrial parks, golf courses, metropolitan parks, and the like, if they are adjacent to dense urban development.

In 1986, 174 million (approximately 73.7 percent) of the total United States population were living in urbanized areas. Less than half this number (74 million) lived in 340 central cities, with roughly 105 million living in the urban fringe (suburbs). The 1980 population counts showed continued growth of urbanized areas with the greatest gains made in the urban fringe. Also of interest is the fact that these areas covered only 36,290 square miles, or about 1 percent of the total land area of the United States.

METROPOLITAN STATISTICAL AREA

Closely linked to the urbanized-area concept is the concept of Metropolitan Statistical Area (MSA). The MSA is used to identify central cities with at least 50,000 inhabitants,[4] the counties in which they are located, known as central counties, and those adjoining counties (known as outlying counties) that have economic or social relationships to the central city. There is no limit on the number of outlying counties in an MSA. The outlying counties in an MSA may even be in different states, as long as a large enough percentage of the employed workers residing in the county commute to the central county (the criteria range from 25 to 50 percent) and the population density of the county is high enough.

The purpose of the Metropolitan Statistical Area is to indicate the extent of the economic and social integration between the central city and outlying densely populated areas. Political boundaries do not adequately delimit cities, because they seldom include the lightly settled areas at the fringe of urbanized areas. In general, urbanized areas are the thickly settled core of the MSA. The balance of the MSA is the area of low-density settlement often considered the suburban fringe. (The relationship between the urbanized areas and MSA can be seen in Figure 2.1).

Metropolitan Statistical Areas are also categorized into levels based on total population. Level A is MSAs of 1 million inhabitants or more; Level B is MSAs with between 250,000 and 1 million; Level C is MSAs with between 100,000 and 250,000 inhabitants; and Level D is MSAs with fewer than 100,000 inhabitants.

PRIMARY METROPOLITAN STATISTICAL AREAS (PMSAs)
AND CONSOLIDATED METROPOLITAN STATISTICAL AREAS
(CMSAs)

In Level A Metropolitan Statistical Areas, Primary Metropolitan Statistical Areas may be identified. Each PMSA consists of a large urbanized county or cluster of counties that demonstrates very strong internal economic and social links, in addition to close ties to neighboring areas. When PMSAs are defined, the MSAs of which they are component parts is redesignated a CMSA. Not all PMSAs, however, have a central city.

In the 1970 census, the two largest metropolitan areas in the United States, New York and Chicago, were designated by the Bureau of the Census as Consolidated Statistical Areas (later renamed CMSAs). These areas were large metropolitan complexes and are viewed by some students of the city as the settlement pattern of the future—the

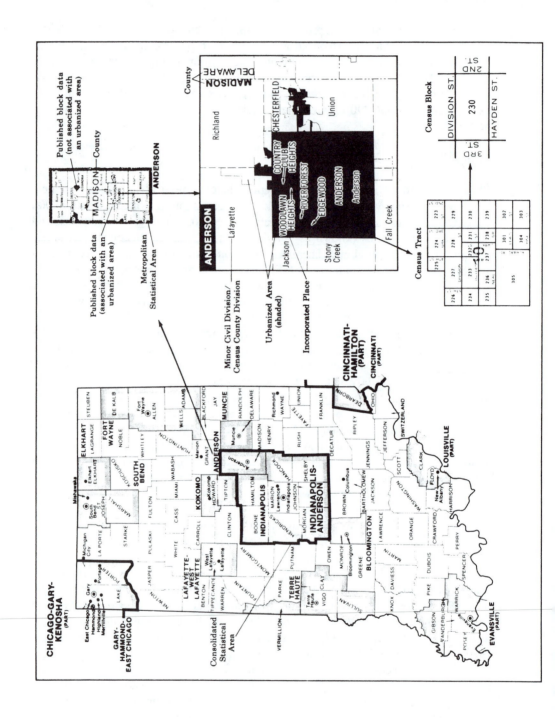

megalopolis. By 1987, the Census Bureau had identified a total of 21 CMSAs. The population of the 261 MSAs, combined with those in the 21 CMSAs and 73 PMSAs of which they are a part, contain approximately 185 million people or 77 percent of this nation's population (Bureau of the Census, 1987, Table 31). See Figure 2.2.

USEFULNESS OF THE U.S. CENSUS DEFINITIONS

The definitions and practices of the United States Census Bureau are not without faults. Obviously, many of the criteria used by the Census Bureau are arbitrary and could lead to inaccuracies in classification. For example, a single incorporated place could conceivably have 49,999 inhabitants, and it would not be considered an urbanized area. Most of the classification practices are largely dictated by practical considerations such as time and cost. The question for social scientists is whether the Census's categories are useful in research. In other words, can these relatively simple measures based on population size, density, and employment be used to analyze more complex and social economic phenomena? The answer is yes. The definitions reflect a long dialogue between the users of the data and the Census Bureau. The Census Bureau appears to provide reliable data that are applicable to the study of a wide range of phenomena.

This is especially true of the 1990 U.S. Census, the most sophisticated ever conducted. Employing TIGER, an acronym for the bureau's Topologically Integrated Geographic Encoding and Referencing System, the bureau produced the first complete, large-scale computer-based map set in U.S. history (Marx, 1986).[5] The TIGER computer files included every known road, river, railroad, boundary feature, and address in the United States and its territories. These address files can be matched by the computer with data collected from other sources—utility and tax records, credit card information, hospital records, and the like—through a process called *geocoding*. These matched files have become a powerful research tool in fields as diverse as area marketing to the epidemiology of AIDS. These developments will be discussed in greater detail in Chapter 8, "Social Area Analysis and Factorial Ecology."

The United States census is the best in the world. Comparative studies of urban phenomena in other nations are far more difficult because the definitions employed by the United States Census Bureau are not used worldwide, and census terminology differs among countries. Nevertheless, in many countries census officials delimit urbanized and metropolitan areas with criteria similar to those of the United States. In Canada, for example, "census agglomeration" is equivalent to the United States Census term "urban area." The British Standard Metropolitan Labor Area is similar to the Metropolitan Statistical Area (MSA). The problems in developing comparative international data on urbanization are under study by the World Bank, the United Nations, and other international agencies and study groups, but no formal recommendations have been made. At present, every researcher making international comparisons must examine the available data for a correspondence among census units. Although this approach leaves much to be desired, in the absence of universal census definitions it seems likely to continue.

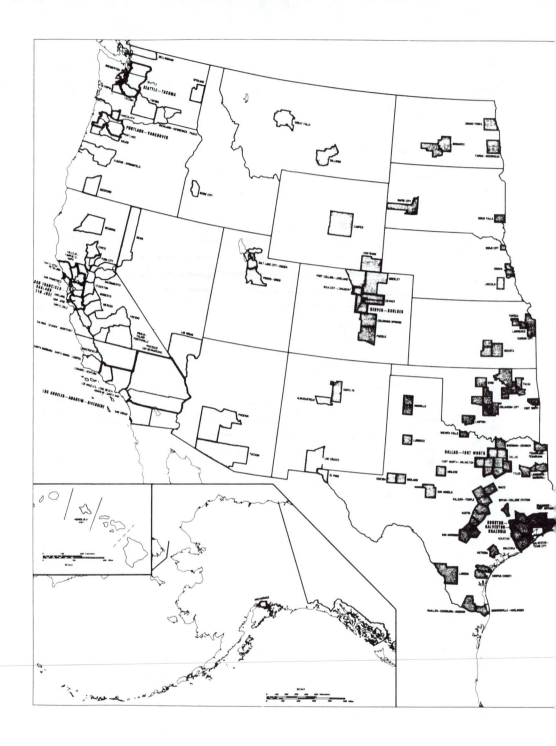

FIGURE 2.2 Metropolitan Statistical Areas (CMSA's, PMSA's, and MSA's). Areas Defined by U.S. Office Management and Budget, June 30, 1985.

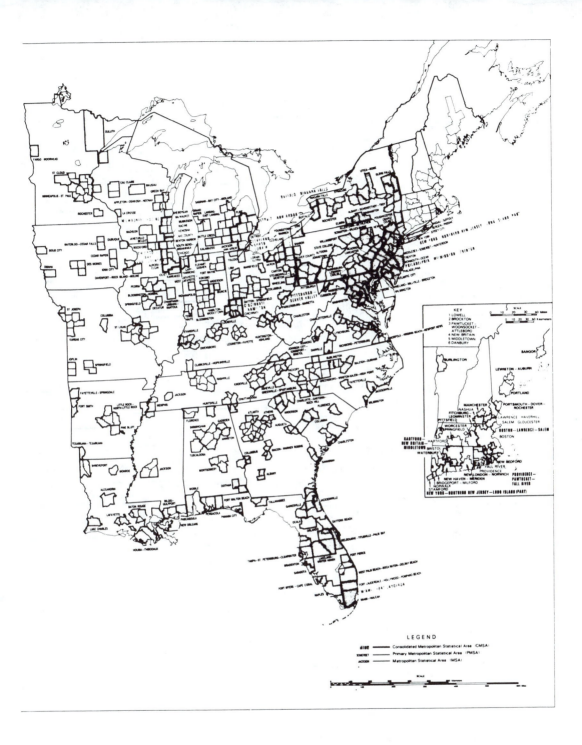

LEGEND

#100 ———— Consolidated Metropolitan Statistical Area (CMSA)

SOMERSET ——— Primary Metropolitan Statistical Area (PMSA)

JACKSON ——— Metropolitan Statistical Area (MSA)

SCALE

PATTERNS OF URBANIZATION

For the purposes of this text, I have chosen a narrow definition of the concept of urbanization—the process of population concentration. We have also reviewed the problems faced by the U.S. Census Bureau in measuring this process, as well as the problems faced by nations in other parts of the world. For practical reasons, I have adopted the criteria used by the United Nations and the World Bank, an arbitrary number—100,000 persons—as the threshold for urban place. Even with these conceptual and measurement problems resolved, there is the problem of presenting data on the urbanization patterns in the more than 250 nations in the world. How does one make sense of the enormous diversity in cultures, economies, and regions? One method is to make a distinction among nations based on their level of development.

Throughout the text, I make a distinction between two types of societies—more developed countries (MDCs) and less developed countries (LDCs). I use these terms in preference to others because they reflect the shifting relationships among nations of the world. Argentina is a country with enormous natural wealth, and 70 years ago it was considered a more developed country. Mismanagement by a succession of military governments during the past 30 years has left its economy in ruins, and today Argentina is considered a LDC.

The twentieth century has been America's. For the past 90 years, the United States has dominated the world's economic order. Our preeminence, however, is under attack. The United States still has the world's largest economy and its most productive industry, but other nations are catching up. In 1980, Japan displaced the Soviet Union as the world's second largest economy, and the economic unification of Europe in 1992 will create a market of 350 million people spanning much of the continent. Therefore, all nations are developing, some faster than others, and over time, the relative position of each nation changes. Today, it is generally agreed that MDCs include the United States, Canada, the nations of Europe, the Soviet Union, Japan, New Zealand, and Australia. Transitional nations include the Republic of China (Taiwan), South Korea, and Singapore. The remaining nations of the world are considered LDCs. This chapter describes the urbanization process in more developed nations. In the chapter that follows, the special problems faced by less developed nations will be explored.

Definitions of urbanization may differ, but one thing is certain: urbanization cannot be achieved without an increase in economic development. Economic development is usually measured by increases in per capita income. This figure is calculated simply by dividing a nation's gross national product (or gross development product) by population. An arbitrary figure, say, $5000 in 1986 U.S. dollars, can be used to divide the nations in the world into more and less developed.

Social scientists generally agree that the process of urbanization and the process of economic development are linked (Bairoch, 1988). But does economic development cause urbanization, or is it the other way around? The study of economic development, like the study of urbanization, is complicated by a definition that is less than clear. For example, one finds the terms *modernization, economic development,* and *industrialization* used interchangeably in the literature. In general, the term economic development is used to refer to the constellation of changes in the social and economic structure of a society as it moves from an agricultural/rural to an industrial/urban economy. Modernization, in contrast, refers to the social/psychological side of this process—the changing norms, values, institutions, and behaviors of a population as it adapts to an emerging industrial/urban way of life. As you can see, there is considerable overlap in the two definitions. Before exploring the relationship between urbanization and economic development, one must attempt to define what economic development means.

DEFINING ECONOMIC DEVELOPMENT

Of the dozens of definitions for economic development, the most common is based on technological criteria. From this perspective, economic development is viewed as occurring simultaneously with industrialization, which is "the extensive use of inanimate sources of power for economic production and all that entails by way of organization, transportation, and communication, and so on" (Moore, 1963, p. 92). Industrialization requires the reorganization of the labor force into more efficient forms that provide a greater output of goods and services for consumption by society. An example is the emergence of the factory system and the gradual elimination of the artisan—the silversmith, the shoemaker, and the like. The shift of the labor force into a factory setting and the transformation of, say, shoemaking, from a single skilled worker fabricating a single pair of shoes to a group of unskilled workers assembling shoes on a line, increase efficiency. It is this increase in efficiency or output resulting from the reorganization of the labor force that is considered economic development.

Different social scientists have focused on the social implications of economic growth. Greer (1962) sees these increases in efficiency and output as leading to increasing differentiation of the social structure—the specialization of its functions. Davis (1972b) views economic growth as leading to more complex new forms of social integration. Both writers see changes in the economic sphere of society reflected in a greater social complexity—the emergence of new occupations, interest groups, institutions, and businesses—as well as in more elaborate ways that these new social structures are linked together. Development, then, is one element in a complex process that leads to fundamental modifications of the fabric of society (Smelser, 1963). It is these changes in the fabric of society that sociologists call modernization.

Daniel Lerner (1958) discusses modernization, which he defines as the process of social change whereby the less developed societies acquire characteristics common to more developed societies. As a society undergoes modernization, a change occurs in its members' world outlook, values, norms, consumption behavior, and so on.

A final set of theories links economic development to energy sources. In one view, economic development is the extent to which a society's members use inanimate sources of power and/or tools to multiply the effects of their effort (Levy, 1967). Others have defined it as the process of using more energy to increase the productivity and efficiency of human labor (Meadows, 1972).

The various definitions suggest that the term economic development can be used to describe numerous broad changes in a society. First, a society's structure changes to permit the more efficient use of resources (the production of greater output). Changes also occur on the social-psychological level, in individuals' attitudes and values. Economic development also entails a change in the sources and the quantity of energy used by the society.

In this text, economic development and modernization are used synonymously and defined as increases in the aggregate output of a society and the social and cultural changes that occur in the development process. Economic development is a continuing process. Some countries are slowly changing their methods of production and social forms, whereas other countries are rapidly devising new production techniques and forms of organization. There are no such things as "developed" countries, only "more developed" and "less developed." The development scale is a relative one; as noted earlier, the position of a country on this continuum changes not only in response to internal changes but in response to the changing positions of other countries. For example, subsequent progress in the rest of the world caused Argentina to become a relatively less developed country (Hagen, 1968).

IRWIN'S MODEL OF MODERNIZATION

Patrick Irwin (1975) has employed our definition of modernization in a model. Irwin argues that a more developed country uses tremendous amounts of energy (coal, gas, oil, and hydroelectricity) in producing goods and services, but these countries use their energy more efficiently than could a less developed country. In other words, during economic development a country undergoes fundamental changes in its social organization that lead to the use of increasing quantities of energy and increased per capita output. The higher the country is on the development scale, the more complex its social organization and the more efficient its use of resources. Rather than studying economic development in terms of organizational complexity, division of labor, and the like, Irwin examines the total input of energy to a country's economy and the resulting output of goods and services. The greater the efficiency of a country's economy, the higher the level of development (see Figure 2.3). The Irwin approach thus links resources and technology to broad changes within society. It measures modernization; however, it really does not specify what is involved in gaining increased efficiency. Irwin's research explores the broad social changes taking place within a country that permit its people to utilize resources more efficiently. Irwin, however, does not examine the relationship between urbanization and modernization.

In Figure 2.3 GNP and energy consumption figures are plotted for 15 countries, providing the basis for some interesting comparisons. For example, find the points for Poland and Japan in the figure and notice that the two countries have approximately the same per capita energy usage. Now, run an imaginary line from the points to the y-axis and note that Japan has a per capita GNP that is more than three times greater than Poland's. France and the United Kingdom, and Greece and Spain are two other examples. In this scheme, the nation with the greatest output with the least input of energy would be the more developed.

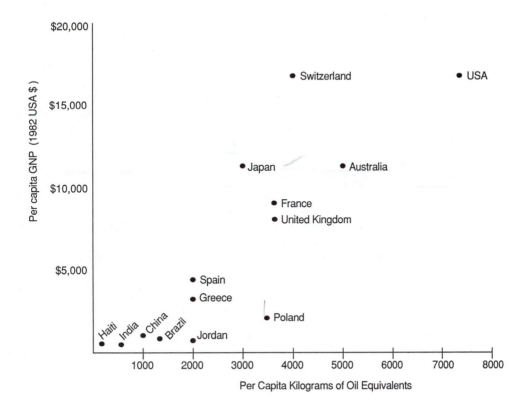

FIGURE 2.3 Per Capita GNP by Per Capita Energy Consumption in Fifteen Selected Countries.
Source: World Bank, *World Development Report 1987.* New York: Oxford University Press, 1987, Tables 1 & 31.

RELATING MODERNIZATION AND URBANIZATION

Several social scientists have examined the relationship between modernization and urbanization. Gibbs (1958) takes an ecological position, stating that in the final analysis all societies are organized to provide for material sustenance. That is, a society must provide food, clothing, shelter, and other items of consumption for mere physical survival. However, a country's natural resources are seldom in one place, and are usually widely dispersed. Because no one region is self-sufficient, the country's population must organize itself to exploit the resources and convert them into consumption items for nationwide distribution. One possible approach is to build a complex and expensive road system linking each resource area to all other areas. An alternative is to build a center to act as a transportation hub for the country. This city becomes a place of trade, a center of control over extractive industries, and a locale for processing and combining raw materials. Of the infinite number of ways in which societies can organize for survival, urbanization—organizing into cities—is the most efficient, as is demonstrated by the present dominance of this form.

Gibbs and Martin (1958) considered another situation: the country in which most of the raw materials are close to a single center. Such a city would be less dependent on a transport center and as a result this center's population would decline. This situation is fairly common. In general, the degree of urbanization in a country varies directly with the extent of the dispersion of the items it consumes. In agricultural societies, for example, raw materials are evenly dispersed, and the relatively few items of consumption can be produced locally. Thus there is less need for urbanization. Countries that consume many more items and have widely dispersed natural resources will have high levels of urbanization. Urbanization contributes to the efficiency of a society by bringing together at one place the people, capital, and natural resources necessary to manufacture the items consumed. Moreover, the transportation and communication systems centered in cities facilitate the eventual distribution of these objects of consumption.

The link between urbanization and modernization arises from this notion of objects of consumption. The total number of objects produced by a country is its output, which is measured by gross national product (GNP). Modernization or economic development is societal change that permits increased output and increased energy efficiency. It is in the city that this social change takes place; therefore, modernization and urbanization are inseparable processes. The expansion of a country's economy through technological development marks a fundamental change in the way a society organizes itself for sustenance.

This relationship can be seen in the data presented in Table 2.2, "Per Capita GNP and Percent Urban." Note that the 55 countries in the sample have been grouped according to per capita income ranging from low-income countries like Ethiopia, India, and China, through middle-income countries like Bolivia, Nigeria, Costa Rica, and Brazil, to industrial market economies like Japan, Canada, and the United States. First, these data show the enormous income disparities that exist in the world. Ethiopia, the poorest nation in the world, has an annual income per capita of only $110. At the other extreme is the United States with the world's highest per capita income of $16,690. Using the arbitrary figure of $5000 per capita per year as the dividing line between more developed and less developed, we see that the vast majority of nations in the world are less developed: 88 of the 119 countries for which the World Bank has data.

A perusal of the data in the last column of Table 2.2 suggests the crucial role that urban places play in the development process. Note that as the per capita income of a nation increases, so too does the percentage of that nation's population that lives in cities. I have summarized the average GNP and percent urban figures for each income category in Table 2.3. Note that there is a direct correspondence between the two sets of figures. Low-income countries with an average per capita GNP of only $270 also have the lowest percentage of their total population living in urban places—22 percent. Without fail, as per capita GNP increases the percentage of a country's urban population increases. Industrial market economies with an average per capita GNP of $11,800 have 75 percent of their populations living in urban places.

TABLE 2.2 GNP Per Capita and Percent Urban for 55 Selected Countries.

LOW-INCOME ECONOMIES	GNP PER CAPITA	PERCENT URBAN POPULATION	PERCENT URBAN CITIES OVER 500,000
Ethiopia	110	15	37
Bangladesh	150	18	51
Zaire	170	39	38
India	270	25	39
Kenya	290	20	57
Sudan	300	21	31
China	310	22	45
Pakistan	380	29	51
Sri Lanka	380	21	16
Zambia	390	48	35
MIDDLE-INCOME ECONOMIES			
Bolivia	470	44	44
Indonesia	530	25	50
Philippines	580	39	34
Egypt, Arab Rep.	610	46	53
Zimbabwe	680	27	50
Nicaragua	770	56	47
Nigeria	800	30	58
Thailand	800	18	69
El Salvador	820	43	0
Paraguay	860	41	44
Peru	1,010	68	44
Turkey	1,080	46	42
Ecuador	1,160	52	51
Tunisia	1,190	56	30
Guatemala	1,250	41	36
Costa Rica	1,300	45	64
Colombia	1,320	67	51
Chile	1,430	83	44
Jordan	1,560	69	37
Brazil	1,640	73	52
Uruguay	1,650	85	52
Hungary	1,950	55	37
Portugal	1,970	31	44
South Africa	2,010	56	53
Poland	2,050	60	47
Yugoslavia	2,070	45	23
Mexico	2,080	69	48
Panama	2,100	50	66
Argentina	2,130	84	60
Korea, Rep. of	2,150	64	77
Greece	3,550	65	70
Israel	4,990	90	35

TABLE 2.2 (cont.) GNP Per Capita and Percent Urban for 55 Selected Countries.

HIGH-INCOME OIL EXPORTERS	GNP PER CAPITA	PERCENT URBAN POPULATION	PERCENT URBAN CITIES OVER 500,000
Libya	7,170	60	64
Saudi Arabia	8,850	72	33
Kuwait	14,480	92	0
United Arab Emirates	19,270	79	..
HIGH-INCOME INDUSTRIAL MARKET ECONOMIES			
Spain	4,290	77	44
Italy	6,520	67	52
United Kingdom	8,460	92	55
France	9,540	73	34
Australia	10,830	86	68
Germany, Fed. Rep. of	10,940	86	45
Japan	11,300	76	42
Canada	13,680	77	32
United States	16,690	74	77

Source: World Bank, *World Development Report 1987.* New York: Oxford University Press, 1987, Tables 1 and 33.

TABLE 2.3 Average per capita Income and Percent Urban for Countries grouped by Income.

	GNP PER CAPITA IN U. S. DOLLARS	PERCENT URBAN
Low-income countries (37)	270	22%
Lower-middle-income countries (23)	820	30%
Middle-income countries (13)	1,290	48%
Upper-middle-income countries	1,850	65%
High-income oil exporters (4)	9,800	73%
Industrial market economies	11,810	75%

Source: World Bank, *World Development Report 1987.* New York: Oxford University Press, 1987, Tables 1 and 33.

The growth of GNP and the increase in a country's urban population reflect, as Irwin and Gibbs and Martin suggest, a fundamental restructuring of a society. This is reflected in the figures in Table 2.4, which show the contributions of the three major sectors of an economy—agriculture, industry, and services—to a nation's gross development product (GDP). The findings are as predicted. As the per capita GNP increases, the importance of agriculture to a nation's economy declines, and the industrial and service sectors expand accordingly. As we have seen, industrialization, economic development, and urbanization work in concert to bring about a fundamental change in the way societies organize themselves to overcome the problems of survival. These three processes, however, are interrelated in convoluted and complex ways, and researchers are still trying to unravel the relationships.

URBANIZATION IN MORE DEVELOPED COUNTRIES

NORTH AMERICA

Unlike the United States, which has three cities—New York, Chicago, and Los Angeles—on the list of the world's 40 largest cities, Canada has none. Nor should one expect it to. Canada has only 25 million people, compared to the nearly 250 million people in its neighbor to the south. This is not to say that Canada is without large cities. Montreal, Toronto, and Vancouver all have metropolitan populations of over 1 million. Montreal is expected to grow to the 8–9 million range early in the next century. Canada is one of the largest nations in the world, but highly urban—77 percent of Canada's population live in urban places; approximately one-third of this number live in cities of over 500,000 inhabitants. Canada has also been able to achieve a high rate of industrial development, which provides its people with one of the highest per capita incomes in the world. By any measure, the quality of life in Canadian cities is superior to that found in cities in the United States (Simmons and Bourne, 1984).

The United States is not quite as urban as Canada—74 percent versus 77 percent—but three-fourths of this urban population is concentrated in large cities. The United States has eight of the world's 100 largest cities—New York, Los Angeles, Chicago, Philadelphia, Detroit, San Francisco, Boston, and Washington, D.C. The only states with less than 50 percent urban populations are Alaska, Mississippi, North Carolina, Virginia, North Dakota, South Carolina, South Dakota, Vermont, and West Virginia. The five most urbanized states are California, New Jersey, Rhode Island, New York, and Massachusetts. Of course, individual states vary in the number of large cities they contain.

Urbanization, industrialization, and the United States are synonymous. Unfortunately, America's urbanization is also associated with drugs, crime, congestion, unemployment, homelessness, and despair. Many studies have shown the quality of life

TABLE 2.4 Contribution of Major Economic Sections to Gross Development Product for Countries Grouped by GNP.

	AGRICULTURE	INDUSTRY	SERVICES
Low-income countries	32	33	35
Lower-middle-income countries	22	32	47
Middle-income countries	14	34	52
Upper-middle-income countries	10	35	54
Industrial market economies	3	36	61

Source: World Bank, *World Development Report 1987.* New York: Oxford University Press, 1987, Table 3.

in most American cities to have declined steadily since the 1960s as the role of the federal government has diminished. Since much of this book focuses on American cities, the discussion of these topics will be reserved for later chapters of this book.

EUROPE

Only four European countries—West Germany, the United Kingdom, Italy, and France—have populations of over 50 million. As late as 1950, four of the world's ten largest urban agglomerations—London, the Rhein–Ruhr, Paris, and Moscow—were found on this continent. By 1990, these cities were eclipsed by U.S. cities and by cities in the less developed world. In four decades, London dropped from second to seventeenth; the Rhine–Ruhr from third to eighteenth; Paris from sixth to fourteenth; and Moscow from ninth to twenty-third.

The urbanization patterns of Europe can be neatly divided by what was previously known as the iron curtain. Most of the countries in Western Europe (with the exception of Spain and Portugal) have urbanization levels equal to or higher than those of North America. The United Kingdom is 92 percent urban; France, 73 percent; West Germany, 86 percent; Sweden, 86 percent; the Netherlands, 88 percent; and Belgium, 96 percent. There is, however, great diversity in the settlement patterns found in these nations. In the United Kingdom over half of its urban population lives in large cities of over 500,000 inhabitants, but in Belgium, although 96 percent of its population is urban, only 24 percent live in large cities (see Table 2.5) (Carter, 1984; Dalmasso, 1984; Hall and Hay, 1980; Grimm, 1984).

In Eastern Europe, the level of urbanization is considerably lower. In Hungary only 55 percent of the population is urban; in Poland, 60 percent; in Yugoslavia, 45 percent; in Czechoslovakia, 66 percent; and in East Germany, 76 percent. Moreover, there are fewer large cities. In Hungary, only 37 percent of the urban population lives in places over 500,000 inhabitants; in Yugoslavia, 23 percent; in Czechoslovakia, 12 percent; and in East Germany, 17 percent. Planned, centrally controlled economies have prevented the agglomeration of economic activity in large cities and the population growth that follows. Most of these nations have pursued a national policy that disperses industrial activity and administrative functions across the entire country (Dziewonski et al., 1984; Grimm, 1984; Lappo and Pivovarov, 1984).

Although the two Germanies have been united for more than a year, they are still two very different societies. Germans are only now beginning to appreciate the human and economic costs of reuniting the two countries politically, socially, and economically. The old East–West division will continue to divide Germany into starkly different regions for generations to come because of their different urban patterns.

Former West Germany. Since the end of World War II, West Germany (the Federal Republic of Germany as of 1990) has experienced phenomenal growth. There is a strong relationship between the expansion of West German cities and national market forces. This relationship can be seen by the fact that almost seven out of ten homes in West Germany have been built since 1945, and there has been great industrial

TABLE 2.5 Urbanization Patterns in Europe.

WESTERN DEMOCRACIES	PERCENT URBAN	PERCENT URBAN IN LARGEST CITY	PERCENT IN CITIES OVER 500,000
Portugal	31	44	44
Spain	77	17	44
Ireland	57	48	48
Italy	67	17	52
Belgium	96	14	24
United Kingdom	92	20	55
Austria	56	39	39
Netherlands	88	9	24
France	73	23	34
Finland	60	27	27
Germany, Fed. Rep. of	86	18	45
Denmark	86	32	32
Sweden	86	15	35
Norway	73	18	62
Switzerland	60	22	22
FORMER EAST BLOC			
Hungary	55	37	37
Poland	60	15	47
Yugoslavia	45	10	23
Albania	34	25	0
Bulgaria	68	38	38
Czechoslovakia	66	12	12
Germany, Dem. Rep. of	76	9	17
USSR	66	4	33

Source: World Bank, *World Development Report 1987.* New York: Oxford University Press, 1987, Table 33.

development in the cities at the expense of rural development. The pursuit of an industrial market economy has meant a high rate of rural to urban migration especially to the job-rich industrial cities. Cities like Munich, West Berlin, Stuttgart, and Frankfort have grown rapidly since the war. Today, the Rhine–Ruhr is over 10 million; Hamburg, Stuttgart, and Rhine–Main over 2 million, and Hannover, Nuremberg, Munich, and Rhine–Necker over 1 million (see Figure 2.4) (Scholler et al., 1984).

Former East Germany. The urbanization of East Germany (formerly the Democratic Republic of Germany) has also advanced rapidly since the end of World War II. Much of this urbanization can be explained by "push factors," which drove unemployed rural inhabitants to the cities in the search for employment. This is in sharp contrast to the "pull factors" at work in West Germany, which precipitated rapid urban development.

The urban patterns in East Germany represent the attempt of the GDR to carry out a truly national program of development. Rather than allowing market forces to determine settlement patterns, planning principles have prevailed. There has been a concern for the specialization, cooperation, and integration of the nation's system of cities; stabilizing the

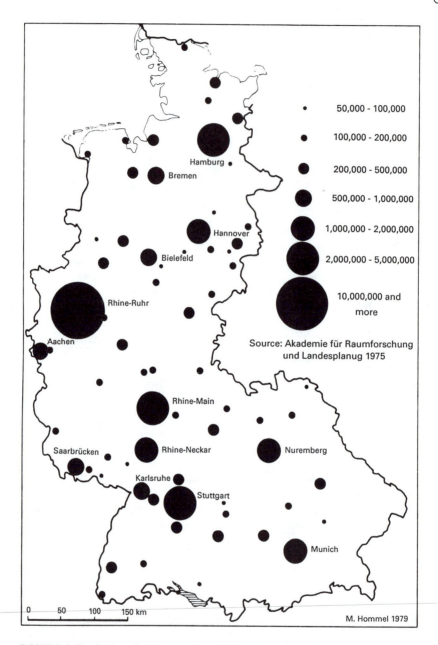

FIGURE 2.4 The Federal Republic of Germany: Metropolitan Areas by Population, 1970.

Source: Reproduced from *Urbanization and Settlement Systems* edited by L. S. Bourne, R. Sinclair, and K. Dziewonski, © International Geographical Union 1984, by permission of Oxford University Press.

urban network and the rank-size relationships between cities and towns; increasing the development and industrialization of the backward rural regions in the north and east of

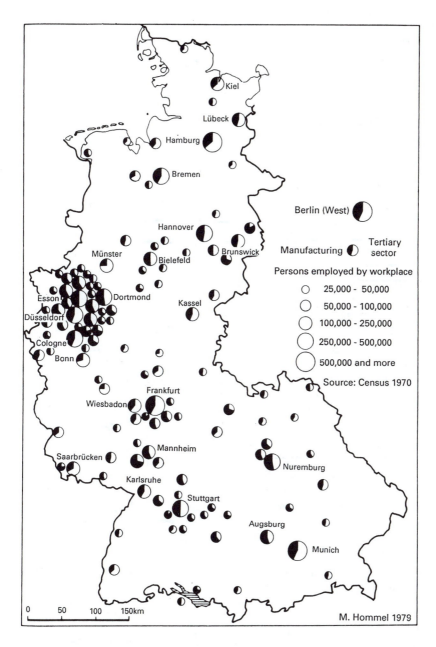

FIGURE 2.5 The Federal Republic of Germany: Classification of Urban Settlements in the GDR According to Their Importance to Their Hinterlands.

Source: Reproduced from *Urbanization and Settlement Systems* edited by L. S. Bourne, R. Sinclair, and K. Dziewonski, © International Geographical Union 1984, by permission of Oxford University Press.

the country; slowing the growth of population in agglomerated regions; strengthening the role of political administrative centers and their districts; and transforming rural settlement systems through the restructuring of agriculture. If one compares the maps of what was formerly East and West Germany (Figure 2.4 and 2.5), one sees a more even distribution of urban places with a clear functional and administrative structure in East Germany. When one considers the recent economic and political problems faced by all East Bloc nations, one wonders how well this comprehensive development strategy has worked (Grimm, 1984).

JAPAN

Of all the countries outside the West, Japan most closely resembles western nations in the level of economic development and urbanization. In 1987 its per capita GNP was sixth in the world at $11,300, but its gross development product was second only to the United States at over $1.3 trillion. The U.S. GDP was over $3.9 trillion (World Bank, 1987). Japan is also one of the most urbanized nations in the world, with more than 77 percent of its population living in urban places. A disproportionate share of this population lives in large cities—44 percent of its urban population reside in cities of over 500,000 inhabitants. In 1990, the Tokyo–Yokohama urban agglomeration was the largest in the world, with a population of 23.4 million people (World Bank, 1987).

The study of urbanization in Japan has been difficult because of the ambiguities associated with the definition of the term *city*, changes in this definition, and in the methods used to compile census data on urban population. Prior to the 1950s, the census used the term *shi*, translated "city" to define urban populations, but "shi" refers to an urban administrative district, which is usually much larger than the actual city. The Japanese Bureau of the Census recognized these problems and adopted for the 1960 census an urban delimitation called "densely inhabited district (DID) that corresponds well to real urbanized areas (Yamaguchi, 1984).

As with other Asian cities, Japanese cities have a history that stretches back to the middle ages. There were four types of cities which have their origins during this feudal period. These are castle towns, post towns, temple and shrine towns, and free ports and markets. The castle and post towns were the most numerous, and over the centuries they were intentionally evolved into political-commercial as well as cultural central places. In the massive urbanization that occurred in the seventeenth century, much of this growth was concentrated around these castle towns. By 1700, one of the more important of these castle towns, Edo, had grown to nearly one million inhabitants—one of the largest cities in n the world. During the same period Osaka and Kyoto had populations over 300,000. By the beginning of the nineteenth century, Japan was already one of the most urbanized nations in the world, with more than 10 percent of its population living in cities of 10,000 or more (Black, 1975).

In the first half of this century, the six metropolises of Tokyo, Osaka, Kyoto, Nagoya, Kobe, and Yokohama formed the social, economic, and political backbone of Japanese society. Although these cities were destroyed during World War II, they emerged in the post-world war period as the major urban foci of urban growth. Today, most of Japan's population is concentrated in a 100-kilometer-wide by 500-kilometer-long corridor running from Fukuoka in the south to Tokyo in the north (see Figure 2.6). Although we are bombarded with the economic miracle of Japan, Japanese cities face serious problems of overcrowding, pollution, and crime. Rapid industrial and urban expansion has not kept pace with the demand by city dwellers for adequate transportation, sewerage, and other services. An antiquated land tenure system linked to the powerful farm lobby has kept land prices artificially high and housing prices out of the reach of many Japanese families. Consequently, the cost of living in Japanese cities is the highest in the world and the quality of life of its urbanites is below that of many countries in the West (Yamaguchi, 1984).

SOVIET UNION[6]

Urbanization in the Soviet Union is ancient, some cities have histories that stretch back to the first centuries of the Christian era. As early as 1550, European Russia had 160 cities. By 1708, this number had more than doubled to 336. Like Japan, much of this growth was centered on palace/castle settlements, and the functions of most of these cities were ceremonial or religious. Under Peter the Great, commercial links were opened to the West, and many Russian cities began to take on a commercial character.

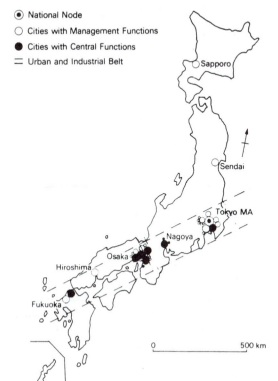

FIGURE 2.6 Specialized Cities in Japan's Urban-Industrial Core.

Source: Reproduced from *Urbanization and Settlement Systems* edited by L. S. Bourne, R. Sinclair, and K. Dziewonski, © International Geographical Union 1984, by permission of Oxford University Press.

Even with this growth in commerce, Russia remained a peasant society. In 1800, Russia was only 4 percent urban; in 1860, 10 percent. These percentages were comparable to most of the world, but lagged far behind the burgeoning commercial-industrial nations of Western Europe. One reason was the feudal character of Russian society. The growth of a strong, prosperous middle class spearheaded development in Western Europe; this group was slow to develop under the strictures of Tsarist Russia. Without the skills of this class, Tsarist Russia was relegated to a peripheral role in European development—condemned to the role of a supplier of raw materials rather than a producer of finished goods (Black, 1975).

In 1861, Tsar Alexander II abolished serfdom, freeing millions of peasants. The restructuring of Russian agriculture that followed set up a massive rural to urban migration. The size and scope of this migration is reflected in the growth of cities. In 1859 there were 619 cities; by 1910, 2681, a 333 percent increase. In 1863, 10 percent of Russia's population was urban; by 1897 it had grown to 12.9 percent; on the eve of the revolution, to 18 percent. Overnight old cities were transformed into industrial metropolises, and the pace and scope of urbanization overwhelmed the government's capacity to cope. More than one author has argued that the success of the Bolshevik revolution was due, in part, to the deplorable conditions found in the cities of Tsarist Russia (Murvar, 1967; Roland, 1976).

When the Bolsheviks took power in 1917, Russia resembled a less developed country. The cities held more people than jobs, and the majority of the population lived in slums similar to the ones found in much of the less developed world today. Japan turned outward for development. Soviet Russia turned inward. In order to avoid entanglements with Western capitalist nations, the Soviet Union withdrew from international trade and developed the natural resources of their nation, which spanned an entire subcontinent. This catch-up strategy was done at enormous human cost—forced collectivization of Soviet agriculture, the murder of millions by Stalin, and the use of slave labor subsidized the rapid industrialization and urbanization of this nation. Much of this development was focused on the interior region east of the Ural Mountains. This legacy continues to shape the course of Soviet urban development (Black, 1975).

The Soviet Union today is a nation of contradictions, it is once both a more and a less developed nation. In the areas of military science and space exploration it is a world leader; in agriculture, manufacturing, and high technology it has more in common with LDCs than with more developed nations. Recently these contradictions have forced basic change in the political and economic organization of this nation as reflected in the two words "perestroika" and "Glasnost"—restructuring and openness.

The Soviet Union is the largest nation in the world, spanning an entire subcontinent and ten time zones. The territory of the USSR has a diversity of natural, historic, demographic, and national conditions which has profoundly influenced development. Geographically, the Soviet Union has five major zones of settlements: the extreme north, the middle and economically active region, the desert, the piedmont; and the mountains. Overlaid is the political geography of the nation: a federation of 15 republics, each having its own economic and cultural development. As a centrally planned society, much of the nation's political and economic activities are centered in the capitals of the republics. It is also an ethnically diverse nation with more than 100 recognized ethnic groups, each with its own language and customs (Lappo and Pivovarov, 1984).

Because of the size of the country and the enormous distances that must be spanned, large cities and powerful lines of transportation have been built and provide the framework within which most urban development takes place. Figure 2.7 shows the major tendencies in development in the USSR. Note the line of settlement (the dark line), which corresponds with the route of the Trans-Siberian Railroad. Planned cities are used as spearheads for the development in the interior (dashed line). Note also that the most urbanized region remains to the west along the border with the Soviet Union's East Bloc neighbors.

Table 2.6 summarizes the major demographic and geographical regions of the Soviet Union. In 1987, 66 percent of the Soviet Union's total population lived in urban places and roughly a third of this number in cities with more than 500,000 inhabitants. These data show that there is major regional variation in these settlement patterns. The Baltic republics, the Urals, the Ukraine, and the Volga River valley exhibit a level of urbanization comparable to the rest of Europe. Siberia and the Asian republics more resemble their Asian counterparts (Lappo and Pivovarov, 1984).

SUMMARY

This chapter explores a number of issues associated with the process of urbanization. For the purposes of this text, urbanization is considered to be the process of population concentration. Measuring this process has proven to be quite difficult.

More than thirty different definitions are used in the world to define a population concentration as urban. The most widely used criterion is population size, followed by legal and government criteria. In making international comparisons, the degree of urbanization frequently is considered simply the percentage of a country's population living in urban areas, according to that country's own definition of urban. This approach presents numerous problems, so most international comparisons use the percentages of each country's population in cities of 100,000 or more inhabitants. In our study of urbanization in the United States, however, we have used the definitions employed by the U.S. Bureau of the Census.

Most of the chapter explores the relationship between urbanization and the processes of economic development, modernization, and industrialization. For the purposes of this text, economic development and modernization were used synonymously and defined as a society's increased output and the social and cultural changes that occur in the development process. Economic development is, therefore, a complex process that leads to fundamental modification of the fabric of society; urban centers are the places where this change takes place. Throughout this text, a distinction is made between more developed and less developed countries of the world. These

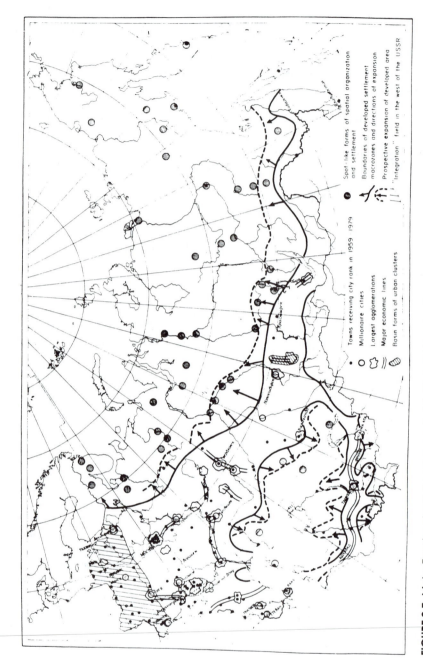

FIGURE 2.7 Major Tendencies in Development of Settlement in the USSR.

Source: Reproduced from *Urbanization and Settlement Systems* edited by L. S. Bourne, R. Sinclair, and K. Dziewonski. © International Geographical Union 1984, by permission of Oxford University Press.

TABLE 2.6 Demo-geographical Regions of the USSR

REGIONS	AREA		POPULATION IN 1979		POPULATION DENSITY 1979 (PERSONS/KM²)	
	THOUSANDS OF KM²	%	THOUSANDS	%	TOTAL	RURAL
Baltic	275.0	1.2	14,299	5.4	52.0	12.0
Byelorussian	207.6	0.9	9,559	3.6	46.0	20.7
European North	1320.6	5.9	4,286	1.6	3.3	0.8
Northern old agricultural	437.2	2.0	5,348	2.0	12.2	4.7
Central	435.5	2.0	29,584	11.3	67.9	13.8
Southern old agricultural	232.0	1.0	10,051	3.8	43.3	20.3
Volga-Kama	258.3	1.2	10,689	4.1	41.4	17.3
Lower Volga	387.9	1.7	9,336	3.6	24.1	6.7
North Ukraine	183.6	0.8	12,508	4.8	68.1	30.8
Southwestern Ukraine and Moldavia	126.3	0.6	10,350	3.9	82.0	48.9
West Ukraine	70.4	0.3	7,123	2.7	101.2	58.6
Black Sea	113.4	0.5	7,134	2.7	62.9	23.7
Southern mining	244.5	1.1	20,671	7.9	84.5	17.6
Urals	710.9	3.2	16,842	6.4	23.7	6.5
West Siberian	1132.2	5.1	13,140	5.0	11.6	3.9
Middle Siberian	1539.8	6.9	5,518	2.1	3.6	1.0
South-Siberian	1045.9	4.7	2,572	1.0	2.4	1.1
Far Eastern	1441.3	6.5	5,136	2.0	3.6	0.9
Asian North	7677.7	34.5	2,650	1.0	0.4	0.1
North Caucasian	254.3	1.2	11,406	4.4	44.9	22.5
Transcaucasian	186.1	0.8	14,075	5.4	75.6	33.8
North Kazakhstan	489.0	2.2	3,740	1.4	7.7	3.9
Central Kazakhstan	738.8	3.3	2,537	1.0	3.4	0.9
West Kazakhstan	728.5	3.3	1,832	0.7	2.5	1.2
East Kazakhstan	395.4	1.8	2,311	0.9	5.8	2.9
South Kazakhstan	365.6	1.6	4,265	1.6	11.7	5.9
Soviet Central Asian	1277.1	5.7	25,480	9.7	20.0	11.8
USSR	22274.9	100.0	262,442	100.0	11.8	4.4

TABLE 2.6 (cont.) Demo-geographical Regions of the USSR

REGIONS	URBAN POPULATION IN THE REGIONAL TOTAL (%)			POPULATION OF CITIES IN URBAN TOTAL (%)			POPULATION DYNAMICS (1979 AS PERCENTAGE OF 1959)		
	1959	1979	ABSOLUTE CHANGE	1959	1979	ABSOLUTE CHANGE	TOTAL	URBAN	RURAL
Baltic	65	77	12	67	71	4	127.9	151.8	84.1
Byelorussian	43	55	12	38	60	22	118.7	212.1	77.1
European North	63	77	14	30	45	15	129.8	157.9	82.0
Northern old agricultural	36	61	25	27	49	22	92.1	159.4	55.1
Central	63	80	17	60	65	5	113.6	144.0	62.2
Southern old agricultural	27	53	26	49	57	8	99.1	193.1	63.7
Volga-Kama	35	58	23	46	65	19	111.8	187.3	71.7
Lower Volga	55	72	17	61	72	11	130.4	169.7	81.4
North Ukraine	34	55	21	37	56	19	114.4	186.6	77.9
Southwestern Ukraine and Moldavia	22	40	18	23	44	21	110.6	205.3	84.3
West Ukraine	29	42	13	29	39	10	119.0	174.4	96.7
Black Sea	49	63	14	57	57	0	140.6	181.9	101.5
Southern mining	71	79	8	54	62	8	123.7	138.7	87.6
Urals	61	73	12	48	59	11	110.9	132.8	77.0
West Siberian	50	67	17	67	69	2	110.4	146.5	74.0
Middle Siberian	54	72	18	43	56	13	124.6	167.4	74.7
South-Siberian	45	56	11	38	42	4	126.2	157.6	100.4
Far Eastern	69	75	6	33	50	17	132.0	144.4	104.2
Asian North	59	73	14	15	46	31	205.1	252.2	136.5
North Caucasian	37	50	13	40	52	12	137.6	185.8	109.4
Transcaucasian	46	55	9	58	64	6	148.1	178.7	122.1
North Kazakhstan	32	49	17	15	60	45	142.5	216.7	107.2
Central Kazakhstan	65	73	8	40	51	11	172.2	192.5	133.4
West Kazakhstan	42	52	10	–	63	63	171.2	212.7	141.2
East Kazakhstan	45	50	5	39	48	9	133.1	148.6	120.4
South Kazakhstan	43	50	7	70	71	1	178.4	206.3	157.5
Soviet Central Asian	35	41	6	44	56	12	186.2	217.2	169.7
USSR	48	62	14	51	60	9	125.7	163.6	90.8

Source: This table was compiled on the basis of the data from: *Naselenie SSSR (USSR Population). Po dannym Vsesoiuznoi perepisi naselenia 1979 goda.* M.. Politizdat, 1980; *Naselenie SSSR (USSR Population). 1973,* M.. 'Statistika', 1975; *Narodnoie khoziaistvo SSSR v 1978 (National economy of the USSR in 1978).* M.. 'Statistika', 1979. Data on absolute movement of population are absent in the table, since the above sources give their relative values only (as per 1000 persons). This prevents us from recalculating them for larger regions.

terms are used in preference to others because they reflect the shifting relationships among nations of the world.

The last section of this chapter describes the urbanization patterns found in the more developed countries of the world—Canada and the United States in North America, Eastern and Western Europe, USSR, and Japan. These nations share industrial-based economies, high rates of urbanization, and high per capita incomes by international standards. Canada, the United States, Western Europe, and Japan have industrial market economies, the highest per capita GNPs in the world, and the highest level of urbanization. The centrally planned economies of the East Bloc and the USSR have lower levels of urbanization because of national development strategies that have prevented the operation of agglomeration economies of scale. Industries have been dispersed across nations, and across the urban hierarchy. Centrally planned economies have also meant lower productivity and lower per capita GNP. The democratic reforms combined with emerging market economies now occurring in these nations may fundamentally alter the urbanization process in these societies.

NOTES

1. For a detailed discussion of problems of urban definitions, see *Growth of the World's Urban and Rural Population, 1920–2000* (United Nations publication, E.69.XIII.3, pp. 7–10; *Manual VIII. Methods for Projections of Urban and Rural Population* (United Nations E.74.XIII.3, pp. 9–13); and *Patterns of Urban and Rural Population Growth* (United Nations ST/ESA/SER.A/68).

2. The geographic concepts used by the United States Bureau of the Census employ complicated criteria. For those interested, I suggest "Geographic Concepts and Codes" in U.S. Bureau of the Census, *State and Metropolitan Area Data Book, 1986*. Washington, D.C.: U.S. Government Printing Office, 1986, pp. 625–632.

3. The United States Census was one of the first modern censuses, beginning in 1790. Today it is considered one of the best in the world. The United States Constitution originally required the federal government to take a census every ten years in order to reapportion the seats in the House of Representatives. Today, census figures are widely used by business and industry to determine the future locations of factories, stores, and other facilities. In addition, government at all levels utilizes the census in formulating land use plans, public policy, and the administration of federal programs. The census is also a major tool of social scientists. Urban sociologists and ecologists depend on these public data for their research. The definitions used and the accuracy of the census are therefore of vital interest to many spheres of society.

The importance of these data to the country is reflected in the cost of the national census. The cost of the 1990 census will be more than five dollars for every man, woman, and child in the United States, or nearly 1.5 billion dollars.

4. If an MSA's largest city has less than 50,000 population, the area must have a total population of at least 100,000.

5. For more information about TIGER products, I suggest phoning your state census office for more details; a convenient 800 number is available. For a simple nontechnical description of the TIGER files, see the Bureau of the Census's *Tiger Tales: A Presentation of the Automated Geographic Support System for the 1990 Census,* available free from the census bureau. For a more

detailed technical description, review the article by Robert W. Marx, "The Tiger System: Automating the Geographic Structure of the United States Census," *Government Publication Review* 13 (1986), pp. 181–201. For a description of the products available through the TIGER system, see Robert A. LaMacchia, Silla G. Tomasi, and Sheldon K. Piepenburg, "The Tiger File Proposed Products," available from the census bureau.

6. The Soviet Union ceased to exist on September 5, 1991. What government emerges in its wake is anyone's guess. As an author with a book ready to go to the printer, I'm in a dilemma. Do I rewrite this section to reflect the changes in the former Soviet Union as of today, or do I let what I've written stand. My guess is that regardless of what I write, civil war, another coup, or some other event will overshadow a new section anyway. But sociology tells us that the past constrains the present and shapes the future. The past 74 years of centrally planned Communist rule over the urban patterns of the Soviet's 15 republics will shape urban patterns for generations to come. Thus, my presentation of urban patterns is, and will continue to be, relevant for many years to come. Please accept my caveat in the following section.

URBANIZATION IN THE LESS DEVELOPED WORLD

INTRODUCTION

Reading the paper, listening to the evening newscast, or scanning the covers of *Time* or *Newsweek*, we are assaulted with the world's problems. Death and misery come in many guises—famine in Ethiopia, civil war in Somalia, typhoons in India, earthquakes in Russia, floods in Bangladesh, squatters in the Philippines, and the homeless in Central America. Through the miracle of modern communication, the sights and sounds of these horrific events can be brought into our homes along with a sanitized background report on the proximate cause of the disaster—a two-year drought, a massive earthquake, a force five typhoon, battling religious factions. Seldom do the sources of our daily news explore the causes of these problems. The trail of events that led to the disasters often appears beyond the scope of human understanding or solution. There is one thread that ties all these events together, however: world population growth. But when was the last time you were told you are living through the most significant demographic event in history? When were you last reminded that the world's population will grow from 2.5 billion people in 1940 to over 6 billion in the year 2000 (Repetto, 1987)? When were you reminded that these demographic changes bedevil us today but loom over our future?

Demographic change cuts across societies, but population problems are becoming increasingly urban problems. In 1950, 275 million people were living in cities in the developing world—38 percent of the world's total urban population. By 1975, the world's urban population reached 1.6 billion, with more than half of this number living in the metropolitan areas of the developing world. By the year 2000,

65

2.2 billion of the world's 3.3 billion urban dwellers (66 percent) will live in the cities of the developing world. In the 25 years from 1975 to 2000, the cities of the developing world will have to accommodate nearly 1.3 billion new inhabitants. More often than not, these numbers are moving to the world's largest cities. In 1950, only one city in the developing world had more than five million inhabitants. By the end of this century, some forty cities are expected to be this size. In today's world, population problems have become synonymous with urban problems (Todaro, 1984, Table 1, p. 10).

Urbanization cannot be studied in isolation. It is not only related to population change, but it is also linked to processes of economic development and modernization. The purpose of this chapter is to explore the urbanization process in the developing world. The chapter focuses on the three major facets of the urbanization process: demographic, economic, and social/cultural change. First, global population and urban patterns are presented and the underlying demographic patterns are discussed. Fertility, mortality, and migration patterns are explored, the theory of demographic transition is presented, and the impact of these changes on cities is assessed.

Second, issues surrounding economic development are presented. The relationship among the more and less developed countries of the world is discussed, along with the relationship between the cities and their rural hinterlands. Primacy, the phenomenon in which the population of a country's largest city outstrips that of all others, is explored. The formal and informal economies found in these cities are discussed.

Urbanization and economic development change the way people organize and live their lives. A third section explores the revolutionary changes in society's norms, values, and roles which accompany the development process. The contrasts between the old and the new values and the formal and informal economies of these societies are explored in the context of the spontaneous settlements found in the cities of the developing world. Special attention is given to spontaneous settlements and the role they play in the development process.

The chapter ends with a discussion of the major theories that are used to explain the world patterns of urbanization, economic development, and modernization.

WORLD POPULATION GROWTH

I was born in 1947. In that year, the earth's population was a mere 2.5 billion people. By the time I reached 30, the earth's population had nearly doubled to 5 billion. On my fiftieth birthday, near the year 2000, the world's population will exceed 6 billion (Repetto, 1987). In the course of my lifetime, one of the greatest events in the planet's history will occur: the domination of the earth by a single species, homo sapiens. This domination has had disastrous consequences for the earth's ecosystem. Population pressure has led to the extinction of thousands of species, the destruction of the ozone layer, global warming, the destruction of the world's rain forests, decertification, widespread famine, and a host of other ills. The media identify chemicals like chlorofluorocarbons, atmospheric CO_2, and acid rain as the culprits, but in reality the increase in these chemicals in our atmosphere is linked to the unprecedented growth of human population.

Population growth does not take place in a vacuum, but within societies. A useful tool in the analysis of population trends is to group nations by their levels of economic development. More developed countries (MDCs) have very different population characteristics than less developed countries (LDCs). MDCs include the United States, Canada, the nations of Europe, the Soviet Union, Japan, New Zealand, and Australia. Transitional nations include the Republic of China (Taiwan), South Korea, and Singapore. The remaining nations of the world are considered LDCs. This distinction between more and less developed is used in the following analysis of population trends.

LEVEL OF DEVELOPMENT AND POPULATION GROWTH

How is population growth related to a nation's level of economic development? Figure 3.1 shows the contributions of the more and less developed regions to world population growth. Until 1900, the population growth of MDCs equaled or exceeded LDCs. This pattern began to change in the 1930s, and by the end of World War II enormous differences existed in the growth rates of the two regions.

Today, the less developed countries of the world contain approximately three-quarters of the world's five billion people. Since the end of World War II, these nations have grown from two to three percent per year. On average, their populations double in size every 27 years. Contrast this pattern with the experiences of more developed countries. Most MDCs grew no more than one to one and one-half percent a year during their period of most rapid population increase in the nineteenth century. Today, their growth rates are below one percent and their populations double, on average, every 111 years (Repetto, 1987, pp. 1–9).

Why the differences in the growth rates of MDCs and LDCs? The population growth of LDCs in the postwar period can be attributed to one factor—the importation of death control technology from MDCs. DDT and other insecticides, first introduced 40 years ago in the tropical regions of the world, have controlled one of the great scourges of humankind—malaria. Universal smallpox vaccination, improved water supplies, childhood immunization programs, and other public health measures have dramatically lowered mortality rates in LDCs (Boserup, 1981; Taeuber, 1962).

This decline in death rates in LDCs, however, has not been offset by a decline in birth rates. The gap between these two vital events has lead to rapid population growth. The most optimistic projections predict a world of over six billion people by the year 2000; five billion of these people will live in the less developed countries of the world. Nations like India will grow from 835 million to 1 billion; Brazil, from 147 million to 180 million in the last decade of this century (Population Reference Bureau, 1989).

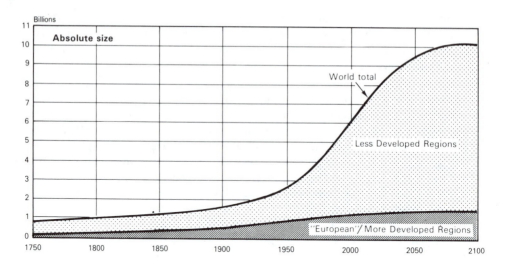

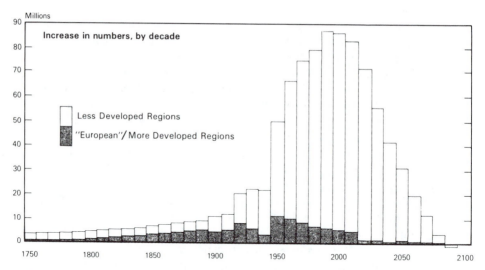

FIGURE 3.1 World, developing and developed regions, population growth: 1750–2100.

Source: Thomas W. Merrick, with PRB staff, "World Population in Transition," *Population Bulletin* 41, No. 2 (April 1986): Figure 1, p. 4.

THEORY OF DEMOGRAPHIC TRANSITION

A number of competing theories describe these demographic processes, but by far the most important is the theory of demographic transition introduced by Kingsley Davis nearly 50 years ago (Davis, 1945).[1] The theory of demographic transition posits that there is a close relationship among economic development, modernization, and demographic processes. As societies move from less developed to more developed—from traditional to modern—conditions are created encouraging low fertility. The theory suggests that people in modern societies have fewer children because they no longer want large families. One reason is that mortality has been greatly reduced, especially the deaths of infants and children. Couples no longer need to have large families to ensure that several will reach adulthood. Other changes in modern societies, including mandatory education and child labor laws, have greatly diminished the economic value of children. Children no longer are economic assets but economic burdens. Therefore, fertility patterns follow mortality patterns. Mortality usually declines first, and, then, after several generations, fertility declines to a level close but never as low as mortality (Davis, 1945, 1963).

STAGE 1

The transition process is graphically depicted in Figure 3.2. In Stage 1, one finds traditional societies with high and stable rates of fertility and high and unstable rates of mortality (Famine and epidemics periodically kill thousands.). Since the rates are both high, they tend to balance each other out, and the size of the population remains stable. These societies have high growth potential because any improvement in the food supply or death control technology can lead to a rapid increase in population.

The vital events in Stage 1 societies profoundly influence all aspects of life—their institutions, values, norms, and roles. Life is short; life expectancies range between 25 and 40, and as a result these societies use ascribed status to fill key positions. Orphans and widows are common, so these societies have extended families; only in this way can society be assured that children will be cared for if their parents die. The values, norms, and roles of the extended family ensure high fertility. Women in these societies have few options to the roles of mother and homemaker, and the social pressure to have children is intense. It is not a question of if a wife will bear children, but of how many children she will bear (Goldscheider, 1971).

STAGE 2

Stage 2 is a phase of transitional growth. The industrialization that accompanies economic development improves the quality of life. Improved diets, cheaper and more abundant clothing, fuel, and shelter, as well as public health measures lead to dramatic declines in death rates. Figure 3.3 provides the birth and death rates for Mexico from 1895 to 1985. Note the decline of mortality from 40 per thousand in 1920 to 7.1 per thousand in 1985, but also note the high and stable birth rate, which only begins to dip in 1976. The difference is natural increase on an unprecedented scale. The explanation for this lag is that institutions change slowly. The values and norms of an extended family continue to encourage high fertility, but as parents learn most of their children will survive to adulthood, as the nuclear family becomes the dominant family form, and as women find alternatives to the role of mother and homemaker, birth rates decline. Most LDCs are in this transition stage, and they are experiencing unprecedented rates of natural increase.

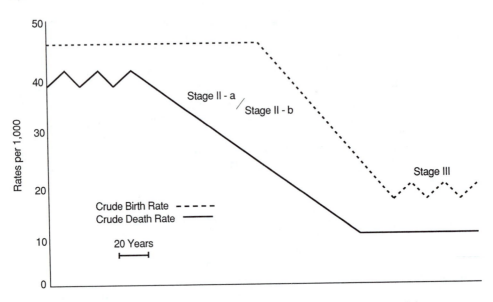

FIGURE 3.2 Graphic representation of the classical demographic transition model.

FIGURE 3.3 Birth and death rates: Mexico, 1895–1976.

Sources: Francisco Alba, *La poblacion de Mexico: evolucion y dilemas* (Mexico, D.F.: El Colegio de Mexico, 1977), Table 3.2. Mexican National Fertility Survey, 1976, advance data supplied by World Fertility Survey, London, and director of the Mexican survey. United Nations Statistical Office. *Population and Vital Statistics Report*, Statistical Papers, Series A, various issues. Thomas W. Merrick, *Population Pressures in Latin America* (Washington, D.C.: Population Reference Bureau, Inc., 1986), Table 2, p. 8.

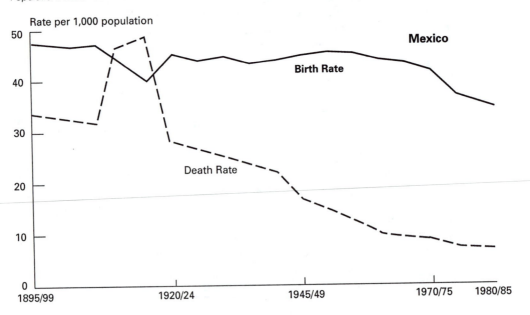

STAGE 3

In Stage 3 societies have low and stable death rates and low but unstable birth rates. (Remember the post-World War II baby boom and the much-touted baby bust.) The result: populations are stable in size or change slowly. Life expectancies are long, over 70 years, which permit new social patterns. Achievement rather than ascription is used by society to fill key positions. The extended family is supplanted by the nuclear form. Women have alternatives to the roles of mother and homemaker, and the values and norms of the nuclear family encourage smaller families. Therefore, the values, norms, institutions, and other patterns in society are intertwined with its vital events (Goldscheider, 1971).

The theory of demographic transition has been tested and refined over the past 50 years. In general, the theory reasonably describes the course of vital events in most industrialized nations, but it has never been able to predict levels of fertility and mortality or the timing of these events. This is because the theory is based on the experiences of societies that have already experienced the transition—more developed countries. The conditions under which MDCs developed in the nineteenth and early twentieth centuries are very different from those that LDCs face today. Few MDCs had birth rates as high as those of LDCs, nor were their levels of mortality as high. And, as we have already noted, mortality decline in MDCs was the result of economic development created through innovation and invention from within, not through technology introduced from outside the society (Boserup, 1981; Goldscheider, 1971).

Importing technology rather than creating the technology internally suggests that the demographic transition in LDCs will differ from MDCs. The United Nations reports that public health measures in LDCs have reduced mortality to a minimum, and in the future these efforts will have little impact on population growth. Therefore, any attempt to bring about significant reductions in the rate of population growth in these countries must focus on changing fertility.

The problem is that death control can be applied without the knowledge of the individual through public health; birth control requires the participation of individuals. In the past, fertility decline was correlated with the development process. As development proceeded, there were fundamental changes in the underlying fertility and mortality patterns of a society. In the Western world this was true; in the developing world, the relationship is not as clear-cut. The improvement in birth control technology over the past 40 years has lowered its cost and simplified its distribution. The result: the fertility rate in LDCs has declined faster than economic development. Whereas in England it took 100 years to reach low rates of fertility, in some LDCs the same transition is being compressed into a single generation. Although there is hope for future trends in world population growth, a major gap still exists between birth and death rates (Birdsall, 1980).

When one examines the demographic data for the world's LDCs, one finds enormous differences within and between countries. In Latin America, infant mortality for women with no education is five times higher than for women with eight years of education (Merrick, 1986). Therefore, one must not only understand the general demographic patterns shared by LDCs, but, in addition, appreciate the variation in vital events within the nations we refer to as less developed.

EFFECTS OF RAPID POPULATION GROWTH

The economic growth experienced by European nations during the nineteenth and early twentieth centuries was associated with the first sustained population growth in history. Population growth then was viewed as good, because more people meant larger markets for newly burgeoning industries. The population that could not be absorbed in cities emigrated to the sparsely populated regions of the world—North and South America, Australia, and New Zealand. Growth rates were moderate by today's standards, seldom exceeding one percent, and the process was gradual, spanning a century (Tilly, 1974).

The situation is different today. Growth rates in LDCs run between two and three percent per year; populations double in less than 30 years. Rapidly growing populations distort the age structure of a society, and one finds in LDCs a disproportionate share of a society's population in the young, unproductive age categories. Consequently, less developed countries face enormous service burdens. Children require schools, hospitals, housing, food, clothing, and other services, but they are not old enough to work and make contributions to the nation's economy. More seriously, LDCs cannot export their surplus populations; there are no virgin, undeveloped territories left in the world. In addition, LDCs must compete in a world dominated by the advanced economies of the more developed nations. Thus, at a time when LDCs must expand their technology, improve their infrastructure of roads, communications, and public facilities, and modernize their agriculture to compete in world markets, they are saddled with enormous service costs to a young, unproductive population (Birdsall, 1980; Stockwell and Laidlaw, 1981).

Research shows that high population growth slows economic growth and exacerbates the inequality between more and less developed nations in at least two ways. First, an increase in population means an increase in the numbers of workers. More workers mean that on the average each worker produces less per worker in relationship to the land and other resources available in the society. Second, as the number of children per worker increases, there are fewer savings to go into industry and technology to increase productivity. Resources go to schools, health care, and food instead of roads, electrical systems, factories, and other parts of the capital stock necessary for competition in world markets. Thus, many of the problems faced by LDCs are linked to their underlying vital events (Birdsall, 1980; Stockwell and Laidlaw, 1981).

WORLD URBAN GROWTH

In the last half of the twentieth century, the world's population problems have become the world's urban problems. Underemployment and unemployment, poor public services, inadequate housing, nonexistent medical care, and poor nutrition are now concentrated in their most visible and pernicious forms in the cities of the world. In LDCs, population growth on the national level is unprecedented; urban growth is astounding. In 1950, 275 million people—38 percent of the world's urban population—were living in the cities of the less developed world. By 1975, the world's urban population had reached 1.6 billion, and more than half these numbers were living in the cities of LDCs. By the year 2000, in less than a decade, the world's urban population will exceed 2.1 billion and 66 percent of this population will be in the cities of the developing world. Therefore, between 1975 and 2000, a span of just 25 years, the cities in LDCs must absorb 1.3 billion people—a task that would strain the managerial talent of any nation, much less an LDC (Todaro, 1984, Table 1, p. 10). Figure 3.4 shows these population trends for the more and less developed regions of the world.

Contrast this with the urbanization experience of MDCs. In the nineteenth and early twentieth centuries, during their period of rapid urbanization, population growth was relatively low, incomes were high, rural to urban migration was manageable, and the diffusion of innovations was slow by today's standards. The process was painful, but the adaptation of our political, economic, and social institutions was carried out over the span of a century. Urbanization in LDCs will be different. First, the rate of natural increase and the magnitude of rural to urban migration are much higher than in the past.

Second, in the nineteenth century, rural to urban migration reduced the population pressure on agricultural land in MDCs. In LDCs, high rates of natural increase in both urban and rural areas have kept the ratio of population to arable land high.

Third, unlike MDCs, innovation and technology in LDCs is imported and it diffuses rapidly throughout the society. Imported communication technology informs farmers and villagers of the opportunities in cities, and imported transportation technology lowers the cost of migration to these centers.

Fourth, in MDCs when rural to urban migration threatened to overwhelm the absorption capacity of cities, there was a safety valve—emigration. North and South America and the far-flung colonies of the European empires provided virgin territory for settlement. Today, international migration is closed, and in LDCs cities, not colonies, have taken on the role of absorbing surplus rural population.

Therefore, the urbanization in LDCs will be both qualitatively and quantitatively different from MDCs. These societies will be forced to absorb more people in less time than any societies in history. Experiences will vary from country to country, but, in general, the vast majority of this urban population will be poor with few skills, and LDCs will be saddled with two problems—absorbing this growing population and carrying out economic development (Gilbert and Gugler, 1982).

CURRENT AND PROJECTED GROWTH

The above are general patterns. There is enormous variation between and within the world's regions. Table 3.1 provides estimated and projected urban populations for selected countries in the world's regions. Note that as late as 1950, 60 percent of the

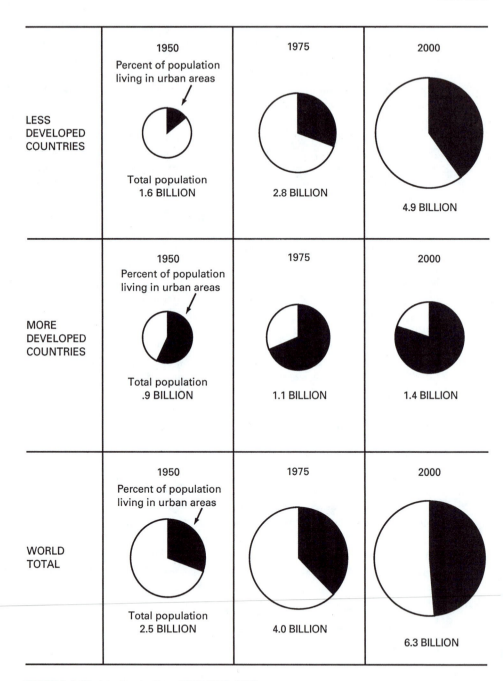

FIGURE 3.4 World urbanization: 1950, 1975, 2000.

Source: United Nations Population Division, "Trends and Prospects in Urban and Rural Population in 1973–74," ESA/P/WP 54 (New York: United Nations, April 25, 1975), Table C, medium variant.

TABLE 3.1 Size of Urban Population in Major World Regions and Selected Countries, 1950–2000 (in thousands)

	1950	1960	1970	1975	1980	1990	2000
WORLD TOTAL	724,147	1,012,084	1,354,357	1,560,860	1,806,809	2,422,293	3,208,028
Developed regions	448,929	572,730	702,876	767,302	834,401	969,226	1,092,470
Developing regions	275,218	439,354	651,481	793,558	972,408	1,453,067	2,115,558
Africa	31,818	49,506	80,373	103,032	132,951	219,202	345,757
Algeria	1,948	3,287	6,529	9,024	12,065	19,714	28,021
Egypt	6,532	9,818	14,080	16,346	19,119	26,604	37,048
Ethiopia	761	1,284	2,315	3,273	4,562	8,555	15,140
Ghana	727	1,575	2,511	3,193	4,104	6,830	10,843
Kenya	336	597	1,145	1,592	2,223	4,314	8,125
Morocco	2,345	3,412	5,236	6,551	8,265	13,126	19,704
Nigeria	3,595	5,642	9,009	11,449	14,811	25,665	45,041
Senegal	563	704	930	1,070	1,265	1,896	3,002
South Africa	5,261	7,424	102,281	11,934	14,154	20,417	30,109
Sudan	572	1,212	2,571	3,722	5,305	10,014	16,551
Zambia	428	742	1,290	1,704	2,235	3,802	6,260
Latin America	67,511	106,559	162,355	198,366	240,592	343,304	466,234
Argentina	11,205	15,172	18,616	20,436	22,300	25,818	28,875
Brazil	19,064	32,996	53,253	66,621	82,172	119,271	163,027
Chile	3,558	5,145	7,048	8,044	9,116	11,390	13,460
Colombia	4,334	7,665	13,209	16,946	21,212	31,102	41,779
Ecuador	911	1,490	2,384	2,971	3,707	5,735	8,564
Guatemala	921	1,317	1,889	2,269	2,763	4,193	6,384
Mexico	11,348	18,458	29,706	37,318	46,660	71,069	102,293
Nicaragua	397	609	930	1,163	1,457	2,256	3,396
Paraguay	474	631	853	1,003	1,205	1,800	2,708
Peru	2,811	4,265	7,605	9,619	11,942	17,498	24,132
Venezuela	2,739	5,084	8,048	9,795	11,776	16,364	21,125

TABLE 3.1 (Continued) Size of Urban Population in Major World Regions and Selected Countries, 1950–2000 (in thousands)

	1950	1960	1970	1975	1980	1990	2000
Asia	175,618	283,026	407,646	490,570	596,609	885,544	1,297,719
Bangladesh	1,786	2,649	5,150	6,838	9,531	18,192	32,095
India	59,247	76,575	106,994	127,177	154,524	235,837	360,688
Indonesia	9,362	13,522	20,395	25,079	31,293	49,477	76,612
Iran	4,087	7,249	11,601	14,959	19,209	30,162	43,138
Iraq	1,819	2,937	5,461	7,272	9,414	14,525	20,366
Nepal	183	285	440	550	708	1,245	2,275
Philippines	5,695	8,350	12,387	15,244	18,902	29,198	43,988
South Korea	4,347	6,843	12,766	16,682	20,921	29,915	37,807
Sri Lanka	1,106	1,772	2,736	3,359	4,108	6,090	8,660
Syria	1,071	1,677	2,708	3,393	4,290	6,776	10,105
Turkey	4,441	8,181	13,536	17,106	21,482	32,684	45,482

Source: United Nations, Population Division, Department of Economic and Social Affairs, *Estimates and Projections of Urban, Rural and City Populations, 1950–2025: The 1980 Assessment.* New York: United Nations, 1982.

world's urban population lived in MDCs. By 1975, however, the world's 1.6 billion urban population was equally divided between more and less developed countries. Thus, between 1950 and 1975, the urban population of LDCs grew 189 percent, from 275 million to 794 million. Africa grew 222 percent, from 32 to 103 million; Latin America, 191 percent, from 68 to 198 million; and Asia, 163 percent, from 218 to 574 million.

Between 1975 and the year 2000, urban populations in MDCs are projected to grow by 42 percent or 325 million, while the cities in LDCs are expected to grow by 166 percent, or 1.3 billion people. Some regions will grow faster than others. African cities are expected to expand by 236 percent, an additional 242 million inhabitants; Latin America, by 135 percent, an additional 268 million inhabitants; and Asia, by 146 percent, an additional 838 million inhabitants.[2]

Table 3.2 provides another view of this urbanization process—annual growth rates. Annual growth of the world's urban population has not fluctuated a great deal since 1960 and is not predicted to change much before the turn of the century, but this summary measure masks the enormous variations in growth rates in the world's regions. The growth of urban populations in MDCs will drop by half between 1950 and 2000 to 1.2 percent. The rate for LDCs will decline but not as rapidly. There is regional variation. Africa's urban growth peaked in the late 1970s at 5.1 percent per year (the highest ever recorded), and it is projected to remain high and decline to only 4.6 percent by the end of the century. Rates in Asia and Latin America, in contrast, peaked around 4.6 percent a year in the late 1950s and early 1960s, but are projected to decline to 2.9 percent by the of the century.

Where do these people come from? A society's urban population comes from three sources: reclassification (a town's population grows large enough to be considered an urban place by the nation's census), migration, and natural increase (births exceeding deaths). United Nations data suggest that most urban growth in LDCs comes from the high fertility of urban residents. In 1988, only 39 percent of urban growth in LDCs was attributable to rural-to-urban migration and reclassification; 61 percent came from natural increase. In MDCs the pattern is reversed; 58 percent of urban growth is due to urban migration and reclassification, and only 42 percent from natural increase (Todaro, 1984). These percentages are correct, but misleading, because they ignore the selective nature of migration. The characteristics of migrants whether in more or less developed nations are similar—young, better educated, and more skilled than those who do not migrate. The selective nature of migration is important, because those who move are in their prime reproductive years. Therefore, the unprecedented growth of cities in LDCs is attributable to both the high rate of rural-to-urban migration, and the high fertility of these new migrants to the city (Goldscheider, 1971).

MIGRATION

Two questions remain: Why do people migrate to the city when conditions there are often so deplorable? What cities are they likely to choose? The answer to the first is simple: People relocate because it is rational for them to do so. Just as in this country,

TABLE 3.2 Annual Growth Rates for Selected Countries

URBAN AREA	1950	AVERAGE ANNUAL GROWTH RATE	1975	AVERAGE ANNUAL GROWTH RATE	2000
Developing Countries					
Type 1		(Percent)		(Percent)	
Mexico City	2.9	5.4	10.9	4.4	31.6
Buenos Aires	4.5	2.9	9.3	1.6	14.0
Sao Paulo	2.5	5.7	10.0	3.9	26.0
Rio de Janeiro	2.9	4.4	8.3	3.5	19.4
Bogota	0.7	6.5	3.4	4.2	9.5
Type 2					
Cairo	2.4	4.3	6.9	3.5	16.4
Seoul	1.0	8.3	7.3	3.8	18.7
Manila	1.5	4.4	4.4	4.3	12.7
Type 3					
Kinshasa	0.2	9.7	2.0	6.2	9.1
Lagos	0.3	8.1	2.1	6.2	9.4
Type 4					
Shanghai	5.8	2.6	10.9	2.3	19.2
Peking	2.2	5.6	8.5	3.3	19.1
Jakarta	1.6	5.1	5.6	4.5	16.9
Calcutta	4.4	2.4	8.1	3.6	19.7
Bombay	2.9	3.7	7.1	4.0	19.1
Karachi	1.0	6.2	4.5	5.2	15.9
Developed Countries					
New York	12.3	1.3	17.0	1.3	22.2
London	10.2	0.2	10.7	0.7	12.7
Paris	5.4	2.1	9.2	1.2	12.3
Tokyo	6.7	3.9	17.3	1.7	26.1

Source: George J. Beier, "Can Third World Nations Cope?" *Population Bulletin,* Vol. 31, No. 4, 1976, Table 2 reproduced by permission Population Reference Bureau.

migrants move from low-wage to high-wage areas of a nation. The young are in a strategic point in the life cycle to recoup the cost of migration, and research shows that migrants seem to be better off, on average, than those who stay in the countryside.

The answer to the second question is that migrants usually choose the largest city in the region. Transportation networks are usually keyed on the largest city of a nation, with the result that transportation costs to the primate city are low. Second, migration does not occur randomly but along clearly defined migration streams. Kin and neighbors from the old village are usually found in neighborhoods within the large city and can aid the migrant in her or his transition to urban life. This network helps the migrant find employment, housing, and financial support. In general, when a primate city has reached 20 percent of the nation's total population, everyone will have at least one relative in the capital city (Gilbert and Gugler, 1982).

A TYPOLOGY OF URBANIZATION PATTERNS IN LDCS

I have been making generalizations about urban patterns throughout this chapter. As I have already noted, there are enormous differences in the demographic patterns among the major regions of the world, and there are also enormous variations within a region. One way to study the urbanization of LDCs is to ignore region and identify similar underlying demographic patterns. Four patterns of urbanization in the LDCs can be identified, and the characteristics of a sample of countries of each type is presented in Table 3.3.

Type 1. This group includes countries like Argentina, Mexico, Colombia, and Brazil, where the urbanization process is well under way. The population is already half urban, incomes are high by international standards, and there are abundant natural resources for their populations. It is projected that urban growth will stop in these countries by the end of the century, when 75 percent of their populations will be urban. By then, rural areas will be experiencing absolute declines in population.

Most Type 1 societies are in Latin America. They have been undergoing industrialization and economic development for most of this century, and these processes have encouraged rural-to-urban migration. These societies are characterized by enormous inequality in both the cities and the countryside. The benefits from development, especially in the area of public services, is directed to middle- and upper-income families. As a result, one finds massive numbers of poorly housed, poorly educated, and poorly serviced people in both rural and urban areas (Beier, 1984).

Type 2. This group includes the nations of East Asia and North Africa—Algeria, Egypt, Korea, and the Philippines. In these societies urbanization is more recent, and today over half of the population is urban. Incomes are low by international standards, but these countries have been successful in creating employment and raising incomes. Urban services are improving but still below those found in MDCs. In general, these nations have few natural resources, and their success in the future depends on careful population control (Beier, 1984).

Type 3. These countries include the sub-Saharan nations of Senegal, Ivory Coast, Nigeria, Sudan, Kenya, and others. They are predominantly rural but urbanizing at a tremendous rate—between 4 and 5 percent a year. Even at this rate, these societies still will be rural in the year 2000 because of high birth rates in their rural populations. It is unlikely that per capita income will rise in these societies as population growth outstrips agricultural, oil, and other natural resources (Beier, 1984).

Type 4. India, the Peoples Republic of China, and Pakistan dominate this group of countries. These nations are predominantly rural, subsistence-level societies. They are experiencing severe pressures on their land and other natural resources. Although their cities are growing at high rates, general population growth is also high, so in the year 2000 half their populations will still be rural, living in absolute poverty. Although these nations will continue to have massive rural populations, urbanization is occurring on an unprecedented scale. India, for example, will absorb 210 million people in its cities and

TABLE 3.3 Urbanization Patterns in a Sample of Less Developed Countries

COUNTRY	PER CAPITA GNP LEVEL (IN 1972 U.S.$)	SIZE OF POPULATION (IN MILLIONS) 1975 URBAN	1975 RURAL	2000 URBAN	2000 RURAL	PERCENTAGE OF POPULATION URBAN 1975	2000	COMPOUND GROWTH RATE (URBAN) 1970–1975	1990–2000	COMPOUND GROWTH RATE (RURAL) 1970–1975	1990–2000
Type 1											
Argentina	1290	20.3	5.1	29.3	3.6	80.0	89.2	2.0	1.2	-1.1	-1.6
Mexico	750	37.4	21.8	103.6	28.7	63.2	78.3	4.6	3.8	1.3	0.9
Colombia	400	16.0	9.9	40.4	11.1	61.8	78.4	4.8	3.2	0.9	0.2
Brazil	530	65.2	44.5	162.2	50.3	59.5	76.3	4.5	3.3	0.9	0.3
Type 2											
Algeria	430	8.4	8.4	26.0	10.7	49.9	70.8	5.7	3.9	1.0	0.7
Egypt	240	17.9	19.6	41.5	23.1	47.7	64.3	3.9	3.1	1.2	0.4
Korea	310	16.1	17.9	36.0	16.0	45.9	67.0	4.8	2.5	-0.1	-0.6
Philippines	220	16.0	28.5	45.6	47.1	36.0	50.9	4.8	3.9	2.7	1.2
Malaysia	430	3.6	8.4	9.9	12.1	30.2	45.1	4.7	3.5	2.2	0.8
Type 3											
Senegal	260	1.3	3.2	3.5	4.7	28.4	42.7	4.1	4.1	1.8	1.4
Ivory Coast	340	1.0	3.9	3.7	5.9	20.4	38.7	6.5	4.8	1.7	1.6
Nigeria	130	11.4	51.5	40.9	94.0	18.2	30.3	5.0	5.2	2.2	2.4
Sudan	120	2.4	15.9	8.9	30.0	13.2	22.9	5.5	5.1	3.0	2.9
Kenya	170	1.5	11.8	6.4	24.6	11.3	20.7	6.1	5.8	3.0	2.9
Upper Volta	70	0.5	5.6	1.7	9.2	8.3	15.7	5.2	4.9	2.1	2.0
Type 4											
Pakistan	130	19.0	51.6	62.3	84.6	26.9	42.4	5.3	4.4	2.4	1.5
India	110	131.7	481.4	342.1	717.2	21.5	32.3	3.7	3.7	2.1	1.2
Indonesia	90	26.2	109.8	74.7	162.8	19.3	31.4	4.7	3.9	2.2	1.2
China, People's Republic of	170	196.9	641.9	414.1	733.8	23.5	36.1	3.3	2.9	1.2	-0.4

Source: United Nations Population Division, Department of Economic and Social Affairs, *Urban and Rural Projections from 1950 to 2000.* New York, 1982. Table reproduced from Beier, Table 2.

236 million people in its countryside between 1975 and 2000. China, in contrast, has been able to stabilize its overall population growth, has controlled rural to urban migration, has increased per capita income, and has reduced inequality. China is still a poor country, but its few resources are more equitably distributed to its billion-plus population. One measure of its success is that average life expectancy in China now approaches those of most MDCs (Beier, 1984).

This typology is a convenient tool for grouping the urbanization patterns of the world's LDCs. What they do not show is the patterns of urbanization found in these societies. If one were to make one generalization, the populations of societies around the world—MDCs and LDCs—are increasingly being accommodated by large cities—cities that dwarf all others in the country (see Figure 3.5). This urbanization pattern is known as *primacy.*

THE QUESTION OF PRIMACY

The post-World War II period has experienced the explosive growth of cities in the LDCs of the world. Already large at the end of the war, they have experienced explosive growth in the 40 years that have followed. Mexico City, with just 2.9 million inhabitants in 1950, is expected to grow to 31.6 million by the end of the century. Sao Paulo, 2.1 million in 1950, will not be far behind, with 29 million in that same year. In 1950 there were only 90 cities in LDCs with populations over one million; by the year 2000 there will be 300 (Beier, 1984).

This rapid growth of cities in the less developed world demonstrates a second trend—the continued concentration of population in the largest cities in the more and less developed world. If we define urban as cities of more than 100,000 inhabitants, the pervasive trend has been the growth in population in cities of over 1 million. Between 1950 and 2000, the proportion of those living in these large urban centers will grow from 38 to 65 percent in the cities of LDCs. Most of this population will be absorbed in cities of over 5 million. In 1975 million-plus cities already contained 13 percent of the world's population; by century's end this figure will be much higher. Moreover, most of this population growth will be concentrated in already existing cities (Beier, 1984).

The growth of one large city at the expense of other cities is called primacy. The terms *primacy* and *primate city* were introduced by Mark Jefferson in 1930; they refer to one large city that dominates all other cities in a country and through time "draws away from all of them in character as well as size" (Jefferson, 1939, p. 227). Primacy is measured simply by comparing the population of the largest city with that of the second largest city.

PRIMACY'S RELATIONSHIP TO DEVELOPMENT

The nature of primate cities and their relationships to economic development has been studied by historians, geographers, ecologists, and demographers for the past 50 years. Many of these researchers believe that primate cities in developing nations are "parasitic" and hold back economic development. Why parasitic? Many of the world's

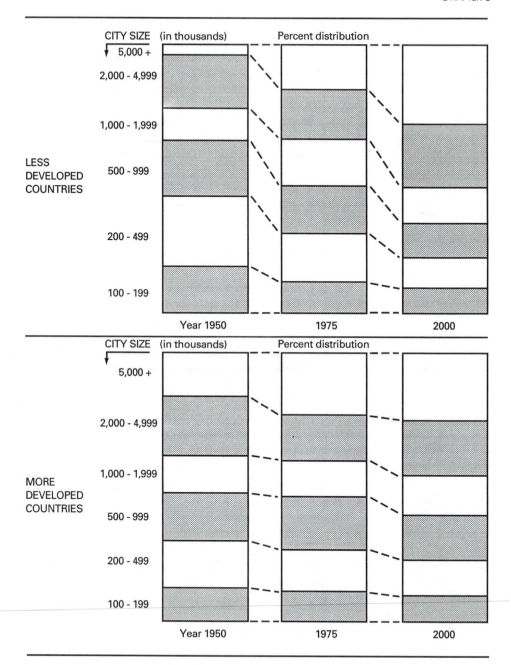

FIGURE 3.5 Distribution of population in cities over 100,000 in 1970: 1950, 1975, 2000.

Source: United Nations Population Division, "Trends and Prospects in the Populations of Urban Agglomerations, 1950–2000 as Assessed in 1973–1975." ESA/P/WP 58 (New York: United Nations. November 21, 1975), Table C.

primate cities are in countries that have economies based on agriculture rather than industry. Traditional agriculture differs from industry because it does not produce large profits that can be reinvested in other areas of the economy for development. Cities are expensive to build and maintain; they also tax the limited financial resources of these nations. In other words, money that might have gone into industry, tractors, mining, or irrigation projects is spent on the support of a large urban place (Graves and Sexton, 1979; Gugler, 1982).

Another aspect of primate cities exacerbates this problem—the primate city's power to attract migrants. Large numbers of the rural population, especially the young, are drawn to the city by the prospect of jobs and other opportunities. Although some find jobs, most remain unemployed or underemployed, continuing the drain on the nation's resources. The term *overurbanized* refers to those nations whose urban population is too large in relation to the level of economic development (Davis and Golden, 1954; Sovani, 1964). The cost of providing food and shelter for this nonproductive population also detracts from economic growth.

Lowering the rate of economic development, however, is not the only consequence of high primacy. Uneven economic development occurs as a government makes large investments in the primate city while ignoring the needs of the other regions of the country. This large investment in the primate city encourages industrial and commercial activities to locate there. Through time, a vicious cycle develops; industrial growth means more jobs, but new jobs also increase the attractiveness of the primate city to new migrants from other parts of the country. This population movement detracts from the growth that might occur in other cities, and economic development in other regions of the country stagnates.

Primacy also has political ramifications. Many primate cities are national capitals and become governmental, educational, and religious, as well as industrial centers. The concentration of a nation's political, business, and religious elites in one city leads to major social and political division within a country. The primate city becomes the center of wealth and power, and the countryside becomes the habitat of the poor and powerless.

Thailand is one example of a country that has a small percentage of its population in urban places, but a disproportionate number of urban dwellers in a single primate city. In 1990, 19.0 percent of Thailand's population was living in urban places, but a disproportionate number of these inhabitants were living in one city, the capital and its twin city, Bangkok–Thomburi. Bangkok–Thomburi had a population of almost 5 million in 1990, but the second largest city, Chiengmai, had a population a little more than 100,000. Thailand's primacy index was 51: The nation's largest city was 51 times larger than the second largest one. The rapid urbanization of Thailand and its capital is occurring faster than the rate of change in its economic and social institutions, leading to what some consider overurbanization.

Sociologists call the uneven rate of change in various elements of a society *cultural lag*. William F. Ogburn introduced the concept in 1922 and summarized it as follows:

> The thesis is that the various parts of modern cultures are not changing at the same rate, some parts are changing much more rapidly than others; and that since there is a correlation and interdependence of parts, a rapid change in one part of a culture requires readjustments through other changes in various correlated parts of culture (Ogburn, 1922, p. 200).

The problems of primacy and overurbanization are good illustrations of the concept. Medical technology has been introduced into LDCs, but it has not been accompanied by comparable institutions for handling the ensuing population growth. Vast numbers of peasants have been pushed off their land through the introduction of high-yield grains and other farm technology. This new technology requires a higher capitalization per acre, and fewer farmers are needed to produce more food. Traditional handcrafts and indigenous industries are unable to absorb the surplus population, and nearby villages, towns, and small cities offer few jobs opportunities. With nowhere else to go, the surplus rural population migrates to the city, where institutions of government often find it impossible to provide basic city services. The city is only one part in the larger encompassing society, and change in one part of this system will inevitably have an impact on the city. The urbanization patterns of Thailand and its massive urban problem are not an isolated phenomenon but one shared by many developing nations.

AN ALTERNATIVE VIEW: PRIMACY A SOLUTION

There is an alternative view. If LDCs are going to develop, they must shift population from rural/agriculture to urban/industrial employment. If LDCs are going to industrialize, they must compete in a world market, and if they are going to compete in a world market, they must take on the financing, marketing, and management patterns that the world economic community demands. In many cases, LDCs have no choice. Large multinational corporations dictate industrial development. The World Bank, the International Monetary Fund, and the General Agreement on Tariffs and Trade frame the economic relationships among nations, and they are all controlled by more developed countries. Thus, MDCs set the rules and control the playing field. But LDCs are just that: less developed. They have not yet developed the transportation, communication, finance, marketing, management, and the host of other corporate services that international corporations demand. More importantly, their educational systems have not produced the managers, bankers, accountants, computer experts, and other specialists necessary to support a modern industrial society. Since there are so few skilled people, the only way that these societies can provide the manpower necessary for modern enterprises is to concentrate millions of people in one primate city. Additionally, only in the primate cities of LDCs does one find the transportation, communication, and other corporate services upon which these operations depend. Finally, there are agglomeration economies. The location of a large industry in a primate city attracts a constellation of other enterprises—suppliers, utilities, banks, and corporate service firms. The presence of these firms creates an environment favorable for additional growth: Growth feeds growth (Gilbert and Gugler, 1982).

Many researchers feel that the social, economic, and political costs of this process are unacceptably high, and therefore, LDCs must pursue alternative policies of rural and urban development. The idea is simply that if opportunities were available in other parts of a country, rural migration could be directed there instead of the primate city (Rondinelli, 1983).

However, migration is an efficient way to reallocate the human capital of a society. All societies need to know the best location for new industry, jobs, and housing. In some cases, it may be a second city in another region of a nation; in others, rural areas; in still others, the primate city. The question is who can best make this decision.

Locational decisions are individual decisions: individuals responding to the perceived economic and social situation in their present community versus others. If the information given citizens accurately reflects the true costs of a move, then people will make rational decisions, and the population redistribution will be cost effective for the society. This is seldom the case, because there is a very important public policy overlay that distorts this process. We are all aware of the growth of the Sunbelt in the United States. Millions of Americans have migrated from Snowbelt states to the South and West. Few Americans are aware of the massive federal subsidy that made this migration possible—the subsidy hidden in military budgets and in an implicit industrial policy buried in the tax code (Rondinelli, 1983; Gugler, 1982).

In general, public policy in LDCs favors primate cities over smaller cities and rural areas. Public services are usually better in primate cities. Industrial protection policies, price controls on agriculture products, and national budgets usually favor cities. Taken as a whole, they motivate rural residents to migrate to the city.

Large cities, therefore, exist because they provide an environment conducive to industrial production. There are certain agglomeration economies of scale for industries locating in cities: the clustering of suppliers and customers, as well as access to a wide range of corporate services—financing, legal services, advertising, and the like. Substantial savings on transportation, communication, and training further reinforce the tendency for these cities to grow.

There are also disadvantages. As the size of city grows above a certain size, transportation, land, and service costs increase. Size increases the distance between place of residence and place of work, and the time and cost of transportation increases. Increased size and population increases congestion, pollution, and a host of other costs for consumers. Cities grow as rapidly as they do because people are rational, and cities usually have higher incomes and opportunities not found in the small towns or the rural hinterlands.

INTERNAL STRUCTURE OF THE CITY

The timing, scope, and magnitude of urbanization vary from region to region, and we have explored this process by grouping nations by their levels of economic development—more and less developed—and by the magnitude of their vital events—Types 1–4. We however, have said nothing about the internal structure of cities in LDCs. How are these cities organized? Where are business and industry located? Where do the people live? Are these cities organized in the same way as the ones in MDCs? The answers to these questions are complex. Just as in the case of the urbanization process, enormous variation is found in the urban patterns in the major regions of the world. There are, however, underlying similarities in the physical form of these cities, because cities reflect the characteristics of their societies and are, therefore, shaped by similar social, economic, and ecological forces.

The physical form of the city can be described along two dimensions. There is the physical dimension—the streets, buildings, neighborhoods, and commercial, industrial, and political areas of the city—and there is also an organizational dimension—the family, ethnic, class, and associational groups found there. A complex interrelationship exists between the social structure and the physical reality of the city. In general, social change that takes place on the societal level is manifested first and most clearly in the use of space within cities. One can tell a great deal about a society by exploring the characteristics of its cities.

THE PREMODERN CITY

Large cities are not new to the less developed world; they originated there. Only since the sixteenth century have European cities gained prominence. Before that time, the world's major cities were in LDCs, and some of these cities reached remarkable size and organization. Many were ancient religious and political centers, including cities like Bangkok, Mecca, Mandalay, and Kabul. Others developed after the sixteenth century and were established by European empires. Outposts like Capetown, Bombay, Calcutta, Hong Kong, Singapore, and many Latin American cities played a crucial role in the exploitation of these societies by the colonial powers (Abu-Lughod and Hay, 1977). The empires of France, Great Britain, Germany, and other colonial powers were dismantled after World War II, and their colonies were replaced by self-conscious nation-states, but one still finds remnants of these much older cities at the core of many of the largest cities in the less developed world.

There are four distinct patterns associated with the premodern city. First, these cities were compact and densely settled. Houses were packed together along an irrational street pattern. They were pedestrian cities. Since everything had to be within walking distance, the spatial patterns of these cities were constrained by the transportation technology. Transportation still constrains cities in LDCs because per capita income is so low that automobile and mass transportation is beyond the reach of the average city dweller (Abu-Lughod and Hay, 1979; Sjoberg, 1960).

Second, people were segregated into precincts based on tribe, caste, or ties to a rural village. Even today in India caste plays an important role in determining the residential structure of the city. In Africa, the tribe plays a similar role.

Third, there is the absence of specialized areas of the city based on function. Premodern cities had ceremonial centers and quarters that housed the elite, but the rest of the city was a hodgepodge of homes, shops, and industry.

Finally, these cities had an inverse distance–status gradient: The wealthy lived near the city's center and the poor at its periphery.

In general, the premodern city can be characterized as dense, compact, and residentially segregated on the basis of tribe, caste, or village. There is little functional specialization of land use and an inverse status gradient with the wealthy living at the city's center and the poor at the periphery. This pattern characterizes all societies where the transportation technology is poorly developed. This was the case in the nineteenth- and early twentieth-century American city, and this pattern is found in the cities of the less developed world in the twentieth century (Sjoberg, 1960; Abu-Lughod and Hay, 1977).

THE MODERN CITY

Improved transportation and communication technology permits an entirely different type of spatial organization in the modern city. Population densities decline, and residential segregation is based on social class, family type, and ethnicity. Specialized subareas emerge according to economic function; areas of the city are specialized in industry, education, banking and finance, and government activities. There is also a direct distance–status gradient—the poor live near the city's center, the wealthy at the periphery.

Although societies around the world differ in history and culture, research suggests that as development proceeds, the spatial patterns of cities move from the premodern to modern form. Primate cities are the first to take on the modern spatial form because they are the portals for change. Over time these innovations to modern urban forms diffuse to other cities. Change does not occur smoothly. In most cities in the less developed world, one usually finds elements of both forms—areas of the city that look and feel like any city in the West, and vast areas of the city that have a premodern form. This is especially true of the spontaneous settlements found in the largest cities of most of the less developed world (Stockwell and Laidlaw, 1981; Gilbert and Gugler, 1982; Linn, 1983; Schwirian, 1974, Part V).

SPONTANEOUS SETTLEMENTS

Housing is the most visible problem facing less developed countries in their struggle to develop and modernize. Sprawling shanty towns, slums, and squatter areas are permanent features of most large cities in the less developed world. In primate cities, one finds square mile after square mile of dilapidated structures patched together from scraps of cardboard, corrugated iron, and discarded wood. In general, these areas lack even the most basic services—safe drinking water, sanitation, and drainage. Electricity, schools, clinics, and police protection are unimaginable. Any Westerner passing through a squatter settlement would agree that something needs to be done. But what is the appropriate way to attack the urban housing problem in the developing world? How can the housing and service needs of over a billion new urbanites be accommodated in a single generation? What are the alternatives to spontaneous settlements when the average incomes of most of the people in the world is less than $3000?

Shanty towns are not the only type of housing found in the cities in LDCs. There are spacious suburbs, luxurious high-rises, and large and prosperous working-class neighborhoods, but spontaneous settlements are the primary housing for the poor. Most owners, squatters, and renters in the less developed world live in homes and neighborhoods that started out as spontaneous or unplanned settlements. LDCs are not the only places where one finds spontaneous settlements. We all too quickly forget our own less prosperous past and our shameful present. Hoovervilles graced the Mall in Washington, D.C. and other American cities during the Great Depression, and today this nation's 2.5 million homeless inhabit the streets, abandoned buildings, culverts, and overpasses, as well as spontaneous settlements in virtually every major American city. These settlements vary enormously in size and form, and it is difficult to generalize from one society to another. Moreover, the terms—squatter settlements, squatments, shanty towns, slums, and spontaneous settlements—are value laden and represent the biases of those who use such terms. The term "squatter settlement" is misleading because many of these structures are built on purchased land. "Shanty town" is inappropriate because many middle-class homes started out as shanties but have been upgraded into nice homes. "Spontaneous settlement" is misleading because many of these developments have been carefully planned by community leaders in cooperation with politicians. Even with these qualifications, I still prefer the term "spontaneous settlement" because it represents the innovation that the poor bring to their housing problems.

SPONTANEOUS SETTLEMENTS DEFINED

There are four basic types of spontaneous settlements: invasions, when structures are built without permission on another's land; pirate settlements, where the land is purchased but lacks planning permission; rental settlements, where the structure is built on rented land; and usufruct settlements, where the tribe, local government, or owner has given permission to build (Gilbert and Gugler, 1982, p. 89). Regardless of type, spontaneous settlements share two or more of the following characteristics: First, most dwellings have been built and are occupied by the original settlers. Second, the settlement was built on another's land or lacked planning permission. Third, the settlement was built without basic services and in many cases still lacks services. Fourth, the settlement is occupied by the poor. Fifth, there is usually an element of self-help: Much of the construction is carried out by the occupants, although some of the work is contracted out (Gilbert and Gugler, 1982, p. 89).

Table 3.4 gives a general idea of the scope of spontaneous settlements in the major regions of the world. Note that the incidence rate in cities in sub-Saharan Africa range from as high as 90 percent in Cameroon and Ethiopia to a low of 33 percent in cities in Kenya and Madagascar. In North Africa and the Middle East the rate ranges from as high as 70 percent in Casablanca to a low of 1.5 percent in Beirut. (This figure has changed with the onset of the civil war.) The cities in low-income Asian nations like India, Indonesia, and Pakistan have rates that range from 20 to 30 percent. Cities in Korea, the Philippines, and other middle-income Asian nations are in the 30 percent range. Cities in Latin America and the Caribbean display a wide range from as low as 13 percent in Porta

TABLE 3.4 Incidence of Slums and Squatter Areas in Selected Cities

REGION AND COUNTRY	CITY	SLUMS AND SQUATTER SETTLEMENTS AS PERCENTAGE OF CITY POPULATION	YEAR
Sub-Saharan Africa			
Cameroon	Douala	80	1970
	Yaounde	90	1970
Ethiopia	Addis Ababa	90	1968
Ghana	Accra	53	1968
Ivory Coast	Abidjan	60	1964
Kenya	Nairobi	33	1970
	Mombasa	66	1970
Liberia	Montovia	50	1970
Madagascar	Tananarive	33	1969
Malawi	Blantyre	56	1966
Nigeria	Ibadan	75	1971
Senegal	Dakar	60	1971
Somalia	Mogadishu	77	1967
Sudan	Port Sudan	55	1971
Tanzania	Dar es Salaam	50	1970
Togo	Lome	75	1970
Upper Volta	Ouagadougou	70	1966
Zaire	Kinshasa	60	1969
Zambia	Lusaka	48	1969
North Africa and Middle East			
Iraq	Baghdad	29	1965
Jordan	Amman	14	1971
Lebanon	Beirut	1.5	1970
Morocco	Casablanca	70	1971
	Rabat	60	1971
Turkey	Ankara	60	1970
	Istanbul	40	1970
	Izmir	65	1970
Low-income Asia			
Afghanistan	Kabul	21	1971
India	Calcutta	33	1971
	Bombay	25	1971
	Delhi	30	1971
	Madras	25	1971
	Baroda	19	1971
Indonesia	Jakarta	26	1972
	Bandung	27	1972
	Makassar	33	1972
Nepal	Katmandu	22	1961
Pakistan	Karachi	23	1970
Sri Lanka	Colombo	43	1968

TABLE 3.4 (Continued) Incidence of Slums and Squatter Areas in Selected Cities

REGION AND COUNTRY	CITY	SLUMS AND SQUATTER SETTLEMENTS AS PERCENTAGE OF CITY POPULATION	YEAR
Middle-income Asia			
Hong Kong	Hong Kong	16	1969
Korea	Seoul	30	1970
	Busan	31	1970
Malaysia	Kuala Lumpur	37	1971
Philippines	Manila	35	1972
Singapore	Singapore	15	1970
Latin America and the Caribbean			
Brazil	Rio de Janeiro	30	1970
	Belo Horizonte	14	1970
	Recife	50	1970
	Porto Alegre	13	1970
	Brasilia	41	1970
Chile	Santiago	25	1964
Colombia	Bogota	60	1969
	Cali	30	1969
	Buenaventura	80	1969
Ecuador	Guayaquil	49	1969
Guatemala	Guatemala City	30	1971
Honduras	Tegucigalpa	25	1970
Mexico	Mexico City	46	1970
Panama	Panama City	17	1970
Peru	Lima	40	1970
	Arequipa	40	1970
	Chimbote	67	1970
Venezuela	Caracas	40	1969
	Maracaibo	50	1969
	Barquisimeto	41	1969
	Ciudad Guayana	40	1969

Note: Definitions of "slums" and "squatter areas" vary from region to region and from city to city; therefore, these data only present the roughest of impressions of the housing problem in these cities.

Source: O.F. Grimes, "Urban Land and Public Policy: Social Appropriation of Betterment," World Bank Staff Working Paper No. 179, Washington, D.C., 1976.

Alegre, Brazil to as high as 80 percent in Buenaventura, Colombia. Half the people in the world's largest city, Mexico City, live in spontaneous settlements. Percentages mask the tremendous number of people who live in these areas. If we multiply these percentages by the populations of these nations, we are looking at hundreds of millions of people who are housed in vast unplanned areas of cities (Grimes, 1976).

Spontaneous settlements are significant and permanent features of most cities in LDCs. They represent the only way that developing nations can absorb the millions of new inhabitants of their cities. On the surface, they may appear to be squalid and pathological, but researchers have found complex social systems below the surface.

Within the boundaries of such settlements are support networks of family and kin; employment, education, and banking cooperatives based on the caste, tribe, or the village of the residents; mutual aid societies; schools; churches; retail and wholesale establishments; factories; and industries. In some countries a significant proportion of the nation's food supply comes from these settlements. For example, in Brazil over 50 percent of the pork production comes from spontaneous settlements (Skinner and Rodell, 1983; Turner, 1976).

LIFE CYCLE OF SPONTANEOUS SETTLEMENTS

Research in Latin America and the Caribbean also shows that spontaneous settlements follow a life cycle that sometimes results in middle-income housing. In the first stage, known as the *bridgehead*, recent migrants, renters, and the poor invade land that they do not own, or land that they own but have been denied planning permission; to build homes there is an element of illegality. There is strength in numbers, and the invasion is often highly organized by community leaders with the tacit permission of local politicians. The invaders are taking a calculated risk; they are betting that once settlement takes place, local officials will be unwilling or unable to evict them. In the bridgehead stage, the areas lack basic services, and the structures are usually shanties. As the area gains political strength, and a quasi-official identity, the area moves into the second stage—consolidation. Political clout means that local authorities can be pressured into supplying water, electricity, waste disposal, paved streets, schools, police, and clinics. With the threat of eviction removed, homeowners slowly replace the cardboard and scraps with more substantial materials. Slowly the spontaneous settlement moves into the final stage—an area with the characteristics and identity of an ordinary suburb (Gilbert and Gugler, 1982).[3]

WHY PEOPLE SETTLE THERE

Why do people choose spontaneous settlements? What would you rather be, a renter or an owner? Given the choice, would you rather slowly develop equity in a home or pay rent to a slumlord? People living in spontaneous settlements are as rational and as economically sophisticated as we are. The consolidation process has been found to be slow but consistent. When money is available, residents improve their dwellings. When times are hard, they do not have to worry about eviction and can use their money to buy food. When the prices of food, fuel, and clothing rise, the cost of housing remains the same. Therefore, in the best of circumstances, spontaneous settlements provide a cheap and flexible way to house the poor of the less developed world. In the worst of circumstances, crowding and a lack of basic services mean high infant mortality, chronic illnesses, and lowered life expectancies. The absence of schools, bus service, and employment diminishes life chances and perpetuates inequality, just as the slums in this nation diminish the life chances of our poor. The dilemma for the less developed world is that there is probably no other alternative to this pattern of urban development.

In the past 20 years there has been a dramatic change in policy on spontaneous settlements by governments in LDCs. In the past, spontaneous settlements were seen as a blight to be removed from the city as soon as possible. Borrowing planning principles from the MDCs, urban renewal removed spontaneous settlements and replaced them with showcase projects. As in the United States, these short-sighted plans, designed to help the poor, actually exacerbated their conditions.[4] In recent years, the World Bank and other international agencies have funded projects that harness the spontaneous settlement process. The Indonesian government with the help of the World Bank has pursued a program to provide spontaneous settlements with basic city services. As a result, 62 percent of households in Jakarta have basic city services. Currently 22 nations are experimenting with preemptive planning with funds from the World Bank. Undeveloped urban land is subdivided into small lots and provided with basic services. Lots are provided at little or no cost to the poor and building regulations are relaxed so that the slow consolidation process can occur (Linn, 1983, pp. 120–190; Rondinelli, 1983; Blair, 1984; Choguill, 1987).[5]

When one studies the social, economic, and physical characteristics of the major cities in less developed countries, one often finds two cities sharing the same site. In those cities that were once colonial outposts, one still finds the old European quarter: broad, tree-lined streets; Western-style homes; and spacious administrative centers and country clubs. These areas stand in sharp contrast to the native quarters developed with their own vernacular architecture and chaotic street plans. There are literally two worlds: one native and one European.

The nineteenth-century city continues to affect the present. The society's elites have replaced the colonialists, central business districts look like those in MDCs, middle- and upper-class citizens have taken over the high ground, and the poor are segregated in vast areas of the city—often spontaneous settlements.

These spatial divisions are reflected in political, economic, and social divisions as well. The local labor market usually has two sectors—one formal and one informal. The formal sector is modeled after those found in MDCs and employs well-educated middle- and upper-income people in industry, business, and government. These are usually high-paying jobs requiring high levels of skill; entry is restricted by educational level or family connections, and the activities are regulated and taxed by government. The informal sector, in contrast, employs the poor and very poor who have recently migrated to the city. They are employed in a variety of occupations ranging from native crafts, street vending, and shoeshining to small-scale retailing and manufacturing. These small-scale operations often are carried out in the household. People working in this sector are self-employed or family-employed and have low skill levels, and their enterprises are unrelated to and untaxed by government (Linn, 1983).

The social structures also differ. The prosperous areas often reflect the lifestyles and family form of the middle class found anywhere in the world: nuclear families, middle-class value systems, a concern for the education and experiences of children, and middle-class consumption norms. One often finds in the spontaneous settlements traditional lifestyles followed by the most recent migrants to the city. In some cases, the social structure of the village has been effectively transferred to the center of the city. Therefore, there are two physical realities, two economies, two social structures—two worlds—inhabiting the same city at the same time (Gilbert and Gugler 1982, pp. 116–133; Linn, 1983).

The physical and social realities of these two worlds have sobering implications for their respective inhabitants. Table 3.5 presents the characteristics of nonsquatter

TABLE 3.5 Characteristics of Nonsquatter and Squatter Urban Settlements in Manila, Philippines

PARAMETER	NONSQUATTER	SQUATTERS	NOTES ON SQUATTER SETTLEMENT
School dropouts before high school (percent)	20	35	
Hospital-bed-to-population ratio	1:300	1:4000	Squatter settlements surveyed are Tondo, Malabon, and Navotas (pop. 714,924)
Infant mortality rate (per 1000 live births)	76	210	Tondo and Navotas Port area (pop. 2100)
Birth rate (per 1000 pop.)	33	177	Tondo and Navotas Port area (pop. 2100)
Neonatal mortality rate (per 1000 live births)	40	105	Tondo and Navotas Port area (pop. 2100)
Tuberculosis rate (per 100,000 pop.)	800	7000	Greater Tondo area (pop. 0.4 million)
Gastroenteritis rate (per 100,000 pop.)	780	1352	Greater Tondo area (pop. 0.4 million)
Third-degree malnutrition (percent of population surveyed)[a]	3	9.6	Tondo area nutrition survey of 6000 households (Operation Timbang)
Second-degree malnutrition (percent of pop. surveyed)[a]	21	37.5	Tondo area nutrition survey of 6000 households (Operation Timbang)
Anemia (percent of pop. surveyed)	10	20	Tondo area nutrition survey of 6000 households (Operation Timbang)
Per capita energy intake (calories)	1700	1550	Tondo area nutrition survey of 6000 households (Operation Timbang)
Typhoid rate (per 100,000 pop.)	33	135	Tondo area
Diphtheria rate (per 100,000 pop.)	48	77	Tondo area
Measles rate (per 100,000 pop.)	130	160	Tondo area
Clinical signs of vitamin A deficiency (percent of pop. affected)	50	72	Cebu City

[a] Malnutrition is defined according to the standard weight-for-age classification (also referred to as Gomez classification).

Source: Samir S. Basta. (1977). Nutrition and Health in Low Income Areas of the Third World. *Ecology of Food and Nutrition* Vol. 6: pp. 113–24.

and squatter settlements in Manila, Philippines. Regardless of the social indicator, the health and quality of life of those living in squatter settlements are poorer. School dropout rates are 75 percent higher; hospital-bed ratios are 1:300 for nonsquatter, 1:4000 for squatter; the infant mortality rate is nearly three times higher for squatter, and the birth rate six times higher; the tuberculosis rate is nine times higher. Although data are sparse, these patterns reflect the gulf that exists between the people who live in the spontaneous settlements of the cities of the world and those who live in traditional areas (Linn, 1983).

This is the reality. It is a pattern tied closely to the tremendous population pressures that exist in these societies because of high birth rates and low death rates. Spontaneous settlements reflect the momentous shift of population from rural to urban areas and the difficulty that LDCs have in absorbing massive numbers of people in their cities. Spontaneous settlements are ubiquitous in the cities of the world because these societies and the governments that lead them have no alternatives. The World Bank and other international agencies are recognizing spontaneous settlements as one of the few ways LDCs have to house their people. Demonstration projects have shown the feasibility of harnessing this process, but the question remains: Are things getting better or worse?

ARE CONDITIONS GETTING WORSE?

A review of the literature suggests that things have gotten worse. A perusal of UN data shows that housing construction in LDCs has fallen behind population growth. Spontaneous settlements continue to grow unchecked. Unfortunately, many students of housing equate the growth of spontaneous settlements with a decline in the quality of urban life, but as we have seen, spontaneous housing may be the first step on a long process of consolidation. As time passes and these areas receive water, electricity, and other services, conditions improve. I am not trying to diminish the population, housing, health, and service problems that the vast majority of nations in the world face, but it should be noted that the biases of researchers, either Westerners or those trained in the West, lead us to apply inappropriate standards to these societies. This problem, combined with the lack of valid and reliable data, makes it impossible to accurately assess conditions in the cities in LDCs. One must also remember that, regardless of how appalling the conditions are in the cities, more people have access to potable water, sewerage, drainage, electricity, clinics, and hospitals than those who live in rural areas (Linn, 1983; Blair, 1984; Gilbert and Gugler, 1982).

Development is a process that brings change across a society. The United States is undergoing a painful adjustment to the emergence of an integrated world economy. Millions have lost their high-paying manufacturing jobs because plants have been moved overseas and our society has shifted employment to the service sector. American society reels, trying to cope with a $3.0 trillion deficit and intractable social problems. Imagine the problems faced by societies in the first stages of the development process. Imagine the problems of transforming a traditional/rural economy to a modern/urban one in a single generation; trying to improve agricultural productivity at just the right pace so that people can be shifted to more productive industrial activity, but not so fast that cities are overwhelmed by migrants; attempting to create an infrastructure of roads, rail, telecommunications, and electricity upon which modern enterprises depend; creating a system of universal education, health, and social services that can produce the trained people needed to run modern enterprises; providing housing and other services and a humane standard of living for those who live in the cities and the countryside. It is a herculean task, which would strain the human and economic resources of any society, much less a less developed one.

THEORIES OF DEVELOPMENT

In more developed countries economic development and urbanization were linked together in the process of industrialization and modernization. As I have shown, in the less developed world, urbanization is occurring at an unprecedented rate, but economic development lags far behind. This state—population growth without economic growth—was not supposed to happen.

PREDICTIONS GONE ASTRAY

After World War II, theorists from a number of disciplines developed a tidy scenario on how LDCs would change. These theorists considered LDCs underdeveloped because they were agricultural and rural. They argued that development would occur with industrialization. Moreover, industrialization requires shifting labor away from farming, mining, and forestry to manufacturing, and because industries are located in cities, a massive redistribution of population from rural to urban centers was required. Thus industrialization and urbanization were viewed as inseparable: linked together, one supporting and facilitating the other. Manufacturing, however, requires a population with higher levels of skills and literacy than does agriculture. Therefore, one of the prerequisites for economic growth was the creation of a national system of mandatory education and the inculcation of a value system that supports an industrial economy. New values, new norms, new roles supporting things like entrepreneurial personality types, a money economy, achieved status, and the nuclear family were viewed as both prerequisites and facilitators of rapid social change. These theorists assumed that the rise of cities and an urban way of life would quickly replace the rural/traditional way of life found in these societies.

Development requires a revolutionary change in the economic, social, and cultural patterns of developing societies. Many of these changes were expected to be generated internally as the process of development proceeded; however, implicit in this argument was the assumption that much of the innovation would come from the West. Innovation would first diffuse from more to less developed societies. Cities would be the portals of change from which this innovation would be diffused to the rest of the society. Therefore, cities, especially primate cities, played a central role in this development model.

Economic development and modernization in LDCs has not occurred as predicted. Two theories—Modernization Theory and World Systems—exist in the literature which explain why less developed societies have not developed as predicted.

MODERNIZATION THEORY

Modernization is an ethnocentric concept which refers to the social and political changes that accompanied the industrialization and modernization process in Europe and North America (Bendix, 1964). Among these changes are urbanization, achieved status, a money economy, wage labor, universal education, representative government, and a concern for individual rights. Modernization involves the diffusion of these characteristics from more developed to less developed regions, and built into the concept is the notion of a time lag. It is argued that urban areas tend to change first and rural areas tend to lag far behind. The result is that two cultures coexist in the same society: a modern one associated with large primate cities and urban areas, and a traditional one associated with rural areas. Modernization theorists argue that development has not occurred as predicted because the modern is in conflict with the traditional. They maintain that the only reason a modern sector exists at all is because colonial powers imposed their alien system upon a traditional order through military coercion. Thus, there is a dualism in these societies—urban/modern versus rural/traditional—and modernization theorists argue that the inconsistency in the development process (the state of population growth without development) results from the resistance of traditional segments of less developed societies to industrialization and urbanization (Horowitz, 1977; Hermassi, 1978; Chirot, 1986).

There are many sources of resistance. The first comes from the people themselves. Culture is a blueprint for living—values, norms, roles, and institutions—that permits a people to deal with the problems of day-to-day living. There are many who prefer the traditional to the new and refuse to adopt the modern way of life, impeding the development process (Horowitz, 1977; Chirot, 1986).

A second source of resistance comes from the traditional elites: those whose power, wealth, and prestige are linked to the traditional social order—large landowners, clerics, village elders, and so on. Development changes the social structure: Achievement replaces ascription, rationality replaces tradition, and change undercuts the power and prestige of the old order. Therefore, both forces, the masses who resist the imposition of an alien culture and the elites who have a vested interest in maintaining the old system, work in concert to encapsulate the change in the major urban areas and prevent its diffusion into the larger society. Therefore, growth without development is the result of this duality—two incompatible cultural systems sharing the same society (Horowitz, 1977).

There are numerous examples in history of colonial powers intruding into the traditional societies in Latin America, Africa, and Asia, setting up modern sectors with cultural and economic ties to the motherland and few with the indigenous population. The smoldering resentment of subjugated peoples toward colonial powers led to dismantling of empires in the post-World War II period. In most cases independence has not resolved the conflict between the modernists and traditionalists. The Iranian revolution, in which Mullahs, Bazarine merchants, and peasants overthrew the Peacock Throne, is a recent example of the resolution of this dialectic. To many Iranians, the revolution cleansed the nation of the corrupting influences of the West, as thousands of would-be modernizers were executed or expelled, with the result that Iran was returned to theocratic traditionalism (Abrahamian, 1986).

DEPENDENCY THEORY/WORLD SYSTEMS THEORY

Dependency Theory, or World Systems Theory, is more recent than modernization theory. Its advocates are usually neo-Marxian, and often are citizens of developing nations. Modernization Theory blames the traditional social system for resisting modernization; Dependency Theory blames the world capitalist system for underdevelopment. The model of the class system used to describe the stratification system in a single society is used by dependency theorists to describe the relationship between nations in the world economic system (Harvey, 1973).

Dependency refers to an imbalanced economic relationship in which one side enjoys advantageous economic control over another. The dominant nations in the world, core nations found in North America and Europe, have diversified economies and are modern and highly industrialized. Although their populations are small, the size and power of their industrial economies, and their control of the organizations that control world monetary relationships (for example the World Bank, the International Monetary Fund, GATT) allow them to hold economic sway over peripheral nations—the less developed nations on the bottom of the world stratification system (Frank, 1969; Wallerstein, 1974; Chirot, 1986).

Peripheral nations often have little industry, swelling populations, and economies specialized in the export of a narrow range of raw materials—coffee, cotton, ore, hemp, and petroleum. A few nations in the world display the characteristics of both core and peripheral nations, and they are known as *semiperipheral* nations, for example, South Korea and Taiwan. Therefore, we find a world community in which a relatively small number of nations in the core, because of their economic, political, and military might, exploit peripheral nations for their own ends. Moreover, resistance by peripheral nations to this exploitation is met with resistance by the core nations through overt military force or covert political and economic action.

How does this exploitation take place? The fundamental mechanism is the domination of peripheral nations by foreign firms and investors who control their economies. This, in turn, has several consequences. First, profits from overseas investments flow back to the core nations, denying the peripheral nations development capital. Second, foreign investors are in a key position to control the types of industries that are carried out in a peripheral country. Core nations have a vested interest in selling high value-added manufactured goods to peripheral nations, and therefore, invest in agricultural and extractive processing rather than in plants that produce manufacturing goods. This leads to a situation where peripheral nations are forced to depend on an export economy—an economy that condemns them to poverty. Why? Raw materials are subject to the vacillations of a world commodity market. Commodity sales depend on the demand by consumers in the core nations. A drop in consumption in core nations can devastate a peripheral nation's economy. The recent health craze in the United States reduced the demand for palm and coconut oil overnight, which devastated the economies of a number of peripheral nations. Similarly, world coffee prices recently dropped 50 cents a pound, throwing the Brazilian and Colombian economies into turmoil. Economic recession and energy conservation in core nations have wreaked havoc in the OPEC nations (Frank, 1969; Wallerstein, 1974; Chirot, 1986).

According to dependency theory, peripheral nations that have specialized export economies have distorted economies. Their development tends to be concentrated in relatively few sectors of their economy, often centered in primate cities, and low capital returns mean that there is little money or motivation to develop other regions of the nation.

Dependency is implicit in colonialism, and the mechanism by which colonial powers exploited their colonies is well understood. The political and economic exploitation of colonialism ended for the most part with World War II (Frank, 1969). Dependency theorists argue that the economic exploitation of neocolonialism in the postwar period is its successor. The principal agents are large multinational corporations headquartered in core countries. AT&T, General Motors, Ford Motor Company, and mammoth oil companies are all examples of corporations headquartered in core nations which have more employees and larger budgets than most nations in the world. These corporations use their economic power to influence the political and social life of the societies in which they operate to their own benefit, not necessarily that of the host nation.

THE THEORIES COMPARED

The two theories, modernization and dependency, posit different explanations for growth without development. Modernization stresses the continuing resistance of traditional cultures and elites to economic development. Large landowners, privileged families, clerics, and a rural population holding traditional values are the central culprits that cause underdevelopment in LDCs. Dependency theory, on the other hand, stresses the hegemony of Western nations over the world economic order, and the ability of their proxies—multinational corporations—to perpetuate inequality. The two theories, however, explore different aspects of the same problem. Whereas modernization theory describes the social and cultural factors within societies that inhibit development, dependency theory explores those factors external to LDCs that profoundly affect the course of development. A clearer understanding of the development process requires a fusion of the two perspectives.

SUMMARY

Change is occurring at an unprecedented rate on this planet, and much of this change is related to the unprecedented population growth. From 1950 to the year 2000, the world's population is expected to grow from 2.5 billion to over 6 billion people. Increasingly, this population is being absorbed in the world's cities.

Population growth must be studied within the social, economic, political, and cultural context of society. Throughout this text, a distinction is made between more developed countries (MDCs) and less developed countries (LDCs), reflecting the fact that all societies are developing, some more rapidly than others. These two categories of nations are used to explore the relationship between urbanization and economic development.

The Theory of Demographic Transition describes the relationship between economic development and demographic processes. The theory argues that as societies move from less developed to more developed, conditions are created encouraging low fertility. Families in more developed nations have fewer children because it is in their economic interest to limit fertility. The theory suggests a three-stage transition process from traditional societies in Stage 1 with high fertility and mortality and stable populations; through societies in transitional growth with high fertility and declining mortality and rapidly growing population; to societies in incipient decline with low fertility and mortality and stable populations. Most LDCs are in Stage 2, and imported death control technology has dramatically reduced mortality but not fertility. Death control technology can be applied without the consent of the individual through public health. Birth control technology requires the cooperation of couples. Equally important is the persistence of the values in traditional families which encourage large families. The consequence of rapid population increase in LDCs is the retardation of the development process, as money that would go into development is invested in a large, unproductive, young population.

In the last half of the twentieth century, the world's population problems have become the world's urban problems. Underemployment and unemployment, poor public services, inadequate housing, nonexistent medical care, and poor nutrition are now concentrated in the cities. Two approaches were used to examine these patterns. The first employed level of development—more developed versus less developed. The second grouped less developed nations into four types based on the characteristics of their demographic patterns. Applying the first criterion, we observed that urban growth in LDCs is unprecedented. In 1950, 275 million, or 38 percent, of the world's urban population lived in the cities of the less developed world. By 1975, the world's urban population had reached 1.6 billion, and half this number were living in the cities of LDCs. By the year 2000, the world's urban population will exceed 2.1 billion, and 66 percent of this population will be in the cities in the developing world. The experiences of LDCs differ sharply from those of MDCs in the timing, scope, and magnitude of urbanization.

Four types of societies were examined. Type 1 societies are in Latin America. They have been undergoing economic development for most of this century, and they will end the urbanization process by the end of the century with 75 percent of their populations in cities. Type 2 nations are found in East Asia and North Africa; more than half of their populations are in cities. Urban life in these societies is slowly improving as economic development proceeds. Type 3 nations are located in the Subsahara. They are rural but urbanizing rapidly. Even at this rate, most will still be rural by the turn of the century. Population growth in these nations will outstrip the resources of these societies, leading to a declining standard of living. Type 4 nations include India, China, and Pakistan; the rapid population growth in these subsistence-level societies exerts tremendous pressure on the natural as well as the urban environment.

Increasingly, the urban population of the world is being accommodated in large cities. This is true for both the more and less developed countries of the world. The situation in which the population of one city in the world outstrips that of all other cities is called *primacy*. Primacy has been studied by social scientists for more than 50 years. Two schools of thought have developed around this concept. The first group views primate cities as parasitic. The argument made by these scientists is that primate cities often exist in societies based in agriculture. Cities are expensive to build and maintain, and these large urban populations drain away the limited financial resources of an entire nation. Primate cities also polarize a nation politically, socially, economically, and culturally because the major institutions of these nations tend to locate in the primate city.

The second group argues that primate cities operate to create a critical mass of talent necessary for development to take place. They argue that there are so few people with the skills necessary to run modern enterprises, the only way to bring the necessary people together is to concentrate millions of people in one place. Additionally, only in primate cities does one find the infrastructure—banking, finance, transportation, and communication—necessary for modern enterprises to exist.

The internal structure of the city can be described along two dimensions—a physical dimension and a organizational dimension. The physical dimension includes the streets, buildings, neighborhoods, and commercial, industrial, and political areas of the city. The organizational dimension includes the family types, ethnic, class, and associational groups found there. A complex interrelationship exists between the two. In general, the characteristics of the larger society are reflected in the physical structure of the city. A distinction is made between the structure of the premodern city and the modern city. Premodern cities are densely settled, compact, and residentially segregated on the basis of tribe, caste, or village. There is little functional specialization of land use and an inverse status gradient. This pattern was related to the low level of transportation technology. Modern cities, in contrast, have lower population densities, residential segregation based on social class, family type, and ethnicity, and specialized areas based on function. There is also a direct distance–status gradient, with the poor living near the city's center and the wealthy at the periphery. Although societies around the world differ markedly in history and culture, research suggests that as development proceeds, the spatial patterns of the city move from the premodern to modern form, with primate cities the first to experience change in the society.

Spontaneous settlements are a permanent and visible element of most cities in LDCs. Spontaneous settlements around the world share at least two of the following characteristics: Most are occupied by the original settlers; most have been built illegally; most lack basic services; most are occupied by the poor; and most are built with an element of self-help. The number of people housed in spontaneous settlements varies from region to region, but the number is in the hundreds of millions. Research suggests that many spontaneous settlements follow a life cycle from an initial settlement or bridgehead, through a period of consolidation in which the area gradually improves, to a final stage when the area takes on the characteristics of an ordinary suburb. These settlements, once viewed with alarm by government officials and often destroyed by urban renewal, are now viewed by many as the only way LDCs can provide housing for their citizens.

Two physical and social systems usually share the same city in LDCs. The modern sector shares the economic and social characteristics of cities in MDCs: nice housing, wage employment, and middle-class value systems. There is also a traditional sector, often spontaneous settlements, that houses the poor: poor housing, high unemployment, and lifestyles that resemble village life. Therefore, there are two physical realities, two economies, two social structure—two worlds inhabiting the same city at the same time in much of the less developed world.

In more developed countries economic development and urbanization were linked together in the process of industrialization and modernization. In less developed countries population growth is occurring without development. This pattern goes against many of the theories developed after World War II to predict the course of development in LDCs and to guide the spending of development funds.

Two theories have been developed to explain this deviation—Modernization Theory and Dependency, or World Systems Theory. Modernization refers to the social and political changes that accompanied the industrialization and modernization process in the West. Modernization involves the diffusion of these changes from more developed to less developed regions of the world. This process began in the sixteenth century and continued into the twentieth as European powers subjugated native populations into their empires. These powers imposed an alien culture on a traditional one and set up a dualism between the modernists and traditionists—a source of conflict even today. This theory argues that underdevelopment is the result of the resistance of traditional elements of less developed societies to industrialization and urbanization.

Dependency Theory is more recent than modernization theory, and it is neo-Marxian. Modernization theory blames the traditional social system for resisting modernization; dependency theory blames the world capitalist system for underdevelopment. Dependency Theory argues that core nations, MDCs, have used their economic and military might to control the world economic order and structure economic relationships in a way to perpetuate dependency. During the colonial period, this domination was direct in the form of political and economic control. In the neocolonial period the control is indirect and is carried out by large multinational corporations, headquartered in core nations, which exert economic sway over peripheral nations. Multinationals exert this control by targeting investments, manipulating foreign governments, and perpetuating export economies in peripheral nations. All these techniques distort local economies, which facilitates the exploitation of peripheral nations over time.

Thus, the two theories posit different explanations for growth without development. Modernization stresses the continued resistance of traditional cultures and elites to economic development. Dependency theory emphasizes the hegemony of Western nations over the world economic order and the actions of their proxies in perpetuating inequality between nations.

NOTES

1.   The concept of a demographic transition was first introduced in 1929 by Warren Thompson to describe patterns of population growth he had discovered in data collected in the first

quarter of this century. Thompson described three groups of countries. Group A were countries in northern and western Europe and the United States. These nations had moved from very high rates of natural increase to very low rates between the late nineteenth century and 1927. Thompson felt that these nations should be moving into a period of stable or even declining population growth. Group B were countries in central Europe, Spain, and Italy. These countries had rapidly declining birth and death rates, but death rates were declining at a faster rate than birth rates. Therefore, Thompson expected these countries to grow rapidly in the future. He suggested that they lagged 30 to 50 years behind Group A nations in their demographic progress. Group C countries were countries we now call LDCs; he saw little evidence that these societies had any control over either births or deaths. In his opinion, natural events like bumper harvests, famine, and epidemics would control their numbers, not human intervention.

There was little academic interest in population problems through the 1930s and it was not until 1945 that Frank Notestein used Thompson's ideas to formalize and name the pattern *demographic transition.* It was not yet a theory, but Notestein labeled the Group A pattern *incipient decline,* the Group B pattern, *transitional growth,* and the Group C pattern, *high-growth potential.* Moreover, as the world grew smaller and more demographic data became available, researchers found that most countries followed the transition process.

Thompson and Notestein described empirical regularities, an evolutionary process in the demographic foundations of most societies. Kingsley Davis, one of the century's most important sociologists, was responsible for formalizing this empirical regularity into the Theory of Demographic Transition, which has now become a central theme in demography.

2. Although Africa is experiencing the largest percentage growth, and Asia the lowest, the population bases are different. Until 1950, the level of urbanization in Africa was low. Asian countries, in contrast, notably India and China, already had large urban populations.

3. Most of the research on spontaneous settlements has been done in Latin America and the Caribbean. A question that has not been resolved is what the odds are that an area will experience consolidation, and what conditions are necessary for a bridgehead to move through the consolidation process to become a middle-income suburb.

There are no clear-cut answers to these questions because the research is preliminary and incomplete. One factor that seems to be a good predictor is the security of land tenure. The less secure the land tenure, the slower the consolidation process. Invasions of another's land involve risk, and bridgeheaders are unwilling to make investments in a structure until they are sure their investment is not going to be torn down. In general, the more secure the land tenure, the faster the rate of consolidation. A second factor is the price of land. In rapidly growing cities, invasions may be impossible because there is no available land. The poor, therefore, are forced to buy land, and its price is set by a complex set of private and public policies. Finally, the price of building materials in relationship to average family income is also crucial. The building products are often a government monopoly in LDCs, and government policies often keep prices artificially high, dampening the consolidation process. The crucial question is whether this process is limited to the relatively prosperous Latin American region, or is it one that is repeated in other LDCs, especially subsistence societies like India and Pakistan. This question has not yet been answered.

4. Experience has shown that rarely do large public housing projects work in LDCs. First, these projects, modeled after those in the West, drain off a disproportionate share of the scarce resources these societies have for housing. Second, the housing all too often goes to those with political connections—middle-class citizens—not the poor they were designed to help. Third, these projects are often built on centrally located sites, recently cleared of low-rise spontaneous settlements. The destruction of housing exacerbates the tight housing markets in which the poor

must operate. Finally, high-rise apartments are often inappropriate living space for recent immigrants to the city. The transition from village to urban life is made more difficult in a high-rise setting.

5. I do not want to give the impression that preemptive planning and the elimination of construction standards are the panacea to the housing problems in LDCs. For a plan that failed miserably in implementation, see C. L. Choguill's book, *New Communities for Urban Squatters: Lessons from the Plan That Failed in Dhaka, Bangladesh.* A complete citation of the work may be found in the bibliography.

the Origin of Cities is
the Origin of Civilization

*T*HE ORIGINS OF CITIES

INTRODUCTION

People often ask, "Who am I?" and "Where did I come from?" This concern with origins and identity is a common theme in the comic and tragic literature of many cultures; it is evident today in the growing popularity of genealogy, as well as in the increasingly frequent attempts of adoptees to uncover the identities of their true parents.

The same questions motivate social scientists who are exploring the physiological and social origins of the human species. Research by these scientists during the past 30 years has revolutionized thinking on the evolution of humankind. For example, in the area of research concerned with physical evolution, fossilized remains of early humanoids found at Olduvai Gorge and other sites in Africa indicate that the human species originated two to three million years ago—much earlier than previously estimated (Halloway, 1974; Leakey, 1967). Similarly, archeological finds from more recent human history have greatly expanded knowledge of these earliest societies and settlements (Clark, 1965; Jacobsen, 1976; Lamberg-Karlovsky, 1971; Schild, 1976; Smith, 1976). Generally, these studies have illuminated the process by which human settlements have evolved to more complex urban forms.

This chapter traces the growth of cities from a historical perspective. Examination of the first agricultural villages 8000 years ago and their evolution into cities is followed by discussion of the social, political, economic, and ecological characteristics of these early cities and their similarities with other preindustrial cities, whether in Mesopotamia in the third millennium B.C. or in western Europe in the

Middle Ages. The emphasis in this section is not on the chronology of historical events per se, but rather on the patterns and processes of urban development. Next, the Industrial Revolution and its impact on urban form and function are explored with emphasis on contemporary urbanization. Finally, the role of the city in American social history is surveyed.

The premise of this chapter is that an understanding of the origins and functions of cities in the past will lead to an understanding of contemporary urbanization. Consequently, the focus is on the broad social changes that made possible the emergence of a unique form of social organization—the city.

COLLECTION OF EVIDENCE

Until recently, knowledge of the origin of cities was based on data gathered from the durable remains of partly explored sites, fragments of writing dating from 3500 B.C., and eyewitness accounts of Mesoamerican cities written by the Spanish during their conquest of the Inca and Aztec empires in the sixteenth century.

Since World War II, new technology has greatly expanded archaeology's data base. Carbon-14 dating techniques, introduced in the 1940s, enable archaeologists to place evidence in proper chronological order (Renfrew, 1971). Microscopic analysis of pollen left in storage containers centuries ago gives an inventory of the early human diet (Bender, 1975, pp. 37–64). Rigorous statistical analysis of the frequency and distribution of artifacts at a site, made possible by the high-speed computer, gives insight into the social structure of prehistoric people (Adams, 1966, pp. 1–37). Most important has been the change in the conception of archeology as natural history—the collection, description, and classification of artifacts through inductive reasoning—to a view of it as a deductive social science concerned with theory construction and hypothesis testing (Polgar, 1975). A case in point is the present research on prehistoric societies. The new archeology views human beings as a species of animal and explores the adaptation of this animal to its environment. This ecological approach analyzes the complex interaction among early humans, their technology, and a changing environment and provides a description of the ways social organization has evolved.

PRECONDITIONS FOR CITIES

The impact of cities on the modern way of life is so great that it is difficult to realize how "new" cities are in human social history. Archeological evidence shows that the first cities did not appear until about 3500 B.C. (Adams, 1960; Davis, 1973; Sjoberg, 1972). To place the evolutionary process in perspective, one must realize that humankind in its present form, Homo sapiens, has existed for approximately 40,000 years but has lived in cities for only 5500 years, or a little more than 10 percent of the span of human existence (Halloway, 1974; Adams, 1966).

TECHNOLOGICAL AND ENVIRONMENTAL CONDITIONS

The emergence of cities, therefore, is a benchmark in an evolutionary process lasting many thousands of years. During these millennia humans gradually accumulated the technical and social inventions necessary for the formation of cities (Harrison, 1954). One of these was the technology to produce a food surplus so that individuals could be freed from food production. This elaborate technology included agriculture, animal husbandry, and a host of related inventions. Also needed was a complex social organization, beyond the ties of family and kinship, to allow the distribution of surplus food for valued social ends. Finally, there was one precondition over which humans had no control—a mild climate. The level of technology in early societies was so low that only the most favorable climatic conditions would allow large permanent population concentrations. Such conditions did not prevail until about 10,000 B.C., when the last stage of the Ice Age came to an end in Europe (Davis, 1973, pp. 11–13).

NECESSARY SOCIAL CHANGE

Pondering these preconditions, one might think that the invention of agriculture would be synonymous with the urban revolution. It is true that permanent settlements require a reliable and intensive agricultural base, but it is incorrect to think of the urban revolution and the agricultural revolution as the same process. Abundant evidence suggests that they were separate processes. For example, the agricultural technology necessary to support an urban population probably had developed several thousand years before the emergence of cities (Adams, 1966, pp. 38–78). The availability of a food surplus, therefore, does not adequately explain the development of urban forms of human settlement. Cities require not only a food surplus but also the means for its transportation, storage, and distribution for socially valued ends. Thus, a complete change in the structure of society was necessary before cities could evolve. To understand this change one must examine human social evolution prior to the emergence of cities.

HUMAN PREHISTORY

Archeologists have divided human prehistory into three time periods: the Paleolithic or Old Stone Age, lasting from 500,000 to 10,000 B.C. in the Near East, the Mesolithic or transition period of the Stone Age, lasting from 10,000 to 8000 B.C. in the Near East, and the Neolithic or New Stone Age, lasting from 8000 B.C. to the appearance of the first cities in the Near East around 3500 B.C.

PALEOLITHIC PERIOD

During the half-million years of the Paleolithic period humans lived as nomads—wandering hunters and gatherers with no permanent settlements and a level of technology so low that every individual was required to participate in food gathering.

Probably no other form of social organization was possible during this period. The climate during most of the Paleolithic period was much colder than it is today; much of northern Europe, Asia, and North America was covered by glaciers, and the environmental conditions necessary for agriculture were not present.

Technology set limits on both the size and form of Paleolithic societal organizations. Even during the late Paleolithic, when humans were producing flint and bone tools, cave paintings, and sculptured figurines, technology permitted only 0.025 person to be supported per square mile (Deevy, 1960, p. 196). Paleolithic people therefore were forced to live in small, homogeneous groups. Because there was no surplus of food, there could be no specialized labor beyond that based on age and sex, and without specialization there could be no social classes or other forms of complex human organization (Clark, 1965; Jacobson, 1976; Smith, 1976).

MESOLITHIC PERIOD

The last main glacial period in Europe, the Wurm, ended around 10,000 B.C., when dramatic climatic changes occurred. As a result of a milder climate, new plants and animals appeared. With the climate change came the onset of the Mesolithic or transition period in human prehistory. The most significant occurrence of this period was the emergence of the first villages. They were based not on agriculture but on a new subsistence strategy of intensive collecting of plants and animals. These villages became a dominant form of human settlement during the Mesolithic period and were widely dispersed from as far north as the Baltic Sea to as far south as India.

Excavation of Mesolithic sites has uncovered improved bows, scrapers, reapers, and a variety of other specialized tools. Archeologists have concluded, however, that the technology used by each village was related directly to the foodstuffs found in the immediate vicinity. For example, near the Baltic Sea people subsisted on shellfish; in southern Germany, elk; in western Greece, the red deer and plant life; in western Iran, grain. Each population concentration developed a variety of specialized tools to use in exploiting the resources in their environment. Improved technology combined with climatic changes meant that the population that could be supported per square mile increased sixfold—to fifteen persons (Deevy, 1960, p. 196).

The Mesolithic-village form of life was an important step in human social evolution. Sedentism, or permanent village life, based on the intensive exploitation of plants and animals, gave people an intimate knowledge of their local environment. Their accumulated experiences with wild wheat, barley, and other food plants, as well as with wild goats, sheep, pigs, cattle, and horses, and the ecological niches where these plants and animals existed, formed the knowledge base from which agriculture would develop (Adams, 1966, pp. 38–78).

NEOLITHIC PERIOD

The Neolithic period began with the appearance of agriculture. The agriculturally based village originated in about 8000 B.C. in an area of Asia known as the Fertile

Crescent, which encompasses present-day Israel, Lebanon, Jordan, Syria, northern Iraq, and western Iran. It is a region with a dry climate, plentiful sunshine, mild winters, and abundant water. In addition, in the highlands of the Fertile Crescent were found the ancestors of modern wheat, barley, sheep, goats, and cattle.

The importance of climate cannot be overstated. Neolithic technology was poorly developed, but plentiful sunshine and mild winters provided two or more growing seasons each year, a dry climate permitted the safe and long-term storage of grain and other staples, and abundant water made possible intensive agriculture. Therefore, most early Neolithic settlements of both the Old and the New World were in the tropical latitudes where such conditions prevail.

THE AGRICULTURAL REVOLUTION

By 8000 B.C. the inhabitants of the hills of the Fertile Crescent had come to know their habitat so well that they were beginning to domesticate the plants and animals they had been collecting and hunting.[1] The food-producing revolution was therefore not an event but a process that occurred gradually and followed different courses of development according to different local conditions, even within the Fertile Crescent (see Figure 4.1) (Adams, 1966, p. 41). The distinction between plant gathering and plant breeding, moreover, is not based just on the sowing of seeds. For instance, first people had to take wheat from its narrow ecological niche in the highlands and mountains of the Fertile Crescent to open flat areas to which it was not adapted. Second, the removal of certain pressures of natural selection led to strains of wheat more suitable for agriculture. By 7000 B.C. domesticated wheat had been bred, and grain culture had emerged. The domestication of cereal grains expanded the environmental range within which these crops could be grown and increased substantially the size and reliability of yields.[2] An important quality of grain is its ability to be stored for long periods of time. A large, reliable source of easily stored foodstuffs added physical and, more significantly, social stability to the Neolithic farm village (Bender, 1975; Braidwood, 1960; Harris, 1967; Kimber, 1972; Renfrew, 1973; Solheim, 1972).

Agriculture and animal husbandry were not the only inventions making village life possible. Over the centuries an array of tools, utensils, and cooking techniques had developed to make the plant tissue palatable. In the plow, as well as the versatile use of wood, hides, and bones, formed a technological complex that augmented the cultural evolution made possible by a food-producing technology.

One question remains: What motivated hunting and gathering societies to become agricultural? The work by archaeologists and anthropologists suggests that agriculture is an undesirable alternative to hunting and gathering. Undesirable alternative? Many of us harbor images of hunting and gathering societies eking out a bare existence, deprived of home and culture, condemned to an endless, mindless wandering. This image is far from the truth. Anthropologists who have studied the few remaining hunting and gathering societies show that an enormous array of foodstuffs can be gathered with far less work than most of us imagine. The truth is that people in these societies did not have to work very hard. There were seasons when life was hard

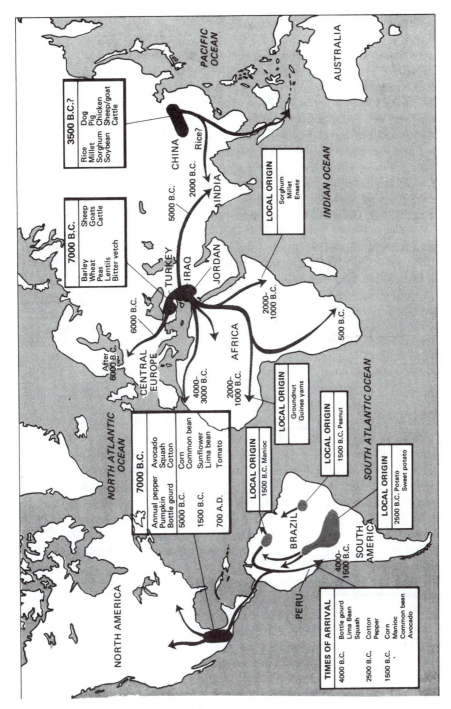

FIGURE 4.1 Agriculture—where it began and how it spread.

Source: ©1967/72 by The New York Times Company. Reprinted by permission.

and food collection became a full-time job, but for most of the year leisure, not work, characterized tribal life. The artifacts that remain suggest a rich, varied, and in all likelihood, satisfying way of life. This life was made possible because hunters and gatherers had few material needs, and there were no elites or specialists to be supported by others. What would motivate people to adopt a way of life where they would have to work harder (Sanlins, 1968)?

There are a number of competing theories; all are controversial. Gordon Childe (1957) and others stress the role of climate (Meyers, 1971). As we have already noted, about 10,000 B.C., the last of the major glaciers receded, and the climate in the Middle East became drier. This climatic change reduced the supply of game and plants and compelled hunters and gatherers to adopt agriculture. Critics are quick to point out that similar climatic crises have occurred throughout time without triggering an agricultural revolution, and available evidence suggests that the cradle of agriculture in the hills that flank the Fertile Crescent did not experience the dramatic climate change Childe suggests (Braidwood, 1972).

Archaeologists have put forth a second theory—population pressure. They contend that an increase in population density compelled hunters and gatherers to adopt agriculture. Analysis of skeletal remains show that life expectancies gradually improved throughout prehistory, and we know from present-day experience in the less developed world that population increase has the same impact on food supply as climatic change (Flannery, 1972). Historically, migration has been the way societies rid themselves of surplus population. We know that colonization was used by ancient Greece to lower population density on their arid peninsula, and in recent history, the Americas, Australia, and New Zealand were colonized for the same reasons. However, by 10,000 B.C. humans inhabited every continent except Antarctica, and migration no longer served to keep population densities low. Therefore, population pressure may have forced hunting and gathering societies into agriculture. There is evidence in the Near East of food shortages resulting from changes in the physical environment as well as increasing density of population (Flannery, 1972).

Others point out that population density and climatic change alone cannot explain the change from hunting and gathering to agriculture. Braidwood (1972) offers a cultural explanation. Over hundreds of generations, hunting and gathering societies slowly gathered the technology and knowledge of the environment to support a settled way of life. A triggering event, either climatic change or population pressure or a combination of the two, set these ancient peoples on a course to settled agriculture. Since the process was repeated by different peoples in different regions, Braidwood asserts, the Agricultural Revolution was a predictable outcome of a long historical process of cultural accumulation.

AGRICULTURE AND CITIES

In the course of many centuries, the basic elements of the food-producing revolution spread west across the entire eastern end of the Mediterranean and as far east as the Caspian Sea. Eventually the new way of life reached the Aegean and spread into

Europe. As in previous ages, indigenous populations selectively borrowed elements of the new technology and adapted them to the conditions of the local environment (Bender, 1975, pp. 89–106; Braidwood, 1960; Harris, 1967; Harrison, 1954). Neolithic villagers, however, did not work at highest efficiency and grew only enough food for their own needs. In order for cities to be formed, both the technology to produce a surplus and the institutional mechanism to motivate farmers to grow and relinquish their surplus were required. By about 4000 B.C. the people of southern Mesopotamia had developed the agricultural technology to produce a large food surplus. Seasonal flooding of Tigris and Euphrates Rivers and small-scale irrigation had led to a new form of intensive agriculture. Trade appears to have been a major factor in motivating villagers to produce more food than they needed for their own use.

EARLIEST CITIES

ROLE OF TRADE

Although Neolithic villages were separated by hundreds of miles of mountains and water, archeological evidence shows that the settlements throughout the Near East were in active communication. Geological studies, for example, indicate that the entire Fertile Crescent region is devoid of obsidian deposits. Nevertheless, substantial amounts of this material have been found at the excavations at Jarmo (more than 450 pounds) and other Neolithic sites. "From this it appears that well before 6000 B.C. Jarmo must have been conducting a thriving trade across the mountains that brought it into contact with the communities to the north of Armenia" (Dixon, 1968, p. 44).

Obsidian was not the only material traded in prehistoric times. Soapstone, textiles, pottery, and probably perishable items also were traded. By examining artifacts at widely dispersed sites, archaeologists are now reconstructing the trade routes of prehistoric peoples. "These routes, some of which cross the most inhospitable terrain in the world, linked the early settlements in a communication network that must have influenced their development profoundly" (Dixon, 1968, p. 45).

THE OVERGROWN VILLAGE

Only a few villages out of hundreds had the right combination of terrain, climate, technology, and location in relation to trade routes to become trade centers. The wealth brought to a village through trade permitted it to increase its population and allowed some individuals to become part-time specialists in production and trade. These "overgrown villages covering five to six acres and supporting upwards to 5,000 people began to emerge between 4000–5000 B.C. and became the containers in which the social changes necessary for the emergence of cities occurred" (Davis, 1973).

The overgrown village represents a transition stage in the emergence of the first cities. They were up to ten times larger than the surrounding agricultural villages, and their size permitted a more complex social structure in which the chances for innovation were enhanced. Some of the innovations that indicate a city was forming include: (1) permanent settlement in dense aggregations, (2) nonagriculturalists in specialized functions, (3) taxation and capital accumulation, (4) monumental public building, (5) a ruling class, (6) the technique of writing, (7) the acquisition of predictive sciences—arithmetic, geometry, and astronomy, (8) artistic expression, (9) trade, and (10) replacement of kinship by residence as the basis for membership in the community (Childe, 1950, pp. 4–7). Childe's list is interesting because social innovations rather than technical inventions predominate. Many social forms connected with cities make their first appearance in the overgrown village.

EVOLUTION OF SOCIAL ORGANIZATION

The social innovations made possible by the trade surplus in the overgrown village were crucial in the development of cities. For instance, the "cradle of civilization"—Mesopotamia—is not homogeneous in climate, terrain, or rainfall, but forms an environmental mosaic. Some areas are well suited for grain cultivation, others for orchards, herding, and fishing. Each ecological niche supported its own specialists, and an early function of the overgrown village was to provide a marketplace for exchange of the diverse agricultural products. Adams (1966) reports that a number of pre-Hispanic cities in Central America became "hyperdeveloped" markets that had really no other function. More than 60,000 people would gather daily in these cities to exchange and barter (p. 53).

EARLY FORMAL INSTITUTIONS

Early formal institutions had their beginnings in the relationship among the different agricultural specialists. Early temple records suggest that one of the earliest functions of priests was to control and formalize these relationships and even set rates of exchange, for example, fish–grain equivalents (Adams, 1966, p. 48). The priests, in all likelihood, were also involved in other forms of social control, including keeping herdsmen out of fields during seasonal shortages of fodder and controlling the construction and maintenance of irrigation systems, as well as the distribution of water. In each case, submitting to the control of a centralized authority and paying that authority part of one's agricultural production was an early exchange relationship beneficial to all parties.

FULL-TIME SPECIALISTS

The continued growth of trade and local exchange enabled part-time specialists to become full-time artisans, priests, officials, and warriors. The concentration of these full-time specialists in one place not only encouraged technical innovation but also enabled them to organize and extend their social control. The invention of writing by those specialists led to accurate record keeping that aided commerce. More importantly, it allowed more complex administrative and legal systems and more rigorous thought. Organizationally, these developments resulted in systematized religious control, linkage of religious institutions with a centralized government, property rights bound to land as a quasi-governmental institution, and an expanded division of labor that facilitated the exchange of goods and services (Adams, 1966). Hence, the cumulative social and technical innovations fostered in the expanded-village environment transformed these villages into the first cities. By 3500 B.C., southern Mesopotamia had evolved specialized groups of producers whose relationships followed the lines of the dominant urban institutions—the palace and the temple. Ultimately, the combination of a trade surplus and social specialization ushered in the structured inequality of a more complex social order.

CHARACTERISTICS OF MESOPOTAMIAN CITIES

Among the earliest cities were Erech, Eridu, Ur, Lagash, and Larsa in the southernmost valley of the Tigris–Euphrates Rivers and Kish and Jemet Nasr in the north (Sjoberg, 1960, p. 34). The first cities were small by modern standards, rarely exceeding 8000 to 25,000 persons. The city of Ur, for example, covered only 220 acres and had an estimated total population of 24,000. However, these cities were ten to twenty times larger than the Neolithic villages that previously had been the largest settlements, and they must have been awe-inspiring to the rural people of the day.

ECOLOGICAL AND ORGANIZATIONAL CHARACTERISTICS

Interestingly, these cities were very similar in their ecological and organizational characteristics. First, each city was ruled by a king who was also considered a representative of the city's deity, and thus its chief priest. Second, they had similar cultures including wheat and barley cultivation; bronze metallurgy; use of wheeled vehicles; the raising of sheep, goats, cattle, and horses; the use of oxen as draft animals; and the production of luxury goods by local artisans from metals and precious stones. Third, these cities were similar in physical appearance. The city's center was a walled zone containing a temple–palace complex devoted to the city-god and the king-priest. Surrounding this core were houses made of dried or fired mud brick, "jumbled together forming an irregular mass broken at intervals by open spaces in front of a temple or governmental building" (Sjoberg, 1960, p. 35). Streets were narrow, winding, unpaved, and inadequately drained. Sanitation was poor; offal and other refuse were simply thrown into the streets. Subareas of the city appear to have been inhabited by various groups of specialists. Agriculturalists lived just outside the city's wall within walking distance of their fields. At the periphery of the city, but inside the wall were the poorest inhabitants, who lived in mud and reed hovels. Merchants and artisans lived closer to the city's center, where the nobility, priests, and warriors resided.

Ironically, the opposite pattern characterizes most modern metropolises. High-status groups live at the city's periphery, while the poorest inhabitants live closer to the city's center. This relationship between space and social status will be analyzed in Chapter 9.

VULNERABILITY

These cities shared one other characteristic—vulnerability, both internal and external. Their general tendency to be located on flood plains meant periodic destruction by water. Cooking fires frequently set off conflagrations that leveled large areas of the city. Sanitation was almost totally lacking, and the streets became open sewers, tainting water supplies and breeding disease. The trade on which all the earliest cities relied spread epidemics. Social and economic decay also affected these settlements. Archeological evidence suggests that many of these early cities fell victim to disease and natural disaster and simply ceased to exist.

The earliest cities were vulnerable to attack from without. Agricultural technology during antiquity was inefficient by modern standards, and an enormous number of agriculturalists were needed to support a small urban population. Hawley (1971) estimates that only three or four percent of a local population could be supported in urban settlements during this period. Urban populations could grow only when more farmers and producers were brought under the influence of the city. The rise and fall of cities, therefore, corresponded to the rise and fall of their empires. A city could continue only as long as the ruling elite had the political power to ensure that agriculturalists would give up part of their yield to support city dwellers. The rulers could accomplish this process benignly through trade and taxation or, as was more often the case, through military coercion and the exaction of tribute. Because the urban populations were so greatly outnumbered by the people in the countryside, these settlements were vulnerable to rebellion by angry peasants. The cities also were vulnerable to conquest by other peoples and periodic attack by nomadic raiders. As a result a foe who could seize and destroy the empire's capital city normally brought an end to the empire. Figure 4.2 shows the growth and decline curves of empires from 600 B.C. to 700 A.D. The curves measure the physical area of political empires in million of kilometers. Note that the rise and fall of cities parallels the rise and fall of empires.

WHY THE URBAN REVOLUTION?

To this point, I have described where, when, and how the earliest cities originated. But why did cities evolve? There are a number of competing theories, but all, to a degree, are controversial. One theory argues that cities evolved because they contribute to human efficiency. People often think of an invention as a material thing, when in fact the inventions that have had the most pervasive influence on human life have been social in character. Of the numerous ways of defining the term *city*, one of the more interesting is to describe a city as a time-saving device that enables diverse groups of people to come together to exploit each other. "Some scholars regard the city as second only to agriculture among the significant inventions in human history" (Sjoberg, 1960, p. 1). The

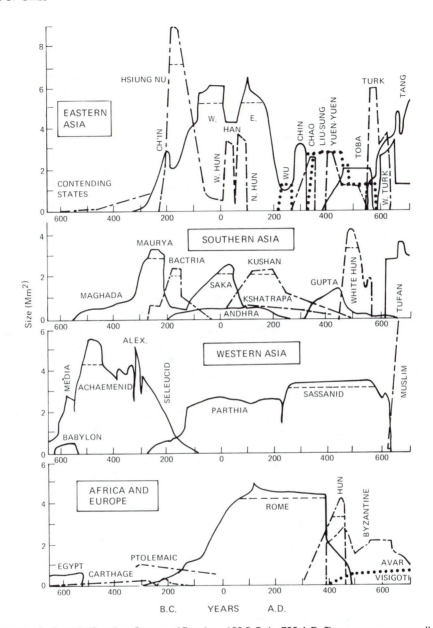

FIGURE 4.2 Growth/Decline Curves of Empires, 600 B.C. to 700 A.D. The curves measure the physical area of political empires in millions of square kilometers.

(*Source:* Rein Taagepera. "Size and Duration of Empires: Systematics of Size." *Social Science Research* 7 (1978): 118. Reproduced by permission.)

major obstacle to exchange and production is distance, and cities reduce this obstacle by concentrating a large population at one place. Thus, they facilitate specialization and exchange and allow for increased productivity at less cost. Farmers, therefore, grew and brought their surplus to cities to trade for the goods and services available only there. Since cities were a superior adaptation to their environment, they displaced the Neolithic farm-village as the dominant form of organization (Davis, 1973, pp. 14–16).[3]

Surplus theory is another answer to the question, "Why the Urban Revolution?" According to this theory, the creation of a city depends on an agricultural surplus that permits a society to support nonagricultural workers. Through most of the Neolithic period agricultural technology was so primitive that everyone—men, women, and children—had to participate in agriculture in order to survive. As in the case of the agricultural revolution, Neolithic peoples slowly accumulated the knowledge and technology to produce a small surplus, and the first cities emerged. Mesopotamia was the first region in the world where agriculturalists were able to produce a large enough surplus to support cities (see Figure 4.3). As the peoples in other regions of the world began to produce a surplus, they too developed urban civilizations (Childe, 1950; Davis, 1973; Braidwood, 1972).

Why did the villages grow a surplus in the first place? Why would they give it up? Who collected, transported, and distributed the surplus? The surplus theory doesn't answer these questions. Archaeological evidence shows the ancient state as the collector and distributor of the food surplus, and the seat of the ancient state was the city. The state is a politically organized body of people, and from this perspective, cities were the only mechanisms available to organize and support the constellation of specialists—priests, merchants, soldiers, scribes, nobility—necessary to carry out state activities. This raises still another question: What are the origins of the state? There is still much controversy about this point, and two schools of thought have developed—conflict and integrative theories (Service, 1978). Conflict theorists assert that the state and social inequality did not occur by accident but because one group had the power to impose its will on others. Over millennia, a nomadic tribe or a local kinship group was able to coerce the surplus from the local farmers. Over time this pattern of expropriation became institutionalized, and the farmer was forced to grow a surplus to pay taxes or tribute. Just as the agricultural revolution preceded the development of cities, these theorists argue that social inequality predates the formation of the first cities. Privileged groups, whether conquerors or dominant local kinship groups, formed the state to exploit the weak and the unprivileged. These theorists argue that just as the Agricultural Revolution must predate cities, so too must social inequality (Carneiro, 1970; Cohen and Service, 1978). There is some evidence for their assertion. In Egypt and other ancient societies the state existed before cities, but as far as we know, cities never existed before the state (Kemp, 1977).

Integrative theorists, in contrast, emphasize the benefits that the state conferred. The ancient world can be divided into two camps—settled agriculturalists and nomads. The wealth of the earliest cities and the farmers upon which they depended must have been tempting targets for nomadic peoples. In the sites of most ancient cities, archaeologists find layer after layer of ruin—one city built on top of the remains of another. Interspersed in these gray-brown mud brick tells are dark bands: the charred remains of ancient cities. In some cases, the destruction can be correlated with historical

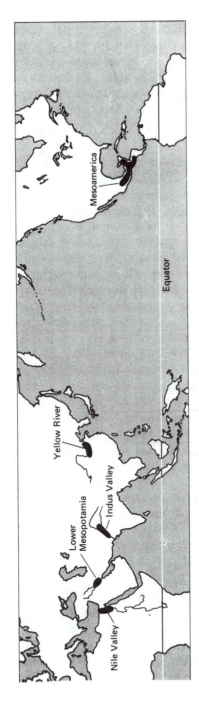

FIGURE 4.3 The world's earliest cities first evolved from villages in the lower Mesopotamia. Thereafter cities arose in similar valleys in other parts of the world.

Source: Gideon Sjoberg. "The Origin and Evolution of Cities." Copyright © 1965 by Scientific American, Inc. All rights reserved.

records that chronicle the clashes between enemy city-states and empires; others are the result of raids by nomadic tribes after the plunder of the city. It is possible that early agriculturalists banded together for military security. It is also possible that ancient villagers petitioned the leader of a local nomadic tribe for protection. Foodstuffs were traded for protection. Impressed with the tribe's military prowess, the relationship became institutionaized over time in the form of taxes paid in grain or raw materials. Over time the ancient state began to carry out other beneficial functions, including the building and maintenance of irrigation and flood control projects (Carneiro, 1970; Cohen and Service, 1978). Both Adams (1960) and Childe (1950) agree that in Mesopotamia irrigation encouraged city growth and only through state mechanisms could large bodies of men be organized to build projects on such a vast scale.

The integrative and conflict theories are not mutually excluding, but describe the contradictory elements found in all social systems—integration/stability versus conflict/change (Service, 1978). Theories are speculative, and a truer picture of the rise of the state and early civic cultures may be a combination of the two. It is clear that the role of state in ancient civilization was complex. On the one hand, the military power of the state ensured peace and prosperity. The state's ability to build large-scale irrigation and flood-control projects provided a reliable food supply. The resolution of internal conflict, the regulation of commerce, and the maintenance of a state religion were other functions that contributed to the integration and stability of ancient civilizations. On the other hand, these activities led to specialization, and specialization led to inequality. Over time priests and warriors were able to consolidate their power into a ruling elite, which used the state to exploit their subjects for their own ends. Therefore, when we scan the history of these ancient civilizations, we are confronted with the contradiction: Ancient agricultural societies needed the state's protection and public works, but the emergence of ancient societies is synomous with the invention of war, the systematic exploitation of agriculturalists, slavery, and the creation of class differences in lifestyle and consumption (Adams, 1966). Naturally, agrarian people resented and struggled against exploitation by urban interests, and this conflict, which is a recurring theme in the history of the ancient world, is one very much with us in the modern era.

OTHER EARLY URBAN DEVELOPMENT

The pattern of evolution of the earliest cities in Mesopotamia was repeated in at least four other places in antiquity—in the valleys of the Nile, the Indus, and the Yellow rivers and also in Central America. It is generally agreed that Mesoamerican and Mesopotamian cities arose independently, whereas the emergence of cities in other regions of the Old World probably was influenced by Mesopotamian cities.

EARLY CITIES IN EGYPT

Agriculture, animal husbandry, and other technologies diffused from the Fertile Crescent southwest into the Nile Valley. Cattle, wheat, and barley not indigenous to

Africa were incorporated into the Neolithic villages that arose along the lower Nile and its delta around 4000 B.C. By 3500 B.C., a number of these farm villages had grown to the overgrown-village stage and were clustered into several politically independent units, each containing large cooperative irrigation projects (Sjoberg, 1960, p. 37). The transition from settled agricultural communities to cities appears to have occurred around 3300 B.C., when the lower Nile was unified under the first pharaoh, Menes.

The archeological record of Egypt's earliest cities is sketchy before 2000 B.C. The few remaining temples, secular buildings, and written records suggest that Egyptian cities were generally not as large or as densely settled as those of Mesopotamia. One reason for this difference is the early dynastic "practice of changing the site of the capital, normally the largest settlement, with the ascendancy of a new pharaoh" (Sjoberg, 1960, pp. 38–39). Cities simply were not given the opportunity to grow in size or become complex in structure. Another reason was the security provided by the Nile Valley. The Nile is buffered on both the east and west by desert, which was a barrier to invasion. Once the Nile Valley was unified politically, Egyptian cities, unlike Mesopotamian cities, did not require elaborate fortifications and garrisoned troops to protect them from invading armies.

Another factor was the combination of the religious and political leadership of Egypt in one god/king, the pharaoh. In Mesopotamian cities, political rule and religious rule were interrelated but not identical. Power was fragmented further by the dispersal of population in city-states. In Egypt, where religious and political power was concentrated in the hands of one person, most full-time specialists were attached to the pharaoh at his capital. Hence, the development of a full civic culture in other urban settlements was retarded (Coulburn, 1959, pp. 67–82).

The combination of environmental and organizational factors in Egypt led to the emergence of cities that diverged from the pattern of those in the lower valleys of the Tigris and Euphrates Rivers. Though it is likely that city-building technology diffused to Egypt from the Mesopotamian city-states, Egypt's indigenous population selectively borrowed items and combined them with the local culture to produce a unique early civilization.

THE HARAPPA CIVILIZATION

The next center of civilization appeared around 2500 B.C. in the Indus River system, in what is now western Pakistan. This civilization, known as the Harappa culture, imposed a uniform culture over an area in excess of one half-million square miles. The civilization was distinguished by twin capitals—a northern one, Harappa, in the Punjab, the tributary region of the Indus, and Mohenjo-daro, 350 miles south on the Indus. The uniformity of these cities in layout, size, and population is remarkable.

Each city was laid out in a gridiron pattern with straight, wide streets running north–south and east–west, forming rectangular blocks roughly 1200 feet by 800 feet. These blocks composed precincts, each inhabited by a specific group—potters, weavers, brick makers, metal workers, and working people. Working people's quarters, for example, consisted of rows of identical two-room dwellings next to the granary and milling works. The elite also were segregated and lived in houses built around courtyards with windowless exterior walls broken only by essential doors. Many of these homes were multistoried and were provided with wells and complex drainage systems. The use of refuse collection bins and a complex underground drainage system suggests a concern for sanitation not shared by other contemporary urban societies.

The cities covered roughly a square-mile area and housed approximately 20,000 persons (Piggott, 1962, p. 167). Centered on the western edge of both cities was a raised citadel, 1200 feet by 600 feet, topped by buildings that appear to have been used for ceremonial or public purposes. The buildings included a great ceremonial bath, a collegiate building, and a pillared hall. This citadel indicates a religious or administrative life of a significant scale.

Centralized control and planning extended beyond the cities to the entire kingdom. After 2500 B.C. the Harappa culture featured a standard of weights and measures, fired bricks of uniform size, mass-produced pottery, and towns and villages with standardized layouts. The extreme uniformity of material culture throughout the territory suggests that the Harappa kingdom was ruled by a single "priest-king, wielding autocratic and absolute power" from two capital cities 350 miles apart but linked by a river thoroughfare (Piggott, 1962).

This civilization was obliterated by invaders in about 1500 B.C. after being remarkably stable for 800 to 1000 years. It adopted few material innovations during the millennium of its existence. There is some evidence of trade with the Sumerian states via the Dilmun empire by 2000 B.C., but the unchanging material culture suggests isolation. The writing of this civilization is still undecipherable and is unrelated to Mesopotamian languages. The evidence taken as a whole suggests that the Harappa culture emerged independently. If city-building elements were borrowed by the people of the Indus valley, these people gave them a special cultural flavor (Sjoberg, 1960).

EARLY CITIES IN CHINA

The valley of the Huangho (Yellow) River is regarded as the birthplace of another civilization, the Shang, which arose around 1800 B.C. Before 1950, the earliest known city in China was Yin, dated at 1300 B.C. Its ruins are north of the Huangho at the site of the present city of An-yang. From 1928 to 1937, fifteen seasons of scientific excavations were undertaken in this region by the National Research Institute of History and Philology of China. Archaeologists discovered at this site a high culture with mature urbanism and related institutions—class differentiation, trade and currency, chamber burials with human sacrifices, highly developed bronze metallurgy, writing, advanced stone carving, and elegant pottery (Chang, 1968, pp. 209–226). Yin, however, was an enigma to archaeologists because it contained no signs of a primitive phase; the material culture was in a highly developed state with no ties to China's Neolithic past. Scholars argued that China's early urban development was the result of advanced technology's being diffused from the Near East, where civilization had existed 1500 years before it came to China.

Since 1950, theories on the evolution of China's early civilization have been reinterpreted on the basis of findings from several sites north and south of the Huangho. The discovery of Shang remains in 1950 south of the Huangho and about 100 miles from An-yang filled some of the gaps dating from 1650 B.C. with evidence of a large population and a complex social order. The most interesting conclusion from this and other Shang sites of the same period is that individual cities were composed of an organized group or network of villages that shared a single political and ceremonial center. Surrounding but linked to this center were industrial quarters for specialists in bronze, pottery, and bone as well as farm-villages, all of which used the administrative center for exchange and redistribution (Chang, 1968, pp. 240–241). The settlement pattern is without precedent in the early civilizations of Mesopotamia, the Nile, and the Indus. These Shang settlements, however, performed all the essential functions of a city. They represent an organizational nexus that contrasts sharply with the Neolithic villages and can be classified as urban.

Still older sites have been identified since 1960 in an area near the Yi and Lo Rivers, tributaries of the Huangho. The primitive pottery and bronze works found there are unlike the elegantly worked artifacts found at Yin and Cheng-chou. These sites represent "the earliest verifiable phase of a full-fledged Shang civilization with bronze metallurgy, advancing forms of symbols on pottery, a Shang art, large hang-t'u structures, a highly stratified burial pattern, and specialized handicrafts" (Chang, 1968, p. 200).

The remains of these early Shang settlements have been dated at approximately 1850 B.C. Although they are not considered urban settlements, they are indicative of a highly stratified and complex society. More importantly, the findings at these sites demonstrate the close relationship between the Neolithic culture of the area and the early Shang culture.

Although cultural items possibly were diffused from the Near East to the valley of the Yellow River, the distinct phases of the Shang civilization suggest that the transformation from Neolithic to civic culture in China was a gradual one rooted in the cultural history of the Huangho valley.

URBAN DEVELOPMENT IN THE NEW WORLD

In comparison with the time spans of the archeological epochs in the Old World, human history in the New World is very brief. Archeological evidence suggests that people migrated to the Western Hemisphere via Siberia and the Bering Strait a little more than 15,000 years ago. These prehistoric people slowly fanned out from the arctic region to populate both Americas by 1300 B.C. (Clark, 1965). In the southward migration, they came into contact with species of plants and animals very different form those of the Old World. The adaptation of these people to the virgin land led to the emergence of cultures and civilizations that differ markedly from those of the Old World.

MESOAMERICA

The earliest cities in the New World first appeared around 200 B.C. in Mesoamerica, specifically the area that includes southern Mexico, Guatemala, Belize (formerly British Honduras), and the western parts of Honduras and El Salvador. Domestication of plants began in this region as early as 7000 B.C., but the first agricultural villages did not emerge until 1500 B.C. Mesoamerican peoples, therefore, were entering the Formative Era (a stage roughly equivalent to the Neolithic of the Old World) at a time when Mesopotamian cities had been in existence for nearly two millennia. The nature of New World agriculture was one factor in this late development (Clark, 1965, p. 171). The corn, squash, beans, peppers, and gourds on which the villages depended were more difficult to domesticate than the wheat and barley of the Near East.

THE MAYA

Of the several civilizations—Olmec, Teolihucan, Toltec, Aztec, and Mayan—that evolved in Mesoamerica, the Mayan was unquestionably the most culturally developed. The origin of the Mayan civilization is still not well understood, but recent excavations in Belize and other parts of Central America are rapidly expanding knowledge of this culture. It flourished between 300 and 1000 A.D. and featured mathematics, astronomy, an accurate calendar, a complex hieroglyphic script, and painting, sculpture, and architecture rivaling those of ancient Greece and Rome (Hammond, 1977). Tikal, Vaxactun, Chichén Itzá, Mayapán, Copán, and other cities were the centers of small states ruled by a leader drawn from the priesthood. These city-states appear to have been combined into some sort of loose confederation.

The layout of these cities conforms to the internal structure of cities in the other civilizations of early antiquity. At the center were the palaces or temples housing priests and nobility, surrounded by the residences of the wealthy and influential. Toward the periphery were the homes of the lower class. The overall population appears to have been very small, so small that some scholars have argued that these were not cities at all but simply "ceremonial foci to which the rural population flocked on special occasions" (Sjoberg, 1960, p. 47). Maya specialists, however, are coming to believe that they were true urban centers. The highly stratified society that included priests, nobility, soldiers, merchants, and artisans and this society's ability to mobilize the resources necessary to construct ceremonial centers of immense size suggest an urban-based civilization.

THE AZTEC

The Aztec civilization, centered in the high plateau region of southern Mexico, emerged in the 500-year period after the decline of the Mayans around 1000 A.D. The Aztec capital, Tenochtitlan, at the site of Mexico City, probably had a population in excess of 100,000 at the time of Spanish conquest in 1521. This civilization was derived from and was similar to the Mayan in many respects.

THE INCA

The only other known New World civilization was the Inca of South America, centered in what is now Peru, Bolivia, and Colombia. Agriculture had diffused from Central to South America by 2500 B.C., but at least another 1000 years elapsed before an extensive pattern of farm-villages appeared there. The diffusion of city-building elements is also likely, but the Incan civilization differed in other significant ways from the Mayan and the Aztec.

Between 100 and 1400 A.D. the Incas conquered most of the central and northern regions of South America, unifying it into an empire linked by more than 10,000 miles of road converging at the Inca capital at Cuzco, in present-day Ecuador. The empire was administered by a centralized governmental bureaucracy under a god-king. This civilization created elaborate public works such as bridges, canals, terrace systems, and roads and conducted large-scale social, economic, and city planning. Of interest is the fact that the Inca did not develop writing, although they did have a system of numerical notation using the "quipu," a knotted string. Consequently, mathematics, astronomy, and calendar making were poorly developed. The Incas were conquered in a few months by the Spanish in 1532 (Sjoberg, 1960).

THE SPREAD OF THE URBAN REVOLUTION

The valleys of the lower Tigris, Euphrates, Nile, Indus, and Huangho Rivers and Mesoamerica were the birthplaces of civilization. In succeeding centuries their agricultural, material, and social innovations diffused outward from these centers, profoundly affecting the course of social development in the rest of the world. By the first centuries of the Christian Era, the continents of Europe, Asia, Africa, and the Americas were urbanized to a degree. In Africa, for instance, cities had emerged in the Sudan region by 700 A.D. and were followed in the next 1000 years by urban-based empires in most of the other parts of the continent (Davidson, 1966).

In Europe, those regions closest to the Middle East and most similar to it in climate were predictably the first to develop cities. Trade with the Near East and raids by barbarians on the urban settlements of that region promoted the diffusion of essential city-building elements on the European continent. Mycenaean cities on the Greek mainland and Minoan cities on the island of Crete emerged around 2000 B.C.

By 800 B.C. urban settlements such as Sparta, Corinth, Megara, and Athens dotted the Greek mainland. Urbanization was disseminated to the rest of the Mediterranean Sea basin through the practice of these Greek city-states of establishing sister colonies once the mother-city population exceeded a manageable size. Concurrently, the Etruscans in southern Italy had established urban settlements that eventually led to the most famous civilization of antiquity—Rome.

Rome greatly expanded the scope of urbanization by establishing forts and administrative centers throughout its extensive empire. Modern cities of Europe whose urban beginning can be traced in name, situs, and/or traditions to Roman influence include York, London, Brussels, Ghent, Utrecht, Granada, Seville, Cologne, Strasbourg, Paris, Toulouse, Bordeaux, Basel, Vienna, Zagreb, Sofia, and Belgrade (Sjoberg, 1960, p. 57).

With the fall of the Roman Empire in the fourth century A.D., much of Europe entered a long period of cultural and economic stagnation with subsequent decline in urban populations. Although the Roman Empire ceased to exist, city-building knowledge lingered on to reemerge in the Renaissance cities of Florence, Genoa, Venice, Pisa, and others on the Italian peninsula. Although 5000 years of urban development preceded the rise of these cities, it is interesting to note that cities of the Renaissance have more in common with the earliest cities of Mesopotamia than they do with cities in today's urban-industrial societies. The reason is that Renaissance cities were a part of agricultural societies with a feudal form of social organization.

THE INDUSTRIAL REVOLUTION

In England during the mid-eighteenth century, a long series of changes began that would profoundly affect the course of that nation and the rest of the world—the Industrial Revolution. The Industrial Revolution commonly is thought of in technological terms—the invention of complex machines and the tapping of inanimate sources of energy—but important cultural, organizational, and population elements also were involved.

REASONS FOR THE INDUSTRIAL REVOLUTION

The exact reasons for this revolution are still a source of major debate among social scientists. Sjoberg (1960) emphasizes the role of technology in both requiring and making possible certain social forms. He posits that technology is linked to surplus, and the presence or absence and the size of a surplus prescribe the nature of a society.

Weber (1958), Mumford (1961), and others examine nontechnological factors in this change. Weber, in *The Protestant Ethic and the Spirit of Capitalism*, suggests that a fundamental change in Western values and outlook was a prerequisite for the Industrial Revolution. For example, among the artisans in medieval Europe, the notion of profit was an alien concept. The price of an object was set by adding to the cost of materials the fair value of one's labor. Without profit, which is an excess of the selling price of goods over their cost, there could be no large capital formation and hence no industrial societies as they are known today.

The Protestant Reformation fostered a new set of values that stressed rationality, hard labor (the work ethic), and the material rewards of labor. This ethic, originating in small religious sects in northern Europe in the sixteenth century, spread throughout Western society and influenced all religious groups to a degree. This new ethic predates the Industrial Revolution and may have been a necessary precondition for it.

Mumford (1961) suggests a constellation of changes in Western societies originating in the fourteenth and fifteenth centuries as the underpinnings of the

Industrial Revolution: the destruction of the feudal order and the rise of nationalism and the modern nation state; the erosion of class barriers and the emergence of an urban-based middle class as a potent force in society; changes in values and outlook; centralized political and economic control; uniformity in taxes, currency, law, and rule; and the rapid expansion of urban population.

The following sections describe the changes in English agricultural technology, manufacturing, and social structure brought about by the Industrial Revolution. These changes form the basis for the emergence of the present-day urban-industrial world.

CHANGES IN ENGLISH AGRICULTURE

In the preindustrial world, only a small percentage of the population was urban, and the cities themselves were small by modern standards. The level of agricultural technology was a major determinant of this patterning, for without an increase in the food supply there could be no growth in the percentage of the society's population in cities. The American colonies provide a good example. Just before the American Revolution only one out of 26 Americans lived in cities, 85 to 90 percent of the labor force was engaged in agriculture, and nine farm families were needed to support just one urban family. In contrast, by 1970, one American farmer supported 45 other people, and less than 5 percent of the total work force was engaged in agricultural occupations. Clearly an important precondition for urban-industrial societies was the removal of the constraints placed on population concentrations by the food supply.

Changes in English agriculture began to occur at a rapid rate during the first half of the eighteenth century. At the beginning of that century, the average English farmer practiced three-crop rotation, whereby fields were divided into fourths and one parcel was left fallow each year to replenish itself. Pasture lands were held in common by the local village, as were woods and water rights. Moreover, the average farm was small. The farmer grew only for his own needs and had little left over for sale.

One of the many agricultural innovations during this period was the discovery that three-crop rotation could be replaced if farmers would replenish their soil by periodically planting nitrogen-fixing crops. This new practice spread rapidly, and within a few decades the amount of acreage in crops increased substantially. At the same time, the selective breeding of animals and the practice of storing silage for winter fodder brought about striking increases in the number and the average weight of farm animals.

The revolution in English agriculture was hastened by Parliament's passage of the infamous Enclosure Acts. In this series of acts, Parliament deeded the common lands historically held by villages to the nobility that held ancient title to the land. Farmers, herdsmen, and squatters whose families had lived off this land for generations found themselves without homes or livelihood. Though social costs were staggering, the small inefficient farms were replaced by more efficient large farming estates (Mantoux, 1961, pp. 136–185).

The changes in agriculture had a pervasive effect on all of English society. First, in the course of 50 years the quality and quantity of food improved dramatically. The higher quality and greater reliability of the food supply brought about significant declines in mortality that, combined with the high birth rate of the period, caused England's population to grow rapidly.

A second outcome of the changes in agriculture was a reduction in manpower needs in the countryside. The small farmer and the peasant had little choice but to migrate to nearby cities and towns.

Third, the expanding food supply and the rural-urban migration of population stimulated urban growth and development. Finally, the growth of cities and towns and the rationalization of agriculture stimulated a dramatic improvement in England's transportation network. Throughout the eighteenth century, canal and toll-road construction crisscrossed the English countryside to provide a transportation network for moving agricultural produce to urban markets (Pahl, 1970, Mantoux, 1961).

Viewed as a whole, these changes in English society formed the foundation from which an industrial society could arise. A reliable, high-quality food supply supported greater numbers of people in cities. An expanding population provided for the labor force for industry, and an efficient transportation system provided essential linkage.

CHANGES IN MANUFACTURING

At the same time as the revolution in English agriculture, inventions were being made that could tap the new manpower, food surpluses, and transportation improvements. The revolution in industry—essentially the substitution of machines for hand tools and the tapping of new sources of energy—evolved over a period of decades.

Cottage Industry. Before 1750, manufacturing was done on a small scale, often in the form known as cottage industry, whereby an entire family worked as a unit within their home, handcrafting objects with their own tools. In the manufacturing of a woolen garment, for example, a middleman would purchase the wool from a merchant and in turn "let it out" to a farm or village family who would clean, dye, and spin the wool into yarn. The middleman would purchase the yarn and have it woven into cloth by another family and in turn would have the cloth fabricated into a garment. Thus the fabrication of one item was costly and inefficient, requiring the coordination of the activities of a large number of families scattered over a large geographic area. Concentration of population at one place was impractical if not impossible because of the lack of an adequate food supply, labor pool, and transportation network. Even during the early stages of the Industrial Revolution, when factories were operated by water-driven machinery, the need for factories to be near running water precluded their expansion (Mantoux, 1961, pp. 47–185).

Production in Factories. James Watt's invention of the first practical steam engine in 1769 was a major breakthrough. The steam engine harnessed to the machine dramatically broadened the economic capacity of society and made possible the fabrication of many more commodities than the cottage system could produce. More importantly, steam power removed the locational constraints of earlier factory-towns. Rather than eliminating jobs, the machines rapidly increased the demand for an urban work force. The increase in manufacturing output stimulated the creation of jobs in other spheres of the economy (Mantoux, 1961, pp. 311–338).

The technological breakthroughs in agriculture, energy, and manufacturing made possible the transfer of all types of cottage industries to factories in urban settings. By 1800, London was the largest city in the world with a population in excess of 900,000. Birmingham, Leeds, Manchester, and Sheffield also grew rapidly, drawing vast numbers of people to work in the factories concentrated there. Living and sanitary conditions, never good in the preindustrial city, reached new lows. Filth, crowding, and disease typified the new industrial centers. The peasant, released from the tyranny of the feudal order, endured the regimentation, low wages, and oppressive working conditions of the factory.

CHANGES IN SOCIAL STRUCTURE

England before 1700 was like any other preindustrial feudal society—class permeated the entire social order. Society consisted of two classes, the elite and the masses, and was characterized by ascribed status, little social mobility, and the domination of the political, economic, educational, and religious institutions by the elite.

Class in industrial society, although important, is not the all-pervasive force that it was in the preindustrial world. The most distinguishing characteristic of the social structure of industrial England was the growth of a large, influential middle class. The social structure was relatively flexible, and social mobility was not only possible but relatively common. The political, economic, religious, and educational institutions, although still influenced by social class, began to evolve into rational bureaucratic forms wherein one's position within the organization was based on training and expertise—achievement rather than ascriptive criteria.

CONCLUSIONS

Many people narrowly define the word *revolution* as an armed confrontation with the establishment, but in sociology this word refers to any rapid change in a society's institutions. In this sense, the word *revolution* accurately describes the scope of change in English society in the eighteenth and nineteenth centuries. In terms of its overall effect, the Industrial Revolution in England was similar to the French and American Revolutions of the same period. It brought about fundamental change in the structure and character of English society and in so doing changed the course of development in all societies.

AMERICAN URBAN HISTORY

In the sixteenth century, when the first English colonists arrived in North America, they found a continent without cities. Except for the Indians of the Northwest, the North American Indian population was nomadic or lived in small agricultural villages.

At this time the native population of the entire continent was estimated to be fewer than one million persons.

In the nearly five centuries that have followed, the virgin continent has become the site of the leading urban-industrial society in the world. In 1990, more than 70 percent of the United States population lived in urban places that occupied less than 2.0 percent of the land area. The history of America's social, economic, and technological changes during the last 500 years is important to other societies that hope to follow its development pattern or to avoid its mistakes.

In the following sections, the history of America's transformation to an urban society is explored. First, historians' theories on the city's role in American history are described briefly. Then, the urban transformation is examined in terms of five groups of cities—the Atlantic coast cities, the river cities, the lake cities, the southern cities, and the cities of the Southwest. Each group is composed of cities that are similar in time of settlement, transportation dependence, and social and economic characteristics. Each group played an important role in the development of this nation.

HISTORIANS' PERSPECTIVES

For the past 40 years, historians have been involved in a controversy over the role of the city in the history of America's national development. For much of the last century and the first quarter of this century, the original colonies of the Atlantic coast region were considered the mainspring in this development. In 1893, Fredrick Jackson Turner suggested a new interpretation of American history and declared, "the true point of view in the history of this nation is not the Atlantic Coast, it is the Great West."[4] Turner noted that the United States during the nineteenth century, in comparison with Europe, had been relatively free of communal social unrest, and he contended that the availability of free land in the West acted as an escape valve contributing to domestic tranquility. Turner reasoned that people who became dissatisfied with the conditions in the urban East could simply move out and homestead in the West (Schlesinger, 1941).

CRITICS OF THE TURNER THESIS

Arthur M. Schlesinger in the 1940s questioned the Turner thesis and suggested that an urban reinterpretation of American history was needed. Schlesinger (1940, 1949) and others (Holt, 1953; Thernstrom, 1968) noted that the massive immigration of farmers to the cities in the last half of the nineteenth century not only contributed to the tremendous growth of cities, but also was a major factor in national development. The reason for this urban migration was the state of American farming during that period. The price of commodities fluctuated widely on the world market, and currency was periodically deflated. Consequently, the nineteenth-century farmers who had secured long-term loans in good times were forced some years later to repay them in deflated dollars, that is, dollars with much greater buying power. Because the real cost of these loans had increased substantially, many farmers were no longer able to meet their obligations and were forced to sell out and move to the cities.

A noneconomic factor in the migration from farm to city was the general undesirability of farm life. The magazines and popular writings of the late nineteenth century describe the backbreaking labor involved in farming on the Great Plains and the months of deadening isolation without outside contact.

AN URBAN REINTERPRETATION OF AMERICAN HISTORY

Turner's thesis, therefore, may be wrong, and the reverse may be true: the city rather than the Great West may have been the escape valve, not for the urbanite but for the disenchanted farmer. One reason for the general absence of social unrest in the nineteenth-century city may have been that the difficult living and working conditions of the city were still better than those on the farm.

Critics have accused Schlesinger of confusing urbanization with related phenomena such as industrialization, failing to identify the forces that created the city and making the same mistake as Turner by attributing causality to a single factor—the city (Diamond, 1969; Lampard, 1969; Lubove, 1969). Schlesinger's work, however, marks the beginning of a major dialogue among social scientists and a new direction in the field of American historiography. It is now generally agreed that urban life rivaled frontier life from the beginnings of the nation and that to understand America's history one must understand its urban history.

ATLANTIC COAST CITIES

The Atlantic coast was the original frontier, and cities and towns had a key role in its settlement. For example, the first successful English settlements at Jamestown and Plymouth were in fact small towns. The small towns and villages that eventually dotted the landscape east of the Appalachian Mountains provided mutual protection as well as the population necessary to support a variety of occupations. In addition, these towns contributed to the settlement of the surrounding countryside. New colonists normally would spend their first months in one of these communities, gathering provisions and learning the ways of the new land before moving into the countryside. Once settled, these colonists continued to depend on urban places for markets and for manufactured goods. The standard of living of the colonial farmer was greatly improved by the nails, hinges, cloth, and medicines sold in these places (Bridenbaugh, 1938, 1955; Chudacoff and Smith, 1988).

As a result of this settlement pattern, by 1690 almost 10 percent of the colonial population was concentrated in the five coastal cities of Boston, New York, Philadelphia, Newport, and Charleston.

Similarities. These cities, although different in geography, were similar in time of settlement and in social, economic, and physical characteristics. First, all were seaports and became commercial centers for trade between Europe and the colonies. Second, not only goods entered these ports but also new ideas from Europe. Early in American history, the intellectual activities in science, literature, medicine, and the arts were centered in the colleges (Harvard, the College of Charleston), libraries, museums, and professional and scientific organizations of these cities. Although small by modern standards, these preindustrial cities exerted an influence on the colonies far out of proportion to their size. Third, not surprisingly, they faced similar urban problems. Fire was always a serious threat; these cities enacted building codes and other ordinances for the common welfare. Public disorder, pauperism, sanitation, and other problems led all five cities to adopt similar solutions, not by innovation but by borrowing from the great cities of Europe (Bridenbaugh, 1938). Finally, these cities were similar in social structure, which was greatly influenced by the absence of an ancestral feudal order in the New World. On the whole the leadership was Protestant, and the cultural values were drawn from the new middle class of Europe (Main, 1965).

In sum, the cities, towns, and villages of the East Coast spearheaded the settlement of the American frontier; without them colonization of the New World would not have been possible.

THE RIVER CITIES

The settlement pattern in the East continued in the region west of the Appalachian Mountains. Forts and trading posts were established in advance of permanent agriculture, and the outposts pushed the frontier into the Old Northwest. By 1800, the sites of every major metropolis in this region except Chicago, Milwaukee, and Indianapolis had been cleared and surveyed (Wade, 1969, p. 100). The settlement of this region occurred in waves. In the early decades of the nineteenth century the cities along the Ohio River underwent rapid economic and population growth. Later in the century cities on the Great Lakes displaced the river cities in dominance of the political and economic affairs of the region.

The urban history of this region is marked by "city-making mania" and intense intercity rivalry. Many of the new towns were speculative ventures, the land purchased and the town platted by investors in the East. Others, with names like New London, New Baltimore, and New Philadelphia, reflected the hopes and aspirations of their founders. Some of these communities flourished briefly and then failed, leaving behind the West's first ghost towns. Wheeling, West Virginia; New Albany, Indiana; and Zanesville, Ohio are examples of towns that at one time had chances to be major metropolises but were surpassed by rivals such as Pittsburgh and Cincinnati and became subordinate to them (Wade, 1957; Abbott, 1981a).

The winners of this intense and often brutal competition were Pittsburgh, Cincinnati, Louisville, and St. Louis—the river cities. All of these cities were founded in the eighteenth century as forts or trading posts prior to the use of their land for settled agriculture. They were remarkably similar in economic, social, and physical characteristics. Each of these cities was a winner in the urban rivalry because of its strategic location on the interior river system. Pittsburgh, for example, is at the site where the Allegheny and Monongahela Rivers converge to form the Ohio River. Cincinnati was strategically located with respect to a road system in Ohio, Kentucky, and Indiana. Louisville was founded at a major series of falls on the Ohio River, and the stevedore operations that grew up there were later expanded into other areas of commerce. Finally, St. Louis is near the mouth of the Missouri River where it enters the Mississippi.

In the eighteenth century these cities were small towns with populations of fewer than 1000 inhabitants. After 1800 growth of these cities accelerated. By 1815 Pittsburgh was a thriving center of 8000. Cincinnati estimated its population to be 4000, and Louisville and St. Louis were half that size. The real growth of these cities came after 1820 with the introduction of the steamboat, which permitted upriver shipment of goods for the first time. Consequently, 50 years of growth was compressed into a single decade (Wade, 1964b, p. 102).

The importance of the river cannot be overstressed. Roads during this era were unpaved, and few were wider than a single wagon. Rivers were the major transportation arteries, and the trade and commerce that spread through the interior river system were the economic lifeblood of the river cities. Later, such industries as glass and iron manufacturing at Pittsburgh and meat packing and brewing and distilling at Cincinnati expanded their local economies.

The river cities were laid out in a gridiron pattern with streets running perpendicular and parallel to the river. The river bank was dominated by docks, warehouses, businesses, mills, and granaries; little or no land was set aside for recreational uses. These cities were compact and densely settled and had many of the same urban problems as their eastern counterparts. Like the great cities of the East, they were not innovators but borrowers. Their forms of government and solutions to the problems of fire, public safety, pauperism, and sanitation were copied largely from those of eastern cities, especially Philadelphia (Wade, 1957).

Class consciousness emerged early in the river cities. Business leaders headed the social structure, followed by professionals, working people, freemen, and slaves. A leisure class was lacking, and the dominance of the business community was reflected in all aspects of the city, especially its physical characteristics—that is, the commercial use of the river bank.

In time, the river cities came to dominate the political and economic institutions of the region. Wade (1957) suggests that early in the history of this region two cultures emerged, one urban and the other rural. In religion, urban populations largely attended formal mainstream churches; rural populations were drawn to the tent revivals and more expressive religions. In politics, the cities provided leadership for the major state and national offices; rural constituencies controlled the state legislatures. Finally, the colleges, libraries, professional societies, museums, and theaters in the cities were dynamic cultural forces influencing the outlying rural areas.

THE LAKE CITIES

Another wave of urbanization occurred in the north in the so-called lake cities of Buffalo, Cleveland, Detroit, Chicago, and Milwaukee. Their period of rapid economic and population growth was the 1850s, when tens of thousands of people poured into the upper Mississippi River valley. These cities were shaped by similar social, economic, and transportation forces, particularly the latter. All five cities are lake ports and owe their existence to the development of the transportation technologies of the canal and railroad. Buffalo, Cleveland, and Detroit, for example, are the end points of major canal systems; Chicago and Milwaukee grew as railroad centers (Taylor, 1951). The fact that the initial success of these cities was based on commerce led to serious economic problems because the canals and lakes were impassable during the winter months. However, the resultant high seasonal unemployment eventually led to an increase of manufacturing and industry in all these cities (Still, 1941). The economic growth of the lake cities was spectacular, and they soon displaced the river cities in importance. For example, Chicago had surpassed St. Louis in population by 1885 (Belcher, 1947).

The lake cities were also similar in social and political characteristics. Like the river cities before them, they were borrowers and not innovators. Their nineteenth-century charters, for example, differed only in the name of the city in the title. Local governments were of the strong mayor/council form based on Jacksonian democracy, and each city underwent a subscription stage in which voluntary groups performed the vital municipal services.

The lake cities revered the "common man," and local governments passed ordinances protecting every aspect of daily life from the sizing of bread to the cleanliness of markets and the purity of milk. Moreover, their populations were more cosmopolitan than those of the river cities; more than 50 percent of their inhabitants were foreign-born in the 1860s and 1870s. This cosmopolitan character is still evident in the rich ethnic mixture of neighborhoods in these cities (Still, 1941).

Today, these cities share similar forms of government, physical characteristics, and urban problems as a result of the forces that shaped their initial development.

THE SOUTHERN CITIES

Until the 1960s, there were few works on the urban history of the South. This changed in 1964 with the publication of Richard Wade's (1964a) book, *Slavery in Cities*. This influential book along with the spectacular growth of the Sunbelt has inspired a generation of historians, political scientists, sociologists, and journalists to study the urban growth in this region.

Wade was one of the first to comment on the unusual pattern of cities in this region. If you examine the map in Figure 4.4, you will notice that the cities are situated along the region's periphery with little urban development in the core. Wade refers to this pattern as the South's "urban perimeter"; others have likened it to a horseshoe. This imaginary horseshoe is oriented from northwest to southeast with the open end in the Carolinas and is composed of the cities of New Orleans, Memphis, Mobile, Savannah, Charleston, Baltimore, and Louisville. These cities dominated the commerce of the region through the antebellum period and acted as administrative centers for the settlement of the southern interior. This pattern persisted into the nineteenth century, although the size of the horseshoe contracted as cities in the border states, like Baltimore and Louisville, were integrated into the regional economies of

FIGURE 4.4 Major cities of the South prior to the Civil War.

the Northeast and Midwest. Surprisingly, one could still find the horseshoe configuration as late as World War II by running a line westward from Richmond through Nashville and Memphis to Dallas, and back through Houston and New Orleans to roughly Jacksonville, Florida (Brownell and Goldfield, 1977, p. 7). Since World War II, cities in the South's core have expanded rapidly, but one wonders why this spatial pattern persisted for nearly three centuries. The answer lies in the early history of the region.

By 1700, a string of cities stretched the length of the Atlantic Coast from Boston to Charleston. However, as early as the Colonial Era the distinctive climates, geography, and agriculture of the North and South had set these regions on very different paths of urban development. In the region south of the Chesapeake Bay, broad navigable rivers reached deep into the interior. The fertile alluvial soils of the lowlands along with a benign climate permitted the growth of staple crops like tobacco and rice on large plantations. In addition, large land holdings and staple crops were the conditions necessary for the use of slave labor. As a result, ships with small drafts could navigate up the inland rivers and dock at the wharves of plantations. Development of the interior, therefore, could be completed with few interior cities. Coastal cities like Charleston and Savannah prospered as commercial cities, marketing and shipping the agricultural wealth of the interior. This was in sharp contrast to the North with its poor soils, harsh climate, few navigable rivers, and small farms. Cities in this region acted as staging areas, spearheading the development of the frontier, which led to a fairly dense pattern of urban settlement (Goldfield, 1982, pp. 12–27; Earle and Hoffman, 1977).

Thus, a number of interrelated patterns emerge from the Colonial Era which were to shape the urban development of the region to the present day: first, the region's dependence on agriculture, especially staple crops like tobacco, rice, and later cotton; second, the creation of a biracial society through the institution of slavery; third, low density of urban settlement in the interior and large commercial cities on the periphery.

These patterns persisted into the Antebellum Era. The region was rapidly urbanizing during this period, but most of this growth was captured by small urban places with fewer than 4000 inhabitants. Cities like New Orleans, Charleston, Mobile, and Savannah prospered, but these cities were not cities in the Northern sense; rather, they were giant market centers which boomed in late summer and fall and fell into the doldrums the rest of the year. Atlanta, Dallas, and other cities in the interior remained quiet backwaters because of the region's dependence on exports. Wade's explanation for this pattern was that the antebellum South had ties to a capitalistic society—the North—but was itself a feudal society. The South at this time was dominated by "aristocratic feudal lords," who were concerned not about the return on their investments but with maintaining their social position. Therefore, monies that might have been used for the building of railroads and industry went into land and slaves. In addition, slaves living at or near subsistence did not provide the consumers needed to drive a capitalistic economy (Goldfield, 1982, pp. 28–79).

Although the South exported an enormous amount of agricultural products, the Northern capitalists probably made more money on cotton and other exports than the South. The Northerner provided the shipping, warehousing, insurance, processing, manufacturing, and marketing of these exports, and therein lay the profits. In many respects the South in this period could be likened to an underdeveloped country, and its economic ties to the North could be defined in terms of imperialism.

Because the economies of the Southern cities during this period were based on commerce, changes in transportation technology and world commodity markets greatly affected them. New Orleans, for example, had notable growth between 1820 and 1840 and shared economic prosperity with the river cities. New Orleans was a break-in-transportation city. Goods shipped from the Northeast via the Atlantic and the Gulf of Mexico were transferred to barges there for distribution to the cities in the interior. By 1860, New Orleans was the sixth largest city in the United States, but after 1860 railroads and canals provided a more direct link between the Midwest and the Northeast, and New Orleans sank into economic decline.

The same fate befell Mobile, Savannah, and Charleston. Charleston, for example, was the fifth largest city in the United States in 1810, dropped to twenty-second in 1860, and after 1860 underwent both economic and population decline. Richmond, Virginia, the only Southern city with an industrial base before the war, was leveled by the Union armies and failed to regain its economic importance in the postwar period (Wade, 1964a).

The economy of the South was destroyed by the Civil War, but the themes that run through its history persisted in the postwar period. After the war the region desperately needed cash and capital, and it quickly returned to the patterns of the past. Although the Civil War brought slavery to an end, Southern whites quickly reestablished a biracial society through sharecropping, wage peonage, and political disenfranchisement. The continuation of a biracial society kept nearly half the South's population living at the subsistence level, and a low standard of living meant few consumers and a retarded regional economy. Staple crops continued as the stalwart of the region's economy, and the boom/bust cycles on world commodity markets plagued the region's financial planning and development. Technology changed. Rail displaced water as the major means of transportation, and once small, dusty rail towns like Dallas and Atlanta prospered. After the war an integrated national economy emerged, and the South continued in its subordinate role to the Northeast. A classic example can be found in the development of the railroad. At a time when the North had developed a complex, integrated rail system, the South's rail system usually linked only two cities. The end result was that the South never developed a balanced regional economy. The absence of rail network and the communication, finance, marketing, and distribution infrastructure made it virtually impossible for the industries in southern cities to compete with the North. More importantly, the North had the wealth and the political and economic tools to perpetuate the South's subordinate position. For example, Andrew Carnegie, fearful of the competition of southern steel manufacturing centered in Birmingham, neutralized the threat by purchasing the steel works. J. P. Morgan controlled the development of the South's rail system by buying all the major railroads in the region (Goldfield, 1982, pp. 80–196; Rabinowitz, 1977).

As late as the 1960s, students of the city estimated that the South lagged 15 to 20 years behind the urbanization in the North. Few would make that argument today. The impressive economic and population gains in this region in the post-World War II period have rapidly reduced this differential. How did the South in the course of two generations overcome centuries of retarded economic development? The answer can be found in the policies of the federal government. The federal government began to exert an influence on the region's economic development as early as World War I when a number of major military bases were opened or expanded in the region. The Great Depression with its New Deal programs brought the first great infusion of federal dollars into the region. Public housing, public works projects, rural electrification, and a host of other federal programs began to address the serious social problems of the South. However, it was World War II that changed the region forever. The South benefited more than other regions from the most massive military buildup in history. Millions of people and billions of dollars poured into the region, and the South's cities were overwhelmed. The business community geared up to provide the housing, transportation, and other services necessary for the war effort at government expense. After the war, the business community cringed at the thought of a bust, but it never came. An infrastructure now existed, and the climate and other place amenities meant investment would continue. Growth fed growth, and a growth inertia developed. But again, much of this growth occurred at government expense—the interstate highway system linked the cities of the South, federal grants subsidized the region's sewers, water systems, and roads, the Cold War kept military budgets high, and money continued to pour into the military bases and aerospace industry of the region (Goldfield, 1982, pp. 80–196; Hass, 1977; Abbott, 1981b; MacDonald, 1984).

The patterns that shaped the South's early history continue. It is still very much a biracial society. The region still suffers from boom/bust cycles because of its dependency on agriculture, oil, and gas. The South still is unable to raise its own capital and still turns to Northern banks for its capital needs. The corporate headquarters and banking and financial institutions situated in the North still hold sway over much of the development in the South. And critics argue that the investment of billions of dollars by the federal government has managed to transform the South from a poor agricultural region to a poor industrial region. The past continues to exert a powerful influence over the people, the economy, and the urban patterns of this region.

CITIES OF THE SOUTHWEST

The South through much of its history served as an economic hinterland for America's industrial core, providing the major Atlantic coast, river, and lake cities with raw materials, labor, and new markets. Since World War II, a new relationship has become apparent. Increasingly, large numbers of people and resources have been siphoned away from the older and now declining regions of the Northeast and North Central United States. This process has by no means been a uniform one. Some northern cities continue to grow, especially their suburbs. In some cases, northern cities have been able to hold and even increase their populations, and the sheer inertia of historical patterns should ensure that this region continue to hold the major financial, government, and industrial centers of the United States. Many observers now, however, point to the dramatic growth and development mentioned above in the "Sunbelt"—a region extending roughly from Virginia through the Southeast and Southwest to southern California (Goldfield and Brownell, 1979, p. 335) (see Figure 4.5). Nowhere has population and economic growth been more spectacular than in the cities of the Southwest.

Southwestern cities include this nation's most rapidly growing metropolitan areas—Phoenix, Tucson, Dallas, and Houston. Between 1940 and 1980, growth in and around these cities was remarkable. Phoenix grew 1107 percent, Tucson grew 825 percent, and Albuquerque 836 percent (Luckingham, 1983, p. 317). The important point is that these cities differ from those in other regions in that, after years of being stable and small in size, they grew to metropolitan status after World War II. For

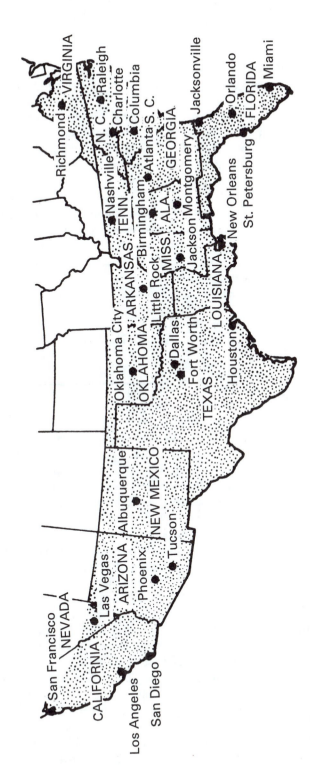

FIGURE 4.5 Map of U.S. sunbelt.

Source: Goldfield, David R. and Blaine A. Brownell, *Urban America: From Downtown to No Town* First Edition. Copyright © 1979 Houghton Mifflin Company. Used by permission.

example, in 1940 Tucson and Albuquerque each had populations of approximately 35,000. Phoenix was larger, but still had a population of under 70,000 in 1940. Then came the great influx of immigrants. By 1980 the city of Phoenix approached a population of 800,000 (the metropolitan area was over 1.5 million), and the Tucson and Albuquerque metropolitan areas had more than 450,000 people (Luckingham, 1983, p. 321). These cities have been shaped by the transportation, communication, and industrial technology of the twentieth century, and they differ from the older cities of other regions in their physical form, population composition, and economic base.

Many factors are responsible for the growth of cities in the Southwest, but none are more important than the effects of the microelectronics, computer, and aerospace industries. Some observers have argued that this technology is as important to twentieth-century societies as industrialization was to the nineteenth century (Gordon, 1978, p. 107).

The implications of these industries for urban places lie in the fact that the transportation, communication, and service needs of industries based on this technology differ from those that developed at earlier stages of our industrialization. For example, the new industries operate at much higher levels of efficiency and require a small but highly skilled and well-educated work force. Smaller work forces mean that these industries no longer need to be located near the cities of the Northeast and North Central regions with their large populations of unskilled labor. Instead, a plant can be located on the basis of markets, prevailing wage and tax rates, and benign climate. This is readily apparent when examining Figure 4.5. Note the strategic location of the southwestern cities in relation to the growing markets of Southern California, the South, and the lower Midwest.

Other factors recognized as influencing the growth of cities in this region include the following: (1) the growth of government military spending: (world nuclear strategy has made military bases in this region vitally important to our national security); (2) the migration of large numbers of retirees (often on government pensions), drawn to the cities of the region by the warm climate and low cost of living; (3) a changing American lifestyle and an improved standard of living, which have resulted in fewer hours at work and more time at leisure—the mild climate permits year-round outdoor activity; and (4) entrepreneurship and boosterism, qualities of the political and economic leadership of these cities that have motivated these leaders to take economic risks to draw industry and other economic activities into these regions (MacDonald, 1984; Lotchin, 1984; Abbott, 1981b; Perry and Watkins, 1977; Sale, 1975; Nash, 1973;).

The factors shaping the cities of the Southwest mean that they have a form and character quite different from cities of other regions. Their population mix is different, with a relatively highly skilled work force. Moreover, the physical form of these cities is different. Shaped by the automobile, they have no need for a downtown central core; rather, these cities sprawl over the landscape and have low population densities. Finally, these cities face their own urban problems arising from the shortage of water, delicate arid or semiarid ecosystems, and large indigenous populations of Indians and/or Mexican Americans.

In sum, the rise of cities in the Southwest, and for that matter in all of the Sunbelt, is not an anomaly in United States history; rather, it is a part of a long process that has continuously transformed this nation's system of cities. This urban development cannot be understood in a vacuum. Changes in our economic system and the emergence of the computer age have changed the nature of regional economic and urban growth. For many reasons, cities in the Southwestern region have been better suited to take advantage of these changes. Because of the importance of this region to the nation's urban development, the growth and change in the Sunbelt will be explored in greater depth in Chapter 7, "The System of Cities."

SUMMARY

The first cities appeared more than 5500 years ago; they represented a revolutionary change in the way humans adapt to their physical environments. The emergence of these first cities was the outcome of a long evolutionary history in which the social and technological innovations necessary to support a large population at a permanent site were accumulated. This process began in the Mesolithic period, when climatic changes enabled people to live in permanent villages through intensive hunting and gathering. The skills and knowledge of the environment gained in this epoch led to the formation of the first agricultural villages during the Neolithic period, which began around 8000 B.C. The Agricultural Revolution was an important prerequisite for the emergence of the first cities, but not the only one. Human societies also needed the ability to store, transport, and distribute a food surplus and to use the surplus for varied social ends before the first cities could develop.

Therefore, the earliest cities arose as a result of the convergence of organizational and technological innovations and environmental conditions in areas of benign climate, such as the valleys of the lower Tigris and Euphrates, Nile, Indus, and Huangho Rivers. Technology modified the barriers to city building imposed by the environment, and, as city-building and agricultural technology improved, cities spread to other regions of the world where conditions were less favorable. By the early centuries of the Christian Era, most of the world's continents had urban populations. The cultures of these cities differed, but, as Sjoberg has shown, their ecological, institutional, and technological characteristics were similar whether they existed in early antiquity or in more recent times.

The Industrial Revolution, which began in England during the mid-eighteenth century, was a historical force that profoundly affected the course of humankind. Technological breakthroughs in agriculture, energy, and manufacturing during the eighteenth century led to the rapid growth of urban populations and the transfer of all types of cottage industries to factories in urban settings. The ability to draw upon vast numbers of people to work in factories contributed greatly to the level of human efficiency and brought about a fundamental change in the fabric of society. Class is not now the all-pervasive force that it was in the preindustrial world. A large and influential middle class arose during the Industrial Revolution, as well as social structure in which social mobility was common. The major institutions of society, although still influenced by social class, began to evolve into the rational bureaucratic forms common today in more developed societies.

The exact role of cities in the development of the United States has been a source of major debate within the field of American social history for much of this century. It now appears that the role of the "true pioneer" of folklore, who escaped the restrictions of society by carving a homestead out of the wilderness, has been exaggerated. The settlement of the West was accomplished mainly by groups. Many settlers who moved west across the Appalachian Mountains were "in search of promising towns rather than good land, their inducement being urban opportunities rather than fertile soil" (Wade, 1969, p. 100). Moreover, the settlement process was extremely conservative; most of the new settlers attempted to reproduce their old institutions as closely as possible.

The role of cities in the settlement of the United States is explored by examining five groups of cities—the Atlantic coast cities, the river cities, the lake cities, the Southern cities, and the Southwestern cities. The cities in each group were settled at about the same time, were dependent on the same type of transportation, and had similar local economies.

NOTES

1. The Agricultural Revolution may have occurred 5000 years earlier in southeast Asia. Solheim and his associates have excavated artifacts from sites in Thailand that suggest the domestication of plants of a type very different from those of the Fertile Crescent may have begun around 13,000 B.C. See W. G. Solheim, "An Earlier Agricultural Revolution," *Scientific American* 226, no. 4 (1972): 34–41.

2. For two excellent works on the transition to food production, see B. Bender, *Farming in Prehistory: From Hunter-Gatherer to Food Producer* (New York: St. Martin's Press, 1975) and the collected work edited by Stuart Stoeuver, *Prehistoric Agriculture* (Garden City, N.Y.: American Museum of Natural History, 1971).

3. This explanation is similar to central place theory, which is described in detail in Chapter 5. Central place theory argues that early agriculturalists grew a surplus and transported it to cities out of self-interest. Archaeological evidence shows an extensive trade network throughout the Middle East during the Neolithic Period; cities facilitated the exchange of locally produced goods for those imported from outside the region. For more information, see the citations for the works of Childe, 1957; Mayer, 1965; Oates et al., 1977, and Price, 1978 in the bibliography.

4. For a discussion of the Turner thesis, see "Epilogue: The City and the Historians," in *American Urban History: An Interpretive Reader with Commentaries,* ed. A. B. Callow, Jr. (New York: Oxford University Press, 1969).

THEORIES OF LOCATION

INTRODUCTION

One of my favorite pastimes is exploring the countryside by car. I have a county map in the glove compartment, but I never use it. I drive to the end of my street and make a snap decision. Right? Left? It doesn't make any difference. Usually, I'll start out on a familiar highway, drive until there is a side road I haven't been on before and then just follow it until it comes out somewhere. Through this random driving, I've found wonderful country restaurants, auctions, a wildflower seed company, marijuana fields, a commune, and some of the friendliest and most hostile people I've ever met.

My dad started me in this pernicious habit. On a rainy Saturday or Sunday afternoon, he would make some frivolous excuse for getting out of the house, and he usually took me along. We'd drive around and land up at a greenhouse, an orchard, a junk shop, a used book store, or a decrepit restaurant, and when we got back home three or four hours later, my mother would always ask, "Where have you two been?" We would look at each other and smile and say in unison, "No place special." We all knew the places weren't special; our time together was.

One trip has always stayed with me. I must have been eight or nine, and we had just driven through our fourth or fifth tiny village. They were those little places we all are used to. Just before you get to one, there's a road sign, "Speed zone ahead" closely followed by one announcing the village's name, usually tacked onto a "25 MPH" speed sign. There is a smattering of small houses—one usually stands out because of its size or upkeep—an old gas station, small store, and a church at the center, and before you know it you're doing 55 mph again. I remember asking, "Dad, what are these little towns doing here?" He thought a second and said, "I suppose the farmers need to buy groceries, and seed, and other things." And for some reason, he said, "Let's see how far the next one is." It was 6.2 miles. The next one was 4.8 miles. The next one, 5 miles or so. We played this odometer game for the rest of the trip, and all these tiny places were spaced about the same distance apart. I always wondered about the spatial regularity of these villages. I was in graduate school before I found an answer—central place theory.

The location and distribution of human settlements have been of interest to geographers, economists, and human ecologists for more than a century. In this chapter, the "how" and "why" of the location of cities are explored. Three of the most important theories on city location are presented. The break-in-transportation theory focuses on the role of transportation in determining the location of cities. Specialized function theory emphasizes the presence of raw materials as a determinant of city location. Central place theory, the most general of the three models, is based on the role of trade and the relationship of a city to its hinterland or trade area. Although the theories are presented separately, and each theory provides a different explanation for the location of cities, the three theories complement rather than conflict with each other. Together, they provide a theoretical framework that describes the location of such diverse places as Buffalo, New York, Las Vegas, Nevada, and Warrensburg, Missouri.

BREAK-IN-TRANSPORTATION THEORY

LOCATION AND TRANSPORTATION

The break-in-transportation theory was one of the earliest theories of city location. It can be traced to the works of a sociologist, C. H. Cooley (1984), who emphasized the importance of transportation in the location of cities. He observed that population and wealth tend to collect wherever there is a break-in-transportation (p. 313). A break-in-transportation occurs in the shipment of goods from one place to another when it is necessary to load a shipment from one form of transportation, say, an oceangoing vessel, onto another, such as a train or truck. Interrupting the shipment of goods is expensive, and specialized equipment and workers are required. Therefore, a city is likely to emerge at the point where one form of transportation intersects another, for example, where deep-water shipping intersects land transportation.

BREAK-IN-TRANSPORTATION CITIES

The section of Chapter 4 on American urban history illustrates the importance of transportation in the emergence of cities. In that section the earliest American cities are categorized as either Atlantic Coast, river, or lake cities; these titles reflect the dominant forms of transportation on which the cities were dependent. New York, Philadelphia, Boston, and Charleston, South Carolina—the Atlantic Coast cities—owe their existence to excellent deep-water harbors. The cargoes in incoming oceangoing vessels were loaded onto either wagons for surface transport or onto smaller sailing vessels that could navigate the inland rivers. The ability of these cities to provide a linkage between different forms of transportation ensured their economic survival.

Until the advent of the railroads, the most important highways in the American interior were the rivers. Roads in the eighteenth and nineteenth centuries were poor, and travel was slow and expensive. In general, roads were passable in summer but turned into quagmires during the spring and fall rains. Because of the difficulty of land travel, rivers and other waterways were used as the primary transportation network (Wade, 1964, p. 39). The river cities of Pittsburgh, Cincinnati, Louisville, and St. Louis emerged at the points where river transportation met the primitive road system of the trans-Allegheny area.

Louisville, Kentucky, exemplifies the break-in-transportation concept of city location. From Pittsburgh to the port of New Orleans, the Ohio and Mississippi Rivers flow more than 1000 miles with only one major obstruction—a series of falls on the Ohio River. In the twentieth century, locks were built to allow smooth movement of barge traffic past the Ohio Falls. In the eighteenth and nineteenth centuries, however, barges were forced to unload above the falls and reload below. Of the four possible settlement sites at the falls, only one afforded a natural harbor and an area of flat ground well above flood stage suitable for settlement. The stevedore operations that initially developed there eventually led to the emergence of Louisville as a commercial center (Wade, 1964, pp. 13–18).

The lake cities that developed somewhat later owed their economic success to new modes of transportation—the canal and the railroad. Buffalo and Cleveland are at the points where major canals meet Lake Erie; Chicago and Milwaukee connect lake and railroad transportation.

EFFECTS OF TECHNOLOGICAL CHANGE

The commercial cities of the nineteenth century were much more competitive with each other than they are today. The river cities, for example, were settled at roughly the same time, had similar residential populations, depended on the same forms of transportation, and were involved in the same types of trade. Thus, it is not surprising that gains in commerce by one city were viewed with alarm by its competitors. With the development of new forms of transportation, such as the canal or railroad, a city's ability to lock itself into the new transportation network was viewed by civic leaders as a matter of economic survival. A work by Julius Rubin, "Canal or Railroad?" (1961), outlines the lengths to which cities would go to stay abreast of changing transportation technology.

The Erie Canal. Rubin outlines the response of three commercial cities, Philadelphia, Baltimore, and Boston, to the competitive influences brought about by the completion of the Erie Canal in 1825. The Erie Canal stretches 364 miles from Albany to Buffalo, New York. It was not simply a success; "it was an enormous, astounding, almost unbelievable success" (1961, p. 5). New York City had access to the canal through the Hudson River and thus became the Atlantic terminus. Overnight, the canal displaced both the turnpikes and the rivers as the dominant form of transportation in America and placed the cities in New York State in a position to dominate the trade of the entire northern Midwest.

Note in Figure 5.1 that wherever a break-in-transportation occurred in the canal route, a major city developed. Cargoes from New York City were shipped to Albany, where they were broken down for barge shipment along the canal to the lake port at Buffalo. There the cargoes were reassembled and loaded on sailing vessels for distribution by lake to the upper Midwest. The eastern flow of goods from the Midwest was probably more important. Cheap water transportation made possible for the first

FIGURE 5.1 The Trans-Appalachian projects.

Source: From Julius Rubin, "Canal or Railroad? Imitation and Innovation in the Response to the Erie Canal in Philadelphia, Baltimore, and Boston." *Transactions of the American Philosophical Society* vol. 51, p. 7 (1961).

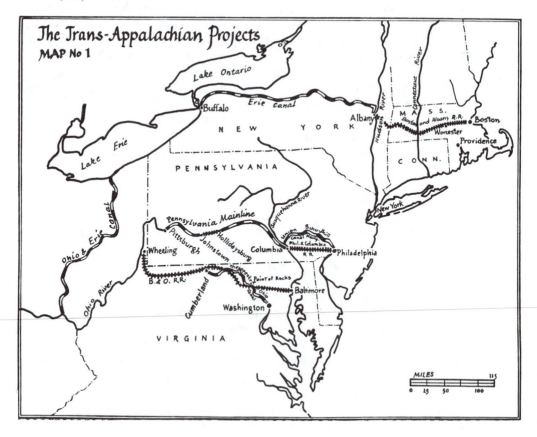

time the bulk shipment of agricultural produce to eastern markets, and thus encouraged the rapid westward expansion of the United States.

Canal and railroad technology. Philadelphia, Boston, and Baltimore were forced to react to this revolution in transportation. Failure to develop competitive transportation to the West would have meant economic stagnation and ruin. All three cities faced geographic obstacles very different from those encountered by the builders of the Erie Canal. Figure 5.2 gives elevation profiles for six trans-Appalachian projects. Note that the route of the Erie Canal is over relatively flat terrain, requiring only 84 locks to overcome a total rise and fall of 675 feet. In contrast, all the other projects involved crossing a mountain range that in one case required a rise and fall of more than 9460 feet! All three cities, besides being confined by mountain ranges, were commercialized coastal areas, subject to the competitive pressures created by the Erie Canal; all had access to almost identical technical information on canals and railroads; all made their construction decisions at almost the same time. Yet despite the many similarities among these cities, their reactions to the transportation crisis were entirely different.

By 1825, canal-building technology had been well tested. Railroads, though sufficiently developed in England to indicate their engineering feasibility, had not been adequately tested. In 1825, for example, a wide, flat, cast-iron rail was used rather than the modern narrow steel ribbon rail. These early rails, besides being difficult to mass-produce and lay, were brittle and prone to fatigue and fracture. This problem was exacerbated by the practice of attaching them directly to solid stone supports rather than to wooden ties, set in gravel ballast, that absorbs shock and vibrations. Baltimore, like the other two cities, could have cautiously employed proven technology by building a canal or could have gambled with new technology by building a railroad through the mountains. In an atmosphere in which the public viewed with alarm the slightest delay in making a decision, the leaders of Baltimore panicked and decided to build both (Rubin, 1961, pp. 29–35).

Baltimore's canal and railroad. Construction on both the Chesapeake and Ohio Canal and the Baltimore and Ohio Railroad began in the summer of 1828. Predictably, both projects were plagued with technical and financial difficulties, and both required more than twenty years to complete. After many years the Baltimore and Ohio Railroad did become a financial success. The canal, however, was from the beginning a financial disaster. The maintenance costs and the low volume of freight on the canal made it impossible to repay the bonds that had financed its construction. The State of Maryland, a major financial backer of the project, was brought to near financial collapse (Rubin, 1961, pp. 48–62).

The Pennsylvania mainland canal. By 1826 the leaders of Philadelphia, with the backing of the state of Pennsylvania, decided to build a canal to compete with the Erie. The Pennsylvania Mainland and Union Schuykill Canals were completed eight years later, and, as was the case in Maryland, both canals became an immediate financial liability. The reason was simply that the terrain and water resources were not suitable for the construction of a canal. Allegheny Mountain, elevation 2891 feet (Figure 5.2), was the

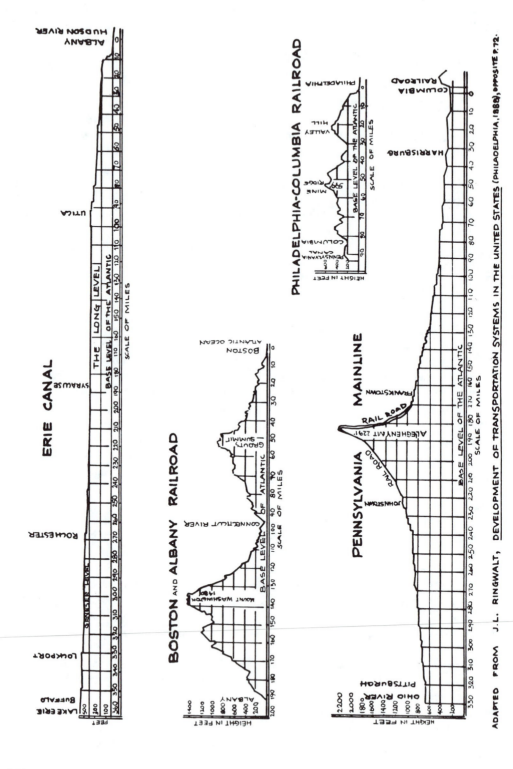

ERIE CANAL

BOSTON AND ALBANY RAILROAD

PHILADELPHIA-COLUMBIA RAILROAD

PENNSYLVANIA MAINLINE

ADAPTED FROM J.L. RINGWALT, DEVELOPMENT OF TRANSPORTATION SYSTEMS IN THE UNITED STATES (PHILADELPHIA, 1888), OPPOSITE P. 72.

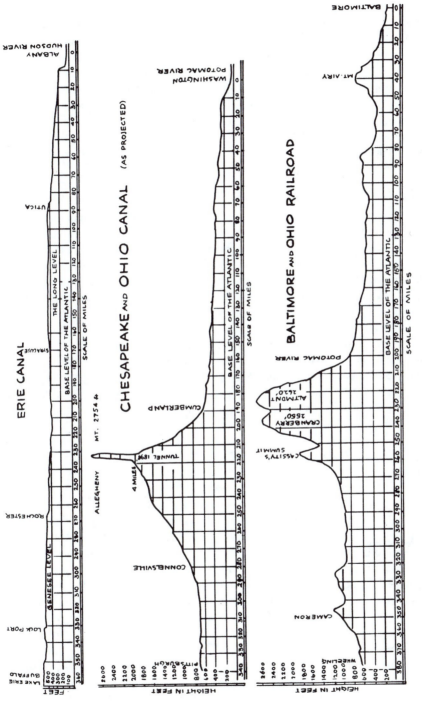

FIGURE 5.2 Profiles of the Trans-Appalachian projects.
Source: From Julius Rubin. "Canal or Railroad? Imitation and Innovation in the Response to the Erie Canal in Philadelphia, Baltimore, and Boston." *Transactions of the American Philosophical Society* vol. 51, pp. 10–11 (1961).

147

most formidable obstacle. Early engineering studies had shown that a lock system could not economically lift a barge over the summit of this mountain. Therefore a complicated inclined plane system was developed. Cargoes, after traveling the length of the Mainline Canal, were unloaded onto flatcars. A stationary steam engine at the top of Allegheny Mountain pulled the cars to the summit and then lowered them to the other side, where the cargoes continued their journey to Pittsburgh. The expensive handling of goods, as well as water shortages and freezes that closed the canal for much of late summer and winter, made the canal a money loser. The enormous capital outlays for the construction of the canal and the yearly operating losses brought the state of Pennsylvania to the brink of financial ruin (Rubin, 1961, pp. 63–79).

The Boston and Albany railroad. In the third city, Boston, the leaders took a more cautious approach and decided to delay their decision on building a canal or a railroad. Engineering studies strongly suggested that a canal through the mountains was simply not reasonable. Moreover, the leaders of this community realized that railroad technology had to be improved and tested before it could be applied to western Massachusetts. Boston and the state of Massachusetts waited until 1832 to begin construction on the Boston and Albany Railroad, and it was completed ten years later. The railroad linked Boston to Albany, New York, and gave the city of Boston access to the Erie Canal. The construction delay allowed for the improvement of railroad technology, and, unlike the projects of the other two cities, the Boston and Albany Railroad was a financial success (Rubin, 1961, pp. 80–94). Rubin points out in the analysis of these three locales the complex interplay among new technology, geography, economic competition, and public opinion that led to irrational decision making in both Baltimore and Philadelphia. Although both cities survived their folly, the financial losses on their projects crippled their economies for many years.

EFFECTS OF TECHNOLOGICAL CHANGE IN THE TWENTIETH CENTURY

The close relationship between changing transportation technology and patterns of human settlement is further illustrated in a classic ecological study by Cottrell (1951), "Death by Dieselization." Cottrell explores railroad technology and the changeover from steam to diesel locomotives. During the steam era, locomotives were required to stop at fixed intervals for fuel and water. These stops brought into being many small towns whose existence was wholly dependent upon the railroad. After World War II, when the railroad industry changed to diesel locomotives, many of these stops were eliminated, and large numbers of small railroad towns simply ceased to exist. Other communities that had developed other functions through the years continued to exist but at a smaller size.

Today, truck and air transportation is influencing the patterns of urban settlements. Akron, Ohio, for example, because of its proximity to both the large industrial centers of the East and the interstate highway system, has become a major truck transfer and dispatching center. Similarly, Atlanta's geographic location has made it the southern hub of the air transportation industry. Most commercial flights in the South and Southeast make an intermediate stop at Atlanta's Hartsfield International Airport.

A more recent example is the federal deregulation of much of the trucking and air transportation industry. Prior to the 1980s, air and truck carriers were required to file detailed route and fare schedules with federal regulatory agencies (for example, the Interstate Commerce Commission and the Civil Aeronautics Board). Proposed changes in these schedules required a lengthy and complicated regulation procedure that was often avoided by the carriers because of the expense. With deregulation, carriers have had wide latitude in determining routes and fares, and one result has been that major trucking and air carriers have dropped unprofitable routes. Chattanooga, Tennessee, provides one example. Prior to deregulation, this city was serviced by several major airlines. Since deregulation, these airlines have either dropped or drastically reduced service. The end result is that Chattanooga is now less competitive in drawing industry and business to its area. Executives faced with the prospect of depending on small and often unreliable commuter airlines for business travel will likely choose a different location, one with good air service.

POPULATION GROWTH

The foregoing examples explain the reason for the location of break-in-transportation cities, but not for the high population concentrations at those locations. In the early history of all break-in-transportation cities, a dockworker or stevedore class made up a large percentage of the city's population. Through time, however, these cities attracted additional residential populations employed in other economic activities. Because these cities are often the termini for many shipping lines, they are natural locations for the construction and servicing of transportation vehicles. Moreover, auxiliary services to the transportation industry, such as warehousing, brokering, financing, managing, and insuring, employ additional people.

Because large bulky cargoes—coal, ores, and agricultural produce—are expensive to transship, processing plants are often built at break-in-transportation locations. Normally, at these locations costs of transportation and costs of materials are at a minimum, and it becomes cheaper to ship a finished product than to reship raw materials. Pittsburgh, for example, because of its proximity to coal and ore fields and the availability of cheap water transportation, grew as a steel-producing center. Similarly, food-processing and flour-milling operations were established in Chicago as a result of the city's strategic location with respect to water and rail transportation and its proximity to the nation's major food-growing area, the Great Plains.

The families of the various classes of workers support secondary and tertiary functions in the local economy in the areas of retail and wholesale trade and professional and other services. Thus, the combination of developmental forces referred to as growth inertia leads to the concentration of large populations at break-in-transportation locations.

In summary, changes in transportation technology greatly influence the patterns of urban settlements. The rise and economic decline of many cities can be attributed in part to changing transportation technology. In America's urban history, chance is often listed as the major cause for one city's growing at the expense of another. More often than not, however, a city's strategic location combined with its willingness to invest heavily in innovative transportation technology offers a more meaningful explanation.

Shipping continues to be an important element in the local economies of cities originally settled as break-in-transportation centers. Today the nation's economic well-being is inextricably tied to participation in global markets. In particular, the nation must balance the costs of massive oil imports with overseas sales of finished manufactured goods and agricultural products. In the area of agricultural exports, technology has opened up large regions of the United States to international markets. Tulsa, Oklahoma, for example, was landlocked prior to 1960. With the completion of the Kerr-McClellan Waterway Project along the Arkansas River, Tulsa has become an international port with a growing grain export business serving several inland states.

SPECIALIZED FUNCTION THEORY

LOCATION AND RESOURCES

Specialized function theory provides another explanation for the location and distribution of cities. The model, however, is not a general one and applies to those cities that are tied closely to environmental conditions or the high concentration of raw materials at one location. It applies to certain types of cities that do not fit the explanatory frameworks provided by the general theories of location. The specialized function theory, therefore, supplements rather than competes with the central place and break-in-transportation theories.

SPECIALIZED FUNCTION CITIES

The location of some cities was deliberately predetermined. For example, many state capitals—Columbus, Ohio; Indianapolis, Indiana; Jefferson City, Missouri; Springfield, Illinois—are at the geographic centers of their states. Their location was the result of a political compromise that ensured that the capital was equally accessible from all points within the state. Similar reasoning was used in the selection of county seats. In many states, statute mandated that the county seat be located at a point in the county that was accessible by all persons in the county within a half-day's wagon travel. This location enabled farmers to travel to the seat, complete their business, and return home in one day.

The location of certain other communities was totally dependent on the resources found at one strategic place. Ely, Minnesota, is a specialized mining center near massive iron ore deposits. Similarly, Scranton, Wilkes-Barre, and certain cities in western Pennsylvania are coal-mining centers wholly dependent on the nearby anthracite coal deposits. Such resort cities as Miami, Florida, and Las Vegas, Nevada, emerged mainly as the result of their climate.

SUBSEQUENT DEVELOPMENT

Edward Ullman (1941) raises the point that once a city emerges as a result of a specialized function, it develops much differently than break-in-transportation or other cities. First, there is little diversity in the local economy because of the city's dependency on one industry. Even secondary services are highly specialized and directly related to the nearby resources. Mining-equipment manufacturing and repair, ore processing, and other related activities typify these specialized-function cities. As a result the fortunes of such cities are tied to the health of one industry. When the one industry fails, the consequences can be catastrophic for the city. In the last century, Virginia City, Nevada, almost became a ghost town when the nearby gold deposits were exhausted. Today, Youngstown, Ohio, is suffering major financial dislocations due to the closing of the city's steel plants. Similarly, Miami, Florida, in recent years has had financial problems caused by a downturn in the local tourist industry. Many specialized-function cities, therefore, are attempting to diversify their functions so that their local economies are protected from the financial failure of a single employer.

CENTRAL PLACE THEORY

By looking at a road map of your state, you can see that there is a more or less uniform distribution of villages, small towns, cities, and metropolises. And if you look more carefully, you will find that they are organized into a hierarchy. On the first level there are many villages with small populations, and they are fairly evenly distributed across the countryside. On the next level you will find towns with larger populations, but they are fewer in number, and they seem to be at the center of a cluster of villages. As you move up the hierarchy to cities and metropolises, the pattern repeats itself—fewer places, larger populations, centered in larger territories. Central place theory explains the location and size of these towns. Central place theory can be traced to the works of two German geographers, Christaller (1933) and Lösch (1958),[1] who were interested in providing a theoretical explanation for the location and size of cities in the plains area of Germany. Since they introduced the theory, it has been tested in many parts of the world—Europe, the Soviet Union, North America, Australia, and New Zealand—and has been shown to have wide applicability. Interestingly, the model fits the plains states of Kansas, Iowa, and Nebraska better than it fits the plains area of Germany.

The theory of central place states that a certain amount of productive land is necessary to support an urban place. The size of an urban place and the types and number of services it can support are, therefore, a function of the size of its trade area or, as it is often called, its *hinterland*. Services oriented toward the people in the surrounding countryside are termed *central functions,* and places performing those functions are known as *central places.*

From your day-to-day living, you use rules to guide your consumer behavior which explain the central place hierarchy. If you're out of milk, bread, or Coke, do you go across town to buy it? No. You go to the nearby convenience store. Need to do your weekly grocery shopping? Willing to pay the exorbitant prices at the convenience store? Probably not. Most likely you will drive to a more distant grocery store. Preparing Chinese food for a dinner party? You're probably going to have to drive across town to the oriental market to get your bean paste, soy, rice wine vinegar, and egg roll skins.

The location and size of these stores are guided by two principles—threshold and range. First, if a store is going to stay in business, it must sell enough goods and services to cover operating costs and make a profit. Most new businesses lose money for a few months until their volume of sales exceeds costs. This critical level is called the *threshold.* The threshold is the minimum size of a trade area from which people must travel to make a firm profitable. The threshold for a convenience store may be a few hundred customers living in the neighborhoods within a half mile of the store. The threshold for a large grocery may be an entire side of a city from which it draws the thousands of customers necessary to make the operation profitable. Because of the low demand for Chinese food, an ethnic grocery may need a trade area the size of an entire city. The thresholds for selected central functions are presented in Table 5.1. Note that filling stations have a low threshold: only 196 consumers are needed. Health practitioners are at the other extreme; they need a much larger trade area to attract the 1424 patients necessary to stay in practice.

The second principle is the range of a good. The range is the optimum service area of a store. Using the example of the convenience store again, if you live next door, the cost of your groceries is the same as the purchase price, because there are no transportation costs. However, if you live a mile away, the true cost of the goods will be the price of the goods plus the time and cost of your travel. These cost are not insignificant: a late-model car costs between 25 and 30 cents per mile to operate. Therefore, the true cost of goods to a consumer increases with distance from a store, and, as a result, demand declines with distance. At some distance from the store demand will drop to zero; travel costs are so high that consumers will simply shop elsewhere. Therefore, range is that distance from a store where demand is zero. If any firm is to stay in business, the threshold must be met within the range of their goods and services. If the threshold cannot be met within the range, the firm goes out of business.

In Figure 5.3a, the threshold and range are superimposed on each other. Since the threshold is the minimum territory necessary to make a profit, the area between the threshold and range of a good represents excess profits. Over time, other convenience stores will move into the area to soak up excess profits, forming an interlocking cluster of trade areas (Figure 5.3b). Some will earn profits, and some will lose money and go out of business, but according to microeconomic theory, the system of convenience stores will move toward equilibrium with all firms earning normal profits.

TABLE 5.1 Economic activities found in three classes of central places—Snohomish County, Washington.

POSITION IN CENTRAL PLACE HIERARCHY	ECONOMIC FUNCTION	THRESHOLD POPULATION
First-order	Filling stations	196
	Food stores	254
	Churches	265
	Restaurants	276
	Taverns	282
	Elementary schools	322
Second-order	Physicians	380
	Real estate agencies	384
	Appliance stores	385
	Barber shops	386
	Auto dealers	398
	Insurance agencies	409
	Bulk oil distributors	419
	Dentists	426
	Motels	430
	Auto repair shops	435
	Drug stores	458
	Beauticians	480
	Lawyers	528
	Apparel stores	590
	Banks	610
	Farm implement dealers	650
	High schools	732
	Jewelry stores	827
	Sporting goods stores	928
Third-order	Sheet metal works	1076
	Department stores	1083
	Optometrists	1140
	Hospital and clinics	1159
	Undertakers	1214
	Public accountants	1300
	Health practitioners	1424

Source: Adapted from Brian Berry and William Garrison, "The Functional Bases of the Central Place Hierarchy." *Economic Geography*, April, Vol. 34, No. 2 (1958): p.150.

ASSUMPTIONS OF THE THEORY

There are no theories in science that can be applied indiscriminately; scientists normally specify the exact conditions under which a theory should work. The central place theory is no different, and four assumptions are associated with it:

1. The geographic area under study is assumed to be flat with few geographic disturbances, such as large rivers or mountains.

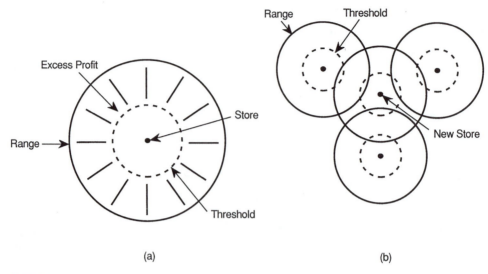

FIGURE 5.3 Threshold and range combined.

2. The geographic area under study is assumed to have an agricultural rather than an industrial economy, and the dominant economic function of urban places is assumed to be trade.

3. The principle of least effort is assumed. That is, a consumer with the choice of shopping at two trade centers will normally exert the least effort and trade at the closest trade center. A trade center may be a village, town, or city that supplies goods and services to residents of its surrounding countryside.

4. The size of the trade area of an urban place is assumed to be a function of transportation technology. The automobile, for example, would allow a city to serve a wider area than would the horse and buggy.

The concepts of threshold and range along with the limiting assumptions of the theory explain the size and location of many small communities. To maximize profits, firms will locate themselves as close to as many customers as possible and as far from competitors as possible. If the assumptions of the model are met, and the territory is flat, the result is a series of tightly packed market areas, each supplier having a monopoly over a given trade area. Economic activities with low thresholds, like filling stations and restaurants, will tend to cluster together in small trade centers, and there will be many of these trade centers evenly distributed over the countryside. Activities with higher thresholds may try to locate in a small trade center but will be forced to move to a city with a larger population. Since people will use the principle of least effort, they will tend to go to the closest city to obtain a good or service, and over time trade areas will tend to be nested. If you are a farmer and need gas, you will probably go to the nearby village; for weekly shopping, to the nearest town; and if you need a medical specialist, to the nearest city with a medical center. These nested trade areas are known as first-, second-, and third-order central places, and their complex economic relationship forms the central place hierarchy. The types of economic activities that are usually found in these central places are presented in Table 5.1.

THE CENTRAL PLACE

The notion of central place and its limiting assumptions, combined with a related concept, the urban hierarchy, explain the size and location of many small communities. Urban places develop symbiotic (mutually beneficial) economic relationships with the surrounding productive farm land. Farmers find it expensive and difficult to ship their agricultural produce by road to distant markets. Small trade centers, therefore, develop to buy and transship agriculture products. The farmer benefits in finding a nearby market, but in turn the trade center benefits economically by supplying its surrounding trade area with goods and services.

The first order. These small towns and villages are known as first-order central places, a category of towns and villages similar in size and in the type and number of services they offer. As the frontier was settled, such communities sprang up across the countryside. Normally their small size permitted them to carry out only a few economic functions; one finds in them today only a grocery, gas station, and possibly a hardware or implement store. Moreover, their small size enables them to draw customers from only a small trade area. Therefore, the first tier of the urban hierarchy consists of a large number of first-order places with small trade areas, more or less evenly distributed across the landscape. These places form the foundation upon which still larger urban places depend.

The second order. Certain economic functions, such as wholesaling, banking, and grain storage, cannot be carried out economically in small first-order places. Through time a few of the first-order centers, because of their strategic locations in space, grew in population and took on additional economic functions. These second-order functions include wholesaling to the groceries and other stores in the first-order trade centers, and also the provision of services directly to customers in the trade areas of the first-order centers. Thus the trade areas of the second-order centers overlap the trade areas of the surrounding towns; however, first- and second-order trade centers do not directly compete with each other. Second-order centers provide those goods and services that are not available in the smaller trade centers.

The third order. In turn, certain activities, such as milling and meat packing, require even larger trade areas to be economically profitable. Third-order central places emerge because of their strategic locations, and their expanded trade areas overlap the trade areas of urban places lower in the hierarchy. Again, none of these different orders of cities directly compete with each other, even though they have overlapping trade areas. Each center has its own economic niche that permits it to survive and flourish.

Figure 5.4 gives a picture of the overlapping trade-area patterns suggested in the central place theory. The distribution of central places resembles a pyramid. On the first tier is a large number of first-order places with small trade areas of equal size. The

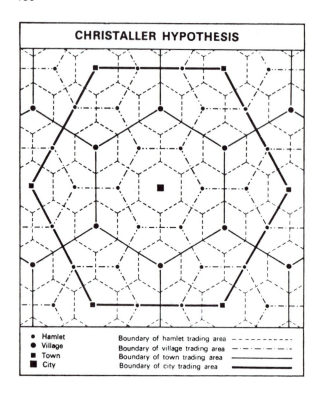

FIGURE 5.4 The hexagonal network of urban places.

CHRISTALLER HYPOTHESIS

• Hamlet   Boundary of hamlet trading area   — — — — — — — —
• Village   Boundary of village trading area — · — · — · — · —
■ Town   Boundary of town trading area   ————————
■ City   Boundary of city trading area   ————————

number of central places declines, however, as the size of their trade areas expands. Moreover, the trade areas of lower-order central places fit neatly (nest) inside the trade areas of higher-order centers. If a state were the unit of analysis, the capstone of the urban hierarchy would be the one city with a trade area the size of the entire state.

EFFECTS OF REGION AND TECHNOLOGY

The distance between cities of the same order is a function of the transportation technology at the time of settlement and the nature of the agriculture carried out in the region. First-order places in the Southwest, for example, are on the average farther apart than those in the Midwest. Part of the explanation is that the Midwest was settled earlier than the Southwest, and transportation technology at the time of settlement was at a different stage of development. Another factor is the nature of the region's agriculture. The agriculture of the semiarid Southwest is based on the cattle industry. The low rainfall and sparse vegetation require enormous tracts of land to support the cattle herds. Ranches are large and support relatively few people. Therefore, the demands for services are such that central places tend to be few in number and far apart. The agriculture of the Midwest, in contrast, is based on intensive farming of the land in wheat, corn, and other grains. The rainfall and soil conditions permit smaller farming units, and the region supports a larger farm population. Larger populations mean greater demand for goods, and more central places that are closer together.

Once an urban place is settled and its trade niche is established, its future is determined by its location in the central place hierarchy. The Midwest is dotted with New Londons and New Philadelphias, whose founders saw their new communities as the future great metropolises of the West. However, unless these settlements were located at some strategic point in the emerging pattern, they were destined to become lower-order places.

TESTS OF THE THEORY

The central place theory has been tested in several countries.[2] The works of both Christaller (1931) and Lösch (1958) suggest that the theory roughly fits the plains but not the mountainous areas of Germany. Ullman (1941) reports that "many nonindustrial regions of relatively uniform land surface have cities distributes so evenly over the land that some sort of central-place theory appears to be the prime explanation." Similarly, Thomlinson (1969) states that "research indicates that the scheme is not too different from existing urban networks in many of the Midwest and Great Plains states in the United States."

The concept of urban hierarchy. Other researchers have tested specific elements of the theory to determine its validity. Both the notion of central places and the notion of an urban hierarchy have been systematically explored. According to the central place theory, the number of cities declines at each successively higher tier in the urban hierarchy as their trade areas expand. Duncan (1960) and Zipf (1949) explored this postulated pattern and found it to be mathematically constant—as the size of cities increases, their frequency decreases. Duncan tested this proposed relationship with data from the 1950 census on cities with populations of 100,000 persons or more. Note in Table 5.2 the close agreement between the predicted and actual numbers of cities in each category.

TABLE 5.2 The predicted* and actual number of urbanized areas of 100,000 or more in the United States, 1950.

SIZE OF COMMUNITY	CALCULATED	ACTUAL
1,000,000 +	12.5	12
500,000 +	12.1	13
300,000 +	15.3	17
200,000 +	20.8	18
150,000 +	19.8	22
125,000 +	15.9	16
100,000 +	23.6	21

*Predicted values from the Pareto Formula $y = 10^6 \times 9.8528X^{-0.98356}$, where X = number of inhabitants, Y = number of cities of X size or larger.

Source: O. D. Duncan et al. *Metropolis and Region.* Baltimore, MD: The Johns Hopkins Press for Resources for the Future, 1960, p. 53.

Duncan and his colleagues also found the expected relationship between the number of functions and the size of urban places. The authors concluded that in the four regions of the United States, the position of an urban place in the urban hierarchy and the magnitude and scope of its economic functions are "more or less adequately indicated by city size" (1960, p. 56). The authors state, however, that the central place theory cannot explain all of the specialized functions that develop in the largest cities. They note that some urban centers are so large that they generate "needs and tastes not typical of small cities." Moreover, certain specialized services emerge solely for the inhabitants of that city and do not reach out into the trade area. This phenomenon suggests that inertial forces not explained by central place theory come into play once cities in the hierarchy exceed a certain population.

The size and shape of trade areas. The second test of the theory has focused on the size and shape of the trade areas themselves. Note in Figure 5.4 that the trade areas of places in the urban hierarchy are represented as hexagons with a central place at the center of each. According to von Thunen's (1826) original formulation, trade areas took the form of a circle. Later Lösch (1958) argued that the shape that best fills all of a geometric form is the hexagon.

Studies of the trade areas of various places have shown that neither shape is valid. Moreover, the size and shape of the trade area of an urban place seem to change with the type of service being studied and with the technique used to measure that service. Thus, if one were looking at wholesaling and repair services for the same city, two overlapping trade areas would probably be evident. Green (1955) showed that the areas of influence of Boston and New York City, as measured by newspaper circulation, were irregular in shape but did not overlap (see Figure 5.5).

A work by Swedner (1960), "Ecological Differentiation of Habits and Attitudes," is a study of the trade areas of urban places in Sweden. The author concludes that different urban places of the same size are related differently to their hinterlands, and that the size and shape of trade areas are a function of the place under study and the specific function measured. Ullman (1941) and Pfouts (1962) found essentially the same phenomenon in the United States. Some services extend geographically much farther into the countryside than others, and their trade areas in no case could be described as either circular or hexagonal. Figure 5.6 represents the department store retail trade areas for five cities in the Piedmont area of North Carolina. The trade areas are not only irregular in shape, but in many cases overlap.

CRITICISMS OF THE THEORY

The following criticisms have been made of the central place theory:

1. Central place theory is not a general theory for the location of cities. Break-of-transportation and specialized function theories are required to explain the location of certain cities.

2. The hexagonal trade areas postulated are not found in reality.

3. The assumptions of the theory limit its use in the study of much of the developed world.

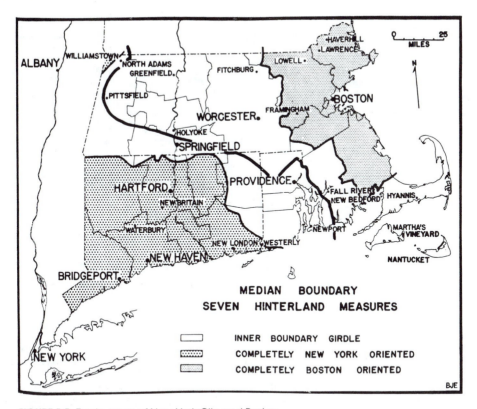

FIGURE 5.5 Trade areas of New York City and Boston.

Source: H. L. Green, "Hinterland Boundaries of New York City and Boston in Southern New England." *Economic Geography* 31 (October, 1955): p. 300.

4. The services carried out in the larger centers of the urban hierarchy cannot be explained fully by the central place theory. In large urban places inertial forces arise that are not related to the trade function.

Many of the criticisms are of recent origin, and their appearance can be explained in part by changes that have occurred in American and other societies during the last century. The present patterns of urban places in the United States were determined between 100 and 300 years ago at the time of settlement of the various geographic regions. During the past 75 years there has been a revolution in transportation technology and a transformation of this society's economy from an agricultural to an industrial base. These changes have had a profound impact on human settlements and have set up forces not accounted for in the central place theory.

CENTRAL PLACE THEORY REEXAMINED

These changes in human settlement patterns are explored in a work by Harold Mark and Kent Schwirian (1969), "Ecological Position, Urban Central Place Function, and

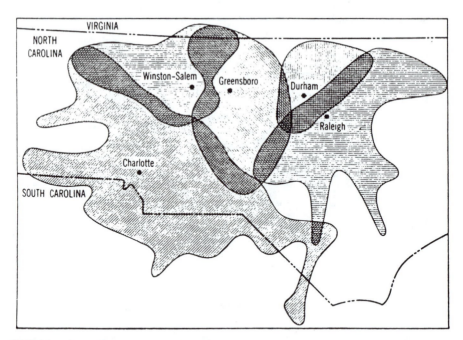

FIGURE 5.6 Out-of-town accounts for selected department stores in Raleigh, Durham, Greensboro, Winston-Salem, and Charlotte. Each shaded area represents the generalized shape of the charge-account area of the indicated city based on the locations of towns of 500 or more population with at least 20 charge accounts per 1000 inhabitants.

Source: R. W. Pfouts, "Patterns of Economic Interaction in the Crescent." In R. S. Chapin and S. R. Weiss, eds., *Urban Growth Dynamics.* New York: John Wiley and Sons, 1962, p. 37. Reprinted by permission of John Wiley and Sons, Inc.

Community Population Growth," using Iowa as their subject of study. Iowa fits the central place model extremely well, and Schwirian and Mark were interested in assessing the impact of changing transportation technology on the central place pattern.

Changing transportation technology. After World War II, Iowa, like many other midwestern states, undertook a program to improve the state's road system. Much of this work simply involved widening and paving highways. However, the state's master plan also called for building bypasses around many small trade centers. The highway improvements and bypasses greatly increased the distance a driver could travel in an hour. The end result was that an entirely new transportation network was superimposed over the old central place pattern.

A farmer, for example, with access to the high-speed modern highway could avoid the high prices at the local store and travel 30 or 40 miles to the supermarket in the city. During the 1950s many of the merchants in the small trade centers simply did not understand why their business was declining. Finding their town a mile or two off the main highway after the bypass had been built, they often responded by erecting a billboard on the highway—"Smallville, Nice People and a Nice Place to Shop." This gesture was fruitless because their position with respect to the new transportation network was such that they were doomed to economic decline. The new transportation technology permitted higher-order places to expand their services and trade areas to compete directly with the small trade centers. Economies of scale—the ability of high-order places to buy in volume and minimize transportation costs—dramatically changed the pattern of competition.

Effects of industrialization. Industrialization was another force modifying the locational patterns of cities and towns in Iowa. Industrialization brought about the improvement of the transportation system as well as rapid economic and population growth. Mark and Schwirian found that this growth was not uniform across the state and that certain ecological classes of cities expanded but others did not. In general, cities at the top of the old urban hierarchy had a competitive edge over lower-order cities. These places already had large labor pools, good rail transportation, and other services that made them attractive to new industry. Therefore, they became the focal point for regional development at the expense of smaller trade centers.

These changes are summarized in Table 5.3, which gives the ecological position of a sample of Iowa's cities and the changes in their populations and retail trade volume between 1950 and 1960. Note in column 1 that most of the population growth in the state during these years was centered in metropolitan areas. Growth in central cities was moderate; the suburbs absorbed most of the state's population increase. The category *metropolitan neighbors* refers to small first-order trade centers that came under the economic influence of their large neighbors. For the most part, they grew in population because they became satellite bedroom communities. Because they were within the expanding trade area of the metropolis, they ceased to be trade centers. As the metropolitan centers in Iowa continue to expand, these communities ultimately will be surrounded and absorbed into the suburban ring.

TABLE 5.3 Community ecological position by population and trade function changes 1950–1960.

COMMUNITY ECOLOGICAL POSITION	POPULATION CHANGE 1950–1960 (%)	CHANGE IN TRADE VOLUME 1950–1960 (%)	NUMBER OF PLACES
Central cities	10.0	9.1	6
Suburbs	40.4	41.5	5
Metropolitan neighbors	12.4	2.4	17
Noncompetitive trade centers	3.8	.7	14
Competitive trade centers	0.5	.7	48

Source: Adapted from H. Mark and K. P. Schwirian, "Ecological Position, Urban Central Place Function and Community Population Growth." *American Journal of Sociology* 73 (July 1967): pp. 37–38. Reprinted with permission of The University of Chicago Press.

Competitive and noncompetitive trade areas are lower-order central places that have not yet come under the economic influence of the metropolitan areas. They still function as trade centers, but they have made only slight gains in population.

This analysis is further strengthened by the trade volume figures in column 2 of Table 5.3. These figures give the percentage change in retail trade sales between 1950 and 1960. The metropolitan neighbors and the competitive and noncompetitive trade centers have shown large increases in dollar sales, but their economies have been stagnant and have made no real growth. They have merely kept up with inflation.

The downtown areas of central cities in Iowa have held their own and have had small increases in their total volume of sales. Suburbs, in comparison, have achieved rapid expansion of their retail markets. Growth in suburban retail trade reflects the emergence of the shopping mall on a large scale in the post-World War II period. The location of malls at the periphery of the city enabled them to tap the suburban middle-class market, and their location combined with the high-speed highway system allowed them to serve a greatly expanded rural trade area. These retail sales patterns, however, are not shared by all regions. The downtown areas of many cities, including Cleveland, Detroit, Toledo, and Louisville, have had dramatic declines in the volume of sales as a result of peripheral shopping mall development.

CHANGE IN THE HIERARCHY IN THE 1980S

The Mark and Schwirian work was completed more than twenty years ago, but its message is clear. First, the central place hierarchy represents a process: The economic relationships among villages, towns, and cities are always evolving. Second, changes in transportation technology or the character of the economy will affect the nature of cities and their relationships to each other.

These two principles are particularly true when we discuss the plight of rural America in the 1990s. For more than a decade, the state of the American farm economy has received the attention of the nation's media, government officials, and policy makers. Although there is sharp disagreement on the causes and consequences of the downturn in the farm economy, most agree that the current recession is the worst since the Great Depression, and now as then painful adjustments have occurred. Every economic indicator bears testimony to the scope and magnitude of the farm problem: Farm income, when adjusted for inflation, dropped 32 percent in the decade ending in 1988; the number of farm foreclosures reached a post-World War II high in 1985; the number of farm operators dropped a third between 1976 and 1986; and during this same period the government's farm subsidy program swelled to $26 billion. If central place theory is correct, this economic upheaval will lead to a spatial upheaval in the central place hierarchy because first-order central places are dependent on the farmers living in their rural hinterland.

The state of Arkansas was hard hit by the farm crisis, and I was interested in the impact of the recession on the state's urban hierarchy. A rural sociologist, Frank Farmer, and I replicated Mark and Schwirian's earlier work with data collected between 1977 and 1984 on Arkansas. We used the same categories of central places, as well as the variables population and per capita retail sales to measure central place functions.

The effect of the crisis on the state's economy and central place hierarchy can be seen in the changes in population and retail activity presented in Table 5.4. The rate of population growth for the state was 8.4 percent for this period, but central places grew by 10.7 percent. Therefore, Arkansas followed the national pattern of population redistribution, with urban places growing and hinterland populations declining. But note, growth was not uniform across the hierarchy: The growth of suburbs, metropolitan neighbors, and noncompetitive centers was above average, the others below average.

The effect of the farm crisis on Arkansas's predominantly agricultural economy was devastating. Between 1977 and 1984, per capita retail activity for the trade centers fell 11.9 percent, and like population change this decline was not uniform. Suburbs and noncompetitive trade centers, because of their unique position in the urban hierarchy, experienced modest declines in sales, while central cities, metropolitan neighbors, and competitive trade centers experienced declines exceeding 18 percent. Everyone lost, but some communities fared better than others.

More importantly, we found much the same thing that Mark and Schwirian had before us: Certain communities, because of their unique ecological positions, were able to capture population and economic activity better than others. As in the past, suburbs continued their economic expansion and population growth at the expense of central cities and metropolitan neighbors (old trade centers in the process of becoming bedroom communities). The communities most affected by the farm crisis in Arkansas were the same as those that suffered the most during the economic reorganization of Iowa—competitive and noncompetitive trade centers. However, different mechanisms were involved. In Iowa, the redistribution of population and retail activity represented the emergence of an integrated urban economy, which buffered the state to a degree from the volatility of the farm sector. Arkansas has little industry, and the modification of the central place hierarchy was brought about by the loss of buying power of farm producers and processors. As a result, no one was left unscathed.

TABLE 5.4 Community Ecological Position and Rate of Population Change, 1977–1984

	POPULATION CHANGE (1977–1984)	CHANGE IN TRADE VOLUME (1977–1984)	NUMBER OF PLACES
Metropolitan	3.4	-18.3	6
Suburbs	16.5	-3.7	20
Metropolitan neighbors	12.7	-20.0	43
Competitive trade center	7.4	-22.1	69
Noncompetitive trade center	34	-4.3	225
Total Municipalities	10.7	-11.9	

Source: Adapted from Frank Farmer and William A. Schwab, "Economic Recession and Community Change: An Analysis of an Agricultural Region's Central Place Hierarchy," Tables 1 and 2, forthcoming.

In our study, the communities most dependent on the farm economy suffered the most. Noncompetitive trade centers (small isolated communities) experienced robust population growth (34 percent) and modest declines in retail activity, but this change was the result of immigration from the trade center's hinterland: bankrupt farm families, who added population but little purchasing power to the community. The real losers were competitive trade centers. Because they were close to other trade centers, few of these communities grew in population, and this category experienced a 22 percent decline in retail sales.

Criticisms of the central place theory result from the inability of the theory to predict modifications of the original central place patterns caused by economic and technological changes during the last 75 years. The preceding discussion shows how new locational influences cause the growth and expansion of one center and the decline of another. With modifications of the basic assumptions of the theory, however, the central place theory can continue to be used in the historical analysis of the present and future patterns of human settlement.

In general, any change, whether it be technology, the climate, or the economy, will result in a change in the spatial order of a region's urban hierarchy. Many of the weaknesses identified in central place theory result from ignoring the dynamic and ever-changing relationship between cities in the urban hierarchy.

SUMMARY

The three theories of location examined in this chapter demonstrate the utility of the ecological perspective in examining the why and how of the location of cities. The three theories complement each other because each theory explains the concentration of a population at a particular point in space in terms of different elements of the ecological complex or POET framework noted in Chapter 1.

The Break-in-transportation theory combines environmental and technological factors to explain why cities arise in a certain place. A favorable environment—a location along a navigable river or lake—is important, but the level of transportation technology at the time of settlement and at later dates is more important to this theory. The river cities, for example, came into existence because of poorly developed road transportation technology. The growth of the lake cities was closely tied to new transportation technology—the canal and the railroad. The specialized function theory explains the initial settlement and consequent growth of a population in terms of the resources available in the environment. Subsequent growth of the economies (organization) of these cities is linked to the environmental factors responsible for their initial settlement. The Central place theory is the most general of the three because it explores the complex interaction of environment, transportation, technology, and economic organization to predict the location, size, and functions of human settlements across a region. Recent improvements in automobile technology and shifts of regional economies from agriculture to industry have caused major modifications in central place patterns.

In general, when the theories are used in conjunction with each other, they explain the reason for a location but do not explain changes in the pattern that occur through time. Combined with concepts of metropolitan growth and dominance—as in the Mark and Schwirian work—the location theories can be helpful in predicting the future direction of growth.

NOTES

1. Christaller's and Lösch's works are now available in translation, and I would suggest to anyone interested in central place theory to read these benchmark works. General reviews of central place theory are available in three works: B. J. L. Berry's 1967 monograph, *Geography of Market Centers and Retail Distribution;* and a general review and annotated bibliography is available in B. J. L. Berry and Allen Pred's, *Central Place Studies: A Bibliography.* For a complete citation of each work please see the bibliography.

2. There are two monographs in Prentice-Hall's "Foundations of Economic Geography Series," that I would recommend. The first, Brian Berry's monograph, *Geography of Market Centers and Retail Distribution,* provides a general overview of central place theory. The second, James E. Vance, Jr.'s *The Merchant's World: The Geography of Wholesaling,* deals with the question really never addressed by central place theory: How did the central place hierarchy develop in the first place. The monograph is only 170 pages, and its emphasis on the evolutionary character of settlement patterns is a fine ancillary to one's reading on this topic. For a complete citation of this work please see the bibliography.

3. In the original formulation of central place theory by Christaller, seven orders of central places were hypothesized. The base of the hierarchy was composed of small trade centers (Marktort) with a range of 4 kilometers to one large central place (Landstadt) at the top with a range of 108 kilometers. For the purposes of discussion, only three orders are presented here.

4. A thorough review of the tests, as well as, specific criticisms of central place theory are beyond the scope this book. The best general review of these issues that I have found is Chapter 4, "Central Place Functions and Central Place Theory" in Harold Carter's text, *The Study of Urban Geography.* For a complete citation of this work please see the bibliography.

CHAPTER 6

THE CLASSIFICATION AND RATING OF CITIES

INTRODUCTION

Every spring, with the predictability of the swallows returning to Capistrano, salespeople from the major textbook publishers descend on the nation's college campuses. This past spring, I was working in my office when I heard a firm, confident knock on my door, and, as I was yelling, "Come in," a bright, cheerful, young man strode into my office with his hand extended and the following introduction on his lips, "Hi, I'm Greg, and I'm your new rep. I hear we have something in common; we're both Cincinnati boys."

"Really," I said, thinking to myself that it's been years since anyone had referred to me as a boy, but I really needed an excuse not to write. And it would be fun to play the name game for a few minutes and see what books he was pushing. So I waved him toward the chair near my desk, and as he was sitting down and getting settled I gave my normal disclaimer, "I'm not really from Cincinnati, I was raised in a town about 20 miles north. Ever hear of Hamilton?"

"Hamilton! Hamilton! Do I know Hamilton!" he said. "It used to be part of my old territory. I used to have to drive through that pit to get to Miami University. I bet you're glad you don't live in that toilet anymore?"

He actually used the word *toilet* to describe the place I was born. The town where I had spent the first half of my life. The town my family has lived in for the past 200 years. The town I associate with some of the best moments in my life. The town that shaped me. The town that is still an important part of my life. I felt my blood pressure rise, the hair on the back of my neck prickle, and my face flush. I thought to myself, "You fool, you just blew a sale," and I lowered my head, looked over the top of my glasses, and with irritation in my voice said, "Yep, that toilet's my hometown, what are you selling?"

Hometowns are funny things. They're like your children. You can say something critical about them, but nobody else had better. I like Hamilton, Ohio. My family and some of my closest friends still live there, and it hurts my feelings when someone says something bad about it. I, like the majority of Americans, have a sense of place—that one spot on earth where you feel you belong—and although I've lived in Fayetteville, Arkansas, for the past decade, it's still not home. Hamilton is.

In the 1980s there have been a lot of bruised feelings in cities around the nation, not at the hands of insensitive people, but at the hands of the media. Because it was the decade of city ratings. It seems that at least once a month, someone—a national magazine, a university researcher, a newspaper, or a publisher—releases a new study rating the nation's cities. Of course, the cities are ranked from best to worst, and the public, like an addict waiting for a fix, eagerly scans the lists, looking to see how their city fared. If you call Pittsburgh, Atlanta, Danbury, Connecticut, or one of the other top-ranked cities home, you're saying, "I knew it all along; it's time everybody knew it. I wonder if this is going to help property values?"

But what if you live in a city labeled the worst place to live in America? A Yuba City, California? A Pine Bluff, Arkansas? Your feelings are hurt. There is an understandable sense of outrage. You are probably mumbling to yourself, "What does that Eastern establishment know anyway?" Why? Because who you are is tied to where you live. And the residents of these poorly ranked cities haven't sat idly by. The citizens of Yuba got together and had a bonfire with the maps sold by the publisher of one study. (It's a good thing the authors weren't nearby.) Pine Bluff put on a public relations blitz after another study ranked them last. And Tulsa sued the authors of a third study for $26 million when they admitted that computational errors had led to the low rankings of that city. The leaders of these communities take these studies seriously because classification and rating schemes are used by business and government in decision making. Businesses use ratings to decide where to open or expand new plants, and governments use a form of ratings in dispersing community development, welfare, and other funds. This is why you should know more about this research.

The classification and rating of cities is not new. The first city classification scheme was developed a century and a half ago, and city ratings have been done since the 1930s. Although these two bodies of literature share many things in common, they were developed independently by different branches of the social sciences, and they have been used for different purposes. For this reason, this chapter explores the literature on the classification and rating of cities separately. Each section walks you through the process of developing a classification or a rating scheme. Studies key to the development of each approach are presented. The data problems and methodological weaknesses of each approach are explored, and examples of classification and rating schemes are presented.

CLASSIFICATION OF CITIES

In Chapter 4, theories of location were discussed, and it was noted that cities at different locations differ in the nature of their local economies, the socioeconomic characteristics of their populations, and their physical features. These differences can be explained by the technology available at the time of their settlement, the local resources on which their early growth depended, regional differences in climate and resources, and changes in the competitive advantage of cities caused by changes in the national and regional economy. Simply, what a city does is closely related to where it is. For example, the Atlantic Coast cities are deep-water ports largely involved in commerce and trade. The concentration of the petrochemical industry in Houston, Dallas, and Tulsa is a result of their proximities to gas and oil fields. Processing and distribution of agricultural products are centered in Kansas City and Omaha because these cities are in the farm belt. Location and function are the opposite sides of the same coin; in this section we explore city functions and the attempts by researchers to classify cities into typologies.

WHY CLASSIFY?

Language is the ability to communicate symbolically, and we are the only species with the ability to use language. Classification is a basic procedure used in language to structure and give meaning to the world. Symbols such as *man*, *woman*, *child*, and *book*, give meaning to an entire category of things and permit the transmission of information about these things from one person to another. Without classification, language would be cumbersome, and science—the collection and classification of knowledge—would be impossible. Little is gained from classification alone, however; it must serve some purpose. The purpose of classifying cities into groups or types is to learn more about the basic processes that shape them and in turn gain insight into urban problems and their possible solution. Specifically, city classification is done for the following reasons:

First, classification helps to bring order out of the enormous amount of information on cities that the Census Bureau and other public and private agencies collect. By identifying key dimensions of certain types of cities, classification can make sense out of an otherwise incomprehensible mass of data.

Second, classification enables the researcher to group the hundreds of cities in this and other societies into a manageable number of categories to better understand basic urban and economic processes. Our understanding of the changes that have brought about the growth of the Sunbelt and the decline of the Snowbelt is based on research which has grouped these cities by region and function and then identified changes in their populations and economies (Nelson, 1988; Noyelle and Stanback, 1984; Bickford, 1980).

Third, the classification of cities aids in the assessment of urban problems and can contribute to better policy formation and decision making (Bickford, 1980). With a looming $3 trillion deficit, the federal government does not have the money to address all the nation's problems. The effectiveness of federal programs in the areas of health, housing, and poverty, however, can be enhanced by determining the types of cities where specific programs are cost-effective.[1]

CRITERIA USED IN CLASSIFYING

City classification has been done informally for centuries. When early chroniclers wrote in their journals that they had traveled through a "market town," a "seaport," a "religious center," or a "capital," they were, in effect, creating a city classification based on function. These informal schemes were replaced with formal ones during the Industrial Revolution as the number, size, and complexity of cities increased. As early as 1840, the British Government's Committee on the Health of Towns (1840) in Great Britain found it necessary to create a classification scheme to report their findings. Their scheme included five categories: the metropolises, manufacturing towns, populous seaport towns, great watering places, and inland nonmanufacturing towns. As with the early chroniclers, the committee classified cities by function, and it represents one of the first attempts by a society to systematically classify its cities (Carter, 1981).

Hundreds of classifications have been published since then, and many different criteria have been used. An important point to remember is that any criterion can be used to classify cities as long as two conditions are met. First, the measure must permit every city in the study to be placed in only one category—the categories must be mutually exclusive. Second, the categories chosen must be all-encompassing, so that every city can be classified. Such factors as age, size, region, demographic characteristics, economic function, and government structure have been used in developing city typologies, but basically all of these schemes are of two kinds—single-dimension and multidimensional (multivariate) typologies (Berry, 1972, Bickford, 1980).

SINGLE-DIMENSION TYPOLOGIES

The simplest way to classify cities is on the basis of a single characteristic such as population size, density, or types of employment. As an example, a city typology can be constructed from the figures in Table 6.1. Table 6.1 lists the percentage of the labor force employed in four types of nonagricultural jobs for eight United States SMSAs. Other categories of employment could have been included, but these four represent about 70 percent of the labor force in these cities. By scanning the table, one can see that these cities vary significantly in their employment profiles. This variation forms the basis for a classification on the single dimension of employment.

A classification scheme based on these employment figures is presented in Table 6.2. Philadelphia, Pittsburgh, and Cleveland are classified as "manufacturing type," because durable goods manufacturing is the dominant employer in each of these cities. The employment in New York city is evenly dispersed across the categories in Table 6.1; this city is labeled "diversified type." Government is the major employer in Washington,

TABLE 6.1 Employment in nonagricultural jobs for selected U.S. SMSAs (in percent).[*]

SMSA	MANUFACTURING		WHOLESALE & RETAIL TRADES	FINANCE	GOVERNMENT
	DURABLE GOODS	*NONDURABLE GOODS*			
Philadelphia, PA	25.4	8.0	21.8	6.0	16.2
Pittsburgh, PA	28.5	4.9	21.3	4.7	13.6
New York, NY	16.5	12.4	19.8	12.1	17.6
Washington, DC	3.5	4.2	18.8	5.8	38.5
Sacramento, CA	7.2	4.2	22.1	4.3	40.9
Miami, FL	13.7	8.2	26.3	7.6	13.9
Columbus, OH	14.0	6.5	23.5	6.9	21.2
Cleveland, OH	30.2	7.8	23.0	5.1	13.1

[*]Italics added.

The figures in this table show that there are similarities and differences in the employment characteristics of these cities; these similarities and differences form the basis for a classification scheme. For instance, in column 1, "durable goods manufacturing," Pittsburgh, Philadelphia, and Cleveland stand out, with significantly higher percentages of their labor force in this category than other cities. Pittsburgh and Cleveland are known for the production of steel and fabricated metal products, and Philadelphia is a major producer of machinery, electrical equipment, and other durable goods (Duncan et al., pp. 279–327). Note that New York is ranked fourth, but it is nine percentage points below Philadelphia and would not be included within this city type.

In column 2, New York is the only city with major employment in "nondurable goods manufacturing." Employment in "wholesale and retail trades" is about equal in all eight cities; the category would not be useful in classifying these cities. In column 3, New York is the only city with a high percentage of its labor force in "finance." In the last column, Washington, D.C., Columbus, Ohio, and Sacramento, California, lead the other cities in the percentage of their labor force in "government service."

On the basis of these employment figures, three types of cities are identified—manufacturing, diversified, governmental.

Source: Bureau of Labor Statistics. Employment and earnings, states and areas, 1939–75. Washington, D.C.: U.S. Government Printing Office, 1977.

D.C., Sacramento, California, and Columbus, Ohio, these cities are classified as "governmental." Interestingly, Miami, Florida, does not fit into any of these categories, and this fact reflects some of the difficulties in constructing city typologies. Miami is heavily dependent on the tourist industry; if "service employment" had been included as a category in Table 6.1, Miami would have been so classified.

TABLE 6.2 A single-dimension typology constructed with nonagricultural employment data from Table 6.1.

MANUFACTURING TYPE	DIVERSIFIED TYPE	GOVERNMENTAL TYPE	?
Philadelphia Pittsburgh Cleveland	New York	Washington, D.C. Sacramento Columbus	Miami

HARRIS'S CITY CLASSIFICATION

The foregoing simple example shows how a single-dimension typology can be constructed. Harris (1943) applied the same rationale in an early classification of 605 American cities, using employment and occupation figures from the 1930 census of population and the 1935 census of business.[2] He faced many of the same problems noted in the example. In Table 6.1 each metropolitan area has some employment in each category. Harris recognized that all large cities are multifunctional to a degree and that the classification of a city as "commercial" does not indicate the absence of other employment functions. The major goal of Harris's study was to identify "critical levels" of employment that would separate cities into clearly defined functional types. As in the above example, Harris constructed his classification framework by scanning the employment profiles of cities and then intuitively setting minimum levels of employment for each functional type. At the end of this process Harris had classified 605 American cities into nine functional types.

City Types. Table 6.3 lists the criteria used by Harris in identifying city types. The figure at the right of each subheading is the percentage of the cities of that type in his sample. Not surprisingly, manufacturing cities were the most numerous type, comprising 44 percent of the metropolitan areas and 43 percent of the smaller cities. The high number of manufacturing cities led Harris to divide this category into two subtypes; Mé type (19.5 percent), overwhelmingly manufacturing cities, and M type (23.1 percent), manufacturing cities with large numbers of people employed in support activities such as trade and wholesaling. In 1930, as today, most manufacturing cities were in an area east of the Mississippi and north of the Ohio Rivers. Harris also noted some clustering of manufacturing cities in the Piedmont region of the southeastern United States. (See Figure 6.1.)

Harris found fewer cities of the other functional types, but each city type had unique locational characteristics linked to its function. The majority of retail centers, R type (17.2 percent), were outside the manufacturing belt, along a narrow band that is the eastern boundary of the farming area of the Great Plains.

Diversified cities, D type (21.5 percent), in which neither trade nor manufacturing was clearly dominant, were well distributed but "were particularly numerous in the transitional area between the manufacturing belt and the band of retail centers" (p. 91). The largest metropolitan areas in the nation, New York, Chicago, and Boston (each a preeminent break-in-transportation city), were included in this category.

Wholesale centers, W type (4.5 percent), were of two kinds: smaller centers engaged in the assembling, packing, and marketing of agricultural products and large centers (usually the largest cities in their regions) that furnished durable and nondurable goods to their surrounding areas.

Most transportation centers, T type (5.3 percent), railroad centers and ports, were at break-in-transportation points. Mining towns, S type (2.3 percent), were near the source of raw materials. University towns, E type (2.8 percent), were the seats of large

TABLE 6.3 Criteria used by Harris in classifying cities.

Manufacturing Cities (M)—19.5%. Principal criterion: Employment in manufacturing equals at least 74% of total employment in manufacturing, retailing, and wholesaling (employment figures). Secondary criterion: Manufacturing and mechanical industries contain at least 45% of gainful workers (occupation figures). Note: A few cities with industries in suburbs for which no figures were available were placed in this class if the percentage in the secondary criterion reached 50. The largest city in this group was Detroit, Michigan. The smaller cities with heavier dominance of manufacturing were Fulton, New York, and Thomasville, North Carolina.

Manufacturing Cities (M)—23.1%. Principal criterion: Employment in manufacturing equals at least 60% of total employment in manufacturing, retailing, and wholesaling. Secondary criterion: Manufacturing and mechanical industries usually contain between 30% and 45% of gainful workers. Philadelphia was the largest city of this type. Pittsburgh and Rochester, Syracuse, and Albany, New York, are other examples.

Retail Centers (R)—17.2%. Employment in retailing is at least 50% of the total employment in manufacturing, wholesaling, and retailing and at least 2.2 times that in wholesaling alone. Tulsa, Oklahoma, Wichita, Kansas, and Shreveport, Louisiana, were the largest cities classified as retail centers.

Diversified Cities (D)—21.5%. Employment in manufacturing, wholesaling, and retailing is less than 60%, 20%, and 50% respectively of the total employment in these activities, and no other special criteria apply. Manufacturing and mechanical industries with few exceptions contain between 25% and 35% of the gainful workers. New York, Boston, and Chicago were the largest cities in this category. Smaller cities include Indianapolis, Columbus, Ohio, and Minneapolis-St. Paul.

Wholesale Centers (W)—4.5%. Employment in wholesaling is at least 20% of the total employment in manufacturing, wholesaling, and retailing and at least 45% as much as in retailing alone. Cities of this type were usually the largest city in their region and include such cities as Salt Lake City, Denver, Memphis, Oklahoma City, and Dallas.

Transportation Centers (T)—5.3%. Transportation and communication contain at least 11% of the gainful workers, and workers in transportation and communication equal at least one-third the number in manufacturing and mechanical industries and at least two-thirds the number in trade (occupation figures). (This applies only to cities of more than 25,000 for which such figures are available.) Harris identified rail centers and ports; among the better-known port cities were New Orleans and Portland, Maine.

Mining Towns (S)—2.3%. Extraction of minerals accounts for more than 15% of the gainful workers. (This applies only to cities of more than 25,000 for which such figures are available.) For cities between 10,000 and 25,000, a comparison was made of available mining employment by counties, using employment in the cities within such mining counties. Published sources were consulted to differentiate actual mining towns from commercial and industrial centers in mining areas. Scranton–Wilkes-Barre and Johnstown, Pennsylvania are among the best-known mining centers.

University Towns (E)—2.8%. Enrollment in schools of collegiate rank (universities, technical schools, liberal arts colleges, and teachers' colleges) equaled at least 25% of the

TABLE 6.3 (*continued*)

population of the city (1940). Enrollment figures are from *School and Society*, vol. 52, 1940, pp. 601–619. Oxford and Oberlin, Ohio, State College, Pennsylvania, and Chapel Hill, North Carolina, are among the most notable university towns.

Resort and Retirement Towns (X)—3.6%. No satisfactory statistical criterion was found. Cities with a low percentage of their population employed were checked in the literature for this function.

Source: Harris, C. D., "A Functional Classification of Cities in the United States." Reprinted from *The Geographical Review* 33, no. 1 (1943): p. 88, with the permission of the American Geographical Society.

state universities. Finally, resort and retirement towns, X type (3.6 percent), were either summer or winter resorts in warm southern locales, along seacoasts and lakes, or in the mountains. Harris mentioned political cities, garrison cities, professional centers, and fishing, lumbering, and farm centers, but did not include them in his typology.

Harris's typology was a bench-mark work, and it has been used as a model by other researchers in the construction of their own classification frameworks. In the research that followed, the number of variables included in studies increased, and the computational techniques became more sophisticated, but the goals remained the same—understanding the structure of the city and the forces which shape it.

USES OF CITY CLASSIFICATION SCHEMES

By the early 1970s, critics argued, and justly so, that the development of different classifications had become an end in itself (Berry, 1972; Hadden and Borgatta, 1965; Keeler and Rogers, 1973). Cities had been classified, but the classifications had not been used as a point of departure for further analysis. In addition, these schemes usually used economic variables. Some researchers claimed that since cities were now less specialized, economic characteristics were less important than their social characteristics (Alford, 1972). This was also the decade that the nation lost the War on Poverty and admitted that the spending of billions of dollars had done little to improve the conditions of the central city. It was also a decade of stagflation, economic recession, and the emergence of the so-called "me generation": a cohort who, some claimed, were more concerned about themselves than others. This change in the national tenor was reflected in changes in federal urban programs, which now required communities to demonstrate need before funding. In this environment classifications became a tool—a first step—in the analysis of urban problems and processes. Beginning in the 1970s, four types of studies using classifications appeared in the literature: fiscal strain studies, regional migration studies, urban hardship studies, and federal impact studies (Bickford, 1980).

FIGURE 6.1 The spatial distribution of cities in the United States by city types, Harris's 1943 city classification of 605 American cities.

Source: Harris, C. D., "A Functional Classification of Cities in the United States." Reprinted from the *Geographical Review* 33, 1 (1943): p. 92, with the permission of the American Geographical Society.

FISCAL STRESS

There are as many definitions of fiscal stress as there are researchers. The major reasons for studying fiscal strain, however, are to classify cities according to their degree of stress, explain why fiscal stress occurs, and identify cities at risk so that they can be helped before a financial emergency. These studies proliferated in the mid-1970s after the near default of New York City and Cleveland, which required massive bailouts by federal and state governments. These studies were often utilitarian: The results were used by banks, businesses, and government to assess the risk of doing business with certain cities.

How do you define fiscal strain? There are dozens of definitions, but one of the first was presented by Stanley (1976), who felt that a city is facing a fiscal crisis if it doesn't have the cash or credit to meet its obligations or if it is experiencing a long-term decline of its economic or social conditions.

Most researchers use a similar concept, but there are problems with this approach. First, is the cash crisis a short- or a long-term problem? Many Sunbelt cities have short-term financial problems because of rapid growth, but as their economies grow, so will their tax base; money eventually will be available to solve their problems. Snowbelt cities, in contrast, have long-term financial problems attributable to basic structural problems in their economies. Population and industries are declining along with the tax base, and the problems facing Snowbelt cities are different and intractable (Bickford, 1980).

A second and in many respects a more serious problem facing researchers is the lack of data or incompatible data. Budget and reporting practices vary from state to state and from city to city, and comparing the fiscal health of cities, say, in the Northeast with those in the West is difficult. Also, the cost of providing services varies enormously from region to region, as well as the expectations for services. I live in a low-tax state, but there are few city services. What would be considered minimal services in Massachusetts would be considered high-quality services in Arkansas. Therefore, all studies make relative comparisons.

It was the looming New York City financial crisis that focused national attention on a 1973 study, *City Financial Emergencies* (Advisory Commission on Intergovernmental Relations, 1973). The study examined the finances of the nation's 30 largest cities in an attempt to identify the specific factors contributing to municipal fiscal stress. The researchers identified several indicators that predicted problems: a significant gap between revenues and expenditures, large deficits, inability to pay short-term operating loans, rising property tax delinquencies, and a sudden decline in the assessed valuation of property.

Other researchers applied the same methods and came up with other stress indicators. Thomas Muller (1976) presented his findings to Congress and identified a somewhat different set of danger signals: out-migration, loss of jobs, high tax burdens, an increase in the number of high-service-cost, low-income, and minority families, and low per capita income.

The most comprehensive analysis of fiscal stress, however, was published in a series of articles by Terry Clark and others (Clark and Rubin 1976a; Clark, 1976;

Clark, 1977a; Clark and Ferguson, 1977b; Clark and Fuchs, 1977c). Clark analyzed the characteristics of 51 cities and developed 29 fiscal strain indicators that were grouped into four categories: socioeconomic characteristics, legal responsibility for high-cost services (welfare, education), leadership and decision-making patterns, and large debts due to earlier construction projects. Clark found that cities that were fiscally strained were often the large, older cities of the Northeast, which had declining populations, a high proportion of high-cost citizens—poor, old, minority—and a declining tax base. These findings reinforced most people's conception of a troubled city, but what is interesting is that the highest correlations in the studies were between fiscal strain and government structure. Specifically, cities experiencing fiscal strain were usually ones in which local decisions were made by a local government dominated by a strong mayor. Moreover, these were cities where the business community was so diffused, ineffective, or incompetent that they provided no checks to the power of the city. But, in the final analysis, Clark concluded that government structure and high-service-cost residents were only contributing factors. More important were the national processes of population redistribution and economic change over which local communities have no control. Certainly, when the mayor of a major city caves in to the demands of the unions, he or she is saddling the city with long-term obligations, but a mayor has no control over trade legislation, a leveraged buyout of the city's major employer, or the nation's periodic recessions. By classifying cities, Terry Clark and the other researchers showed that national forces along with local factors must be taken into consideration when examining the fiscal stress of cities.

REGIONAL MIGRATION STUDIES

Regional migration studies document the changes taking place in the nation by studying the flow of population and economic activity. By classifying cities, we gain clues as to why the cities in one region are losing population and employment while others are gaining (Noyelle and Stanback, 1983; Nelson, 1988; Taub and Sawyers, 1984). The population and economic changes in the Sunbelt versus the Snowbelt have received the greatest attention by the popular press. The popular image is that there has been an exodus of our best and brightest from northern to southern cities in pursuit of high-paying jobs in the nation's footloose, high-tech industries. The argument goes: As the tired industrial cities of the Snowbelt decay, the young, vibrant cities of the Sunbelt glimmer. But is this image correct? Have Sunbelt cities been the only winners and Snowbelt cities the only losers?

In an important study by Noyelle and Stanback (1983), *The Economic Transformation of American Cities,* the authors grouped 140 U.S. metropolitan areas, using a "location quotient" which measures the share of a metropolitan area's population in a given industry as a percentage of the share of employment in the same industry within the total U.S. economy. If a metropolitan area has the same percentage of its work force in, say, manufacturing, as the nation, then the location quotient is 100: fewer workers, the quotient falls below 100; more workers, the quotient is over 100. For example, Memphis's location quotients for wholesaling and manufacturing are 158 and 77, respectively. Therefore, Memphis is considered to be relatively specialized in wholesaling, not in manufacturing (Noyelle and Stanback, 1983, p. 52). (The classification is more sophisticated but similar to the earlier works of Harris.)

Using this technique, the authors identified four major types of cities: diversified service centers or nodal centers, specialized service centers, consumer-oriented centers, and production centers. Noyelle and Stanback's classification scheme is presented in Table 6.4. **Diversified service centers** are high-order central places, which provide goods and services to the nation or its major regions. They are the centers of complex corporate activities. They provide distribution services, and they are frequently centers of government and nonprofit activities.

Specialized service centers are places that are narrowly specialized in government, education, and manufacturing activities. They are smaller in size then the diversified service centers and are usually dominated by a single institution. For example, manufacturing centers are usually dominated by the central offices of corporations; educational centers, by a major university and related nonprofit activities; and government centers, by a strong pubic service sector.

Consumer-oriented centers include residential and resort–retirement metropolitan areas; they are specialized in providing services to individuals.

Finally, **production centers** are specialized in manufacturing, industrial-military, and mining activities; they produce goods for export. In general, their small service sectors provide services to local residents (Noyelle and Stanback, 1983, pp. 51–92).

Using the classification system as a point of departure, the authors examine the shift of a wide variety of activities through this hierarchy of places, as well as the flow of people and economic activities within and between cities in different regions. For example, the authors explored who had lost or gained the headquarters of Fortune 500 corporations, the change in total deposits in the major commercial banks in different cities, changes in the distribution of assets, employment, and revenues of cities, changes in national and international air traffic through metropolitan airports, and the list goes on.

In reporting their findings, the authors do not deny that the Sunbelt has been growing faster than the Snowbelt, but when they probed more deeply and took into consideration city types, a different picture emerged. First, there has been a reshuffling in the cities where large companies are headquartered, but for the most part the northern cities have done well—losing some, winning others. In general, northern cities continue to be the home of the nation's largest corporations, and although there has been an erosion in the number of regional and divisional headquarters located there, northern cities are still dominant.

Second, the authors support the popular notion that there has been a relocation of manufacturing: first from the central city to the suburbs and then from the suburbs to smaller nonmetropolitan communities. However, Noyelle and Stanback show that the popular press has ignored changes that have occurred in manufacturing. Footloose industries are involved only in assembly, and other divisions of a corporation or outside suppliers supply parts. The profits are not in assembly but in the production of high-value-added parts. These producer services are concentrated in good-sized cities,

TABLE 6.4 140 Largest SMSAs Classified by Type and Size under Four Major Groupings, 1976

DIVERSIFIED SERVICE CENTERS

NATIONAL NODAL
1	New York	1
2	Los Angeles	1
3	Chicago	1
7	San Francisco	1

REGIONAL NODAL
4	Philadelphia	1
6	Boston	1
10	Dallas	1
11	Houston	1
12	St. Louis	1
14	Baltimore	1
15	Minneapolis	1
17	Cleveland	1
18	Atlanta	2
21	Miami	2
22	Denver	2
23	Seattle	2
26	Cincinnati	2
28	Kansas City	2
30	Phoenix	2
32	Indianapolis	2
33	New Orleans	2
34	Portland	2
35	Columbus	2

SUBREGIONAL NODAL
41	Memphis	3
45	Salt Lake City	3
46	Birmingham	3
52	Nashville	3
53	Oklahoma City	3
56	Jacksonville	3
58	Syracuse	3
65	Richmond	3
66	Charlotte	3
69	Omaha	3
91	Mobile	4
101	Little Rock	4
106	Shreveport	4
110	Des Moines	4
114	Spokane	4
120	Jackson MS	4

SPECIALIZED SERVICE CENTERS

FUNCTIONAL NODAL
5	Detroit	1
13	Pittsburgh	1
16	Newark	1
24	Milwaukee	2
31	San Jose	2
36	Hartford	2
38	Rochester	3
40	Louisville	3
44	Dayton	3
47	Bridgeport	3
50	Toledo	3
51	Greensboro	3
57	Akron	3
62	Allentown	3
63	Tulsa	3
67	New Brunswick	3
70	Jersey City	3
75	Wilmington	3
78	Paterson	4
86	Knoxville	4
96	Wichita	4
100	Fort Wayne	4
103	Peoria	4
137	Kalamazoo	4

GOVERNMENT-EDUCATION
8	Washington, DC	1
39	Sacramento	3
48	Albany	3
77	Raleigh-Durham	4
81	Fresno	4
82	Austin	4
84	Lansing	4
85	Oxnard-Ventura	4
88	Harrisburg	4
89	Baton Rouge	4
99	Columbia, SC	4
111	Utica	4
112	Trenton	4
113	Madison	4
117	Stockton	4

EDUCATION-MANUFACTURING
54	New Haven	3
64	Springfield	3
90	Tacoma	4
130	South Bend	4
140	Ann Arbor	4

TABLE 6.4 (continued)

PRODUCTION CENTERS

MANUFACTURING

27	Buffalo	2
42	Providence	3
59	Worcester	3
60	Gary	3
61	N.E. Pennsylvania	3
71	Grand Rapids	3
72	Youngstown	3
73	Greenville	3
74	Flint	3
80	New Bedford	4
92	Canton	4
93	Johnson City	4
94	Chattanooga	4
98	Davenport	4
104	Beaumont	4
107	York	4
109	Lancaster	4
115	Binghamton	4
116	Reading	4
119	Huntington	4
124	Evansville	4
125	Appleton	4
131	Erie	4
134	Rockford	4
136	Lorain	4
123	Huntsville	4
126	Augusta	4
127	Vallejo	4
128	Colorado Springs	4
132	Pensacola	4
133	Salinas	4

INDUSTRIAL–MILITARY

20	San Diego	2
37	San Antonio	3
49	Norfolk	3
87	El Paso	4
97	Charleston, SC	4
102	Newport News	4
121	Lexington	4

MINING–INDUSTRIAL

83	Tucson	4
105	Bakersfield	4
118	Corpus Christi	4
129	Lakeland	4
135	Johnstown, PA	4
138	Duluth	4
139	Charleston, WV	4

CONSUMER-ORIENTED CENTERS

RESIDENTIAL

9	Nassau	1
19	Anaheim	2
76	Long Branch	3

RESORT–RETIREMENT

25	Tampa	2
29	Riverside	2
43	Fort Lauderdale	3
55	Honolulu	3
68	Orlando	3
79	West Palm Beach	4
95	Albuquerque	4
108	Las Vegas	4
122	Santa Barbara	4

Note: Number preceding city indicates 1976 population rank; number following city, 1976 population size group (see text).

Source: Noyelle, T. J., and Stanback, J. T. M. (1983). *The Economic Transformation of American Cities.* Totowa, NJ: Rowan and Allanheld. Adapted from Table 4.2, pp. 56–57. That table is based on data from U.S. Bureau of the Census, *Current Population Report,* Series P-25, and Appendix A.

and most of these cities remain in the Snowbelt. For example, Tennessee may have won the competition for the new General Motors Saturn assembly plant, but the engine and other high-value-added parts—radios, computerized controls, fasteners, and sheet metal parts—are manufactured elsewhere.

Third, the authors found that the banking and service industry continues to be concentrated in the Snowbelt, as well as other high-paying service activities in advertising, accounting, and other producer services. Moreover, the authors detail the role of government and nonprofit institutions in the restructuring of the U.S. economy, especially the role of higher education and research in transforming northern and southern cities.

In general, this work is important because it calls into question the deeply entrenched views on the U.S. economy held by businessmen, economists, government officials, and the general public. It shows the important use of city classification in sorting out the complex process of economic restructuring and population redistribution, and the classification scheme developed by Noyelle and Stanback has been used by Nelson (1988) and others to study other aspects of migration and economic reorganization.

HARDSHIP STUDIES

Hardship studies compare cities on the basis of some definitions of need. The first studies were developed for the Department of Housing and Urban Development (HUD) to target federal aid funds, especially Community Development Block Grant funds. The studies vary, but most use widely available government data on unemployment, income, the location of high-service-cost citizens, welfare and education costs, poverty, and housing to classify cities. These data are then used to compare differences between metropolitan areas, as well as differences between a metropolitan area's central city and suburbs (Bickford, 1980).

It is not surprising that the majority of the studies show cities in greatest need concentrated in the central cities of our largest cities: cities usually found in the upper Midwest and Northeast. Large sums of money are involved, and the findings of many of these studies have been hotly disputed; some have even been challenged in court (Nathan and Adams, 1976; Garn, 1977a, 1977b).

While fiscal studies explore the long- and short-term financial problems of cities, hardship studies look to the social costs of our urban problems. They ask how well we clothe, house, educate, and feed the most disadvantaged segments of our society and how scarce federal funds can be spent best.

FEDERAL IMPACT STUDIES

When the Congress passes housing, employment, welfare, and tax legislation, the effect is not neutral; some cities and regions benefit more than others. Now that government itself at all levels generates about 25 percent of the nation's GNP, it is not surprising that interest has grown in the impact of federal spending on local economies.

Direct grants and aid to local governments are easily traced, and during the Carter administration urban impact statements (similar to environmental impact statements) were required for federal urban programs. Interestingly, much of this research showed that many federal programs had unintended consequences and in some cases actually hurt the cities they were designed to help (Catsambas, 1978; Noyelle and Stanback, 1983; Macdonald, 1984; Vaughan, 1977).

These are direct effects, but there are also hidden or latent consequences of federal policy. The most infamous were the unintended consequences of the Highway Trust Fund Legislation, which paid for the nation's interstate highway system, FHA and VA mortgages, which made new home construction on the fringe cheaper than the rehabilitation of dwellings in the central city, and federal grants-in-aid, which subsidized suburban water and sewerage systems. Taken as a whole, these programs represent a massive, hidden subsidy of suburban development by the federal government which spurred the exodus of people from central cities to the suburbs after World War II.

More recent studies have shown that there is a pronounced regional impact of federal spending. For example, in 1979, 78 percent of the military payroll and 58 percent of the prime military contracts went to the Sunbelt states, and this disparity increased during the massive military buildup during the Reagan Administration. If one examines all federal payments between 1975 and 1980, Snowbelt states sent Washington $165 billion more in taxes than they received in federal aid, while Sunbelt states sent Washington $112 billion less in taxes then they got back in aid (Macdonald, 1984, pp. 24–27).

Investment tax credits are not targeted regionally, but they favor those regions where growth is occurring—the South and the West. Similarly, depreciation allowances for major capital investments favor new construction and cities in the South. Only now are researchers beginning to gain a grasp on this topic, and once again city classifications are a tool used in their analyses.

In summary, there is a long history of city classification, and hundreds of studies have been published. City classifications were first developed by geographers and later diffused into other disciplines. Once merely an academic exercise, classifications have become an indispensable tool in urban research. They are used to study urban problems and processes, and they have become an important element in the creation, implementation, and managing of urban policies and programs. We now turn to the related topic of city ratings, which have their beginnings in sociology and that discipline's attempt to develop social indicators and to measure quality of life.

CITY RATINGS

America has a national obsession: the need to know who, where, and what is the best. In professional sports and in collegiate basketball and baseball it's easy; we have months of playoffs. Think about it. In professional baseball, we have teams that play more than 160 games, and we still don't know which is America's best team at the end of the regular season. Nonfans suffer through weeks of playoffs and then a week of the World Series to pick a world champion.

Think of the nightmares college football causes our national psyche. Football fans suffer through months of consternation as members of the National Sports Writers Association crown a national champion. "Too imprecise," say some. "What we need is a national playoff series," say others. Imagine: football games during graduation.

We don't just rank things and people; we also rank places. The popular press's interest in ratings began in 1931, when Charles Angoff and H. L. Mencken ranked the best and worst states in which to live. They used 63 variables to rank the 48 states and the District of Columbia. Massachusetts won. Mississippi lost. More recently, the press picked up on a United Nations study on the ratings of countries. Much to their consternation, the United States was ranked eleventh in the world in the physical quality of life, and we were not even in the top 20 in social progress. The winners? Iceland and Norway.

The public's interest in city ratings began in 1981, when Rand McNally published *Places Rated Almanac* (Boyer and Savageau, 1981). Sales exceeded all expectations, and the book was reprinted four times in the first six months. Other publishers scurried to come out with copycat books, and others have gotten in the act (Bowman et al., 1981; Conway, 1981; Garwood, 1984; Marlin and Avery, 1983). Magazines like *Money* and *Inc.* now have annual ratings of cities (Baer-Sinnott, 1987; Eisenberg and Englander, 1987, 1988). The results are picked up by AP and UPI, and the ratings are reprinted in most of the nation's newspapers. There is also the case of unsuspecting academics, who receive instant notoriety after they release a new rating study. When the press heard that Robert Pierce was presenting his ratings to the annual meeting of the American Geographic Society, the press bombarded the convention site with over 400 phone calls.

What the public doesn't know is that these popular city ratings represent the accumulation of 40 years of scientific research. In the 1950s, sociologists began to develop social indicators to measure the social health of the nation; in the 1960s, this evolved into an interest in social well-being and the quality of life; in the 1970s and 1980s, this research was applied to the rating of cities. Therefore, the second half of this chapter explores how city ratings evolved and how they are constructed. Important studies are reviewed, and their strengths and weaknesses are assessed. The section ends with a discussion of how individuals might use city ratings in their own lives.

BACKGROUND

It is impossible to listen to the news, read a paper, or browse a *Time* or *Newsweek* without being bombarded with government statistics. We are used to the blizzard of statistics on agricultural production, AIDS victims, the homeless, the percentage in poverty, unemployment, inflation, and GNP growth. But many of these statistics have been available only recently. The federal government has always gathered information on the characteristics of our population and economic conditions. During the Hoover administration the executive branch even published a report on the social conditions in the nation (Research Commission, 1930), but for most of our history statistics were confined to the general economic health of the nation—GNP, unemployment, and inflation figures. Little was available on the social health of the nation. Few asked how well we housed, educated, and provided for the basic needs of our people.

This changed after World War II. The postwar housing boom was responsible for the first interest in social indicators. During the 1950s, mass-produced suburbs and other residential forms first appeared. Social scientists became interested in these new residential forms, and a need developed to know how satisfied people were with them. In addition, the expanding role of the federal government in slum clearance, urban renewal, and public housing led many policy makers to demand more data on the conditions of central city housing and the poor and minorities who lived there (Cutter, 1985; Campbell et al., 1976; Duncan, 1964, 1984; Myers, 1987; Wish, 1986a).

The role of government expanded even more during the Johnson administration. Lyndon Johnson's Great Society was responsible for the most sweeping social legislation since the Great Depression. The federal government became the great equalizer in this society, and problems previously left to the states became the target of federal programs. Today many federal programs in health, nutrition, housing, and education can trace their origins to the 1960s. This was also the decade when sociologists and other social scientists embarked on a large-scale research program to gather more and better data for social planning and policy development. The reason was simple: Policy makers could not develop and evaluate programs without concrete data of their effectiveness (Duncan, 1964, 1984).

In the process of evaluating programs, comparisons were made on the social well-being of regions and states. The study of the quality of life—the consequences of different living environments and people's satisfaction with them—was, therefore, a natural evolution of the work on social indicators. Soon two different lines of measurement emerged—one focused on individual well-being and the other on urban quality of life. Studies on individual well-being were based on subjective data gathered through surveys and interviews. These studies accessed the quality of life from the perspective of the individual, not the group. In some of the large national studies, respondents were clustered by residential type—central city, suburb, small town—but the small size of the samples made comparisons of specific cities impossible (see Campbell et al., 1976).

Studies in urban quality of life, in contrast, were based on objective data gathered by the Census Bureau or other bureaucracies in their normal course of doing business. Massive amounts of data were available, and modern high-speed computers permitted detailed comparisons of hundreds of cities on dozens of variables. The focus of these studies was not the individual, but the collective experiences of a community. An early study by the Urban Institute by Flax (1971) showed that detailed comparisons of cities, using social indicators techniques, were feasible; dozens of studies soon followed (Cutter, 1985; Myers, 1987).

WHAT IS QUALITY OF LIFE?

Quality of life (QOL) refers to the individuals happiness and satisfaction with life and the environment. In evaluating the quality of life, individual needs, desires, aspirations, lifestyle, and stage in the life cycle influence one's feeling of overall well-being (Campbell et al., 1976). Humans are social beings and don't live in isolation but in a web of social relationships. These social relations include family, friends, coworkers, and a complex of relationships among the individual and the community's institutional structure—schools, churches, factories, offices, stores, hospitals, and other elements in the local economy. The physical environment—climate, scenic beauty, topography, and environmental quality—also exerts a powerful influence on people's definition of their quality of life. Quality-of-life research is based on the assumption that the institutional structure and the physical environment are the major determinants of an individual's quality of life. Therefore, analyzing and rating places rather than individual experiences makes sense because the community in which we live is the envelope which shapes our experiences and our definition of the quality of life (Bayless and Bayless, 1982; Wish, 1986a, 1986b).

Researchers involved in the study of QOL are actually measuring indirectly the differences between two mental states—a goal state and an appraisal state. A goal state asks, "What institutions should be in the community? What should the environment be like?" It is a state of mind of a community—a collective impression. It's subjective and similar to that nebulous term, community spirit. Moreover, it is a state shaped by history, culture, and individual tastes (Campbell et al., 1976; Campbell, 1981).

The appraisal state measures the actual environment—what is actually there. It, too, is shaped by history and culture, and it, too, involves a subjective evaluation of objective conditions. Quality of life is the difference between what should be and what is in a community—the difference between the goal and appraisal states. Therefore, for the purposes of this text, quality of life is defined as the measurement of the conditions of place, how those conditions are experienced and evaluated by individuals, and the relative importance of each of these to individuals. From this perspective, the measurement of quality of life requires the analysis of objective conditions, as well as subjective assessments of these conditions between and within places. (Cutter, 1984, p. 2). As we will see, one of the major criticisms of this literature is that objective conditions are examined; little attention has been given to the subjective evaluations that people make about the places they live.

CONSTRUCTING A CITY RATING

Although city ratings differ in the number of variables included in their analysis, as well as how the variables are weighed, they are similar in the way they are constructed. In Table 6.5, 11 cities have been listed along with their values on three variables—the number of drug stores, service stations, and restaurants per 100,000 inhabitants. The first step is to make certain assumptions on what the figures mean. I am going to assume that the more drug stores, service stations, and restaurants, the more available and convenient these services, and the better the quality of life—the larger the figure the better.

The first step is to order the cities by rank, using the raw data presented in the first three columns of the table. Pursuing the data on drug stores in the first column, note that Dallas is first with 36 stores per 100,000 inhabitants, New York second with 33, San Francisco third with 31, and the process continues until the last city is ranked, Washington, D.C., eleventh with 19. This same process is repeated for the data on service stations and restaurants. The rank order of the cities is presented in columns 4 through 6 of the table.

I don't consider drug stores to be more important than gas stations in quality of life, so I'm not going to weigh the rankings. I'm simply going to sum the rank order figures. In the case of New York City, note that the city was ranked second in drug stores, eighth in service stations, and fourth in restaurants for a total score of 14. The sums range from a 4 in Dallas to a 32 in the nation's capital.

The final step is simply to rank order the sums; the city with the lowest score will have the highest ranking. In this example, Dallas is ranked first with a score of 4—it was first in drug stores and service stations and second in restaurants—San Francisco is second with a score of 8, Houston is third with a score of 10, and New York and Los Angeles are tied for fourth, so there is no fifth. At the other end of the spectrum, Cincinnati, Philadelphia, Chicago, and Washington, D.C.—eighth through eleventh.

Although the process has been simplified, this is the methodology used in city classification studies. It is important to recognize that the cities chosen for the analysis, the concepts used, the variables chosen as indicants of the concepts, and the decision on how the variables are used in constructing a rating scheme are subjective decisions made by the researcher. These decisions are shaped by the discipline, education, region, race, and sex of the researcher, and they influence the final results. Therefore, it is important to recognize the subjective nature of all city rating studies. Keep this in mind when reading about the rating studies in the following section.

SELECTED STUDIES

Interest in urban places by researchers and the general public has stimulated a large number of empirical studies on the quality of life. These studies range from studies that have rated cities on stress to others that have rated cities on their potential for

TABLE 6.5 SCHWAB'S SERVICE RATING

| METROPOLITAN AREA | SERVICES PER 100,000 | | | RANK ORDER | | | | |
	DRUG STORES	SERVICE STATIONS	RESTAURANTS	DRUG STORES	SERVICE STATIONS	RESTAURANTS	TOTAL	RANKING
New York	33	62	213	2nd	8th	4th	14	4
Los Angeles	29	70	231	5th	6th	3rd	14	4 tie
Chicago	25	45	153	9th	11th	10th	30	10
San Francisco	31	75	294	3rd	4th	1st	8	2
Dallas	36	107	254	1st	1st	2nd	4	1
Houston	30	79	211	4th	3rd	5th	12	3
Cleveland	23	74	199	10th	5th	6th	21	7
Cincinnati	27	63	174	7th	7th	8th	22	8
Philadelphia	26	52	155	8th	9th	9th	26	9
Washington, DC	19	49	132	11th	10th	11th	32	11
Jacksonville, FL	28	86	188	6th	2nd	7th	15	6

Source: U.S. Department of Commerce, Bureau of the Census. *The State and Metropolitan Area Data Book.* Washington, D.C.: U.S. Government Printing Office, 1983.

economic growth. Four studies are described below. They were selected because they were either important in the development of the literature or they have been widely reported in the press.

Ben-Chieh Liu's Study. The modern era for urban quality-of-life research began with the publication of Flax's study for the Urban Institute, which demonstrated the feasibility of using social indicators in city ratings (Flax, 1971). However, it was Ben-Chieh Liu's research (1975) on the quality of life done for the Environmental Protection Agency that became the benchmark for all other studies. The purpose of Liu's study was to assess the quality of life in 243 standard metropolitan areas. One hundred twenty-three variables were used in the study, and to reduce the complexity of the analysis, a technique called *factor analysis* was used to summarize the variables into five composite indices. They were economic, political, environmental, health and education, and social indices.

Previous research had shown that city size was inversely related to people's sense of well-being (Elgin, 1974), so Liu grouped SMSAs into small (under 200,000), medium (200,000 to 500,000), and large (500,000 and greater) metropolitan areas. Liu ranked the three categories of cities on each of the five dimensions, and in addition, calculated a general score and used it to assign a letter grade for each city ranging from A (outstanding) to E (substandard). Liu published maps with the study showing the distribution of cities on each of the indices as well as the summary measure. Figure 6.2 shows the geographic distribution of ratings on the overall quality of life for large cities.

Several generalizations can be made from looking at the maps; the most obvious is that the quality of life gets better as you move away from the South. Whether it be the social, political, or summary index, cities in the South are ranked consistently worse than any other region. The far West, upper Midwest, and selected cities in the East fared best in this study.

Ben-Chieh Liu's work was important for many reasons. The sheer complexity, comprehensiveness, and the quality of the scholarship separated it from others. Second, Liu was able to incorporate data on environmental quality, previously absent in these studies. Third, some subjective data were included in the study: Community leaders were polled on the amenities in their communities—parks and recreation. In addition, for the first time indicators on environmental quality—air and water quality, noise, and solid waste—were included in a city ratings study.

The Liu study has been replicated and used as the basis of other studies. In the studies that followed specific questions were addressed, including the quality of life in small cities and the role quality of life plays in migration. For these reasons, it had a profound affect on the development of the literature on city ratings.

Places Rated Almanac. In 1981, Boyer and Savageau published their *Places Rated Almanac,* which combined statistical information, place profiles, and other information on 277 metropolitan areas. Using 53 variables, the authors created nine indices on metropolitan areas' climate, housing, health care and environment, crime, transportation,

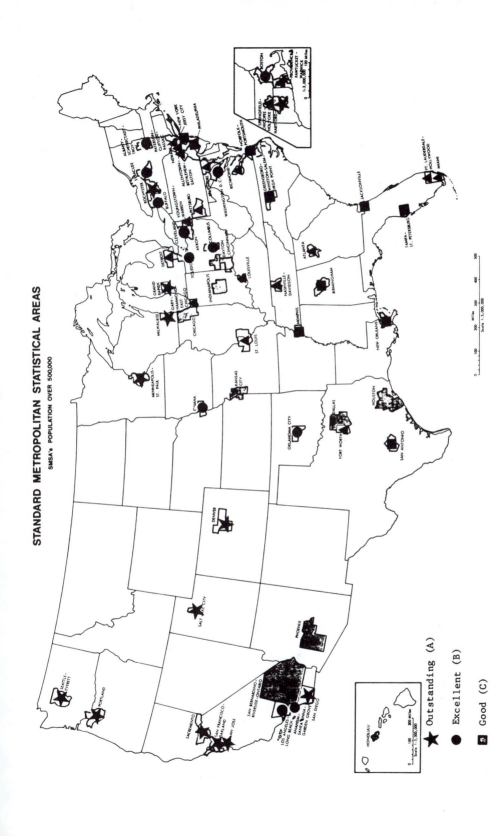

FIGURE 6.2 Geographic Distribution of Ratings: Overall Quality of Life (L)

education, recreation, arts, and their economies. The 277 places were ranked on each dimension. Individual scores were then summed and the city with the lowest score (the highest overall ratings on each dimension) was rated first, the second lowest score, second, and so on. No weight was given to one dimension over another.

The success of the book led the authors to publish *Places Rated Retirement Guide* in 1983 and to revise and release second and third editions of their popular *Places Rated Almanac* in 1985 and 1989. Table 6.5 lists the 25 cities rated the best and the worst in 1981 and 1985. Atlanta was rated the best place in the nation to live in 1981, but dropped to eleventh in the 1985 almanac. Washington, D.C. was second in 1981 but fifteenth in 1985. Can a place change that much in four years? The authors note in their 1985 study that three factors were responsible. First, there were more cities in the study in 1985—329 versus 277—the data were updated and improved, and one index had been modified.

Some interesting patterns emerge. In Liu's study, no southern city, regardless of size, was in the top ten. Ben-Chieh Liu found top-rated cities clustered in the far West, upper Midwest, and the Northeast. Boyer and Savageau, in contrast, found the best

TABLE 6.5 BOYER AND SAVAGEAU'S RATINGS, 1981 AND 1985

	1981	
TOP TWENTY-FIVE		*BOTTOM TWENTY-FIVE*
1 Atlanta, GA	253	Paterson–Clifton–
2 Washington, DC		Passaic, NJ
3 Greensboro–Winston–	254	Killeen–Temple, TX
Salem–High Point, NC	255	Fort Smith, AR
4 Pittsburgh, PA	256	Lafayette, LA
5 Seattle–Everett, WA	257	Meriden, CT
6 Philadelphia, PA	258	Modesto, CA
7 Syracuse, NY	260	Stockton, CA
8 Portland, OR		New Britain, CT
9 Raleigh–Durham, NC	261	Brockton, MA
10 Dallas–Fort Worth, TX	262	Decatur, IL
11 Knoxville, TN	263	Sherman–Denison, TX
12 Nashville–Davidson, TN	264	Macon, GA
13 Anaheim–Santa Ana	265	Rockford, IL
GardenGrove, CA	266	Waterbury, CT
14 Cleveland, OH	267	Vineland–Millville–
San Francisco–Oakland, CA		Bridgeton, NJ
16 Denver–Boulder, Co	268	Texarkana, TX
17 Cincinnati, OH	269	Lawton, OK
18 Boston, MA	270	Greeley, CO
19 Louisville, KY	271	Bristol, CT
20 Miami, FL	272	Fresno, CA
21 Chicago, IL	273	Panama City, FL
22 San Diego, CA	274	Lowell–Nashua, NH
23 Minneapolis–St. Paul, MN	275	Pine Bluff, AR
24 St. Louis, MO	276	Fitchburg–Leominster, MA
25 Utica–Rome, NY	277	Lawrence–Havermill, MA

TABLE 6.5 *(continued)*

	1985		
	TOP TWENTY-FIVE		*BOTTOM TWENTY-FIVE*
1	Pittsburgh, PA	305	Dubuque, IA
2	Boston, MA	306	Wichita Falls, TX
3	Raleigh–Durham, NC	307	Janesville–Beloit, WI
4	San Francisco, CA	308	Sherman–Denison ,TX
5	Philadelphia, PA–NJ	309	Decatur, IL
6	Nassau–Suffolk, NY	310	Bradenton, FL
7	St. Louis, MO–IL	311	Baton Rouge, LA
8	Louisville, KY–IN	312	Greeley, CO
9	Norwalk, CT	313	Mansfield, OH
10	Seattle, WA	314	Sheboygan, WI
11	Atlanta, GA	315	Anniston, AL
12	Dallas, TX	316	Fitchburg–Leominster, MA
13	Buffalo, NY	317	Texarkana, TX–AR
14	Knoxville, TN	318	Laredo, TX
15	Baltimore, MD	319	Victoria, TX
16	Washington, DC–MD–VA	320	Anderson, IN
17	Cincinnati, OH–KY–IN	321	Rockford, IL
18	Burlington, VT	322	Casper, WY
19	Albany–Schenectady–Troy, NY	323	Gadsden, AL
20	Syracuse, NY	324	Benton Harbor, MI
21	Albuquerque, NM	325	Albany, GA
22	Harrisburg–Lebanon–Carlisle, PA	326	Dothan, AL
23	Richmond–Petersburg, VA	327	Modesto, CA
24	Providence, RI	328	Pine Bluff, AR
25	New York, NY	329	Yuba City, CA

Source: Boyer, R., and Savageau, D. (1981). *Places Rated Almanac.* Chicago, IL.: Rand McNally; Boyer, R. and Savageau, D. (1985). *Places Rated Almanac.* Chicago, IL: Rand McNally.

places to live in 1981 concentrated in the Mid-South—Tennessee, North Carolina, and Georgia—with a few cities on the West Coast and in the states of Illinois, Ohio, Pennsylvania, and New York. In the 1985 study, the Mid-South lost its dominance to the Mid-Atlantic states. Obvious differences exist between the Liu and the Boyer and Savageau studies.

Although the *Places Rated Almanac* received widespread media attention, it was not well received in the academic community. In fact, it was ignored. Unlike Liu's work, which has been replicated, there have been few attempts to build on the work of Boyer and Savageau. One reason is that Richard Boyer is best known as a mystery writer, and David Savageau is not a researcher, but the director of a personal relocation consulting firm. Another reason was the audience; the book was written for the general public, and it had not gone through a vigorous peer review process, which research publications must.

Robert Pierce's Study. A geographer named Robert Pierce (1984) was one of the few to replicate Boyer and Savageau's findings. One reaction to the Rand McNally study was a sharp disagreement between the public's perception of the quality of life in certain cities and the ratings based on objective data. Robert Pierce argued that part of the problem might be in the way Boyer and Savageau constructed their overall index: They simply summed the nine indices for each city—they didn't weigh one index more heavily than another. Robert Pierce argued that people don't rank all aspects of their lives the same; some elements are more important than others. To test this hypothesis, he sampled 1100 New York state residents and asked them to rank the nine criteria used by Boyer and Savageau according to their importance in their lives. The respondents rated economics, climate, and crime the highest and recreation, transportation, and the arts the lowest. Robert Pierce then reworked Boyer and Savageau's data by assigning a weight to each index. For example, the rankings on the economic measure were multiplied by nine, because the respondents felt this was the most important dimension. At the other end, because most people felt the arts were unimportant to their quality of life, these rankings were multiplied by only one. The products were then summed, and the places reranked.

Robert Pierce's (1984) findings are presented in Table 6.6. First, he found a positive correlation between his weighted rankings and the unweighted ones employed by Boyer and Savageau. He also found a concentration of top-rated places in the South.

TABLE 6.6 PIERCE'S RATINGS, 1984

	TOP TWENTY-FIVE		BOTTOM TWENTY-FIVE
1	Greensboro, NC	253	Pittsfield, MA
2	Knoxville, TN	254	Corpus Christi, TX
3	Asheville, NC	255	Kankakee, IL
4	Nashville, TN	256	Peoria, IL
5	Raleigh, NC	257	Waterbury, CT
6	Charleston, WV	258	Meriden, CT
7	Wheeling, WV	259	Gary, IN
8	Evansville, IN	260	New Britain, CT
9	Anaheim, CA	261	Bristol, CT
10	Atlanta, GA	262	Lewiston, ME
11	San Jose, CA	263	St. Joseph, MO
12	Galveston, TX	264	Macon, GA
13	Portland, OR	265	Jackson, MI
14	Louisville, KY	266	Bakersfield, CA
15	Seattle, WA	267	Great Falls, MT
16	Lexington, KY	268	Patterson, NJ
17	Eugene, OR	269	Lowell, MA
18	Ft. Wayne, IN	270	Rockford, IL
19	Washington, D.C.	271	Texarkana, TX
20	Huntington, WV	272	Pine Bluff, AR
21	New Brunswick, NJ	273	Stockton, CA
22	Pittsburgh, PA	274	Lawton, OK
23	Salem, OR	275	Fitchburg, MA
24	Utica, NY	276	Lawrence, MA
25	Johnstown, PA	277	Fresno, CA

Source: Pierce, R. M. Rating America's metropolitan areas. Used with permission, © American Demographics, July 1985.

Greensboro, North Carolina, ranked first, followed by Knoxville, Tennessee, Asheville, North Carolina, and Raleigh, North Carolina. Only three cities, Atlanta, Greensboro, and Raleigh, appear on both lists. In general, Pierce found the best places to live on the Pacific Coast and in the Southeast. The worst places were concentrated in the old mill towns of New England, agricultural communities in California's Central Valley, and in industrial cities like Gary, Indiana, located near Chicago.

In response to the revised *Places Rated Almanac*, Pierce (1985) also recalculated his earlier rankings. Using the same system, Pierce found Nassau–Suffolk, New York, to be most livable metropolitan area followed by Raleigh–Durham, North Carolina, and Norwalk, Connecticut. Although the relative position of many of the previously rated cities changed, the regional pattern of the best and worst cities remained.

The major contributions of the Pierce study was the introduction of perceptual components into the ratings of cities. His study showed the value of using perceptual indicators to weigh the objective indicators used in the rating of cities.

City Ratings from the Editors of* Money *Magazine. Rand Mcnally's *Places Rated Almanac* and the Pierce studies identified the most livable metropolitan areas in the United States, but a number of popular magazines felt that they failed to provide appropriate information for their readers. The result was that the editors of *Money* decided to construct their own city rating. *Money* published their first rating in 1987 and followed it with a second in 1988. However, the methodology they used in both studies was the same. A sample of subscribers (mean age, 42, mean income, $61,000 in the 1988 report) were asked to score 60 variables on a scale of 1 to 10. The most important variables were a low crime rate, the likelihood that their houses would appreciate, and the availability of doctors. The editors used census data and a computer software package called *Places, U.S.A.*, along with two other subject measures: weather—rated against San Diego's—and civic pride—measured with the percentage of adults registered to vote in each metropolitan area. Three hundred cities were ranked on nine dimensions by summing the rankings of each city on each dimension. The city with the lowest score was ranked first, and so on.

The ratings of the highest- and lowest-ranked cities are presented in Table 6.7. Danbury, Connecticut, was the top-rated city, but it had its drawbacks; the cost of a three-bedroom house averaged more than $175,000. Dramatic swings in the ratings took place in a single year. Cincinnati moved up from 104th to 31st and Cleveland moved from 83rd to 22nd because of improved local economies. Cities that dropped the most between 1987 and 1988 were low-crime, low-housing-cost cities but with foundering local economies—Houma/Thibodaux, Louisiana (11th to 128th), Scranton/Wilkes-Barre, Pennsylvania (9th to 114th), and Wheeling, West Virginia. Some have questioned the reliability of a study that experiences such wild swings in ratings in a single year.

CRITICISM OF THE METHODOLOGY

The literature on city ratings range from the Liu's broad, comprehensive, and complex research to *Money* Magazine's simple and straightforward study. Although these studies differ in their focus and audience, they share one thing in common: They assume that the

TABLE 6.7 *Money* Magazine's Ratings, 1988

	TOP 25			BOTTOM 25	
1	Danbury, CT	(5)	276	Greeley, CO	(289)
2	Central New Jersey	(13)	277	Poughkeepsie, NY	(152)
3	Norwalk, CT	(2)	278	Mansfield, OH	(291)
4	Long Island, NY	(6)	279	Jacksonville, NC	(222)
5	San Francisco, CA	(12)	280	State College, PA	(79)
6	Nashua, NH	(1)	281	Visalia, CA	(214)
7	Los Angeles/Long Beach, CA	(17)	282	Modesto, CA	(191)
8	Orange County, CA	(10)	283	Odessa, TX	(295)
9	Boston, MA	(45)	284	Lima, OH	(262)
10	Bergen/Passaic, NJ	(39)	285	Stockton, CA	(226)
11	Seattle, WA	(60)	286	E. St. Louis, IL	(244)
12	Boston's North Shore, MA	(8)	287	Fayetteville, NC	(285)
13	Monmouth/Ocean, NJ	(23)	288	Albany, GA	(273)
14	Stamford, CT	(25)	289	Fall River, MA	(172)
15	Bridgeport/Milford, CT	(37)	290	Muskegon, MI	(299)
16	Chicago, IL	(48)	291	Des Moines, IA	(278)
17	Riverside/San Bernardino, CA	(29)	292	Rockford, IL	(296)
18	Orange County, NY	(38)	293	Flint, MI	(300)
19	New York City, NY	(82)	294	New Bedford, MA	(272)
20	Pittsburgh, PA	(43)	295	Janesville/Beloit, WI	(265)
21	Oxnard/Ventura, CA	(7)	296	Battle Creek, MI	(287)
22	Cleveland, OH	(83)	297	Yuba City, CA	(246)
23	Houston, TX	(120)	298	Benton Harbor, MI	(298)
24	Newark, NJ	(68)	299	Jackson, MI	(294)
25	Beaver County, PA	(4)	300	Atlantic City, NJ	(297)

Note: Figures in parentheses, rankings in 1987 study.

Source: Eisenberg, R., and Englander, D. W. (1988). The best places to live in America. *Money* (August): 76–84. This article is reprinted from MONEY magazine by special permission; copyright 1988 The Time Inc. Magazine Company.

quality of life is based on the sum of the well-being of many individuals. Moreover, since it is impractical to monitor large numbers of individuals, these studies use proxy variables with data collected by educational, political, and economic organizations. These similarities have led to similar criticism of all these studies. First, city ratings are not based in theory but rather are driven by the availability of data. Related is the criticism that they use ill-defined concepts that are often poorly or haphazardly operationalized. These problems can be seen in Table 6.8, which presents the variables included in the political component of Liu's study. First, what is an "informed citizenry?" Is it a person who can identify the local leadership and list the problems facing the community, or is it a citizen who is politically active, or is it a citizen who is aware of the problems in her or his neighborhood or block? The problem is that the concept is never defined in the study. Equally important, do variables like "local Sunday newspaper circulation per 1000 population," "percent of occupied housing units with TV available," and "local radio stations per 1000 population" measure an informed citizen? They may not. For example, you may get the paper for the sports page, comics, and classified ads. Your town may be wired for cable, and you may watch Chicago's evening news rather than a local station's. Or you may listen only to rock stations which seldom carry local news. These variables are tenuous at best, and no one has demonstrated that they are indicants for the ubiquitous concept, "informed citizenry."

TABLE 6.8 VARIABLES USED IN THE CONSTRUCTION OF LIU'S POLITICAL COMPONENT

FACTORS

I. Individual Activities
    A. Informed citizenry
        1. Local Sunday newspaper circulation per 1000 population
        2. Percent of occupied housing units with TV available
        3. Local radio stations per 1000 population
    B. Political activity participation-ratio of presidential votes cast to voting age population

II. Local Government Factors
    A. Professionalism
        1. Average monthly earnings of full-time teachers ($)
        2. Average monthly earnings of other full-time employees ($)
        3. Entrance salary of patrolmen ($)
        4. Entrance salary of firemen ($)
        5. Total municipal employment per 1000 population
        6. Police protection employment per 1000 population
        7. Fire protection employment per 1000 population
        8. Insured unemployment rates under state, federal, and ex-servicemen's programs
    B. Performance
        1. Violent crime rate per 100,000 population
        2. Property crime rate per 100,000 population
        3. Local government revenue per capita
        4. Percent of revenue from federal government
        5. Community health index
        6. Community education index
    C. Welfare assistance
        1. Per capita local government expenditures on public welfare ($)
        2. Average monthly retiree benefits ($)
        3. Average monthly payments to families with dependent children ($)

Source: Liu, B. (1975). *Quality of life indicators in U.S. metropolitan areas, 1970: A comprehensive assessment.* Washington, D.C.: U.S. Environmental Protection Agency.

    Second, the studies cannot be compared. The findings in one study usually do not agree with another. Scan the results in the studies presented in the previous section. Find much overlap in the top 5? Top 10? Top 25? Note that there is more agreement on which cities are at the bottom. Naomi Wish (1986a) carried out a simple correlation of the ratings between the Liu and the Boyer and Savageau's and found a correlation of only 0.08—no relationship.

    Third, these studies use data for an entire metropolis. From your own experiences, you know that every city has prestigious neighborhoods and distressed neighborhoods. In general, suburbs are nicer than the central city. But all these differences are ignored when a city is rated on variables for the entire metropolis (Cutter, 1985).

Fourth, city ratings use objective data and, for the most part, have not used subjective data gathered from surveys and interviews. The reason is cost. This problem can be seen clearly in the city ratings on climate. The evaluation of climate is a personal thing. However, *Places Rated Almanac* rated climates poorly if they were hot and humid or very cold, with the result that cities in the deep South or upper Midwest rank poorly. In my opinion, there are some aberrations. Seattle, Washington has only 57 clear days a year, yet it is ranked the twelfth best climate. Buffalo, New York, with 90 inches of snow a year, is ranked 111th best climate. Austin, Texas, with hot and humid summers and mild winters, is ranked 281st. Yet, when the citizens of Austin were asked if the weather in July and August detracted from the quality of life, only 15 percent thought so. The evidence is clear that one of the major reasons the Sunbelt has grown so rapidly is that people prefer heat and rain over cold and snow (Myers, 1987). Only recently have studies begun to explore the subjective side of these objective indicators (Pierce, 1985).

Fifth, every community has some feature that is special to residents—features unknown to outsiders unless locals are interviewed. They seldom are (Myers, 1987).

Finally, it's said that you can be happy anywhere as long as you have a good circle of family and friends, and this statement is supported by research (Fischer, 1985). You may call New York, Boston, Chicago, or San Francisco home, but in your day-to-day life you use very few of the facilities these cities have to offer. In the final analysis, you live in a network of family, friends, neighbors, and colleagues, and the institutional framework of a community either facilitates or impedes this interaction. These networks are, at least, as important as the institutional structure in determining an individual's sense of well-being, and these subjective evaluations must be incorporated into city ratings (Campbell et al., 1976; Campbell, 1981).

Therefore, improving quality-of-life studies will require the following: First, quality-of-life studies must incorporate social and environmental elements as well as people's perceptions of these elements. Second, they must include both objective and subjective data. Third, concepts should be clearly defined and carefully operationalized. Indicators should actually measure what they say they are measuring. Fourth, more thought should be given to the units of measure. Is the use of the Metropolitan Statistical Areas the most appropriate areal unit? Maybe central cities or suburbs should be compared instead.

Fifth, the purpose of a study should be clearly stated. When these studies are written for the public, the public should be told of the inherent problems and limits to this type of research.

The literature on city ratings is evolving. Research has been published that addresses many of these issues. For example, Austin, Texas, is carrying out an ambitious project to measure its residents' perception of the quality of life. The study is based on the following premises: First, quality of life is a local experience, and most people experience life in a single community; second, people judge the quality of life through changes they experience over time; and third, leaders need to know these perceptions for decision making. The study used interviews to measure subjective trends, and the researchers found that residents perceived improvements in Austin's restaurants/shops, entertainment, income, education, and recreation, and declines in housing affordability, crime, traffic, and water quality. The research is fine for Austin, but the question remains: How does Austin compare with other cities (Myers, 1987)?

Several attempts have been made to use subjective data for city comparisons. Recently, researchers attempted to compare the quality of life in a small sample of cities, using subjective data from HUD's Annual Housing Survey (Dahmann, 1981). The results are preliminary and based on a small sample, but they show promise in incorporating subjective data into city ratings.

Finally, even with the problems with city ratings, they do provide a point of departure for other efforts. Whether we approve or disapprove, city ratings are used by business and government in decision-making. Moreover, millions of Americans have purchased books like *Places Rated Almanac,* so they have become an important part of our popular culture. This research also shows the dynamic nature of social science research and its efforts to develop reliable and valid ratings of America's cities.

SOCIOLOGICAL IMAGINATION AND CITY RATINGS

The concept of a sociological imagination was introduced by C. W. Mills nearly 40 years ago. It refers to the ability to understand our own experiences by using a broad sociological perspective. It refers to the realization that our experiences and life chances are shaped not only by our intelligence and skills but also by cultural, historical, economic, and social forces of which we have no control. Although unemployment, divorce, marriage, and success are intensely personal experiences, each is shaped by society. For example, if I lose my job, I'll probably think of myself as a failure. I may have self-doubt. I may think there must be some flaw in my character or some other weakness. But if I step back and look at this event from a broader perspective—with a sociological imagination—I may see that the firing was due to an economic recession, or the restructuring of the economy because of foreign competition, or a leveraged buyout of my company because of a change in federal tax laws. Unemployment is an intensely personal experience, but it is one shared by millions of others and shaped by larger societal and historical forces. One of the goals of this book is to help you develop a sociological imagination. Let's apply the literature of city ratings to a problem many of you share—what do you do after graduation?

Urban sociology is usually taught on the junior and senior level, so most of you are probably facing graduation in the next year or so. Since entering college you have learned many skills, the most important being the skill to solve problems. But most of us use these analytical skills to solve other people's problems. Sadly, we seldom apply them to our own.

As you near graduation and begin interviewing, you will be making two interrelated decisions that will profoundly influence your life. One is your choice of a first job. The other is the choice of a community within which to live. The job and in turn the city you choose will influence many things: your general happiness, the friends you will make, the person you will marry, your chance of being victimized by crime, your chance of dying of cancer, your chance of surviving an accident or heart attack, and your children's chances of being well educated and successful. Therefore, these two interrelated decisions are among the most important you make. Interestingly, most of us approach them haphazardly.

The city has been likened to a giant sorting device that matches people with similar characteristics—lifestyle, stage in the life cycle, income, ethnicity—with an appropriate subarea of the city. There is a large literature on how people search for a new home, and it can tell us much about the way people search for a new city. Purchasing a home is one of the largest investments we make, but research suggests that people chose a new home and a neighborhood in a nonrational way. It has been called an intendedly rational decision. Why? Our intention is to make a rational decision, but in reality it is made with incomplete and distorted information. It has been found that every source of information about housing and neighborhoods, whether it be from realtors, friends, coworkers, the newspaper, or the general impressions we all have on the good and bad places in a city to live, has its biases. These biases often lead house-hunters to choose a home in one part of town, when in fact they might be better off in another.

In searching for a new city, decision-making is also distorted and intendedly rational. The reason: Choices are structured. Campus interviews are often arranged by the university's office of career planning and placement, and companies in the region are usually overrepresented. Moreover, you have little if any information on cities, and most people have distinct biases that distort locational decisions. For example, this spring I discussed city ratings in my large general sociology class, which has over 400 students. When we finished the discussion on city ratings, I asked, "Where are you moving after graduation?" Ninety percent were going out of state; when I polled their destinations, they were Dallas and Houston, followed by Tulsa, New Orleans, and Atlanta, and a few indicated Phoenix and Los Angeles. Not a single person mentioned a northern city. I asked, "Isn't anyone going North? Look, it's a seven-hour drive to Dallas from here and only four hours to Kansas City and five hours to St. Louis. Has anyone even considered these other cities? Every study we have looked at today ranks northern cities higher than southern cities. Why not consider Kansas City? St. Louis? Cincinnati?" I scanned an auditorium of dumb faces. The thought of going North never crossed their minds, even though a northern city might provide a better quality of life than a southern one. I asked, "Can anyone give me one reason not to consider a northern city?" There was a long and painful silence. Then from the back a student shouted, "Yankees! Who wants to live next to a Yankee!" It brought the house down, but while we were all laughing, there were plenty of nods of approval. So much for the science of city ratings: The outcome of the Civil War seems to influence locational decisions in this part of the country.

There are a number of lessons that come from the decision-to-move and city ratings literature. Try to be more rational in your decisions by finding as much information about potential communities as possible. First, don't bypass the career planning and placement office, but be aware of the regional biases built into their interview schedules and pursue other job-searching strategies. Second, make an inventory of those things important to you. If you're not married and don't plan to have children, then the quality of schools is irrelevant. Hate opera, ballet, museums? Then cultural amenities don't need to be considered. Concerned about your personal safety? Excited about professional sports? Enjoy parks and recreation? Want to pursue graduate or law school at night? Information on all these things is available in the city rating studies and from reference books found in your library, or you can invest $49 in a computer program like *Places, U.S.A.* that will do it for you. You can never take all the risk out of any decision, but it is far more reassuring to know that you have stacked the odds in your favor by being well informed.

The social sciences have much to offer society in helping it grapple with its problems; city ratings and classifications are one tool. They also have much to offer individuals in providing them with tools and perspectives to better understand their lives.

SUMMARY

This chapter explores the classification and rating of cities. The first city classifications were developed in the mid-eighteenth century, and city ratings have been done since the 1930s. Although these two bodies of literature share many things in common, they were developed by different disciplines—geography and sociology—for different purposes.

Geographers developed city classifications. Their general purpose for classifying cities was to learn more about the basic processes that shape cities and in turn to gain insight into urban problems and their solutions. Other specific reasons for classifying cities include: providing a framework to summarize the enormous body of data from the U.S. Bureau of the Census and other agencies, providing a framework that permits the systematic study of hundreds of cities at the same time by grouping them by type, and aiding researchers in the assessment of urban problems and policy formation.

Hundreds of classification schemes have been developed, based on a wide variety of criteria. Any criterion can be used to develop a classification scheme, as long as two conditions are met. First, the measure must permit every city in the study to be placed in only one category. Second, the categories chosen must be all-encompassing so that every city can be classified.

Beginning in the 1970s, four types of studies using classifications appeared in the literature. They were fiscal strain studies, regional migration studies, urban hardship studies, and federal impact studies. Today, city classification has become an indispensable tool in urban research. It is used to study a wide variety of urban problems and processes, and has become an important element in the creation, implementation, and management of urban policies and programs.

City ratings have a different history. City ratings have their beginning in the social indicators movement of the 1950s and 1960s. As the role of the federal government grew to include amelioration of some of the nation's long-standing social problems, a need developed for valid and reliable measures of social conditions. In the process of evaluating programs comparisons were made on the social well-being of regions and states. The study of the quality of life—the consequences of different living environments and people's satisfaction with them—soon developed into two lines of research. One focused on individual well-being and was based on subjective data gathered through surveys and interviews. The other was concerned with urban quality of life and was based on objective data collected by the Census Bureau and other bureaucracies.

Urban quality of life is defined as the measurement of the conditions of place, how those conditions are experienced and evaluated by individuals, and the relative importance of each of these to individuals. Researchers attempt to measure the institutional and environmental factors that affect the collective experiences of people living in a community. The factors that researchers feel are important and can be measured are used as the basis for comparing cities. The process is straightforward. Factors that the researcher feels are important in contributing to the quality of life are developed into concepts (abstractions on the theoretical level), variables or indicants are used to operationalize the concept, and data are collected on the variables. The scores on the indices are calculated, sometimes weighed, and then summed to form a composite index. Cities are then ranked from high to low on this single measure.

Four studies are presented, but they all share similar problems. First, the studies tend to be driven by the availability of data, not theory. Second, the studies are incomparable. Third, these studies rate an entire metropolis and ignore the enormous differences in the quality of life that exists within any community. Fourth, ratings have not used subjective and perceptual data—there are questions of the validity of the studies. Fifth, researchers seldom visit the cities they rate and are unaware of those things that are special and important to residents. Finally, there is evidence that kin, friends, and neighbors are as important as the community in which one lives in determining the quality of life.

Even with these problems, I argue that city ratings are useful to society and individuals. I propose using a sociological imagination to understand how your own locational decisions influence your life. Understanding how the community in which you live structures experiences suggests that, used judiciously, city ratings can aid each of us in the search for a new residence in a new city—a choice which, we will see in later chapters, can have profound effects on your life chances and sense of well-being.

NOTES

1. A review of the literature on city typologies shows that these objectives have not always been met. Critics have argued that the development of different schemes has become an end in itself. In other words, critics have been classified, but the classifications have not been used as a point of departure for future analysis (Smith, 1965, pp. 539–540). Other writers recognize the usefulness of these typologies and note that classification schemes have been sadly underemployed in urban research. Schnore and Winsborough suggest that carefully developed city typologies could be used to illuminate "the determinants, concomitants and consequences of city functions" (Schnore and Winsborough, 1972, p. 125). This advice has been taken, and the current uses of city typologies are reviewed in a later section of this chapter.

2. William Ogburn (1937) published a similar city classification six years before Harris's typology. In many respects, Ogburn's scheme is more sophisticated in methodology, but it has received scant attention in the literature on city typologies. For this reason, the better-known Harris work is examined here.

*T*HE SYSTEM OF CITIES

INTRODUCTION

The 1970s and 1980s were a fascinating time to be an urban sociologist, and the reason can be summed up in two words—Sunbelt and Snowbelt. The changes occurring in these regions during these decades dominated our national discussion of urban problems, altered our political landscape, reshaped the nation's economy, and changed our tastes, fashion, food, and language. The reason can be seen by scanning population and economic data for the regions. In the 40 years between 1945 and 1985, the Sunbelt grew from 40 million to over 100 million people—a population shift representing one of the greatest migrations in history—while during this same period, population growth in the Snowbelt slowed, stagnated, and in some areas declined. The population shifts between cities were even more dramatic. Between 1970 and 1980, the central cities of Snowbelt metropolises like Cleveland, Chicago, Detroit, Buffalo, and St. Louis lost an average of 28 percent of their central city populations, while Sunbelt cities like Dallas, Miami, Houston, Atlanta, Phoenix, and Los Angeles grew an average of 121 percent. Demographic change was accompanied by an equally striking shift in the economic fortunes of the regions. Ninety percent of all new manufacturing jobs were created in the Sunbelt, while employment in the stalwarts of the Snowbelt economy—autos, steel, glass, and rubber—dwindled. Shifts in other sectors of the nation's economy—retail and wholesale sales, construction, and agriculture—reflected the profound changes in the economic, political, and social relationships between these regions.

In the opening years of the 1980s, the growth of the Sunbelt seemed to be invincible. Images of Sunbelt cities shaped in the popular culture by shows like *Dallas* portrayed the glamour of new wealth created for the few by rapid growth. And the gleaming new skylines of the region's major cities attested to this new-found prosperity. By the end of the decade, however, this image had tarnished. The region's economy, tied to cyclical industries like agribusiness, oil, defense, real estate, technology, and leisure, shuttered when boom turned to bust. Like a house of cards, one sector of the region's economy after another faltered. In the early 1980s, a downturn in agribusiness was followed by the collapse of the oil industry, which led to the fall of a bloated real-estate market, which precipitated a crisis in the region's banking and savings and loan industry. During these same years, disturbing pictures emerged of the squalor behind the glamorous facade of Sunbelt cities. Long described in the professional literature, the media began to report the sordid conditions found in the region's cities. The squalor of the barrios, the exploitation and neglect of minorities, unemployment and underemployment, and hopelessness, despair, and misery—conditions long associated with Snowbelt cities—were found to be of a pernicious and particularly nasty form in the cities of the Sunbelt.

At the same time, new images of Snowbelt cities began to filter into the American consciousness. Wrung dry by recession in the early 1980s and by a restructuring of the region's industry, Snowbelt states emerged as examples of how state economies should diversify for the future. In addition, new words like gentrification, revitalization, and urban renaissance entered our vocabulary to describe the changes taking place in the central cities of most of the region's metropolises.

How does one make sense of these bewildering and often contradictory descriptions of the cities in the two regions? Sort through the myriad of population, economic, and political data to discover what is really going on? One way is to recognize that these regional changes cannot be studied in isolation because cities are elements in the economic, social, and political organization of the nation. Cities in the Sunbelt and Snowbelt are interdependent and form an integrated and mutually dependent system of cities. As a result, change in one group of cities will have a mutual and reciprocal influence on cities throughout the entire national system. This chapter, therefore, focuses on the profound changes that have occurred in the system of cities which span both the Sunbelt and Snowbelt, building on the concepts and theories introduced in the previous two chapters. The concepts of threshold and urban hierarchy from central place theory, and the concept of functional types of cities introduced in the presentation of city typologies are used to describe the changes in the nation's system of cities.

The first half of this chapter the concepts of economic base, initial advantage, and economic multiplier are introduced to show why some cities, because of their size, unique location, access to resources, or dominance of a form of transportation, are in a strategic position to shape growth and development in the future. In the second half of the chapter, our attention turns to the Sunbelt/Snowbelt controversy. The Sunbelt is not a figment of someone's imagination; it is a relatively homogeneous region—a region to which population and resources have poured since World War II. Why the growth of the Sunbelt cities? Why the relative decline of the Snowbelt? Most discussions of the Sunbelt focus on the growth of population and manufacturing in the region, but the restructuring of the nation's economy has been far more complex. As we will see, the Sunbelt has gained in some areas, but the Snowbelt continues to dominate other spheres of the economy. The chapter ends with a presentation of the major theories that have been posited to explain the changes in these two regions.

THE SYSTEM OF CITIES

The process of urbanization cannot be studied in isolation because urban places are spatial elements in the economic, social, and political organization of regions and nations. In a sense, there is no such thing as a nonurban place anymore. First, 74 percent of the U.S. population lives in urban places, and second, even if you live in Crosses, Arkansas, Ross, Ohio, Nashville, Indiana, or Lebanon, Missouri, your economic well-being is inextricably tied to the markets and decisions made by people living in urban places. There is an interdependence between places. We have already alluded to this interdependence in our discussion of city typologies. Single-dimension typologies emphasize the functional specialization of cities; the classification of a city as a retail center implies the city's dependency on other centers (manufacturing, transportation, and wholesaling) for the goods it supplies to its trade area.

In an attempt to ferret out the complex relationships among cities, researchers have combined the concept of functional specialization from classification studies with the concept of an urban hierarchy from central place theory. The pyramid-shaped hierarchy, which has been used to describe the economic relationship between small villages, towns, and cities in agricultural regions, has been expanded to the nation to describe the complex economic relationships among cities in a system of cities. It works fairly well. Look at Table 7.1. Edgar Dunn (1980) has applied the central place model to 4381 trade centers, and they fall into the predicted hierarchy. Note that the actual pattern roughly corresponds to the expected pattern. Also notice that the only deviation from the predicted pattern occurs in the category "small full-convenience centers" at the bottom of the hierarchy, where there are fewer places than expected, and in the categories "wholesale–retail" and "complete shopping urban centers" at the top of the hierarchy, where there are more places than expected. The number of places, however, tells us little about the distribution of population (Dunn, 1980, pp. 71–72). The lower panel of Table 7.2 presents the population predicted by central place theory and the actual U.S. population in each of category of places. These data show that there are potent forces at work in our economy which lead to the concentration of economic activities and people in metropolitan places at the top of the hierarchy (Dunn, 1980, pp. 74–75).

THE ECONOMIC BASE

To explore the changes in the economic relationship between cities, researchers have used a number of related concepts—economic base, initial advantage, and the multiplier effect. Economic base refers to the fact that the growth of a city depends on

TABLE 7.1 Comparison of the frequency distribution of trade-center types with the theoretical expectations of central place theory

PANEL A. U.S. UPPER MIDWEST (1960)

TRADE-CENTER CLASS	CENTRAL PLACE THEORY EXPECTATION	UPPER MIDWEST ACTUAL	RATIO OF ACTUAL TO EXPECTED
Metropolitan	1	1	1.00
Primary wholesale–retail	2	7	3.50
Secondary wholesale–retail	6	10	1.67
Complete shopping	18	79	4.39
Partial shopping	54	126	2.33
Full convenience shopping	162	112	0.69
Minimum convenience	486	379	0.78
Hamlet	1458	1539	1.05
Total	2187	2253	

PANEL B. TOTAL U.S. (1970 POPULATION, 1960 TRADE CENTER CLASSIFICATION)

TRADE CENTER CLASS	CENTRAL PLACE THEORY EXPECTATION	U.S. ACTUAL	RATIO OF ACTUAL TO EXPECTED
Metropolitan	70	70	1.00
Wholesale–retail	140	248	1.77
Complete shopping	420	1313	3.13
Partial shopping	1260	1289	1.02
Full convenience	3780	1461	0.39

Source: Dunn, Edgar S. *The Development of the U.S. Urban System: Volume I—Concepts, Structures, Regional Shifts.* Baltimore, MD: The Johns Hopkins University Press for Resources for the Future, 1980, Table 3, p. 74.

TABLE 7.2 Comparison by trade center type of a hypothetical population array (based on central place theory) with the actual population array (based on population averages), 1960 (number of persons)

HYPOTHETICAL TRADE CENTER CLASS	AVERAGE POPULATION U.S.	ACTUAL POPULATION
Metropolitan centers	500,000	1,388,452
Wholesale–retail centers	149,678	175,543
Complete shopping centers	45,577	13,164
Partial shopping centers	14,450	3,885
Full convenience centers	5,090	2,104

Source: Dunn, Edgar S. *The Development of the U.S. Urban System: Volume I—Concepts, Structures, Regional Shifts.* Baltimore, MD: The Johns Hopkins University Press for Resources for the Future, 1980, Table 4, p. 75.

its ability to sell goods and services beyond its borders. The more goods and services it sells, the more growth occurs, and the more active the local economy becomes. Thus a city's economy can be divided into two parts: the basic sector, consisting of the goods and services produced locally but sold beyond its borders, and the nonbasic sector, consisting of those goods and services produced and sold locally. The basic sector, then, is the sector of the local economy that must expand if the city is to grow (Blumfield, 1970).

The process of urbanization in the United States in many respects is a history of urban places' attempts to expand the basic sector of their economies. These efforts are exemplified by the intense competition among cities and the attitude commonly held by the leaders of those cities—boosterism. Boosterism is the belief that the more manufacturing and commerce going on in a city, the more growth; the more growth, the larger the city's trade area; and the larger the trade area, the better the local economy. In short, growth for growth's sake. Julius Ruben's (1961) *Canals or Railroads?* describes boosterism during the nineteenth century. Boosterism in the twentieth century has guided the growth of many cities in Texas and the Sunbelt. Unfortunately, experience has shown that unbridled optimism, entrepreneurship, and risk capital are not always enough to insure economic success because, in a sense, there is a stacked deck in growth and development (Macdonald, 1984).

CONCEPT OF INITIAL ADVANTAGE

The stacked deck results from the initial advantage some cities have. Allan Pred (1966) introduced this concept; it included three related ideas. First, certain already established places have economic inertia. Inertia allows them to compound their advantage over time. Second, existing places are the seedbed for innovations, and their institutional structures permit them to influence subsequent growth. Third, once an economic activity is concentrated in a location, it has a self-perpetuating momentum (Pred, 1966, p. 15). In short, some urban places, because of rapid industrialization, generate their own conditions for growth into large metropolises, and these places are usually those possessing an initial advantage (Pred, 1966, p. 15). New York City is a wonderful example. First settled on one of the best natural harbors in the world, its link to the interior via the Hudson River permitted the city to dominate the early commerce of the region. The city's location at the top of the urban hierarchy in this earlier era permitted it to control the emerging new technology of the canal. The opening of the Erie Canal allowed New York to expand its hinterland to cover the entire Great Lakes region of the Upper Midwest and to ensure that it stayed at the top of the hierarchy. Whether one looks at commerce, industry, finance, banking, communication, or transportation, New York's large population and diverse labor force have made it a fertile seedbed for innovations, and its size and wealth has placed it in a strategic position to shape and control future development (Pred, 1966, pp. 86–142). Indeed, the harsh truth is that the system of cities mirrors society—the rich get richer. Put another way, development is a cumulative process that enables certain cities with an initial advantage in transportation, communication, and industrial technology or proximity to resources to shape growth and change in such a way as to maintain their advantageous position.

THE MULTIPLIER EFFECT

Allan Pred (1966) uses another concept, the multiplier effect, to explain this cumulative character of advantage. There is a close relationship between urban growth and changes in the structure of urban activities. Cities differ in their economic bases and the structure of their labor forces, and out of this dynamic soup comes innovation—say, a new manufacturing process. As you can see in Figure 7.1, the new industry will have an initial multiplier effect; that is, demand for goods and services will be created by the factories and by the purchasing power of their labor force. New businesses will be created or old ones expanded to meet this demand. In addition, roads, houses, streets, water and sewer systems, schools, hospitals, and businesses must be built to meet the demand created by the new firm, and this activity creates new jobs in other parts of the labor force. Buildings are not the only things in demand; services expand and the number of doctors, lawyers, dentists, nurses, teachers, accountants, police, firemen, and the myriad of other occupations needed to keep the metropolis functioning increases. As the original manufacturer grows, suppliers spring up to supply the intermediate parts necessary for the process. The transportation network expands to move the new people and products within the city and its hinterland. Changes in the economic base of a city modify the structure of the labor market and the infrastructure of the city, and these changes along with the growth of population mean that the city reaches a new threshold that allows a second multiplier to kick in that permits still newer forms of manufacturing and service activities. There are limits to growth. Eventually, a metropolis will outstrip its transportation, communication, and industrial technology or exhaust nearby resources, and growth during this stage in its history comes to a close. In short, there is the tendency in cities for growth to feed on itself. Moreover, since cities are linked economically, there is also the tendency for cities at the top of the hierarchy to maintain their position over time. New York, for example, was the largest city in the United States in 1860, 1910, and 1990. Chicago was ranked eighth in 1860, second in 1910 and 1980, and third in 1990. Philadelphia was ranked second in 1860, third in 1910, fourth in 1980, and sixth in 1990. Over the years there has been shuffling and reshuffling of cities in the urban hierarchy, but certain cities, because of their initial advantage and their strategic position in the urban hierarchy, maintain their advantageous position; others with less advantage have declined (Pred, 1966, pp. 24–37).

CONDITIONS FOR GROWTH IN THE BASIC SECTOR

In general, the experience of a city is determined by the potential for growth in its basic sector. This potential is determined by (1) the city's location with respect to natural resources and other cities; (2) the transportation and resource exploitation technology at the time of settlement and in later periods; (3) the nature of the regional and national economy; and (4) the size and composition of the regional and national

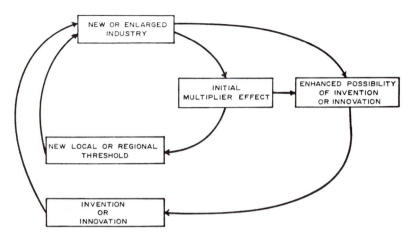

FIGURE 7.1 Circular and cumulative process of industrialization and urban-size growth.
Source: Pred, A. R. *The Spatial Dynamics of U.S. Urban Growth, 1800–1914.* Cambridge, MA: MIT Press, 1966, Table 2.1, p. 25.

population. These conditions indicate that the system is not static but dynamic, changing in response to economic and technological changes that occur over time (Dunn, 1980, pp. 37–43).

Whereas some cities have grown and prospered because of their initial advantage and location near resources, other cities, because of their position in the urban hierarchy or their inability to adapt to new situations, have declined. Charleston, South Carolina, was the 20th largest city in 1860, dropped to 77th by 1910 and to 286th in 1980. In recent years, the much-touted growth of the Sunbelt can be attributed to cities that have flourished because of changes in the national economy which created a new set of demands for natural and human resources. Cities like Houston, Dallas, and Phoenix have grown from near oblivion in the pre-World War II era to among the largest in our system of cities.

A DEVELOPMENTAL PROCESS

The foregoing discussion suggests a developmental sequence. The problems and solutions created in one stage of this evolutionary sequence create new problems and in turn new solutions in the next stage. This problem–solution process is portrayed by Dunn (1980) in his description of the evolution of the problems faced by England in the development of steel processing.

Problem: the expanding scale (in England) of metallurgical processes, combined with the exhaustion of wood fuel reserves.
Solution: the replacement of charcoal with coal.

New problem: coal carried chemical impurities that compromised the quality of the product.
Solution: the development of coke.

New problem: the expansion of coal production used up open pits.

Solution: the development of methods for locating hidden seams and the development of shaft mining.

New problem: water in the mines.

Solution: the development of the pump.

New problem: previous generalized sources of power (dams, windmill-, human-, or animal-powered turnstiles) were difficult to apply in that they all generated rotary motion and tended to be insufficiently available in the right location.

Solution: the invention of the piston steam engine...and so forth (Dunn, 1980, pp. 49–50).

The developmental sequence that Dunn uses to describe the development of modern steel metallurgy is also useful in describing the evolution of our system of cities. The problems faced at one point in our history set the stage for the problems and solutions in the next. Therefore, the dominant technologies of a particular point in our history are useful markers to frame the various stages in the development of the nation's system of cities.[1]

EVOLUTION OF AMERICA'S CITY SYSTEM

The emergence of a system of cities and the changing relationships within this system can be understood best by examining urban and regional growth in the United States during the past 200 years. As already noted, the growth of an urban center depends on its ability to expand the basic sector of its economy, or, in other words, its ability to collect, process, and distribute raw materials and finished goods to its hinterland. The growth of these centers, therefore, is closely tied to the natural resources in their hinterlands and the levels of technology in the transportation and processing of these resources. These two factors are interrelated, however. The level of industrial technology determines the size of an urban center's trade area. For example, the invention of the steam engine and later the internal combustion engine created the need for coal and oil exploration. Demand for coal and oil led in turn to the growth of new urban centers to exploit these natural resources. Similarly, changes in transportation technology (the emergence of the automobile as the primary mode of transportation, for example) have permitted urban centers to greatly expand their trade areas.

PRESENT TRENDS

Examining these changes in manufacturing, the labor force, and transportation, one can anticipate future modification of America's urban system. Most important is the massive movement of population and retail manufacturing activities from central cities to their fringe areas. This movement in turn has led to the physical sprawl of metropolitan centers, to the point that in some regions adjacent metropolitan areas have coalesced into one massive urban agglomeration. Jean Gottman (1961) introduced the term *megalopolis* to describe those massive urban agglomerations.

Nowhere is this new megalopolitan form more visible than along the unbroken urbanized seaboard of the United States between Boston and Washington, D.C. Officially running from Rockingham County, New Hampshire, to Prince William County, Virginia, the Boston–Washington megalopolis is of staggering dimensions. Ranging in width between 100–150 miles, it runs over 600 miles in length, embracing part or all of ten states and the cities of Boston, New York, Philadelphia, Baltimore, and Washington, D.C. (See Figure 7.2). In 1978, the Boston–Washington megalopolis had a population of nearly 42 million, or roughly one-fifth of the United States population. In addition, a significant proportion of the nation's industry, business, financial, government, and educational resources was concentrated in this megalopolis.

Through most of the 1970s and early 1980s, however, the picture in much of this region was one of economic and population decline or, at best, stagnation. Some 1.2 million more people left the area than moved in between 1970 and 1977. This declining population reflects the loss of large segments of important industries, such as textiles and transportation. Bearing the brunt of this decline are New York City, Philadelphia, and Newark, New Jersey. New York City alone lost nearly 10 percent of its population between 1970 and 1978 (*U.S. News and World Report,* 1980, p. 55).

One factor that contributes to the population decline in the Boston–Washington megalopolis is the age of its central cities—the oldest of any region in the United States. Associated with city age are the problems of congestion, dilapidated and deteriorating housing, obsolete factories and industries, shortages of open space and recreation facilities, and a general decline in the quality of city services. This is especially characteristic of New York City. And it is, of course, in the central cities of the Northeast that one finds the greatest concentration of blacks and other deprived groups—people with the greatest need for services but with the fewest resources to pay for them. Not surprisingly, the most serious urban and social problems faced by our society are concentrated in the 55,000 square miles of this megalopolis.

There is a second major factor contributing to the population decline of this megalopolis. Since World War II, America's industry has shifted from the manufacture of basic goods, such as steel, to the manufacture of light, high-technology goods. The manufacture of light and complex products is normally limited to the final assembly of parts built by suppliers; very few components are made inside the plant. The transportation cost of such products as calculators and computers is low in comparison to the high value of the finished item. Therefore, with transportation constraints lessened, the manufacturer can select a plant location on the basis of other factors, such as labor and plant construction costs, climate, and amenities for workers—for example, education. The result has been a spectacular growth of metropolitan centers in Florida, the Southwest, and Southern California—the so-called Sunbelt states.

In these regions megalopolitan growth is well under way. Figure 7.2 shows the location of 26 emerging megalopolises in which two out of every three Americans is expected to live by the year 1980. The cities in the South and West are enjoying a tremendous boom in population. Southern Arizona—the area around Phoenix and

FIGURE 7.2 This is a satellite photograph taken at night showing the eastern half of the United States. Note the emerging megalopolitan centers along the Atlantic Coast, Lake Michigan, and Lake Erie.

Source: U.S. Air Force Photo.

Tucson—led the nation in the 1970–1980 period with a 35 percent increase. Metropolitan population gains in excess of 10 percent were in the southern and western regions of the United States. Stagnant or declining population growth was limited to the north-central and northeastern regions of the United States. Clearly, the complex interaction of environmental resources and technological innovations has profoundly affected the relationships within the system of cities, resulting in a major redistribution of population and economic activities within and among this nation's metropolitan centers. Moreover, megalopolitan growth has emerged as the new order in the organization of inhabited space.

THE SUNBELT/SNOWBELT

Recently, a Gallup poll reported that for the first time in their 50-year history a majority of Americans indicated that they no longer believed that the future will be better than the present. Other polls report that parents no longer think their children will live as well as they do. These polls suggest an uneasiness in the land—a vague

1. Metropolitan Belt
1A Atlantic Seaboard
1B Lower Great Lakes
2. California Region
3. Florida Peninsula
4. Gulf Coast
5. East Central Texas —
   Red River
6. Southern Piedmont
7. North Georgia —
   South East Tennessee
8. Puget Sound
9. Twin Cities Region
10. Colorado Piedmont
11. St. Louis
12. Metropolitan Arizona
13. Willamette Valley
14. Central Oklahoma —
   Arkansas Valley
15. Missouri — Kaw Valley
16. North Alabama
17. Blue Grass
18. Southern Coastal Plain
19. Salt Lake Valley
20. Central Illinois
21. Nashville Region
22. East Tennessee
23. Memphis
24. El Paso —
   Ciudad Juarez

FIGURE 7.3 Megalopolises, year 2000. This map shows the 26 growth areas of the United States that now are exhibiting megalopolitan patterns. Population projections suggest that the urban strips depicted in the map will characterize many parts of the United States in the year 2000.

Source: Adapted from *Population Growth and American Future.* Washington, D.C.: U.S. Government Printing Office.

feeling that events are out of our control. There is an awareness that fundamental changes are occurring in this society: changes that may not be for the best. What is troublesome to some is that America has always embraced change. At the center of our national ethos has been a belief in progress—a faith that the future will be better than the present. Today, many Americans look to the future, not with unbridled optimism, but with trepidation.

This shift in attitude is not baseless. Look at the events of the past decade. As a nation, we have mortgaged our future with a three-trillion-dollar federal deficit. Our leaders in Washington lack the will or the courage to deal with the nation's problems, and, as a result, our cities are in decay and millions of our citizens are homeless, hungry, and unemployed. Our educational system fails to prepare our children for a world of high technology. Our nation's industry is no longer competitive, and yearly we rack up $150 billion trade deficits. Our economy has been shaken with the collapse of the stock market and the savings and loan industry. Our medical institutions offer no hope for the AIDS epidemic. Our courts and police have lost the war on drugs. Our religious institutions have been tainted with greed, sex, and sectarian division. And even our family, the most basic and important of all our institutions, is troubled by divorce, violence, and abuse. Regardless of where one looks, one finds institutions grappling for solutions to new and intractable problems. Changes in some of these institutions are so extensive that they have been viewed as revolutionary.

The term *revolution* conjures up an image of an armed overthrow of a government—the American Revolution, the French Revolution, or the Russian Revolution. Sociologists, however, define revolution far more broadly: as simply rapid change in the institutions of a society. Applying this definition, we see that the most important revolutions for humankind—the agricultural revolution, the urban revolution, and the industrial revolution—have not involved an armed insurrection but rather a profound change in the way societies structure themselves to solve recurring problems. At first glance, America's problems appear to be unrelated. They are not. They are indicators of the basic changes occurring in our institutions in an attempt to cope with the problems posed by events in the last quarter of the twentieth century. The dominant institution in this process has been the economy, and the changes in this one institution have been so basic and extensive that, some have argued, they rival the industrial revolution in scope.[2]

CHANGE IN THE NATIONAL ECONOMY

What are these economic changes? First, there has been the rising importance of service activities in the U.S. economy. Between 1970 and 1988, 34 million jobs were added to the American economy, but over 90 percent of this growth was in the service economy. Manufacturing is still important, but technology has permitted more goods to be produced with fewer people, and today nearly 80 percent of our work force is white-collar. Moreover, most of this growth in white-collar employment is concentrated in services to corporations—banking, insurance, advertising, legal counsel, and services carried out in the headquarters of major corporations.

Second, markets have changed. After World War II, the size of markets increased first from local to regional, then from regional to national, and finally from national to international.

Third, changes in market size were made possible by changes in transportation, communication, and industrial technology, which permitted organizational forms heretofore impossible. The size of organizations has increased, and the span of their control is now worldwide.

Fourth, government and nonprofit organizations have expanded their roles in society, especially in the areas of medical care, research, and education.

Finally, very large, multiproduct, multinational corporations have emerged as a dominant economic force in our economy. Employment in corporate headquarters, research and development centers, and national, regional, and divisional offices, along with allied support services, now exceeds the numbers in manufacturing (Noyelle and Stanback, 1984, pp. 13–26).[3]

ROLE OF INNOVATION IN URBAN CHANGE

These changes have been national in scope, but it is important to remember that cities are economic machines, inseparable from our national economic system. In fact, the economic activities centered in cities are the dominant way in which nations accumulate wealth. The changes and technological innovations like those outlined above have been long recognized as a critical element of capitalism. Karl Marx in the nineteenth century and Joseph Schumpeter in the twentieth century noted that in dealing with capitalism one is dealing with an evolutionary process, a system that not only never is but never can be stationary. From this perspective, innovation is an inextricably element of capitalism and one of the engines of change within the capitalistic system. Schumpter writes:

> ...innovation's role as the source of supranormal profit makes it the fundamental impulse that sets and keeps the capitalistic engine in motion...The process of industrial mutation—if I may use that biological term—that incessantly revolutionizes the economic structure from within, incessantly creating a new one. This process of creative destruction is the essential fact about capitalism (Schumpeter, 1947, p. 82).

According to this argument, technological innovation may cause the destruction of an entire industry, like steel in Pittsburgh and Birmingham or tire manufacturing in Akron, but if a city has a diverse economic base, then, as one activity dies out, there will be enough creative energy and innovation in the local economy to create new firms to take over the idle factories and labor. Therefore, technological innovation alters urban economies and in turn modifies the relationships among cities in our system of cities. In the evolution of the American system of cities, transportation, communication, and technological innovations create economic change, which leads to spatial upheaval in our system of cities. At each stage of this evolutionary process, some cities, because of their strategic location or economic base, have prospered; others have declined. Today, the change in the relationship among cities in the Sunbelt and Snowbelt is nothing new. It is merely the newest chapter in the long evolutionary process that has created our system of cities.

GEOGRAPHY OF THE SUNBELT/SNOWBELT

Where is the Sunbelt? The Snowbelt? The Sunbelt is usually defined as those states within the tropical and semitropical climatic zones of the nation—the region with average daily temperatures above 60 degrees during the winter and above 80 degrees in the summer. At the front of most seed catalogs is a map of planting zones, and you can find the Sunbelt by following the northern boundary of the semitropical zone. The zone begins on the northern border of North Carolina in the East, and snakes its way through Memphis to Oklahoma City, before jumping to Albuquerque and then winding its way through southern Nevada before it ends at San Francisco in the West. This region enjoys between 250 and 350 days of sunshine a year, hence the name Sunbelt. Geographers use a different approach; they include in the region the states that fall below the 37th parallel: North and South Carolina, Georgia, Florida, Tennessee, Alabama, Mississippi, Arkansas, Louisiana, Oklahoma, Texas, New Mexico, Arizona, Nevada, and California. A few include Virginia; others include the border states of Kentucky and West Virginia. But climate and geography are not the only things these states have in common. The region was remarkably homogeneous in its population until the end of World War II. Free of the massive European migrations of the nineteenth and early twentieth centuries, it was dominated by the Anglo–Saxon subculture. Moreover, it is a region dependent on agriculture and resource exploitation for its livelihood, as well as dependent on the cheap labor provided by its black, brown, and red populations. Historically, there was little manufacturing in the Sunbelt; rather, the Sunbelt was the source of raw materials that were shipped to the industrial core of the nation—the Snowbelt.

The Snowbelt is usually defined as the area east of the Mississippi River and north of the Mason–Dixon Line, and in much of the literature it is also known as the heartland. Fourteen New England and Great Lake states are included: Maine, New Hampshire, Vermont, Massachusetts, Rhode Island, Connecticut, New York, New Jersey, Pennsylvania, Ohio, Michigan, Indiana, Wisconsin, and Illinois. Since the nineteenth century, it has been the manufacturing belt of the nation, and manufacturing is still important to the region's economy. Its population is the most heterogeneous in the nation, having absorbed wave after wave of immigrants in the nineteenth and early twentieth centuries. Like the Sunbelt, the Snowbelt shares a similar climate, geography, culture, settlement patterns, history, and economy (Sale, 1975, pp. 3–15).

SHIFTING RELATIONSHIPS BETWEEN THE SUNBELT/SNOWBELT

What happened in these regions after World War II? How do you explain the dramatic shift of people and resources from the Sunbelt to the Snowbelt? It is a complicated story, but it tells us much about the complex interplay between the economic, political, and social forces at work in the nation's system of cities.

Through most of our history, the Snowbelt was the only region of the nation with the transportation, communication, finance, and marketing infrastructure to support large-scale industry. States outside the Snowbelt—called the hinterland—were subordinate and supplied raw materials and markets for finished goods. It was a mercantile system—the Snowbelt enjoyed the prosperity created by the production and sale of high-value manufactured goods, and the hinterland was less prosperous because of its dependence on mining and agriculture. As a result of this relationship, the economies of cities in the Snowbelt became highly specialized. Even today, when one thinks of northern cities, one associates steel with Pittsburgh, rubber with Akron, and stockyards and manufacturing with Chicago. Not only were the economies of Snowbelt cities specialized, but the dependence of this region on rail transportation meant that industrial activities were concentrated in their central cities. High specialization meant high vulnerability. After World War II, when manufacturing and transportation technology changed, the central cities of the Snowbelt reeled when manufacturing left for the suburbs, and soon entire metropolises suffered when industry left the suburbs for the Sunbelt and overseas (Norton, 1979, pp. 17–30).

IMPORTANCE OF METROPOLITAN AGE

Why this dramatic decline? In a nutshell, Snowbelt metropolises are nineteenth-century cities existing in a late twentieth-century economy. The crucial period in shaping today's metropolises was the 1920s, when automobile and airplane technology began to shape cities. Those cities that gained great size before 1920—shaped by the technology of an earlier era—will differ from those that gained great size after 1920. Industrial cities in the Snowbelt reached metropolitan size (50,000 or more inhabitants) in the nineteenth century and were shaped by the dominant industrial and transportation technologies of that century—steel and the railroad. A major theme of this book is that the past shapes the present and constrains the future. Metropolitan age has an important affect on the density of settlement, the city's transportation network, the racial and occupational mix of its population, and its institutional endowments such as schools, hospitals, museums, libraries, as well as the quality of its infrastructure—streets and sewer and water systems. In other words, cities of different age will differ in their institutional endowments and infrastructures (Norton, 1979, pp. 17–39).

Table 7.3 presents data on the nation's 30 largest metropolitan areas in 1970. Column 1 ranks these cities by their size in 1910. Column 2 is the percentage of each urbanized area's work force in manufacturing in 1950 (1950 was the year this nation reached its industrial zenith). Column 3 is the percentage change in each city's population for the 30-year period 1950–1980. The final column is the percentage change in the population of each metropolitan area for the same period.

As hypothesized, the year when a city reaches metropolitan status appears to be an excellent predictor of the other variables. First, notice that 12 cities have been grouped at the top of the table and have been labeled "industrial"; the 12 at the bottom of the table have been labeled "young." Notice that, for the most part, young metropolises are in the Sunbelt, and industrial metropolises are in the Snowbelt. Presented at the bottom of each column are averages for the two city types and the percentage difference between the two. Note that in 1950 industrial/Snowbelt cities had nearly 35 percent of their work force in manufacturing—a historical high. Young cities, in contrast, had only 19 percent of their work force in these occupations; in 1950, the majority of these cities were service centers. Now examine the figures in columns 3 and 4. Whereas industrial cities lost an average of 27 percent of their central city populations between 1950 and 1980, young cities had impressive growth—an increase of 143 percent. The same pattern exists for metropolitan growth (Norton, 1979, pp. 1–30).

DECLINE IN MANUFACTURING

Table 7.4 gives the change in total employment, manufacturing, service, and central city population for the years 1948–1982. These figures are sobering. Industrial cities in the Snowbelt lost an average of 19 percent of their total work force over this 35-year period,

TABLE 7.3 *1950 Employment Structure and Post-1950 City and SMSA Growth*

AGE CLASS	CITY, BY 1910 METROPOLITAN SIZE	PERCENT URBANIZED WORK FORCE MANUFACTURING 1950	PERCENT CHANGE CITY POPULATION, 1950–1980	PERCENT CHANGE SMSA 1970–1980
Industrial	New York	30.8	-10.3	- 8.6
	Chicago	37.7	-17.0	+ 1.8
	Philadelphia	35.6	-18.5	- 1.25
	Boston	28.7	-29.8	- 4.68
	Pittsburgh	38.0	-37.4	- 5.72
	St. Louis	33.8	-47.1	- 1.53
	San Francisco	19.4	-12.4	+ 1.05
	Baltimore	30.9	-17.2	+ 4.5
	Cleveland	40.5	-37.3	- 8.0
	Buffalo	39.7	-38.3	- 7.88
	Detroit	46.9	-34.9	- 1.84
	Cincinnati	33.4	-23.5	+ 1.01
Anomalous	Los Angeles	25.6	+50.5	+ 1.07
	Washington	7.4	-20.4	+ 5.1
	Milwaukee	42.9	- 0.2	- 0.5
	Kansas City	24.5	- 1.9	+ 4.1
	New Orleans	15.6	- 2.3	+13.4
	Seattle	19.8	+ 5.6	+12.9
Young	Indianapolis	33.1	+64.1	+ 5.0
	Atlanta	18.3	+28.3	+27.2
	Denver	16.8	+18.4	+30.8
	Columbus	25.0	+50.3	+ 7.4
	Memphis	20.5	+63.2	+ 9.5
	Nashville	22.9	+161.4	+21.6
	Dallas	18.4	+108.2	+25.1
	San Antonio	11.6	+92.4	+20.7
	Houston	21.4	+167.6	+45.3
	Jacksonville	13.1	+164.5	+18.6
	San Diego	15.7	+161.8	+37.1
	Phoenix	10.4	+639.3	+55.3

Means and Significance of Mean Differences			
Industrial cities	34.6	- 27	- 2.6
Young cities	18.9	+143	+24.8
Difference	15.7	170	27.4
Significance	p<0.001	p<0.01	p<0.001

Source: Column 1: U.S. Bureau of the Census, *1950 Census of Population, Vol. II, Characteristics of the Population, United States Summary,* 1952. Column 2 and Column 3: U.S. Bureau of the Census, *Current Population Reports,* Series P-25, No. 709, 1982. The original analysis of these data based on the work of R.D. Norton. *City Life-Cycles and American Urban Policy.* New York: Academic Press, 1979.

TABLE 7.4 Percentage Changes in Central-City Employment in Trade, Services, and Manufacturing: 1948–1982

AGE CLASS	CITY BY 1910 METROPOLITAN SIZE	TOTAL EMPLOYMENT, 1950–1982	PERCENTAGE CHANGE IN MANUFACTURING, 1950–1982	PERCENTAGE CHANGE IN SELECT SERVICES, 1950–1982
Industrial	New York	- 2	- 42	+ 87
	Chicago	- 14	- 53	+ 85
	Philadelphia	- 12	- 57	+ 31
	Boston	- 7	- 36	+151
	Pittsburgh	- 34	-29	+59
	St. Louis	- 46	- 47	+ 10
	San Francisco	+ 21	- 6	+211
	Baltimore	- 12	- 48	+ 27
	Cleveland	- 37	- 44	+ 54
	Buffalo	- 39	- 57	+ 1
	Detroit	- 39	- 70	- 6
	Cincinnati	- 5	- 3	+ 98
Anomalous	Los Angeles	+107	+ 79	+272
	Washington, D.C.	- 12	- 39	+114
	Milwaukee	+ 7	- 35	+ 70
	Kansas City	+ 20	+ 11	+146
	New Orleans	- 5	- 28	+104
	Seattle	+ 6	+ 75	+145
Young	Indianapolis	+108	+ 26	+182
	Atlanta	+ 55	+ 67	+336
	Denver	+ 68	+58	+228
	Columbus	+103	+ 30	+155
	Memphis	+100	+ 39	+160
	Nashville	+208	+184	+315
	Dallas	+222	+239	+612
	San Antonio	+206	+162	+338
	Houston	+284	+239	+851
	Jacksonville	+256	+136	+418
	San Diego	+354	+369	+539
	Phoenix	+1289	+1688	+1174

Means and Significance of Mean Differences

Industrial	- 19	- 41	67
Young	271	270	442
Difference	290	311	375

Source: U.S. Bureau of the Census. *City and County Data Book, 1950,* Washington, D.C.: U.S. Government Printing Office, 1950. U.S. Bureau of the Census, *City and County Data Book, 1988,* U.S. Government Printing Office, 1988. The original analysis of these data based on the work of R.D. Norton. *City Life-Cycles and American Urban Policy.* New York: Academic Press, 1979.

whereas the employment in young Sunbelt cities grew by an average of 271 percent—a 290 percent difference. Therefore, the decline in population and employment in the Snowbelt and the growth of the Sunbelt can be contributed to one factor—the movement of manufacturing activities from the cities of one region to another. In less than two generations, the Snowbelt cities in this sample lost 41 percent of their manufacturing employment, while manufacturing in Sunbelt cities grew by 270 percent. Although not presented here, data for the entire metropolitan area show the same pattern.

An argument frequently made is that the United States is becoming a post-industrial society: an economy driven by service, not manufacturing. Maybe what we are seeing is a reshuffling of people from manufacturing to service jobs. The last column of the table shows this not to be the case. Although service employment in Snowbelt cities grew by 67 percent (Sunbelt cities by more than 442 percent), the growth in the service sector was not large enough to offset losses in manufacturing: Industrial cities lost 19 percent of their total employment in a little less than two generations.

Why this drastic decline in manufacturing employment? During the 1960s and early 1970s, many economists thought that Snowbelt cities had local economies vigorous enough to act as seedbeds for new industry. Through the process of creative destruction, they would create new industries to take advantage of the city's unused human and other resources. Our review of employment data shows this not to be the case. Although there was a healthy increase in service employment, the increase in this sector was simply not large enough to offset the losses in other sectors.

What is often overlooked is that Snowbelt cities have experienced a loss of manufacturing jobs for most of this century. Shoes, textiles, and apparels left the Snowbelt for the Sunbelt before World War II; automobiles, tires, glass, and heavy manufacturing, after the war. The trend is clear. Snowbelt cities controlled 73 percent of all manufacturing jobs in 1909, 68 percent in 1947, 56 percent in 1969, and below 50 percent in 1979. Consequently, we know that long-term job losses can be traced to the industrial eclipse of Snowbelt metropolises. In the nineteenth century there were potent forces that led to the concentration of economic functions in the core of industrial cities; now there are potent forces bringing about the decentralization of production. The most visible impact of these changes has been in the Snowbelt, but as a nation are painfully aware that the process is national in scope as America loses millions of jobs to Japan and other nations of the Pacific rim (Norton, 1979, pp. 95–118).

LAW OF INDUSTRIAL GROWTH

The decline of the Snowbelt can be attributed to the very character of capitalism and the element referred to by Schumpeter as *creative destruction.* Our system works because of the seedbed function. The nation's economy and those of its cities must be diverse and dynamic enough so that as one industry dies the seedbed will produce a replacement. On the national level, we are now suffering from a failure to produce new exports to replace those now on the decline. The nation's multibillion-dollar trade deficit bears testimony to this fact. Norton and others argue that this same thing happened to the Snowbelt cities.

Industries that grow from the seedbed follow a life cycle called the law of industrial growth. The stages are as follows:

Stage 1	Period of experimentation
Stage 2	Period of rapid growth
Stage 3	Period of diminished growth
Stage 4	Period of stability or decline

Innovation takes place in Stage 1 in a rich and diverse urban climate. Whether we look at the early history of automobiles, airplanes, television and radio, or computers, what we find are new activities concentrated in only a few cities. Why? The problems of production are so difficult and the available talent so limited, that only by concentrating people in one place can technical hurdles to production be overcome. The early history of the automobile was played out in Detroit, airplanes in Southern California, TV and radio in New York City, and the early computer industry in New York City. Today, the microelectronic industry is concentrated in a few square miles in the Silicon Valley near San Jose, California (Norton, 1979, pp. 124–126).

Once an industry becomes well established and the problems of production are overcome, production becomes routine. In the process of building a new industry, a cadre of managers, technicians, and workers are trained to carry out the manufacturing activity. In Stage 2 and in subsequent stages, the manufacturing activity diffuses elsewhere to take advantage of cheaper labor and other lower costs. As we know from our own experience, a mature industry can move from the city of its origin to cities in other regions or overseas. Therefore, one of the major reasons for the decline in the Snowbelt is that concentrated within its borders were many industries at the end of their product cycles—automobiles, steel, glass, rubber, and electronics. In the years that followed World War II, the economies of the cities of this region were devastated by the exodus of standardized operations to the suburbs, the Sunbelt, and overseas. A number of researchers feel that this exodus has been so great that the seedbed upon which all cities depend has been destroyed (Norton, 1979, pp. 119–130).

THE SNOWBELT AND CORPORATE SERVICES

Are Snowbelt cities doomed? Has the erosion of their industrial base crippled them forever? Up to this point the discussion of the Sunbelt/Snowbelt has been cast in terms of growth—growth of population, growth of manufacturing, growth of cities. Absent from this discussion has been an analysis of the changes that underlie this growth. When you look at these changes from a broader perspective, a different picture emerges.

SECTORAL CHANGES IN THE ECONOMY

The shift in population and manufacturing that has occurred since World War II reflects the transformation of the national economy upon which both Sunbelt and Snowbelt cities depend. The dimension of this change can be seen in the figures

TABLE 7.5 Percentage distribution of full-time equivalent employment and gross national product (in 1972 dollars) by industry, 1947, 1969, 1977, and 1987.

	1947		1969		1977		1987	
	EMPLOYMENT	GNP	EMPLOYMENT	GNP	EMPLOYMENT	GNP	EMPLOYMENT	GNP
Agriculture, Extractive, and Transformative	43.39	37.38	35.09	35.99	31.60	32.81	26.10	27.80
Agriculture	4.31	5.57	1.74	3.06	1.90	2.87	1.58	2.10
Extractive and Transformative[a]	39.08	31.81	33.35	32.93	29.70	29.94	5.57	6.75
Manufacturing	32.27	24.53	27.66	25.60	24.10	24.18	18.95	19.94
Services	56.61	62.68	64.91	64.03	68.40	66.09	73.90	72.20
Distributive services	13.54	13.36	10.97	15.00	11.36	16.51	11.02	16.00
Retailing services	12.57	11.06	13.00	9.78	14.18	9.89	15.69	9.49
Nonprofit services	2.61	2.67	4.67	3.58	6.34	4.04	4.88	1.87
Complex of corporate activities[b]	6.06	15.50	10.03	18.26	11.96	20.12	6.47	17.21
Mainly consumer services	7.67	5.47	5.75	3.35	4.99	3.11	18.02	15.75
Government and government enterprises	14.16	14.62	20.48	14.07	19.57	12.43	17.82	11.88
	100.00	100.00	100.00	100.00	100.00	100.00	100.00	100.00

[a] Includes mining and construction (not shown).

[b] Because of data limitations, this grouping includes only the producer services (See Table 1.1). Employment and GNP originating from the Central Administrative Offices (COA&A) are not disaggregated and are included in their respective categories: e.g., distributive services, retailing services, manufacturing, and so forth.

Source: U.S. Department of Commerce, Bureau of Economic Analysis, The National Income and Product Accounts of the United States, 1929–74 Statistical Tables, Survey of Current Business, July 1978, and Survey of Current Business, July 1988, Vol. 68, No. 7.

presented in Table 7.5, "Percentage Distribution of Full-Time Employment and GNP by Industry, 1927–1987." First, note the drastic decline in the number of people employed in manufacturing since the end of World War II. Also notice that manufacturing makes the same contribution to GNP (24 percent) in 1987 as it did in 1947. This was made possible by the nation's massive investment in technology and the subsequent increases in productivity. Although Snowbelt cities have lost one-third of their industrial base, other sectors of the economy have become more important (Noyelle and Stanback, 1984, pp. 15–17).

In general, employment has shifted to service—it now accounts for over two-thirds of all employment—but it is a mistake to think of service as an undifferentiated category. Within the service category one finds jobs as diverse as fast-food workers, domestics, pilots, accountants, and leverage-buyout specialists. Within the service sector, employment in some areas has grown while in others employment has declined. For example, the employment in distributive services—trucking, rail, air transportation, warehousing, and the like—has declined since 1947, but its contribution to GNP has increased slightly because of improved productivity. Contrary to popular belief, employment in retailing has increased only slightly since 1947, and its contribution to GNP has actually declined. The biggest shifts have been in the growth of nonprofit services, government, and corporate activities. Nonprofit services refer to the wide range of services provided by universities, nonprofit hospitals, health care providers, foundations, and nonprofit research centers. This is the sector that provides for the health and education of this society's population. Government refers to federal, state, and local government employment, as well as quasi-government agencies like the FSLIC. Finally, the complex of corporate services refers to the broad range of services necessary for the production and distribution of goods and services. This category includes corporate financing, management and marketing consulting, accounting, advertising, and the host of service activities carried out in corporate headquarters. Of the three, the complex of corporate services has had the greatest impact on the nation's economy, and its contribution to GNP now rivals manufacturing in importance. Therefore, the growth of large, multiproduct, multinational corporations is central to understanding the regional restructuring of the Sunbelt/Snowbelt. This element, however, is often overlooked (Noyelle and Stanback, 1984).

SECTORAL SHIFTS AND REGIONAL GROWTH

Changes in what our economy produces, how it produces it, and where it is produced have a spatial as well as a social impact. As employment in this society shifted away from manufacturing to government, nonprofit organizations, and corporate services, the occupational structure of the nation changed. In turn, the shift in the occupational structure affected cities, and the effects differed depending on the city's institutional endowments. Sunbelt cities, because of lower labor costs, available land, huge federal subsidies, a benign climate, and access to cheap oil, gas, and other resources, were in a strategic position to attract manufacturing activities. The region is now in the process of building an infrastructure of distributive, retail, and other services. Northern cities, in contrast, because of their size, their universities and research centers, their historical domination of financing, marketing, and management, have been able to hold onto the corporate and producer services that have been the largest growing sector of the economy. In other words, Snowbelt cities may have lost manufacturing, but they have been quite successful in holding onto national corporate headquarters, research and development centers, and the finance, advertising, management consulting, accounting, and the host of other services demanded by modern large, multinational corporations (Noyelle and Stanback, 1984, pp. 13–50). Why this is so is examined in the next section.

CITY CLASSIFICATION'S USE IN REGIONAL ANALYSIS

From central place theory, we know that the mix of economic activities will vary among places. Cities that have achieved large size can support certain activities that smaller places cannot. Moreover, we know from our earlier discussion that metropolitan economies differ in the activities found in their economic bases, and these differences can be used as the basis of classification. Two urban economists, Noyelle and Stanback, used employment data to develop a city classification scheme, which they organized into a hierarchy (See Figure 7.4.). They then used this typology to describe the changes occurring in the system of cities. There are four broad categories of places: diversified service centers, specialized service centers, production centers, and consumer-oriented centers. At the top of the hierarchy are diversified service centers, which are composed of nodal centers specialized to provide a variety of distributive and corporate services. In this scheme, there are four metropolises (New York, Los Angeles, Chicago, and San Francisco) classified as national nodal. The four national nodal cities have the most diverse range of services, and they provide services to lower-order nodal centers in the hierarchy. The national nodal centers are among the largest cities in the United States, and their influence spans the nation and the world. Moreover, these are the only cities that can support international banking, financing, and marketing, and corporations found in other cities in the hierarchy depend on the services found there. Lower in the hierarchy are regional nodal centers (for example, Philadelphia, Boston, Dallas, Houston, St. Louis, and so on) and subregional nodal centers (Memphis, Salt Lake City, Charlotte, and so on) which supply similar services to the cities in their trade areas.

Specialized service centers are composed of three types of cities: Functional nodal places (for example, Detroit, Pittsburgh, San Jose, Rochester, and Akron) are older manufacturing centers in which major corporations carry out headquarters, research and development, and other nonproduction activities. They are, however, underrepresented in finance, corporate, and producer services. For these activities, they turn to the nodal places. Government–education centers are the seats of government (for example, Washington, D.C., Austin, and Albany) and are often the home of major state universities. Education–manufacturing MSAs are cities that have a double life.

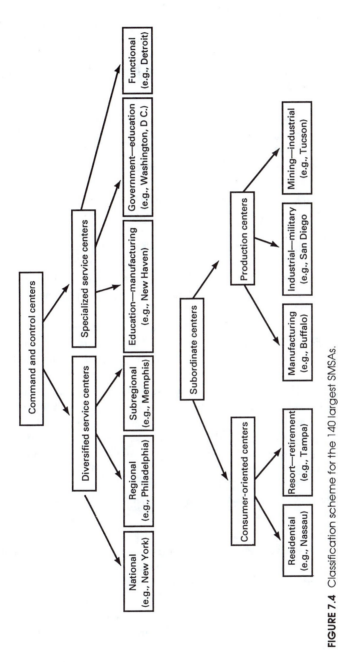

FIGURE 7.4 Classification scheme for the 140 largest SMSAs.

Source: Hanson (1982), adapted from Noyelle and Stanback (1983). From Nelson, K.P. *Gentrification and Distressed Cities: An Assessment of Trends in Intrametropolitan Migration,* p. 85, Figure 4.1.

They are old industrial centers that are also the sites of major universities (for example, New Haven, Yale, and Ann Arbor, University of Michigan).

There are three types of production centers: manufacturing (for example, Buffalo, Gary, and Binghamton), industrial–military (San Diego and Norfolk), and mining–industrial (for example, Tucson, Arizona, and Johnstown, Pennsylvania). These are metropolitan areas whose economies are organized to export goods to other markets, and they have weak service sectors.

Finally, consumer-oriented centers are residential and resort–retirement metropolitan areas. These cities share one thing in common; they provide services to individuals (Noyelle and Stanback, 1984, pp. 51–92).

IMPACT OF TECHNOLOGY ON REGIONAL GROWTH

Noyelle and Stanback found a number of interrelated changes in transportation, communication, and manufacturing technology, which facilitated the rapid dispersion of manufacturing, first from the central city to the suburbs, then from the Snowbelt to the Sunbelt, and then from the Sunbelt overseas. These changes include the following: First, the construction of the interstate highway system, which led to the rise of the trucking industry and the decline of railroads. As a result, industrial location was no longer constrained by the availability of rail lines, and management could locate plants anywhere.

Second, automation simplified manufacturing, and computer technology permitted automation to be applied to previously untried areas. This permitted the management of a product to be separated from the plant where the production was actually taking place.

Third, automated production requires one-floor factories, which in turn increases the demand for large undeveloped tracts of land. The land demands of modern production forced factories to locate in the suburbs or in the less developed regions of the nation.

Finally, for many corporations labor costs and labor strife were a motivation for moving. The Sunbelt's attraction of open shops and right-to-work laws provided a climate that many CEOs found attractive.

ECONOMIC CHANGE AND REGIONAL RESTRUCTURING

Noyelle and Stanback argue that the spatial organization of manufacturing has changed as the inputs have changed, but in their analysis the authors discovered an interesting pattern. Although manufacturing moved to the Sunbelt to take advantage of lower costs, the corporation headquarters and research and development centers did not follow. Snowbelt cities have done quite well in holding onto their corporate headquarters, research and development centers, and the producer services upon which these activities depend, as well as employment in high-skill, high-value-added types of manufacturing—scientific instruments and the like.

The changes in technology that transformed manufacturing also altered corporate structure from simply producing to controlling. Corporations now have markets and a span of control that are national and international in scope. An enormous array of producer services—attorneys, advertising, finance, and public relations experts, management consultants, junk bond specialists, and the like—is now required to manage an enterprise of this size and range. For this reason, national headquarters continue to be concentrated in the large nodal centers at the top of the hierarchy because only there can one find the range of services necessary for the modern corporate world. A perusal of Table 7.6 shows that most of the cities classified as national and regional nodal are in the Snowbelt. Although Snowbelt cities have lost much of their manufacturing base, they are holding onto corporate headquarters, research and development centers, high-skill, high-value-added manufacturing (for example, scientific instruments, computers), and producer services.

This finding should not be surprising. Research using central place theory shows that cities at the top of the hierarchy have the most diverse economies and are in a position to offer the widest range of service to the cities in their hinterlands. Moreover, remember that the nodal centers were the seedbeds from which much of the innovation responsible for the regional restructuring originated. These cities, therefore, were in a strategic position to control and direct change (Noyelle and Stanback, 1984, pp. 51–92).

THE FUTURE

What of the future? Which cities in the hierarchy will do best? I would argue that the diversified and specialized service centers near the top of the hierarchy have the brightest future. Why? First, if we extrapolate the economic trends since the end of World War II, there will be fewer jobs in manufacturing and consumer services and more jobs in corporate and producer services. As we have shown, these are activities already well established in higher-order centers, and they should continue to grow through inertia. Second, the corporate headquarters, research and development centers, producer services, and public institutions are already concentrated in these higher-order centers. These are the groups that created innovation, and they are in a strategic position to control its dispersal to other centers.

Whenever there is change, there are winners and losers. The restructuring of the American economy has meant growth in some sectors and decline in others. There is a spatial element to this economic change. Some cities, because of their unique developmental histories, institutional endowments, or strategic position in the urban hierarchy, have prospered; others, dependent on a single industry with obsolete infrastructures, or positioned at the bottom of the hierarchy, have foundered. Economic change has transformed local economies and has rippled through our system of cities. Noyelle and Stanback's research suggests that effects of economic change have affected the Sunbelt and the Snowbelt differently. Sunbelt cities have gained population and employment in manufacturing, high technology, recreation, and energy industries. Snowbelt cities, after a period of painful readjustment, have been able to hold corporate headquarters and the producer services associated with them.

TABLE 7.6 140 Largest SMSAs Classified by Type and Size under Four Major Groupings, 1976

DIVERSIFIED SERVICE CENTERS

NATIONAL NODAL

1	New York	1
2	Los Angeles	1
3	Chicago	1
7	San Francisco	1

REGIONAL NODAL

4	Philadelphia	1
6	Boston	1
10	Dallas	1
11	Houston	1
12	St. Louis	1
14	Baltimore	1
15	Minneapolis	1
17	Cleveland	1
18	Atlanta	2
21	Miami	2
22	Denver	2
23	Seattle	2
26	Cincinnati	2
28	Kansas City	2
30	Phoenix	2
32	Indianapolis	2
33	New Orleans	2
34	Portland	2
35	Columbus	2

SUBREGIONAL NODAL

41	Memphis	3
45	Salt Lake City	3
46	Birmingham	3
52	Nashville	3
53	Oklahoma City	3
56	Jacksonville	3
58	Syracuse	3
65	Richmond	3
66	Charlotte	3
69	Omaha	3
191	Mobile	4
101	Little Rock	4
106	Shreveport	4
110	Des Moines	4
114	Spokane	4
20	Jackson, MS	4

SPECIALIZED SERVICE CENTERS

FUNCTIONAL NODAL

5	Detroit	1
13	Pittsburgh	1
16	Newark	1
24	Milwaukee	2
31	San Jose	2
36	Hartford	2
38	Rochester	3
40	Louisville	3
44	Dayton	3
47	Bridgeport	3
50	Toledo	3
51	Greensboro	3
57	Akron	3
62	Allentown	3
63	Tulsa	3
67	New Brunswick	3
70	Jersey City	4
75	Wilmington	4
78	Paterson	4
86	Knoxville	4
96	Wichita	4
100	Fort Wayne	4
103	Peoria	4
137	Kalamazoo	4

GOVERNMENT-EDUCATION

8	Washington, DC	1
39	Sacramento	3
48	Albany	3
77	Raleigh–Durham	4
81	Fresno	4
82	Austin	4
84	Lansing	4
85	Oxnard–Ventura	4
88	Harrisburg	4
89	Baton Rouge	4
99	Columbia, SC	4
111	Utica	4
112	Trenton	4
113	Madison	4
117	Stockton	4

EDUCATION-MANUFACTURING

54	New Haven	3
64	Springfield	3
90	Tacoma	4
130	South Bend	4
140	Ann Arbor	4

TABLE 7.6 (continued)

PRODUCTION CENTERS

MANUFACTURING

27	Buffalo	2	116	Reading	4
			119	Huntington	4
42	Providence	3	124	Evansville	4
59	Worcester	3	125	Appleton	4
60	Gary	3	131	Erie	4
61	NE Pennsylvania	3	134	Rockford	4
71	Grand Rapids	3	136	Lorain	4
72	Youngstown	3			
73	Greenville	3			
74	Flint	3			

80	New Bedford	4	123	Huntsville	4
92	Canton	4	126	Augusta	4
93	Johnson City	4	127	Vallejo	4
94	Chattanooga	4	128	Colorado Springs	4
98	Davenport	4	132	Pensacola	4
104	Beaumont	4	133	Salinas	4
107	York	4			
109	Lancaster	4			
115	Binghamton	4			

INDUSTRIAL–MILITARY

20	San Diego	2
37	San Antonio	3
49	Norfolk	3
87	El Paso	4
97	Charleston, SC	4
102	Newport News	4
121	Lexington	4

MINING–INDUSTRIAL

83	Tucson	4
105	Bakersfield	4
118	Corpus Christi	4
129	Lakeland	4
135	Johnstown, PA	4
138	Duluth	4
139	Charleston, WV	4

CONSUMER–ORIENTED CENTERS

RESIDENTIAL

9	Nassau	1
19	Anaheim	2
76	Long Branch	3

RESORT–RETIREMENT

25	Tampa	2
29	Riverside	2
43	Fort Lauderdale	3
55	Honolulu	3
68	Orlando	3
79	West Palm Beach	4
95	Albuquerque	4
108	Las Vegas	4
122	Santa Barbara	4

Note: Number preceding city indicates 1976 population rank; number following city, 1976 population size group (See text.).

Source: Noyelle, T. J., and Stanback, J.T.M. (1983). *The Economic Transformation of American Cities.* Totowa, NJ: Rowan and Allanheld. Adapted from Table 4.2, pp. 56–57. That table is based on data from U.S. Bureau of the Census, *Current Population Report*, Series P-25, and Appendix A.

PLIGHT OF THE SNOWBELT'S CENTRAL CITIES

The Noyelle and Stanback research hints of urban prosperity, not urban malaise. Reading my description of their work, you would think that Snowbelt cities are in the midst of an urban renaissance. Still, there are the nagging images of abandoned buildings and people that we hold of the Bronx, Harlem, Hough, East St. Louis, and the ghettos of all our Snowbelt cities. The major weakness of the Noyelle and Stanback work is that it is based on data for the entire metropolis. They have lumped together in a single figure the experiences of both the central city and the suburbs. They did this out of necessity because these were the only data available, but in doing so they have masked the economic plight of the central cities.

SELF-REINFORCING AND SELF-LIMITING PROCESS OF DECLINE

Kathryn Nelson (1988) in her book, *Gentrification and Distressed Cities,* employs the city classification system developed by Noyelle and Stanback to analyze distress in the central cities. Her work focuses on the effect of the selective migration of whites and blacks to the central cities and the impact this migration has on the economic and social health of these cities. Table 7.7 presents data on the same 30 SMSAs used in the other sections of this chapter, and the cities have been ranked according to their metropolitan size in 1910. As we have seen, the infrastructures and institutional endowments of a city are shaped by the era in which the city reached metropolitan status. The older industrial cities of the Snowbelt have endowments different from young cities, and these are reflected in population change, migration, income characteristics, and distress. Notice in the first column of the table that older industrial cities experienced dramatic declines in their white populations between 1970 and 1980. Migration estimates also show a significant outmigration of whites from the central city. Young cities, in contrast, have had very different experiences. Although many central cities have lost white population, this migration has not been of the magnitude of older industrial cities. Notice the averages at the bottom of the columns. Whereas the white population of industrial cities dropped 30 percent, the decline for young Sunbelt cities was only 8 percent, a 22 percent difference. The estimates of net migration show the same outmigration of whites from the central city but at a substantially lower rate. At the same time that whites have left the central city, the black population has grown. Whether using population change or net migration, these data show that the racial character of the cities in the Snowbelt is changing more rapidly than the Sunbelt.

The migration patterns have a social and economic component. The fifth column of the table gives the city/suburban income ratio. A value of 100 means that the residents of the central city and the suburbs have the same average income; an index greater than 100 means that central city residents have incomes higher than their counterparts in the suburbs, and an index below 100, the opposite. Note that the average for older industrial cities is 84—the typical central city resident earns 84 percent of the typical suburbanite's

TABLE 7.7 Net Migration, Income Ratio, and Distress Indexes for Selected Metropolitan Areas, 1970–1980.

AGE CLASS	CITY BY 1910 METROPOLITAN SIZE	PERCENTAGE CHANGE IN POPULATION 1970–1980[1]		ESTIMATED NET MIGRATION CENTRAL CITY[2]		CITY SUBURB INCOME RATIO[3]	DISTRESS[4] RANK
		WHITE	BLACK	WHITE	BLACK		
Industrial	New York	-29	+ 4.1	-14	38	77	I
	Chicago	-32	+ 7.1	-24	14	78	II
	Philadelphia	-23	+ 4.2	-17	7	83	II
	Boston	-25	+ 6.1	-18	39	82	I
	Pittsburgh	-23	+ 3.8	-20	- 6	93	II
	St. Louis	-34	+ 5.3	-34	0	81	I
	San Francisco	-28	- 0.7	-18	29	101	II
	Baltimore	-28	+ 8.4	-24	10	80	I
	Cleveland	-33	+ 5.5	-33	- 1	68	I
	Buffalo	-31	+ 6.2	-24	12	83	II
	Detroit	-51	+19.6	-33	20	80	I
	Cincinnati	-23	+ 6.2	-27	- 2	96	II
Anomalous	Los Angeles	5	-0.9	- 3	30	100	III
	Washington	-18	- 0.8	-40	9	na	I
	Milwaukee	-23	+ 8.4	-19	35	83	III
	Kansas City	-20	+ 5.3	- 7	16	91	III
	New Orleans	-27	+10.3	-23	- 4	92	I
	Seattle	-14	+ 2.4	-11	21	111	V
Young	Indianapolis	-11	+ 3.8	-11	15	100	V
	Atlanta	-43	+15.3	-27	18	85	II
	Denver	-20	+ 2.9	- 9	34	104	IV
	Columbus	- 2	+ 3.6	- 3	12	89	IV
	Memphis	-14	+ 8.7	-18	14	118	II
	Nashville	- 8	+ 3.7	-12	11	109	IV
	Dallas	-11	+ 4.5	6	36	111	IV
	San Antonio	-15	- 0.3	- 2	20	79	IV
	Houston	8	+ 1.9	9	26	101	IV
	Jacksonville	-10	+ 3.1	14	9	119	IV
	San Diego	8	+ 1.3	5	39	108	V
	Phoenix	18	0	17	22	100	V
Industrial cities		-30	6.3	-24	13	84	1.5
Young cities		- 8	4.0	- 3	21	102	3.9
Difference		22	2.3	21	8	18	2.4

Data Definitions and Sources: (1) Percentage change in SMSA population—U.S. Bureau of Census, 1971, 1981; (2) estimated net migration adopted from Table 4.2, p. 79, Nelson (1988); (3) adapted from Table 2.2, p. 21, Norton (1979); (4) distress index in quintiles from Bruce and Goldberg (1979). I = greatest distress; V = least distress.

earnings. Note also the figure for the young cities in the Sunbelt, an average score of 102. Income translates into tax dollars, and the prospect for the central cities of Snowbelt cities is quite different from those of the Sunbelt.

Finally, city age is highly correlated with measures of distress. The distress ranks presented in the last column are in quintiles. Roman numeral I refers to the quintile of cities in the greatest distress; V, the quintile in the least distress. Without exception, the central cities in older industrial metropolises are ranked I or II; young cities, with one exception, IV or V.

Therefore, Nelson's findings suggest that the outmigration of high-income groups leads to a concentration of low-income and high-service-cost citizens in the central cities of the Snowbelt. At a time when low-income residents are in the greatest need for services, the exodus of the white middle class means that there is a declining tax base. At a time when a larger and larger proportion of city budgets goes to meeting the needs of their most disadvantaged citizens, less money is going to the very services needed to attract and hold the upper-income citizens in the city. The process has been labeled a self-reinforcing and self-limiting cycle of decline. For the past 40 years, higher-status residents have moved away from the central cities of our largest cities. Studies have shown that the process is even more pronounced in cities in distress. The problem has been further exacerbated by the regional shifts in population, which have drawn higher-income and better-educated people from the Northeastern and North Central regions to the Sunbelt. The selective outmigration of white and higher-income groups is self-reinforcing because the decline in the number of high-income residents means that there is less wealth to tax for needed services. Selective migration also means that there is an erosion of the critical mass of higher-income and educated people necessary to support retail and other service activities. The decentralization of business and industry means a loss of the critical mass of businesses needed to support producer services. The end result has been the declining political and economic power of central cities, poor maintenance of residential property and the city's infrastructure, and a drop in housing and land prices. The self-limiting nature of the process is that at some point prices will fall so low that people will return and reinvest—the process of gentrification and neighborhood reinvestment. This is indeed what has occurred in the central city neighborhoods of most Snowbelt cities. But it has been a selective process. Table 7.8 shows the winners and losers. Cities at the top of the urban hierarchy have been able to build upon the growth in the corporate service complex and have stabilized or reversed decline. Cities further down the urban hierarchy continue to decline (Nelson, 1988, pp. 99–159).

CONCLUSIONS

In the last half of this chapter I have tried to show you the variety of research that has focused on the changes in the Sunbelt/Snowbelt. Norton's analysis suggests the fall of the Snowbelt as a result of the eclipse of the region's industry and the loss of the seedbed function. Noyelle and Stanback's broadened analysis includes change in other sectors of the economy. They show that although the Snowbelt has lost manufacturing, it has done well in other rapidly expanding sectors of the economy. Out of necessity, they used aggregate metropolitan data that ignored the plight of central cities. Kathryn Nelson combined the study of the urban hierarchy with a sensitivity to the movement of people within and between metropolitan areas to give a more complete process of urban change.

TABLE 7.8 Patterns of Change in City Selection Rates of Upper-Income Movers, 1970–1980, for Distressed Cities by Economic Type

DOWNTURN	STABILITY	UPTURN
	National Diversified Service Centers	
Chicago	San Francisco	New York
		Los Angeles
		Washington, DC
	Regional Diversified Service Centers	
Atlanta	Boston	Cincinnati
Baltimore	Kansas City	
Cleveland	Minneapolis–	
Miami	St. Paul	
New Orleans		
Philadelphia		
St. Louis		
	Subregional Diversified Service Center	
Birmingham		
	Functional Specialized Service Centers	
Detroit	Rochester	
Louisville	Milwaukee	
Newark		
Paterson		
Pittsburgh		
	Government-Education Specialized Service Center	
	Albany	
	Manufacturing Centers	
	Buffalo	Providence

Source: Nelson, K. P. *Gentrification and Distressed Cities: An Assessment of Trends in Intrometropolitan Migration.* Madison, WI: The University of Wisconsin Press, Ltd., 1988, p. 99, Table 4.7.

She shows the potent force of urban structure and how those cities at the top of the hierarchy have been able to stem decline. Unfortunately, even with the favorable economic and demographic conditions during the past decade, the conditions of the nation's most distressed central cities have not improved. The migration of high-income groups continues setting up the self-reinforcing and self-limiting problems that we have discussed.

THEORIES OF REGIONAL CHANGE

A POLITICAL MODEL OF REGIONAL CHANGE

There have been numerous theories put forth to explain the regional changes in the Sunbelt and the Snowbelt. The first is really not a theory but an assertion backed by empirical evidence. Historically, there have been two stalwarts of the Southern political system: the dominance of the Democratic Party and safe House and Senate seats. Little turnover in Congressional seats means seniority, and seniority translates into the chairmanships of the most powerful committees in Congress—Ways and Means and the Defense Appropriations Committees. Therefore, some argue that a major reason for the growth of the Sunbelt was the ability of Southern senators and congressmen to direct the growth of the military to bases in the region during World War II and the Cold War. As a result, millions of servicemen entered basic training, served, and were mustered out at bases in the Sunbelt. Millions stayed and retired in the region to take advantage of the generous military retirement benefits—free medical care and post exchanges.

Other forces were at work in society, which influenced the migration of millions of additional Americans—retirees. Social security, Medicare, and generous company pensions gave millions of older Americans the freedom to relocate to other parts of the country to take advantage of warm climates and lower costs of living. Others moved to the Sunbelt to join friends and relatives who had already moved there.

The growth of the military and the growth of retirement communities created a self-reinforcing cycle that drew millions from the Snowbelt to the Sunbelt. Population growth translated into political clout. Table 7.9 presents the regional breakdown of membership in the U.S. House of Representatives for the years 1940–1980. In the span of 40 years, House membership from the Sunbelt grew from 132 to 167 seats, and the region is expected to gain additional seats after the reapportionment that follows the 1990 census. The Snowbelt in contrast has watched its representation drop from 207 seats in 1940 to 183 seats in 1980 as the relative proportion of the region's population declined.

The argument made by some students of regional growth is that political clout led to a bias in federal spending to the Sunbelt; that in effect the federal government has provided a massive subsidy to the Sunbelt at the expense of the Snowbelt. The evidence for this assertion, however, is mixed. Table 7.10 presents the per capita expenditure by the federal government for the two regions for the year 1986. The state receiving the most federal money is Massachusetts, a Snowbelt state, receiving $4283 per capita in 1988. The state receiving the fewest federal dollars was Michigan, also a Snowbelt state, receiving only $2571 per capita in 1988. The average federal per capita expenditure in 1988 for the Snowbelt was $3219, for the Sunbelt, $3450. There doesn't seem to be a subsidy here.

TABLE 7.9 MEMBERSHIP IN U.S. HOUSE OF REPRESENTATIVES BY REGION, 1940–1980

	1940	1950	1960	1970	1980
Sunbelt	132	139	146	154	167
Florida	4	8	12	15	17
Texas	21	22	23	24	26
Arizona	2	2	3	4	6
California	23	30	38	43	48
Snowbelt	207	202	196	190	183

Source: U.S. Bureau of the Census, *Statistical Abstracts, 1987.* Washington, D.C.: U.S. Government Printing Office, 1987.

TABLE 7.10 Per capita federal expenditure by state (fiscal year 1988).

REGION AND STATE	PER CAPITA	INDEX
Frostbelt		
Connecticut	$4228	123
Maine	3391	97
Massachusetts	4283	123
New Hampshire	3026	87
Rhode Island	3618	104
Vermont	2828	81
New Jersey	3126	90
New York	3404	98
Pennsylvania	3315	95
Illinois	2760	79
Indiana	2677	77
Michigan	2571	74
Ohio	3108	89
Wisconsin	2731	78
Mean	$3219	93
Sunbelt		
Alabama	$3516	101
Arkansas	3134	90
Florida	3576	102
Georgia	2965	85
Louisiana	2843	81
Mississippi	3770	108
North Carolina	2767	79
South Carolina	3192	91
Tennessee	3235	93
Arizona	3617	104
New Mexico	5790	166
Oklahoma	3289	94
Texas	2947	84
California	3700	106
Nevada	3405	98
Mean	$3450	99

Source: Advisory Commission on Intergovernmental Relations, *Significant Features of Fiscal Federalism 1989 Edition, Volume II.* Washington, D.C.: 1989, Table 29, p. 44.

If you look at the total number of dollars returned to each region, the Snowbelt receives the most money, but a different picture emerges when one looks at relative expenditures—the amount a state puts in and gets out of the federal treasury. When one makes this comparison, a different picture emerges. In general, states in the Snowbelt receive less than they pay into the federal treasury; Sunbelt states receive more. In the years 1980 to 1985, this amounted to more than $200 billion (ACIR, 1989).

In addition to the long-term spending patterns of the federal government, the federal government has provided a hidden subsidy through our tax system. The Sunbelt's economy is tied to six industries—agriculture, defense, high technology, oil and natural gas, real estate, and retirement and recreation. In all six areas, industries receive preferential tax treatment. The intent of the Congress may not have been to subsidize Sunbelt industries, but in just two areas, investment tax credits and accelerated depreciation, the rapidly expanding industries in the Sunbelt benefited far more than the mature industries in the Snowbelt. In addition, the federal government provided massive subsidies to the aerospace and microelectronics industries, which are two of the most dynamic and fastest-growing industries in the society; they are concentrated in the Sunbelt.

Therefore, one cannot ignore the political dimension of regional growth. Whether done intentionally or as an unintended consequence of military and tax policy, the federal government has been a major player in the movement of people, money, and other resources from the Snowbelt to the Sunbelt (Sale, 1975; Macdonald, 1984; Norton, 1979).[4]

CONVERGENCE THEORIES OF REGIONAL DEVELOPMENT

There are dozens of theories on regional development, but one of the more important is the convergence theory, which argues that within any system, parts become more alike over time. Unlike many nations in the world, people and capital are free to move anywhere within our nation. There are no federal or state laws, unlike those in Western European and socialist nations, to prevent, say GM, from closing a plant in Flint and opening a new one in Nashville. They are not legally or financially responsible for the backwash of problems—unemployment, a devastated local economy, a falling real estate market—created when they leave town. In such a system, a rational decision would be for people to move to the region with the highest wages and standards of living and capital to move to the region with the highest returns on investment. Eventually, however, disparities in income and returns on investments are removed, and the shift of people and capital will slow.

There is evidence that this is what has already occurred in the Sunbelt and Snowbelt, and not just in economic realms. Whereas the per capita income of the Old South was only 48 percent of the national average in 1930, it had risen to nearly 80 percent in 1986. Although the wages received for manufacturing employment are still lower in the Sunbelt, the difference is shrinking. In occupations requiring advanced training or higher education, little disparity now exists. As these regional disparities have declined, migration to and economic growth in the Sunbelt have slowed. In addition, there is mounting evidence that as economic differences are removed, cultural differences are being erased too. Mass advertising, mass marketing, mass education, and the mass media have created a mass society (Watkins and Perry, 1977).

MARXIST THEORIES OF REGIONAL INEQUALITY

Marxist scholars have proposed a different set of explanations for the shift of people and capital from the Snowbelt to the Sunbelt. We have already discussed the work of Marx and Schumeter, the role of innovation, and the process of creative destruction in the capitalistic system. There are other theorists who focus on the role of capital in regional inequality. These theorists argue that capital has a social as well as a spatial component. The division of labor is not uniform across the nation, and the control of capital is concentrated in the hands of financial institutions found in a few cities. Moreover, capital accumulates at different places at different times in the evolution of a capitalist system.

The inequality between regions, which has characterized most of our history, did not occur because the North intentionally exploited the South and the West; rather, it resulted from the division of labor. Since cities have different locations in relation to resources, modes of transportation, and labor, they have different use-values. Since, cities have different mixes of occupations in their division of labor and different mixes of businesses and industries in their local economies, unequal regional development occurs. In short, spatial inequality is a reflection of class inequality built into the economic structure of cities. Just as there are class differences between neighborhoods in a city, there are class differences between cities and regions.

Capital is mobile. When we place our savings in a local bank, buy insurance, or invest in a retirement plan, banks, insurance companies, and other financial institutions invest this capital where it will receive the highest return. Capital does not float around in space; it is invested in office buildings, plants, shopping centers, industrial parks, homes, and apartments, and these investments are locked in space in a specific part of a specific city in a specific region. If you happen to live in a community where there is a low probability of profit, chances are that there will be no outside investment and the well-being of your community will fall in relation to others. Uneven development occurs as capital continually circulates to take advantage of new opportunities in new places. As investment capital becomes concentrated in the hands of fewer and fewer institutions, Marxist theorists argue that uneven spatial growth will continue. In short, uneven development is central to the capitalist system. Regional inequality eventually will be addressed in capitalist societies as investors take advantage of lower labor and other cost in less-developed regions, but in doing so they create new regional imbalances. This backwash of problems is evident in the research of Kathryn Nelson on central cities in the Snowbelt (Walker, 1978).

There is no overwhelming evidence to support any of these theories, but on a close reading they make the same arguments using different perspectives. It is important that you be familiar with these theories because they, whether explicitly or implicitly, are at the bottom of our national discussion on the growth and development of the Sunbelt/Snowbelt.

SUMMARY

This chapter is intended to provide an understanding of the structure of cities and their interrelationship within a system of cities. The first half of the chapter examines the dynamic character of the system of cities. The concepts of economic base, initial advantage, and multiplier effect are introduced to explain the relationship between economic change and growth of a city. The economic base refers to the goods and services a city creates within its borders. The economic base is divided in two: The basic sector refers to those goods and services produced locally but sold outside its borders; the nonbasic sector, those goods sold locally. City growth is tied to the expansion of the basic sector, and the history of this nation's cities is a description of cities' attempts to expand their basic sector. Some cities, because of their location, access to transportation or raw resources, or the characteristics of their population, have an initial advantage in the competition for businesses in their basic sector. This initial advantage gives these places a growth inertia, which creates the multiplier effect. The multiplier effect simply means that growth is cumulative. Growth in one industry causes growth in other areas of the economy, which in turn creates opportunities for new businesses, and so on. The thrust of this argument is that some places, because of their initial advantage and their ability to expand their economies through the multiplier effect, are in a strategic position to guide growth and change into the future and maintain their position in the urban hierarchy.

The second half of the chapter discusses changes in the cities of the Sunbelt/Snowbelt. The purpose of this section is to explore changes in the national economy that have profoundly affected the relationship of cities within the national system of cities. The geography of the two regions is described, and the implications of the shift of the national economy to services in the post-World War II era are discussed. The work of three groups of researchers are presented. Norton found that city age, a decline in heavy manufacturing, and the slow growth of service employment were a major cause of the decline of the cities in the older industrial cities of the Snowbelt. According to Norton, these same changes in the national economy had a positive effect on the younger, service-oriented cities of the Sunbelt. The role of innovation in urban growth, the concept of creative destruction, and the law of industrial growth were introduced to raise questions about the viability of the Snowbelt cities' seedbed and the future of the central cities in this region.

Noyelle and Stanback expand the discussion of the problems in the cities of the Sunbelt/Snowbelt by focusing on the broad changes in the national economy. These researchers make a convincing argument that although the cities in the Sunbelt have done well in attracting manufacturing and related activities to their region, cities in the Snowbelt have done remarkably well in holding onto corporate headquarters, research and development centers, and the host of corporate services necessary for multinational, multiproduct corporations. The urban hierarchy and city classification were used by the authors to show that certain cities, because of their position at the top of the hierarchy, have been able to maintain their preeminence because they are responsible for both the creation and the diffusion of innovation. Although the

Snowbelt has lost much of its manufacturing base, it still retains its control function by the domination of banking, finance, and decision-making from the major corporate headquarters found in the cities of this region.

The major weakness of the Noyelle and Stanback research is its dependence on metropolitan data. Kathryn Nelson employs the classification scheme used by Noyelle and Stanback but looks at the plight of central cities in the Snowbelt. She found that the continuing outmigration of white middle-class residents of the central cities in the Snowbelt has set up a self-reinforcing and self-limiting process of decline in central cities. The loss of affluent households means a concentration of high-cost citizens in the central city and a declining tax base. Nelson shows that only a few cities have been able to stem this outmigration, and they are cities found at the top of the urban hierarchy.

The chapter ends with the presentation of three perspectives on regional change—a political model, a convergence theory, and a Marxist theory. There is no convincing evidence that supports one theory over another, but on closer examination the theories complement rather than conflict with each other. Each in its own way contributes to our understanding of the growth and change in our system of cities.

NOTES

1. The most comprehensive discussion of the evolution of the U.S. urban system is Edgar S. Dunn, Jr.'s two-volume work, *The Development of the U.S. Urban System,* the first volume published in 1980 and the second in 1983 by Johns Hopkins Press. For an undergraduate this is a very difficult book to understand, but, in my opinion, the rewards are well worth the effort. In the opening chapter, he introduces an alternative approach to studying urban system—for that matter, all social phenomena—by examining observational options available to the researcher. Social science tends to study the effects of behavior; Dunn suggests that the effects are the result of behavior guided by rules that are modified by social change. Traditionally, social sciences study the classification of these phenomena, but Dunn argues that the relations among these levels of analysis are an alternative and powerful way to study change in urban systems. In the chapters that follow, he looks at the problems in placing boundaries on urban activity systems, examines the sources and sequence of urban change, and then devotes the remainder of the two volumes to examining the changes in the national economy and its impact on the U.S. urban system from World War II to the present.

2. Two books have been written for the popular press that you may find interesting. The first, Kirkpatrick Sale's *Power Shift,* is written in a journalistic style; some say that this book was responsible for the present interest in the Sunbelt/Snowbelt. The major premise of the book is that the growth of the six pillars of the Sunbelt's economy—agribusiness, defense, technology, oil, real estate, and leisure—permitted the region to challenge the Eastern establishment. He then uses the examination of these regional changes as a backdrop for the Nixon-Watergate debacle. Sale argues that Nixon's questionable ethics are a reflection of the questionable business practices of the Sunbelt region. Extrapolating to the 1980s, the same might be said for the Reagan administration. The book was written in 1975, and the fortunes of the region's economy have changed, but the savings and loan and real estate crises in the region lend credence to his analysis.

The second book, Michael C. D. Macdonald's *America's Cities,* is also written in a journalistic style, and it paints a depressing picture of urban conditions in selected Sunbelt and Snowbelt cities. The problems in Sunbelt cities have received far less attention than the Snowbelt, and this book outlines what urban researchers have said for years: We have national urban problems that transcend regions.

3.   For those interested in pursuing the topic of change in the national economy and the impact of these changes on the system of cities, I recommend two books. The first is Thomas M. Stanback, Jr. and Thierry J. Noyelle's *Cities in Transition.* This book examines the rise of services in the national economy and its impact on urban economies. The authors look at the labor market characteristics of service industries, use data from the Social Security Administration to map out these changes in detail, and, finally, explore the implications of these changes in the transformation of seven metropolitan labor markets.

The second book I recommend, *The Economic Transformation of American Cities,* is by the same authors. Much of the second half of this chapter is based on this work, and it expands on the earlier research presented in *Cities in Transition.* This work examines shifts in employment patterns in the national economy and the transformation of the entire U.S. system of cities.

4.   For those interested in a reader on the Sunbelt/Snowbelt, I recommend Larry Sawers and William K. Tabb's *Sunbelt/Snowbelt: Urban Development and Regional Restructuring.* The book is written from a Marxist perspective, but on the whole is a balanced book. Chapter 7 by Anna Lee Saxenian, "The Urban Contradictions of Silicon Valley," is a must reading. Although tax policy has changed since 1982, Michael I. Luger's "Federal Tax Incentives as Industrial and Urban Policy" makes a convincing argument for the federal subsidy of Sunbelt growth. The backwash of problems caused by regional restructuring is sensitively discussed in Bennett Harrison and Barry Bluestone's chapter, "The Incidence and Regulation of Plant Closings."

CHAPTER 8

SOCIAL AREA ANALYSIS AND FACTORIAL ECOLOGY

INTRODUCTION

Are your neighborhood streets lined with Tonka toys and Lego blocks? Has your corner bar and grill gone butcher block and brass? Whether you live in the shadow of a grain silo or an eighty-story skyscraper, your neighborhood speaks volumes about who you are, where you've been and where you're going. Michael J. Weiss's new way of looking at the nation—not as fifty states but rather forty neighborhood types, or clusters—is based on the PRIZM marketing system developed by the Claritas Corporation. Using U.S. Census Bureau data and a host of consumer surveys and public opinion polls, Claritas devised lifestyle portraits of the nation's 250,000 neighborhoods, classifying every block into forty clusters with names such as Blue Blood Estates, Hard Scrabble, Shotguns & Pickups, Bohemian Mix, Young Influentials and more. In *The Clustering of America*, Weiss draws on these clusters—which are used by corporations, political parties and many others for influencing consumer and voter decisions—to explore America's diverse lifestyles. He identifies the residents of each cluster by where they work, how they spend their money, which cars they drive, what they read, which television programs they watch, who they vote for and where they travel. Each cluster claims distinct boundaries, consuming habits, political beliefs and values: residents of Heavy Industry buy lottery tickets, for example, while the people of Furs and Station Wagons keep their money in brokerage accounts; unlike the retirees of Golden Ponds, who shun materialistic status symbols, the affluent elderly of Grey Power communities have a passion for Cadillacs and foreign travel; and though the people of Towns and Gowns and Urban Gold Coast are highly educated, the cities where they live have little in common.

With information gathered from visits to cluster communities across the country, Weiss paints a vivid portrait of American society, the dynamics of today's changing neighborhoods and tomorrow's emerging lifestyles. Taken together, the forty clusters celebrate the remarkable diversity of how Americans really live.

(Advertisement, Michael J. Weiss, *The Clustering of America*. New York, Harper and Row, Publishers, 1988)

The ad for Michael Weiss's book describes the hot marketing concept of the 1980s: area marketing, or target marketing. There is an enormous amount of information out there on each of us, and today's computer technology allows this information to be collected cheaply. Census and other data gathered by the federal government permit researchers and marketers to describe in detail the housing, race, occupation, and income characteristics of this nation's neighborhoods. When we apply for loans and credit cards, use credit cards, sign the waiver at the bottom of our insurance form, apply for life insurance, buy property, pay taxes, subscribe to magazines, receive a traffic ticket, have a wreck, marry, divorce, get sued, or are late with the house payment, this information floats around in a vast computer network. Through a process called geocoding, any list that includes names and addresses, and I mean any list—AIDS victims, registered Democrats and Republicans, members of special interest groups, Toyota owners, subscribers to *Field and Stream,* and the list goes on—can be matched with the census data tabulated for the neighborhood in which we live. (An even faster way is to use zip codes.). Lists are produced, computer maps drawn, and marketers, politicians, and a host of other interested parties put these data to use, in some cases, insidious uses. Until Proposition 51 in California, car insurance premiums were not based solely on the age of the driver or the car owner's driving record, but rather on her/his zip code. Gas, electric, water, and telephone companies require hefty security deposits for some would-be customers and not others. Why? Is it their credit history? Usually not. It's their neighborhood. A colleague of mine whose specialty is geographical information systems told me of one of the most sophisticated and in some ways insidious use of this approach. Ever receive free store coupons in the mail? Look at the next one that comes in the mail, and look at the Uniform Product Code: those benign-looking bar codes. In the vast majority of cases, the bar codes are used by the supermarket to process their refunds from the manufacturer. For a small sample, the bar code is also coded for a residence. When scanned in certain markets, the marketing firm knows when you received the coupon, when you used it, and everything else you purchased in your shopping cart. They then match your consumer behavior on this supermarket trip back to a master file which covers your credit history, the car you drive, whether you own or rent, your occupation, the size and composition of your household, and the characteristics of the neighborhood in which you live. Remember, this is all done without your knowledge and consent. A little scary, isn't it?

In the 1990 census, the Bureau of the Census used the TIGER system. There now exists a computerized base map for the entire United States. Every street, street address, intersection, railroad, lake, stream, and natural barrier have been identified in a vast computer map. All the data collected in the 1990 census is coded back to this base file. These base maps can also be used for geocoding any other type of information. In the 1990s there will be a quantum leap in geographical information systems, and every American will be affected.

What most Americans don't realize is that all this amazing technology has been made possible by the work of social scientists. The burgeoning field of geographical information systems didn't just appear out of the ether; it has been made possible by basic research done by sociologists, human ecologists, and geographers over the past

75 years in their effort to describe the internal structure of the city. Much of the literature in urban sociology is concerned with the distribution of population characteristics, organizations, activities, and behaviors across the urban landscape. This literature explores not only the spatial distribution of characteristics but also the processes by which these patterns emerge. This chapter presents social area analysis and factorial ecology—two related approaches used to describe the internal structure of the city. Geographical information systems have their roots in this ecological approach.

ORIGINS OF SOCIAL AREA ANALYSIS

THE CONCEPT OF NATURAL AREAS

Social area analysis was an outgrowth of the work of the Chicago ecologists Park, Burgess, and others, who during the 1920s and 1930s were among the first social scientists to be concerned with the internal structure of cities. In their studies of Chicago, they discovered that the city was made up of distinct areas, each one relatively homogeneous in population, housing, and other characteristics. What particularly struck the Chicago ecologists was that these areas had not been planned by a builder or large developer. Rather, the areas had evolved as the result of millions of individual decisions made by people who had different moral, political, economic, racial, and ethnic characteristics. Each "natural area" had its own special qualities, the result of its unique ethnic and racial mix, physical characteristics, and other factors, including the income and occupation of its residents.

The major difference between social area analysis and the more general factorial ecology is in the quantity of data each uses. Social area analysis is limited to seven variables that measure the social-status, family, and ethnic characteristics of subareas. Factorial ecology greatly expands the number of variables used, from seven to several dozen. This more general approach was made possible by the modern high-speed computer that became available to researchers in the 1960s.

Social area analysis was first presented in a series of books and articles written by Eshref Shevky, Marilyn Williams, and Wendell Bell in the late 1940s and early 1950s. These researchers maintained that the use of space within cities, as measured by the seven variables in their analysis, was closely related to the degree of economic development of the larger society. Shevky and Bell introduced the concept of "societal scale" to refer to the extent of the division of labor within the society and the complexity of its organization and institutions. As a society modernizes or increases in scale, its degree of societal complexity increases and is reflected in increasing specialization of urban land use. In a high-scale society, neighborhoods become specialized in terms of their social-status, family, and ethnic characteristics. In a low-scale society where social organization is relatively simple, social-status, family, and ethnic characteristics are interrelated, and urban land use is less specialized.

Social area analysis is important because it relates the process of urbanization to the more general process of economic development. Thus, it is based on a general theory that can be applied to the analysis of cities in both more and less developed societies. Factorial ecology, which developed out of social area analysis in the 1960s, is more inductive with little or no associated theory.

I have traced the development of social area analysis and factorial ecology for two reasons: First, I believe social area analysis (SAA) and factorial ecology show the accumulative nature of the scientific endeavor, be it a social or a physical science. Second, social area analysis and related techniques are used today in very practical ways from measuring the extent of the AIDS epidemic, catchment areas of hospital emergency rooms, and the concentration of the disadvantaged to the marketing of products ranging from autos to bath soap. Read the following chapter with care because the spinoffs from social area analysis and factorial ecology affect every aspect of your day-to-day life.

Members of the Chicago School thought of *natural areas* as concrete entities that really existed—places that could be searched for, identified, and described scientifically.[1] Yet they never agreed on how to define the boundaries of an area. McKenzie and Wirth, for example, stressed population characteristics such as race, language, income, and occupation; Zorbaugh, in contrast, was concerned largely with the areas' physical characteristics. Burgess provided the most inclusive definition of a natural area by focusing on the forces responsible for its emergence. Out of these varied approaches, three important components of a natural area emerged: (1) It is the result of the operation of ecological and social forces, (2) it is unplanned, and (3) its boundaries can be discovered by measuring the income, occupation, ethnicity, and housing characteristics of its residents.[2]

While members of the Chicago School were identifying hobohemia, the ghetto, the Gold Coast, and other areas in Chicago, researchers in Cleveland and other cities began dividing their own communities into natural areas. In the early 1930s, statistician Howard Whipple Green set out to identify areas of Cleveland that were "functionally homogeneous with histories and heritages of their own" (1931, p. 7). The 28 Social Planning Areas (SPAs) Green delineated are still in use in Cleveland for reporting police, fire, city health, and census statistics (See Figure 8.1.), although the areas today are much different in character than when first studied by Green.

Initially, Green's goal was to use natural areas as planning units, a basis for more effective allocation of the city's limited financial resources. But the detailed housing, population, and health statistics he compiled had another important application—they could be used to describe the internal structure of the city. Data for various subareas allowed researchers to group areas into types: the slum, the ethnic enclave, and the working-class and middle-class areas. Once a city's various areas had been categorized and plotted on a map, their spatial distribution gave researchers insight into the city's structure.

The concept of natural areas and the theory associated with it had limitations, however. For one thing, the natural areas concept was not consistently defined: In one study, natural areas were viewed as spatial units bounded by major streets, lakes, rivers, and parks; in others, emphasis was placed on the community—aspects of the population living in an area. Some critics claimed it was impossible to find culturally

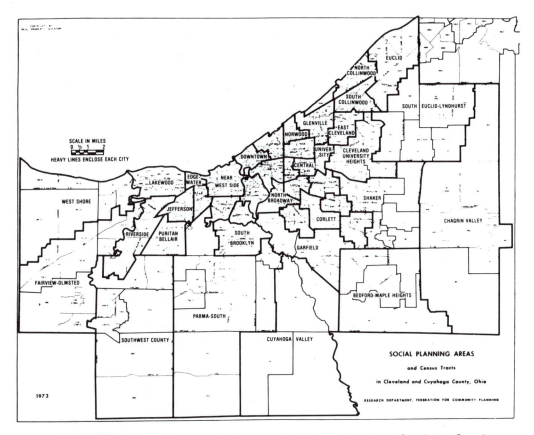

FIGURE 8.1 Social Planning Areas and census tracts in Cleveland and Cuyahoga County, Ohio. The bold lines in this map are the boundaries of Cleveland's Social Planning Areas (SPAs). SPAs were identified by the researcher Howard Whipple Green in the 1930s, and they continue to be used to report fire, police, and welfare statistics. Census tract boundaries are the lighter lines that divide the SPAs into smaller units. In the city of Cleveland there are 28 SPAs but more than 200 census tracts.

Source: Research Department, Cleveland, Ohio: Federation for Community Planning, 1974.

homogeneous areas in cities on the East and West Coasts.[3] The most significant weakness of the work of the Chicago ecologists was that, while concentrating on areas within the city, they ignored the social, economic, and cultural changes taking place in the larger society. This problem was to restrict the usefulness of area-oriented research for nearly two decades.

The move to relate urban process to a wider range of forces and the characteristics of the larger society began as an attempt to develop a typology of subareas of the city. When, in 1940, the United States Bureau of the Census began publishing data for most large American cities by census tracts, urban researchers were faced for the first time not with too few data but with too many. The problem was that although census tracts were similar to natural areas, they were much smaller, averaging only 4000 inhabitants. Thus, instead of 28 Social Planning Areas to classify, for example, in Cleveland, social scientists were confronted with hundreds of census tracts (See Figure 8.1.). A large metropolitan area might contain thousands of tracts. Urban researchers found it necessary to divide the census tracts within a city into larger categories. The approach to be known later as *social area analysis* had its beginning in one such attempt.

THE CONCEPT OF SOCIAL AREAS

In 1949, Eshref Shevky and Marilyn Williams published *The Social Areas of Los Angeles: Analysis and Typology.* There was an important difference between this study of the social areas of Los Angeles and earlier research by members of the Chicago School. The Chicago ecologists were interested in how a city's social organization was manifested spatially: where the very wealthy, the poor, and other groups lived in relationship to the city's center. Shevky and Williams, in contrast, were interested in the position of census tracts in "social space," regardless of their geographic location. That is, Shevky and Williams were interested in the people in the tracts, not the tracts themselves.

Social area indexes. Shevky and Williams attempted to measure and describe the social differences among census tracts according to residents' scores on three indexes—social status, family status, and ethnic status.[4] Each index score represents scores for several variables combined into a single value. The indexes thus enabled the researchers to examine complex data in the form of just a few summary scores. Shevky and Williams further contended that each of their indexes tapped a basic social trend in the emerging urban society—the changing occupational structure, the declining proportion of children in the population, and the patterns of internal migration. These changes taking place in the larger society were measurable by the indexes because they were reflected first and most clearly in the distribution of tracts in social space within the city.

Social status index. The *social status index* is based on various socioeconomic attributes of American households. The most important attribute is the social value of the occupation of the head of the household. Physicians, for example, have higher occupational prestige than lawyers, lawyers higher prestige than factory workers, factory workers higher prestige than garbage collectors (See Table 8.2.). Education is the second element of this index, and it is closely related to occupational prestige. Education not only provides a means of entry into occupations (A person needs a medical degree to become a licensed physician.), but the status of an occupation usually is related to the amount of education required for it.

In most societies, people with similar social status tend to live near each other in fairly homogeneous areas. When these areas are classified into census tracts, they can be ranked from high to low on social status. Because of the strong relationship between status and occupation, changes in the occupation and employment characteristics of the society at large are reflected in the changing distribution of tracts according to social status. The social status index reflects the changing occupational structure in the United States and other developed nations. At present, a growing number of workers are employed in service occupations, and fewer in farming and extractive industries such as mining and forestry.

Family status index. The second index, *family status,* is based on variables such as the fertility ratio, the number of women in the labor force, and the number of single-family dwelling units in a tract. This index can be used to measure the changing economic role of the family. In the past, the extended family (more than two generations living together) was typical, and it operated as a production unit. This arrangement still can be seen on a farm: Grandparents, parents, and children each contribute to the economic well-being of the family. In the city, because children have been prevented from working by child labor laws, children are no longer economic assets but economic liabilities. Today, the typical family is a consumption rather than a production unit, and its form is nuclear parent(s) and children. One can think of each nuclear family as passing through a series of stages. The "family formation" stage occurs when grown children leave their parents' household and set up households of their own, either as singles or as young married couples. Children are born into these new families and are raised to maturity—the child-rearing stage. Finally, grown children leave home, and the death of the parents brings the original family to an end. At each stage of the life cycle, families have different space needs—parents with grown children no longer need a home with four bedrooms. Housing suited to these different space needs tends to be in different areas of the city: Most large cities, for example, have certain areas that consist largely of apartments and are inhabited mainly by singles, retirees, or young couples with small children. In reflecting changes in the distribution of various types of living space, the family status index indicates a shift from the extended family to the nuclear family and the emergence of numerous life-styles, each with its own space needs.

Ethnic status index. The third index, *ethnic status,* is based on variables such as the percentage of a tract's population that is foreign-born or black. The index measures the tendency of new migrants to the city to locate—voluntarily or not—near people of their own background in a homogeneous ethnic or racial enclave. Thus, the index reflects trends in internal migration whereby large numbers of members of various ethnic minorities—blacks and immigrants—concentrate in certain areas of the city. Rural to urban migration of blacks and ethnically diverse immigration from overseas were the trends described and measured by Shevky and Williams.

Shevky and Williams used the three indexes in developing a typology of social areas. First, index values for each of Los Angeles's 568 census tracts were calculated. Second, each census tract was plotted as a point on a scattergram according to its values on each of the indexes. Third, a *social area diagram* was created by adding dividing lines to the scattergram. Figure 8.2, the Los Angeles social space diagram, delineates socially homogeneous subareas within the city. Figure 8.3 shows the population and census tract distribution by social areas.

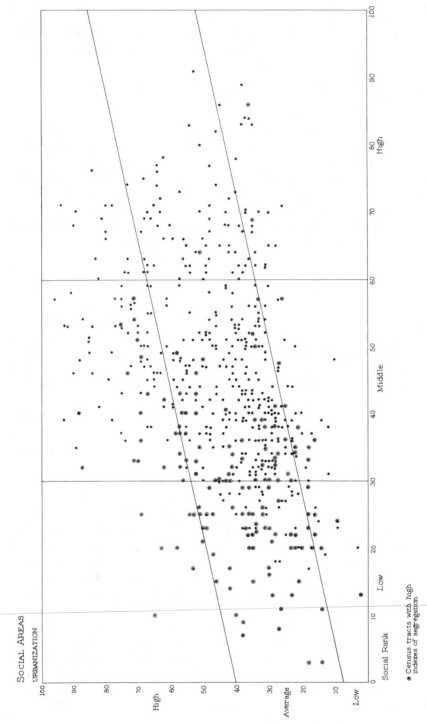

FIGURE 8.2 The figure demonstrates the process Shevky and Williams used in developing a typology of social areas. First, index values for each of Los Angeles's 568 census tracts were calculated. Second, each census tract was plotted as a point on this scattergram according to its values on the indexes. Third, a social area diagram was created by adding dividing lines to the scattergram. In this figure the horizontal and vertical axes are the two dimensions of social status and family status; tracts scoring high on the third dimension, ethnic status, are represented by the symbol ⊙. Note that nine types of social areas were identified by this process.

Eshref Shevky, Marilyn Williams, *Social Areas of Los Angeles: Analysis and Typology.* Copyright © 1949 The Regents of the University of California.

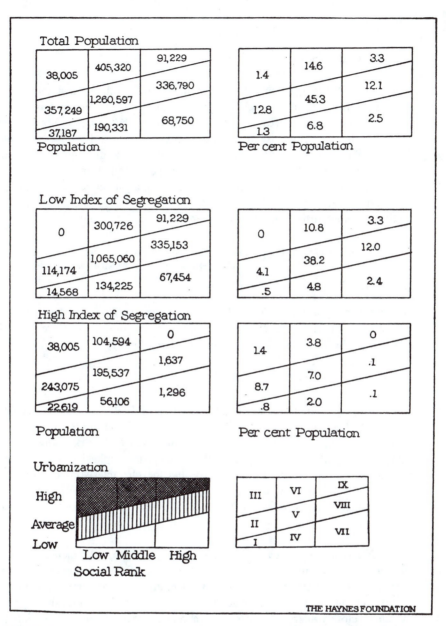

FIGURE 8.3 Distribution of Los Angeles's population by social areas. This figure shows the population and census tract distribution of Los Angeles by the social areas identified in Figure 8.2. Social Area I, low in social status and family status, would be similar to hobohemia in Chicago—single males and females with no children living in apartments in a state of poverty. Social Area IX, in contrast, would be characterized by high social status, few working women, large numbers of small children, and a predominance of single-family dwellings—an upper-middle-class, child-oriented suburb. Social Area V, tracts with average social and family status measures, was the most common social area type, followed by Social Areas VIII and VI.

Source: Eshref Shevky, Marilyn Williams, *Social Areas of Los Angeles: Analysis and Typology.* Copyright © 1949 The Regents of the University of California.

REVISIONS BY SHEVKY AND BELL

Shevky and Williams's approach was attacked on both theoretical and methodological grounds. Although Shevky and Williams did discuss general trends in society and the relationship of their indexes to these trends, the discussion was not presented in the form of a theory. Critics asked why these three indexes had been used. Why not some other mix of variables? Why use indexes at all? These questions were addressed six years later in a work by Eshref Shevky and Wendell Bell (1955).

In their restatement of the social area analysis approach, Shevky and Bell overcame the early narrow focus of the Chicago School by examining the sociocultural context in which urban communities are embedded. They stated:

> We conceive of the city as a product of the complex whole of modern society; thus the social forms of urban life are to be understood within the context of the changing character of the larger containing society (p. 3).

In other words, there is a close relationship between changes in the society as a whole and changes that take place in the use of space in cities. To explore this relationship, Shevky and Bell introduced the concept of *societal scale.*

THE CONCEPT OF SOCIETAL SCALE

The concept of societal scale was introduced in the 1950s to refer to the complex set of changes that accompany the development process. The term *high-scale societies* refers to more developed nations, and *low-scale societies* to less developed nations of the world. Shevky and Bell introduced the concept to emphasize the close relationship between the form or structure of a city and the characteristics of the encompassing society. This was a relationship often ignored by students of development. The changes that accompany an increase in the scale of a society are linked to the use of space within cities.

Effects of an increase in societal scale. As a society increases in scale, basic changes occur in its organization and structure. First, economic functions become increasingly differentiated. Second, organization and structure grow more complex. Third, a change occurs in the range and intensity of human relationships. These changes, which are closely interrelated, can be seen in many areas of American society today.

Economic differentiation. A good example is the changing organization of business and industry. As the scale of American society has increased, people and machines have been integrated into a complex system for the production and transportation of goods. Sophisticated communication and transportation technology has been crucial to this development. For example, members of an organization no longer need to be in face-to-face contact to coordinate their activities; they can communicate by telephone, fax, or computer even when they are separated by thousands of miles. Freed from many of the old spatial limitations, organizations have become more complex, and employees have become highly specialized in their skills. One result of these changes is an increase in the range and a decrease in the intensity of relationships among people in an organization. That is, people interact over greater distances, but their relationships are of an impersonal and superficial (secondary) nature.

For businesses to operate effectively and efficiently in such a high-scale society, they must depend on large numbers of people who are geographically widely dispersed. This pattern has come to characterize all of society. For example, throughout the country, one out of every six Americans is employed directly or indirectly in automobile production—extraction and refinement of raw materials, fabrication and assembly of automobiles, marketing and sales, servicing, road construction, insurance, and financing. To a degree, what happens to the automobile industry influences the economic well-being of every American.

This is especially true of the American economy in the 1990s. The domestic automobile industry is in decline. General Motors began the decade of the 1980s with control of a little over 50 percent of the domestic market. By 1990, its market share had dropped to 34 percent. Ford and Chrysler have done a little better, but the Japanese with their high-quality products now control 28 percent of our market. Japan's big three, Honda, Toyota, and Nissan, now manufacture cars or light trucks in plants in Ohio, Kentucky, Tennessee, and California, but many of the high-value-added components—electronics, engines, and transmissions—are manufactured in Japan or some other country and then assembled here. This nation's recent experience suggests that there is not only an interdependency within a nation but among nations on a global scale. The automobile and petroleum industries and grain producers are three of dozens of examples of this international interdependence.

Increased complexity. Other areas of society also are influenced by its changing scale. As a society's scale increases, so do the range and intensity of its communication flow. In high-scale societies, mass communication—television, radio, newspapers—can influence a whole nation's tastes, ideas, and values. In the United States and other countries, the growth of mass communication combined with the power of large, complex organizations has widened society's span of control over the individual.[5] The increasing sophistication of the computer has facilitated intrusion into people's personal lives by such organizations as the Internal Revenue Service, the FBI, and private credit bureaus. Increases in societal scale also have led to a loss of personal control over important choices that traditionally were individual decisions. The popular press provides numerous examples of parents who have been prevented by courts from rearing their children according to their deeply held religious or moral beliefs, terminally ill patients who have been kept alive against their will and farmers and small businessmen who have come increasingly under the control of regulatory agencies.

Changes in human relationships. Increasing scale has also changed the form and structure of the neighborhood and the family. Neighbors and neighborhoods no longer carry out many of their traditional functions. In the past, during times of family crisis—death or unemployment—neighbors would often pitch in to help a family through their time of need. Today many of these functions have been taken over by public agencies. Similarly, the family has lost a large part of its role in the education and rearing of children. A number of social programs even bypass the family altogether to give benefits directly to children or to protect a child from his or her family.

CHANGES IN USE OF SPACE

The preceding examples show how changes in the scale of society have brought about fundamental changes in the way society is organized and in the way individuals live. Urban ecologists have discovered that these social changes are reflected clearly in the use of social and physical space in cities.

Louis Wirth (1938), in his famous article "Urbanism as a Way of Life," discussed many of the changes then taking place in society. Wirth argued that increases in the size, density, and heterogeneity of America's urban populations had brought about these changes. As Table 8.1 shows, Wirth's research suggested that an increase in the size of a settlement beyond certain limits brings about a shift from primary to predominantly secondary relationships among its residents. Similarly, an increase in a population's heterogeneity leads members to depend increasingly on formal rather than informal means of social control. Wirth concluded that cities were the "prime mover" in the transformation of western society from "traditional-rural" to "urban-industrial."

TABLE 8.1 Louis Wirth's sociological definition of the city in relation to size, density, and heterogeneity

A SCHEMATIC VERSION

	The greater the number of people interacting, the greater the potential differentiation
	Dependence upon a greater number of people, lesser dependence on particular persons
Size An increase in the number of inhabitants of a settlement beyond a certain limit brings about changes in the relations of people and changes in the character of the community	Association with more people, knowledge of a smaller proportion, and of these, less intimate knowledge
	More secondary rather than primary contacts; that is, increase in contacts that are face to face, yet impersonal, superficial, transitory, and segmental
	More freedom from the personal and emotional control of intimate groups
	Association in a large number of groups, no individual allegiance to a single group
	Tendency to differentiation and specialization

TABLE 8.1 *(continued)*

A SCHEMATIC VERSION

Density Reinforces the effect of size in diversifying people and their activities, and in increasing the structural complexity of the society	Separation of residence from work place
	Functional specialization of areas—segregation of functions
	Segregation of people: city becomes a mosaic of social worlds
	Without common background and common activities, premium is placed on visual recognition: the uniform becomes symbolic of the role
	No common set of values, no common ethical system to sustain them; money tends to become measure of all things for which there are no common standards
Heterogeneity Cities are products of migration of peoples of diverse origin	Formal controls as opposed to informal controls. Necessity for adhering to predictable routines. Clock and the traffic signal symbolic of the basis of the social order
Heterogeneity of origin is matched by heterogeneity of occupations	Economic basis: mass production of goods, possible only with the standardization of processes and products
Differentiation and specialization reinforce heterogeneity	Standardization of goods and facilities in terms of the average
	Adjustment of educational, recreational, and cultural services to mass requirements In politics, success of mass appeals—growth of mass movements

---

Source: Reprinted from *Social Area Analysis: Theory, Illustrative Application and Computational Procedures,* by Eshref Shevky and Wendell Bell, with the permission of the publishers, Stanford University Press. Copyright © 1955 by the Board of Trustees of the Leland Stanford Junior University.

Shevky and Bell agreed with Wirth that size, density, and heterogeneity are important measures in describing the character of urban life. However, they disagreed with his conclusions about causality. To them, the qualities of urbanism that Wirth attributed to the influence of size, density, and heterogeneity were not limited to cities but were characteristic of the total society. Cities simply mirror changes taking place in the society at large. In other words, increases in the scale of society bring about changes in the nature of the society's productive activity, in the distribution of occupations in the labor force and in the composition and distribution of the society's population. These broad, society-wide changes ultimately are responsible for the emergence of a predominantly urban way of life. The United States is a high-scale, urban-industrial society. Even its small towns and villages reflect this fact. In a town of 10,000 people, the tastes, consumption patterns, and norms and values are urban in character. Neighbors, rather than talking over the back fence, communicate by telephone. Acts of delinquency may no longer be handled informally but by the police. The unemployed and retired residents of the community collect unemployment benefits or social security rather than depending on neighbors for financial assistance. The dress, manners, and even language of people reflect the character of the encompassing society. Most importantly, the community's financial well-being is tied inextricably to the national and, increasingly, to the world economy. Therefore, although the community is small in size, low in density, and relatively homogeneous in population, it has characteristics that are attributable to the high-scale society of which it is a part.

From their abstract theoretical arguments, Shevky and Bell moved to indexes that measure changes on the community level. Their presentation remained similar to the earlier work of Shevky and Williams, but it was framed in more general theoretical terms. Shevky and Bell's postulates about the changes brought about by an increase in the scale of society referred to change in the range and intensity of interpersonal relations, differentiation of economic functions, and increase in the complexity of the society's organization. Figure 8.4 shows how these changes are reflected in certain social trends.

Changing distribution of skills. The first trend Shevky and Bell identified is the changing distribution of skills in a society. As a society increases in scale, a fundamental change takes place in its system of stratification. For example, in the preindustrial city, members of the upper stratum—the governing elite—derived their station in life from inherited wealth, most of which was based in land ownership. As society increased in scale, the role of income-producing property was altered: Wealth derived from land ownership became less important than wealth derived from manufacturing and commerce. Today, with the growth of stock ownership of companies, ownership of a company is less important than one's position within the enterprise. The chairman of the board of AT&T does not own the company he is directing; the shareholders do. Inherited wealth continues to be important, but the skills of the working population are the basis of the complex organization of high-scale society. Occupations within such a society have been regrouped and have been organized into a hierarchy along levels of skill, income, and prestige. This regrouping of skills mirrors the way consumption items are produced and distributed. In high-scale societies, automation has reduced the need for low-skilled workers and has increased the demand for people with clerical, supervisory, and management skills.

As a result, the importance of a specific skill to the society is reflected in the prestige associated with it. Table 8.2 shows the ranking of occupations in the United States by their social prestige. The most prestigious occupation is U.S. Supreme Court Justice, followed by physician and scientist, and ending with the least prestigious, shoe shiner. In this high-scale society, no other single characteristic tells us more about the

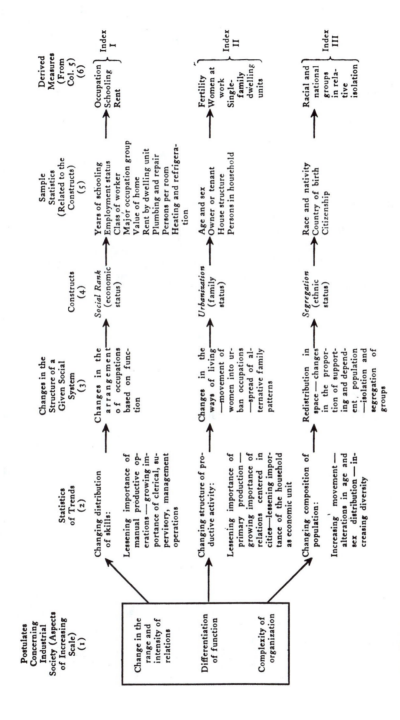

FIGURE 8.4 Steps in construct formation and index construction.

Source: Reprinted from *Social Area Analysis: Theory, Illustrative Application and Computational Procedures,* by Eshref Shevky and Wendell Bell, with the permission of the publishers, Stanford University Press. Copyright © 1955 by the Board of Trustees of the Leland Stanford Junior University.

TABLE 8.2 The prestige of selected occupations in the United States

OCCUPATION	1963 SCORE	1947 SCORE	OCCUPATION	1963 SCORE	1947 SCORE
U.S. Supreme Court Justice	94	96	Newspaper columnist	73	74
Physician	93	93	Policeman	72	67
Scientist	92	89	Radio announcer	70	75
State governor	91	93	Insurance agent	69	68
Cabinet member in the federal government	90	92	Carpenter	68	65
College professor	90	92	Manager of a small store in a city	67	69
U.S. representative in Congress	90	89	Local official of a labor union	67	62
Chemist	89	86	Mail carrier	66	66
Lawyer	89	86	Railroad conductor	66	67
Diplomat in U.S. foreign service	89	92	Traveling salesman for a wholesale concern	66	68
Dentist	88	86	Plumber	65	63
Architect	88	86	Automobile repairman	64	63
Psychologist	87	85	Barber	63	59
Minister	87	87	Machine operator in a factory	63	60
Member of the board of directors of a large corporation	87	86	Owner/operator of a lunch stand	63	62
Mayor of a large city	87	90	Corporal in the regular army	62	60
Priest	86	86	Truck driver	59	54
Civil engineer	86	84	Clerk in a store	56	58
Airline pilot	86	83	Lumberjack	55	53
Banker	85	88	Restaurant cook	55	54
Biologist	85	81	Singer in a nightclub	54	52
Sociologist	83	82	Filling-station attendant	51	52
Instructor in public schools	82	79	Dockworker	50	47
Captain in the regular army	82	80	Night watchman	50	47
Accountant for a large business	81	81	Coal miner	50	49
Owner of a business that employs about 100 people	80	82	Restaurant waiter	49	48
Musician in a symphony orchestra	78	81	Taxi driver	49	49
Author of novels	78	80	Farmhand	48	50
Economist	78	79	Janitor	48	44
Official of an international labor union	77	75	Bartender	48	44
Railroad engineer	76	77	Soda-fountain clerk	44	45
Electrician	76	73	Sharecropper	42	40
Trained machinist	75	73	Garbage collector	39	35
Farm owner and operator	74	76	Street sweeper	36	34
Undertaker	74	72	Shoe shiner	34	33

Source: Adapted from data presented in Robert Hodge, Paul Siegel, and Peter Rossi, "Occupational Prestige in the United States, 1925–63." *American Journal of Sociology* 60 (1964): 290. Reprinted by permission of the University of Chicago Press.

individual and his or her position in society than the person's occupation (Shevky and Bell, 1955, p. 9). Knowing a person's occupation permits one to predict with a high degree of accuracy the person's income and education.

Therefore, *social status,* as measured by the characteristic occupation, education, and rental expenses of a society's population, indicates the scale of the society under study. In a low-scale society where technology is low and the economic system relatively simple, few types of occupations are needed, and the overall skill level of the labor force is low. Moreover, because of the dominance of the elites in these societies, occupational prestige is not closely related to income and education. As the society's scale increases, the number and types of occupations increase, as does the general skill level of its labor force. As specific skills become functionally more important to a society, the level of education needed to acquire these skills increases, as does the reward for acquiring them.

Finally, changes on the societal level are manifested in the use of space within cities. Therefore, tracts high in social status have residents high in the measurable characteristics of occupational prestige, years of schooling, and rental expenses; tracts low in social status are low on all three variables.

Changes in the structure of productive activity. The second trend Shevky and Bell found that resulted from scale-related social changes is change in the structure of productive activity. As societies increase in scale, fewer people are needed in production. Today, because one American farmer can produce enough food to feed 54 other people, less than three percent of the labor force is employed in agricultural occupations. Because of automation, fewer workers are needed in other primary spheres of the economy, such as mining and forestry. These changes in the primary sector have led to rapid expansion of the secondary (manufacturing and industry) and tertiary (service) spheres of the economy. These economic activities require a centralized communication and transportation infrastructure that only an urban area can provide. Therefore, cities in high-scale societies assume a wider range and number of functions for the society as a whole: Shevky and Bell cited "co-ordination and control, service and promotion, and innovation" (1955, p. 12).

This transformation of productive activity affects all parts of society, but according to Shevky and Bell the family has borne the brunt of this change. In traditional agrarian or low-scale societies, the family carried out the functions of economic production, distribution, and consumption, but today, in high-scale societies, the family depends on other institutions for most of these functions.

The changing functions of the family have also changed the role of women in society. Freed from large numbers of children and obligations to kin, more women enter the labor force. Consequently, women have adopted different styles of life and ways of living in high-scale societies. Specifically, in low-scale societies with their extended family forms, an unmarried female of marriage age would live with her family until she married. Today, she would probably be labeled "strange" or "peculiar" if she did not leave home, find employment, and set up her own apartment after high school or college.

Because the nuclear family is often isolated with no ties to kin in the surrounding community, a myriad of life-styles are possible in high-scale societies for the single, the retiree, the young couple with children, the childless yuppies, DINKS (dual income, no children), and the single parent, and each life-style is accommodated by a different part of the city. Shevky and Bell's family status index uses measures of fertility, the number of women at work, and the number of single-family dwellings in a tract to mirror these broad changes in society. A tract low on the family status index would have few young children, many working women, and mostly apartment housing; tracts high on the family status index would have large numbers of small children, few working women, and predominantly single-family dwellings.

Changes in population composition. The third trend Shevky and Bell found related societal scale to changes in society's population composition. As a society increases in scale, the physical mobility of its population increases. This redistribution of a society's population over its territory is closely tied to changes in the distribution of skills and changes in the structure of productive activity. The major factor contributing to this mobility is the restructuring of productive activities. With the mechanization of agriculture, the demand for farm labor declines, and surplus labor migrates from the rural to the urban areas. Similar readjustment takes place within and between cities: As industry declines in one region, opportunities may expand in another, and workers can respond to these opportunities by moving. The growth of the Sunbelt is a recent example. The United States has one of the most mobile populations in the world. Roughly 20 percent of the population moves annually. This massive movement of people suggests that the labor force is closely tuned to the ebb and flow of the national economy.

Persons who migrate normally differ in important ways from the general population. Some migrants are compelled to move by "push" factors; that is, conditions where they have been living have become so bad that migration appears to be their only alternative. The "Famine Irish" who immigrated to this country in the nineteenth century were faced with the grim choice of starving in Ireland or leaving it. Recent examples include the large-scale immigration of Vietnamese to the United States with the fall of Saigon, the Cuban boat lift, Haitian immigration, and the massive migration of people from Central America. In general, migration that results from push factors is much less selective than migration due to pull factors. The young and the old, the skilled and the unskilled overcome the obstacles of migration because their survival or the quality of their lives depends on it.

Migration caused by "pull" factors is very selective. The migrants are normally younger with higher levels of education and training than the general population. They are drawn from an area because of greater opportunities elsewhere. Younger workers just entering the labor market are better off economically if they "shop around" for employment. If a local employer is unwilling to pay an adequate salary, the worker can increase or maximize the return on his or her investment in education and training by moving. Many factors may impinge on an individual's decision to move—the available information on destinations, the efficiency of the search, and the monetary and psychological costs of the move. Migration because of pull factors has been dominant in the United States for much of this century; thus, it has had a considerable effect on the composition of the cities' populations. It causes the percentage of the economically productive part of the population living in cities to increase and the percentage of dependent—the very young and old—to decrease.

The same forces that brought about the massive rural-to-urban migration in this country during the nineteenth and early twentieth centuries were at work in other countries as well. Most of these nations solved the resulting urban problems by exporting their surplus populations to such countries as the United States, Canada, New Zealand, and Australia. Since the United States began as a nation in 1776, more than 40 million Europeans have been added to its population.

The United States's first wave of immigrants, arriving before the Civil War, came from Northwestern Europe—Great Britain, Germany, Sweden, Norway, Denmark, Finland, Belgium, the Netherlands, France, and Switzerland. For the most part these immigrants have long been assimilated. The second wave of immigrants came much later, in the last quarter of the nineteenth and first quarter of the twentieth centuries. These people came predominantly from Southern and Eastern Europe, Poland, Hungary, Italy, the Balkan nations, and Russia. The second wave of immigrants, because they were predominantly Catholic or Jewish, rather than Protestant, with language and customs much different from those of other immigrant groups, were not assimilated as easily into society and formed very durable ethnic enclaves within many large cities. They lived together for mutual support, and they aided each other in learning the language and customs of this country. Rather than being exclusionary, such enclaves gave immigrants a means of adapting to a new culture.

More recently, rural-to-urban migrants' adaptation has followed a similar pattern. These migrants have also been transported to a foreign land—the city—where the customs and even the language are different. Blacks from the rural South migrating North often seek out friends and relatives in the cities to help find employment and housing. Prejudice and discrimination have prevented this group from moving out into other areas of the city, however. In most large cities, sizable ethnic and racial enclaves still exist as viable and dynamic subcommunities. The ethnic status index reflects the racial and national groups who live in relative isolation in cities. The ethnic groups included are, for the most part, Eastern and Southern Europeans. A census tract high on the ethnic status index has large numbers of blacks and foreign-born residents within its borders; tracts low on this index have few of these residents.

TESTING THE SOCIAL AREA MODEL

The most persistent criticism of social area analysis is directed to the validity of the indexes themselves.[6] First, are Shevky and Bell's three indexes—social status, family status, and ethnic status—adequate to account for the social differentiation among areas of the city? Second, do the variables used to calculate these indexes result in a single dimension unrelated to the other indexes as their originators claimed? In other words, if census tracts were ranked from highest to lowest on the family status index, would their order be different—and independent—from their rank by social status?

FACTOR ANALYSIS

To test the validity of the social area model, Bell (1955) used a mathematical technique known as factor analysis. Factor analysis identifies clusters of similarly related variables by sorting variables, identifying their underlying similarities, and summarizing them on a single factor or index score. In the multidimensional typologies discussed in Chapter 6, factor analysis was used in an exploratory fashion. Large numbers of variables were factored to identify the underlying characteristics of metropolitan areas. Shevky and Bell used factor analysis in a different way—to test their original hypothesis.

Shevky and Bell calculated a social status index by combining a census tract's scores on the variables of occupation, education, and rental expense. The family status index was calculated from the variables fertility ratio, number of women in the labor force, and percentage of single-family dwelling units in the tract. The ethnic status index was calculated from variables measuring the concentration of ethnics and blacks in census tracts. Bell reasoned that if the social area dimensions were valid, then the seven variables used to calculate the indexes, if factored, would yield a three-factor solution, each factor identifying a cluster of variables corresponding to the social area dimensions. Bell made 21 predictions on the factor solution he would expect if the social area analysis approach were valid. He predicted that the variables of occupation, education, and rent would be summarized by Factor I; Factor II would identify the variable cluster combining fertility ratio, women in the labor force, and single-family dwelling units; and Factor III would identify only one variable, segregation. (See Appendix A for a general discussion of factor analysis.)

BELL'S PREDICTIONS AND FINDINGS

Using factor analysis, Bell identified three clusters of variables (See Table 8.3.). Factor I identified a cluster of three variables: occupation (0.482), education (0.319), and rent (0.653). The remaining variables were not related to this factor as indicated by their low and insignificant loadings. Factor II identified a second cluster of three variables: fertility (0.562), women in the labor force (0.617), and single-family dwelling units (0.727). Again, the other variables had near-zero loadings. Factor III, interestingly, picked up two variables, segregation (0.576) and education (0.282), but the segregation variable has the highest loadings. The loading of the second variable, education, was not predicted by Bell.

By referring to Table 8.4, one can see that Bell made 21 predictions (A plus sign means a significant loading, zero an insignificant loading.), and that, in his factor analysis of Los Angeles's data, 20 of the 21 predictions were correct. Three factors were identified that corresponded to the three indexes developed theoretically by Shevky and Bell. Therefore, the three factors do appear to be both adequate and

TABLE 8.3 Bell's rotated factor matrix—Los Angeles, 1940.

	MEASURES	I	II	III
1	Occupation	(0.482)	0.193	-0.094
2	Education	(0.319)	-0.044	0.282
-3	Rent	(0.653)	-0.192	-0.189
4	Fertility	0.109	(0.562)	0.176
-5	WLF	0.148	(0.617)	-0.193
6	SFDU	-0.147	(0.727)	0.015
7	SEG	-0.109	0.004	(0.576)

I	Economic Status	WLF Women in the Labor Force
II	Family Status	SFDU Single-Family Dwelling Units
III	Ethnic Status	SEG Segregation

Source: Bell, W., "Economic, Family and Ethnic Status: An Empirical Test." *American Sociological Review* 20 (1955): p. 47. Reprinted with permission of The American Sociological Association.

necessary to account for the social differentiation of the social areas of Los Angeles. In other words, each index has been shown to measure a different thing. Bell's factor analysis of the 1940 census data for the San Francisco Bay Area had similar results.

Van Arsdol, Cammilleri, and Schmid (1958) replicated Bell's research on an additional ten regionally diverse United States cities.[7] The researchers concluded that the Shevky system had high generality for the cities included in their study, although minor variations were observed in the clustering of variables on the three factors.

TABLE 8.4 Bell's hypothesized factor matrix and the observed factor matrix—Los Angeles, 1940.

		PREDICTED			OBSERVED		
	MEASURES	I	II	III	I	II	III
1	Occupation	+	0	0	+	0	0
2	Education	+	0	0	+	0	+
-3	Rent	+	0	0	+	0	0
4	Fertility	0	+	0	0	+	0
-5	WLF	0	+	0	0	+	0
6	SFDU	0	+	0	0	+	0
7	SEG	0	0	+	0	0	+

I	Economic Status	WLF Women in the Labor Force
II	Family Status	SFDU Single-Family Dwelling Units
III	Ethnic Status	SEG Segregation
0	Small Factor Loadings	
+	Large Factor Loadings	

Source: Bell, W., "Economic, Family and Ethnic Status: An Empirical Test." *American Sociological Review* 20 (1955): p. 47. Reprinted with permission of The American Sociological Association.

STUDYING THE AIDS EPIDEMIC

Your place in society is defined in a number of ways. Your socioeconomic, ethnic, and family status define your position in that intangible thing we call the social structure, and where you live—your home and neighborhood—locks you into the physical structure of the city. The two interact in predictable ways, and you use your knowledge of the physical/social space of a city all the time. Let's say you meet a new person at a party. One of the first things you ask in the normal banter at a party is "What do you do?" "You don't happen to know so-and so?" and "Where do you live?" With answers from two or three simple questions along with the person's appearance, use of language, and props, all of us can come up with a fairly clear picture of where this person is in the social structure.

As we have seen throughout this text, human behavior does not occur at random but in fairly predictable ways because behavior is structured and our cities reflect this structure. The interaction between the structure of society and the structure of cities is used by social scientists to study a variety of human behavior; it can be seen clearly in the AIDS epidemic. We have all been bombarded by public health announcements that AIDS is a preventable sexually transmitted disease, and public health officials have known for almost a decade that certain groups—homosexual men, women who have had sexual relations with homosexual or bisexual men, hemophiliacs, children born to HIV-infected mothers, and intravenous drug users—are at particular risk. Since the disease is concentrated in particular groups, we should expect that the disease should be concentrated in specific parts of our cities. It is. Epidemiologists, sociologists who study epidemics, have mapped the distribution of AIDS victims in most American cities. In Los Angeles, for example, researchers found the reported AIDS cases are not evenly distributed across the city but are concentrated in a relatively small number of census tracts northwest of downtown Los Angeles and in Long Beach. Remember, if we know the census tracts where AIDS patients are concentrated, we also know the economic, ethnic, and family status characteristics of the area too. The federal government's Center for Disease Control (CDC) uses this critical information to follow the spread of HIV infection. They have also used this information to project the scope and size of HIV-infected individuals in this society.

There is also an insidious side of the spatial distribution of the AIDS epidemic. Health and life insurance carriers now regularly use zip codes to determine insurability. If your home address should happen to fall within one of the high-risk zip code neighborhoods, you won't get insurance. There are laws pending in California and New York which will make these business practices illegal.

SOCIAL AREA ANALYSIS AND BEHAVIOR

Other studies confirmed the general empirical validity of the Shevky and Bell indexes. However, a more practical question still remained: Is the social character of the subareas within a city, as defined by social, family, and ethnic characteristics, useful in predicting individual attitudes and behaviors? Shevky and Bell saw social area analysis not as an end in itself, but as a point of departure for other types of research. First, the authors saw the rigorous and systematic delineation of the subareas of a city as having great descriptive value for social scientists and city planners alike. Second, Shevky and Bell believed the use of the social area diagram could have practical benefits in providing a sampling frame for urban research. In other words, the type of behavior taking place in Social Area VII could differ in a predictable way from the behavior in Area III (Shevky and Bell, 1955, pp. 20–22).

A number of researchers subsequently used the social area diagram to study a wide variety of behavior, including voting behavior and neighboring.[8] Their results suggest that the social character of the local areas within a city, as defined by social, family, and ethnic status, is important in predicting individual attitudes and behavior, subcultural patterns, and social organization. Therefore, in terms of pragmatic social research, the indexes and social areas have validity.

TESTING THE SOCIAL AREA THEORY

Studies by Bell and others focused on the general empirical validity of the three social area indexes. The hypotheses tested were related to the validity of the indexes, not the general validity of the Shevky and Bell theory. Testing the theory's general validity requires examining the theoretical constructs defined in the theory. One possible test of the theory would be to determine whether the theoretical construct societal scale and the Shevky indexes correspond in a predicted way. Simply, changes in the scale of society should be reflected most clearly in the use of space within cities. Therefore, one could argue that for low-scale societies, the characteristics of social, family, and ethnic status are all closely interrelated, whereas in high-scale societies these characteristics separate into independent dimensions. The reason for these differences is the dominance of the extended family in low-scale societies. In such societies the extended family controls most aspects of life. Because more than two generations live together in one dwelling, the variety of life-styles that characterizes high-scale societies is lacking. In addition, family membership also determines one's social and ethnic status. Thus, family status alone provides an adequate basis for classifying subareas of cities in low-scale societies.

In factor analysis terms, if one were to factor the social area variables for a low-scale society, all the variables should cluster around a single factor reflecting the dominance of the institution of the family. In contrast, in high-scale societies one should find three clusters of variables, each cluster identified by the factors of social, family, and ethnic status.

Many studies have been completed to date on a variety of cities in societies at one end or the other of the development scale. High-scale societies studied include the United States, Canada, countries in Europe, New Zealand, and Australia.[9] Low-scale societies studied include India, Egypt, countries in Africa, and Puerto Rico.[10] The quality of data, the number of variables included in the study, the types of cities studied, and the factor technique employed by the researchers differed among the studies. In general, the social and family status factors appear to be the most sensitive to changing societal scale.

In high-scale societies, social and family status factors are independent of each other. The reason is that the family is no longer the dominant, all-encompassing institution that it once was. One's social status in adulthood can differ from the status of the family into which one is born. With the waning influence of the family, many life-styles and living arrangements are possible, and subareas of the city specialize to serve the needs of each group. As a result, one can have two areas of the city inhabited by people high on the social status dimension but different in their family status.

In contrast, the family is the dominant institution in low-scale societies, and this institution touches every aspect of life. The family and social status dimensions are interdependent. In these societies, one normally lives her or his entire life within the same extended family, and as a result there are few alternative life-styles. One's adult social status is normally the same as the family of origin. For these reasons, only one dimension—family status—is needed to rank the subareas in the cities of low-scale societies.

In sum, an enormous body of cross-cultural research has been completed in the past 25 years. This research provides general support for social area analysis, which has become a powerful analytical tool in understanding the close relationship between the form of a city and the nature of the encompassing society. In addition, through its judicious use we have gained a better understanding of present and future urban trends.

HEALTH CARE AND SOCIAL AREA ANALYSIS

Health care providers are second only to marketing firms in using geographical information systems for applied purposes. One group of health researchers has used social area analysis (SAA) to explore a variety of diseases. For a parent, the specter of sudden infant death syndrome (SIDS) is terrifying: You put your baby in the crib for a nap and return an hour later to find a dead child. Epidemiologists have identified a number of factors to identify at-risk babies—low birth weight, a family history of SIDS, illicit drug use by the mother, and so on. Recently, researchers have turned to SAA to explore the social environments in which SIDS deaths are clustered (Fulcomer et al., 1981).

Other health care officials have used SAA to identify the service or catchment areas of hospitals and emergency rooms. This information can be used to locate or expand services in specific high-demand areas of a city (Piasecki and Kamis-Gould, 1981; Pittman et al., 1981; Rosen and Goldsmith, 1981; Scottsamuel, 1977; Stobina et al., 1982; Struentin, 1971). Other health practitioners use SAA to study the distribution of rare diseases and the environmental factors that may have caused them (Goodman, 1981). Social area analysis is also a major tool of environmental health specialists who must separate social factors from environmental factors in assessing environmental links to disease.

FACTORIAL ECOLOGY

Today one of the most frequently used ecological approaches in the study of the internal structure of a city is *factorial ecology*. Actually the term *factorial ecology* refers to a number of different approaches in which factor analysis is used to study small areas (subareas) of cities. Factor analysis is a mathematical technique that summarizes in a small number of factors the underlying similarities in a large set of research data. In social area analysis, factor analysis is limited to seven variables that measure the social, family, racial, and ethnic characteristics of a city's subareas. Factorial ecology, in contrast, is a more general approach made possible in the 1960s as a result of improvements in computer technology. The major difference between the two approaches is that factorial ecology expands the number of variables used in the analysis of a city's subareas from seven to several dozen.

Both factorial ecology and social area analysis relate the structure and form of a city to the scale or level of development of the whole society. Therefore, the approaches can be applied to the cities of societies in both less and more developed countries. In addition, these approaches can be used to predict the changes that will occur in the internal structure of cities as societies undergo the development process.

Several problems are inherent in factorial ecology. The results of any factor analysis will vary according to the data used. The number and types of variables included in the analysis, the units of observation (census tracts vs. social planning areas, for example), the time span of the study, and the factorial model used all affect the results. One of the strengths of social area analysis is that the number and types of variables used, as well as other parameters, are similar from study to study, and, therefore, the results from one study can be compared with those of another. The same is not true of factorial ecology.

Although the number and mix of variables differ among studies, most work in factorial ecology has emphasized the population and housing characteristics of areas; few, if any, measures of the physical and mental characteristics of individuals have been used. In the United States most factorial ecology studies have focused on these two types of variables and have used census tracts as the unit of analysis; thus, they are generally comparable, unlike most studies of cities outside the United States.

STUDIES OF UNITED STATES CITIES

Michael White (1987) recently published an exhaustive study of the internal structure of American cities. In this work, he uses three tools commonly used in ecological research—factorial ecology, measures of segregation, and contour analysis—to provide a comprehensive analysis of 1980 census data for 21 American cities. In the study, White uses 14 variables in his factor analysis. Figure 8.5 is from his book; it shows the percentage of social diversity between census tracts explained by each factor in Atlanta, Boston, Indianapolis, and Seattle. In Atlanta, over 80 percent of the variation between census tracts on the 14 variables can be explained with the four factors: new

A. ATLANTA

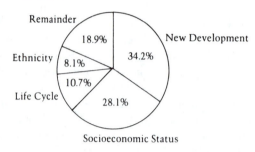

Socioeconomic Status

B. BOSTON

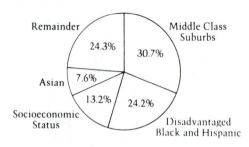

C. INDIANAPOLIS

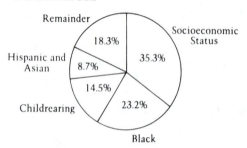

Black

D. SEATTLE

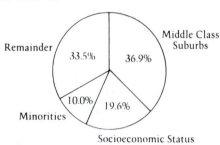

Socioeconomic Status

FIGURE 8.5 Distribution of Principal Components: 4 SMSAs

Source: White, M.J. (1987). *American Neighborhoods and Residential Differentitation.* New York: Russel Sage Foundation, Figure 3.1, p 68.

development, socioeconomic status, life cycle, and ethnicity. In Boston, 75 percent of the variance is explained by a similar group of factors: middle-class suburbs, disadvantaged blacks and Hispanics, socioeconomic status, and Asians. Similar variations can be found in all of the other cities in the sample. Why the variation? Remember, these cities differ in the nature of their local economies, topography, ethnic and racial mix, age, and region and the education, occupation, lifestyle, and life-cycle characteristics of their populations. But although some variation exists, three general factors can be found in each of the 21 cities—socioeconomic status, life cycle, and ethnicity. In the figure, a socioeconomic status factor is identified in the four cities; the factors, middle-class suburbs, child rearing, and life cycle reflect familism or life-cycle, and disadvantaged black and Hispanic, Asian, minorities, and ethnicity reflect the ethnic status differences found in all cities. Some variation should be expected. What is important is that these cities share common factors that reflect the scale of the larger society.

Cities aren't stagnant; they are always in the state of becoming, and, as we stated before, changes in the larger society will reflect themselves first and most clearly in the character and shape of our cities. Most people are aware of important changes in the family and the role of women in American society. The continued decline in fertility, the increased number of women in the labor force, the dramatic rise in single-parent-headed households, and the increasing size and diversity of the suburbs have weakened the traditional relationship between the suburbs and familism, and this is reflected in the morphology of cities.

Although an analysis of 1990 census data is years away, we know the profound changes in American society in the 1980s will be reflected in the organization of cities in the 1990s. Two patterns come to mind. First, one of the most massive shifts of wealth in the nation's history occurred in the 1980s: The upper 1 percent of our population has increased its control of our national income from 8.5 percent to 12.5 percent, while middle-class incomes have stagnated and the poor have lost ground. Consequently, for the first time in our nation's history, there has been a decline in the percentage of our population who own homes. Moreover, the size and type of housing being built in this society has changed dramatically in the past decade. Second, the shift of the American economy, from agriculture and manufacturing to service, and the emergence of an integrated world economy will modify the occupational structure of this society. These two forces will increase the importance of the socioeconomic dimension in describing the morphology of American cities.

Ethnic status will grow in importance. By 2020 black, Hispanic, Asian, and other minorities will make up more than half of our population. Race will continue to be the master status variable in this society, and the segregation of black Americans will continue to be the major social/physical cleavage in the landscape of our cites. Asian Americans are far less segregated, and in many cities they are associated with high socioeconomic areas of the city. As our newest immigrant group assimilates and their high incomes allow them to purchase homes anywhere in the metropolis, their importance in the ecological structure of the metropolis will decline. Hispanics, our largest ethnic group, will be second only to blacks in their importance in defining the ethnic status dimension.

Irrespective of the number of variables included in factorial studies of United States cities, four types of factors have been reported consistently in the literature. Three of the four dimensions correspond to those drawn from the social area analysis model.[11] First, almost all studies in factorial ecology have identified a single *socioeconomic* factor closely related to Shevky and Bell's social status index. Second, one or more *family status* or life-cycle factors normally are reported. In some research, one factor will identify housing types—single-family or apartment areas of a city—and other factors will identify a cluster of variables associated with the characteristics of the population at various stages of the life cycle. Third, factors related to the *mobility* or stability of a residential area's population, or the degree to which an area has undergone recent growth or decline in population, often have been reported. Fourth, most factorial studies have identified a factor associated with the *segregation* of blacks and recently immigrated ethnic people. Studies that have included large numbers of variables on specific ethnic groups (for example, the percentage of Italians or Poles) have identified up to five ethnic factors. In the South, a separate segregation factor has not always emerged because race and socioeconomic status are closely interrelated in that region.

STUDIES OF CITIES IN OTHER HIGH-SCALE SOCIETIES

Factorial studies of Canadian cities show that their structure is described generally by the same factors as the structure of cities in the United States.[12] Studies of Helsinki and Copenhagen have indicated similar factor structures.[13] Socioeconomic status, family status, and mobility factors were identified in Scandinavian cities; ethnicity factors, however, were not identified there, possibly because of the close interrelationship between ethnicity and socioeconomic status or the absence of large numbers of ethnic groups. The factor structure of English cities differs in significant ways from that found in other high-scale Western societies, but the differences are largely due to differences in the census measures and units of analysis employed there (Herbert, 1967; Robson, 1969).

Although the urban structure of the cities in high-scale Western societies can be described in terms of four main factors, one should not assume that socioeconomic status, family status, ethnic status, and mobility provide an unvarying framework for the study of all cities at all times. A detailed analysis of individual studies reveals significant differences in factor structures, reflecting the idiosyncratic characteristics of the society surrounding each city.

STUDIES OF CITIES IN LOW-SCALE SOCIETIES

In many low-scale non-Western societies, subarea data for cities are unavailable or of questionable quality. Egypt, India, and a few other nations do have adequate data, and factorial studies have shown an ecological structure quite different from Western cities. The major finding is that the social and family status factors are not separate but coalesce into a single factor often referred to as *lifestyle*. Additional factors identified in these studies relate to the concentration of large numbers of single males, ghettoized ethnic groups, and social disorganization. But the dominance of the lifestyle factor is the most distinguishing characteristic of these cities. Why the difference? Asked another way, what are the conditions in high-scale Western cities which lead to the separation of family and status factors? First, there must be a social ranking system based on achieved rather than ascribed status, and occupational prestige must be associated with other measures of social status—education and income. Moreover, social differences must be reflected in spatial differences between status groups: the types of housing they consume and their location in relationship to, say, the city's center. Second, differences in family type and level of fertility must vary independently of social status. In the United States, single heads of households and fertility are related to social rank, but the correlation is low. Third, the nuclear family must be the dominant family form, and one must be able to group families by their stage in the life cycle. Fourth, residential neighborhoods must exist which differ in housing type, and the housing and neighborhoods must appeal to families in different stages of the life cycle. Finally, there must be social as well as physical mobility. If any of these conditions are missing, one would expect the ecological structure of a city to differ from those found in Western cities. And they do (Abu-Lughod, 1969, 1971).

In the cities of most low-scale societies, few of these conditions are met. First, the family is still the dominant institution in society, and the family of one's birth has far-reaching effects on one's social status. As a result, one's social status is closely associated with one's family. More importantly, in societies in which the extended family is still dominant, all the stages of the life cycle are carried out in the same household. Housing built for families in a specific stage of the life cycle is rare; if it is built, it is randomly distributed across the city, making its detection difficult. Also consider that low-scale societies are in the early stages of the demographic transition process, and there is often little difference in the fertility and household size of families across social ranks. Also, in traditional, patriarchal families few women work outside the home. Consequently, the variables *single-family dwelling units* and *women in the labor force* have no meaning in these societies. Therefore, the ecological structure of these cities reflects the low level of social differentiation found in the larger society.

One of the first and most influential ecological studies of a low-scale society was conducted by Janet Abu-Lughod (1969, 1971) on Cairo, Egypt. The colonial history of Egypt and the high primacy of Cairo created complications because the city exhibited characteristics associated with cities in low- and high-scale societies. Dr. Abu-Lughod, however, found that the ecological structure of Cairo was relatively simple and only three dimensions—life-style, settlements of migrant male workers, and social pathology—were needed to describe the ecological structure of the city. The most important finding, however, was one factor—lifestyle—a combination of family and social status variables explained most of the differences between areas of the city.

Cairo, like many cities with a colonial history, displayed characteristics associated with both a modern and a preindustrial form. Areas high on the dominant lifestyle factor were associated with a modern, westernized life-style, including nontraditional roles for women, reduced family size, high incomes, servants, and specialized housing. Areas low on this dimension had low incomes, traditional family forms, and high fertility.

On this one factor, Abu-Lughod (1971) identified what she called the 13 cities of Cairo, each different in population, appearance, housing and commercial facilities, and even the dominant dress of the inhabitants. Three of the most important social areas were rural, traditional urban, and modern urban. The rural were urban villagers, recent migrants to the city, who had replicated their rural way of life in the heart of one of the largest cities in the Mideast. This impoverished group was housed on the outskirts of the city, not near the city's center, as is the case in high-scale societies.

The traditional urban population carried out life-styles long associated with the preindustrial city. Merchants and skilled artisans dominated the economic life of these communities. This was a male-dominated society in which women carried out traditional roles, had large families, and lived in permanent poverty. The members of this social area were concentrated in three older, inner-city slum areas.

The westernized populations lived in neighborhoods that Dr. Abu-Lughod labeled modern urban. Residents' life-style, education, roles, household size, fertility, and employment closely resembled the Westerners living in Cairo.

Like most societal processes, the change of a society from low to high scale is not a simple, linear one. A colleague of mine likens it to a drunk staggering back and forth but usually forward. The picture is further complicated by differences—cultural, social, historical, and natural resource—between societies which flavor the development process. These societal differences, combined with the physical legacy of cities, shape the present and determine the future ecology of cities. As noted in Chapter 3, there are powerful norming processes at work in the world today. The emergence of an integrated world economic and monetary system portends a world community in which the characteristics of high-scale societies will dominate the social organization of most societies. The link between the scale of a society and the ecological structure of its cities, however, is well established. The continuing interest of urban sociology will be to see if and how these societal changes manifest themselves in the structure of cities, regardless of their scale.

SUMMARY

This chapter is a detailed review of the origins and evolution of the ecological approaches known as social area analysis and factorial ecology. The dynamic nature of research on the city is demonstrated, beginning with the *natural area* concept introduced more than fifty years ago. This concept, central to the Chicago ecologists' theories of the city, was examined critically by other researchers and was found to have serious theoretical and empirical weaknesses. A more important criticism of the Chicago School was its narrow focus; the theories and models were based on isolated studies of large American cities. The researchers ignored the characteristics of the larger, encompassing society, which now are known to contribute to the form and structure of a society's cities.

Social area analysis is a logical extension of the Chicago School's pioneering work. Shevky, Williams, and Bell's work was not only based on but written in response to the works of the Chicago School. Their aim was to place the urbanization process in a broader perspective, linking the internal structure of the city to the nature and scale of the larger society. They envisioned a more practical use for their theory and methods, however—providing a sampling frame for the systematic examination of human behavior in the urban environment.

Factorial ecology is an extension of social area analysis. Though both approaches relate the internal structure of a city to the society at large, factorial ecology involves the use of many dozens of variables in addition to the seven used in social area analysis.

Used as a whole, the Shevky-Williams-Bell approach has been successful. These researchers used three indexes, social, family, and ethnic status, to classify social areas of cities. For more than twenty years of research, the social, family, and ethnic status factors, combined with a mobility factor, have provided the fundamental dimensions for the differentiation of subareas of cities in high-scale societies. In addition, key concepts such as societal scale have been validated by cross-cultural studies of city structure. The dialogue among researchers in this area has shown social area analysis to be very generalizable and relevant to the study of both high- and low-scale societies.

In this chapter the theoretical arguments associated with social area analysis and factorial ecology are presented. The major emphasis is on the close relationship between the structure of the society at large and the use of social space within cities. Chapter 9 explores how the various social areas of a city are organized into distinctive physical patterns.

NOTES

1. In a sense, Zorbaugh (1929) used this approach in his study of the Near North Side of Chicago, *The Gold Coast and the Slum,* reviewed in Chapter 1.

2. George A. Theodorson (1961) has collected many of the more important articles on the natural area concept in a reader, *Studies in Human Ecology.* It would also be valuable to read the early works of McKenzie (1923), Wirth (1928), Zorbaugh (1961), and Burgess (1964) on this topic. A complete citation for each of these works is given in the bibliography.

3. The major criticisms of the natural area concept are found in the works of Alihan (1964), Davie (1961), Form et al. (1954), and Hatt (1946). A complete citation for each of these works is given in the bibliography.

4. The terminology associated with the three social area indexes has changed over the years. For clarity, the terms *social status, family status,* and *ethnic status* are used in this text.

5. This theme is also explored in a number of popularly written books by Vance Packard, for example, *The Waste Makers* (New York: D. McKay Co., 1960) and *The Hidden Persuaders* (New York: D. McKay Co., 1957).

6. The major criticism of social area analysis is found in the works of the following researchers: Duncan (1955), Bell (1955), Hawley and Duncan (1957), and Bell and Greer (1963). Timms (1971), in his book *The Urban Mosaic,* provides a balanced presentation of the strengths and weaknesses of this approach.

7. Van Arsdol, Cammilleri, and Schmid (1958) replicated Bell's research on ten additional regionally diverse United States cities. Factoring six variables—all the original Shevky variables except rent—these researchers found that three factors were necessary to identify the clustering of variables in all ten cities. Moreover, in eight of the ten cities, the factors identified variable clusters identical to those predicted in Bell's earlier article. For two cities, Atlanta and Kansas City, the fertility variable was more highly correlated with the social status factor than with the family status factor. In these researchers' opinion this deviation was the result of these cities' relatively large proportion of blacks, combined with their location in or near the southern region of the United States. "This fact, combined especially with the unfavorable economic position of the Negroes, may indicate that the range of family forms in these cities, as described by the fertility measure, has not become dissociated from social rank" (Van Arsdol, 1958, p. 291). The researchers concluded that the Shevky system had high generality for the cities included in their study, although minor variations were observed in the clustering of variables on the three factors.

8. Articles by Bell (1959, 1961, 1965), Bell and Boat (1957), Bell and Force (1956a, 1956b), Greer (1956), Greer and Kube (1959), and Kaufman and Greer (1960) represent research in which the social area diagram is used to study neighboring and other types of behavior.

9. The following is a list of some of the more important factorial studies of cities in high-scale societies—United States cities: Anderson and Bean (1961), Anderson and Egelend (1961), Rees (1970), Van Arsdol et al. (1958); Canadian cities: Berry and Murdie (1969), Murdie

(1969), Schwirian and Matre (1974); cities in Europe: McElrath (1962), Herbert (1967), Petersen (1967), Robson (1969), Sweetser (1960, 1965); and cities in New Zealand and Australia: Timms (1971).

10.   The following is a list of some of the more important factorial studies of cities in low-scale societies—Indian cities: Berry and Rees (1969), Berry and Spodek (1971); Egyptian cities: Abu-Lugod (1969), Latif (1974); cities in Africa: Clignet and Sween (1969); and Puerto Rican cities: Schwirian and Smith (1974).

11.   The variable fertility in two of the ten cities in Van Arsdol's study rated more highly on social status than family status. Schwirian and Smith (1974), in their analysis of Puerto Rican data, reported a four- rather than three-factor solution in two of the three cities in their study. Similar patterns were found by Anderson and Bean in their analysis of data from Toledo, Ohio.

12.   The major factorial studies of Canadian cities were conducted by Murdie (1969), Berry and Murdie (1969), and Schwirian and Matre (1974).

13.   The major factorial studies of Scandinavian cities were conducted by Sweetser (1960, 1965) and Petersen (1967).

*T*HE USE OF SPACE WITHIN CITIES

INTRODUCTION

Chapter 8 provides an overview of the approaches known as social area analysis and factorial ecology that link the internal structure of the city to the form of the larger encompassing society. Shevky and Williams (1949) and Shevky and Bell (1955), however, were concerned with the nature of cities' social space, and they used social area analysis as a framework for behavioral studies. Although their books included detailed maps showing the location of various subareas in the cities of Los Angeles and San Francisco, the authors provided little explanation for why one subarea type was concentrated at a city's center and another at its periphery.

The maps do show that social differences existed between subareas and that social distance was reflected in the physical distance between them. In general, the farther apart two areas were on the social area diagram, the farther apart they also were physically. This finding is not new, for as long as humankind has lived in cities, groups have been physically separated. In the preindustrial city, an internal set of walls was erected to form wards and precincts, ghettoizing Jews and other groups. Walls are not erected in the cities of high-scale industrial societies, but barriers still exist. "Living on the wrong side of the tracks" is an example of a popular saying that reflects the existence of important symbolic barriers in modern cities. Moreover, physical distance alone limits the contact between groups, reinforcing the social barriers that Shevky, Williams, and Bell identified as social status, family status, and ethnic status.

Land use patterns are the result of millions of locational decisions made over the life of a city. These decisions are made by individuals, business, and industry in their search for space. Together these decisions determine the broad outline of land uses within a city. Moreover, past decisions determine present urban structure and hence the number of locations available for specific land uses. A decision made by a city's leaders in locating a dump, for example, will preclude the use of adjacent land for other purposes, say, expensive residences.

The purpose of this chapter is to explore the use of space within cities. In the first half of the chapter, the three classical theories of urban land usage—Burgess's concentric zone theory, Hoyt's sector theory, and Harris and Ullman's multiple nuclei theory are examined. Tests of the theories are reviewed—and a modified model of residential land use is presented. In the second half of the chapter, an alternative to the classical models is presented through the work of the political economist, David Harvey. Harvey's case study of Baltimore is used to show the relevance of this approach to the study of American cities.

CLASSICAL THEORIES OF URBAN LAND USAGE

For most of this century, students of the city have tried to develop a general theory that describes the distribution of people and activities across the urban landscape. Three of these theories, Burgess's Concentric Zone Theory, Hoyt's Sector Theory, and Harris and Ullman's Multiple Nuclei Theory have been the starting point for so much research that they are known as classical theories. Three points must be made before the classical theories of urban land usage are considered. First, each theory is based on ideal constructs or a set of generalizations about land use patterns. Because the theories were designed to be general and to describe patterns in many cities, no one city will fit the models perfectly. Secondly, the theories are based on patterns found in American cities, and they do not necessarily describe land use patterns of cities in other parts of the world. Finally, all three theories are concerned with ecological change or how the spatial patterns of cities change as the city grows.

BURGESS'S CONCENTRIC ZONE THEORY

The Burgess theory, first published in 1925, was one of the first attempts to describe and explain general urban land use patterns. Burgess posited that land uses in the modern city assume a pattern of concentric zones. These zones are ideal constructs, and no city will fit the pattern exactly because physical barriers such as rivers, ravines, and hills distort each zone. Major transportation lines further divide the zones into segments. A brief description of each zone in Figure 9.1 follows.

Zone I. Zone I, the central business district or CBD, is the zone that has the greatest accessibility from any point within the city. High accessibility means high demand for land, and only those activities that need a central location and can afford the high land costs are located here. Skyscrapers, department stores, hotels, restaurants,

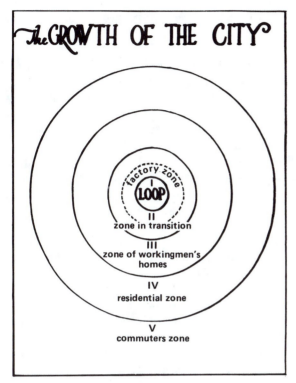

FIGURE 9.1 The Burgess concentric zone model.

Source: Park, R. E., Burgess, E., and McKenzie, R. *The City*. Chicago: The University of Chicago Press, p. 55, Chart II. Reprinted with permission of The University of Chicago Press.

theaters, and specialty stores occupy Zone I. It is an area of retail trade, office and service facilities, light manufacturing, and commercialized recreation.

Zone II. The zone surrounding the CBD is the zone of transition. Unlike the CBD, the zone of transition is residential, populated by groups lower on the socioeconomic scale, immigrants, and rural migrants. The Near North Side described in Zorbaugh's book *The Gold Coast and the Slum* was in this zone, and, except for a small enclave of wealthy people along Lake Michigan, the majority of its population lived in poverty. Interestingly, the land usage in this zone deviates from the type one would expect on the basis of the theory of rents. Theoretically, the proximity of this zone to the CBD should cause the rents in the area to be among the highest in the city; however, its rents are among the lowest. The problem with this explanation of land usage is that it assumes that competition is impersonal. In human societies competition is not entirely impersonal. It is limited by custom and the culture of the larger society. The character of the zone of transition is the result of investors speculating on the future use of the land in the area. Zone II is in the path of business and industrial expansion. Investors buy land in this zone hoping that business and industry will invade the area and buy their property at a much higher price. Because the investors expect the structures they own to be torn down, they have little incentive to pay for their upkeep. The result is blight, and slum conditions prevail as in the Near North Side studied by Zorbaugh. Since the 1920s the rundown housing in that area has been razed and the land has been incorporated into the Loop, the central business district of Chicago.

Zone III. The zone of working people's homes is superior in physical appearance to the zone of transition, but in size and quality its houses fall short of those in middle- and upper-class residential zones. Individuals who live in this zone have relatively low incomes. In comparison with wealthier families, they pay a larger part of their total budget for transportation costs. Low-income working families, therefore, tend to live near their place of employment in or near the CBD. This area also has a large number of neighborhoods made up of second-generation immigrants to the city, people who have escaped the slum conditions of the zone of transition but have not yet joined the ranks of the middle class.

Zone IV. The zone of middle-class homes is the residential area of clerical and managerial people, professionals, and owners of small businesses. The higher incomes of this group permit them to absorb higher transportation costs and therefore escape the noise and pollution of more centrally located housing.

Zone V. The commuter zone is the area of satellite towns and suburbs, sometimes 30 or 40 miles from the CBD in large cities, and normally acting as bedroom communities outside the political boundaries of the central city. In Burgess's time, these were the communities served by commuter railroads that carried commuters to the CBD for employment. Because of the high transportation costs, this area is beyond the reach of most residents of the city, and it is therefore limited mainly to the wealthy.

The dynamic nature of the theory. The foregoing description of the concentric zone theory shows how closely it is related to the theories of the Chicago School. The concentration of the dominant groups in the CBD is the key to the entire model. Burgess noted that as a city grows, so too does the demand for land at the city's center. Through time the CBD expands, invading the adjoining zone of transition, taking over this land for nonresidential usage. Because the property in this area is largely renter-occupied, landlords can turn over their property quickly by simply evicting their tenants. The people displaced by the invading land uses must have housing, so they move outward into Zone III, and the ecological process of invasion and succession continues outward toward the periphery of the city. Burgess, therefore, conceived his theory as a dynamic one that describes the process of city growth and differentiation over time. As a city grows, it must reorganize spatially, and, although transportation lines, rivers, and hills introduce distortions, Burgess believed that a concentric pattern of land usage was discernible in all cities in the United States.

The Burgess theory, although first introduced more than fifty years ago, still is of great interest to students of the city. Literally hundreds of articles have been written to interpret, test, and refute the model. Reasons for this interest are numerous, but among the most important is the fact that Burgess's theory, unlike the works of Hoyt (1939) and Harris and Ullman (1945), is part of a more general theory of the city. Equally important is the fact that it was the first to be published and thus provided a point of departure for other researchers. The theories of Hoyt and of Harris and Ullman were written in response to Burgess's theory.

HOYT'S SECTOR THEORY

The sector theory was an outgrowth of a study conducted by Homer Hoyt (1939) for the Federal Housing Administration during the Depression years of the 1930s. The study was an intensive analysis of the internal residential structure of 142 American cities, and it involved calculating the average residential rental values for each block of every city in the sample. By representing these data graphically on a map as in Figure 9.2, Hoyt found that the general spatial pattern of cities in the United States could be characterized best by sectors rather than concentric zones. Hoyt's study uncovered other important differences from the patterns suggested by the concentric zone theory. Industrial areas tended to develop along river valleys, waterways, and railroad lines rather than around the CBD. Moreover, a significant amount of this industry was at the city's periphery rather than near its center. In addition, the highest-rent areas were not in the last concentric zone but in one or more sectors usually on one side of the city. In general, these high-rent sectors were along the major axial transportation lines, which provided the residents easy access to the city's center. Low-rent areas, in contrast, tended to be more centrally located near the CBD, often in or directly opposite the highest-rent sectors. Middle-income rental areas were generally on either side of the highest rental areas or on the peripheries of low-rent residential sectors (Hoyt, 1939, pp. 72–76).

How Hoyt's theory operates. On the basis of these empirical findings Hoyt rejected the concentric zone theory and proposed his sector theory. As in the case of Burgess's work, Hoyt's theory was dynamic, designed to predict where the city will expand as it grows. The key to Hoyt's theory was the changing location of the city's dominant group—the wealthy. In his analysis of housing rents, Hoyt discovered that the high-rent neighborhoods of the city do not skip around at random in the process of movement—they follow a definite path in one or more sectors of the city (Hoyt, 1939, p. 76) (See Figure 9.2.). These sectors, besides being along established transportation lines, also tended to develop on high ground, free from the risk of floods, or along lake or river fronts not in use by industry. In addition, high-rent residential areas tended to expand toward open country and away from dead-end sections of the city. In general, high-rent areas initially are near the CBD, but as the CBD expands and industry grows, the wealthy abandon these neighborhoods to escape the noise, traffic, and pollution. As this group moves outward in the same sector toward the newer areas at the periphery of the city, their former homes are taken over by members of groups lower on the socioeconomic scale. These homes are often large, multistoried, and prohibitively expensive to maintain as single-family dwellings by anyone but the wealthy. However, they are easily converted into flats and apartments for rental purposes. Because of the age and character of this housing as well as its proximity to the CBD, it is typically investor-owned and is used as described in the discussion of the zone of transition (Hoyt, 1939, pp. 72–76).

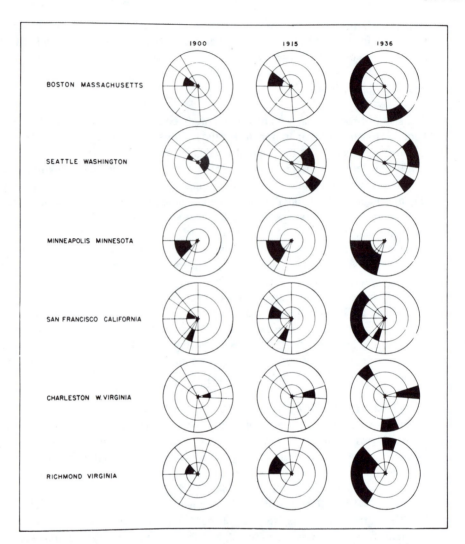

FIGURE 9.2 Shifts in location of fashionable residential areas in six American cities, 1900-1936 (fashionable residential areas indicated by solid black). This figure from Hoyt's original 1939 work shows the shift of high-rent areas at three time intervals. Note that in most cases high-rent districts have moved from the interior of a sector to its periphery. According to Hoyt, this movement was made necessary by the growth of commerce and industry in or adjacent to the central business district. It was made possible by an improved automobile technology.

Source: Hoyt, H., "The Structure and Growth of Residential Neighborhoods in American Cities." Washington, D.C.: Federal Housing Administration, 1939, p. 115, Figure 40.

According to the sector theory, the sorting of various income groups in the city occurs in the following way. The wealthy consume the best land—the high ground in the open areas of the city along major transportation lines. The low-income groups have few or no housing alternatives and either consume the obsolete housing of the wealthy or live in other undesirable areas. The largest group, the working and middle-income people, consume the remaining residential areas of the city. In sum, the theory predicts that cities will grow axially or in only one or two directions at any one time and that the location and movement of high-rent residential areas are the most important organizing principles in this growth. Hoyt's theory also reflects changes in automobile technology that made the rapid expansion of wealthy suburbs possible in the 1920s. A major weakness of this theory is that it largely ignores land uses other than residential, and it places undue emphasis on the economic characteristics of areas, ignoring other important factors such as the race and ethnicity of the residents.

HARRIS AND ULLMAN'S MULTIPLE NUCLEI THEORY

Harris and Ullman (1945) recognized the shortcomings of both the concentric zone and the sector theories and presented an alternative approach known as the multiple nuclei theory. This theory suggests that as a city grows it is differentiated into homogeneous areas or nuclei, but these nuclei do not necessarily form concentric zones or sectors. Harris and Ullman contended that in many cities land use patterns do not focus on a single center, the CBD, but on multiple centers (See Figure 9.3.). These centers include retail areas, warehousing districts, and concentrations of manufacturing and industry, as well as university, governmental, and financial centers. Moreover, these nuclei are often in different parts of the city.

Rules useful in predicting land use patterns. In the presentation of their theory, Harris and Ullman identified several rules useful in predicting the location and future growth of these specialized areas. First, certain activities require specialized facilities and concentrate where these facilities are available. Industry and manufacturing, for example, require transportation facilities, and these activities often locate near rail lines, waterways, and port facilities.

Second, similar activities benefit from being close to each other. Retailers locate near each other to increase the pedestrian traffic in front of their stores and hence their sales.

Third, certain dissimilar activities may be disadvantageous to each other. For example, because of its pollution, industry would be viewed as a nuisance to retailers and residents of high-income residential areas.

Finally, some activities could benefit from a centralized location in or near the CBD but cannot afford the rents. Warehousing or grocery wholesaling are examples of activities that require large structures and would benefit from a central location but must locate elsewhere because of the prohibitively high rents in the city's center (Harris and Ullman, 1945, pp. 9–12).

Harris and Ullman's theory has many of the same shortcomings as the preceding two. It is overly simplistic and does not state the limiting assumptions associated with the model. More importantly, Harris and Ullman are geographers and bring to this theory the unique focus of their discipline—the spatial distribution of specific land

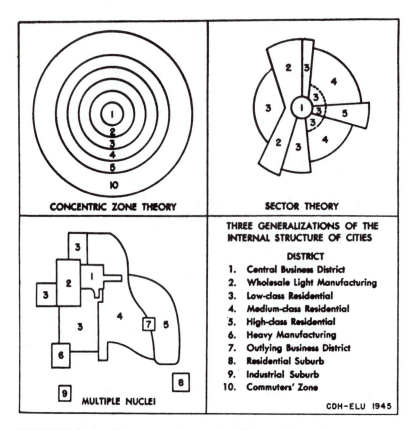

FIGURE 9.3 Concentric zone, sector, and multiple nuclei models.

Source: Reprinted from "The Nature of Cities" by C. D. Harris and E. L. Ullman in volume No. 242 of *The Annals of the Academy of Political and Social Science.* © Copyright 1945, p. 107, Figure 1.

uses. Little attention is given to the process that leads to the sorting of people and institutions across the urban landscape.

TESTS OF THE CLASSICAL THEORIES

The three theories of urban residential structure are an important part of sociological literature. Most introductory texts provide a synopsis of the theories, and urban texts devote at least a part of a chapter to them. The coverage is all the more remarkable when you consider the youngest of the three, the multiple nuclei theory, was published nearly a half-century ago. The reason for the coverage is the number of empirical studies spawned by the theories. All the theories have been tested, but the Burgess model has received the most scrutiny. This is due to the fact that it was the first published; it is the only one of the three tied to a more general theory of the city, and it is the easiest to analyze.

TESTS OF THE BURGESS MODEL

The Burgess model has been tested in two major ways. First, armed with ruler, compass, and map, researchers have tried to find the hypothetical zones or a systematic difference in concentric zones as one moves from the CBD to the periphery. Second, researchers have analyzed status gradients: the tendency for the housing and population characteristics to change as the distance from the CBD increases. Past studies show that many variables—density, socioeconomic status, housing costs, ethnicity—vary with distance. Few studies found sectoral variation. Less attention has been devoted to the multiple nuclei model.

In the minds of many urban researchers, an important breakthrough came in the early 1960s, when Anderson and Egeland (1961) combined social area analysis with the study of urban structure. The result was the creation of the convergence model. Anderson and Egeland found the distribution of census tracts by their social area dimensions corresponded to the hypothesized patterns of each of the theories. Family status characteristics were distributed in a concentric zone pattern, economic status by sectors, and ethnic and racial groups by a spatial pattern resembling multiple nuclei. Studies of U.S. and Canadian cities seem to confirm these findings.

There is a problem. The three major theories were published before World War II, and many of the empirical tests of the theories are one or two generations old. Much has changed since the end of World War II: the emergence of a service economy, the dominance of the automobile, the decline in the size of the American family, the growth of the suburbs, the decentralization of business and industry, the increase in the role of the federal government, and the growth of the Sunbelt, to name a few. Anyone living through these tumultuous times knows that cities today differ from those of the past. How can models conceptualized on cities of the 1920s, 1930s, and 1940s be relevant in the 1990s?

MICHAEL WHITE'S TEST OF THE MODEL

In my opinion, Michael White's *American Neighborhoods and Residential Differentiation* is the best work on urban structure published in the past decade. In his book, White explores the spatial structure of 21 American cities on 34 variables drawn from the 1980 census; he uses techniques ranging from simple mapping to factorial ecology. In his fifth chapter, "The Spatial Organization of the Metropolis," he tests the three models of residential structure. One technique is an analysis of the distribution of characteristics by distance from the CBD. Previous research has shown that distance from downtown is important in understanding a neighborhood's history and current status. To accomplish this, Professor White calculated the average value of social characteristics for four concentric zones around the CBDs of 21 metropolises. Each zone contained 25 percent of the metropolitan area's census tracts. If distance is related to a variable, the average score of the characteristic should increase or decrease as one moves from Zone 1 to Zone 4.

Analysis of Zones. Table 9.1 provides the distribution of population density by the four rings for 21 cities. Note the mean score at the bottom of each column. On average,

TABLE 9.1 Radial Distribution of Population Density*

METROPOLITAN AREA	RING 1	RING 2	RING 3	RING 4	RATIO	ETA
Allentown	7962	3829	2176	1699	0.21[†]	0.25[‡]
Amarillo	2679	3717	3028	1000	0.37	0.28
Atlanta	6202	2750	1470	242	0.04	0.26
Bangor	5531	750	383	790	0.14	0.69
Birmingham	4170	2956	1620	143	0.03	0.43
Boston	21937	13293	5278	2035	0.09	0.45
Chicago	22513	18700	7741	2865	0.13	0.40
Flint	6173	3952	1274	1067	0.17	0.44
Indianapolis	6234	3608	1880	840	0.13	0.48
Lexington	5390	3662	1060	224	0.04	0.59
New Bedford	12855	10702	8189	689	0.05	0.37
New Haven	9988	4498	1726	1361	0.14	0.60
New Orleans	15840	10828	6505	3412	0.22	0.37
Newark	24763	12144	4728	2305	0.09	0.55
St. Louis	7634	5624	2722	1099	0.14	0.40
Salt Lake City	5875	3849	2308	2477	0.42	0.26
San Antonio	6017	4737	2254	648	0.11	0.57
San Diego	7977	6054	4624	2260	0.28	0.29
Seattle	8401	4404	2680	1410	0.17	0.38
Sheboygan	4950	2849	112	93	0.02	0.70
Stockton	4452	3396	2998	1595	0.36	0.16
MEAN	9407	6014	3083	1345	0.16	0.42

*Persons per square mile.

[†]Ratio of Ring 4 to Ring 1.

[‡]Equals the value of eta^2 from an analysis of variance and characteristic on ring.

Source: White, M.J. (1987). *American Neighborhoods and Residential Differentiation.* New York: Russell Sage Foundation, Table 5.1, p 135.

the scores decline from 9407 persons per square mile in Ring 1, to 6014 in Ring 2, to 3083 in Ring 3, ending with only 1345 persons per square mile in Ring 4. There is an inverse relationship between distance and density: As distance increases, density decreases. The last column labeled *Eta* is a statistic that measures the differences between rings. The larger the value of eta^2, the greater the differences among the rings and the more important distance is in explaining the variance of a characteristic. In the case of density, the eta^2 is 0.42, or 42 percent of the variation in the cities' density scores is explained by the ring's distance from the CBD.

Findings from factorial studies have shown consistently the importance of socioeconomic status in describing the urban landscape. One measure of SES is occupational prestige, and a commonly used variable is the percentage of white-collar workers in a neighborhood's work force. If Burgess is correct, then white-collar employment should increase with distance. This is what White found in 19 of the 21 metropolitan areas in his study. In general, the percentage of white-collar workers increases between the first and second rings. Between the second and the third rings, the trend is still upward, but, between the third and the fourth rings, the trend is to decrease. Boston and New Bedford are the only cities in his sample where the white-collar percentage increases across all four rings. We know that there has been a massive movement of retailing, business, and manufacturing to the suburban ring in the past two decades, and this decentralization of business activity is reflected in the mix of status groups in the outermost ring. White-collar workers still commute to the CBD, but they also have jobs in nearby office parks; clerical workers drive to nearby suburban businesses; and high-wage blue-collar workers travel to nearby manufacturing or assembly plants.

The relationship is not as strong as that between distance and density, but distance from the CBD is still important in describing the spatial distribution of groups.

To this point, the Burgess theory is supported, but what about other characteristics? Table 9.2 provides a rank ordering of 34 characteristics for the 21 cities in the study. In general, the physical characteristics of a city—housing age, density, and dwelling type—are the most differentiated by ring. These characteristics are followed by income and poverty measures. In the middle range, there is a complex mixture of life cycle, ethnic, racial, and SES indicators. Found at the bottom of the scale are measures of mobility, several occupational and life-cycle measures; these characteristics are not distributed by zones. Therefore, the relationship between distance from downtown and population and housing characteristics remains an important factor in describing the urban landscape.

Contour Analysis. Statistics and numbers in tables are difficult to visualize, but Michael White employs a far more powerful technique to uncover the spatial structure of cities—contour analysis. Contour analysis creates a social topographical map of the metropolis. Instead of feet above sea level, the height of the contour line is the value of a characteristic at a particular spatial location. Hills drawn as dark and wide lines represent high scores on income, race, density, and other characteristics. Light, thin lines represent valleys, or low scores on a characteristic. You can see the patterns in Figure 9.4. Notice in Figure 9.4 the concentric zone pattern and how the light, thin lines representing low family income are replaced with darker lines representing higher average income as one move outward towards the periphery.

Michael White created over 400 of these contour maps for the 21 cities in the sample. He then examined the maps by eye and grouped them by pattern. White found that the physical features of the city—density, housing age, housing type, and quality—clearly resemble a zonal pattern. Socioeconomic measures varied. Characteristics like income, home value, rent, home ownership, and, to a lesser degree, education were described by concentric zones. Maps reflecting occupational prestige like professionals, clerical, and laborers were more complex. The maps for professionals tended to be nucleated, and those for blue-collar workers often showed a sectoral pattern.

Life-cycle characteristics did not vary much from neighborhood to neighborhood, but the patterns that did exist were zonal. Nucleated patterns were most often seen in the maps of racial and ethnic groups.

TABLE 9.2 Mean Radial ETA for Selected Characteristics

RATIO	MEAN RADIAL ETA^2	
Housing age	45.3*	Most differentiated
Children in single-parent families	43.7	zonally
Low income	43.5	
Population density	42.5	
Median household income	38.8	
Single-family dwellings	36.7	
Owner-occupied dwellings	36.7	
Poverty status	34.9	
Persons living alone	32.4	
High income	30.4	
Mean household income	30.1	
Median rent	27.8	
Recently built housing	27.4	
Home value	25.9	
Elderly	22.9	
Household size	22.5	
Black	22.5	
Foreign-born	21.8	
Support workers	21.3	
Deficient plumbing	21.3	
Education	20.2	
Journey to work (time)	19.8	
Per capita income	19.7	
Spanish origin	18.3	
Vacancy of housing	18.2	
Operative workers	17.3	
Children (0–17 years)	16.7	
Large households (5+ persons)	15.8	
Managerial workers	14.7	
Multifamily units (10+)	14.1	
Female labor force participation	13.3	
Householder's mobility	13.0	
Recent movers	11.7	
Fertility (children ever born to women age 44–49)	8.4	Least differentiated zonally

*Equals the value of eta^2 from an analysis of variance, characteristic on ring.

Source: White, M.J. (1987). *American Neighborhoods and Residential Differentiation.* New York: Russel Sage Foundation, Table 5.5, p. 140.

So what do all these results tell us? Which model is correct? It is clear that the physical characteristics of the metropolis, its housing stock, and population density are quite symmetrical and oriented around downtown, as predicted by the concentric zone theory. Generally, higher-income and status groups live farther from the center than low-income groups, again reflecting the importance of distance in the organizational structure of the city. Neighborhoods differ very little in their life-cycle characteristics regardless of where they are located except for household size, which is related to

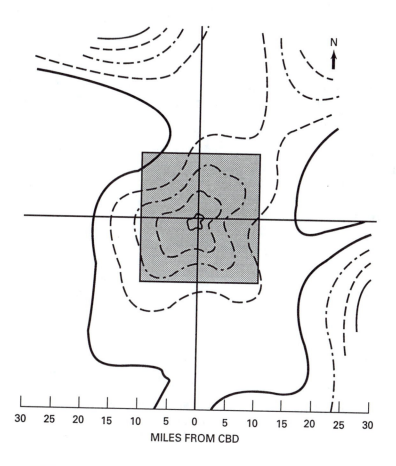

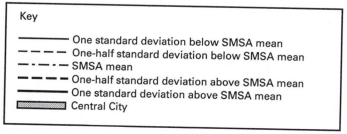

FIGURE 9.4 Contour for Household Income: Indianapolis, Indiana

Source: White, M.J. (1987). *American Neighborhoods and Residential Differentiation.* New York: Russel Sage Foundation, Figure 5.11, p. 144.

distance. Although racial and ethnic groups tend to live in enclaves, none of the models predict their location with any accuracy.

In brief, some characteristics were distributed in a nucleated pattern—high-status groups, minorities, and the poor—a few by sectors, but most by distance from the

CBD. Since we eliminated the sectoral model, the convergence model is also eliminated. If I were to pick a winner, it would be the Burgess model, but the choice isn't that simple.

Social scientists are just that, scientists, and the goal of science is to develop theories. During this century, students of the city attempted to create a general theory of the residential structure of the city. But cities in this society differ in age, size, history, economic base, population, and housing characteristics. Herein lies the problem. As we have already seen in earlier chapters of this text, age and when a city reaches metropolitan status profoundly influence the present character of the city. Streets are the dinosaurs of urban sociology. Even after cities like San Francisco, Chicago, Hiroshima and Nagasaki, Rotterdam, and Leningrad have been leveled by war or fire, they have been rebuilt along the old street pattern. Thus, the past constrains the present and shapes the future. This is why the Burgess theory created 75 years ago is still relevant to the physical structure of the city. Much of the old is still around; it may be underground, but it still shapes the present city. But even this 75-year pattern of a mono-nucleated city is being modified with the emergence of minicities (large malls and office complexes) on the outer belts of our largest cities.

The economic and social structure changes more rapidly than the physical city, and the Burgess model is less relevant to the social side of the metropolis. The number of women in the labor force, fertility, household size, income distribution, occupational structure, and the economy have changed dramatically in this century. The city is not free to accommodate these changes. The housing stock and the clustering of structures into neighborhoods, as well as the location of schools, hospitals, shopping, parks, and other facilities, continue to influence the locational decisions of families. Therefore, social changes must work themselves through the physical city. It takes generations to change these patterns. For this reason, the Burgess concentric zone model will continue to describe the physical characteristics of the city, as well as characteristics like income, housing expenditures, and housing size. The model, however, must be modified to accommodate other characteristics of the city, and this is precisely what Michael White does in the closing chapters of his book.

WHITE'S MODEL OF THE 21ST CENTURY CITY

Michael White (1987) provides a revised model to guide our understanding of the 21st-century city. The model, presented in Figure 9.5, is composed of seven elements.

CORE

The CBD remains the focus of the metropolis. Its functions may have changed over the years, but it still houses the major banks and financial institutions, government buildings, and corporate headquarters. The region's cultural and entertainment facilities—museums, libraries, galleries, zoos, botanical gardens, arenas, and stadiums—are also located here. Retailing has declined over the decades. A few large

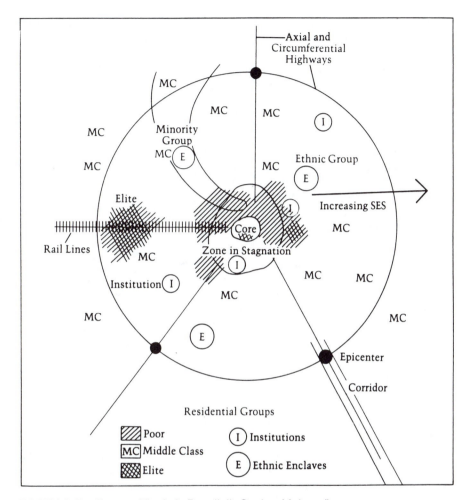

FIGURE 9.5 The Shape of the Late Twentieth-Century Metropolis

Source: White, M.J. (1987). *American Neighborhoods A-D Residential Differentiation.* New York: Russel Sage Foundation, Figure 7.1, p 237.

department stores keep their flagship stores downtown, but most retailing is out where the money is, in the suburbs. Those that remain are specialty stores catering to the daytime commuters.

ZONE OF STAGNATION

Burgess referred to the ring around the CBD as the zone of transition—an area composed of slums, flophouses, red light districts, warehouses, and industry. Back then, the area's dilapidated state was the result of speculation. Investors expected the CBD to expand into the zone, and it was the future, not the present, use of the property that determined its value. Property declined as owners reinvested their money elsewhere.

Burgess was wrong. The CBD did not expand outward, but upward in skyscrapers. Interstate highway construction, slum clearance, and the shifting of warehousing, trucking, and other activities to the suburbs dealt the zone additional blows. In older cities like Cleveland's flats district, warehouses and old factories have been converted into entertainment, shopping, and residential areas. Other cities attempted to convert old ethnic slums into upscale housing: Cincinnati's Over-the-Rhine District is an example of an attempt that failed. Younger cities without nineteenth-century buildings in the zone have abandoned the zone altogether. The first time I drove into Dallas, Tulsa, and Kansas City, I was struck by the vacant land that surrounds the CBD.

POCKETS OF POVERTY AND MINORITIES

Slums are areas that house people with no housing alternatives. In all the cities in his study, White (1987) found highly segregated groups of disadvantaged people living at the fringes of society: addicts, the homeless, and the underclass. They are often members of minorities, and one also finds a concentration of dysfunctional families here. Their surroundings reflect their status—deteriorated housing in blighted neighborhoods. Most of these areas were in the inner city; some skirted the zone of stagnation, but a few were located in older suburbs.

ELITE ENCLAVES

The poor have the fewest housing alternatives, and the wealthy the most. White found that the wealthy were able to insulate themselves from many of the problems of the metropolises, wherever they lived. Most of the elites lived in neighborhoods on the periphery, where expensive houses could be built on spacious lots. Many gilded neighborhoods still existed in the central cities of older, larger metropolises.

THE DIFFUSED MIDDLE CLASS

The largest area of the metropolis is occupied by the middle class. Spatially, this group is concentrated in neighborhoods on the outer edge of the central city extending to the metropolis's fringe. As you will see in our discussion of suburbs in Chapter 12, there has been a massive decentralization of business, retailing, and industry to the suburbs. The social diversity long associated with the central city now describes the suburbs. In the interior sections of the middle-class region, one finds older settled neighborhoods. These neighborhoods are in transition now that the original settlers have raised their children and are either dying off or moving to other dwellings. These older neighborhoods, often adjacent to the central city, are attracting the black middle class. Although African Americans have moved to the suburbs in large numbers in the past decade, they remain highly segregated.

As one moves farther out, one finds the suburban communities described in factorial ecology—married couples with small children living in single-family, detached homes, built on spacious lots. The suburbanization of business and industry means that other groups are present too. Working-class families live in more modest neighborhoods, the elderly live in garden apartments and retirement communities, singles in apartment complexes, and ethnics in their own enclaves. A nucleated pattern describes the location of these groups best.

INSTITUTIONAL ANCHORS AND PUBLIC SECTOR CONTROLS

Hospitals, universities, research and development centers, industrial parks, business and office centers, corporate headquarters, and other large institutional property holders exert an enormous influence over land use patterns and residential development. The location of a large mall complex, for example, can shape the growth of an entire side of a metropolis.

Institutional actors and other members of the growth machine can pressure city government to change zoning, lower taxes, and build highways and sewer and water systems. These concessions often benefit special interests, not nearby neighborhoods. Thus, the location of these activities is important in shaping the residential structure of the city.

EPICENTERS AND CORRIDORS

After World War II, people moved to the suburbs in unprecedented numbers, but, so too, did business and industry. Today, there are more business and industry in the suburbs than in central cities and rural areas.

One of the most distinguishing features of the evolving metropolis of the 21st century is the emergence of epicenters on the periphery of most metropolises. Usually located at the convergence of an outer belt and an axial super highway, epicenters provide a range of services that rivals the CBD—retailing, professional and office services, warehousing, and manufacturing.

Corridor development has also become a permanent feature of the emerging metropolis. Highways connecting the central city to the suburbs and beltways are a focus for intensive economic activity. This corridor development has become part of our vocabulary. How often have you heard the term "beltway bandits" to refer to the consulting firms along Washington, D.C.'s I-495? Silicon Valley near San Jose, Route 128 near Boston, and the Johnson Freeway in Dallas are other examples of corridor development. The residential structure, in turn, is affected because executives and other highly paid workers live nearby in high-status neighborhoods.

This is the White model. It reflects the latticework of high-speed highways built over the past 50 years at government expense which permits the diffusion of population and economic activity to the urban fringe. This transportation system created a new locational calculus, and as a result we have become a suburban nation: More people now live in suburbs than in central cities or rural areas. These technological innovations and federal policies, unforeseen by theorists 50 years ago, have shaped the city. But the research by White (1987) and many others shows that the city is still a giant sorting device that matches people with an appropriate residential environment. Most important, this sorting takes place in traditional ways (White, 1987, pp. 223–250). As we see in White's model, the patterns first identified by Burgess and others in the opening years of this century, with modifications, still describe the city.

POLITICAL ECONOMY: AN ALTERNATIVE APPROACH

In the earlier sections of this chapter we discussed the contributions of Robert Park and other members of the Chicago School to the understanding of the residential structure of the city. Park and his followers saw the city as the end product of ecological processes. The classical models of the city were also presented in an earlier section of the chapter. Regardless of the model, both groups accept the notion that the hidden hand of the market mediates land uses. From this perspective, the city is the accumulation of millions of individual decisions. In each decision people pursue their own self-interest, selecting a location that balances their financial resources with the qualities of a place. In Park's view, this impersonal process creates a natural economy of space; in the economists' view, market forces create an efficient distribution of land uses across the urban scape.

VIOLATION OF THE ASSUMPTIONS OF THE CLASSICAL MODELS

The problem with the classical schools is that they assume a level planning field. They picture a city where there is no interference by government in market operations and a world where social facts like race and ethnicity don't distort the bidding process. More importantly, they ignore the fact that the free competition for privately owned property occurs only in capitalism—an institution created through a political process. They also ignore the fact that certain groups distort the land bidding processes for their own ends through political and economic power.

In all fairness to these early theorists, the conditions in their time were closer to the market conditions they assumed in their models. Beginning in the first decades of this century, a number of political changes violated many of the assumptions of their work. These changes were (1) comprehensive zoning, which regulated land uses in cities; (2) the growth of the role of government in providing the city's infrastructure; (3) an increase in the role of the federal government in the operation of the housing market; and (4) urban renewal and redevelopment. These changes moved the allocation of land away from market to political processes.

ZONING

The first comprehensive zoning ordinance was adopted by New York City in 1916; in the decades that followed, zoning was adopted by almost every city in the United States. At present, Houston is the only major American city without a comprehensive zoning ordinance. In this same decade, Cincinnati adopted the first master plan that not only restricted land use but projected future use of undeveloped land as well. Master plans are also widely used in American cities.

Zoning ordinances change the rules on how land is priced. They freeze parts of the city to a specific land use and in a sense create monopolistic markets. By creating an artificial scarcity of land for a particular use, land costs rise. Changing a parcel from one land use to another is not determined by market forces, but rather by a political process. (Observe the cast of characters at a rezoning hearing sometime.) Money speaks. Citizens with economic clout often manipulate the political process to their own ends.

In short, one of the underlying assumptions of the classical models no longer exists. Disinterested market forces no longer determine land prices; local governments do. Planning commissions, rezoning boards, boards of adjustment, city councils, and planning departments are key actors in shaping the form of the metropolis.

INFRASTRUCTURE

Think of a city without the interstates, water and sewerage systems, schools, universities, police and fire stations, parks, stadiums, and the other facilities and services we take for granted. Think also of the role of government on all levels—local, state, and federal—in creating these facilities.

The connection between these investments and land values is clear. Undeveloped land with utilities is far more valuable than underdeveloped land without them. In this society, we do not tax away the marginal value created by public investments; this money goes to the landowner. Enormous profits can be made if you buy agricultural land with the knowledge that the city is planning to extend services your way. The plots of the movie *Chinatown* and its sequel, *Two Jakes,* explore corruption in Los Angeles and the attempt by members of the growth machine to control public expenditures for private gain. The fiction in movies reflects reality in most cities.

FEDERAL ROLE IN THE HOUSING MARKET

To the degree that government controls the housing market, it controls the sorting and movement of people within the city. The federal government has been involved in the housing market for most of this century. Its first foray was in the 1930s. During the Great Depression cities faced a housing crisis, and Washington provided money for public housing. During these same years, the federal government demonstrated the feasibility of 30-year, fixed-rate mortgages.

After the war, housing subsidizes were expanded to special groups through VA and FHA financing. These low-cost home financing programs, along with federal grants for highway and sewer and water systems, financed the massive suburbanization process in the 1950s and 1960s. There were other hidden subsidies. The most widely used was the provision in the tax law allowing home owners to deduct mortgage interest from their federal income taxes.

The invisible hand of the federal government also appears in the housing market. The Federal National Mortgage Association (Fannie May) and the Government

National Mortgage Association (Ginnie May) are quasi-government agencies that control the amount of money going into the housing sector. The Federal Reserve, by controlling interest rates, indirectly controls the cost of housing for millions of Americans. These benefits are not evenly distributed across our society. They are a welfare program for the middle class. Those who rent—the poor, minorities, recent immigrants, female-headed families, and increasingly the lower middle class—are shut out of these subsidy programs. Subsidies for other groups have dwindled in the 1980s. The homeless problem is attributable to the 80 percent reduction in federal programs for low-income housing during the Reagan years. Therefore, the federal government, through its control of housing financing along with its housing programs, exerts a powerful influence on the residential structure of the city.

URBAN RENEWAL AND URBAN REDEVELOPMENT

After World War II, this nation faced the most serious housing crisis in its history. During the Great Depression, there was little money for housing construction, and during the war money that would have normally gone into the housing market was diverted to the war effort. In an attempt to solve the mounting urban crisis, the Congress passed the Urban Redevelopment Law of 1949. The law allowed cities to create redevelopment authorities with the power of eminent domain to purchase, condemn, demolish, and resell property in blighted neighborhoods. Once large parcels of land were cleared, they were sold to private developers at bargain prices. Developers, in turn, agreed to redevelop the land at higher-intensity uses. The rationale was that intensive uses would increase property taxes and eventually repay the subsidy. There was a provision in the law that required those displaced by redevelopment to be provided safe and affordable housing. Since the federal government didn't provide funds for subsidized housing, those displaced were often given a moving allowance and then quickly forgotten.

The abuses by developers and the unintended consequences of urban redevelopment forced the federal government to abandon the program in the 1960s, but by then the self-reinforcing cycle of inner-city neighborhood decline was established. Critics often point to our lack of a coherent urban policy (or, for that matter, transportation, energy, housing, education, and population policies) as a major contributor to the problems of our cities.

The federal government role in city redevelopment has diminished, but decisions by local and state governments still shape the redevelopment of the city. Downtown commercial anchors, like stadiums and sports arenas, are usually built at government expense. Highway construction, mass transit, and subsidized housing are projects that use government power and money to shape the urban environment.

THE CITY AND THE POLITICAL ECONOMIST

Today, few urban sociologists accept the tenets of classical urban ecology. Rather, they believe that the allocation of space is the result of political and economic power. This alternative perspective is called *political economy;* we explored this approach in Chapter 1, "Theories of the City."

Political economists argue that the value of land is not determined by market forces alone, but in markets shaped by political forces like zoning, tax policies, banking regulations, and redevelopment plans. Some of these theorists focus attention on what they call collective consumption—government-financed roads, sewers and water systems, schools, office towers, hospitals, and the like. These investments benefit some groups and not others and shape urban residential structure.

Other political economists study the class interests of speculators–developers and the role of large institutions, like banking and lending institutions and government, in shaping the built environment.

The works of the leading political economists were summarized in Chapter 1 and are not repeated here. However, I want to present this alternative approach on residential structure by using a case study of Baltimore presented by Harvey in his book, *The Urbanization of Capital*. In this work, Harvey shows how a capitalistic housing market creates housing submarkets housing a specific class. Class segregation, Harvey argues, leads to the exploitation of these groups by landlords and speculator–developers through monopolistic rents.

Harvey argues that speculator–developers can profit only when they control the market system. He shows how this market has come to represent their interests and not those of consumers. Harvey states:

> In the United States, for example, speculator-developers usually realize monopoly rents through the manipulation of zoning decisions. Political control of suburban jurisdictions by speculator-developers is quite general in the United States [and] ... suburban jurisdictions provide one of the most effective of all cartel arrangements with respect to land-use decisions. Political corruption also plays a role which, in a market economy, can be viewed positively, since it frequently loosens up the supply of land from the excessive rigidities of land-use regulation by bureaucratic fiat. Without a certain minimum of governmental regulation and institutional support, however, the speculator-developer could not perform the vital function of promoter, coordinator and stabilizer of land-use change. Without such an interest group to perform these functions, suburban development would degenerate into chaos and finance capital would be forced to withdraw investment from the suburbanization process. The effect of such a withdrawal upon economic growth in general, effective demand in general, and the capitalist market system as a whole, of course, [would] be catastrophic.

Speculator–developers, therefore, play a crucial role in land-use decisions in a capitalist society. Moreover, the role of this group does not occur in a vacuum but in a complex institutional framework involving government and finance. First, there are bureaucratic regulations by federal, state, and local government. From the top, regulations by the Federal Housing Authority and other federal agencies work their way down to the local level. Federal regulations also affect large private institutions like banks and lending institutions, but these organizations also have their own agenda for pursuing profits. Thus, urban submarkets are created by these large public and private institutions; within this matrix landlords and speculator–developers operate.

Figure 9.6 shows the Baltimore submarkets created by the forces identified by Harvey. Each submarket houses a specific social class, and according to Harvey this status segregation allows landlords and speculator–developers to exploit these neighborhoods. Below is a description of a few of these submarkets.

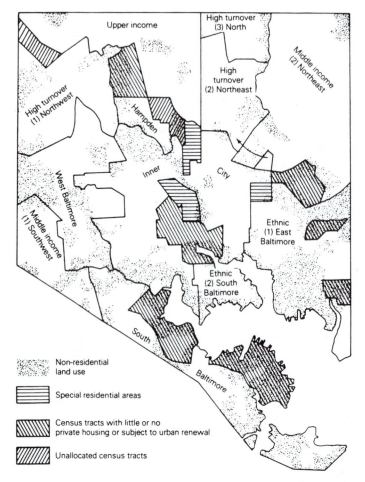

FIGURE 9.6 The Housing Submarkets of Baltimore City, 1970

Source: David Harvey. *The Urbanization of Capital: Studies in the History and Theory of Capitalist Urbanization.* Baltimore, MD: The Johns Hopkins University Press, 1985, Figure 10, p. 73.

The **inner city** houses low-income and predominantly black renters. In the 1970s, banks would not lend in these markets—a practice called *redlining*—and most sales were by private loans and cash transactions. There was little intervention by government, and conflict between landlords and tenants was endemic.

White ethnic neighborhoods were stable, housing was affordable, and most people owned their own homes. Most home sales were financed through locally controlled thrifts, and speculator–developers were kept out of the neighborhood. There was little conflict in these neighborhoods.

West Baltimore housed low- and moderate-income blacks. In the 1970s, banks and savings and loans did not make loans in West Baltimore, and few federally assisted programs operated there. Speculator–developers rose to fill the gap by selling the property they had redeveloped through land contracts. Land contracts are expensive to consumers but profitable to speculator–developers, and this financing became a source of conflict. Local residents resented this "black tax" on housing, and under government pressure land contracts were eventually replaced by other financing schemes.

In the 1970s, **areas of high turnover** were financed through FHA-insured mortgages. The FHA program, along with the enforcement of antidiscrimination laws, created a predominantly black, low-income housing market. Speculator–developers manipulated this market to create high turnover and high profits. Government corruption and poorly administered federal programs contributed to the problems in this submarket.

The **middle-income submarkets** of northeast and southwest Baltimore were owner-occupied areas of the city with housing financed though conventional bank and savings and loan loans. During the time of the study, the inner edges of these neighborhoods were undergoing racial change. Banks withdrew their financing, and speculators moved in to exploit the situation. More affluent submarkets used conventional financing, and their neighborhoods remained stable over the years.

Compare Harvey's map to White's in Figure 9.6, and notice the overlap. The geographical structure of the submarkets in Baltimore around 1970 formed the framework within which individual households made their housing choices. Most people made safe investments and chose already established neighborhoods. What few consumers realized was that the present residential structure represented the accumulated decision making of individuals, groups, and institutions over the preceding centuries.

To Harvey, the creation of urban structure is a continuous process, resulting from the conflicts and struggles of identifiable groups (speculator–developers, landlords, and consumers), public and private institutions, and market forces. Urban structure changes slowly, and in the short run it provides a more or less rigid framework in which different groups pursue their class interests. But according to Harvey, there must always be the realization that urban structure is the end product of capital's search for profit—a continuous process of identifiable groups competing in a city shaped by a capitalist mode of production.

It is an exciting time to be an urban sociologist because of the shift in paradigms in the discipline. Many of Harvey and Castell's ideas, thought radical only a generation ago, are now in the mainstream of urban sociology. In the decade to come, theorists will attempt a synthesis of the theories of ecology and political economy. This effort is underway. The work of Logan and Moltoch summarized in Chapter 1 is one such attempt.

SUMMARY

This chapter explores the social, economic, and ecological processes that lead to the sorting of groups and individuals into homogeneous subareas of cities. In the first half of the chapter, general theories of location are introduced to illustrate the operation of locational forces.

Of Burgess's concentric zone theory, Hoyt's sector theory, and Harris and Ullman's multiple nuclei theory, the Burgess theory was the first published and the most controversial. Burgess posits that land uses are distributed into homogeneous concentric zones through impersonal economic forces. Burgess's theory, however, focuses on the types of people who live in each zone; it has a sociological emphasis. Hoyt's theory, in contrast, is based on an analysis of housing rents; it is more empirical than theoretical and asserts that economic groups are distributed across a city in a sectoral pattern. Harris and Ullman's theory places less emphasis on groups and more emphasis on the distribution of business, industry, commerce, and other economic activities.

The Burgess and Hoyt theories are dynamic, stressing the principle that a city must reorganize spatially as it grows. Burgess points to an expanding CBD as the cause of urban change; to Hoyt, both an expanding CBD and a mobile upper class are causes of change. Harris and Ullman's theory, in contrast, is more static, emphasizing present rather than future land use patterns.

The Burgess theory has come under the greatest scrutiny by students of the city, and the model has been tested in two ways. Some researchers have tried to find the hypothetical zones, and others have analyzed status gradients or the tendency for urban characteristics to change as one moves from downtown to the suburban ring. A test of the models by Michael White from his benchmark work, *American Neighborhoods and Residential Differentiation,* was presented. In general, the study showed physical characteristics of a city, its housing stock and population density to be symmetrical and oriented around downtown, as predicted by the Burgess model. High income and status groups live farther from the center than low-income groups, reflecting the importance of distance in the organizational structure of the city. Neighborhoods differed little in the life-cycle characteristics with the exception of household size, which was distributed radially. None of the models predicted the location of racial and ethnic groups well. High-status groups, minorities, and the poor, however, were found to be segregated from one another in a nucleated pattern. Few patterns were found to be distributed by sectors. In general, distance from the central business district, as described by the Burgess model, is still important in the spatial structure of the American metropolis. The other models fared less well in the analysis.

The city of the past continues to affect the present and shape the future. This is why the physical characteristics of the city still conform to the Burgess model. Social characteristics fit the model less well but are still influenced by the physical city. An alternative to the classical model is presented: Michael White's model of the late twentieth century metropolis.

A summary of the works of political economists was presented as an alternative to the classical approach. Zoning, the role of government in providing the city's infrastructure, the role of the federal government in the operation of the housing market, and urban renewal and redevelopment violate the assumption of the classical theorists. The political economists assume that the allocation of space in the city is the result of political and economic power, not disinterested market forces. A case study on Baltimore by David Harvey was used to demonstrate how housing markets can be manipulated by speculator–developers for their own interests.

CHAPTER 10

THE SUBURBANIZATION PROCESS

INTRODUCTION

Suburb. There are few other concepts in the field of urban sociology which evoke as many contradictory images. To some Americans, the word *suburb* means dreams realized—home ownership, spacious lots, and a good environment to raise the kids. To other Americans, the word conjures up a far less flattering image—tacky bungalows lining treeless streets named Oak, Maple, and Chestnut. To baby-boomers like myself, there is no value judgement associated with the suburb; it was the way everybody lived. Since we were raised in the suburbs, we accepted as normal the child-oriented culture, the convenient schools and shopping, and the dependency on the automobile. Rarely did we visit the central city.

In reviewing the literature on the suburbs, one finds, along with these divergent images of the suburb, a complex overlay of myth and distortion. One myth is that suburbs are something new and unique to the twentieth century. The truth is that as long as there have been cities there have been suburbs. When the elite of the ancient city of Ur wearied of the noise and filth of the city, they retired to their suburban villas. Archaeologists also have found evidence of a suburban region around Rome, Athens, and other ancient cities—again for the benefit of the wealthy. As early as 1820, the U.S. census evoked the category, suburb, to describe the urban development which had taken place on the outskirts of our largest cities. By the census of 1890, most of the nation's large cities had well-developed suburban rings. But the most telling of all census dates are 1890, 1920, and 1970. In 1890, the census bureau could no longer trace a frontier land, and we had become a nation which spanned an entire continent. In

1920, the census bureau reported that more people lived in cities than in rural areas—we had become an urban society. In 1970, the census bureau reported more Americans lived in suburbs than in central cities or in rural areas—we had become a nation of suburbs.

Defined broadly as that area outside the central city but within the boundaries of the Metropolitan Statistical Area, suburbs now hold 102 million of our nation's quarter-billion population (U.S. Bureau of the Census, 1984). Suburbs are not new; the image of the romantic and bucolic suburb has a European rather than an American origin, but America's suburbs share four characteristics that make them unique in the world. Americans live in suburban areas that are far from their place of work, in homes that they own, which are built in the center of yards that are enormous by world standards and which are surrounded by other households of the same social class. Therefore, low population density, home ownership, homogeneous residential social status, and journey-to-work are the elements which make America's suburbs unique.

The process of suburbanization has been studied for most of this century, yet it is still poorly understood. A review of the literature on the suburb shows that at times suburbanization has been viewed as the solution to and at other times the cause of urban ills. For example, as early as 1905, the sociologist Charles Zueblin declared, "The future belongs not to the city but to the suburb." In a little more than fifty years, the process framed as a solution to urban problems was redefined as a problem itself. In the 1950s, authors like Reisman (1958) voiced the concern that the movement of the middle class and their skills and money to the suburbs was draining the vitality from central cities and aggravating the problems of poverty and racism.

In the past three decades, a new generation of sociologists has begun to study suburbs, and they are questioning the images of the suburb developed in the past. They ask: Are suburbs a new phenomenon, or do they represent the normal fringe development of a city? Are the images of the suburb as the bastion of the well-educated, white, affluent middle class and the central city as the home of the poor, uneducated, and minorities correct? Are suburbs all alike, or are there different suburban types? Does suburban growth intensify the political, social, and economic problems of the central cities, or is this a myth? Are the needs of women, the elderly, and minorities met in the suburbs? These questions are addressed in this chapter. The goal of this discussion is to separate the myth of the suburban process from the reality by studying the suburbanization process in the broad perspective of the metropolitan area as a whole.

THE CHANGING IMAGE OF THE SUBURB

Our image of the suburb has changed dramatically over the past century. Once considered a process that would solve urban ills, suburbanization was later thought to contribute to them. This shift in attitude can be explained by changes in the perceived nature of cities and changes in the social and intellectual biases of the researchers conducting suburban studies.

THE SUBURBAN IMAGE OF THE 1920s

Harlan Douglas published one of the first comprehensive books on the suburb in 1925, *The Suburban Trend*. In this work suburbs were viewed positively. To Douglas, the suburbs represented the early states of development of an exciting new urban form—an area that combined the amenities of the city with the low density of the countryside, a place that brought together the best of both worlds. Douglas was writing during a period of history when many of the negative byproducts of industrialization and urbanization were manifesting themselves in cities. The filth and squalor, as well as the crime, political corruption, and social disorganization, found in cities suggested to him that a new urban form was needed. The suburb was thought to be the place where the traditional forms of social control could be brought to bear on these evils. Such an attitude is not surprising. Douglas and many of the other urban researchers of his era had been raised in small towns and rural areas. These were the social forms with which they were most familiar and in which they placed the greatest hope.

THE SUBURBAN IMAGE IN THE 1950s

Ironically, a little more than twenty-five years after the publication of *The Suburban Trend*, the process framed as a solution to urban problems was redefined as a problem itself. After World War II, liberalized lending policies of the Federal Housing Authority (FHA) and the Veterans Administration (VA) made suburban housing affordable to working- and middle-class people. The explosive growth of fringe areas of cities in the decade ending in 1960 led many students of the city to worry about the future of American civic culture. Reisman voices these sentiments in an article written in 1958:

> The city [before World War II] represented the division and specialization not only of labor but of attitude and opinion; by discovering like-minded people in the city, one developed a new style, a new little magazine, a new architecture. The city, that is, provided a "critical mass" which made possible new combinations—criminal and fantastic ones as well as stimulating and productive ones. Today, however, with the continual loss to the suburbs of the elite and the enterprising, the cities remain huge enough for juveniles to form delinquent subcultures; but will our cities be able to continue to support cultural and educational activities at a level appropriate to our abundant economy (p. 382)?

Reisman was part of a new generation of sociologists whose background was not in the countryside but in the great cities. These people were accustomed to the noise, filth, and social disorganization of the city but appreciated its diversity and complexity. Rather than focusing on the negative aspects of urban life, they saw the city as a vital element of American culture. Their work is the basis of the present image of the suburb—single-family homes, crabgrass-free lawns, picture windows, familism, station wagons, backyard barbecues, and neighborliness. Suburbanization meant not only more spacious living but a more gracious lifestyle.

This group was aware that suburbs had existed around the nation's largest cities since the nineteenth century. This group, however, believed suburban growth in the post-World War II period was a unique phenomenon because of rate and magnitude of the growth. Moreover, this group viewed suburban growth as negatively affecting city life in many ways. First, these critics argued that as the middle and upper classes moved to the suburbs, the city would be deprived of its traditional leadership. Second, as these groups moved outward, leaving behind the poor, the old, and the minorities, the problems of poverty and racism in the city would become worse. Third, these critics suggested that the movement of the middle class to the suburbs would cause an erosion of the tax base, and that cities would have fewer financial resources with which to solve their problems. Finally, these sociologists suggested that the financial plight of cities was worsened by suburbanites' practice of living on the city's fringe in politically autonomous communities but working at the city's center, consuming city services but not paying for them. In this sense, the poor in the central city were viewed as subsidizing the affluent in the suburban ring.

These authors also directed their criticism to the structure and lifestyle of the suburbs. Planners argued that suburbs squandered the nation's resources. Because of their low density, suburbs consumed large amounts of land in housing construction. Normally built on a modified grid pattern, they used water, sewer, gas, road, and electrical systems inefficiently. Socially, they were viewed as negatively affecting both men and women—the housewife isolated in the "Cape Cod" with the children by day was ignored at night by the breadwinner exhausted from commuting to the city. Thus, the critics thought the modern suburban lifestyle was unique and inevitably transformed the character of suburbanites.[1]

THE SUBURBAN IMAGE IN THE DECADES THAT FOLLOWED

In the decades that followed, other generations of sociologists began to study the suburbs and to question the prevailing image of suburban life. Scott Greer (1962) in the early 1960s was among the first to interject a cautionary note into the central city–suburban debate. He pointed out that suburbia, in the strictest sense, is only an artifact of the static boundary lines of the central cities. Most new construction takes place outside a city's boundaries because undeveloped land is unavailable in central locations. In addition, Greer noted that the population attributes used by Reisman and others in the 1950s to characterize suburbs (white, middle-class, and familistic) are shared by people living in many of the central city's neighborhoods (1962, pp. 82–85).

In the 30 years since Greer's cautionary remarks, two generations of urban sociologists have explored the suburbanization process. Many of these researchers were raised in the suburbs, and their backgrounds shaped their outlook just as other generations were shaped by theirs. These newer cohorts, however, benefited from hindsight, and by testing the work of others achieved greater objectivity in their research.[2]

THE SUBURBANIZATION PROCESS IN HISTORICAL PERSPECTIVE

As we have seen, in the field of urban sociology a new generation of researchers has built on the work of the past to create a better understanding of suburbanization. This same process is underway in urban history. By far the most important recent history on suburbia is Kenneth T. Jackson's award-winning book, *Crabgrass Frontier: The Suburbanization of the United States,* published in 1985.[3] Housing is one of the most telling artifacts of culture; the theme woven throughout the work is that the way we have chosen to house our people is a reflection of our national character. Jackson argues that the suburbs that ring all our cities reflect our values and preferences—values and preferences that we as a people have always shared. Since colonial time, Americans have preferred detached dwellings to row houses, owning to renting, and rural to urban life. The suburbs represent a confluence of these values along with other technological and political factors. First, new building technology, especially the balloon or stick-built house, lowered the skill level of the labor needed to build homes and thus lowered housing costs. Second, changing transportation technology affected suburbanization. Walking distances determined the size, density, and character of our earliest cities. In the nineteenth and twentieth centuries, a series of transportation innovations—the horse-drawn omnibus and the horse-drawn trolley, then the electrified trolley, and finally the automobile—revolutionized accessibility and cost of land. Third, this nation's abundant resources, especially plentiful land and cheap energy, made suburbs as we know them possible. Finally, there is the often overlooked role of the federal government, whose innovative financing and massive subsidies made suburbanization possible.

According to Jackson, these factors led to the creation of a suburban form unique in the world. The majority of middle- and upper-income Americans live in single-family, detached suburban homes, built in the center of lots that are enormous by international standards and which are located far from one's place of business. The following section traces suburban development from 1800 to the present.[4]

EARLY SUBURBANIZATION—THE COLONIAL PERIOD TO 1890

With the exception of a few years in the 1970s, cities have grown faster than rural areas since 1820, and suburbanization has always been a part of this process. As early as the 1760s, suburbs could be found around major cities like Boston and Philadelphia. These were not the suburbs we know today but a mixture of rural, village, and urban life. Many of these communities provided country homes for the wealthy, but other activities too noxious for the nearby cities—for example, soap making and tanning, along with farming and village life—were found side by side in the urban fringe.

Traditionally, historians and urban sociologists assumed that the fringe simply responded to changes in the central city. Transportation innovation, for instance, might make the fringe more accessible and ripe for development. Henry Binford, in his book on the early suburbs of Boston, found this not to be the case. In the early 1800s,

Binford found suburban entrepreneurs building toll roads, canals, bridges, docks, factories, and warehouses to foster economic development and draw Boston's citizens to their newly platted subdivisions. These early suburbs, therefore, did not simply react but played an active role in their development. More often than not, it was Boston that responded to the capital improvements made in suburban communities.

EFFECTS OF PRIMITIVE TRANSPORTATION TECHNOLOGY

During the years 1800–1890, the United States was undergoing the early stages of the Industrial Revolution. In fact, by 1890 several American cities had become very large. Chicago had grown to 1.1 million, and New York to 1.5 million. Although large, these cities were quite compact. Transportation technology was primitive, and the cost of moving goods and people was very high. In short, transportation technology defined the geographic possibilities of American cities. Because of their dependency on humans and horses as sources of power, cities like Chicago and New York had a radius of densely built-up areas of only four and six miles, respectively (McKelvey, 1963, pp. 35–60; Jackson, 1985).

The limitations imposed on cities by primitive transportation technology affected many other aspects of life. Weber (viz., 1963), writing in this period, remarked with alarm on the appalling congestion of cities. High density combined with the lack of elementary sanitation led to dreadful levels of mortality during the more or less regular epidemics of cholera, typhus, influenza, and other diseases. The visitations of these diseases to New York City can be seen clearly in the graph in Figure 10.1. Note the extreme fluctuations in the graph during most of the nineteenth century and the decline and flatness of the curve in the twentieth century. Public health measures, especially the chlorination of drinking water, greatly influenced this mortality decline, but the lowering of density levels (decongestion) was also an important factor (Rosenberg, 1962).

INTERNAL STRUCTURE OF CITIES

The internal structure of cities was shaped by transportation technology. In the early stages of the Industrial Revolution, only the wealthy and the small middle class could afford a ride on the omnibus or horsecar. Most people lived either in the building where they worked or within a short walking distance of their place of employment. Transportation, therefore, did not permit much spatial separation between social classes. Then, as today, the wealthy could absorb the costs of transportation, and many of them lived in the suburbs or satellite towns serviced by steam railroads. Only a small minority of a city's population could afford to commute; therefore, the railroad had little impact on the spatial structure of the city. The horse-drawn trolley, or horsecar, was a common means of urban transport, but only the middle and upper classes who could afford the fares escaped to other parts of the city. In general, the wealthy, the poor, the artisan, and the factory worker lived near one another and near the factories, wharves, and offices of the city (Warner, 1962).

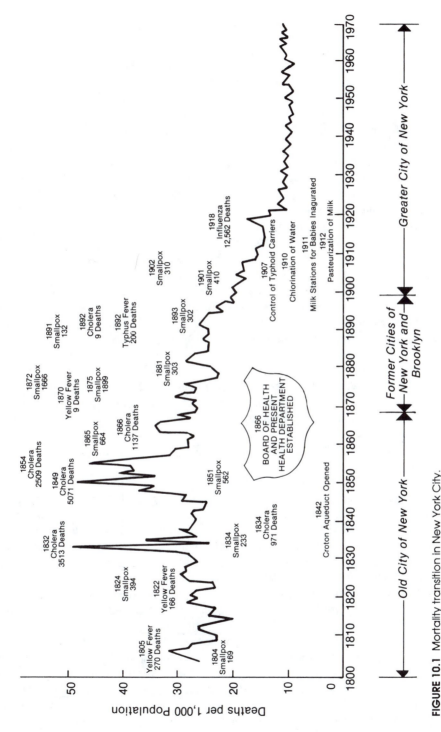

FIGURE 10.1 Mortality transition in New York City.

Source: New York City Department of Health, *Summary of Vital Statistics, 1965: The City of New York.* New York: City Department of Health, 1965.

1890–WORLD WAR I

Before 1890, residential cities were built primarily within the limits of horsepower. This limitation combined with the spectacular growth rates of cities like Chicago and New York led to severe congestion. In 1888, the diffusion of cities' populations was made possible by a technological innovation—the electric streetcar.

The introduction of the electric streetcar on the Richmond Union Passenger Railway in 1888 was so successful that within three years more than 175 systems were in operation in the United States. In 1890, 60 percent of all street railways (by mileage) were operated by horses; by 1902, this figure had dropped to one percent even though the street railway mileage in this country had more than doubled (Tobin, 1976, p. 99). This new and efficient form of transportation lengthened the radius of the densely built-up areas of cities like Boston and Chicago to ten miles.

The United States during the decade ending in 1900 was growing at a rate of 1.3 million persons per year, and most of this growth was centered in cities. New York grew from 1.5 million to 3.5 million inhabitants, and Chicago from 1.1 to 1.7 million. Similar growth rates characterized many other cities in the heartland region of the United States. As these cities grew, so did their suburbs. Warner (1962), in his analysis of the streetcar's impact on Boston's suburban development, gives an estimate of the effect of this new transportation form on population diffusion. In 1850, one of every four Bostonians lived in suburbs; by 1900, more than one-third were suburbanites. Boston's population had grown by fourfold between 1850 and 1900, but the population in its suburbs was six times as large in 1900 as in 1850. This pattern was shared by many American cities. The electric streetcar enabled urban populations to spread out and dramatically reduced residential densities.

INFLUENCE OF STREETCAR TECHNOLOGY

Transportation technology greatly influenced the physical form of cities. Pedestrian cities were usually circular because any place on the periphery could be reached from the center by foot or horse in about the same time. Streetcars, in contrast, ran on rails that were expensive to build and maintain, and they were economically feasible only if they were built between points of ridership demand. Initially, streetcar lines were built to connect the central business district with outlying satellite towns eight to ten miles from a city's center. During the early years of a line's operation, the trolleys would travel outside a densely settled city and pass through several miles of undeveloped farmland before reaching their destination. These satellite communities provided the necessary ridership to justify the lines' initial construction. Through time the undeveloped land between the city and satellite was settled in a pattern prescribed by the transportation technology.

The satellite towns had come into existence originally because of the steam locomotive. Because their economics of operation demanded that a string of cars be pulled, steam engines were not suited to schedules requiring frequent stops. As a result, large expanses of undeveloped land extended between a city and its satellites. Homes in the satellite towns were clustered around a small retail center dominated by the railway station, within easy walking distance. The streetcar, in contrast, was not only based on a more efficient power source—electricity—but was quiet and fast. Cars could be run separately or in tandem, depending on ridership demand. Because power could be applied uniformly to the wheels, frequent stops were possible. Therefore, because of the streetcar's speed and its ability to make frequent stops, residential construction could occur on land adjacent to the line between a city and its satellite towns.

In general, the new streetcar technology led to the emergence of the following spatial pattern. Initially, streetcar lines radiated from a city's center in a pattern resembling the spokes of a wheel. Housing construction in the city's undeveloped fringe was limited to areas within easy walking distance of a trolley stop; the stops were frequent and more or less uniformly spaced along the entire line. Through time, the city changed from a circular pedestrian form to a star-shaped form made up of a densely populated core and appendages of streetcar suburbs. The areas between the built-up streetcar corridors were largely undeveloped; they were inaccessible because of the limitation of this form of transportation technology (Warner, 1962; Ward, 1964).

GROWTH OF SUBURBS

This new transportation technology permitted a much-needed decongestion of American cities. For example, Baltimore grew by 10 percent between 1900 and 1910, but its suburbs grew by 45 percent; Chicago grew by 29 percent, and the area surrounding the city grew by 88 percent; Los Angeles tripled in size during the decade, but its suburbs grew by 533 percent. Many of the nation's cities, especially in the Northeast, underwent similar suburban growth (Tobin, 1976, p. 100).

INTERNAL STRUCTURE OF CITIES

Another and equally important change in the nature of cities resulted from the electrified streetcar—the spatial differentiation of cities according to their social area dimensions. As discussed in preceding chapters, groups that differ in socioeconomic, racial, and ethnic character have always been separated from one another in cities, but primitive technology kept these groups in relatively close proximity to one another. The internal structure of the American city was transformed between 1890 and World War I by several interrelated trends. First, the metamorphosis of society from rural-agrarian to urban-industrial was completed by 1920. This increase in the scale of society was accompanied by changes in the social structure, especially in the percentage of society considered middle class. Second, industrialization brought about more efficient exploitation of natural resources, greater per capita wealth and housing, and other amenities previously impossible to provide. Third, transportation technology permitted the interaction of these two trends and thus led to the greater spatial and functional differentiation of the cities. Therefore, in the quarter of a century ending with the opening years of World War I, American cities were transformed from a preindustrial to a modern metropolitan form.

Suburbanization during this period primarily benefited the middle class, and the city and its fringe began to differ in its social, family, and ethnic characteristics.

Although the suburbanized fringe was predominantly middle class, the housing in the area was graded into price and style groupings. The populations in these suburbs were differentiated spatially by income and occupational characteristics. Cities changed in turn, and, by the start of World War I, American cities were spatially more complex; social distance between groups was reflected in greater physical distance between them, and subareas of the city could be identified by the social area analysis dimensions—a pattern associated with high-scale societies (Warner, 1962).

WORLD WAR I–WORLD WAR II

It is difficult to define specific periods for any process, but in this analysis dates that correspond to cataclysmic national events are used for good reason. During war, resources that normally would go into housing construction and other areas of the economy are diverted to the war effort. In postwar periods, a nation must undergo major economic and social readjustments as industry shifts from war production and millions of men and women leave the military service and join the civilian work force. In the post-World War I years, this readjustment included the most rapid expansion of suburbs that had ever occurred in America. In the 1920s, for example, central cities grew at a rate of 19.4 percent, from 29 million to more than 34 million people, while suburban areas grew by 39.2 percent, from 11 million to more than 15 million inhabitants. This development was nationwide in scope—suburbs grew faster than central cities in 70 percent of all United States metropolitan districts. Tobin (1976), commenting on this suburban growth, writes:

> Many cities experienced rates of suburban growth that would never again be equaled in these urban areas. The central city of Boston grew by 4%, the suburbs by 20%. Cleveland showed a 12% population increase, while its suburbs grew by 125%. New York gained over 1.5 million inhabitants between 1920 and 1930, some 23%, even as the suburbs gained 400,000 persons, a growth of 67%. Saint Louis grew by 5% while the population of the suburbs increased by 107%. (p. 103)

Suburbanization slowed dramatically during the Depression, but the metropolitan growth that did occur followed the patterns established during the previous decade, "with new residential construction primarily taking place in the suburbs" (Tobin, 1976, p. 104).

EFFECTS OF AUTOMOBILE TECHNOLOGY

This large-scale suburbanization occurred simultaneously with the widespread adoption of the automobile. The undeveloped areas between the streetcar corridors in the city's fringe finally were accessible by means of this transportation innovation. The automobile during this period first competed with and then began to displace the streetcar as the dominant form of urban transportation. The reasons were varied, but cost was a major factor. After World War I, mass production lowered the unit cost of the automobile into the price range of the middle class. Cars also became more reliable and convenient. By the 1920s, the electric starter had replaced hand cranks, and technical improvements reduced the number of breakdowns that had so often plagued the automobile a few years earlier. Also, more gas stations and garages had been built, and more mechanics had been trained to keep the machines running.

The automobile was readily adopted by an urban population that disliked public carriers. "Mass transit was characterized by crowding, discomfort and inconvenience.... streetcars remained crowded and dirty, routes were fixed, service was irregular and unpleasant social intermingling persisted" (Tobin, 1976, p. 101). The private automobile enabled the owner to avoid all these problems and provided other benefits as well. It was a multipurpose vehicle that could be used for commuting, recreation, and shopping. Moreover, it gave the owner a high degree of mobility and access to a more varied choice of goods and services, while at the same time providing privacy and segregation from undesirable groups. Most important was the fact that the automobile was fast and comfortable and permitted the owner to schedule his or her activities at will (Tobin, 1976, p. 10).

The automobile became dominant in this period as the major form of intraurban transportation in the United States. Although rates of adoption differed among cities, figures for St. Louis indicate how rapidly this shift from public to private transportation occurred. "In 1916, 83% of the persons entering the central business district of Saint Louis came by streetcar, with 17% coming in automobiles. By 1937, 45% used cars, 12% buses and 27% streetcar" (Tobin, 1976, p. 105). Even earlier, in both Kansas City and Washington, D.C., the majority of persons entering central business districts used the automobile.

POST-WORLD WAR II

In terms of sheer numbers, the post-World War II period was the decade of the greatest suburban expansion in United States history. Most of this suburbanization was based on no other transportation than cars, trucks, and buses. An indication of this dependency is reflected in the number of registered motor vehicles. In 1945, about 25 million motor vehicles were registered in the United States; by 1973, this number had grown to more than 100 million vehicles (Tobin, 1976). It would be wrong to suggest that the automobile and other motor vehicles were solely responsible for this suburban development, however. Cars, trucks, and buses permitted the low-density development of retail, manufacturing, and residential areas in the urban fringe, and thus transportation technology set the broad parameters within which this expansion could take place. Changes in other spheres of society, however, determined how metropolitan areas would develop within these limits.

Specifically, in the post-World War II period several interrelated changes took place in American society in terms of the ecological complex. In population the so-called "baby boom" between 1945 and 1958 generated demands for housing that simply could not be met in the existing housing market. Because little housing construction had taken place during the Depression years and World War II, the nation was faced with a critical housing shortage.

Organizationally, the federal government through the FHA and VA housing programs made long-term, low-down-payment mortgage money available for the first time. These model programs were copied by savings and lending institutions that provided 20-year loans to the general public for the first time. Previously, the purchase of a home had required a large down payment and a loan period of only four or five years. These changes made home ownership a reality to many socioeconomic groups previously priced out of the housing market. The new mortgage availability also permitted the building of the nation's first mass-produced suburbs, suburbs of hundreds and, in some cases, thousands of homes with a standard floor plan and architecture.

Environmentally, the central areas of many older, industrial cities were undesirable in several respects. First, the housing was old and lacked the modern conveniences that the middle class had come to expect in a suburban home. In the city of Cleveland, for example, the average age of a home was 45 years in 1960. Second, the pollution from industry and the high density made a central-city location undesirable in some cities. Third, in many cities the only available land was in the fringe (Schwab, 1976).

Technology affected many aspects of urban life, especially the workplace. A revolution in the technological level of American industry in the post-World War II period enabled fewer workers to produce larger outputs of goods and services, which in turn created higher per capita income. This income provided the additional capital necessary for the rapid expansion of the urban fringe (Jackson, 1985).

SUBURBAN DEVELOPMENT IN THE 1970s AND 1980s

In the past two decades, a process of consolidation and social and economic integration has been underway in the urban fringe (Marshall and Stahura, 1986). The massive decentralization of people and businesses in the post-World War II period created a set of unique problems, and new urban forms emerged to solve these problems. One of the most important is the suburban minicity. According to Peter Muller (1981), a suburban minicity is a major concentration of retailing, employment, entertainment, and other activities formerly found only in the central business district. Usually, a suburban minicity will have at its center a large regional shopping center and on its periphery smaller shopping centers, and retail strips will develop. Over time, office buildings, apartment buildings, hotels, restaurants, and other facilities spring up to take advantage of the large number of consumers drawn to the area. Minicities often have retirement communities, medical complexes, entertainment facilities, and wholesale and professional activities nearby. Many of these minicities have become so large that they have come to rival the CBD.

Peter Muller describes one of these minicities, King of Prussia, Pennsylvania, located 20 miles northwest of Philadelphia (see Figure 10.2).

At the nucleus of the complex is King of Prussia Plaza, the metropolitan area's second largest superregional shopping mall, which contains 1.8 million square feet of selling space, six major department stores...and 200 smaller shops. Distributed about the vicinity within a 5-minute drive of the mall are dozens of highway-oriented retail facilities, including two community shopping centers; one of the region's largest industrial park complexes (over 750 acres), containing the plants and warehouses of Western Electric, GM-Chevrolet, Sears, Borg-Warner, Philco-Ford, three major pharmaceutical manufacturers, and 30 smaller companies; one of General Electric's leading research and manufacturing facilities; a variety of office parks and buildings...the Valley Forge Music Fair, a year-round theater offering top-name entertainers weekly; five first-run cinemas; at least a dozen fine restaurants; one of the area's best known cabarets; numerous superior quality high- and low-rise apartment complexes; and six large motor hotels (198, p. 193).

King of Prussia is not an isolated example; most of our major metropolitan areas have similar complexes. Tri-county near Cincinnati, the Galleria in Dallas and Houston, and the minicities that have developed around the nation's major airports—Harts Field in Atlanta and O'Hare International in Chicago—bear testimony to the emergence of the minicity as a new urban form in the history of our suburban development. Unfortunately, as Muller points out, minicities are seldom planned, so the different activity centers are built without concern for the rest of the center. Since there is no coordination of activities, the consumer must drive from one place to another.

Suburbanization in this society is a complex interaction of the factors. Technology, especially in transportation, set the broad limits for what the city could become. The manner in which the city changed within these limits depended on other spheres in the metropolitan and national system. Suburbanization in the post-World War II period differed from that of early eras in the rate of growth, but not in the kind of growth. In all likelihood, it was the rate of suburban growth combined with the new affluence of society that led Reisman and others to view this growth as something new and unique to the American experience. Since the 1970s, the minicity has emerged as a spatial form that integrates and gives focus to a process that has often been described as amorphous. But what does the past tell us of the future? There are a number of interrelated factors that suggest the rate of suburbanization—which has declined dramatically since the late 1950s—will continue to decline (Denowitz, 1984; Edmonston and Guterbock, 1984). Certain factors—the rising cost of energy, the escalating cost of land, environmental concerns, rising interest rates, rising cost of housing (an end to building innovation), changes in federal policy that reflect the austerity budgets in the post-Reagan era, and the changing structure of the American family, especially the dominance of smaller, two-wage-earner and single-headed families—will slow and eventually bring into equilibrium the expansion of the urban fringe. The consolidation and social and economic integration of the fringe will continue, and these processes are the ones that urban sociologists will study in the decades to come.

THE SUBURBANIZATION OF PEOPLE AND NEARLY EVERYTHING ELSE

SUBURBANIZATION DEFINED

The concept of suburbanization is largely ambiguous and ill-defined. Douglas defined the suburb as "the belt of population which lives under distinctly roomier conditions than is the average lot of city people, but under distinctively more crowded conditions

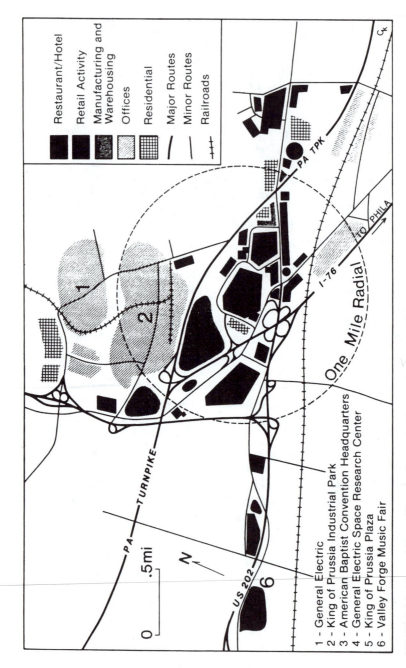

FIGURE 10.2 Map of King of Prussia, Pennsylvania, a suburban minicity.

Legend:
- Restaurant/Hotel
- Retail Activity
- Manufacturing and Warehousing
- Offices
- Residential
- Major Routes
- Minor Routes
- Railroads

1 - General Electric
2 - King of Prussia Industrial Park
3 - American Baptist Convention Headquarters
4 - General Electric Space Research Center
5 - King of Prussia Plaza
6 - Valley Forge Music Fair

One Mile Radial

PA TPK
TO PHILA
I-76
PA TURNPIKE
US 202

N

0 .5mi

than those of the adjoining open country, whether living within or outside the city" (p. 6). In this definition, Douglas stressed one criterion, population density. In more recent research, definitions derived from the United States census have been employed. By one definition, the suburbs are that area located within the Metropolitan Statistical Area (MSA) but outside the central city. On this basis more than 102 million Americans lived in suburbs in 1983 (U.S. Bureau of the Census, 1984). Another more refined census-based definition describes the suburban ring as that area located within an urbanized area but outside the central city. On the basis of this definition, 72 million Americans lived in suburbs in 1983 (U.S. Bureau of the Census, 1984). These definitions employ economic and political criteria in addition to density in delineating suburban areas. The limits of the central cities are defined by their political boundaries, whereas the outer boundaries of urbanized areas and MSAs are based on a complex set of rules for population size, density, and economic dependency (See the discussion of census units in Chapter 2.). Usually the larger the metropolitan area, the smaller the central city, but the use of political boundaries to define the central city introduces distortions. Where city–county governments are consolidated, there are fewer suburbs. Elsewhere, however, a suburban community may be completely surrounded by the central city. San Fernando, California, for example, is surrounded by the city of Los Angeles.

These inconsistencies have led researchers to stress additional criteria such as the housing types in an area and its proximity to the central business district, the rate of workers commuting to the central city, the proportion of an area's residents in the early stages of the family life cycle, the socioeconomic status of residents, and the homogeneity of values and attitudes in the fringe. For the purposes of this book, the deconcentration of activities and population from a city to adjacent fringe areas is called *suburbanization.* This definition refers to the redistribution not only of population, but also of business and industry. Thus, those communities of urban density located near large metropolitan centers are considered suburbs. Suburbs may be either incorporated or unincorporated communities but must be socially and economically dependent on the nearby city. "Their populations are urban and not rural in character; their economies are nonagricultural; their social structures reflect their interdependency with the adjacent city; and their residents usually identify with both their suburb and the city" (Schwirian, 1977, pp. 168–69).

AN OPERATIONAL DEFINITION OF SUBURBIA

The question remains how this definition can be operationalized with available public data. The two major data units available in the United States census are the urbanized area and the MSA. The MSA consists of a group of counties economically and socially dependent on a central city of at least 50,000 inhabitants. MSAs, however, contain many people who hardly fit the common notion of suburbanites. In 1983, nearly 24 million of the more than 102 million people living in MSAs but outside central cities were classified as rural (U.S. Bureau of the Census, 1983, Table 47). An urbanized area, in contrast, is a central city plus the densely populated area at its fringe. This unit of analysis more closely identifies the suburban ring as defined here. Therefore, in the following sections the term *suburbs* refers to that area of the city outside the central city but within the urbanized area.

THE SUBURBANIZATION OF PEOPLE

In the United States, cities have grown faster than rural areas since 1820, and suburbanization was an early part of this urbanization process. As early as the 1760s, suburban areas near Boston and Philadelphia were populated. In 1910, one-quarter of the population of the 25 metropolitan districts defined by the Census Bureau lived in the suburbs (Farley, 1974, p. 99). Weber (viz., 1963), in the first comprehensive study of American cities, found that most older industrial cities in the United States had one or more suburbs as early as 1890. By 1900, the United States was well on its way to becoming an urban–industrial nation, and suburban growth around the larger metropolises during the twentieth century followed the earlier patterns.

Table 10.1 shows interdecade rates of population increases for the total, metropolitan and nonmetropolitan populations of the continental United States for the years 1900–1986. Metropolitan areas are subdivided into central city and urbanized fringe, and separate growth rates are provided for each. A perusal of this table shows that metropolitan areas have captured most of the nation's total population growth in this century. Within metropolitan areas, the urbanized fringe has grown faster than the central city in every decade of this century. The rate of growth, however, has declined steadily since its peak in the 1950s. This decline in growth is expected to continue through the 1990s. The latest census data available shows that suburbs grew by only 5.9 percent between 1980 and 1986, the lowest rate this century.

Table 10.1 indicates that the United States underwent its most rapid suburbanization in the post-World War II period, and the rate of suburbanization has declined since its peak in the 1950s. Table 10.2 provides a somewhat different picture of this process by exploring population change in the central cities and urbanized fringe of the nation's 15 largest urbanized areas in 1980. In 1980, these cities contained more than

TABLE 10.1 Rates of population increase by metropolitan status, 1900–1986

POPULATION STATUS	1980– 1986	1970– 1980	1960– 1970	1950– 1960	1940– 1950	1930– 1940	1920– 1930	1910– 1920	1900– 1910
Total United States	4.2	11.3	13.4	18.5	14.5	7.2	16.1	14.9	21.0
Nonmetropolitan	3.4	3.4	5.8	8.1	6.1	6.5	6.0	6.7	13.6
Metropolitan	4.5	14.5	28.8	47.5	22.0	8.4	27.5	25.5	32.5
Central city	2.7	4.8	9.0	20.8	13.8	5.5	24.2	27.9	37.1
Urbanized fringe	5.9	18.2	45.0	81.0	26.0	8.0	42.6	35.9	49.2

Source: U.S. Bureau of the Census, *State and Metropolitan Area Data Book, 1986.* Washington, D.C.: U.S. Government Printing Office, 1987.

TABLE 10.2 Total population of urbanized areas and decennial growth rates, 1950–1980

ALL URBANIZED AREAS	TOTAL POPULATION (THOUSANDS)				DECENNIAL GROWTH RATES (%) TOTAL		
	1950	1960	1970	1980	1950–60	1960–70	1970–80
New York*							
City	8891	8743	8820	7071	-2	+1	-19
Ring	3405	5372	7387	8513	+58	+38	+15
Los Angeles*							
City	2221	2823	3175	2950	+27	+12	-7
Ring	2147	3666	5177	6528	+70	+41	+26
Chicago*							
City	3897	3898	3697	2970	0	-5	-20
Ring	1024	2061	3017	3741	+101	+46	+24
Philadelphia							
City	2072	2003	1949	1686	-3	-3	-14
Ring	851	1633	2073	2428	+92	+27	+17
Detroit							
City	1850	1670	1496	1192	-10	-10	-20
Ring	810	1867	2475	2617	+131	+33	+6
San Francisco*							
City	1160	1158	1077	674	0	-7	-37
Ring	862	1273	1911	2518	+48	-50	+32
Boston							
City	801	697	641	563	-13	-8	-12
Ring	1432	1716	2015	2115	+20	+17	+5
Washington							
City	802	764	757	635	-5	-1	-16
Ring	485	1045	1725	2127	+115	+65	+23
Cleveland							
City	915	876	751	574	-4	-14	-23
Ring	469	909	1209	1178	+94	+33	-2
Saint Louis							
City	857	750	622	458	-12	-17	-27
Ring	543	918	1261	1390	+69	+37	+10
Pittsburgh							
City	677	604	520	424	-11	-14	-19
Ring	856	1200	1326	1385	+40	+10	+4
Minneapolis*							
City	833	796	744	371	-4	-7	-50
Ring	283	581	960	1416	+105	+65	+48

TABLE 10.2 (continued)

ALL URBANIZED AREAS	TOTAL POPULATION (THOUSANDS)				DECENNIAL GROWTH RATES (%) TOTAL		
	1950	1960	1970	1980	1950–60	1960–70	1970–80
Houston							
City	596	938	1233	1594	+57	+31	+29
Ring	104	202	445	8118	+93	+120	+83
Baltimore							
City	950	939	906	783	-1	-4	-16
Ring	212	480	674	972	+126	+40	+44
Dallas							
City	434	680	844	901	+56	+24	+7
Ring	105	253	494	1550	+141	+96	+214
Average							
City	1797	1823	1815	1523	+1	0	-16
Ring	906	1545	2143	2565	+71	+39	+20

*More than one central city in these urbanized areas.

Source: 1950, 1960, and 1970 data from Farley, R. Components of Suburban Population Growth. In B. Schwartz (Ed.), The Changing Face of the Suburbs. Chicago: The University of Chicago Press, 1976, pp. 6–7. Provisional 1980 data from U.S. Bureau of the Census, 1980 Provisional Metropolitan Data, 1981.

60 million people, half of this nation's population, living in urbanized areas. Because these cities are geographically dispersed, the analysis identifies regional differences that may have been masked in the summary statistics in Table 10.1

A perusal of these data indicates that these 15 cities followed the national trend in population deconcentration for the 1950–1980 period. Between 1950 and 1960, the nation's population grew by 17 percent, but only three cities, Los Angeles, Houston, and Dallas (cities in the so-called Sunbelt), grew in excess of this rate. Note that in all cases the growth of the city's fringe greatly exceeded that of the central city. In fact, the central cities of 12 of the 15 metropolises in the sample declined in population. The Sunbelt cities of Los Angeles, Dallas, and Houston were the only exceptions, but these cities were annexing large portions of their fringe areas during the 1950s. If the figures were corrected for annexation, Dallas and Houston, and probably Los Angeles, would have patterns similar to those of the other cities (Farley, 1976, p. 8).

Between 1960 and 1980, the population grew nationally by 14 percent, but only Houston and Dallas exceeded this percentage. As in the previous decade, central cities on the whole continued to lose population, while suburban rings continued to absorb most of the urbanized areas' population growth (Farley, 1976, p. 8).

One of the stereotyped images of the suburbanization process is that it is the result of white flight to the cities' fringe. This generalization is borne out, since, in both decades, 12 of the cities lost whites and gained blacks. Los Angeles, Dallas, and

Houston were the exceptions; both their white and black populations grew in both the central city and the urbanized fringe (Farley, 1976, p. 8).

SUBURBANIZATION OF BUSINESS AND INDUSTRY

NATIONAL TRENDS

To this point, the discussion of the suburbanization process has focused on the decentralization of the nation's residential population. In the post-World War II period, conditions enabled large numbers of businesses and industries to relocate in the urbanized fringe. This trend is viewed with alarm by the leadership of many cities. Examples of the exodus of major corporations from the city are numerous. New Orleans does not keep statistics on the business and industry it loses, but in the early 1970s it lost the Elmer Candy Company, the Diebert-Bancroft Machinery Works, automobile dealers, and numerous distributors of national products. The city of Atlanta has lost the corporate offices of Sinclair Oil, Shell Oil, Continental Can Company, Avon Cosmetics, Piedmont Life Insurance Company, and Monsanto Chemical Company to suburban office parks (Masetti and Hadden, 1974, p. 88). In the 1970s, St. Louis lost 43 companies to the suburbs. Boston lost 75 firms in two years, and the trend continues in Chicago, Milwaukee, Cleveland, and Detroit (Berry and Kasarda, 1977, pp. 255–256). A more vivid picture of this decentralization of business and industry can be seen in a partial list of companies that in 1974 had moved or planned to move all or part of their operations out of New York City to the surrounding suburbs (Berry and Kasarda, 1977, p. 255):

> **To Connecticut:** American Can Company; Lone Star Cement Corporation; Bangor Punta Corporation; Howmet Corporation; U.S. Tobacco Corporation; Olin Corporation (chemicals division); Hooker Chemical; Chesebrough–Pond's, Incorporated; Technicolor, Incorporated; Christian Dior Perfumes Corporation; General Telephone and Electronics Corporation; Consolidated Oil; and Stauffer Chemical.
>
> **To Westchester County:** IBM, Incorporated; Pepsico, Incorporated; Dictaphone Corporation; General Foods Corporation; Flintkote; and AMF.
>
> **To Northern New Jersey:** CPC International; Union Camp; and the American Division of BASF. Even Fantus Company, the relocation firm that helped plan many of these moves, has taken up new offices in Englewood Cliffs, New Jersey (population 5810), along with COC, Thomas Lipton, Scholastic Magazine, and Volkswagen.

EMPLOYMENT PATTERNS

The pattern of decentralization of business and industry is national in scope, as is apparent in the data in Table 10.3 for the 15 largest metropolitan areas in the United States in 1970. The statistics are sobering. Regardless of region, economic base, and size, there has been a dramatic shift of employment to the suburban ring. In 1960, only 37 percent of total employment was in the suburbs. In 1970, employment hovered near

TABLE 10.3 Percentage increase in total civilian employment in the cities and suburbs of 15 selected metropolitan areas, 1960, 1970, 1988.

METROPOLITAN AREA	CENTRAL CITY PERCENTAGE CHANGE 1960	SUBURBAN EMPLOYMENT PERCENTAGE CHANGE 1970	PERCENTAGE OF TOTAL EMPLOYMENT IN THE SUBURBS 1988
New York	28.8	35.9	—
Los Angeles	47.8	54.3	58.9
Chicago	32.2	47.5	55.8
Philadelphia	37.0	51.8	69.5
Detroit	43.3	61.4	81.9
San Francisco	44.9	50.0	53.6
Boston	55.5	62.2	71.0
Washington, D.C.	36.2	54.9	84.3
Cleveland	28.3	46.0	75.2
St. Louis	39.3	58.0	84.5
Pittsburg	64.0	63.7	69.5
Minneapolis–St. Paul	23.6	41.1	59.6
Houston	15.7	24.4	47.0
Baltimore	34.1	49.9	61.7
Dallas	24.4*	29.0	72.2
Total	37.0	47.6	67.5

Source: 1960 and 1970 data from *New York Times* analysis of U.S. Census Bureau data, October 15, 1972, pp. 1, 58; 1988 data from U.S. Department of Labor, Bureau of Labor Statistics, *Geographic Profile of Employment and Unemployment, 1988.* Washington, D.C.: U.S. Government Printing Office, 1989.

50 percent, and, by 1988, 67.5 percent of all civilian employment in our 15 largest metropolitan areas was in the fringe. In 1988, only Houston had more employment in the central city than the suburban ring, but Houston preemptively annexed large portions of its fringe during the 1970s and 1980s.

But has this decentralization of employment been selective? Has the central city held on to some economic activities and not others? The building boom in the central cities of the nation's largest cities suggests that corporate and service activities may be staying in the central city. The data in Table 10.4 show that this is not the case. By 1988, 62 percent of manufacturing, 57 percent of trade, and 56 percent of service employment had decentralized to the fringe. The only exceptions are Houston, Indianapolis, Phoenix, and San Antonio, all cities that have preemptive annexation policies.

Business and industry have decentralized for many reasons. The most obvious reason has been the development of the motor vehicle. Cars and trucks, combined with the interstate highway and intraurban expressway system, make the entire metropolis accessible. Thus, there is less need for a centralized location near a port or a railhead. Now that travel to most parts of the metropolis is fast and travel time is no longer tied to distance, retailers and wholesalers have more options in finding a location. From

TABLE 10.4 Percentage of Total Civilian Employment in Manufacturing, Trade, and Service in 17 Selected Metropolitan Areas, 1980.

CITY	TOTAL	MANUFACTURING	TRADE	SERVICES
Baltimore	62.0	—	67.7	66.4
Chicago	55.8	57.6	60.4	52.3
Cleveland	75.2	72.2	78.4	78.1
Dallas	72.1	79.1	68.7	69.3
Detroit	81.9	83.6	83.2	80.2
Washington, D.C.	84.3	89.2	87.3	82.4
Houston	46.9*	53.8	40.5	44.5
Indianapolis	38.1*	42.1	34.1	35.3
Los Angeles	58.9	59.4	58.6	55.6
Milwaukee	59.6	63.7	58.7	51.2
New York*	16.1	16.6	19.4	14.6
Philadelphia	69.5	78.4	72.4	63.0
Phoenix	51.5*	55.7	47.9	48.2
St. Louis	84.5	—	—	83.9
San Antonio	32.5*	—	31.5	29.7
San Diego	53.7	56.0	53.5	49.0
San Francisco	53.4	—	55.8	46.9
AVERAGE	58.6	62.1	57.4	56.0

*The New York City DMSA was used in calculating these figures.

Source: U.S. Department of Labor, Bureau of Labor Statistics *Geographic Profiles of Employment and Unemployment, 1988.* Washington, D.C.: U.S. Government Printing Office, 1989, Table 26, p. 120.

your own experience, you know that if you measure your travel costs in terms of time—the time it takes you to drive, find parking, and walk to a retail store—it is probably faster to drive 25 miles on a city's outer belt to a suburban mall than to drive eight miles to a downtown shopping area.

Second, the CBD is no longer the only point within the metropolis where major transportation lines converge. In general, the area around the interchange of two interstate highways is probably as accessible as most downtown locations.

Third, computers, fax machines, overnight mail, teleconferencing, and other technological innovations have drastically changed the way businesses do business. Although nothing will ever replace face-to-face bargaining, a higher proportion of business communication is being conducted electronically. Technology, therefore, has dramatically changed the location calculus.

Fourth, the location of business and industry has been shaped by the revolution in transportation and communication technology; once the process begins, it becomes self-reinforcing—growth creates growth. In the 1950s, people moved to the suburbs to take advantage of low-cost, low-density housing. Manufacturing followed to take advantage of cheap land, low taxes, and the emerging interstate highway system. Manufacturers in turn needed workers, who increasingly chose suburban neighborhoods. Retailers looked to this burgeoning and affluent market and followed their customers to the suburbs. Retailers hired and added more people to the suburbs. All these residents required a range of services—lawyers, dentists, physicians, accountants, veterinarians, pharmacists, teachers, municipal service workers, to name a few—which, in turn, created more demands for retailing and a larger pool of potential employees for manufacturers. Growth fed growth.

THEORIES OF LOCATION

THE WEBERIAN MODEL

A number of theories have been developed to explain this decentralization of retailing, wholesaling, service, and manufacturing industries. The first is called the Weberian model after its creator Alfred Weber (1929). The model is straightforward: A business, in deciding whether to expand at an existing location, relocate, or build on a new site, follows a rational decision-making process in which it attempts to reduce costs and maximize profit. The most obvious factors are the costs of land, labor, transportation, and raw materials; different firms have different needs, and they will key in on different cost elements of their operations. Some firms, especially those manufacturing bulky and difficult to ship products, will probably choose to locate near their markets. Other firms, like steel mills, agricultural processors, and the like, will probably choose a location near the suppliers of their raw materials. Other firms which have a need for a specialized or cheap labor supply will probably opt for a location near a dependable labor supply. Still other firms will choose to locate near other businesses with whom they do business. Parts suppliers locate near auto assembly plants, die makers near plastic and rubber manufacturers, and service firms near the large corporations with whom they do business.

THE INDUSTRIAL LOCATION MODEL

A second model, the industrial location model, has its roots in the work of Ian Hamilton (1967, 1974). Ian Hamilton argues that the Weberian model is too simple; that locational decisions are not entirely rational because they involve human decision makers. The proponents of this model do not underplay the importance of economics in the locational decision of firms, but they feel that these decisions also involve important social, political, and psychological elements. For example, a recent study on the relocation of corporate headquarters from New York City to its suburbs showed that the best predictor of the new location was the suburb in which the CEO's home and country club were located. So much for rational decision making. Numerous studies have shown that zoning laws, political climate, tax rates, and the quality of schools and services play an important role in the location of businesses and industries.

THE PUSH–PULL MODEL

A third model, the push–pull model, suggests that the characteristics of both the suburb and the central city must be considered to understand the relocation decision of firms. This theory includes elements of both the Weberian and Hamilton models. In this more elaborate model, the push factors refer to those characteristics of the central city—high taxes, poor services, crime, and transportation and labor problems—which push leaders of a corporation to begin the search for a new location. The pull factors refer to the characteristics of an individual suburb—its tax rate, labor pool, land costs, services, access to transportation, and other tangible and intangible characteristics. There are intervening obstacles that also affect the decision process. How easily can the firm extract itself from long-term contractual obligations at its present location? Can it sell or lease its building? What are the relocation costs? Severance pay costs? The loss of goodwill with the city?

At present none of these models accurately predict the location of firms. The new industrial model and the suburban characteristics of the push–pull model seem to be the most important elements in the location of firms. Agglomeration effects, the tendency of firms to locate near similar firms, and the persistence of these clusters (identified in the Hamilton model) seem to be one of the best predictors of the location of firms. Retailers cluster in existing malls and strips because of zoning laws and their need for foot traffic. Manufacturers, like parts suppliers, assembly operations, and transportation firms, locate near one another to minimize the cost of transporting inputs and outputs from one another. Wholesaling and service firms usually locate near retail clusters because of their dependence on trade (Stahura, 1982).

STRATIFICATION OF SUBURBS

A social class is a group of people who, over time, develop similar access to the scarce resources of a society. A social class shares similar life chances and life styles, and its members may even have similar biographies. Objective measures, like income, education, and occupation, can be used to group people into social classes. When these classes can be arranged in a hierarchy on one or more of these dimensions, then one has a social stratification system. Measures of social status have been found to be a powerful tool in predicting a wide range of behavior ranging from voting to shopping patterns.

Employing and residential suburbs can be grouped by social status and can be arranged in a hierarchy just like people. In the 1980s, many students of suburbanization became interested in the stratification of the suburbs and the implications of this pattern on the well-being of suburbs at the top and the bottom of the hierarchy. Three competing theories dominate the literature.

THE PERSISTENCE MODEL

The oldest and, in many respects, the dominant theory on the stratification of suburbs is the persistence model. The persistence model argues that in the early stages of settlement a suburb's socioeconomic character and function are fixed and persist through time although the community may undergo rapid population and economic growth at a later date. This model posits the character of a suburb to be shaped initially by its niche in the ecological structure of the metropolis—proximity to transportation lines, the central business district, industry, and amenities such as schools, recreation areas, and cultural facilities. Once secured, the character of the suburb, say, a residential or employing suburb, maintains this character through time. A good example is given by Farley (1974):

> Evanston and Hammond are approximately equal in population size, at the same distance from Chicago's Loop, comparable in age, and both have Lake Michigan frontage. Yet the inhabitants of these suburbs have quite different characteristics. A meat packing plant was the first establishment to attract residents to Hammond, and an excellent rail facility fostered later industrial growth, while the history of Evanston was dependent upon Methodist institutions including Northwestern University (p. 108).

Why the persistence? Researchers have traced the socioeconomic status characteristics of a national sample of suburbs for time periods ranging from 30 to 50 years and have found remarkable stability in status over time (Farley, 1974; Guest, 1978; Stahura, 1984, 1987). The major reason given is the vested interests of homeowners and other users of land, as well as banking and lending institutions. A change in the socioeconomic character of an area would adversely affect the investments of these groups; economic self-interest leads them to preserve the character of the area. Thus, not only are there great differences in the character and function of these communities in the urban fringe, but, once their characters are established, this group argues, they will persist through time.

THE ECOLOGICAL MODEL

The persistence model runs counter to the classic ecological model of Burgess (See Chapter 9.). Ernest Burgess's concentric zone model predicts a continuous cycle of growth and decline of suburbs as higher status households seek newer communities. As older neighborhoods age, they deteriorate through the process of invasion and succession. The ecological model, therefore, predicts a continuous turnover in the status hierarchy of suburbs.

THE STRATIFICATION, OR POLITICAL MODEL

The stratification, or political model, of suburbanization draws upon the conflict perspective to explore the politics of place. As we have seen throughout the text, inherent in the character of place is a conflict between use-value and profit value of property. Suburbs, like all other places, are in economic and political competition for the scarce resources of the metropolis. Just as opportunities are not equally distributed across groups in our society, some suburbs because of the income, education, and occupations of their residents, have special access to the resources of the metropolis. High-income suburbs, therefore, are in a position to mobilize resources to benefit their communities. In the area of public housing, high-status suburbs can use tactics ranging from zoning and building codes to endless legal delays to keep out minorities, the poor, and public housing. Low-income suburbs, especially those adjacent to the central city, have no such access and can be expected to decline in status. In this model, not only would status differences persist, but inequality should increase over time (Logan and Schneider, 1981).

Which theory is correct? The literature is still evolving, and there is no definitive answer. It does appear that variables like time of suburban settlement (pre- vs. post-1950), suburban growth rates, the economic base of the central city, racial composition of the metropolis, and region affect the predictive value of the theories. John Stahura (1987) compared the three models over a 40-year period and reports that, during the period of rapid fringe growth in the 1950s, each model was supported, but, as growth began to subside in the 1960s, each of the models was supported, but to a lesser degree. In the period of slow growth during the 1970s, Stahura reports that none of the models work particularly well. Growth rates in the fringe appear to be the crucial variable. As the growth rate in the fringe continues to decline in the 1990s, one would expect a less dynamic and more static suburban hierarchy—persistence (See also Krivo and Frisbie, 1982.).

Logan and Schneider (1981) found fluidity in the status hierarchy of suburbs under conditions of rapid population growth. This was particularly true of poorer suburbs in southern metropolises that were in the path of rapid fringe development. The low densities of southern cities meant that vacant and underdeveloped property could be purchased and quickly converted to other land uses. In northern metropolises where fringe growth had slowed by the late 1960s, the location of suburbs in the status hierarchy had crystallized and persistence, not fluidity, characterized subsequent decades. As we have seen in earlier chapters of this text, the urban development in the South differed in significant ways from the North. Central cities in the South like Dallas and Houston have used preemptive annexation to bring large tracts of land under their political control, and city/suburban antagonism has been minimized. Northern fringe development has quite a different history.

Suburbs in the North were tools used by middle- and upper-income households to insulate themselves from the politics of the central city. This is also the region where laws passed by state legislatures made it difficult for cities to annex but easy for suburbs to incorporate. Political fragmentation has increased competition between political units and allowed high-status suburbs to use the political system to enhance their position in the hierarchy. It is in the North where exclusionary zoning and a host of related techniques have been used by high-income suburbs to maintain their privileged high-status position (Logan and Schneider, 1981).

THE SOCIAL SIDE OF SUBURBIA

To this point, our analysis has shown that in spite of the major redistribution of population and economic activity since World War II, suburbs remain predominantly white, more affluent, and more likely than the city to contain upwardly mobile families engaged in the process of child rearing. One wonders why this change has not had a greater impact on the suburban way of life. The answer is a complicated one, but it appears that the highly fragmented political structure of the American metropolis has been able to suppress the social consequences of much of this growth and change (Teaford, 1979). In most American metropolises, the central city is surrounded by many suburbs, smaller in size and politically autonomous. In 1980, the 33 largest metropolitan areas contained an average of 200 suburban nonschool-system decision-making bodies. These political units have broad discretionary powers in the areas of taxation, zoning and land-use planning. In other words, suburbs are in a position to control the size and quality of their population and produce a socially homogeneous community. Although suburbs now exhibit the social complexity once only found in the central city, the political structure of the metropolis has minimized these differences by compartmentalizing groups similar in socioeconomic and racial characteristics.

The consequences of these residential patterns are straightforward. The more homogeneous a community, the more likely that a person will find others nearby whose interests and tastes are similar to his or her own. This, in turn, contributes to the development of social networks (coffee klatching, for example) that often lead to the emergence of beliefs, values, and life-style preferences that are associated with suburban living. Therefore, it is not surprising that the behavior of people living in relatively homogeneous suburbs differs from similar groups living in central cities, where they are more exposed to groups that differ in their socioeconomic and racial characteristics (Schwartz, 1976, pp. 330–331).

LIFESTYLES IN SUBURBIA

The compartmentalized character of suburbs permits groups to pursue unique lifestyles. The lifestyle most closely associated with suburbia is familism. Familism refers to a lifestyle that emphasizes activities centered around home and children. The values associated with this lifestyle stand in sharp contrast to alternative American value systems centered on career success and conspicuous consumption. Since American culture stresses all three value systems, there must be a trade-off among them; if a person vigorously pursues a career, he or she will find less time for enjoyable consumption and family life.

Bell (1958) examined these three value systems in a study of several Chicago suburbs. He found that suburban residents placed greater emphasis on familistic values than on the other two value systems. For example, when respondents were asked, "Why did you move from the city?" 83 percent gave responses involving upward social mobility, and only 43 percent gave responses involving consumerism. More recently, Claude Fischer (1982) found many of these same values in the suburbs in the San Francisco Bay Area.

Familism conjures up positive images. M. P. Baumgartner, in his thought-provoking book, *The Moral Order of a Suburb,* explores a less flattering consequence of the suburban environment. Earlier we discussed Claude Fischer's contributions to the discussion on the relationship between social disorganization and the city. In a nutshell, Fischer argues that the city's ecological factors of size, density, and heterogeneity are crucial in creating a critical mass of similar people who, over time, form subcultures. These subcultures have their own value systems, some that reinforce the values of the larger society and some that do not. The conflict and social disorganization of the city, according to Fischer, is the result of an overly rich environment of competing moral communities rather than anomie, as described by Wirth and others.

Baumgartner, a cultural anthropologist, studied a middle-class suburb in the same way that anthropologists would study a preliterate tribe. In the course of the study, the one pattern that struck him was the relative tranquility of middle-class suburbs. He discovered the reason: Rather than a overly rich environment of moral communities, he found what he called *moral minimalism*. Baumgartner found that most of his subjects had shallow, single-stranded relationships with co-workers, church members, and neighbors; when the person moved, the relationship usually ended. The tenuous nature of these relationships, along with the high mobility of Americans, Baumgartner found, led middle-class suburbanites to use avoidance as their major strategy for dealing with the petty day-to-day problems of life. Baumgartner found this to be true of a whole range of relationships. Middle-class families have large homes, and Mom, Dad, and the children live very different lives during the day and often go their separate ways at night and on weekends. Moreover, the nature of the life cycle in middle-class families means that the kids will eventually go away to college and move away from the suburb. Rather than dealing with marital or child-rearing problems, these families often avoid them by staying in their rooms or staying away from home.

Moral minimalism also described the neighboring he observed. He found neighbors ignoring even the most extreme behavior. Baumgartner relates one case in which a man was seen many times running around the neighborhood naked in the middle of the night. The neighbors' response: The kids had to stay away from Mr. X's house. Why wouldn't they do something? One reason is that there are time and emotional costs for intervening; the second, there was a pretty good chance that the problem would simply move away.

Baumgartner cautions that moral minimalism describes middle-class suburbanites living in detached single-family homes. Other class and ethnic groups display very different neighboring activities.

Examining the literature of the suburbs, one is struck by the diversity of lifestyles represented in the fringe. The decentralization of millions of Americans to the suburbs in the postwar period has created suburban ghettoes, suburban ethnic enclaves, and suburban singles' communities, along with the familistic neighborhoods traditionally associated with the fringe, a mosaic of social worlds heretofore found only in the central city.

The question remains whether the suburbs are to be understood simply as the product of ecological processes resulting from metropolitan growth or whether they represent a subculture with distinctive values, beliefs, and lifestyle preferences. In truth, there is probably an interaction between the two. American suburbs are usually age- and class-graded. That is, residents of a suburb will often manifest similar demographic characteristics—age, ethnicity, home ownership, and family life cycle. Young homeowners with children in school will obviously be pursuing familistic lifestyles and have a more direct concern in local rather than national problems. The characteristics of these homogeneous, class-compartmentalized suburbs give rise to suburban values and provide an environment supportive of these attitudes.

Why do people choose suburban housing over locations in the central city? Our discussion suggests that the availability of modern housing and schools unaffected by court-ordered school busing, as well as residential environments insulated from the urban ills associated with more centrally located communities, are major determining factors. Equally important is the presence of a residential environment conducive to a local and/or familistic lifestyle.

CONSEQUENCES OF FRAGMENTATION

There are other consequences of fragmentation for the entire metropolis. In our federal system, land-use controls, such as zoning and the provision and financing of public services, are a local responsibility. In the minds of some researchers, our fragmented governmental structure encourages the suburbanization of high-income households and contributes to the increasing income disparity between the city and the suburban ring. Why? A number of critics argue that political fragmentation creates an incentive for suburbs to pursue exclusionary growth policies. Upper-income families are low-service-cost citizens. The water, sewerage, and waste collection services they need are paid through user fees, and police, fire, and government costs are usually low and are handled through property taxes. High-income households don't need the subsidized housing, day care, and medical and other services required by low-income households. Therefore, it is in the best interest of many suburbs to keep low-income/high-cost citizens out, and they use restrictive zoning, minimum lot size requirements, building codes, impact fees, and other techniques to keep subsidized and low-cost housing from being built within their borders (Logan and Schneider, 1982, Schneider, 1980).

Once a pattern of exclusion is established, it perpetuates itself by influencing the way people choose a residential location. Likes attract, and higher-income households usually settle in suburbs of the same social class. No high-cost citizens means that higher-income suburbanites often receive excellent services at a cost lower than the mediocre ones found in the central city (Logan and Schneider, 1982).

During the 1970s, there was a rapid expansion of federal aid to cities. There were two types of aid: need-based and categorical grant programs. Federal need-based programs used complex formulas to target funds to low-income and minority communities. (This literature was reviewed in Chapter 6, "The Classification and Rating of Cities.") As a result, most of this money went to the central cities and older black suburbs, and these communities became dependent on this federal money to provide basic services to their citizens. Categorical grants, which made up the lion's share of the federal urban development budget, was used to finance capital improvements, like water and sewerage systems. These grants were not formula-based, and higher-income suburbs, because they can hire legal consultants to work through the mire of federal regulations, significantly increased their levels of this funding during the 1970s (Schneider and Logan, 1985). When the fiscal crunch came during the Reagan administration, higher-income suburbs coped well because they had not built federal money into their operating budgets; not so for lower-income suburbs. In these communities, financial problems became financial crises, and the level of municipal services and the quality of life declined (Peterson and Lewis, 1986).

There is a final and far more subtle effect of fragmentation. For most of this century, central cities could dictate policies for the metropolis because they had the largest populations and because most of the region's jobs were within their borders. The massive decentralization of people, manufacturing, industry, and trade in the past 40 years means that central city governments are no longer the dominant player, just another player in the competition for the scarce resources in the metropolis. The loss of this leadership role has wide-ranging implications for the central city's ability to cope with massive human, infrastructure, and fiscal problems it faces (Marshall and Stahura, 1986).

SUBURBIA AND WOMEN, ELDERLY, AND MINORITIES

WOMEN AND THE SUBURBS

In the minds of many feminists, the gender inequality that pervades this society is manifested most visibly and clearly in the use of space within the city. In the 1970s, many writers on the concerns of women argued that suburbs reflect a living environment designed by men for men; little concern had been given to the needs and roles of women in their planning and construction. Janet Abu-Lughod tells of her experience in the 1970s, as the only woman attending a conference on design and the city. The male attenders were excited about a new social model that shortened the work week to three days and allowed husbands to spend long weekends with the wife and kids in the suburbs. Dr. Abu-Lughod objected to the model as one designed by wealthy white males for wealthy white males. Her concern was that this model would further segregate the roles of men and women. The male participants responded to her concerns first with silence and then with embarrassment (Rothblatt, Garr, and Sprague, 1979, p. 55).

In the 1950s and the 1960s, residential suburbs with their single-family houses centered on large lots and zoned from nonresidential activities were thought to be a perfect family environment. Men could commute to the world of work in the nearby city by day and escape from the pressures of the workplace in the bucolic environment of the suburbs at night. Women as mothers and homemakers had a relatively safe and protected environment in which to raise children. So what if the schools, pediatricians, groceries, and dry cleaners weren't nearby; that's what the family station wagon was for.

In the 1970s, this idyllic picture of the suburbs was questioned by a number of studies, which showed that this spatial environment was not all that satisfying for women. Helena Lopata (1980), in a survey of Chicago women, found that young single women traveled to many parts of the city while pursuing their roles at home, school, and work—that is, until they married and the first child arrived. After children, the women felt tied down. If the couple moved to the suburbs for the sake of the children, things worsened. The combination of mortgage, transportation, and child costs—further exacerbated if the mother quit work—pushed many Chicago area families into a smaller and smaller social world often limited to neighbors. Herbert Gans found the same thing a decade earlier in his study of Levittown, New Jersey. He reported that middle-class women, in particular, were frustrated by the isolation of the suburbs and they often turned to neighbors for friendship.

These findings were buttressed by studies that compared the lives of suburban husbands and wives. Husbands, because they lived and worked in different places, had a far more extensive network of friends and associates outside the suburban neighborhood. The networks of wives, in contrast, were often restricted to the neighborhood. As with marriage, husbands were far more satisfied than wives with their suburban lifestyle (Fischer and Jackson, 1976; Michelson, 1976, 1977; Booth and Choldin, 1985).

Wekerle (1980) and others concluded that suburbanization weighs heavily on women. Why? The separation of residential from nonresidential land uses in the suburbs often means that even the most basic services are not nearby. The segregation of families by their age and stage in the life cycle often means isolation from meaningful interaction. Therefore, the low-density suburbs of single-family homes segregated from nonresidential activities was thought to provide an environment for only one role—homemaker and mother. It was thought that the higher density in the central city would provide women greater access to work, shopping, child care, and other services, reducing time pressures and enabling them to better integrate their various roles.

But things have changed, and the image of the suburbs used to shape our attitudes a decade or two ago may no longer be relevant. In 1950, when the first post-World War II suburbs were being built, only 25 percent of our population lived in the suburbs, and the bulk of this nation's business and industry was concentrated in our central cities. In 1970, this figure jumped to 38 percent, exceeding for the first time the population of the central cities (31 percent). By 1980, 45 percent of this nation's population resided in suburbs—only 30 percent in central cities—and, as we have seen earlier in this chapter, this population shift was accompanied by a massive decentralization of manufacturing and retailing. The suburbs now exhibit the diversity long associated with our cities. Peter Muller described the metropolis of the post-1970s as a polycentric city with a declining central city, an inner suburban ring, and an outer ring of suburbs with minicities—multipurpose concentrations of shopping, jobs, and entertainment that were formerly found only in the downtown central city (Muller, 1981). In addition, most of the migrants to the suburbs in the 1950s and 1960s came from the central city. In the 1970s and 1980s, most people living in the suburbs were born and raised in the suburbs. The low-density lifestyle of the suburbs is what they consider normal, not the lifestyle of the central city.

Recently, the thrust of the research has shifted. Donald Rothblatt and associates (1979) studied the suburban environment and its effects on women in San Jose, California. They concluded that environmental factors had little impact on women's overall sense of happiness or psychological well-being. Social influences like the age of women, marital status, the age of children, ethnic identity, and education seemed to be more important than environmental factors. The women in the study, however, reported that older interior suburbs and more distant, comprehensively planned suburbs were more satisfying than mass-produced suburbs. In all likelihood, the sense of place of older and comprehensively planned communities along with greater accessibility to centralized shopping led to this greater sense of well-being.

Christine Cook (1988) studied the needs of women heading single-parent households and found them to be more satisfied with housing in the suburbs than the central city. Lower crime rates and less fear of crime were mentioned most often, but the quality of schools and the peace and quiet of the suburbs were other major factors contributing to the women's sense of well-being.

Daphne Spain (1988) reports similar results from an analysis of housing data. She found that both men and women prefer suburban over central city living. Although shopping, schools, and other services are closer in the central city, so is crime, poor schools, and other urban problems. Professor Spain concluded that neither environment is particularly suitable for the majority of women in their struggle to balance the demands of traditional and newer roles.

Finally, Sylvia F. Fava (1985) shows that there continue to be major gender differences between men and women in their residential preferences. The dramatic shift of employment, retailing, and services to the suburbs now seems to better match the concerns of women with their need for transportation, accessibility, and safety.

In general, research shows that there continues to be a serious mismatch between the lifestyles of many households and the cluster of housing services found in the suburbs. Recent changes in the suburban ring, however, are beginning to give households greater access to a full range of goods and services once found only in the central city.

THE ELDERLY AND THE SUBURBS

Today, eight out of ten Americans can expect to live to retirement age, and, as a result, people over 65 are the fastest growing segment of our population. This population will explode early in the next century when the baby boomers retire, and this society will be faced with a crisis in social security, housing, and medical and other services.

The changing age composition of our population has implications for this society that far exceed those of social services; it also affects the very fabric of our cities. In the past 30 years, not only has the elderly population grown, but their numbers in the suburbs have grown dramatically too. In 1960, only 25.6 percent of the nation's elderly lived in the suburban ring. By 1980, this percentage had grown to 39.4 percent, and 1990 data will show that it exceeds 45 percent. As with the general population, more elderly Americans now live in the suburbs than in the central city or rural areas. Providing the housing, medical, transportation, and other services to the elderly poses special challenges for this society; therefore, the study of the suburbanization of the elderly has important policy implications. Unfortunately, there has been little research on the residential patterns of the elderly in the suburbs; most has been focused on their experiences in the central city (Gutowski and Field, 1979).

We do know from studies of the elderly in the central city that elderly Americans represent a unique segment of the housing market. First, since they have entered the last stages of the life cycle, they need less space but greater access to mass transportation and other social services. In the other stages of the life cycle, families adjust to changing situations by moving, but the elderly are one of the least mobile segments of our population. Often they have strong emotional attachments to the homes and neighborhoods in which they raised their families, and most have built up large home equities that make the sale of a home more difficult. A number of critics have argued for innovative programs that would subsidize the movement of the elderly to smaller units closer to mass transportation, clinics, hospitals, and other services. They point out a second benefit: Housing needed by younger families with children would be freed up (Welfeld, 1986).

A second problem is the segregation of the elderly because most elderly age in place. Many of the elderly purchased their homes in the 1950s, raised and educated their children, and then stayed in their homes even when the home was too big for them. The surrounding communities no longer really served their needs because they were designed for families with children. This mismatch between the space and service needs of the elderly and the homes and neighborhoods in which they live causes problems, but there is a far more subtle and insidious problem often ignored: The segregation of the elderly reduces contacts with other age groups and can result in social isolation.

Much of what we know of the elderly and the city has been gleaned from studies done in the central city. In a landmark study of the suburbanization of the elderly, Fitzpatrick and Logan (1985) found that many of the experiences of the elderly in the suburbs are different from the central city. First, although the suburbanization of the elderly has been dramatic, their segregation in the suburbs is modest and has actually declined over the past 30 years. The only exception is the South, where millions of retirees have settled, often selecting suburban communities that cater exclusively to the needs of older Americans. Second, the researchers found two distinct types of elderly suburbs. In the majority of cases, the elderly tend to be concentrated in denser, poorer, employing suburbs. The second group of suburbs had the highest home values and rents in the suburban ring. In this case, high-income retirees had large equities in their homes and relatively low housing costs, even though they were on fixed incomes.

The policy implications of this research is clear. For many of the suburban elderly, social security, company pensions, savings, and large home equities mean a comfortable retirement in the suburban fringe. For the low-income elderly, the modest levels of segregation suggest that the cost of providing services to them is spread across many communities. The downside of this residential pattern is that the efficiency of providing elderly services is low and the costs are higher than in the central city.

MINORITIES AND THE SUBURBS

BLACK AMERICANS

Suburbanization in the postwar years radically restructured the American metropolis. Once dense and highly concentrated, suburbanization transformed it into a highly decentralized form. No other statistic describes the scope of this change better than the fact that since 1970 more Americans have lived in suburbs than central cities.[5]

Not all Americans shared in this transformation. As millions of whites abandoned the central city for the suburbs, most blacks stayed behind. Black Americans were not completely excluded from this process, but their experiences have been quite different from those of their white counterparts. From a modest beginning in the 1960s, black suburbanization grew rapidly in the 1970s and 1980s, outstripping the rate for whites. Percentages, however, can be deceiving. Since the number of blacks in suburbs was small in 1960, a modest shift in population can lead to large percentage changes. More importantly, the suburbanization of blacks has not dramatically affected the overall segregation patterns in the nation; black Americans are still the most highly segregated group in our society (Logan and Schneider, 1984; Massey and Denton, 1988; Stahura, 1986, 1988a, 1988b).

Statistics on the suburbanization of blacks in key metropolitan areas and the major geographical regions of the nation are presented in Table 10.5. The first three columns give the percentage of blacks in the suburbs in 1970 and 1980, the last three columns give a measure of segregation, the index of dissimilarity. The index of dissimilarity is a measure that we will examine in greater detail in the chapter on segregation. For our purposes in this chapter, all you need to know is that the index has a range from 0 to 100, and it represents the percentage of blacks who would have to move from their present suburb to another to have an integrated community. In 1970, the index of dissimilarity for Chicago was extremely high, 90.6; in other words, 90.6 percent of Chicago's black suburban population would have to move to other suburbs in order to have the same percentage of blacks in every suburb.

Note in Table 10.5 the percentage of blacks in the suburbs ranges from just 7 percent in New York to nearly 60 percent in Miami in 1970. In general, all these metropolises experienced growth in black suburbanization during the decade. Los Angeles and Miami had the largest increases; Chicago, New York, and San Francisco

TABLE 10.5 Black Population Change in Selected Suburbs, 1970, 1980.

KEY SMSAs	PERCENTAGE OF BLACKS IN SUBURBS			DISSIMILARITY BETWEEN WHITES AND BLACKS		
	1970	1980	CHANGE	1970	1980	CHANGE
Chicago	10.0	15.8	6.0	0.906	0.754	-0.15
Los Angeles	31.4	42.1	11.0	0.830	0.789	-0.04
Miami	57.9	68.4	11.0	0.775	0.754	-0.02
New York	7.1	8.2	1.0	0.826	0.704	-0.12
San Francisco	32.1	36.8	5.0	0.681	0.668	-0.01
AVERAGE						
Northeast	18.8	23.3	5	0.737	0.614	-0.12
North Central	12.1	19.3	7	0.758	0.694	-0.06
South	21.8	28.6	7	0.694	0.541	-0.15
West	21.8	33.3	12	0.606	0.493	-0.11
ALL SMSAs	20.6	28.2	8	0.691	0.573	0.12
N = 59						

Source: Adapted from Douglas S. Massey and Nancy A. Denton. "Suburbanization and Segregation in U.S. Metropolitan Areas." *American Journal of Sociology,* 94(3), Tables 1 and 2, pp. 598–600, 602–604. Permission granted by the University of Chicago Press.

had modest ones. This same pattern holds for the regional data. The North Central and Northeastern regions had the lowest percentage of black residents in the suburbs; the South and West considerably more. All metropolises, regardless of region, experienced a significant increase in their black residents in the decade ending in 1980.

Nearly a third of the black population in the metropolises in this study now live in the suburbs, but has the increase in number led to a decrease in segregation? The answer is no. If one examines the last three columns of Table 10.5, one sees segregation indexes on the decline but still the highest of any group in our society. The index scores for all the 59 SMSAs in the study declined from 69 to 57—12 points—but the figures are still sobering.

It was once thought that the deconcentration of our black population to the suburbs would not only reduce segregation but inequality as well. But this has not been the case. Whether we look at the suburbs to which blacks move or the housing they buy, the experience of blacks differs significantly from that of whites. In general, when blacks move to the suburbs, they are more likely to rent than own, and, when they do buy, they are more likely to purchase an older home in poorer condition and of lower value than their white counterparts. Moreover, the homes of black suburbanites are more likely to depreciate than appreciate in value over time.

The suburbs themselves tend to be older residential areas, adjacent or near the central city with high population densities and lower socioeconomic status. They often are industrial suburbs with declining industries, falling tax bases, high taxes, and poor services with a rising number of citizens with high service needs. Black suburbs often mirror the conditions found in many central city neighborhoods.

The majority of black Americans are middle class; why are they still highly segregated? The answer is complex and involves a number of interrelated factors. First, we have long known that color has meant that black Americans are one of the most easily manipulated client systems, and they are often the victims of unfair, undemocratic, and unscrupulous business practices. Through a myriad of techniques, including redlining, market steering, selective use of building codes, and the use of multilist services, real estate interests shut minorities from full participation in the city's housing market. As a result, blacks are at a distinct disadvantage in the housing market, and the cost of a search for a new home is high monetarily and psychologically.[6]

Second, the growth of the suburbs has led to the political fragmentation of the metropolis, the concentration of blacks in the central city, and the deconcentration of business, trade, and industry to the suburban rings. Suburbia is now the dominant form of residence in America. Growth has been translated into political clout and a diminished power base for minorities living in the central city. Gone is the traditional power base of minorities, and gone too is a liberal Congress and White House—political forces that traditionally have provided a counterbalance to the forces at work in the metropolis. The sheer number of relatively well-to-do white middle-class Americans precludes the creation of political conditions that would lead to the deconcentration and decentralization of blacks in the suburbs.

Third, research has shown racial discrimination to be ubiquitous in this society, even in the face of laws that have been written on the national and state level to prevent such behavior. These laws have had little impact on the small markets in which most realtors operate. Open housing laws have few penalties for violation and provide scant legal recourse to plaintiffs who have been harmed by unethical real estate practices. Moreover, the federal government provides little money for enforcement. As a result, black Americans will continue to be one of the most segregated populations in this land regardless of whether they live in the city or the suburbs (Danielson, 1976; Clark, 1979; Lake, 1981).

HISPANIC AMERICANS

Table 10.6 summarizes the same information for Hispanic residents of our major metropolitan areas. Hispanics are much less segregated within central cities than blacks. The average index of dissimilarity between whites and Hispanics in our central cities is only 0.45, 24 points below the average of blacks. There are a number of cities with large and well-known Hispanic barrios—Los Angeles, New York, and Miami among them—but these figures are still considerably lower than blacks. The moderate level of segregation in central cities is even lower in the suburbs—38 in the metropolitan areas included in the sample. There are regional differences. In the Midwest, South, and West, the indexes range between 30 and 40, but in the Northeast the average is 48. The reason is the high proportion of Puerto Ricans, a group which has traditionally had the highest level of segregation among all Hispanic groups. In general, Hispanics have a wider variety of residential options compared to blacks, and they appear to be assimilating rapidly into the American mainstream (Massey and Denton, 1988).

TABLE 10.6 Hispanic Population Change in Selected Suburbs, 1970, 1980.

KEY SMSAs	PERCENTAGE OF HISPANICS IN SUBURBS			DISSIMILARITY BETWEEN WHITES AND HISPANICS		
	1970	1980	CHANGE	1970	1980	CHANGE
Chicago	24.0	26.7	3.0	0.616	0.408	-0.21
Los Angeles	57.1	57.6	1.0	0.611	0.539	-0.07
Miami	49.0	66.1	17.0	0.411	0.477	0.07
New York	4.2	5.8	2.0	0.639	0.399	-0.24
San Francisco	62.2	66.9	5.0	0.498	0.363	-0.14
AVERAGE						
Northeast	48.1	44.6	-4	0.554	0.474	-0.08
North Central	44.3	46.5	-2	0.436	0.344	-0.09
South	38.1	42.3	4	0.412	0.347	-0.07
West	52.7	56.1	3	0.437	0.381	-0.06
ALL SMSAs	46.1	48.2	2	0.450	0.379	-0.07
N = 59						

Source: Adapted from Douglas S. Massey and Nancy A. Denton. "Suburbanization and Segregation in U.S. Metropolitan Areas." *American Journal of Sociology*, 94(3), Tables 1 and 2, pp. 598–600, 602–604. Permission granted by the University of Chicago Press.

ASIAN AMERICANS

The segregation index of Asian Americans is one of the lowest of any minority group's (See Table 10.7.). Their tight-knit families, willingness to sacrifice, strong work ethic, and high regard for education has made Asian Americans one of this nation's great success stories. The sheer numbers of Asian Americans in our universities attest to this success. Academic success translates into economic success, which means more housing options.

There is a problem in measuring the segregation of Asians, because they make up a small percentage of the population in most metropolitan areas. The segregation index of Asians living in central cities is only 41 and drops to 37 in the suburbs. Even in cities like New York, Los Angeles, and San Francisco, where there are large enough populations to have Chinatowns, Japantowns, and Koreatowns, segregation indexes are still moderate (Massey and Denton, 1988; Lam, 1986).

As we discuss in Chapter 12, segregation has social consequences. The assimilation of groups into the mainstream of society is a temporal process with a spatial overlay. An often overlooked aspect of this process is the importance of informal contacts between groups at the grocery, dry cleaner, schools, and churches: contacts circumscribed by the neighborhood in which you live. Segregation limits contact between groups, slows the assimilation process, and slows the movement of groups into the mainstream of American society. The data presented here suggest that the experiences of blacks, Hispanics, and Asians will be very different. The moderate levels of segregation of Hispanics and Asians in the suburbs stand in sharp contrast to those of black Americans.

TABLE 10.7 Asian Population Change in Selected Suburbs, 1970, 1980.

KEY SMSAs	PERCENTAGE OF ASIANS IN SUBURBS			DISSIMILARITY BETWEEN WHITES AND ASIANS		
	1970	1980	CHANGE	1970	1980	CHANGE
Chicago	25.0	49.1	24.0	0.527	0.371	-0.16
Los Angeles	42.4	50.3	8.0	0.506	0.430	-0.08
Miami	66.5	82.5	16.0	0.396	0.301	-0.10
New York	7.7	14.1	6.0	0.498	0.349	-0.15
San Francisco	34.2	48.5	14.0	0.370	0.396	-0.03
AVERAGE						
Northeast	47.0	53.6	7	0.491	0.431	-0.06
North Central	42.7	57.5	15	0.455	0.387	-0.07
South	35.7	47.2	12	0.406	0.382	-0.02
West	46.4	53.5	7	0.338	0.323	-0.01
ALL SMSAs	43.1	53.0	10	0.413	0.376	-0.04
N = 59						

Source: Adapted from Douglas S. Massey and Nancy A. Denton. "Suburbanization and Segregation in U.S. Metropolitan Areas." *American Journal of Sociology,* 94(3), Tables 1 and 2, pp. 598–600, 602–604. Permission granted from the University of Chicago Press.

CONCLUSIONS

Over the years the news media have presented the broad changes in the structure of metropolitan areas as a serious national problem. Is pessimism justified? Are the central cities of the largest and oldest metropolitan areas beyond help? The answers to these questions are neither simple nor definitive, but the tendency to define the changes as an urban crisis is perhaps shortsighted. In addressing these questions one must remember two very important points. First, American cities are in a state of becoming, in a process of continuous change. Second, there is an important difference between the lifespan of a city and the lifespan of an individual. In reference to the first point, the character and spatial form of cities today were shaped by growth during early eras. Schnore (1965) and Berry and Kasarda (1977) have demonstrated that the timing and character of a metropolitan area's suburbanization are tied closely to the period when the city reached metropolitan status. For example, cities that reached metropolitan size in the nineteenth century were shaped by the transportation technology of the horse and the streetcar. These cities were more densely settled in the first place, and when the technology became available, their suburbs grew rapidly. Cities like Dallas and Houston reached metropolitan status in the twentieth century and were shaped by automobile technology. Their initial population densities were lower, and decentralization of their inhabitants was less crucial.

In reference to the second point, people often confuse an institution's time span with personal time frames. The average human lifespan of 70 years is insignificant in comparison with that of cities such as Rome and Athens, which have been in existence for more than three millennia. The suburbanization of the residential population, business, and industry represents the response of these land uses to broad changes in society's transportation, communication, and energy technology, as well as in the size and composition of the population and the organization of society.

SUMMARY

This chapter provides an overview of the changing relationship between the central city and its suburban fringe. Suburbanization is not a new process; it has been a part of this nation's history since its inception more than 200 years ago. However, low population density, home ownership, homogeneous residential social status, and journey-to-work are the elements that make America's suburbs unique.

The suburbanization process is described during four periods spanning nearly 200 years, from 1800 to the present. In the earliest period, early industrialization—1800–1890—most people walked; as a result, one's place of residence and employment were close together. Because of the primitive state of transportation technology, cities were settled at high density and took a circular shape. Moreover, groups that differed in socioeconomic status lived near one another. Only the wealthy could escape to the urban fringe. In the periods that followed, the introduction of new transportation technology, first the electric streetcar and later the automobile, changed American cities into their present-day form. The streetcar era, spanning the years from 1890 through World War I, permitted the first decentralization of the middle class to the suburbs. Later, improvements in automobile technology accelerated the process. In the post-World War II period, in particular, rapid population growth, combined with environmental constraints, organizational changes, and technological breakthroughs in transportation and communication, led to unprecedented growth of urban fringe areas. In the 1980s, suburbanization slowed dramatically, and, in the 1990s, the rate of fringe growth is expected to continue to decline. However, the economic and social integration of the fringe will continue, and new urban forms like minicities will spearhead this process.

There has been a decentralization not only of people but also of business to the suburban ring. In 1970, roughly a third of the civilian work force in this nation's 15 largest cities worked in the suburbs; 20 years later this percentage had jumped to over 60 percent. A number of theories have been developed to describe the decentralization of business. The Weberian model posits that businesses use a rational decision-making process in their attempt to reduce costs and maximize profit. According to this theory, changes in transportation, labor markets, and other factors have led many businesses to seek suburban locations. The industrial location theory expands on these principles by arguing that locational decisions have economic, as well as social, political, and psychological elements. This theory argues that all these elements must be considered when one tries to predict the location of businesses. The third model, the push–pull theory, suggests that the characteristics of the suburbs that attract business, the characteristics of central cities that push businesses out, and the intervening obstacles to a move must be considered in understanding locational decisions. Agglomeration effects and the characteristics of the suburbs that pull businesses to the suburbs appear to be the best predictors of business relocation.

The stratification of suburbs is a major way in which suburbs are studied. Suburbs, like people, can be ranked by socioeconomic status, and the location of suburbs in the stratification system has profound implications for the quality of life of these communities. Three theories were presented to describe changes in the stratification system. The persistence model argues that the socioeconomic character of a suburb is fixed early in its settlement and that a variety of community actors—real estate, banking, businesses—work in concert to maintain the socioeconomic character of the community through time. The ecological model posits that suburbs should experience downward mobility as communities experience the process of invasion and succession. The stratification, or political model, argues that high-income suburbs have the ability to manipulate the system to their advantage because they can afford to hire the skilled professionals necessary to compete for the scarce resources of the metropolis. This model predicts change, not persistence, but with high-income suburbs maintaining or improving their relative position while low-income suburbs decline in socioeconomic status. None of the theories is completely supported in the literature, but time and region appear to be important factors in suburban stratification with older Northern metropolises fitting the stratification model better than metropolises in other regions.

The stratification of suburbs reflects the political reality of the nation's metropolises—political fragmentation. In most American metropolises, the central city is surrounded by many suburbs, smaller in size and politically autonomous. These political units have broad, discretionary powers in the areas of taxation, zoning, and land-use planning and have used these powers to compartmentalize themselves into relatively homogeneous enclaves. These enclaves allow people to find suburbs with a physical and social environment conducive to their particular lifestyle or stage in the life cycle.

In recent years, the experiences of women, blacks, and the elderly have been explored. A common theme in the literature on women and the elderly is that the low density of the suburbs, combined with the lack of crucial social services, creates an environment that makes the lives of these citizens more difficult. Recent research suggests that some of these services are now becoming available in the suburbs. Blacks are highly segregated in the suburbs, and, as a consequence, black Americans receive far fewer returns from their housing dollar than their white counterparts.

Finally, the discussion of the suburbanization process is designed to show how central cities and their outlying fringe areas have become inseparable parts of a single system, a system whose structure can be understood within the general theoretical frameworks provided in Chapters 8 and 9.

NOTES

1. These points of view are expressed not only in the works of Reisman (1958), but also in the works of Spectorsky (1955), Seeley, Sim, and Loosley (1956), Martin (1958), Fava (1956), and Mowrer (1958). A complete citation for each work is found in the bibliography.

2. For a critical review of the problems facing contemporary American suburbia, see M. Baldassare, *Trouble in Paradise: The Suburban Transformation in America,* published by Columbia University Press in 1986.

3. Additional works published in the past decade that have reshaped our image of the historical development of the suburbs include: C. Abbott, *The New Urban America: Growth and Politics in Sunbelt Cities,* published in 1981 by University of North Carolina Press, and "The Suburban Sunbelt," *Journal of Urban History,* 13(3), pp. 275–301; H. C. Binford. *The First Suburbs: Residential Communities on the Boston Periphery, 1815–1860,* published by The University of Chicago Press in 1985; R. E. Foglesong, *Planning the Capitalist City: The Colonial Era to the 1920s,* published by Princeton University Press in 1986; and A. Lees, *Cities Perceived: Urban Society in European and American Thought, 1820–1940,* published by Columbia University Press in 1985. Earlier works by Sam B. Warner, *Streetcar Suburbs: The Process of Growth in Boston,* published by Harvard University Press in 1962, and his work, *The Private City: Philadelphia During Three Periods of Growth,* are classics in the study of urban development and change.

4. There are two books on individual suburbs that I recommend. M. H. Ebner, *Creating Chicago's North Shore: A Suburban History,* published by The University of Chicago Press in 1988, is a beautifully illustrated book. Using hundreds of photographs, period maps, and newspaper illustrations, the author provides a panorama of the development of the North Shore from its founding in the nineteenth century to its rapid growth and development in the twentieth century.

Zane Miller in *Suburb: Neighborhood and Community in Forest Park, Ohio 1935–1976,* published by The University of Tennessee Press in 1981, chronicles the development of a postwar, mass-produced suburb, Forest Park, a suburb of Cincinnati. I grew up a few miles from Forest Park and found this work to be a fascinating account of the attempt by the developer to combine elements of new town planning with the need to make a profit. Forest Park is a predominantly black middle-class suburb, and the experiences of this community in dealing with the issue of racial integration are chronicled in this work.

5.   For the seminal article on the relationship between suburban development and black suburbanization, see John M. Stahura's article, "Suburban Development, Black Suburbanization and the Civil Rights Movement Since World War II," in the *American Sociological Review,* 1986, 52(2), pp. 268–277.

6.   For an excellent overview of the mechanism of racial exclusion, including federal and state legislation, open housing enforcement, and the practices of realtors, see R. W. Lake, *The New Suburbanites: Race and Housing in the Suburbs,* published by the Center for Urban Policy Research at Rutgers University in 1981. M. N. Danielson's *The Politics of Exclusion,* published by Columbia University Press in 1976, remains the benchmark work in the field.

*T*HE COMMUNITY—THE SOCIAL ASPECT OF URBAN LIFE

INTRODUCTION

There are few ideas in Western thought more widely shared than the belief that modern society has destroyed the community. Our literature, movies, criticism, philosophy, social theory, and folk sociology share the belief that we have lost a simpler and better way of life where relationships were based in kin, friendship, and neighborhood. In earlier times consensus reigned, and, when conflict did occur, it was handled informally, in neighborly fashion, over the back fence or in the parlor. Today, critics argue, we find in its place a way of life that is somehow void—void of feeling, void of relevance, void of intimate friendships, supportive kin, and caring neighbors. More disturbing to many is the unsettling feeling that we have lost a sense of belonging, a sense of place, a sense of community. How did this happen? Who is responsible? Theorists and citizens alike blame modern life. Historical forces converged in the twentieth century to create this new way of living, but in its wake tradition was destroyed. Church leaders, politicians, and social critics alike point to the product of this destruction: soaring crime rates, a disintegrating family, a loss of faith in our basic institutions, and the reduction of society to a group of atomistic, selfish, egocentric, and alienated individuals.

Social philosophers argue that the city plays a crucial role in this process of community destruction. It is in the city where modern social and technological innovations were forged. In cities, the factory, the joint stock company, new forms of finance and administration, transportation and communication breakthroughs, modern political arrangements, and new forms of social control were created. Few critics question the role of the city in creating this web of economic, political, and social relationships responsible for the modern way of life. The question is whether this way of life is better or worse than the past.

This chapter explores the community and the social aspects of urban life. What is community? Are the images of the community of the past correct? Has modern society destroyed community? Are the relationships of members of modern societies shallow and superficial? Are there no ties to kin and neighbor? Is the city the villain? We will answer these questions in this chapter by examining the evolution and present usage of the concept of community. In the first section, the contributions of the nineteenth-century community theorists Maine, Tönnies, and Durkheim are explored in terms of the historical factors that shaped their works. Next the works of Robert Park and other members of the Chicago School are discussed in relation to the influence of both the nineteenth-century community theorists and the conditions in American society. In the section that follows, the community as a social unit in contemporary society is examined. In the final section of the chapter, today's most exciting research on community social networks is explored.

EVOLUTION OF THE CONCEPT OF COMMUNITY

Though the concept of community has been of concern to sociologists for nearly 200 years, there continues to be disagreement on its exact definition. Early ideas about community were developed before cities had reached their present-day size and scope, at a time when societies were smaller and less complex and large population centers were few. The early concepts of community focused on the relationship of individuals and groups to their society. How societies maintained order and the forces that produced and maintained rules of conduct were the central concerns in the perspective of the nineteenth-century sociologists.

Societies have changed radically since the nineteenth century, and the concept of community has changed also, but not to the same degree. Though in many respects the nineteenth-century sociologists' concepts of community are not relevant to today's communities, these concepts continue to shape current expectations of the ideal community. This cultural heritage, combined with the fact that what constitutes a "good" or "ideal" community is a subjective evaluation, leads to definitional problems.

The problem of defining the concept of *community* is highlighted in a 1955 article by the sociologist George Hillery entitled, "Definitions of Community: Areas of Agreement." Hillery conducted a thorough review of the sociological literature on community and found 94 separate definitions in use. The only point of total agreement among them was that communities "deal with people!" The diversity of definitions is due to the fact that sociologists work from several different theoretical perspectives, study a wide variety of phenomena, and adopt the definition that is most compatible with their theoretical approach.

Although Hillery concluded that there was no overall agreement beyond the fact that community involves people, he did find substantial agreement among the majority of the authors on three points. First, community involves groups of people who reside in a geographically distinct area. Second, community also refers to the quality of the relationships within this group. The idea that members of a community are bound together by common characteristics such as culture, values, attitudes, and the like was shared by a majority of the authors. Third, community refers to a group of people who are engaged in sustained social interaction—neighboring, for example. Therefore, for the purposes of this text, a *community* is defined as a group of people who share a geographic area and are bound together by common culture, values, race, or social class.

Although an operational definition of community has been established, what level of community is meant? A city? A small town? A neighborhood? The concept of community has evolved from earlier concepts. To understand its present usage and the types of geographic units to which it refers, one must understand its evolution.

The concept of community was a central element in the works of most of the founders of sociology—Comté, de Tocqueville, Maine, Tönnies, LePlay, Marx, and Durkheim (Nisbet, 1966, pp. 47–60). These men were living and writing during the nineteenth century, a period of profound change in western society. Change was so rapid and pervasive that it can best be described as revolutionary. Industrialization, urbanization, and bureaucratization were the forces shaping society. Many negative by-products of transformation were manifested. In this atmosphere, the modern concept of community first emerged. Community during this era was often thought of in romantic terms as a way of life destroyed by the forces of the modern world. Community was equated with the good life, and industrial society was often contrasted with the community of the past. Thus, the concept of community first was used for the purpose of contrast—the past versus the present—and examples of this usage can be found in the works of Maine, Tönnies, and Durkheim (Bell and Newby, 1972, pp. 21–27).

SIR HENRY MAINE: FAMILY VS. INDIVIDUAL STATUS

Maine, an Englishman writing in the middle of the nineteenth century, was primarily interested in the origins of codified or written law.[1] His book, *Ancient Law,* was not concerned with community as such, but his work greatly influenced other thinkers of his age, especially Tönnies. The major contribution of Maine is his demonstration that one cannot understand a society's legal system without first understanding its social system. The contrast he makes between societies of different ages is based primarily on ascribed status and tradition versus achieved status and contract.

The family and tradition. Maine describes these differences clearly in the following statement:

> Society in primitive times was not what it is assumed to be at present, a collection of individuals. In fact, and in view of the man who composed it, it was an aggregation of families. The contrast may be most forcibly expressed by saying that the unit of ancient society was the family, of a modern society an individual (1870, p. 126).

In many ancient societies, the individual was not recognized in law; the family was the legal entity. The individual's position in society was based on the family into which he or she was born. Stated another way, the status of the individual in society was ascribed by family membership. In addition, solutions to the problems of day-to-day living were drawn from the experience of past generations or tradition rather than based on reason.

In contrast, the individual, not the family, is the important unit under law in modern society. Some modern societies even protect the individual from her or his family (for example, in cases of child abuse)—a practice unknown to "society in primitive times." The individual's position in modern society, although influenced by family membership, depends mainly on the person's skills, training, and education. Ideally, the individual rises to a social status based on his or her achievements rather than family membership.

The contract. The contract is another important element of modern society. To Maine, the contract was a revolutionary social invention that made possible an entirely different form of society. A *contract* is simply a binding agreement between two or more individuals or parties. The agreement states certain terms and conditions that, when fulfilled, relieve both parties of any further obligation. It permits two strangers to come together, carry out a business transaction, and then go their separate ways once the terms of the agreement have been fulfilled. Contractualism makes possible an ordered society composed of individuals.

Maine's distinctions between the legal systems of *primitive* and *modern* societies were explicitly recognized and taken into account by sociologists who later attempted to understand and explain change in the social relationships among persons in industrial societies. The influence of Maine is clear in the writings of Tönnies and Durkheim.

FERDINAND TÖNNIES: GEMEINSCHAFT AND GESELLSCHAFT

Tönnies's book *Gemeinschaft and Gesellschaft* (usually translated as *Community and Society*) was first published in 1887. It has provided a constant source of ideas for students of community ever since. Drawing on the earlier works of Sir Henry Maine, Otto von Gierke, and Fustel de Coulanges, Tönnies described several dimensions along which European society had changed (Nisbet, 1966, pp. 72–73). The basic changes were threefold. First, the basis of one's social status had changed from ascription to achievement. In other words, a person's position in society was becoming less dependent on the family into which he or she had been born and more dependent on the individual's accomplishments. Second, the individual was increasingly viewed as the basic unit of society. As Maine noted, by the nineteenth century, the individual was recognized in the legal system of western societies as a person rather than simply a member of a communal organization. Third, the character of societies themselves had changed from sacred-communal to the secular-associational (Nisbet, 1966, p. 73).

Tönnies, like many nineteenth- and twentieth-century theorists, employed a technique known as *ideal types* to structure his analysis. Ideal types do not exist in reality but represent the essential qualities of the phenomenon being studied. Researchers construct ideal types by examining a category of things and then identifying those qualities that set the members of that grouping apart from all others. For example, psychologists use this technique to develop profiles of potential airline hijackers, bank robbers, or child abusers. The ideal type "hijacker" does not really exist; rather, it represents those qualities shared by all persons who are hijackers.

Tönnies employed the ideal types Gemeinschaft and Gesellschaft to describe the characteristics of two different types of societies, the human relationships within those societies, and the process by which society is transformed from one type to another. These ideal types are at polar extremes of a continuum and represent the essential characteristics of traditional versus modern communities. *Gemeinschaft* translates easily into *community*. *Gesellschaft* is more difficult to interpret; its translation is *society*. The problem is that community is a part of society, but the concept becomes clear when one examines the types of societies to which Tönnies was referring.

Gemeinschaft. Gemeinschaft refers to communities that are small and relatively homogeneous. Members of the community normally spend their entire lives in the same locale and have very little geographic mobility. The social structure is relatively simple but rigid. Each person has a clear understanding of where he or she belongs in society; this position is determined by the social status of the family of the person's birth. Gemeinschaft leads to a communal life based on tradition, with strong sentimental attachments to the moral code and conventions of the place. There is nearly universal agreement among the members on the way things should be done. Deviations from this code are punished informally. Because people, places, and things are familiar to everyone, the individual cannot escape this collectivity. The basic unit of the social structure is the family. The individual's life has meaning only in the context of the family and the larger community. Therefore, the moral code is clear, strongly held, and enforced by the family and the church.

The social structure of Gemeinschaft is made possible by the nature of day-to-day interaction among its members. In Gemeinschaft, social relationships are warm and personal, with strong ties among individuals and between the individual and the community. The members of Gemeinschaft are like a family, and, as in a family, the rules of conduct are understood, not codified into law. *Harmony*, *naturalness*, *depth*, and *fullness* are words often used to describe the intimacy and pervasiveness of the relationships among members of Gemeinschaft (Nisbet, 1966, p. 75). Obviously, under these conditions, individualism and privacy are at a minimum.

Gesellschaft. In polar extreme to the ideal type of Gemeinschaft is the ideal type of Gesellschaft. Tönnies saw Gesellschaft as a new phenomenon, the end product of social change occurring in the nineteenth century. Gesellschaft refers to large, complex, heterogeneous societies composed of individuals who differ in their racial, ethnic, and socioeconomic characteristics. The social structure is complex and fluid. The individual has been freed from the constraints of the family and ideally may rise in the social structure to her or his own level of achievement. Gesellschaft is a rational, willed society that one can join or leave at will. The basic unit of the social structure is the individual and as a result the traditional means of social control—the family and the church—are supplanted by what is called *rational-legal authority*, the police and court system, for example. Deviations from the normative order are no longer sanctioned informally but are penalized by formal institutions such as the courts and police.

In Gesellschaft, each individual is guided by her or his self-interest. Human relationships become impersonal; egoism and competition begin to dominate interpersonal relationships. Sharing and concern for others are minimal. Because economic self-interest guides the relationships between individuals, a formal device—the contract—must be used to ensure that both parties abide by an agreement. Moreover, in Gesellschaft, the size and complexity of the social structure make it impossible to know the social status of each person. Tangible symbols of a person's social standing therefore become important, for example, cars, clothing, and homes.

Gesellschaft is a contractual, individualistic society in which the accumulation of property has a greater importance than close personal ties among individuals. Gesellschaft is symbolized best by the modern corporation and its complex economic and legal relationships with the larger society. Relationships are based not on kinship and friendship, but on rationality, calculation, and contractualism.

Gesellschaft refers not just to a concept of society, but also to a process. Gesellschaft describes the process by which society is transformed from one type to another. As a society is transformed from Gemeinschaft to Gesellschaft, the nature of its social organization is changed. Social relationships become more contractual, based on self-interest. Consequently, communal ties are weakened, social solidarity decreases, and the individual is more isolated and potentially more alienated.

Gemeinschaft and Gesellschaft are concepts that reflect a great many factors—legal, economic, cultural, and intellectual—but at the core of each concept is an image of a type of social relationship and a state of mind. As Nisbet (1966) notes, the importance of Tönnies's work is not simply classification of community types but rather his historical and comparative use of these types, which gives insight into the fundamental social change caused by the processes of urbanization, industrialization, and bureaucratization (p. 78).

To Tönnies, Gemeinschaft was humankind's natural habitat, and it was the basis of what he thought modern society should be. Tönnies considered the industrial society of his day to be dehumanizing and artificial, in contrast to the natural structure of Gemeinschaft. This viewpoint was a major source of disagreement between Tönnies and his contemporary, Emile Durkheim, who held that industrial society could be as satisfactory as western societies had been before the Industrial Revolution.

EMILE DURKHEIM—MECHANICAL AND ORGANIC SOLIDARITY

Durkheim shared with Tönnies many concerns about the direction of modern society. He differed from Tönnies, however, in that he believed modern society could be as natural and organic as the Gemeinschaft societies of the past. A major theme in

Durkheim's work is social solidarity. If modern societies are large, complex, and heterogeneous, what is the social glue that holds individuals together to form a functioning society? Durkheim's work covers a broad spectrum of topics, but, for the student of community, his analysis of the types of social solidarity is the most important.

Mechanical solidarity. Durkheim made a distinction between two types of social solidarity—mechanical and organic.[2] Mechanical solidarity is found in small homogeneous societies, similar to Tönnies's Gemeinschaft. In such societies, the division of labor is simple, and each family unit can carry out most of the functions necessary for society. The division of labor is based on the age and the sex of individuals. Moreover, each member knows every other member, and people agree on what society should be. Durkheim called this agreement the *collective conscience*—the values, beliefs, and sentiments held in common by the members of society. The operation of the collective conscience is reflected most clearly in society's norms or rules of conduct and the types of punishment used when these rules are violated. Durkheim agreed with Maine that law reflects the underlying character of society, its institutional structure, and the form of social solidarity.

In societies based on mechanical solidarity, legal rules are repressive; violation of rules demands retaliation and punishment. In general, in such societies, offenses against the collective conscience evoke an immediate and direct response, and this punishment guarantees conformity in other members. Such punishment serves to reinforce the collective conscience. In the context of a Gemeinschaft society, deviants serve a positive social function. Deviation from a norm elicits an immediate response from society. It reinvigorates the collective conscience and increases the solidarity among the members.

Organic solidarity. In small societies, an individual can know the roles of every other member. Modern societies, in contrast, are large and complex, composed of diverse groups of people of which an individual has little or no knowledge. In these societies, the division of labor is complex, based in many cases on specialized skills learned through years of formal training. Because society is composed of diverse groups, there is much less agreement on what society should be. For example, few crimes in these societies would be viewed as "a crime against society." Treason is one, but no one has been tried and convicted of that crime in the United States in more than twenty years. The question posed by Durkheim was, if this type of society is composed of individuals and diverse groups of people and if there is no single unifying collective conscience, what keeps it together? Durkheim suggests that modern societies have a special type of social cohesion—organic solidarity.

In modern complex societies, an individual is dependent on a great many other people for day-to-day existence. An urbanite, for example, depends for basic sustenance—food, clothing, and shelter—on thousands of other people with whom he or she has no personal contact. Organic solidarity occurs in societies in which separate groups perform many different functions. A good analogy of how organic solidarity works is a living organism. The functioning of each organ in the body depends on the functioning of every other part. Each organ is composed of specialized cells that collectively carry out a specific function. All organs work together to accomplish a single purpose—life. A similar interdependency among diverse groups in society (cooperation necessary for survival) provides social cohesion.

The change in the nature of a society's solidarity is reflected in law. With organic solidarity, law is no longer repressive but restitutive. Civil lawsuits, for example, attempt to bring parties together, to reconcile differences so that society can work more smoothly. Contractualism and the legal system that emerges to enforce it exemplify this new form of organic solidarity. However, the collective conscience does not cease to exist. Durkheim notes that although a contract is often made between strangers, a contract cannot exist unless it is built on an explicit social foundation. The parties to a contract know when they enter such a relationship that society will enforce it. Therefore, a collective conscience is present—a set of beliefs and sentiments—but it operates indirectly on an individual through modern society's institutional structure. In societies characterized by mechanical solidarity, the individual is bound directly to society without this intermediary. In addition, mechanical solidarity continues to exist within modern societies, not in society as a whole but within specialized groups. In metropolitan areas, for example, the viability of tight-knit ethnic neighborhoods is based largely on mechanical solidarity.

The preceding brief review of the works of three sociologists of diverse national origins—French, English, and German—shows that each explored the changing nature of human association. Questions raised by these theorists are still central to the discipline of sociology, especially the literature on community. Collectively they had an important influence on all of sociology, but particularly on the works of Robert Park and other members of the Chicago School. The influence of the European social philosophers on Robert Park and the contributions of the Chicago ecologists to the study of community are examined in the following section.

ROBERT PARK AND THE CHICAGO SCHOOL

The preceding section is a brief overview of the theoretical roots of the present concept of community. In general, Tönnies, Maine, Durkheim, and other European theorists documented both the destruction of the small, tightly integrated community and the emergence of community in its modern form. The works of these sociologists give a negative impression of urban life—a life in which egoism, isolation, and anomie pervade the community. Interestingly, early American sociology continued in this tradition, as is particularly evident in the works of Robert Park and other members of the Chicago School.

Wirth, in his 1938 essay, "Urbanism as a Way of Life," summarized the major viewpoint of this school: City growth, with its concomitant increases in the size, density, and heterogeneity of population, leads to a substitution of secondary relations for primary ones and a greater dependency on formal means of social control (See

Chapter 1.). Moreover, the traditional sources of community solidarity and control (the family and the church) were believed to be largely ineffective in the urban setting, and social disorganization was thought to be a predictable outcome of these underlying changes. Through the works of these sociologists, social disorganization became a central theme in the theoretical and empirical works in American sociology for the next two decades. The obsession of the Chicago ecologists with disorganization is reflected in the titles of their works: Thrasher's *The Gang;* Anderson's *The Hobo;* Shaw's *Delinquency Areas, The Jack-Roller,* and *Brothers in Crime;* Zorbaugh's *The Gold Coast and the Slum;* Wirth's *The Ghetto;* and Faris and Dunham's *Mental Disorders in Urban Areas.*

INFLUENCE OF NINETEENTH-CENTURY COMMUNITY THEORISTS

There is an important difference between the sociology of Tönnies, Maine, and Durkheim and that of the Chicago ecologists, however. The nineteenth-century theorists used the concept of community in a broad sense and considered whole societies. The Chicago School was referring to cities, like Chicago. Thus, *community* is synonymous with *city* in much of their work. In addition, the concept of community was defined ecologically as the "patterns of symbiotic and communalistic relations that develop in a population; it is in the nature of a collective response to the habitat; it constitutes the adjustment of organisms to the environment" (Hawley, 1950, p. 2). Although community was defined narrowly by these ecologists, both groups wrestled with essentially the same problem—the problem of order in society. Park's sociology in particular attempted to identify the "control mechanism through which a community composed of several quite different subcommunities can arrange its affairs so that each of them maintains its own distinctive way of life without endangering the life of the whole" (Stein, 1972, p. 17). This statement is reminiscent of Durkheim's work because Durkheim greatly influenced Park. Durkheim addressed the same problem in his interpretation of the transition from mechanical to organic solidarity as the basis for order in society. Like Park, Durkheim saw a role for each type of solidarity in modern society: Subgroups within society were held together by the bonds of mechanical solidarity, whereas in the larger society the cohesive forces of organic solidarity prevailed. Park examined the relationships between subcommunities (natural areas) and the encompassing community. The major thrust of both of their works, therefore, was how organic solidarity can be achieved (Stein, 1971, pp. 17–18).[3]

Achieving solidarity in the modern community. To Durkheim, the integration of complex societies was based on the role of occupational subgroups. Each subgroup—physicians, lawyers, tradesmen, and skilled workers—would develop their own code of ethics through which the behavior of their members would be restricted. Moreover, in order to survive, each subgroup had to integrate its functions with the larger society. In this way, the self-interest of the occupational subgroup and the necessities of organic solidarity could be reconciled (Stein, 1972, p. 20).

Park approached the same problem but from a somewhat different perspective, subcommunities. Subcommunities were simply another type of subgroup in society that were defined spatially. The behavior of the members of these subcommunities could be controlled either through a complex set of social institutions (police, courts, welfare agencies) or through the operation of the informal control mechanisms of the residential subgroups. The operation of these informal control mechanisms within subcommunities was of greatest interest to the members of the Chicago School.

Natural areas. As noted in previous chapters, the urban landscape is not homogeneous and undifferentiated, but is composed of a mosaic of social worlds. These subcommunities, or natural areas as they were called by Park, are often strikingly different in makeup, but most large cities share many of the same types of subareas. For example, every large city has a central business district, slums, ghettoes, and middle- and working-class areas. Most large cities have a "skid row," a "bright lights district," and a "Greenwich Village," where "life is freer, more adventurous and lonely than elsewhere" (Stein, 1972, p. 21). To Park, these areas were the product of unplanned biotic forces; the product of the sorting of individuals and groups into homogeneous subareas based on common culture and language, race, or occupational and socioeconomic status. The reason for their emergence was framed in purely ecological terms. Natural areas emerged simply because they helped a group of people with similar characteristics satisfy "fundamental needs and solve fundamental problems." Park reasoned that as long as the problems remained, natural areas would continue to exist.

There is another important characteristic of natural areas, according to Park. Through time, each natural area develops its "own peculiar traditions, customs, conventions, standards of decency and propriety, and, if not a language of its own, at least a universe of discourse, in which words and acts have a meaning which is appreciably different for each local community" (Park, 1952, p. 201). New residents of the natural areas through time are socialized and take on the norms of their new community. Therefore, once a natural area comes into existence it has a tendency to perpetuate itself. Thus, Park, like Durkheim, saw subgroups—defined spatially within the larger community—as developing a moral code to regulate the behavior of the members. In addition, natural areas must make a contribution to the functioning of the encompassing community. This functional interdependence among subareas of the city was the basis for the integration and solidarity of the larger community.

Why social disorganization was emphasized. The question remains of why Park and the Chicago School emphasized social disorganization. The answer relates to Park's notion of natural area. Natural areas were not viewed as static but as dynamic phenomena. Park reasoned that within a city, individuals, groups, and institutions are constantly being sorted and relocated. During periods of rapid population growth, especially when there is an influx of large numbers of diverse ethnic or racial groups, the stability of certain natural areas is upset as the subareas undergo the invasion–succession process. As a result of this transition, the mechanisms for social control within the natural areas are weakened and social disorganization occurs. Most natural areas maintain their solidarity, but in some areas the control mechanisms break down.

In the 1920s, Chicago gained more than one-half million people. This rapid growth affected all areas of the city to a degree, but nowhere was the effect greater than in the slums. In the slum, ghetto, and hobohemia, the Chicago ecologists saw an absence of any effective means of social control. In these areas, the traditional forms of social control—the family, the church, and the neighborhood—had been undermined and such "secondary agencies as the police, courts, newspapers, schools and settlement houses" had taken their place.

CRITICISM OF THE NATURAL AREA CONCEPT

The image of a community (a city) as a planless outgrowth of ecological segregation, along with the view that homogeneity and stability characterize a city's subcommunities or natural areas, has persisted and influences the present image of community. Is this image correct? Did natural areas, as the concept was advanced by the Chicago School, exist in the 1920s, and, if so, do they exist today?

The social order of the slum and ghetto ignored. A review of the works published by the Chicago School in the 1920s and the research on subcommunities completed since that decade suggests that Park and the Chicago ecologists may have overstated their case. First, were the slums, ghettoes, and hobohemias as devoid of social order and institutional structures as this school suggests? In *The Gold Coast and the Slum* (1929), Zorbaugh begins with this general statement on the slum, which he characterizes as a collection of isolated individuals:

> The slum is an area of freedom and individualism. Over large stretches of the slum men neither know nor trust their neighbors. Aside from a few marooned families, a large part of the native population is transient: prostitutes, criminals, outlaws, hobos. Foreigners who come to make a fortune, as we used to go west, and expect to return to the Old Country as soon as they make "their stake," who are not really a part of American life, and who wish to live in the city as cheaply as possible, live in the lodging-houses of the slum. Here, too, are the areas of immigrant first settlement, the foreign colonies. And here are congregated the "undesirable" alien groups, such as the Chinese and the Negro (p. 128).

Zorbaugh in this paragraph lumps a number of diverse groups under one heading—slum dwellers. Moreover, he implies that they are unorganized. But it is interesting to note that within a few pages he describes the manner in which the immigrant community is organized:

> As the colony grows, the immigrant finds in it a social world. In the colony he meets with sympathy, understanding and encouragement. There he finds his fellow-countrymen who understand his habits and standards and share his life-experience and viewpoint. In the colony he has status, plays a role in a group. In the life of the colony's streets and cafes, in its churches and benevolent societies, he finds response and security. In the colony he finds that he can live, be somebody, satisfy his wishes—all of which is impossible in the strange world outside (p. 141).

Commenting on other areas, Zorbaugh notes:

> The life of this area is far from unorganized. The Gold Coast has its clubs; intimate groups gather in "village" studios; the foreign areas have numerous lodges and mutual benefit societies; the slum has its "gangs...." And these groups may play an enormously important role in the lives of their members (p. 192).

During the same period other researchers, including H. A. Miller (1920), Robert Park, Fredrich Thrasher (1926), and Louis Wirth (1928), identified similar organizations within the slum, but their attention continued to be focused on social disorganization. Why were findings of organization in slums reported by the Chicago ecologists and then ignored? Suttles (1972) and Whyte (1943) suggest that the theoretical and political perspectives, as well as the class and social backgrounds of the researchers themselves, biased their research.[4] Whyte (1943) observes:

> Apparently Zorbaugh began his study with the conviction that the slum represents the Gesellschaft ideal type. [This idea is expressed in the first quote.] His discussion of the evidences of social organization does not fit the ideal type. However, by calling them [organizations] interstitial phenomena, he manages to dismiss them from further consideration (p. 36).

Zorbaugh found that lower-class organizations were closely bound to the local area and had no "community-wide loyalties." Because these organizations were very different from the middle-class ones with which he was familiar, he dismissed them as unimportant. More recent ethnographic works, however, have outlined in detail the social organization and the normative order in these districts. Whyte's *Street Corner Society* (1955), Liebow's *Tally's Corner* (1967), Gans's *The Urban Villagers* (1962), and Suttles's *The Social Order of the Slum* (1968) are four of the dozens of community studies that have reported in detail the social processes operating within slums.

Park's influence on research. Apparently Park's influence at the University of Chicago over both the types of research and the researchers themselves led to biases in the school's works. Park looked back with nostalgia to the days when the family, the church, and the neighborhood provided a natural order for a community. In the present, he looked to secondary institutions such as schools, newspapers, and social agencies as potent forces in reconstituting a community, e.g., a city. Within this scheme, natural areas were viewed as a social unit that could provide a social order similar to that of an earlier and simpler time. Therefore, Park saw the combining of two worlds, the Gemeinschaft in the subcommunity within the encompassing Gesellschaft society.

Difficulty in identifying natural areas. The natural area concept has a second weakness. Natural areas were viewed by the Chicago School as emerging through the operation of basic ecological or biotic forces. To these ecologists, the most distinctive characteristic of these areas was that they were not planned or artificially constructed, but developed out of millions of individual decisions based on different moral, ecological, political, and economic positions. The city from this perspective was a mosaic of social worlds loosely organized by larger political and administrative structures of the metropolis. In other words, each natural area had a unique quality that was the result of the unique combination of the area's ethnic and racial mix, physical characteristics, and other factors, including the income and occupation of its residents.

The reader of this literature is left with the impression that all one needs to do to delineate the boundaries of each natural area is examine the racial, ethnic, income, and occupational characteristics of a city's population or examine its housing and land-use characteristics. That is, a city is seen as a gigantic jigsaw puzzle, and natural areas are the pieces. In this scheme, boundaries do not overlap, and the world is neat and ordered.

In the 1930s, 1940s, and 1950s, research was published that called into question the validity of the natural area concept. For example, Davie (1938), Hatt (1946), and Form et al. (1954) were unable to find clearly bounded, culturally homogeneous areas in the cities they examined. By the mid-1940s, the concept of natural areas and the theoretical foundation of the Chicago ecologists had been seriously undermined.

As a result of these findings, most research since the 1940s has shifted from the physical characteristics of urban subareas to the social character of these areal units. Although the term *natural area* is seldom used, Keller (1968) suggests that many of the key components of this concept have been integrated into the popular term *neighborhood*. Since the 1940s, the major areas of sociological research on the neighborhood have been urban-rural differences in neighborhoods, formal and informal participation in neighborhood activities, family adaptation to new residential environments, social networks in urban areas, propinquity, and neighboring and symbolic communities.

SOCIAL CONSTRUCTION OF COMMUNITIES

Much recent research is directed to identifying the present nature of the communities. Janowitz (1961), Greer (1962), Suttles (1968, 1972), and Hunter (1974) address two questions about the modern community. First, what is the relationship of communities to changes in the scale of the larger society? Second, do local communities have recognizable names and boundaries, and are these names and boundaries known to their residents and members of the larger metropolis as well?

SOCIETAL SCALE AND THE LOCAL COMMUNITY

A consensus seems to have developed about the relationship between societal scale and the nature of a local community. Increasing societal scale—indicated by increasing use of nonhuman energy and increased per capita output—results in a loss of autonomy and fragmentation of local groups and increased dependency on secondary and formal institutions, especially in the area of crisis intervention. Concomitantly, increasing societal scale leads to greater social and physical mobility and a decreasing dependency on the local community.

Separation of physical and social neighborhoods. The validity of this point is found in the research of Morris and Mogey (1965). These authors found in their studies on neighboring a decreasing correspondence between social and physical groupings in urban areas. They concluded that the growth of secondary institutions, such as schools and welfare organizations, and increased physical mobility have led to a separation between physical and social neighborhoods. As Keller (1968) states, these changes have altered the social relationships among neighbors from "neighboring of place to a neighboring by taste" (p. 55). Transportation innovations, in particular, have drastically changed the nature of human relationships within urban areas. In the past, because of poor transportation, people either worked within the home or lived within walking distance of their place of employment. The individual was closely tied to the subcommunity because there were no alternatives. Today, the automobile gives Americans great physical mobility. The place of employment is normally far from one's place of residence. The automobile gives individuals many alternatives. The urbanite has been released from the constraints of the local area, and he or she can be very selective in choosing friends. Ties to the local community have been weakened, but new forms of social relationships have emerged (Meier, 1968; Tobin, 1976).

The community of limited liability. Janowitz (1961) in contrast explored in detail the effect of an increasing societal scale on the subareas of the city. To Janowitz, the most important change brought about by increasing societal scale was the metamorphosis of community from a primary grouping to a more voluntary and less involving institution. Janowitz (1961) introduced the concept of "community of limited liability" to describe this phenomenon and defined it as the "intentional, voluntary, and especially the partial and differential involvement of residents in their local community" (p. 47).

Janowitz discovered this pattern in specific areal units while studying the local community press. He found that neighborhood newspapers sold weekly within the metropolis's subcommunities provided not only an advertising medium for the local merchants, but also a communication mechanism for the social and cultural integration of the local area. During the same period, Hawley and Zimmer (1970), Axelrod (1957), and others found large numbers of voluntary associations operating within local areas, organized to argue their community's position on metropolitan issues. The Clintonville area of Columbus, Ohio, provides a good example. In 1975, the city of Columbus decided to widen and thus destroy a beautiful tree-lined street in the Clintonville area known as Northwest Boulevard. The local area's weekly, *The Booster*, in a series of front-page stories, publicized the city's plans. As a result, several local concerned citizens' groups were formed, monies were collected for attorneys' fees, and the city's plans were blocked in the courts. The point that Janowitz and others have made is that the neighborhood or "the community of limited liability" is no longer a primary group, but it is still an important source of social contacts for a large proportion of the metropolis's residents.

SYMBOLIC COMMUNITIES

*types of
communities*

Suttles (1968, 1972) provides additional support for the concept of the community of limited liability and also addresses the question of whether local communities have recognizable boundaries that are known both to their residents and to members of the larger metropolis.

Suttles's research suggests that the individual simplifies and makes comprehensible the complexity of the metropolis by developing a simplified mental or cognitive map of the city. In large cities, those mental maps were found to consist of three symbolic structures—the face-block, the defended neighborhood, and the community of limited liability.

The face-block. The most elementary grouping in urban areas is a network of acquaintances known as the face-block. "These are acquaintances who are recognized from face-to-face relations or encounters and seen regularly because they live on the same block, use the same bus station, shop at the same stores, and for any number of reasons continually cross one another's pathways" (Suttles, 1972, p. 55). The basis for this association is not ethnicity, race, or socioeconomic status but rather familiarity because in the back of each person's mind "is the knowledge that this person lives close by or uses the same facilities" (Suttles, 1972, p. 55).

Face-blocks are only loosely organized and do not constitute a neighborhood because the boundaries of these units are normally known only to the residents living within them and remain unknown to outsiders. The areal unit is real and important for the people living within its boundaries, however. Parents often use the face-block as the area in which their children are permitted to play. As a result, these units become the basis of the child's peer-group activities. In addition, adults use this unit to organize block clubs, "a common adult form of organization for acquiring better public services" (Suttles, 1972, p. 56).

Social process carried out in the face-block. Thus, the face-block that surrounds the household is an important and inescapable part of any household's environment. Here the problems of social order are clearest because this is the areal unit in which the play of children as well as child–adult and adult–adult, relations must be regulated. If misunderstanding and conflict arise, the orderly performance of the household may be interrupted. In addition, the social interaction that takes place on this level is in many respects determined by the nature of the physical environment. In apartment-house districts, the communication level is low because of the lack of common or overlapping space and a separation of the work and leisure routines of the residents. In these areas, greater dependence generally is placed on the rules of the building and the formal authorities that enforce them.

In familistic areas, social interaction is greater. As Suttles notes, it occurs among persons whose paths must cross—in adjoining backyards, bus stops, schools, on sidewalks, and in playgrounds. Interaction with one's neighbors is unavoidable (Michelson, 1970).

Although the face-block is a social unit for both adults and children, Suttles believes that it is not based on the ties suggested by Park in the natural area concept. Although age, race, and ethnic and socioeconomic status characteristics do bring about the general sorting of individuals into subareas of the city, physical closeness and small area are the basis of the face-block.

The defended neighborhood. The defended neighborhood is composed of numerous face-blocks. It is commonly the smallest area within the metropolis that has an identity known to both its residents and outsiders. Suttles (1972) defines it as that area outside the face-block in which residents have a high degree of familiarity and a relative degree of security on the streets compared to adjacent areas (p. 57). These units vary considerably in size depending on the characteristics of the area's inhabitants, but normally include the schools, churches, and grocery and retail stores that an area's residents use on a day-to-day basis.

Zorbaugh's *The Gold Coast and the Slum* and many of the other works by the Chicago School explored the operation of defended neighborhoods. Park and his followers give the impression that these areas were homogeneous, occupied by a single ethnic, racial, or occupational grouping. Suttles, however, suggests that very few of these defended neighborhoods now have, or ever have had, homogeneous populations and that most inner-city neighborhoods have undergone a continuous process of invasion–succession during the past 40 years. Interestingly, although these areas' populations have completely turned over, the character and boundaries of many of the areas have remained the same. This persistence is due to the fact that these units have been incorporated into the cognitive maps of residents of the larger community. As Suttles remarks:

> [Some neighborhoods] may be known as snobbish, trashy, tough, exclusive, dangerous, mixed or any number of other things. Some neighborhoods may simply be unknown, and reference to one's residence may arouse only puzzlement and necessitate one's explaining one's guilt or virtue by residential association. In any case, neighborhood identity remains a stable judgemental reference against which people are assessed, and although some may be able to evade the allegations thrown their way, they nonetheless find such evasions necessary (1972, p. 35).

These units are also used in the cognitive maps of city residents to guide other types of behavior, specifically travel. In large metropolitan areas, one must be concerned about one's personal safety. In many areas of a city it is not safe to travel day or night. The cognitive map held by individuals simplifies the choices he or she makes on spatial movement within the city, for example, areas of travel, time of day, type of transportation, and appropriate number of people in the group.

Finally, although some people may have strong sentimental attachments to a defended neighborhood, this feeling is not the basis for social cohesion in these areas. Though there may be underlying similarities in race, ethnicity, and income, solidarity appears to be simply a matter of common residence. Defended neighborhoods are a grouping and as in any other grouping "members are joined in a common plight whether or not they like it" (Suttles, 1972, p. 37). The fate of a defended neighborhood often depends on city planners, realtors, politicians, and industry. This common fate and common experience provide the cohesion of the neighborhood. A threat to the neighborhood will lead to a defensive response that generates cohesive solidarity.

Community of limited liability. A defended neighborhood may or may not be known to members of the larger community. A community of limited liability, in contrast, is a unit of analysis that research has shown to be symbolically important to residents of an area and to members of the larger metropolis as well. More important is the fact that in some cities the boundaries of these units are reinforced by governmental agencies on the federal, state, and local levels. Physical and symbolic boundaries of these areas do not always reinforce each other. However, such physical characteristics of a city as parks, railroads, waterways, highways, and major distorting features in the terrain normally lead to a clear demarcation of these areas.

Formation of communities of limited liability. One aspect of the boundary-forming and boundary-maintenance process that Suttles believes has largely been ignored by sociologists is the role of external organizations in defining residential groupings. Both Suttles (1972) and Hunter (1974) report that the boundaries, as well as the names used by residents to identify their communities, have often been imposed by planners, developers, booster organizations, and realtors. "Once symbols and boundaries come into existence numerous external adversaries or advocates…are anxious to claim a constituency or market and keep it intact" (Suttles, 1972, p. 49). Unlike the other cognitive structures identified by Suttles, a community of limited liability has an official identity that requires its name and boundaries to be institutionally secured by governmental acknowledgment. More importantly, although this official identity is imposed by an external force, the boundaries and symbols are often incorporated into the cognitive models of the residents of the neighborhood and the wider metropolis as well (Hunter, 1974, p. 25).

The validity of the concept can be seen in Hunter's research on the community areas first delineated by Burgess and his students in the 1920s. At that time, Chicago was mapped into 75 exhaustive and mutually exclusive areas. Kitagawa and Tauber outlined the criteria used in this mapping process in the introduction to the 1960 edition of *Local Community Fact Book for Chicago Metropolitan Area.* They state:

> …when community area boundaries were delineated…the objective was to define a set of subareas of the city each of which could be regarded as having a history of its own as a community, a name, an awareness on the part of its inhabitants of community interests, and a set of local businesses and organizations oriented to the local community (Kitagawa and Tauber, 1963, p. xiii).

Although the names and boundaries were imposed on these areas nearly fifty years ago, for a large proportion of Chicago's residents these community areas still operate as meaningful symbolic communities or natural areas (Hunter, 1974, p. 25). A significant percentage of the residents sampled were able to name the community area and its boundaries in a way consistent with the *Fact Book.*

In terms of the mechanisms by which these symbols were transmitted from generation to generation, Hunter points to the role of local community organizations, neighborhood newspapers, government agencies, and real estate interests as crucial in maintaining symbolic stability through time. The gradual socialization of a new member of a community into an area through initial contacts with schools, shops, realtors, and neighbors is another dimension of this process. Both Hunter and Suttles provide general support for the existence of these areal units in the city of Chicago. Similar units are found in many other cities. A map of Cleveland's planning areas is provided in Figure 8.1.

A community of limited liability develops when the similar interests of residents are transformed into common interests based on the degree to which the vital resources of a household are involved—for example, public schools and government services. The residents of a community of limited liability are therefore functionally interdependent, often with a single adversary. Communication in a community of limited liability takes place through two channels—the community press and local voluntary organizations. Organizations, such as homeowner associations, are more important in ordering behavior, whereas the press is the more effective channel of communication.

PARTICIPATION IN LOCAL COMMUNITY AFFAIRS

What is the relationship of local voluntary associations and the community press to the residents of an area? The interaction of the community press and the local voluntary associations is examined in detail by Greer and Orleans (1962), Greer (1970), and others in their studies of the participation of residents in local community affairs. These authors suggest that approximately 90 percent of a city's population fits into one of three categories: isolates, neighbors, and community actors.

Isolates. Isolates are people who are literally disengaged from the organizational structure of a local community. They operate as neighbors slightly if at all and belong to none of the voluntary organizations in the area. In general, they rarely vote. They seldom read the local community newspaper except to see the advertisements. As a result, they are generally ignorant of most of the local community affairs. For example, they are unable to name local leaders or important current issues in the community.

Neighbors. Neighbors are the second largest group. They are involved in their immediate social environment. Generally, they live in the small world of the face-block, and their social life revolves around casual social interaction and family friendships. They tend to be young families, and, like isolates, they have low rates of participation in politics, but are likely to read the local community newspaper and to know the names of local community leaders. They participate in the local area, but this participation is limited to their face-block or defended neighborhood.

NEIGHBORING

The intensity of neighboring activity varies considerably from one area of a metropolis to the next. John Ciardi questions the value of neighboring in the metropolis, in general:

If the anonymity New York grants us is a problem, it is also a blessing. In small towns it is natural and easy to be passing friendly with everyone nearby, and in a small town it works. But in New York there are too many people nearby. Just try being friendly to everyone you meet there! Not only would you never get where you are going, but you would be making a nuisance of yourself to thousands of people with their own errands to run. The very multitude of people makes it necessary for us to stare through and beyond one another.

Were I living in an apartment house, I would not care to know who lives above me, below me, or in the next apartment on either side. I want to choose my friends. I do not care to have them thrust upon me by the rental agent. And I do not want people dropping in to borrow whatever people borrow, nor to chitchat whatever neighbors chitchat...It can be lonely at times inside that anonymity, but let a small-town friendliness echo through those canyons and the future would be chaos forever, bumper to bumper and nose to nose from here to infinity.

Source: John Ciardi, "Manner of Speaking," *Saturday Review*, Feb. 12, 1966, pp. 16–17.

Community actors. Community actors are the smallest group but are the most influential because of their involvement in local organizations. Generally they are "joiners" involved in voluntary associations at many levels—a church group, the Chamber of Commerce, or the Lions Club. They are a disproportionately large part of the local electorate (Approximately 70 percent of them vote versus 30 percent of the isolates.), and they are the most knowledgeable on local issues. Interestingly, this group, which carries out most of the public affairs in a local community, is self-selected. Interest in local community affairs is so low that literally anyone who has the time and the interest can be a community leader. Therefore, it is the community actors who speak for the interests of the local community, normally through a community-based voluntary association. This group could be likened to a ruling class who through their influence have a disproportionate role in determining the outcome of local community issues.

The other less interested groups benefit from the actions of these self-chosen community actors, however, and frequently identify with them. The community actors serve an important watchdog function in the community and defend it from outside adversaries. If a threat to the local area is particularly severe, this group uses the local community press and their overlapping memberships in voluntary associations to publicize the problem. In certain circumstances, they can elicit the help of neighbors and, in extreme circumstances, even of the isolates.

TRANSITION IN LOCAL COMMUNITIES

Although face-blocks, defended neighborhoods, and communities of limited liability appear to be present in Chicago and other cities, these units are in a process of continuous change. In a face-block, for instance, a dispute among the block's central clique may cause members to switch their loyalties to other adjacent areas. Likewise, the defended neighborhoods in inner cities regularly undergo the invasion–succession process that may influence both their solidarity and identity. The boundaries and identity of a community of limited liability may also change as groups of advocates and adversaries compete for influence over the constituencies of these areas. The identification of the areas is complicated by the fragmentation of authority on the local level. Municipal governments are often familiar with the natural or symbolic communities but seldom use their boundaries explicitly to determine the jurisdictions of various public agencies. Suttles (1972) and Hunter (1974) found very little overlap in the boundaries of Chicago's community areas, political wards, school districts, and police districts. Residents often are members of more than one community of limited liability. In one case, the boundaries may coincide with a school district, in another an improvement district. The split loyalties that result from the fragmentation of local authority partly explain the high failure rate of local community groups. It is difficult to raise interest in a particular issue when residents of an area are involved in other issues.

In general, when one examines how an urbanite defines and uses space, a somewhat confusing picture of the urban landscape emerges. Boundaries between the various areal units are not clear and sharply delineated but instead overlap and in some cases are superimposed over one another. The pattern contrasts to the neat patchwork that results from social area analysis. Social area analysis provides a tool for examining the broad structural form of a city, but it is less useful in analyzing the actual operation of a city on the social level.

This is not to say that the social area dimensions are unimportant in analyzing the social basis of community life. Family status, ethnic status, and social status have each been identified as important factors influencing social interaction and the size of the various symbolic community units. In lower socioeconomic areas of the city, for example—areas characterized as low in both ethnic and social status—distrust among residents is often high and the defended neighborhood may be a single building (Suttles, 1968). Suburban areas, in contrast, are characterized by high family, ethnic, and social status, and normally their defended neighborhoods are very large, covering many square blocks.

RELATIONSHIP OF A COMMUNITY TO THE LARGER SOCIETY

The discussion of community suggests that local communities, whether they be face-blocks, defended neighborhoods, or communities of limited liability, are best described as partial communities unable to perform within their boundaries all the functions traditionally carried out in Gemeinschaft communities. In the past, the services provided by local merchants, bankers, and schools were important in generating a sense of community. Today, most local communities depend on numerous institutions and organizations outside their borders for basic, day-to-day services. Most local communities, for example, have chain stores, branch banks, schools, and churches that serve the local community but are affiliated with metropolitan or national organizations. These ties that Warren (1978) calls "vertical patterns of integration" are important in that they integrate the local area into citywide and national social and economic systems. There are, however, costs. Because of these ties, subcommunities do not perform a full range of community functions on their own, those functions often necessary to generate a sense of community. However, there are mechanisms and institutions within the local community that promote cohesiveness. Ideally, the community press, local voluntary organizations, and locally based networks of friends and kin, as well as awareness of a common fate bring about the internal integration of a local community. This horizontal pattern of integration combined with vertical patterns leads to the orderly operation of a local community in the metropolitan system.

SOCIAL NETWORKS

> Individuals' bonds to one another are the essence of society. Our day-to-day lives are preoccupied with people, with seeking approval, providing affection, exchanging gossip, falling in love, soliciting advice, giving opinions, soothing anger, teaching manners, providing aid, making impressions, keeping in touch—or worrying about why we are not doing these things. By doing all these things we create community. And people continue to do them, today, in modern society. The relations these interactions define in turn define society, and changes in those relations mark historical changes in community life (Fischer, 1982, p. 2).

This quote from Claude Fischer's book, *To Dwell Among Friends*, demonstrates an exciting alternative approach to the study of community. Whereas Janowitz and Hunter explore community structures like face-blocks, defended neighborhoods, and communities of limited liability, Fischer and other researchers explore the world of intimate social relationships—social networks. Students sometimes have trouble relating to concepts like communities of limited liability because they haven't experienced them in their day-to-day lives. All of us know social networks because we live in them. Take a moment and explore your own social network. From your perspective, personal relationships emanate outward—first to kin and close friends; then to other students, co-workers, and church members; then finally to people in the local community and friends back home. Community from this perspective isn't simply a jigsaw of local structures but a complex web of relationships, a latticework of interpersonal ties.[5]

CREATING SOCIAL NETWORKS[6]

As children our networks are centered in family, and we have no control over this choice. But as we grow older we are free to choose our friends, co-workers, and associates, and by the time we are young adults our social networks have been forged.

An interesting thing occurs in creating our networks: We tend to choose friends, co-workers, and associates from people like ourselves. Social networks are homogeneous. They tend to be inbred: composed of people of the same social class and ethnic and racial group. Why? Because we are not totally free to choose our network. Our alternatives are limited by society. This notion that we make choices from socially constrained alternatives is known as the choice–constraint model. The model assumes that decisions are rational. It recognizes that all relationships have costs and benefits. It accepts the fact that relationships are double-edged; they contribute to our sense of well-being but can also destroy it. More importantly, it reminds us that even in a small town we can know only a minuscule number of people. We have to decide with whom we're going to spend time and whom we're going to ignore. But throughout this analysis is the recognition that we have freedom to make these decisions but freedom within constraints.

Our position in the social stratification system is the most important force in determining our networks. Simply, the higher your social status, the larger your personal network. If you have money, you can buy more long distance telephone calls, plane tickets, and ski weekends with friends, and these investments pay off. Research shows that the wealthier you are, the larger, more encompassing, and supportive your network. At the bottom, you find people with few alternatives: few housing alternatives, few employment alternatives, and few network alternatives. Many of the problems of the poor are linked to their small personal networks. When researchers include other factors—stage in the life cycle, age, gender, race, region, and level of education—in their analysis, they can predict with uncanny accuracy the size and scope of social networks.

Personal networks are constrained by the social structure, and they are constrained by the local community. They are constrained by the schools we attend, the jobs we hold, the places we shop, and by the organizations we join. The location of housing, businesses, jobs, public transit, and public institutions affects networks. And innocuous things like the weather, traffic, and crime also affect the choices and constraints we face in building our personnel networks.

Things get more complicated. We don't sit idly by and simply react to our environment; we interact with it. Americans are the most mobile people in the world. If a neighborhood or community doesn't suit us, we move and find one that does. Self-selection, therefore, affects neighborhoods and communities and in turn our personal networks. Regardless of where you live, you know where the rich, the poor, the working folk, the professionals, and the minorities live. Students are usually segregated in campus dorms or nearby apartment districts. And these areas come into existence because people select these neighborhoods because they meet their needs. Young singles seek out the excitement of central city neighborhoods; retirees seek the quiet of retirement communities and small towns; parents choose suburbs because of the kids. Once a neighborhood takes on a special character, the reinforcing nature of the self-selection process perpetuates it, in some cases for generations. Choices within the constraints of society and community, along with self-selection, explain much of the community-making process.

ALTERNATIVE APPROACHES AND THEORIES OF THE COMMUNITY[7]

Claude Fischer, in *To Dwell Among Friends*, uses social network analysis to explore urban life in the last quarter of the twentieth century. Fischer and his colleagues interviewed 1050 adults living in 50 northern California communities. Residents of San Francisco high rises, Oakland slums, suburban tract homes, and small farm communities were interviewed, and the size and quality of their social networks, measured. Fischer's research gives us a glimpse into personal networks: their links to kin, neighbors, co-workers, and friends; their structure and spatial form; and their role in creating subcultures. He also tests many of the assumptions of the decline-of-community theory.

THE DECLINE OF COMMUNITY THEORY

The decline of community is a theme woven through much of this chapter. These theorists believe that urban life weakens traditional ties of family, kin, and community. In the past, we have lived, worked, and worshiped with the same people, so relationships were rich and multistranded. Today, we live in one area of the city, work in another, and shop in a third, and each one of these roles involves a different set of people. Since few of these relationships overlap, traditional means of social control don't work, and the rich and overlapping network of the traditional community no longer gives people a sense of belonging and a shared commitment to the group. Crime, vice, mental illness, suicide, and social disorganization are predictable outcomes because traditional means of social control cannot work. The public is comfortable with this explanation. It seems to make sense. It explains at a gut level the murder and mayhem in New York, Washington, and Miami.

THE SUBCULTURAL THEORY OF URBANISM

There is an alternative explanation—the subculture theory of urbanism. The theory holds that the diversity of the city—its size, density, and heterogeneity—creates an environment ripe for the creation of subcultures. As we stated earlier, our social networks are inbred and we chose our networks from among those like us. In a large city, you can be choosy because there are more alternatives. If you are a trekkie, an environmentalist, or a gay, there will probably be enough people like you in a big city to form a club, an association, or even a subculture with its own values, beliefs, and norms.

There's more. Cities not only create the critical mass necessary for the birth of subcultures, but they also provide the conditions necessary for subcultures to become a world unto themselves. They provide an environment where Italians, Latinos, or Vietnamese can create a community within a community—communities that have their own cultures, languages, and foods, and their own schools, churches, hospitals, stores, and savings and loans. When subcultures become associated with certain parts of the city—Little Italy, Pole Town, the Castro District—physical as well as social barriers are erected to the outside community. Therefore, rather than a community of isolates, Fischer argues we have a mosaic of social worlds. Cities, rather than being a random collection of isolated individuals, are filled with people with complex attachments to a rich variety of subcultures. From this perspective, the carnage in Washington, D.C. and New York isn't the lawlessness of individuals, but the product of subcultures—gangs, organized crime, and leveraged-buyout artists. The behavior of these groups is normal because it is guided by the goals, values, and norms of subcultures.

Thus, we are faced with two contradictory explanations. Has the community declined, or is the behavior we see the result of competing moral communities? Fischer attempts to resolve this question by testing three assumptions of the decline of community theory. It has long been assumed that urbanism leads to psychological strain, reduced social involvement, and a decline in traditional values. Each assumption is discussed in the following.

A TEST OF THE DECLINE OF COMMUNITY THEORY

PSYCHOLOGICAL STRAIN[8]

Since the heyday of the Chicago School, Americans have believed that large cities are unhealthy places and lead to psychological strain. A casual reading of the statistics would lead many Americans to conclude that this is indeed the case. A cornucopia of social ills are associated with the city—drug use, suicide, murder, crime, vice, and corruption. In the opening decades of this century, Park and Wirth found a higher concentration of personal disorganization in the central city than elsewhere. This is still the case. Most measures of collective mental health—admissions to mental hospitals, outpatient mental health services, drug treatment services, and suicide rates—seem to support the contention that cities are psychologically stressful places to live.

There's another way of looking at these statistics, however. There is a great deal of evidence showing that people already suffering from mental illness drift to the larger cities of a region. Bizarre behavior deemed intolerable in small towns may go unnoticed in a big city. Cities are also the places where you find the region's services—homeless shelters, soup kitchens, the Salvation Army, drug treatment centers—as well as illicit drugs and services. There also may be more admissions to mental hospitals and outpatient programs because cites have larger and better staffed and funded service organizations. So what we may be seeing is a statistical artifact of selective migration and not a link between urbanism and psychological strain.

Fischer's survey of his 1050 respondents was extensive. Interviewers asked respondents 131 questions from a 53-page survey. One series of questions touched on the urbanism–strain hypothesis. Respondents were asked how nervous, worried, and pleased they felt about their lives. These answers were combined in an overall mood scale. Decline of community theory predicts that as urbanism increases, morale decreases. This is not what Fischer and his colleagues found.

Figure 11.1 summarizes the results from the mood scale. Along the x-axis is a measure of urbanism; the four community categories are arranged from semi-rural to the regional core. The y-axis presents the scores on the mood scale. First, note that the mood

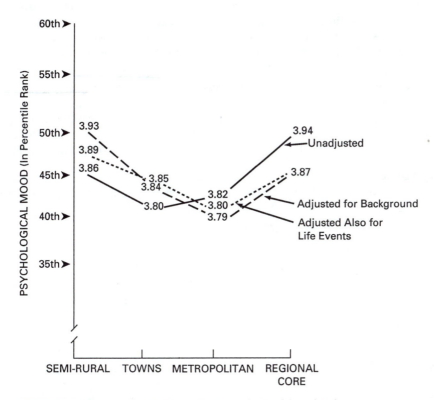

FIGURE 11.1 Mean respondents' psychological mood, by urbanism.
Source: Claude S. Fischer. *To Dwell Among Friends: Personal Networks in Town and City.* Chicago: The University of Chicago Press, 1982, Figure 3, p. 47.

scale doesn't vary much across the four categories of places. The average for all four groups was at the forty-fifth percentile, and semi-rural residents were slightly above it; at the other end of the urban scale, residents of the regional core had the highest score. Respondents living in towns and metropolitan areas had the lowest scores in the study.

We know from our own experiences that certain life events, like the death of a family member, a serious illness, or unemployment, can affect our mood. Fischer was able to statistically correct the data for these life events as well as for background variables that may have biased the scale. These corrected data are represented by the dashed line. Even with these corrections, Fischer found no relationship between urbanism and psychological stress.

URBANISM AND SOCIAL INVOLVEMENT[9]

Community-decline theorists state that the city creates isolated individuals. They argue that the frenzied daily schedules pull urbanites in many directions. We live in one place, work in another, send our kids across town to school, meet with our club or professional association somewhere else. The end result: relationships become superficial and meaningless. They just aren't the social stuff that creates community. Or are they?

Fischer found that urbanites are engaged in a wider variety of activities than their counterparts in other parts of the region. The self-selecting nature of the core accounts for most of these differences. The core attracts young, unmarried, and well-educated people, and they are more active wherever they live. But the idea that they lack meaningful relationships is quite a different matter.

Figure 11.2 is similar to the previous one. The x-axis measures urbanism; the y-axis summarizes the number of persons named by respondents as part of their networks. The two lines at the top are the total number of persons named. The dark line

FIGURE 11.2 Number of persons named, by urbanism.

Source: Claude S. Fischer. *To Dwell Among Friends: Personal Networks in Town and City.* Chicago: The University of Chicago Press, 1982, Figure 4, p. 57.

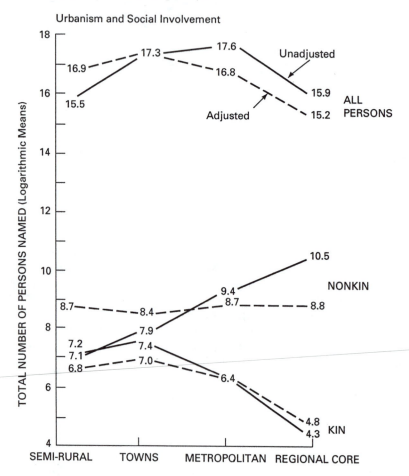

Urbanism and Social Involvement

is the unadjusted figures; the dashed lines are scores adjusted for background factors. Notice that there is no clear linear relationship between urbanism and social involvement. In general, core residents had about two fewer associates than did respondents living elsewhere, but this doesn't represent isolation. The differences aren't great, but they do exist, and self-selection appears to be responsible for much of the difference in the size of the networks. The bottom half of the figure throws some light on these differences. Here, the curves at the top of the table are divided into their kin and nonkin components. Note that those living in the regional core report fewer kin in their networks, but they balanced this out by having more nonkin. The results say something about the relationship between urbanism and familism, but there is no evidence that urbanism produces social isolation.

The destruction-of-community theorists would argue that Fischer has missed the point; it's not the number, but the quality of the relationships. Fischer looked at levels of intimacy and length of friendships and found no evidence that the quality of urban relations was inferior to those of small-town residents. There seems to be little support for the second hypothesis drawn from the decline-of-community theory.

URBANISM AND TRADITIONAL VALUES[10]

The 1980s was rough on small towns. There were a third fewer farmers at the end of the decade than at the beginning, and the communities that depended on the farm economy withered. Scores of small towns closed stores, boarded up schools, and shut down hospitals and other services. The media dutifully recorded these personal and collective tragedies, but it also sparked a national debate about our national character. Commentators insisted that American values were tied to the land, the farm, and the small town. Some critics likened the dying of these small towns to the death of the last member of a species. Some had the unsettling feeling that a thread in the national fabric was lost and the bolt weakened. The media and the public agreed that our modern, urban way of life destroys traditional values.

Urbanism weakens traditional values. Fischer discovered that residents of the regional core were more likely to live out of wedlock, more likely to have no religious identity, and more likely to be gay. The decline-of-community theorists argue that this happens because attachments to kin, friends, and neighbors are the most powerful form of social control. The small town's rich network of overlapping and intertwined relationships is effective in reducing deviance and bringing about conformity. In the city, these all-encompassing networks fall apart, and individuals can be just that, individuals, free to act as they wish. Simply, deviance and nonconformity result from a breakdown of traditional values.

Fischer provides an alternative explanation. Rather than a breakdown of traditional values, he argues for a buildup of competing moral orders. The presence of a critical mass of similar people creates subcultures with their own values, beliefs, and norms. It is not a paucity of values but a rich environment of competing value and normative systems that accounts for the nontraditional behavior. Behavior from the perspective of one subculture is deviant; from another, normative.

Both the decline-of-community thesis and the subcultural argument predict a decline in traditional values as urbanism increases. They then converge. Deviant behavior from the perspective of the traditionalists is a breakdown of traditional means of social control. Subcultural theorists say, first, it may not be deviant, depending on the subculture, and second, it results from the growth of competing moral orders.

Fischer developed a traditionalism scale by measuring respondents' opinions on social issues (sex before marriage, abortion, legalization of marijuana, and allowing homosexuals to teach in public schools). The results are summarized in Figure 11.3. Again, the x-axis measures urbanism, and the y-axis summarizes the scores on the traditionalism scale. The solid line is the unadjusted scores; the dashed and dotted lines are the curves corrected for personal and network traits. The relationship is clear: the more urban a community, the lower respondents' traditionalism scores. It is a strong relationship. The respondents in semi-rural communities were near the seventieth

FIGURE 11.3 Traditionalism, by urbanisrn.

Source: Claude S. Fischer. *To Dwell Among Friends: Personal Networks in Town and City.* Chicago: The University of Chicago Press, 1982, Figure 5, p. 69.

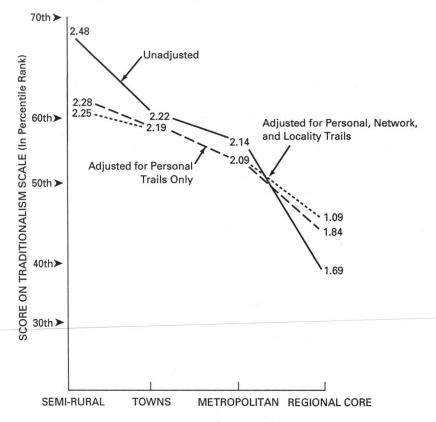

percentile, the ones in the regional core near the fortieth. In a complex analysis of the networks of the respondents, controlling for involvement with kin and nonkin, the pattern is the same, as traditionalism declines with urbanism.

Of the three classic charges against urban life, that it is psychologically stressful, socially isolating, and nontraditional, only the last hypothesis is supported by the study. Urban centers are no more likely to lead to psychological stress than other communities. Nor are people living in cities more likely to be socially isolated. Those living in the urban core have slightly fewer people in their networks, but there is no evidence that these relationships are less intimate. Urbanites, nevertheless, are more tolerant of nontraditional behavior, and it appears that urbanism itself contributes to these rural/urban differences. But is a decline in traditional values such a bad thing? Remember, traditional values include elements of racism, sexism, and intolerance.

Fischer, however, offers another explanation. According to Fischer, the items in his scale on abortion, marijuana, and homosexuality don't just tap permissive behavior, but also the progressive attitudes of our day. In Fischer's mind, it is not individual license that is the key to understanding these results, but the liberal ideology in our popular culture—feminism, gay rights, and personal privacy.

CONCLUSIONS

The work of Fischer and others in network analysis has opened up a new way of looking at the community. Rather than looking at historical forces or community structures, Fischer explores the web of personal relationships that combine to form social structures and, in turn, societies. The complexity of this research is mind-boggling, and the analysis, even with a sample of only 1000 respondents, requires a mainframe computer. The work is valuable because it introduces a new tool for exploring the community and the city. It is also important because it provides another technique for analyzing theories, like the decline-of-community theory.

The present generation always laments what it has lost in the past. Somehow life was always better back then. Time is a powerful filter. It strains out the tension, conflict, and misery of the past. It ignores the tyranny of the majority and the suffering of minorities that have committed no sin other than being different. Fischer's work is indispensable reading for anyone interested in community, because it shows us that we put our lives and communities together as we always have. The setting has changed, and transportation and communication technology has allowed us to organize community differently. But that's the point—the community is different, not better or worse.

We all carry around mental baggage—values, beliefs, and prejudices that sometimes crumble under close scrutiny. We hold to these things because they are comfortable, and public opinion holds dear the belief of community decline. It is interesting to watch our leaders dredge up the decline-of-community theories to justify a new drug policy or a police crackdown. Tragically, public opinion and public beliefs rather than research findings guide social policy. I find Fischer's work exciting because it opens up new vistas on community, and it suggests alternative remedies to the most serious problems facing this society.

SUMMARY

In this chapter the evolution of the concept of community is traced from its use by nineteenth-century social philosophers to its present usage in American community studies. The nineteenth-century community theorists Maine, Tönnies, and Durkheim used the community concept to analyze the changing relationship between the individual and society. Community was also applied as an ideal by which life in industrial societies could be compared with life in communities of the past. Although the concept of community is a theme in many of their works, each theorist explored a different aspect of this phenomenon. Maine explored the legal systems of societies, contrasting the family-centered traditional societies with the individual-centered modern societies.

Tönnies employed the ideal types Gemeinschaft and Gesellschaft to analyze the qualities of past and present societies. Gemeinschaft refers to small, homogeneous communities based on tradition, communities in which an individual is guided by the norms and conventions of the community and is tied to the institutions of family and church. Gesellschaft stands in polar extreme to Gemeinschaft and refers to large, complex, heterogeneous societies composed of individuals. In these societies reason prevails, and contracts define the relationships between people.

Durkheim's concern was with the "social glue" that holds society together. He identified two types of social solidarity: mechanical and organic. Mechanical solidarity is found in small, homogeneous societies in which there is nearly universal agreement on the values, beliefs, and norms of the community—a collective conscience. Organic solidarity prevails in modern societies that have large, heterogeneous populations and a complex division of labor. The all-encompassing collective conscience cannot exist in such societies because of their size, but the functional interdependency that develops among specialists forms the basis for social solidarity.

In general, these sociologists concluded that three basic changes had occurred in community. First, the basis of one's social status had changed from the family's status to one's individual achievement. Second, an individual was increasingly viewed as the basic unit of society. Third, the character of societies had changed from sacred-communal to secular-associational.

Park and the Chicago School were influenced by the writings of the nineteenth-century sociologists. Their interest, however, was not in "community" in a broad sense, but in cities and their subcommunities. Although this school's unit of analysis differed from that used in the earlier works of Durkheim, Tönnies, and Maine, both groups were interested in essentially the same problem—order in society.

Park, in particular, combined the ecological notion of natural areas with Durkheim's concepts of mechanical and organic solidarity to explain how a community composed of several different subcommunities could allow each of them to maintain its own distinctive way of life without endangering the life of the whole community (Stein, 1972, p. 17).

Durkheim greatly influenced Park. Like Durkheim, Park felt that the city was held together by both mechanical and organic solidarity. Park viewed natural areas as homogeneous in their family, social, or racial and ethnic characteristics. Their mechanical solidarity was based on their commonly held norms, values, and beliefs. However, each of these specialized natural areas made a functional contribution to the operation of the entire city, which produced organic solidarity. Major weaknesses in Park's approach have been identified. The natural areas concept has been called into question, as has the emphasis of the Chicago School on social disorganization. These notions, nevertheless, continue to influence the present image of community.

Recent research by Suttles, Hunter, and others suggests that areal units continue to influence life in urban places. Face-blocks, the most elementary grouping in urban areas, are based on the familiarity among people who live on the same block or use the same parks, stores, or other local facilities. This unit is important because it is where children play and where adult–child and adult–adult relationships are regulated.

The defended neighborhood corresponds to the areas identified by Zorbaugh and the other members of the Chicago School. It is the larger area outside the face-block that people use on a day-to-day basis.

The most distinguishing characteristic of the community of limited liability, the largest of the three symbolic communities, is that it is normally known by the people who reside within it and by the larger community as well. These units are normally composed of numerous defended neighborhoods and come into existence through the actions of builders, planners, or booster groups. Most residents of these areas are classified as isolates or neighbors and have little involvement in community affairs. The few community actors who hold membership in many community organizations provide the political direction for the community.

Social network analysis is one of the newer approaches to the study of community. Social networks are often spatially dispersed rather than concentrated in a single locale. These networks of kin, friends, and co-workers and shared memberships in churches and voluntary associations can span an entire metropolitan area. Friends in one network may share friends in another, and a complex, interconnected social network can emerge across the city.

Social networks are homogeneous. They tend to be composed of people of the same social class and ethnic and racial group. Social structure is responsible for this homogeneity, and the choice–constraint model was introduced to describe the selection process. The model assumes that people are rational, that they enter into relationships because they are rewarding, and that the choices they make are from alternatives constrained by the social structure. One's social class is the most important constraint in determining one's network, but other factors like race, stage in the life cycle, characteristics of the local community, and self-selection are also important in limiting alternatives.

The decline of the community is a common theme among the theorists in this chapter. These theorists believe that urban life weakens traditional ties of family, kin, and neighborhood and that social disorganization results. They argue that informal means of social control have been replaced by the police and the courts and people's intimate, close-knit ties to the family, neighborhood, and the community have been replaced by ones in which individuals pursue their own self-interest.

Claude Fischer provides an alternative thesis—the subculture theory of urbanism. Fischer argues that the diversity of the city—its size, density, and heterogeneity—creates an environment ripe for the creation of subcultures. Subcultures are like all cultures: They develop their own goals, values, beliefs, and norms, and through the socialization process they perpetuate themselves. Consequently, rather than seeing the city as a haphazard collection of unattached individuals, subcultural theorists argue for a rich environment of competing moral communities.

Fischer uses network analysis to test three of the basic assumptions of decline-of-community theorists: Urbanism leads to (1) psychological strain, (2) reduced social involvement, and (3) nontraditional values. Fischer found that only one of the three assumptions was supported by his analysis. There was no evidence that urbanism was related to either psychological strain or reduced social involvement. There is a close relationship between urbanism and nontraditional values. Fischer reports profound differences in the values held by urban and rural residents. Urbanites tolerate nontraditional behaviors and accept many of the core values held by the liberal ideologies in our popular cultures—feminism, gay rights, and personal privacy.

The nature, scope, and functions of local communities have changed dramatically in the past century, and these changes mirror the underlying scale of society. The increasing scale of society has brought major improvements in transportation, communication, and energy technology that make the all-encompassing Gemeinschaft communities of the past unnecessary. A common human failing is to remember the past selectively. In many respects, this is what has happened to the concept of community. The Gemeinschaft type of community is romanticized and continues to be described by the words *harmony*, *naturalness*, *depth*, *fullness*, and *family-like*. Such communities, however, are not without their costs. They preclude free expression and individualism. The local community as it is known today in urban America is neither better nor worse than those of the past, just different.

Social critics suggest that the crime, isolation, poverty, and alienation in the urban setting are the result of the destruction of community. Is this a fair criticism? The city is composed of a mosaic of social worlds, each subcommunity serving the needs of a special subgroup in society. Certainly, problems are severe in some subcommunities. They always have been. But for the majority of Americans living in urban areas, the partial communities in which they live provide a satisfactory and satisfying solution to the recurring problems of day-to-day life in large, complex societies.

NOTES

1.   The discussion of Maine, Tönnies, and Durkheim is based in part on the following books: Robert A. Nisbet, *The Sociological Tradition* (New York: Basic Books, Inc., Publishers, 1966); Lewis A. Coser, *Masters of Sociological Thought* (New York: Harcourt Brace Jovanovich, Inc., 1971); David A. Karp, Gregory P. Stone, and William C. Yoels, *Being Urban: A Social Psychological View of City Life* (Lexington, MA: D. C. Heath and Co., 1977), Chapter 1; Larry Lyon, *The Community in Urban Society* (Chicago: The Dorsey Press, 1987).

2.   The following material is based in part on Chapters 3, 4, 5, 6, and 8 of *Emile Durkheim: Selected Writings,* edited and translated by Anthony Giddens, Cambridge, England: Cambridge University Press, 1972.

3.   This material is based in part on Maurice Stein, "Robert Park and Urbanization in Chicago," in *The Eclipse of Community: An Interpretation of American Studies* (Princeton, NJ: Princeton University Press, 1972) (expanded edition).

4.   This material is based in part on an article by William F. Whyte, "Social Organization in the Slums," *American Sociological Review* 8 (1943): 34–39.

5.   The origins of network analysis can be found in an essay published by Georg Simmel in 1922, titled "Social Circles." In this essay, Simmel discusses the different types of relationships possible in modern urban societies and contrasts them to those in rural and premodern societies. Simmel employs the concept of "social circles," what we now call personal networks, to contrast the two. Simmel's article was not published in English until 1955, explaining, in part, the slow introduction of this concept into the urban literature. See Georg Simmel, *Conflict and the Web of Group-Affiliations* (translated and edited by Kurt Wolff and Reinhard Bendix) (Glencoe, IL: The Free Press, 1955).

Interestingly, the first empirical use of network analysis was done in anthropology, not sociology. For an excellent overview of the historical development of this approach, see S. D. Berkowitz, *An Introduction to Structural Analysis: The Network Approach to Social Research* (Toronto: Butterworths, 1982).

6.   This section is based in part on section I, "Networks," in Claude S. Fischer, et al. *Networks and Places: Social Relations in the Urban Setting* (New York: The Free Press, 1977) and Chapter 1, "Personal Community," in *To Dwell Among Friends: Personal Networks in Town and City* (Chicago: University of Chicago Press, 1982).

7.   This section is based in part on Chapter 3, "Personal Networks: An Overview," in Claude S. Fischer, *To Dwell Among Friends: Personal Networks in Town and City* (Chicago: The University of Chicago Press, 1982).

8.   This section is based on Chapter 4, "Urbanism and Psychological Strain," in Claude S. Fischer, *To Dwell Among Friends: Personal Networks in Town and City* (Chicago: University of Chicago Press, 1982).

9.   This section is based on Chapter 5, "Urbanism and Social Involvement," in Claude S. Fischer, *To Dwell Among Friends: Personal Networks in Town and City* (Chicago: University of Chicago Press, 1982).

10. This section is based on Chapter 6, "Urbanism and Traditional Values," in Claude S. Fischer, *To Dwell Among Friends: Personal Networks in Town and City* (Chicago: University of Chicago Press, 1982).

*T*HE SEGREGATION AND LOCATION OF GROUPS IN CITIES

INTRODUCTION

One of my favorite places in Cincinnati is Findley Market. Findley Market was founded in the early 1800s, and it is wedged in the center of one of the city's oldest and densest neighborhoods—the Over-the-Rhine. The Over-the-Rhine district was settled by German immigrants, and the austere red brick homes, apartments, and tenements are set one next to the other on narrow lots with no setback from the sidewalks. The market itself is a shedlike structure that runs the length of two city blocks. The inside is broken into open stalls with butchers, sausage makers, fishmongers, poultry sellers, and grocers specializing in butter and eggs, bread and cookies, pickles, sauerkraut—the list is almost endless. On market days, greengrocers hawk their produce outside from open stands with only a canvas awning to protect them from the weather. Across the street on all four sides of the market are full-time businesses—butchers, groceries, and specialty stores—which meet the needs of Cincinnati's ethnic communities. It is said that if you can't find it at Findley Market, it's probably not available in town.

Wednesday, Friday, and Saturday are market days, and thousands are crammed into the few blocks of Findley Market; the crush of the people and the activities of the market assault every sense. The smell of butchered meat mixes with the sawdust on the floors and blends with the smells of cheeses, breads, produce, diesel exhaust, body odor, and the stink of storm drains—a smell that's both revolting and pleasing. As you push your way through the crowds, you catch sight of people of every description—black, white, rich, poor, yuppie, preppie, German, Greek, Italian, Mexican, Vietnamese, and those in native dress from Africa, India, and other lands.

367

Three days a week one finds concentrated in the few blocks of Findley Market the diversity of the city: the diversity that gives the tang, thrill, and excitement to urban living. And the market is also a metaphor for the diversity that characterizes the entire city. When people leave the market with their purchases they return to the city's neighborhoods, which have grown up to meet their needs. Cincinnati, like all cities, is a collection of neighborhoods—a mosaic of social worlds. For example, in Cincinnati blacks are concentrated in Avondale, Bond Hill, and Oakley and in older suburbs like Kennedy Heights; Jews in Roselawn and Amberly Village; third- and fourth-generation Germans in Mount Lookout; the wealthy in Hyde Park, Indian Hills, and Mariemount; yuppies in Mt. Adams; and the list goes on. Each group is separated from the others by a process known as segregation.

Urban sociologists have studied segregation for almost a century, and they have been as acutely aware as we of the deep racial, economic, and ethnic cleavages in American society. Urban sociologists have recognized that these divisions that shape the nation also shape the residential structure of our cities. We know that the social distance between groups is reflected in the spatial distance between their residential neighborhoods. Blacks/whites, rich/poor, old ethnics/new ethnics live in and use different parts of the city. Knowing where these groups live, why they live there, and how their location changes tells us much about the processes that shape urban structure and our society.

Segregation has social consequences. We know that one's personal safety and accessibility to services such as schools, jobs, and medical care are tied to where he or she lives. Therefore, measures of segregation are the litmus test for evaluating a wide range of social problems ranging from issues of inequality, busing, and fair housing to AIDS.

This chapter explores the three forms of segregation—socioeconomic, ethnic, and racial. We discuss how segregation is measured; the theories that attempt to describe segregation; the ecological, voluntary, and involuntary factors responsible for segregation; and the spatial outcomes of this process. Segregation has its costs and benefits, and we end the chapter by looking at the consequence of this process for the most highly segregated group in our society—black Americans.

SEGREGATION: THE STUDY OF GROUPS

WHY STUDY SEGREGATION?

More than sixty years ago Robert Park stated:

> It is because social relationships are so frequently and so inevitably correlated with spatial relationships; because physical distances so frequently are, or seem to be, the indexes of social distances that statistics have any significance whatever for sociology. And this is true, finally, because it is only as social and physical facts can be reduced to, or correlated with, spatial facts that they can be measured at all (Park, 1926, p. 18).

The notion that the social distance between groups is reflected in the spatial distance between them is a basic ecological principle. This principle is implicit in the studies reviewed in this text, especially the research on the social area analysis model. However, in the discussion of the structural characteristics of cities, little was said about the social implications of these patterns.

In general, the sorting of groups and individuals into homogeneous areas of a city leads to spatial isolation. Segregation reduces the personal contacts between groups and causes social isolation. Without close day-to-day interaction, contact between such groups tends to be formal and is confined to the market and workplace. Therefore, the segregation of a population influences the patterns of relationships between people and can have positive and negative consequences for a community.

Positive effects of segregation. On the positive side, as long as there have been cities, people with similar social position, language, race, and religion have lived together. When this segregation is voluntary, residents may find living with others of similar backgrounds to be satisfying and to contribute to a sense of belonging and security. A group consciousness may emerge based on similar group attributes and common residence. Consequently, voluntary segregation of a group may affect the behavior of the residents positively. Similar characteristics provide a common ground for friendships and neighboring or may lead to the creation of ethnically based groups like fraternal organizations or political action groups.

Negative effects of segregation. The involuntary segregation of groups can cut two ways. Segregation can lead to the emergence of community, but once the community is created it can act as a barrier restricting the life chances of residents. For example, blacks are the most segregated group in American society; many live in the least desirable areas of cities, where housing is poor and public services are inadequate. The children of these families are often forced to attend the worst schools in the city, a practice that has been found to perpetuate inequality (Coleman, 1966; Armor, 1972; Wilson, 1986). In an attempt to overcome the negative aspects of segregation, federal courts have relied on the controversial policy of school busing: a policy actively resisted in many cities.

Another consequence of the group consciousness that emerges in segregated areas is the riots and other forms of collective behavior that have marked the nation's history.

Reasons for studying segregation. Residential segregation is of interest for several reasons. First, the degree of segregation between groups is a good indicator of the degree of social inequality in society. Second, measuring residential segregation gives policy makers an indication of the effectiveness of their programs or social legislation in addressing the problems of social inequality, for example, open housing legislation and the 1964 Civil Rights Act (Clark, 1986; Stahura, 1986). Third, the study of segregation gives sociologists insight into the basic ecological processes that shape the internal structure of the city. Fourth, the segregation or integration of neighborhoods in different parts of a city leads to the emergence of communities with different characteristics and institutional structures and different behavioral patterns among its residents.

Understanding the complex linkages of process, social structure, and behavior is a common goal of all social science.

WHY DOES SEGREGATION OCCUR?

Sociologists and ecologists have been trying to determine why segregation occurs for most of this century, and they have identified three sets of factors that influence segregation—ecological, voluntary, and involuntary.

Ecological segregation. If a population differs in life-style, race, social status, and culture, experience shows that they will separate themselves from others on the basis of some subjectively important criterion. The social scientist looks at the cost and types of housing and its location in relation to the CBD to explain residential segregation. The Burgess concentric zone model (reviewed in Chapter 7) is a good example of a sociologist's attempt to explain and describe the segregation of groups within industrial cities. The model predicts that the operation of impersonal economic forces results in the segregation of groups in various zones of a city.

Voluntary segregation. Another school argues that segregation is the result of voluntary factors of self-selection. A group with a common language or culture will have common problems and needs that can be addressed best if the members live close together. In ethnic enclaves, schools, churches, businesses, and stores spring up to meet the needs of the group. The enclave also serves to socialize the young into the language and culture of the group, perpetuating the subculture from generation to generation.

Alternatively, Timms (1971) suggests that a person's identity is closely interwoven with the people with whom he or she interacts, and a person's peers provide an important reference point for the evaluation of the individual's behavior. Moreover, a person's public identity, the social class to which he or she belongs, is defined by the people with whom he or she associates. Because physical distance between people is a major factor in determining who associates with whom, choosing a proper residential location is a strategy for increasing the probability of desired interaction. People who want to interact will live close to each other in order to lower the time and costs of interaction. People who want to avoid each other will live far apart to minimize the chances of accidental contact (Timms, 1971, p. 100).

Timms's explanation has two implications. First, it describes the psychological factors that influence residential choice. Second, it explains why neighborhoods keep their social character even though people are constantly moving in and out. Once an area becomes associated with a social group, individuals who wish to identify with it move into the area, perpetuating segregation.

Involuntary segregation. Involuntary segregation can occur in several ways. A group may be required by law or custom to live in designated areas of a city. The apartheid policy in South Africa is an example of governmental action that creates a segregated society. Involuntary segregation may also be the result of collective action of individuals or institutions within a community. So-called "white flight" (white individuals moving out of a neighborhood as blacks move in) is an example of how individual acts, when combined, tend to perpetuate racial segregation.

The role of realtors. Institutions also have an important impact on land uses and the levels of segregation in a city. Realtors have traditionally been singled out as a major force in perpetuating segregation (Galster, 1987). As late as the 1950s, the National Association of Real Estate Brokers included in their code of ethics the following statement:

> ...a realtor should never be instrumental in introducing into a neighborhood, by character of property or occupancy, members of any race or nationality, or any individual whose presence would be clearly detrimental to property values in a neighborhood (U.S. Commission on Civil Rights, 1975, p. 11).

This statement no longer appears in the association's code of ethics, but realtors are one of several gatekeepers in modern industrial cities who channel and control the activities of people looking for a new home (Galster, 1987). Normally, a realtor is one of the first persons with whom a new resident comes in contact. The realtor can influence the selection of clients, the houses shown, and the sale prices. The realtor often intervenes into the source and type of mortgage the buyer secures. The literature is filled with examples of tactics used by realtors to match the social class and racial characteristics of buyers to the existing social characteristics of neighborhoods. Although civil rights and fair housing legislation have put an end to many abuses, a recent study conducted for the Department of Housing and Urban Development suggests that these practices are still widespread (Wienk et al, 1979).

The role of government and lending institutions. Other institutions also greatly influence residential segregation. For many years, the Federal Housing Authority (FHA) would not loan money to blacks if their purchase of a home would upset the racial balance of an area. The practice of redlining by banks and lending institutions, as well as the decisions of planning commissions, zoning boards, and other agencies, influences residential land uses and the patterns of segregation. Although most of these practices have ended, their effects still linger in the residential structure of our cities (Clark, 1986; Stahura, 1986, 1988).

Interaction of Factors. These factors do not operate alone, but together in complex and interrelated ways. For example, ecological and voluntary factors may interact and limit the areas of the city in which people of high social status will reside. A wealthy person is not going to live in a slum. Thus, the distribution of housing types combined with the desire of high-status individuals to live near members of their own group contributes to segregation. One goal in the following discussion is to identify those factors that seem to be most responsible for patterns of segregation. These factors interact in different ways, depending on the particular social, ethnic, or racial group.

MEASURING SEGREGATION

Over the past decade there has been controversy surrounding the measurement of segregation. Currently, two measures, the dissimilarity index (D) and the exposure index (P*), are used. The dissimilarity index compares the residential location of pairs of groups, whites and blacks for example, and gives a measure of the net percentage of one population who would have to relocate in order to produce an integrated community. The index (D) has values that range from 0 to 100. (The index is also presented on a scale of 0 to 1.0.) For example, if blacks and whites were evenly distributed in all the census tracts of a city, the index would be 0. No one would have to change their residence to maintain a racial balance. If the city were completely segregated and census tracts were inhabited exclusively by blacks or whites, the index would be 100. For example, the dissimilarity index for New York City in 1980 was 72.8, which means that 72.8 percent of the blacks or 72.8 percent of the white residents of the city would have to move in order to have an integrated community (Sterns and Logan, 1986).

The dissimilarity index was introduced more than 40 years ago, and it has come under attack in recent years. One major drawback of the index is that it has the tendency to register high values even when the minority group under study makes up only a small proportion of a city's population. For this reason, students of segregation have developed a variety of measures, but the alternative measure used most often is the exposure index, P* (Lieberson and Carter, 1982; Farley, 1984; Stearns and Logan, 1986).

The exposure index measures the potential for contact between groups. Using information on the racial composition of census tracts, one can calculate the average percent white in the census tract of a typical black resident, as well as the average percent black in the census tract of a typical white. Like the dissimilarity index, it has a range from 0 to 100. The dissimilarity index for New York City in 1980 was 72.8, but the exposure index for that same year for blacks encountering whites was 16.4, and for whites encountering blacks, 5.6. In New York City, the typical black lives in a neighborhood that is 16.4 percent white, but the typical white lives in a neighborhood that is only 5.6 percent black. Blacks are segregated in the city; they made up 21.3 percent of the city's population in 1980, and the chance for exposure of the two groups in their neighborhoods is low (Clark, 1986).

In contrast, blacks make up only 2.4 percent of the population in Minneapolis/St. Paul, and blacks are highly segregated in the city: The dissimilarity index is 68.3. But the exposure indexes for blacks and whites are 62.2 and 1.7, respectively. A typical black is in the minority in her or his neighborhood; it is 62.2 percent white. In contrast, a typical white lives in a neighborhood that has only 1.7 percent black residents. Fewer blacks in this city mean that the potential exposure of these groups to each other is very different (Carter, 1986).

The dissimilarity and exposure indexes are widely used and give measures of segregation that allow comparisons from decade to decade and from city to city. Therefore, both will be used to describe segregation in this chapter.

SOCIAL STATUS SEGREGATION

The distribution of wealth and income in American society is unequal. Twenty-five million Americans live below the poverty line, and nearly three million are homeless, while at the same time one percent of the population controls more than a third of the nation's wealth, and two percent of private stockholders own about two-thirds of all stocks held by individuals. Changes in the economy and tax system during the 1980s have exacerbated inequality. The fears of some observers are that a two-tier society is emerging: one well educated and well paid in high-skill jobs; the other poorly educated and poorly paid in low-skill jobs and condemned to a life of poverty (Wilson, 1986). Much of the rhetoric in the 1988 presidential election revolved around the issues of wealth and poverty and the future of the middle class.

The data presented in Table 12.1 show the percentage of this nation's income received by each fifth of the nation's families for the years 1947–1986. In 1986, the poorest fifth of the families in the United States received only 4.6 percent of the nation's annual income, whereas the richest fifth received nearly 44 percent. This pattern of income distribution has remained unchanged since the end of World War II, in spite of the massive federal poverty programs carried out over the past four decades. Kolko's (1972) research suggests that this general pattern may not have changed much since the 1920s. Other measures of social status—education and occupation—show similar distributions. Given the gross inequalities in American society, one would expect to find segregation among groups that differ in their occupation, income, and education.

RESEARCH ON STATUS SEGREGATION

Ecological theories. The segregation of status groups was among the first studied by urban sociologists. Ernest Burgess (1925), one of the early Chicago ecologists, described in his concentric zone model that lower-status groups are centralized near the central business district, whereas upper-status groups are decentralized near a city's

TABLE 12.1 Percent of income received by each fifth of families in the United States, 1947–1986

INCOME	RANK	1947	1950	1960	1966	1972	1986
Lowest	Fifth	5.1	4.5	4.8	5.6	5.4	4.6
Second	Fifth	11.8	11.9	12.2	12.4	11.9	10.8
Third	Fifth	16.7	17.4	17.8	17.8	17.5	16.8
Fourth	Fifth	23.2	23.6	24.0	23.8	23.9	24.0
Highest	Fifth	43.5	42.7	41.3	40.5	41.4	43.8
Total Families		100.0	100.0	100.0	100.0	100.0	100.0

Source: Data for years 1947–1972, Executive Office of the President: Office of Management and Budget, *Economic Report of the President.* Washington, D.C.: U.S. Government Printing Office, 1974. 1986 data from Bureau of the Census. *Statistical Abstract of the United States, 1988.* Washington, D.C.: U.S. Government Printing Office, 1988.

periphery. To Burgess, the residential segregation of these groups was the result of impersonal ecological and economic factors operating within the city. The mechanism is straightforward. A family attempts to maximize its housing satisfaction while minimizing its costs by balancing the costs of transportation with costs of rent within the constraints of the family budget. Theoretically, a citywide pattern of land rents would be high rents and low transportation costs near the city's center and the reverse situation at the city's periphery. Only high-status families have true locational freedom because only they have the income to absorb the costs of transportation and rent. Because high-status families prefer large houses on spacious lots in areas where there is little congestion or business and industry, they select locations at the city's periphery. The poor have no choice and live near the city's center, where transportation and housing costs are lowest. The concentric zone model has been widely tested, and it appears to describe older industrial cities (See Chapter 7.).

Test of the theory. If the model is correct, one would expect a close relationship between the characteristics of the social structure and the degree and form of residential segregation. Albert A. Simkus (1978) examined the segregation of occupational groups in 10 metropolitan areas.[2] He used the index of dissimilarity to examine the differences in the residential distribution of eight major occupational groups. The prestige of each occupational category was determined by using national survey data from the National Opinion Research Center studies on occupational prestige (See Table 8.1.), and each category was ranked from highest prestige (professional) to lowest (laborers). Table 12.2 is a summary of Simkus's findings for the decade ending in 1970. Above the diagonal are the indexes of dissimilarity among employed males in each of the eight occupational groups. Below the diagonal are the changes that occurred in the indexes between 1960 and 1970. The figures represent the average scores across the ten urbanized areas included in the study.

The figures above the diagonal show that the most segregated groups are those at the top and the bottom of the occupational hierarchy. Groups in the middle of the hierarchy have relatively low indexes, which means that they tend to live near each other. On the whole, the figures below the diagonal show that segregation patterns among occupational groups has changed little since 1960. The only exception is the change in the index for service workers. Service workers became less segregated from the top five occupational categories during the decade ending in 1970. This shift suggests that the importance of service workers has changed in American society. In general, the table shows that there is only a moderate degree of residential dissimilarity, and this same pattern is found for other measures of status—like education and income.

LOCATION OF STATUS GROUPS

Social status segregation is a universal phenomenon, but the degree and magnitude of residential dissimilarity varies from society to society. The central business district is the benchmark for analyzing the location of status groups. Whether it is the highest or

TABLE 12.2 Indexes of residential dissimilarity among employed males in major occupational groups, averaged across ten urbanized areas, 1970 and change from 1960 to 1970.[a]

MAJOR OCCUPA- TIONAL GROUP	PROFESSIONAL	MANAGERIAL	SALES	CLERICAL	CRAFT	OPERATIVE	SERVICE	LABORERS
Professional		16	16	28	36	45	40	46
Managerial	0		14	30	36	46	42	48
Sales	0	0		27	34	44	39	45
Clerical	-1	0	3		20	25	22	29
Craft	0	1	3	3		20	25	29
Operative	-2	-1	1	0	0		19	19
Service	-8	-7	-6	-9	-8	-4		19
Laborers	-11	-11	-10	-12	-11	-7	-4	

[a]Above diagonal, 1970; below diagonal, change from 1960 to 1970.

The setup of this table permits the reader to find the index value of any pair of occupations. First, note that the left column contains the same categories of occupations as those across the top of the table. Comparing the occupational category "professionals" (the top category in the left column) with the category "managers" (the second category along the top of the table) yields an index value of only 16. Thus, there is very little difference between those two groups in their residential patterning. As one compares professional with other occupational categories across the top of the table, the index scores increase regularly. Under the heading "laborers" the index value is 46. This score means that 46 percent of this occupational group would have to be relocated to eliminate differences in residential patterning between professionals and laborers. The overall pattern in this table suggests that the most markedly segregated groups are those at the top and the bottom of the occupational hierarchy. The fact that those in the middle of the hierarchy (sales, clerical, and craft workers) have relatively low indexes means that they tend to live near each other.

The figures below the diagonal are the changes in the indexes during the 1960s. Note that the degree of segregation between each of the six highest occupational categories remained roughly the same, averaging less than one point of change. The indexes of dissimilarity between service workers and the six higher categories decreased by an average of 7.6 points, whereas the indexes between laborers and the six highest categories averaged an 11.0 point decline. The finding that service workers are less segregated from the five highest occupational categories than operatives suggests that measurable changes in the occupational prestige of these two categories may be observable on the national level in the near future. Except for the changing residential segregation patterns of service workers, Simkus (1978) indicates that the patterns have remained stable since 1950. On the whole, these figures suggest only a moderate degree of residential dissimilarity among groups.

Source: Simkus, A., "Residential Segregation by Occupation and Race in Ten Urbanized Areas, 1950–1970." *American Sociological Review* 43 (1978): p. 84. Reprinted with permission of The American Sociological Association.

the lowest status groups that are concentrated near the city's center depends on the scale of the society, as well as the position of the city in the country's urban hierarchy.

Low-scale societies. In countries undergoing the modernization process, cities at the top of the country's urban hierarchy, especially primate cities, modernize before others. Thus, centralization patterns differ among cities; some cities have an industrial pattern, and others a preindustrial pattern. Kent Schwirian and Jesus Rico-Velasco (1971) studied this relationship in Puerto Rico's three metropolitan areas. The authors found that San Juan follows the pattern of a high-scale society with low-status groups closer to the city's center than high-status groups. However, the smaller outlying cities of Pounce and Mayaguez had the opposite pattern—high-status groups lived near the city's center, low-status groups at the periphery.

High-scale societies. In high-scale societies, variations in centralization are evident. Older industrial cities like Detroit and New York have patterns consistent with Burgess's model, whereas Tucson and Los Angeles diverge and high-status groups are concentrated in the central city, and low-status groups are dispersed in the periphery.

The major reason that these cities diverge from the Burgess model is that they reached metropolitan status in the twentieth century and were shaped by the technology and economic organization of this century. Tucson and Los Angeles have CBDs, but they do not operate as the central organizing element for those cities. Automobile technology has allowed these cities to develop in a way best described by Harris and Ullman's multiple nuclei theory (Schwab, 1982, pp. 377–399). 275 - 276

FACTORS INFLUENCING SOCIAL-STATUS SEGREGATION

Social-status segregation is the result of many factors, and understanding it is confounded by the effects of both race and ethnicity. Blacks and other minorities in American society are overrepresented in the lower socioeconomic strata. As a result, cities with large black and Hispanic populations will have more extreme social-status segregation than cities with small minority populations (Farley and Wilger, 1987).

Ecological and voluntary factors appear to be most important in explaining social-status segregation. Persons of high social status have the income to select houses and neighborhoods in accordance with their tastes. Different neighborhoods have different types of housing, and, to the degree that housing is segregated, status groups will be segregated. Research supports this position, demonstrating that social-status segregation is largely the result of occupation and income (Clark, 1986; Simkus, 1978).

Even if the effects of occupation, income, and education are removed mathematically, a residual segregation remains. Such segregation is probably the result of voluntary factors of self-selection that are difficult to measure statistically.

In sum, residential dissimilarity among status groups appears to be a universal phenomenon. The pattern of residential dissimilarity is U-shaped, the groups at the high and low ends of the status hierarchy being the most segregated. The centralization of high- and low-status groups, however, is difficult to predict. Factors such as city age, position in the urban hierarchy, and the scale of the society appear to influence the centralization or decentralization of particular status groups in the urban landscape.

ETHNIC SEGREGATION

Germans, Greeks, Swedes, Norwegians, Japanese, Koreans, Chinese, Laotians, Vietnamese, Ethiopians, Nigerians, Kenyans, French, British, Irish, Russians, Italians, Croatians, Poles, Czechs, Hungarians, Cubans, Mexicans, Salvadorans, Nicaraguans, and the list goes on. This is a glimpse at the ethnic richness of the nation called the United States. There is no nation in history that has accepted as its citizens, albeit sometimes reluctantly, more people from more backgrounds than the United States. On the one hand, it is one of the nation's strengths; we have brought together the talents and the perspectives of many cultures in defining our national character. On the other hand, immigration has been a source of great division at times, creating cleavages that have weakened our political and social consensus. The American miracle is that such a diverse collection of peoples can live together in peace.

In every city with a sizable ethnic population, one finds evidence of this rich ethnic heritage in the names of the areas in which these groups are segregated—German Town, Pole Town, Little Taipei, Chinatown, the Barrio, the Ghetto. Even when the ethnic group isn't identified in the name of a neighborhood, certain areas of a city come to be associated with certain groups. In Cleveland, eastern European Jews are associated with the suburbs of Euclid and Shaker Heights, Poles with Parma, and Germans with Lakewood. The same is true for the city's other ethnic groups.

Americans carry their ethnic identity inside them. I ask my students the ambiguous question, "What are you?" Most respond with an answer like, "I'm Scotch/Irish." "I'm German." "I'm Afro-American." Research suggests that the majority of Americans are like my students and have kept an ethnic identity. When the National Opinion Research Center asked a sample of Americans about their ancestry, 48 percent replied with the name of a single country, and 42 percent named more than one country. Only 10 percent could not name a single country (Alba and Chamlin, 1983). In spite of rising levels of intermarriage, couples and children of mixed ancestry still identify with one ethnic group. Since ethnicity is an important marker in American society, it is not surprising that these attitudes have been translated into behavior and that ethnic segregation exists. Two factors—time of arrival and region of origin—explain much of the ethnic segregation in this society.

FACTORS INFLUENCING ETHNIC SEGREGATION

Region of origin and time of arrival. Three waves of immigrants came to this country.[3] The first wave spanned the years from the first settlements in the New World through the first half of the nineteenth century, ending with the Depression of 1857. This wave was composed of western and northern Europeans. Their Anglo-Saxon physical features and predominantly Protestant religion reinforced the character of the host society, and little assimilation was required. Most of this group settled on farms, but those who settled in cities chose cities in the Midwest, including the lake and river cities (Smith and Zopf).

Thirty million people immigrated to the United States between 1860 and 1924, forming the second and largest wave of immigration. Although Germans, Scandinavians, and millions of Irish continued to immigrate, the origins of most of this immigration shifted from western and northern Europe to eastern and southern Europe. The majority of these groups settled in Atlantic Coast and lake cities. The new ethnics differed from the native population in physical features, culture, and, most importantly, religion—they were predominantly Catholic and Jewish. To Americans already here, they seemed foreign or alien to the American culture, and prejudice and discrimination led to their segregation into ethnic enclaves and ghettoes (Smith and Zopf).

Three developments shaped the third wave of immigration. First was the passage of the 1965 amendments to the Immigration and Nationality Act of 1952. The 1952 act created a quota system based on national origin, but, in 1965, the act was amended to stress family reunification and the admission of aliens with needed skills. Second was the fall of U.S. client states in Cuba and Indochina and the massive immigration that followed. Third was the appearance of a worldwide pattern of international labor migration from less developed nations to more developed nations. As a result of these changes, the source of the immigration shifted from Europe to Mexico, Central and South America, the Caribbean Basin, and Asia. In addition, the immigration stream no longer was directed to the large cities of the Northeast but to cities across the nation (Massey, 1981, pp. 57–63).

It is now estimated that approximately 25 percent of the nation's annual population growth results from immigration. Not included in this figure are the one to three million aliens who enter this country illegally each year (U.S. Census Bureau, 1982, Table 92). The problem of illegal migration for the nation became so serious in the 1970s and 1980s that Congress responded by passing the Immigration Reform and Control Act in 1986 (PL 86-661).[4] The act provided amnesty for millions of illegal immigrants and imposed penalties on employers who employed undocumented aliens. At this time, the effects of this legislation are unknown.

The influence of technology. Region and time of arrival shaped the experiences of the different waves of ethnics in American cities, but there were other social, economic, and technological factors at work as well. For example, in the first half of the nineteenth century, transportation technology was poorly developed, and people had to be able to walk from where they lived to where they worked. Business and industry were on a much smaller scale, and unlike our cities today these activities were spread across the city. As a result, the Germans and Irish who immigrated before the Civil War were not highly segregated in our cities (Hanlin, 1969).

After the Civil War, industrialization and the transportation revolution brought about by the elevated railroad and the electrified trolley permitted the middle and upper classes to escape the city. For the first time, it was possible for large numbers of people to separate their place of residence from their place of work and to avoid groups they defined as undesirable. Since the second wave of immigrants was more distinctive than the old ethnics—Germans and Irish—greater assimilation was required. The consequence was segregation.

There were other factors at work. Industrialization brought about a growth in the size and scale of factories, and since the factories were dependent on the railroads, specialized industrial centers sprung up in cities. Thus the new immigrants arrived in an entirely different type of city. Most of the immigrants were without money or skills, so they located near their jobs in the zone of transition adjacent to the central business district (Massey, 1985).

In short, the industrialization of the last half of the nineteenth century created structural conditions conducive to high levels of segregation. In turn, high levels of segregation created a critical mass of people that permitted the creation of ethnic enclaves. Within these enclaves, one still finds ethnic stores, churches, schools, hospitals, social clubs, newspapers, and benevolent societies designed to meet the needs of the ethnic group. Over time there emerged a community within a community, and this had major consequences for ethnic segregation. Once enclaves are established they encourage additional immigration, contribute to the group's sense of peoplehood, socialize the young into the subculture, and perpetuate ethnic identity. These are factors that contribute to segregation (Bledea, 1979).

Congress ended the second wave of immigration in 1924 with the passage of restrictive immigration laws. Furthermore, the Great Depression and World War II reduced immigration to a trickle. The third wave of immigration began at the end of World War II. Cities felt the full impact of the automobile in the postwar years. The automobile gave individuals greater locational freedom, accelerated the expansion of the suburbs, permitted the decentralization of business and industry, and reduced the structural pressures for ethnic segregation. The Hispanics and Asians who entered the nation after World War II are less segregated than previous groups. However, in the older industrial cities of the Northeast, and in many Sunbelt cities one still finds high levels of segregation of these groups. As in the past, our newest immigrants are often poor and lack the education and skills necessary for high-paying jobs, so they must keep housing costs down. They tend to locate in older inner-city neighborhoods located near the low-paying service jobs in the central city (Massey, 1981).

THEORIES OF ETHNIC SEGREGATION

An ethnic group is any group that is defined or set off by race, religion, or national origin or some combination of these categories. In addition, these categories have a common social-psychological referent that can serve to create a sense of we-ness—a sense of peoplehood. This label can be used by the group itself or by the larger society. But implicit in our discussion of ethnicity is the notion that ethnicity is the immigration of a group into an already existing social structure. The experiences of the ethnic group, in large part, will be determined by those who control the host society, the charter group (Gordon, 1964).

A *charter group* is usually the first ethnic group to enter a territory. Because they control the key institutions of a society, they make the decisions about who gets in and what their experiences are going to be. In addition, they form the social framework to which the immigrant group must adapt and fit into. If the immigrant group is similar to the charter group, the process will be relatively smooth and rapid; if major differences exist, the process will be slow and erratic. The process of fitting an ethnic group into an already existing social structure is called *assimilation*. There are two types of assimilation—behavioral and structural. Behavioral assimilation is a process whereby members of a group acquire the behavior, attitudes, sentiments, values, language, and history of the host society. Think of behavioral assimilation as fitting into or disappearing into a new culture. Structural assimilation refers to the distribution of ethnics through the social system of a society—the process by which members of ethnic groups move into key decision-making positions in government, business, and other spheres of society. Both types of assimilation are temporal processes, but they can occur at very different rates. A good example is blacks in American society. Blacks

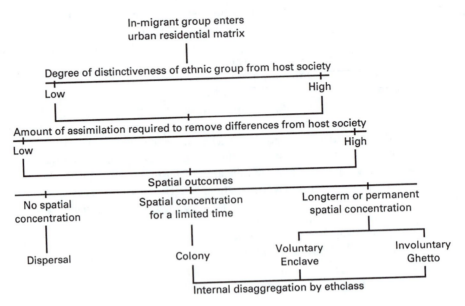

FIGURE 12.1 Ethnic groups, assimilation, and residential spatial outcomes

Source: Adapted from Figure 1 in F. W. Boal, "Ethnic Residential Segregation." In H. Johnston (ed.), *The Geography of Housing.* London: Aldein, pp. 41–77. Reprinted by permission of John Wiley & Sons, Ltd.

have been behaviorally assimilated into American society for centuries; only recently have blacks begun to move into key positions in this society—to be structurally assimilated (Boal, 1981).

Figure 12.1 summarizes the relationship between the forces at work in the society and those at work in cities. In this model, immigrants with few differences from the host society should be rapidly dispersed into the residential structure of the city. For example, I live in a small city in which there are a large number of Australians. Other than speaking English with an accent, their dress, behavior, values, and customs are so similar to American society that they have been dispersed across the city.

There is the other extreme in this model. Immigrants with a high degree of distinctiveness in language, custom, or color require a high degree of assimilation. If these differences are not easily removed (In the case of color, they may never be removed.), long-term or permanent segregation will occur. There are two spatial outcomes—ghettoes and ethnic enclaves. A ghetto refers to the residential area of a city where an ethnic group has been involuntarily segregated. As we see later in this chapter, housing discrimination is responsible for much of the residential segregation of blacks. On the other hand, the term *enclave* denotes an area where an ethnic group has voluntarily chosen to live in order to maintain the group's religion or culture. For example, Russian Jews are one of the nation's most successful ethnic groups, yet they remain highly segregated. Undoubtedly some housing discrimination occurs, but the high income of this group should mean more dispersal. In this case, voluntary factors are probably important in explaining the segregation of this group.

The final case is those ethnic groups who are distinctive but require only a moderate amount of assimilation. They are concentrated for only a single generation into areas called *colonies*. A current example is the large British colony in Southern California. The colony, estimated to be over 30,000 people, preserves the food, customs, and English of Britain. Mick is a friend who lives in Los Angeles. He loves America. He loves the climate, the high wages, the low taxes, and the life-style. He hates Americans. He thinks we are loud, boorish, gross, and ill-mannered. But he doesn't have to deal with Americans. He lives in the center of the British colony, works for a British company, shops at British grocery, drinks his favorite brew at a British-only pub, and plays darts on Tuesdays and Saturdays just as he did in London. Except for the intrusion of an occasional American, Mick and other British expatriates have successfully transported their way of life 6000 miles. But there are some cracks in Mick's idyllic life. His wife is a teacher, and her friends and colleagues are Americans. His children go to American schools and have American friends and accents. The final blow came when his eldest son turned 18, and chose U.S. over British citizenship. Mick may be able to wrap himself in the Union Jack, but his children have not, and the model predicts that the colony will last only a generation.

THE ASSIMILATION PROCESS

Although the model predicts the spatial outcomes of immigrants entering a host society, it does not describe the assimilation process. We normally study ethnic assimilation on the neighborhood level, using the concept of invasion–succession. Invasion–succession refers to the process of neighborhood change that occurs when a new ethnic group enters a residential area and displaces the original inhabitants. Two different models are found in the literature; they predict very different spatial outcomes.

The melting-pot model. The Chicago ecologists felt that ethnic segregation was an aspect of social-status segregation. Ethnic segregation was seen as an artifact of their low social status in American society. Most sociologists thought that this social status was a temporary phenomenon, and, as an ethnic group's standing improved, its segregation would gradually disappear. A four-stage process of assimilation was hypothesized: (1) New arrivals seek cheap accommodations because of their poverty and desire to accumulate savings. The tenements in the zone of transition were cheap and close to jobs and became centrally located ethnic ghettoes. (2) Over time, the immigrants improve their socioeconomic status. Higher incomes permit them to pursue better housing, and they begin to move outward into other areas of the city through the process of invasion–succession. (3) The redistribution of this group in other areas of the city leads to less physical concentration and a breakdown of the old cultural solidarity. (4) Subsequent movements result in further dispersion of group members and their assimilation into the surrounding society. According to the model, ethnic segregation is the result of socioeconomic differences among ethnic groups and the fact that people who differ in socioeconomic status live in different parts of the city. From this perspective, ecological factors independent of ethnicity are responsible for the segregation of these groups (Burgess, 1928).

This ideal pattern is known as the melting-pot thesis. It has been taught in American high school history and civics classes for decades. However, several books written in the 1960s and 1970s called into question the melting-pot notion (Glazer and Moynihan, 1963; Kantrowitz, 1973; Novak, 1971). These authors pointed to the durable ethnic divisions that persist in our cities after many generations and suggested that these groups represent major cleavages within the city—cleavages particularly important in our political process.

The-ethnic status model. The recognition of these unmeltable ethnics has led to the development of a second approach, the ethnic status model. The model argues that ethnic status alone can account for residential dissimilarity among ethnic groups. In short, one's desire to maintain a particular ethnic identity may be translated into a preference to live near others with similar ethnic backgrounds. Once an enclave is formed, a critical mass of ethnics supports an institutional structure of schools, churches, stores, and associations. In turn, these institutions provide the enclave with a means to recruit and hold members and to socialize the young into the ethnic subculture—a means of perpetuating the community. There may be other forces at work. The group's distinctive character may trigger discrimination by other groups in society and prevent the group from participating in a citywide housing market. Thus, the status of an ethnic group may be derived from both processes at work within the community and external societal forces. Regardless of the forces at work, this model predicts a very different spatial outcome. Rather than spatial dispersal and assimilation of the ethnic group as the group improves its socioeconomic status, this model predicts that the group will remain residentially segregated regardless of their social class. The question is, "Which model is correct?"

RESIDENTIAL PATTERNS OF ETHNICS

The 1980 U.S. census was the first to ask a large sample of individuals about their ethnicity or ancestry. Table 12.3 summarizes the dissimilarity index for 12 ethnic groups against America's charter group—people of English ancestry. Note that there were moderate levels of ethnic residential segregation in the 16 cities included in the analysis. Descendants of the first wave of immigration were the least segregated from the English, as illustrated by an average segregation score of 22 for Germans, 23 for Irish, 29 for French, and 30 for Scots (Farley and Wilger, 1987).

RESIDENTIAL PATTERNS OF GREEKS IN CINCINNATI, OHIO

The melting-pot model argues that recent immigrants locate near the CBD, and as their socioeconomic status improves they move to better housing in other parts of the city—often the suburbs. According to the theory, the move to the suburbs is accompanied by the diffusion of ethnic families, the destruction of their subculture, and the assimilation of the group into the mainstream of society.

Figures 1–3 are from the research by Bongkotrat Techatraisak (1978) on the changing residential patterns of Greeks in Cincinnati, Ohio, from 1910 through 1976. Mr. Techatraisak uses a mapping technique called *centrography* to analyze the clustering and diffusion of this ethnic group. Note the points, ellipse, and cross hairs in Figure 1. One point represents one household; the ellipse, the boundary which describes the cluster of Greek families. The center of the cross hairs is the center of the ethnic community.

Figure 1 shows that in 1910 Greeks were concentrated in a tight cluster adjacent to the CBD. However, over the next 66 years the group has dispersed. In Figure 2, notice that the size of the ellipse has grown progressively larger, and the center of the community has moved directly north of the central business district. According to the theory, the spatial diffusion of the Greeks should be accompanied by their assimilation. The evidence is otherwise. As the Greek community has moved to the better housing on the periphery, it has taken its institutions along. Figure 3 shows the movement of the Greek Orthodox Church from 1908 to the present. Located in downtown Cincinnati in 1908, it is now located in the suburbs along with its members. Research in other cities has shown that ethnic groups maintain their ethnic identity after many generations, even when the ethnic neighborhood no longer exists. Ethnic churches, fraternal organizations, and family ties provide cohesiveness without propinquity (Agocs, 1981; Chrisman, 1981; Golant and Jacobsen, 1978; Klaff, 1977).

FIGURE 1 Distribution of Greek Households, 1910.

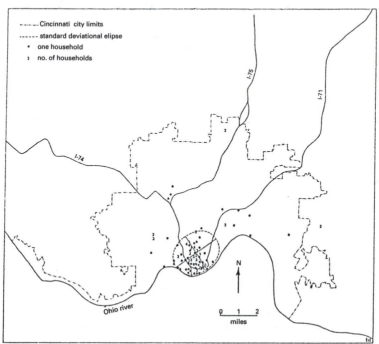

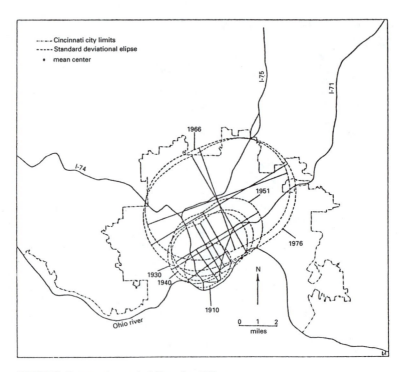

FIGURE 2 Comparison of all Standard Ellipses.

FIGURE 3 Movement of the Greek Orthodox Church in Cincinnati.

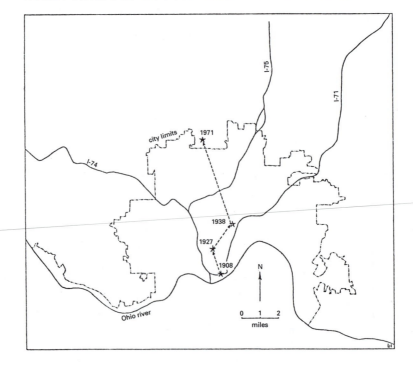

TABLE 12.3 Measures of the Residential Segregation of Blacks and Selected Ethnic Groups from the English Ethnic Group: Metropolitan Areas in 1980[*].

	BLACKS	GERMANS	IRISH	FRENCH	SCOTS	SWEDES	DUTCH	ITALIANS	POLES	HUNGARIANS	GREEKS	RUSSIANS
Atlanta	75	19	12	22	26	38	26	34	37	n.a.	n.a.	63
Baltimore	73	24	21	30	32	n.a.	37	34	45	48	56	73
Chicago	80	28	35	33	32	30	52	49	52	44	55	64
Cleveland	83	24	27	35	33	n.a.	n.a.	41	47	33	55	60
Dallas	77	16	14	23	27	33	28	33	37	n.a.	n.a.	n.a.
Detroit	85	21	20	27	28	36	37	45	42	44	52	66
Houston	73	17	17	22	31	35	33	29	35	n.a.	n.a.	n.a.
Los Angeles	78	14	17	24	28	25	34	25	37	41	46	55
Miami	71	18	17	27	29	32	37	29	50	48	44	61
New Orleans	63	27	23	31	n.a.	n.a.	n.a.	37	n.a.	n.a.	n.a.	n.a.
New York	67	39	43	40	n.a.	n.a.	n.a.	55	52	52	64	49
Newark	77	25	26	36	30	33	39	41	44	42	48	48
Philadelphia	77	27	32	35	32	n.a.	41	41	40	44	62	64
St. Louis	78	26	20	24	35	35	31	39	35	44	n.a.	75
San Francisco	71	15	21	26	25	25	32	30	28	41	45	43
Washington, D.C.	68	15	17	25	27	36	33	25	29	41	46	51
Average	75	22	23	29	30	33	35	37	41	44	52	59

[*]These are indexes of dissimilarity calculated from census tract data. Data are shown for all metropolitan areas with 250,000 or more black residents in 1980, except Memphis. Each group is compared to the residential distribution of those who gave English as their only ancestry. Blacks are defined by the race question. Ethnic groups consist of individuals who reported one specific ancestry, such as German or Irish.

n.a. = Indexes were not calculated if the group size was less than ten times the number of census tracts.

Source: U.S. Bureau of the Census, *Census of Population and Housing: 1980,* Summary Tape File 3. Reynolds Farley and Robert Wilger. *Recent Changes in the Residential Segregation of Blacks from Whites: An Analysis of 203 Metropolises (Report 15).* Ann Arbor, MI: Population Studies Center, 1987, Table G.

Descendants of groups in the second wave of immigration—Italians, Poles, and Hungarians—were more distinctive, required more assimilation, and even today are more segregated from the charter group. Their scores range from 37 for Italians to 59 for Russians.

As noted earlier, structural changes in our cities have meant lower levels of segregation for the third wave of immigrants. Table 12.4 summarizes the dissimilarity index for our newest group of ethnics—Hispanics and Asians—for the period 1970 and 1980. Hispanic population growth varied considerably across urban areas, so the average level of dissimilarity changed very little, falling from 44.4 to 43.4 between 1970 and 1980. Although not shown here, the largest Hispanic communities located in the Northeast and West experienced the greatest immigration, the fastest growth, and the largest increases in spatial dissimilarity over the decade. In contrast, small, slowly growing Hispanic communities in the north central and southern regions experienced small declines in dissimilarity. In general, Hispanic immigration and population growth

TABLE 12.4 Average Residential Dissimilarity of Hispanics and Asians from Anglos in Five Key Metropolitan Areas and Regional and Metropolitan Size Differences for 60 SMSAs

	HISPANICS			ASIANS		
	1970	*1980*	*CHANGE*	*1970*	*1980*	*CHANGE*
Metropolitan Area						
Chicago	58.4	63.5	5.1	55.8	43.9	-12.0
Los Angeles	46.8	57.0	10.2	53.1	43.1	-10.0
Miami	50.4	51.9	1.5	39.2	29.8	-9.4
New York	64.9	65.6	.7	56.1	48.1	-8.0
San Francisco	34.7	40.2	5.5	48.6	44.4	-4.2
Regional Differences						
Northeast	51.5	54.0	2.9	48.2	41.8	-6.4
North Central	46.9	43.6	-3.4	44.8	35.7	-9.1
South	42.4	38.4	-4.0	43.5	30.8	-12.7
West	40.2	41.7	-1.5	39.5	31.5	-8.0
SMSA Population						
Largest	69.9	60.8	-9.1	47.9	39.0	-8.9
Bigger	74.2	67.6	-6.6	40.0	31.5	-8.5
Smaller	78.6	73.2	-5.4	42.8	34.1	-8.7
Smallest	61.0	55.4	-5.6	43.9	32.1	-11.9
Average						
60 U.S. Cities	44.4	43.4	-1.0	43.7	34.2	-9.5

Source: Adapted from Douglas S. Massey and Nancy A. Denton. "Trends in the Residential Segregation of Blacks, Hispanics, and Asians, 1970–1980," *American Sociological Review* 52 (1987), Table 1, p. 807, and Table 3, p. 813.

appear to be the driving force behind changes in Hispanic residential segregation (Massey and Denton 1987, pp. 813–817).

Asians also experienced significant immigration and population growth in the decade ending in 1980, but on a much smaller scale. Only three cities, San Francisco, Los Angeles, and New York, had large enough populations to support Asian enclaves, so most Asians entering this country moved into predominantly Anglo neighborhoods. As a result, Asian residential dissimilarity declined between 1970 and 1980 to an average value of only 34.2. This is remarkably low for an immigrant group and roughly equal to the index for first-wave ethnics (German and Irish) in 1970 (Massey, 1987, pp. 816–817). However, if this group continues to grow at its present rate, at some point a critical mass of Asians will be reached, and enclaves will emerge in our cities and segregation of this group will likely grow.

ETHNIC SEGREGATION IN OTHER SOCIETIES

CANADA

Canada, like the United States, is a nation of immigrants, and, like the United States, Canada experienced three waves of immigrants. The first wave arrived before 1940 and included people from Britain, Poland, Scandinavia, and Russia. The second wave occurred in the 1950s and included French, Germans, and Dutch. The latest wave includes Italians, Asians, and Caribbean groups who entered Canadian society in the 1960s. Patterns of ethnic segregation parallel those found in the United States, except that the overall level of segregation is lower. The dissimilarity index between immigrants and native Canadians range between the 20s and 50s, with an average of 30. As in the United States, northern and western Europeans have lower index scores than eastern and southern Europeans. In general, patterns of assimilation are similar to the United States. Ethnics locate in central city enclaves; as time passes and their income improves, they move to other parts of the city, where other factors become important (Massey, 1985).

AUSTRALIA

Australia is also a nation of immigrants, but, until World War II, the majority of immigrants were of British or Irish extraction. After the war, the government pursued a program to encourage immigration. Initially, most of the immigrants were from Britain, Ireland, and northern and southern Europe. In the past 20 years, immigration has shifted to Asia, the Middle East, and Oceania. Today, 20 percent of Australians are foreign born, and Australia's major cities are ethnically diverse.

The cleavage between northern and southern European immigrants that characterizes Canada and the United States is also found in Australia but on levels comparable to Canada. The major ethnic division is between English-speaking and non English-speaking groups. English-speaking immigrants have moved into white-collar occupations and tend to live in the suburbs; non English speakers tend to be blue-collar and live and work in the central city. The ethnic enclaves are dispersing in a manner similar to those in Canada and the United States (Massey, 1985).

BRITAIN

Until the end of World War II, Britain was a homogeneous society with few ethnics, and, unlike the United States, Canada, and Australia, it was a nation of emigration not immigration. After the war, Britain experienced two waves of immigration from within the commonwealth—West Indians (1947–1970) and Indians and Pakistanis (1960–1980). Today, ethnics make up approximately 5 percent of Britain's total population, but the majority of the ethnic population is concentrated in Britain's largest cities. The factors affecting segregation in Britain were also different from those in the other nations discussed. The number of immigrants is smaller, there is less suburbanization, economic growth is slower, and government plays a larger role in housing than in the other three nations. The dissimilarity index ranges from the 30s to the 50s, with an average for both groups of around 50. Ethnicity has not been well studied in Britain, but ethnic enclaves are found in the central cities of most cities, and their persistence is closely associated with the social status of their residents (Prandy, 1980).

WESTERN EUROPE

After World War II, western European nations launched a massive rebuilding program, and this effort combined with rapid economic growth led to chronic labor shortages. By the 1960s, many western European governments were recruiting guest workers from Spain, Portugal, and Italy. When this source of labor dried up they turned to Yugoslavia, Turkey, and North Africa. Guest workers were seen as a temporary solution to a short-term labor problem, but, as labor shortages persisted, temporary immigration became permanent. By the 1970s, Western Europe contained 11 million foreign residents, comprising about 5 percent of the total population. As with immigrants in other societies, these groups gravitated toward the continent's largest cities, and, by the late 1970s, the percentage of foreign-born residents in Brussels was 16 percent, in Paris 12 percent, in Berlin 18 percent, in Munich 15 percent, and in Amsterdam 5 percent.

Ethnic segregation has not been widely studied in Europe, but research in Germany shows that dissimilarity indexes range from 10 to 40. As in other societies, the index scores are tied to the similarity between the immigrant group and the host society. Generally, these groups live in the oldest housing in the central city near the industries where they work and in isolated neighborhoods near suburban industrial centers (Massey, 1985).

ETHNIC SEGREGATION DUE TO SOCIAL STATUS FACTORS

How does one account for the continued segregation of these ethnic groups? Is it the result of their income and occupational characteristics, as the melting-pot model predicts, or are other factors involved, as the ethnic status model predicts? Sharon Bledea (1978, 1979) was interested in finding the degree to which the segregation of ethnic groups in 15 U.S. cities was the result of social status factors. Using census data, she was able to determine, through a process known as *indirect standardization,* the percentage of an ethnic group's segregation that was the result of their educational, income, and occupational characteristics. Table 12.5 is a summary of the data for six of the 15 cities in her study. The first column of the table for each city is the dissimilarity index for each group. Note that groups from western Europe have lower scores than groups from eastern and southern Europe. The second through fourth columns in each table give the percentage of each ethnic group's residential segregation that can be explained by the group's educational, income, and occupational characteristics. Note that these percentages are low: Only a small percentage of the segregation scores can be attributed to status characteristics. These results support the ethnic status model.

Unfortunately, the method of indirect standardization tells us only the percentage of the discrimination index score that can be attributed to social factors. It does not address the question, "Is ethnic segregation inversely related to social status?" Douglas Massey (1979, 1981b) examined residential dissimilarity between Hispanics and whites in ten metropolises, and he was able to compare the residential dissimilarity of Hispanics and whites through a process called *direct standardization:* He directly compared the scores of whites and Hispanics of different levels of education. He found that as income and years of education increase, the index of dissimilarity decreases—an inverse relationship as predicted by the melting-pot model.

To this point in the chapter, we have explored the rich ethnic heritage of the nation, the waves of ethnics who have molded our national character, the ecology of our cities, which has shaped their experiences, and the forces at work on the societal level which have shaped the residential structure of our cities. But questions remain: Does ethnicity make a difference? Are there substantial ethnic differences in achievement in the United States? Have some ethnic groups done better or worse than others?

In an exploratory study, Neidert and Farley (1985) examined the assimilation process of first-, second-, and third-generation ethnics from 21 ethnic groups. The researchers looked at the educational, income, and occupational characteristics of men aged 20 to 64 in each ethnic group and compared them to members of the charter group—men of English an ancestry. Table 12.6 summarizes the data for foreign-born men (first generation) and men born to native-born parents (third generation). Among first-generation men, no group exceeds the occupational score of the English, and southern and eastern Europeans have scores below the English. The only exception to this pattern is Asians. In general, those groups who have been here the longest and who are most similar to the charter group have the highest incomes and occupational prestige.

What about the third generation—does ancestry still make a difference? The second half of the table shows that most groups of European origin have scores about the same as the charter group. Note, too, that by the third generation, western Europeans and Italians are no longer at a disadvantage in the competition for good jobs. Russians and other eastern Europeans, often of Jewish ancestry, have made remarkable gains and by the third generation exceed the occupational prestige of the English. Asians have been even more successful in converting education into

TABLE 12.5 Indexes of Residential Dissimilarity Between Selected Ethnic Groups Versus Native Whites and Percentage of Actual Residential Dissimilarity Due to Educational, Income, and Occupational Characteristics of Each Ethnic Group[1]

NATIONAL ORIGIN	BOSTON DISSIMILARITY INDEX	PERCENT FROM: EDUCATION	INCOME	OCCU-PATION	CHICAGO DISSIMILARITY INDEX	PERCENT FROM: EDUCATION	INCOME	OCCU-PATION
Canada	17	40	20	15	25	4	6	15
Ireland	28	20	10	5	41	4	3	5
United Kingdom	16	24	19	4	23	3	7	14
Sweden	29	13	14	5	30	12	3	8
Germany	28	12	4	8	22	43	18	4
Poland	35	11	18	5	43	22	4	10
Czechoslovakia	66	4	4	5	43	18	2	6
Austria	45	5	14	7	31	16	10	2
Hungary	62	6	11	9	37	10	12	2
Italy	33	29	20	15	39	20	10	6
U.S.S.R.	51	6	21	11	56	7	16	13

NATIONAL ORIGIN	CLEVELAND DISSIMILARITY INDEX	PERCENT FROM: EDUCATION	INCOME	OCCU-PATION	NEW YORK DISSIMILARITY INDEX	PERCENT FROM: EDUCATION	INCOME	OCCU-PATION
Canada	25	9	9	13	34	12	11	8
Ireland	35	6	6	5	45	9	13	7
United Kingdom	22	5	5	9	30	4	8	9
Sweden	45	3	4	10	28	23	8	3
Germany	21	37	21	4	24	46	28	9
Poland	39	20	6	10	43	19	3	6
Czechoslovakia	33	22	5	9	40	20	2	6
Austria	25	25	6	9	40	21	3	5
Hungary	27	18	13	6	57	44	6	2
Italy	32	19	12	5	45	44	14	3
U.S.S.R.	50	7	16	13	48	4	17	11

NATIONAL ORIGIN	SAN FRANCISCO DISSIMILARITY INDEX	PERCENT FROM: EDUCATION	INCOME	OCCU-PATION	WASHINGTON DISSIMILARITY INDEX	PERCENT FROM: EDUCATION	INCOME	OCCU-PATION
Canada	21	8	3	23	25	18	13	15
Ireland	40	6	2	5	32	2	7	14
United Kingdom	22	3	10	11	23	10	17	16
Sweden	31	7	3	6	43	9	16	12
Germany	24	19	6	6	25	6	5	10
Poland	39	5	12	12	37	14	23	16
Czechoslovakia	49	5	7	2	39	3	19	7
Austria	37	5	10	8	39	7	20	13
Hungary	49	1	8	7	44	6	20	11
Italy	33	20	15	8	26	5	23	7
U.S.S.R.	38	10	20	17	50	13	24	17

[1] Derived through indirect standardization.

Source: Adapted from Sharon Estee Bleda, "Intergenerational Differences in Patterns and Bases of Ethnic Residential Dissimilarity," *Ethnicity* 5 (1978), Table 3, pp. 100–101.

TABLE 12.6

| | FIRST GENERATION | | | | THIRD GENERATION | | | |
| | *MEDIAN YEARS OF SCHOOL* | *PERCENT WITH SOME COLLEGE* | *MEAN OCCU-PATIONAL SCORE* | *PER CAPITA INCOME* | *MEDIAN YEARS OF SCHOOL* | *PERCENT WITH SOME COLLEGE* | *MEAN OCCU-PATIONAL SCORE* | *PER CAPITA INCOME* |
ANCESTRIES								
English	13.2	43%	50	$9,400	13.3	50%	44	$8,600
British Isles Not England	13.6	52	47	10,500	13.6**	53	45	8,250
Germany	13.2	48	42	9,900	12.9*	42*	41*	7,700
Other northwestern European	13.4	52	44	9,600	13.1*	45*	41*	7,825
Italian	10.0*	15*	32*	6,000*	13.2	48	41*	7,700*
Other southern European	10.2*	17*	28*	5,000*	13.5	50	42	8,800
Russian/eastern European	13.1	47	44	8,800	14.1**	62**	49**	8,875
Asian	14.2*	64**	44	5,200	14.8**	69**	51**	11,800**
Spanish	11.1*	28*	31*	4,800*	11.1*	37*	32*	4,825*
Mexican	6.9*	9*	18*	2,700*	11.7*	29*	32*	5,200*
African-American	n.a.	n.a.	n.a.	n.a.	11.5	26	28	5,600

*Mean is significantly smaller than mean for English ancestry group.

**Mean is significantly larger than mean for English ancestry group.

Source: Adapted from Lisa J. Niedert and Reynolds Farley. "Assimilation in the United States: An Analysis of Ethnic and Generation Differences in Status and Achievement," *American Sociological Review* 50 (December 1985), Table 1 and Table 3, pp. 840–850.

prestigious jobs. The groups at a disadvantage are the descendants of the three groups who have had the greatest difficulties in removing differences from the charter group—Mexicans, native Americans, and blacks.

Is the melting-pot model or the ethnic status model correct? If the melting-pot model holds that third-generation ethnic groups will be indistinguishable from the charter group in education, occupation, or income, then the answer is no. In the third generation, significant differences exist between groups. But the thrust of the ethnic-status model is that the ethnic status of some groups puts them at a disadvantage in a society dominated by a charter group. The results do not support this position, either. Among European-origin ancestries, only Russians and eastern Europeans are significantly different from the charter group, and they are more successful.

Which model is correct? I would argue that parts of both models are correct. Ethnic identification is an important factor in the persistence of ethnic segregation. But maybe we are using the wrong time frame, or possibly ethnic divisions may always be a part of American society, as the ethnic status model suggests. There is support for this position in other societies. The ethnic Chinese in Vietnam, Jews in the Pale of eastern Europe and Russia, and Korean ethnics in Japan have maintained their language, customs, and culture for centuries. Nevertheless, there has been an underlying preoccupation in much of the research on ethnicity in the United States on the eventual and inevitable assimilation of racial and ethnic minorities into the mainstream of society, and this preoccupation has clouded how we study ethnicity (Klaff, 1980). The mass media and a mass popular culture are potent forces at work in American society bringing about conformity, but the countervailing forces of ethnic identification mean that ethnicity will continue to be important to understanding our cities and our society well into the twenty-first century. Rather than an assimilated society, it may be more valuable to think of America as a pluralistic one and work toward a time when ethnic divisions are recognized, protected, and appreciated.

The literature on ethnicity is evolving. In the 70 years this topic has been studied, we have learned much about the process by which immigrants become members of a new society. We have learned much, but we still have much to learn.

RACIAL SEGREGATION

The 26 million black Americans are this nation's largest and most segregated minority group. Americans of African heritage have roots that reach back to the founding of the nation, yet today the residential segregation of this group is higher than our most recent immigrants—Hispanics and Asians. Understanding why black Americans remain segregated after centuries reveals something about the forces that shape our cities, as well as our society.

RURAL-TO-URBAN MIGRATION OF BLACK AMERICANS

Through much of our history, America's black population has been mostly rural and southern. However, during the past 80 years, a major redistribution of population occurred in America as blacks moved to urban areas in the North and the South. The size of this migration can be seen in the figures in Table 12.7. In 1900, 76 percent of this nation's black population lived in rural areas and nearly 90 percent in the South. By 1980, only 18 percent of this nation's black population lived in rural areas, and 47 percent lived in regions outside the South.

The reasons for this movement are reflected in the figures in Table 12.8, which gives the percentage change in the racial makeup of populations of metropolitan areas for the years 1900–1980. The first significant out-migration of blacks from the South began with World War I and continued through the 1920s. The primary attraction of northern cities to southern blacks was jobs. The war cut off the immigration of cheap European labor to northern industries, creating a labor shortage. At the same time the mechanization of farming was creating a surplus of unskilled farm labor in the South. Therefore, black Americans in the 1920s and the decades that followed became a new source of cheap industrial labor.

The Depression of the 1930s dramatically lowered the growth of blacks in metropolitan areas. Later, with the rapid expansion of American industry during World War II, the flow of migrants accelerated, and this trend continued into the 1950s and 1960s. During the 1970s and 1980s, migration slowed, and the regional distribution of population by race has stabilized.

TABLE 12.7 Population location by race, 1900–1970 (percentage distribution).

	NORTHEAST	NORTH CENTRAL	SOUTH	WEST
White				
1900	30.9	38.5	24.7	5.8
1920	30.5	35.0	25.4	9.0
1940	29.2	32.7	26.8	11.3
1960	26.2	30.3	27.4	16.1
1970	25.0	29.1	28.4	17.4
1980	22.4	20.2	31.3	18.7
Black				
1900	4.4	5.6	89.6	0.3
1920	6.5	7.6	85.2	0.8
1940	10.6	11.0	77.0	1.3
1960	16.0	18.3	60.7	5.7
1970	19.2	20.2	53.1	7.4
1980	18.4	20.2	53.0	8.4

Source: Irene B. Taeuber, "The Changing Distribution of the Population of the United States in the Twentieth Century." In Vol. 5 of Commission Research Reports, *Population Distribution and Policy,* ed. Sara Mills Mazie, U.S. Commission on Population Growth and the American Future. Washington, D.C.: U.S. Government Printing Office, 1972, pp. 44–45.

TABLE 12.8 Racial change in metropolitan areas in the twentieth century (% change).

DECADE	INSIDE CENTRAL CITIES		OUTSIDE CENTRAL CITIES	
	WHITE	BLACK	WHITE	BLACK
1900–1910	36.2	46.3	25.2	19.3
1910–1920	24.7	93.7	39.0	33.7
1920–1930	25.9	107.8	67.4	77.9
1930–1940	4.2	27.6	17.1	20.8
1940–1950	4.4	74.2	42.3	62.3
1950–1960	-6.9	55.7	70.4	73.3
1960–1970	-7.6	41.7	24.7	57.6
1970–1980	-24.0	16.5	23.6	18.5

Source: Irene B. Taeuber, "The Changing Distribution of Population in the United States in the Twentieth Century." In Volume 5 of Commission Research Reports, *Population Distribution and Policy,* ed. Sara Mills Mazie, U.S. Commission on Population Growth and the American Future. Washington, D.C.: U.S. Government Printing Office, 1972, p. 89. 1970–1980 from U.S. Bureau of the census (1987). *State and Metropolitan Area Data Book 1986.* Washington, D.C.: U.S. Government Printing Office, Table 11.

Migration streams. Enclaves and ghettoes serve many functions—they give a group a sense of peoplehood; they allow a group to avoid a hostile host society; they provide a safety net of kin and friends; they support stores, shops, schools, and other enterprises; they provide a haven to new immigrants; once they reach a critical mass, they encourage additional migration. How? Through a network of old friends and relatives in the sending society. Money, letters, calls, and people pass back and forth between the sending and the receiving societies, and over time migration occurs in streams. One of the largest migrations in our history is the Famine Irish, who entered this country in the second half of the nineteenth century. Ward in his book, *Boston's Immigrants*, describes the factors that confined much of this immigration to a stream between Ireland and Boston. Recently, Douglas Massey (1981c, 1986, 1987; Massey and Schnabel, 1983) examined Mexican immigration and described the network of kin and friends, the lines of communication, and the economic ties between Mexico and the United States, which shape the size and direction of this migration to the United States.

One of the greatest migrations in history occurred between 1900 and 1980, when over 5 million blacks left the South, largely for the cities of the North. As with other groups, this migration did not occur at random but in well-defined streams. Blacks from the South Atlantic states of Virginia, North and South Carolina, Georgia, and Florida migrated to the metropolises of the Northeast and Middle Atlantic states, including Washington, D. C., Philadelphia, New York, and Boston. Blacks from Alabama, Mississippi, Tennessee, Arkansas, and Louisiana tended to follow migration streams along the valleys of the Mississippi and Ohio Rivers to the lake and river cities. Blacks from Texas and western Louisiana usually chose cities in the West (Smith and Zopf, 1976, pp. 141–145).

RESIDENTIAL PATTERNS IN THE 1970s AND 1980s

By 1980, 82 percent of all blacks were urban, a percentage that exceeds that of their white counterparts—71 percent. The black migration from the South was predominantly a migration to the central cities of metropolitan areas. By 1980, the population of metropolitan areas had become 15 percent black, and blacks made up 7 percent of these areas' suburban rings (Stahura, 1988). The shift of more than five million blacks during this century must be viewed in perspective, however. Although this is an enormous number of people, it pales when compared to the magnitude of European immigration during the opening years of this century. In just ten years, from 1901 to 1911, 8.8 million European immigrants entered the United States (U.S. Census Bureau, 1975, Table 153).

Rural-to-urban migration of black Americans has ceased to be an important factor in metropolitan growth. Today, the majority of moves made by blacks are within and between metropolitan areas, and the growth of the black populations within metropolitan areas is due to natural increase (births exceeding deaths). This population increase, however, has been contained in well-defined areas of the city. Even as black Americans begin to move to the suburbs, the suburbs to which they move are usually older and adjacent to the traditional black area of the central city. Black suburbs are politically autonomous but share many of the housing, employment, and service problems of central city neighborhoods. As a result of the forces at work in our cities, blacks continue to be the most segregated group in American society (Stahura, 1988; Sterns and Logan, 1986; Logan and Schneider, 1984).

TRENDS IN RACIAL SEGREGATION

In the nineteenth century, the few blacks who lived in urban areas were not separated from whites. Residential land use in the preindustrial city was not like the modern metropolis. Industry and commerce were dispersed across the city, and most people lived near where they worked (Hershberg, 1979). The cities were heterogeneous, but different populations lived side by side despite the ethnic, racial, and social-status differences that separated them in other aspects of urban life. Table 12.9 presents dissimilarity indexes for free blacks in 15 cities in 1850. Note that the scores range from a high of 59.2 in Boston to a low of 15.8 in Louisville. But these indexes are based on ward data, and they can be deceiving because they mask some segregation. We know from studies in Cincinnati, Detroit, and Philadelphia that if segregation patterns are analyzed on the street and block level, one finds that blacks were not evenly distributed within wards but tended to be concentrated on a few streets within each ward (Katzman, 1973; Hershberg, 1979; Taylor, 1981). For example, Taylor in his study of Cincinnati found that 52 percent of the black population of Cincinnati in 1850 resided on just 3 percent of the city's streets. When he examined these clusters, blacks were found to live together regardless of nativity, sex, household structure, stage in the life cycle, or occupation. (Taylor, 1981, pp. 48–53).

In the twentieth century, the size of the black urban population has grown, the forces shaping the city have changed, and the scale of urbanization has increased. But have segregation patterns changed? This question is answered by a study conducted by Reynolds Farley and Robert Wilger for the National Academy of Sciences (1987). The authors analyzed the changes in the residential segregation of blacks from whites for 203 metropolitan areas for the years 1960 through 1980. Table 12.10 presents their data on the 29 metropolitan areas with black populations of 150,000 or more in 1980. The black

TABLE 12.9 Free black indexes of dissimilarity for fifteen cities, rank ordered for 1850.

CITY	BLACK POPULATION	PERCENT TOTAL POPULATION	INDEX OF DISSIMILARITY
Boston	1,999	1.46	59.2
Philadelphia	10,736	8.85	49.3
Pittsburgh	1,959	4.20	46.3
New Orleans	9,905	8.51	45.1
Cincinnati	3,137	2.67	37.5
New York	13,815	2.68	37.2
St. Louis	1,398	1.80	35.8
Brooklyn	2,424	2.50	31.8
Buffalo	675	1.60	25.1
Albany	860	1.69	25.1
Providence	1,499	3.61	24.2
Baltimore	24,442	15.05	21.4
Charleston	3,441	8.01	20.5
Washington, D.C.	8,158	20.39	20.4
Louisville	612	1.34	15.8

Source: L. P. Curry. *The Free Black in Urban America: The Shadow of a Dream.* Chicago: University of Chicago Press, 1981, p. 56.

TABLE 12.10 Measures of Residential Segregation for Metropolitan Areas with Largest Black Populations in 1980[a]

	POPULATION IN 1980 (IN THOUSANDS)		INDEXES OF BLACK-WHITE RESIDENTIAL SEGREGATION[b]			INTERRACIAL CONTACT MEASURES[c]			
	TOTAL	BLACK	1980	1970	1960	% BLACK FOR WHITES	% WHITE FOR BLACKS	% WHITE FOR WHITES	% BLACK FOR BLACKS
New York	9120	1941	78	74	74	9%	28%	84%	64%
Chicago	7104	1428	88	91	91	4	15	90	84
Los Angeles	7478	944	79	89	89	6	30	79	61
Detroit	4353	890	88	89	87	5	20	93	80
Philadelphia	4717	884	78	78	77	7	28	92	70
Washington, D.C.	3061	853	71	81	78	12	30	84	69
Baltimore	2174	557	75	81	87	9	26	89	73
Houston	2905	529	74	78	81	8	31	85	66
Atlanta	2030	499	78	82	77	9	26	90	73
Dallas	2975	419	78	87	81	5	30	90	67
Newark	1966	418	80	79	73	8	27	89	70
St. Louis	2356	408	83	87	86	5	24	94	75
San Francisco	3251	391	71	77	79	7	42	81	51
New Orleans	1187	387	73	74	65	14	27	85	72
Memphis	913	364	71	79	73	16	24	83	76
Cleveland	1899	346	88	90	90	4	18	94	81
Miami	1626	280	79	86	90	7	30	89	68
Birmingham	847	240	75	68	64	10	26	89	74
Norfolk	807	224	63	77	77	14	36	83	63
Pittsburgh	2264	176	73	75	74	4	44	96	55
Richmond	632	221	66	77	75	13	34	86	66
Cincinnati	1401	174	79	82	83	5	36	94	59
Kansas City	1327	173	79	87	83	5	30	93	69
Nassau–Suffolk	2606	162	77	n.a.	n.a.	3	49	95	49
Greensboro	827	160	69	75	67	9	37	90	63
Boston	2763	160	77	79	81	3	40	95	55
Jacksonville	737	158	68	82	78	10	35	89	65
Indianapolis	1167	152	80	84	79	5	33	94	67
Milwaukee	1397	151	84	90	90	4	29	95	70
Average	2617	472	77	81	80	8	31	89	68

[a]These measures are calculated from data for census tracts. No adjustments have been made for changes over time in the boundaries of metropolitan areas.

[b]These are indexes of dissimilarity comparing the distributions of the white and black populations across census tracts. If individuals were randomly distributed, the index would approach its minimum value of zero. In a situation of absolute apartheid, the index would equal 100. The 1970 and 1980 indexes compare blacks and whites; the 1960 indexes, whites and nonwhites.

[c]These measures of potential interracial contact for 1980 show the percentage black in the census tract of the typical white, the percentage white for blacks, the percentage white for whites, and percentage black for blacks.

Sources: (1980 Data): U.S. Bureau of the Census, Census of Population and Housing: 1980, Master Area Reference File (tape file). (1960 and 1970 Indexes): Thomas L. Van Valey, Wade Clark Roof, and Jerome E. Wilcox, "Trends in Residential Segregation: 1960–1970," American Journal of Sociology, 82, 4 (January) 1976. Reynolds Farley and Robert Wilger, Recent Changes in the Residential Segregation of Blacks from Whites: An Analysis of 203 Metropolises (Report 15). Ann Arbor, MI: Population Studies Center, 1987, Table A.

TABLE 12.11 Metropolitan Areas with the Highest or the Lowest Racial Residential Segregation in 1980

METROPOLITAN AREAS	INDEXES OF BLACK–WHITE RESIDENTIAL SEGREGATION			INTERRACIAL CONTACT MEASURES			
	1980	1970	1960	% BLACK FOR TYPICAL WHITE	% WHITE FOR TYPICAL BLACK	% WHITE FOR TYPICAL WHITE	% BLACK FOR TYPICAL BLACK
Highest Levels of Residential Segregation							
Gary	89	88	89	5	19	92	78
Chicago	88	91	91	4	15	90	84
Cleveland	88	90	90	4	18	94	81
Detroit	88	89	87	5	20	93	80
Fort Myers	88	n.a.	n.a.	2	25	96	74
Flint	86	86	83	5	25	94	73
Bradenton	85	n.a.	n.a.	4	35	95	61
Fort Lauderdale	84	95	n.a.	3	27	95	73
Milwaukee	84	90	90	4	29	95	70
Midland, TX	83	86	n.a.	5	49	90	44
Saginaw	83	84	82	6	32	91	62
St. Louis	83	87	86	5	24	94	75
West Palm Beach	83	85	n.a.	5	29	94	70
Buffalo	80	86	87	4	34	95	65
Newark	80	79	73	8	27	89	70
Lowest Levels of Residential Segregation							
Lawrence, KN	29	50	n.a.	5	93	90	6
Danville	33	n.a.	n.a.	25	59	74	41
Jacksonville, NC	34	n.a.	n.a.	18	68	79	31
Anchorage	39	n.a.	n.a.	6	89	86	10
Fayetteville	39	45	n.a.	25	52	71	47
Lawton, OK	40	53	n.a.	14	67	77	31
Clarksville, TN	43	n.a.	n.a.	18	65	80	34
Victoria, TX	43	n.a.	n.a.	7	82	83	14
Vineland, NJ	43	54	n.a.	11	60	83	38
Lynchburg	44	48	n.a.	16	60	84	40
Texarkana	44	39	n.a.	17	57	82	43
Bloomington, IL	45	54	n.a.	4	91	95	9
Colorado Springs	45	55	n.a.	6	85	89	13
Anderson, SC	46	n.a.	n.a.	14	65	86	35
Columbia, MO	46	60	n.a.	5	78	93	21

Source: Reynolds Farley and Robert Wilger. *Recent Changes in the Residential Segregation of Blacks from Whites: An Analysis of 203 Metropolises (Report 15).* Ann Arbor, MI: Population Studies Center, 1987, Table B.

populations range from 1.9 million in New York to 151,000 in Milwaukee, and these metropolises held over half of the nation's black population. Note that the dissimilarity index varies from a high of 88 in Cleveland, Chicago, and Detroit to scores in the 60s in the cities of Norfolk, Richmond, and Jacksonville. In general, the larger the black population, the higher the dissimilarity index. In cities with a large black population, the index averaged 77; cities with the smallest black populations averaged 64.

There is a great variation in residential segregation from metropolis to metropolis. Table 12.11 presents data on the 15 metropolises with the highest and the lowest dissimilarity indexes. Notice that older northern industrial cities, like Gary, Chicago, Cleveland, and Detroit, and several rapidly growing retirement communities in Florida—Fort Myers, Bradenton, and West Palm Beach—have the highest levels of segregation. Cities with low levels of residential segregation are often tied to nearby military bases—Jacksonville, North Carolina and Camp Lejune; Fayetteville, North Carolina and Fort Bragg; Lawton, Oklahoma and Fort Sill; Clarksville, Tennessee and Fort Campbell—or university towns—Lawrence, Kansas and the University of Kansas; Charlottesville, Virginia and the University of Virginia; Columbia, Missouri and the University of Missouri; Athens, Georgia and the University of Georgia; Ann Arbor, Michigan and the University of Michigan. The small size of these communities and the transient character of their populations seem to affect residential segregation.

Does region or the size of the metropolis make a difference? Considering the racial history of the South, one might expect this region to have the highest levels of segregation, but it does not. Table 12.12 shows that the cities in the Northeast and Midwest had the highest levels of segregation: The average metropolis in the South was on the average 9 points lower. In the West, blacks were even less residentially segregated than in the South. Size also makes a difference. Places with a population of 800,000 or more had an average index of 75; those of less than one-quarter million, only 65 (Farley and Wilger, 1987. p. 7).

These are interesting patterns, but has residential segregation changed in recent years? The last column of Table 12.12 shows that during the 1970s, black residential segregation decreased, regardless of region or community size. Have civil rights legislation and fair housing laws helped to lower the residential dissimilarity between blacks and whites? The index of dissimilarity suggests that they have, but this index is a general measure of segregation; it does not tell us what is happening in a typical neighborhood. For this we turn to the exposure index, P^*, which gives a measure of racial isolation.

The exposure index gives us the composition of the census tract of the typical white or the typical black resident of the city. If people live near each other, they are likely to have contact because they use the same stores, parks, schools, and theaters. Contact leads to interaction, and social interaction is at the basis of the assimilation process. Conversely, segregation and isolation limit the contact between groups, inhibit interaction, and perpetuate segregation. The likelihood of contact between groups is measured by the exposure index, and it gives a general impression of the future direction of racial relations.

TABLE 12.12 Measures of Black-White Residential Segregation for Metropolitan Areas

	NUMBER OF METROPOLITAN AREAS IN 1980	INDEXES OF DISSIMILARITY			
		1980	1970	1960	Change 60–80
Total United States	203	66	73	76	
Regions					
Northeast	29	69	74	74	-5
Midwest	53	72	77	80	-8
South	106	63	71	74	-11
West	15	60	72	79	-19
Metropolitan Population Size in 1980					
Under 250,000	88	60	68	74	-14
250,000 to 499,000	50	65	71	74	-9
500,000 to 799,000	24	72	77	75	-3
800,000 or More	41	75	81	80	-5
Percentage of Population Black in 1980					
Under 6%	29	64	73	77	-13
6% to 14%	94	69	76	78	-9
15% to 23%	50	64	71	76	-12
24% or More	30	62	69	71	-9
Percentage of Dwelling Units Built After 1969					
Under 19%	22	74	76	74	0
19% to 28%	85	69	76	77	-8
29% to 39%	72	60	69	74	-14
40% or more	24	65	72	81	-16

Source: Reynolds Farley and Robert Wilger. *Recent Changes in the Residential Segregation of Blacks from Whites: An Analysis of 203 Metropolises (Report 15).* Ann Arbor, MI: Population Studies Center, Table C.

The last two columns of Table 12.10 give the P^* indexes for the metropolitan areas with the highest and the lowest racial residential segregation in 1980. The figures show that whites are isolated from blacks, but many blacks live in neighborhoods with large white populations. In all 203 metropolitan areas, the typical white lives in a neighborhood where 7 percent of her or his neighbors are black, but for a typical black 34 percent of her or his neighbors are white. In older and larger cities that have large black populations, blacks live in census tracts with majority black populations, but in smaller and younger cities and in cities in the West, blacks are usually a minority in their neighborhoods (Farley and Wilger, 1987, p. 14). Therefore, blacks have a much greater array of racial experiences than whites, and this has consequences for race relationships in this society.

The Farley and Wilger study suggests the following: First, in the decade ending in 1980, the residential segregation of blacks decreased in all regions and in metropolises of all sizes. Second, although there has been a decline, black residential segregation is much higher than white ethnics, even Hispanics and Asians, who have recently arrived. Third, there has been little change in the residential patterns of whites; they continue to live in neighborhoods with few blacks. In contrast, blacks live in neighborhoods where there is considerable racial variation. Fourth, the highest levels of black residential segregation are in the large industrial cities of the North—the terminus of the massive rural-to-urban migration of earlier in this century. Fifth, low levels of segregation are often found in small and moderate-size communities where the military or a university is the major employer (Farley and Wigler, 1987, pp. 1–2).

A COMMUNITY WITHIN A COMMUNITY

Segregation forces blacks of widely different social status to live closer to each other than their white counterparts. Because of the persistence of segregation in American society, the black community in most large American metropolises has taken on some of the characteristics of the total metropolis of which it is a part. The most interesting of these is residential segregation according to class within the black community. The pattern is shown clearly in Table 12.13, in which indexes of residential dissimilarity for employed males are listed by occupation and race. These figures, calculated from the 1970 census, are the average index scores of ten urbanized areas. In the top third of the table, the residential patterns of whites of different occupational status are compared. As noted in the discussion of social-status segregation, as the social distance between any two status groups increases, the average physical distance between their residences as reflected in the indexes of dissimilarity also increases. In comparing white professionals with other white occupational groups across the top line of this table, one sees that the index scores increase in a regular fashion as social-status differences increase.

In the middle of the table, the indexes of dissimilarity for nonwhites are presented. The same patterns are observed, but these index scores are consistently higher than the white scores. In other words, although blacks are segregated as a group, their racial communities are clearly differentiated internally with respect to social status.

The bottom of the table compares whites of different occupational status with blacks in the same occupational categories. Comparing blacks and whites of the highest occupational status—professionals—produces a score of 70. The rest of the table shows that within the ten urbanized areas included in the study, two communities exist—one white and one nonwhite.

Social consequences of these patterns. The figures in Table 12.13 show that indexes of dissimilarity between socioeconomic groups were roughly the same for whites and nonwhites in 1970. What the figures do not show is the physical closeness (propinquity) between the various occupational groupings. The dissimilarities between white occupational groupings are spread out over an entire city; black occupational differences are accommodated within the ghetto. Erbe (1975) investigated this relationship among different status groups in both the white and black populations in

TABLE 12.13 Indexes of residential dissimilarity calculated between employed males categorized by occupation and race, averaged over ten areas, 1970.

		PROFESSIONAL	MANAGERIAL	SALES	CLERICAL	CRAFT	OPERATIVE	SERVICE
			WHITE					
A.	Professional		15	15	26	36	43	34
	Managerial			14	28	36	43	35
	Sales				25	33	40	32
	Clerical					19	25	18
White	Craft						14	18
	Operative							20
	Service							
	Laboring							
			NONWHITE					
B.	Professional		43	45	38	46	46	44
	Managerial			46	39	42	42	43
	Sales				37	40	39	40
	Clerical					26	25	28
Nonwhite	Craft						18	24
	Operative							21
	Service							
	Laboring							
			WHITE					
C.	Professional	70	80	79	77	79	78	76
	Managerial	84	86	85	84	85	84	83
	Sales	89	90	89	88	89	88	87
	Clerical	87	88	87	85	85	84	83
Nonwhite	Craft	87	87	86	84	83	82	81
	Operative	88	89	88	86	86	84	83
	Service	87	88	87	84	84	82	81
	Laboring	89	89	89	87	86	84	81

Source: Adapted from Table 3 in Simkus, A. A. "Residential Segregation by Occupation and Race in Ten Urbanized Areas, 1950–1970." *Sociological Review* 43 (1978), p. 86. Reprinted with permission of The American Sociological Association.

Chicago. She discovered that the residential propinquity between high- and low-status persons differed dramatically between racial groups. Although white professionals and managers lived in census tracts with others of comparable status, black professionals and managers "lived in tracts with occupational composition comparable, on the average, to that of tracts where unskilled white workers live" (Erbe, 1975, p. 811). For the black middle class in Chicago, social-status segregation meant avoiding the inner ghetto and public housing, but it did not mean isolation from the black lower class. Unlike whites, middle-class black families shared schools, parks, and other facilities with lower socioeconomic groups, and, since the neighborhood environment affects things like children's school performance, these findings suggest that propinquity may have consequences for social mobility.

Much has changed in the past decade. Average family income for black Americans has grown, and blacks in increasing numbers have moved to the suburbs. Although most of this suburban growth has been contained in older suburbs, adjacent to traditional black areas of the city, this movement has increased the physical distance between the black lower and middle classes. The black middle class has been able to do what whites have done all along—avoid groups that they define as undesirable—and isolate themselves in politically autonomous suburbs. The move to the suburbs may serve the interest of the black middle class, but it has consequences for those left behind.

William Wilson (1987) in his controversial book, *The Truly Disadvantaged,* explores the consequences of these changes in the black community. He makes an argument that is the opposite of Erbe's: The lower class may have hindered the social mobility of the middle class, but the middle class has traditionally provided the leadership, role models, and values and norms for the entire black community. This occurred because blacks of all social classes shared the same area of the city. During the 1970s and 1980s, blacks experienced upward social mobility, and the black middle class abandoned the traditional community for other parts of the city. According to Wilson, the people left behind are the most disadvantaged element of the black community: the underclass.

The black underclass is a heterogeneous grouping of families and individuals outside the mainstream of the American occupational system. They lack training and skills; they suffer from long-term unemployment or have never worked; they engage in street crime and other aberrant behavior; they have a long history of welfare dependence. They share similar problems: low income, poor health, broken homes, inadequate housing, poor education, and cultural and linguistic differences that separate and isolate them from the mainstream of society (Wilson, 1987, pp. 6–8). Is the outward migration of the black middle class the only reason for the emergence of the underclass? The answer is no. Structural changes in America's economy have contributed to the problem. Chicago and other northern industrial cities have changed from manufacturing and distribution centers to administrative, information, and service centers. Gone are the highly paid factory jobs. Gone are low-paying, entry-level jobs. Growing are jobs that require high levels of education and training. Wilson argues that racism and discrimination have led to the overrepresentation of black Americans in lower occupational groupings, and these jobs are vulnerable to changes in the economy. Not only has there been a decline in the number of jobs in the low wage sector, but the ones that still exist are no longer found in the central city; they are in the suburbs. There is a mismatch between where people live and where the jobs are.

Therefore, structural changes in America's economy, combined with the suburbanization of industry and the black middle class, have led to the segregation and isolation of the most disadvantaged citizens in this society. According to Wilson, this isolation has contributed to the destruction of the black family, the growth of female-headed families, and the emergence of a set of values and norms that perpetuate inequality. For example, at a time when education is vital for success, the children of the underclass are going to the worst schools in the city. At a time when intact black families are experiencing upward social mobility, the pool of employed males available for marriage is shrinking. At a time when the fastest-growing segment of the poor is female-headed households, the stigma on unwanted pregnancy and illegitimacy in the ghetto is on the decline. And at a time when an intact family—one in which both the father and mother are present—has been found to be a major deterrent to illegitimacy, these families have become rare in the neighborhoods of the underclass.

Solutions? Wilson explores the failed programs of the past—the War on Poverty, Model Cities, and Job Corps—and claims that they failed because they were not broadly based. He contends that a program that will work is one that addresses structural problems: problems faced by all Americans, not just those of color.

The work of Wilson has been corroborated by the research of others on occupational inequality. For more than 30 years, researchers have investigated patterns of racial socioeconomic inequality in cities. Occupation is one of the most important dimensions of social status because it is related to so many other factors. One's occupational status is correlated with one's education, income, life-style, social roles, and life chances. As with residential segregation, occupational status is an important indicator of racial inequality in American society.

Researchers have shown that in the last 40 years there has been a steady decline in socioeconomic differences between blacks and whites. They have documented the growing equality in schooling, earnings, and access to employment (Fossett and Swicegood, 1982; Fossett, Galle, and Kelly, 1986; Farley, 1987). But major differences still exist. Why? Because of the ecology of place. People living in different places face different opportunity structures. Since the end of World War II, changes in transportation and communication technology have permitted the decentralization of industry from the central city to industrial parks and commercial centers on the fringe. When blacks are segregated in the central city, they tend to be cut off from information on outlying labor markets. The time and cost of commuting is an additional barrier to employment. Segregation means isolation, and blacks are cut off from labor markets in the suburbs.

This is what Lewin-Epstein (1986) found in unemployment among black and white youths. In the past decade there has been a growing disparity in labor-market standing of black and white youth. While the employment of white youth has increased, unemployment rates among blacks have risen to twice that of young whites. Adolescents live with their parents, and they have no choice in residence. Few black youth own cars, and poor mass transit makes commuting costs to the suburbs prohibitive. The isolation of black youth "from life outside their communities and neighborhood restricts their ability to receive, organize, and put to use diverse labor market information" (Lewin-Epstein, 1986, p. 561). It appears that residential segregation not only inhibits contact between groups, lessening the chances of interaction and eventually assimilation, but it is also a major factor in the perpetuation of inequality in our society. One's life chances are circumscribed not only by your position in the social structure but also by your residential location within the city.

WHY RACIAL SEGREGATION?

Ecological factors. In the discussion of ethnic segregation three factors—voluntary, involuntary, and ecological—have been identified as being responsible for the segregation of these groups. The assimilation model presented in this section argues that the segregation of ethnic groups is an artifact of the groups' social status. In the case of blacks, if ecological factors are responsible for segregation, then poor blacks should live near poor whites, and rich blacks should live near rich whites. Table 12.15 presents measures of racial residential segregation for 16 metropolitan areas, controlling for income and education. A perusal of these data show that even with the effects of income and education removed, the dissimilarity index remains high and near the national average of 77. In the cities of Chicago, Los Angeles, and Detroit, the indexes are consistently higher than the national average. Therefore, blacks are segregated from whites regardless of income or education. Even among the highly educated, where you would expect to find racial tolerance, residential segregation is high. Therefore, it appears

TABLE 12.15 Measures of Racial Residential Segregation, Controlling for Income and Education, 1980.

	AVERAGE FOR 16 METROPOLITAN AREAS[a]	FIVE LARGEST METROPOLISES IN TERMS OF BLACK POPULATION				
		NEW YORK	CHICAGO	LOS ANGELES	DETROIT	PHILADELPHIA
Family Income In 1979						
Under $5,000	76	70	80	82	79	76
$5,000 to 7,499	76	74	81	82	79	77
$7,500 to 9,999	76	75	81	83	79	76
$10,000 to 14,999	75	75	80	81	79	74
$15,000 to 19,999	75	77	81	81	79	75
$20,000 to 24,999	76	78	81	81	81	75
$25,000 to 34,999	76	79	82	81	82	74
$35,000 to 49,999	76	80	82	81	82	73
$50,000 or more	79	78	82	83	83	77
Educational Attainment of Persons 25 and Over						
Less than 9 years	76	72	82	83	79	76
High school, 1–3 years	77	76	83	84	81	78
High school, 4 years	76	78	83	82	83	76
College, 1–3 years	74	77	81	78	82	74
College, 4 years or more	71	72	76	73	80	68

[a]These residential segregation scores are averages for all metropolises containing one-quarter million blacks or more, with the exception of Memphis. The index shown for $20,000 to $24,999, 76, compares the residential distribution of black families in this income category to that of whites in the identical category.

Source: U.S. Bureau of the Census, *Census of Population and Housing: 1980,* Summary Tape File 3A. From Reynolds Farley and Robert Wilger. *Recent Changes in the Residential Segregation of Blacks and Whites: An Analysis of 203 Metropolises (Report 15).* Ann Arbor, MI: Population Studies Center, 1987, Table F.

that the improving social status of blacks is unlikely, in and by itself, to alter the prevailing patterns of racial segregation.

Voluntary and involuntary factors. Even if involuntary and ecological factors in residential patterning could be eliminated completely, the segregation of races would persist for voluntary reasons—blacks would choose to live near blacks. However, the evidence is strong that involuntary factors are responsible for much of the segregation. The nation's history is replete with examples of how violence, rumor, prejudicial insinuation, and racial threats of declining property values and block busting have been used to segregate black Americans. Racial minorities, because of their high visibility, are the most easily manipulated real estate client groups. Because their housing options have been limited by prejudicial feelings, a segregated market, and the undemocratic rules to which they are subject, racial minorities have traditionally had little choice in the matter of residential location. Nearly a century ago William Graham Sumner, a founder of American sociology, stated, "Stateways cannot change folkways." It is true that federal legislation cannot change attitudes (prejudices), but it can stop overt behavior (discrimination). The 1964 Civil Rights Act and subsequent legislation have had a measurable impact on the economic well-being of black Americans—these laws have reduced discrimination in the economic sphere. And several empirical studies suggest that most whites endorse the ideal of equal opportunities for blacks in the housing market. Yet changes in attitude have not been translated into behavior. Whites still choose to live in neighborhoods that have few or no black residents, and blacks continue to live in a community within a community in the nation's urban places.

SUMMARY

This chapter addresses the segregation and location of socioeconomic, ethnic, and racial groups in cities. Urban sociologists have discovered that the social distance between groups is reflected in the spatial distance between them in their residential locations. These patterns can have positive and negative consequences for society. Voluntary segregation can positively affect society by contributing to the solidarity of groups and directly enhancing the individual's sense of belonging and security. However, segregation can also lead to the physical and social isolation of a group and form a barrier to their full participation in society.

Segregation is studied for several reasons. First, the degree of segregation between groups is an indicator of the degree of social inequality in society. Second, understanding residential segregation gives policy makers an indication of the effectiveness of social programs and government policies in reducing segregation. Third, the study of segregation gives the sociologist insights into basic ecological processes that affect the overall structure and functioning of society.

Three sets of factors have been identified as influencing the segregation process. Ecological factors include impersonal economic and ecological forces, such as the location of housing types and the socioeconomic characteristics of groups. Voluntary factors are ones of self-selection. Individuals of common culture face common problems and needs and willingly choose to live near each other. Involuntary segregation occurs as the result of laws or customs that prescribe where certain groups can live. These three types of factors can operate alone but are usually interrelated.

The degree to which members of different status groups are residentially segregated from each other has been of long-standing interest to students of cities. Social-status segregation is a universal phenomenon; the gross inequality in the distribution of income in the United States is reflected in the residential patterns of its status groups. When the indexes of dissimilarity are plotted, a U-shaped curve is produced that shows that the members of the highest and lowest status groups are the most segregated. The location of these groups depends on the scale of the society and the age and region of the city under study. Voluntary and ecological rather than involuntary factors are indicated in the segregation of status groups.

Ethnic segregation continues in many U.S. cities in spite of theories that predict the assimilation of ethnic groups. Three waves of immigrants came to this country, and their region of origin, time of arrival, and the dominant transportation and industrial technology in cities at the time of their arrival influenced their segregation. In general, those groups who were similar to the society's charter group—core English ancestry—were the most rapidly assimilated and least segregated. Two models were presented to describe the assimilation process—the melting-pot model and the ethnic-status model. The melting-pot model argues that ethnic assimilation is a function of the low socioeconomic status of recently arrived ethnics. As the socioeconomic status of the groups improves, their segregation will decline. The ethnic-status model argues that a group's ethnicity operates independently of socioeconomic status, and ethnicity acts as a marker affecting segregation. Although, ecological factors such as income, occupation, and education explain some of this residential segregation, voluntary factors appear to contribute to the durability and resiliency of ethnic enclaves in American cities.

Black Americans are the largest and most segregated minority group in the United States. Blacks lived in mostly southern and rural areas until this century, when more than 5 million black Americans left the rural South for the cities. A majority of these migrants moved to the central cities of the North, where they formed durable racial communities. These communities have isolated black Americans, and this isolation has social consequences. The concentration and isolation of the poorest of this group has led to the emergence of an underclass. The values, levels of education, and demographic and family structures make the participation of this group in the mainstream of American society difficult. The problems of the underclass have been exacerbated by the decentralization of jobs to the suburbs. Although nationally there were declines in the segregation of blacks in the decade ending in 1980, black Americans remain the most segregated group in our society.

Finally, although voluntary factors cannot be eliminated, research has shown that ecological factors have little effect. In all probability, racial segregation in the United States is due to involuntary factors. Although the 1964 Civil Rights Act has increased economic opportunities for black Americans, it has not increased the number of housing alternatives. Therefore, racial segregation will persist in the United States for the foreseeable future.

NOTES

1. The mathematics of the dissimilarity index and the exposure index are beyond the scope of this book. For those interested in the calculation of the indices and the debate that has developed around them, I would suggest the following articles. First, the work by Stanley Lieberson and Donna K. Carter, "A Model for Inferring the Voluntary and Involuntary Causes of Residential Segregation." This is the work that began the most recent debate on the indices.

Second, a short article by John E. Farley, "P[*] Segregation Indices: What They Tell Us about Housing Segregation in 1980?" In this work, Farley explains in clear language the usefulness of the indices in describing a group's potential exposure and the different information the exposure indices provide in comparison to other measures.

Third, the Douglas S. Massey and Nancy A. Denton article, "Trends in the Residential Segregation of Blacks, Hispanics, and Asians: 1970–1980," gives the exposure and dissimilarity indices for these three groups in 60 metropolitan areas. They also describe changes in the residential patterns of these groups over the decade ending in 1980.

Finally, W. A. V. Clark, "Residential Segregation in American Cities: A Review and Interpretation," explores the policy implications of these indices from the perspective of a geographer. He brings together data from divergent sources to describe the segregation patterns of blacks in American cities. Moreover, he explores the policy implications of these indices and discusses their use in court cases and their importance in the formation of public policy. Refer to the bibliography for a complete citation of each article.

2. The Simkus's study included the cities of Hartford, Syracuse, Chicago–Gary, Cleveland, Columbus, Indianapolis, Fort Worth, Atlanta, Memphis, and Richmond.

3. Smith and Zopf identify five distinct periods in the history of immigration to the United States. "The first embraces the years from establishment of the first settlements to the emergence of the national state in 1783; the second period of free immigration ended about 1830; the third, extending until 1882, was the period of state regulation; the fourth, beginning with the passage of the first national immigration act in 1882 and lasting until 1917, was a period of federal regulation with individual selection; and the fifth, the present stage of restricted immigration, began in 1917" (Smith and Zopf, 1976, p. 473). For the purposes of this text, waves of migration have been classified according to the region of origin; this classification reflects the work of Douglas Massey and other students of ethnicity and assimilation.

4. The nation's current immigration law still follows the framework of the Immigration and Nationality Act of 1952, which established a national quota system. However, with major revisions in 1965, the national-origins emphasis in this law was replaced by the governing themes of family reunification and the admission of aliens with needed skills. The Immigration Reform and Control Act of 1986 (P.L. 99-603) is built on the earlier legislation but addresses the control of illegal immigration by employer sanctions for the employment of unauthorized aliens, legalization of some undocumented aliens, and the legal admission of alien agricultural workers.

$\mathcal{U}$RBAN PROBLEMS

INTRODUCTION

America felt good about itself in the 1980s—none of that doom and gloom of the Carter administration. If we just unleashed capitalism by lowering taxes, slashing domestic spending, and building up our military might, America would be great again. Americans bought into the dream, and at first blush the plan seemed to work. Following the 1981–1982 recession, the nation experienced the longest peacetime expansion in our history; unemployment dropped, record numbers of Americans joined the ranks of the employed, and disposable income rose. In 1986, Ronald Reagan was reelected by one of the largest margins in history.

Trouble lurked just under the surface. By 1990, the federal deficit exceeded $3 trillion. In the span of ten years, the nation was transformed from the largest creditor to the largest debtor nation in the world, and millions were hungry, millions were without health insurance, and millions of middle-class Americans were squeezed between stagnant wages and inflation. We now know that this prosperity was bought with a sea of red ink; we now know that few benefited and many suffered; and we now know that the 1980s were witness to one of the largest transfers of wealth in our history.

Poverty is a national problem, and so too is AIDS, crack cocaine addiction, and violent crime. But national problems in more developed societies like ours are played out in our cities. In the last few years, it seems that you can't open a *Time* or *Newsweek,* turn on a TV, or read a paper without being assaulted by an urban horror story: Medical wastes wash up on Jones Beach; AIDS overwhelms San Francisco's health system; homeless freeze to death in Chicago doorways; six are dead in Los

Angeles after gang shooting; and a woman jogger is raped and beaten by gang wilding. The headlines have a backdrop of stories on crumbling roads and bridges, deteriorating sewers, ineffective schools, incompetent police, and city governments that can't govern.

This entire book could be devoted to urban problems, but I have chosen three that touch on the major functions carried out by municipal government—maintaining the infrastructure, providing services, and maintaining social control. The problem of the homeless is used to explore the problems of urban infrastructure. It is estimated that anywhere between 350,000 and 2 million Americans are homeless, and millions more live in substandard dwellings. Why? What can be done?

AIDS is an epidemic that most Americans would like to forget. We can't. The virus which first appeared in American's gay communities in the late 1970s is affecting other groups in the 1990s. Intravenous drug users, women, and the poor are now the high-risk groups. We explore the etiology of the disease, its spread through our population, and its impact on our cities.

Public safety is one of the most intractable problems facing city governments, and the fear of crime is one of the factors motivating millions of Americans to leave the central city. Urban crime and the attempts to control it is the third urban problem discussed in this chapter.

All of these problems are national in scope, but are played out in urban places. As we will see in the final chapter of the book, these national problems require federal solutions, but, tragically, this nation lacks a coherent urban policy to deal with them.

HOMELESSNESS

INTRODUCTION

Home. *Home* is a powerful word: a word full of meaning. I've been sitting here thinking about the word. Home is, of course, the place where I eat, sleep, and carry out my private life. It's where I keep my furniture. My things. My home is not just a structure; it's memories. There is the patch in the wall where my two-year-old rammed his toy. There is a dark spot on the carpet where Vicky Sloan spilled her red wine. There is my bookcase filled with my father's books. My wife and I picked the paintings together.

My mother recently sold my boyhood home. Every nook and cranny of that home had meaning. I told my mother on the day of the sale, "This was a happy house; I hope the new owners have as much joy."

Home is other things. It is where I carry out my most important roles—husband, father, and friend. Home is my refuge. It's where I go to get away from the office. It's where I go during the day to think and write. It's that one place on earth where I can let my hair down and be me. Home is where I welcome and entertain my kin and close friends. My home also locks me into the community's social structure. The location of our home determines where my children go to school. The safety and the quality of our lives are tied to the location of our home. Home. *Home* for most people is a word pregnant with meaning and social consequences. This is why being homeless is so devastating. It's not only not having a place to put your stuff. It means separation from friends and kin. It means disengagement and isolation from all those things that give our lives meaning and direction.

Beginning in the late 1970s, police, social workers, and citizens alike began to see an increase in the number of homeless. Some were sleeping in doorways; others wandered the streets; still others hung out behind buildings, in alleys, parks, and bus depots. Some came to our attention by panhandling, others by their disheveled and dirty appearance, and a few by their bizarre behavior. The most vivid images were those homeless heaping all that they owned in a shopping cart. Our individual experiences soon filtered into newspaper stories. Finally, newspaper stories soon began to show up in official statistics. Homelessness became a major social problem in the 1980s.

Although the Congress, the press, and the academic community have examined homelessness for more than a decade, we still have difficulty in defining the concept, measuring the numbers of people affected, describing the types of homeless, or developing solutions. In this section, we look at the history of homelessness in the United States and how the homeless are defined and measured. We ask, "Who are the homeless, and how did they get this way?" Finally, we ask, "What can be done?"

A BRIEF HISTORY OF THE HOMELESS[1]

The homeless in the nineteenth century. Homelessness is not new. One can find homelessness in one form or another throughout our history. Prior to the Civil War, America was a rural nation, and poverty and homelessness were defined as a moral failure. The relatively small number of homeless were housed in almshouses or communal workhouses. Philadelphia's Bettering House was typical. Its operation was based on the premise that the poor chose their idleness, and required the discipline of organized labor to stem their indolence.

After the Civil War, the rapid expansion of the national economy required a mobile work force of unsettled laborers. Hundreds of thousands of transient workers, known as tramps, roamed the states looking for work in lumbering, herding, harvesting, and common labor. Tramps played an important role in the economic development of the nation. This was also the period of massive rural-to-urban migration, massive immigration, and explosive urban and industrial growth. It was also a period of shameful economic exploitation of the working classes. Meager wages, injuries, and illness combined with periodic economic downturns led to this society's first experience with massive homelessness. Police were used to control the rising number of homeless. Idle men were arrested and housed in police stations and poor houses. The numbers were staggering. Between 1867 and 1883, it has been estimated that one out of every 23 males experienced a station house arrest. On average, one out of every five American families had at least one member arrested for idleness. New York City alone provided over 150,000 lodgings per year.

During these years, the press created an image of the homeless as dangerous tramps. These public perceptions carried over into reform. Reformers embracing Social

Darwinism argued that charity and church relief only made things worse, and they influenced state legislatures. By 1900, all but four states had enacted tramp acts: Tramping became a criminal offense. The tramp acts required the homeless and idle to be imprisoned at hard labor in the nearest penitentiary. The police, unable to cope with the massive number of homeless, turned their backs on the problem, and, by the first decade of this century, municipal lodging houses and rescue missions became the predominant way the destitute and homeless were sheltered.

The homeless in the twentieth century. In the opening decades of this century, the election of populist and socialist candidates to state and local offices, the rise of organized labor, the influence of muckraker journalism, and the creation of social work as a profession brought a new perspective to the problem of homelessness. The muckrakers showed that great wealth was often the result of exploitation, greed, and political manipulation. They also showed that poverty and homelessness were often the results of economic cycles and social injustice. Social workers demonstrated that the problem of homelessness was tied to social conditions rather than flawed characters.

Other forces were at work. The tractor and the combine dramatically reduced the need for farm workers. Mechanization revolutionized the lumber and mining industries. Automation meant more permanent jobs, and less need for itinerant labor. These changes improved the conditions of the working class, and dramatically reduced the number of tramps. As labor changed, so too did the nature of homelessness. By the 1920s, social workers began to characterize the sheltered homeless as individuals who were crippled, mentally ill, drug addicts, alcoholics, runaways, and epileptics unable to master the problem of self-support.

The Great Depression once again changed the character of the homeless. The number of poor and homeless exploded in the 1930s. Politicians and professionals were forced to acknowledge for the first time that homelessness was linked to economic cycles. Local governments were unable to cope with the swelling population of homeless. San Francisco sheltered 6902 families in 1929; by 1932, the number had jumped to 55,789. The Roosevelt Administration's New Deal programs brought the federal government to bear on the problem of poverty and homelessness for the first time. In a series of programs like the Civilian Conservation Corps (CCC) and the Works Progress Administration (WPA), jobs, shelter, social insurance, and work projects were created. These projects along with other programs like social security, unemployment insurance, and public housing created the modern welfare state in the United States. These emergency programs evolved into permanent programs. By the 1940s, a two-tiered welfare system had emerged in the nation. Citizens who paid into programs like social security received benefits they were entitled to—thus the name *entitlement programs.* Other welfare programs were designed specifically for the poor and were based on need.

The draft and the demand for industrial labor during World War II and the expanding economy in the postwar period dramatically reduced the incidence of homelessness. Rapidly rising mean family income between 1950 and 1970 reduced the ranks of the homeless. The homeless became associated with older single men surviving on pensions and marginal employment housed in flophouses and missions on skid row.

The homeless once again came to the nation's attention in the early 1980s with the worst economic recession since the 1930s. However, things had changed.

DEFINING AND MEASURING HOMELESSNESS IN THE 1980S

During the 1980s, the press played a central role in shaping our image of the homeless. Two images emerged in the national consciousness. There were the vivid images of the age-old problem of the skid row drifter—drunks, drug addicts, broken men with failed dreams. There was also the image of the new homeless: victims of a changing economy and indifferent government.

In the professional literature, an even more diverse set of definitions of homelessness emerged. A variety of criteria were used, including: transiency—itinerant persons using shelters; frequency—the chronically homeless; ecology—those who lived in shelters or on the streets and alleys in rundown parts of town; spatial marginality—people who live in alleys, dumps, under bridges, and behind buildings; and social marginality—people who are isolated and detached from the social structure, family, and friends (LaGory et al., 1989). Which definition do you use to measure the homeless? Should you include the homeless who are doubling up with friends and relatives? Should you include women and children in battered-women shelters, who will most likely return to their homes? Do you include those who live in intolerable living conditions? Should you include prisoners? Those in mental hospitals? We have problems measuring homelessness because we have trouble defining the concept.

There is also a political dimension. Public agencies and government researchers tend to define homelessness in line with their agency's objectives or the administration's political ideology. Private groups often have a vested interest in making the problem as big as possible. Some censuses include only those who are living in public and private shelters. Others have included sheltered people and street people plus a guesstimate on the hidden population. Some counts have been used to minimize the problem; some have been used to make it a problem of crisis proportions (Jahiel, 1987). At the low end, the U.S. Department of Housing and Urban Development (HUD) estimates the population to be between 250,000 and 350,000 people (a figure which has drawn sharp public criticism). At the high end, the Community for Creative Nonviolence, a Washington, D.C.-based advocacy group, has suggested that 2.2 million Americans are homeless at any given time. Thus, the number moves up and down depending on the definition used, the group doing the counting, and the motives of the counters. Therefore, the problem can be either a national crisis of historical significance or a temporary problem that will improve as the economy improves (Caton, 1990a).

Table 13.1 is a summary of 1984 data which estimates the homeless population using four techniques employed by HUD. The figures range from as low as 192,000 to 586,000 homeless. The most reliable range, according to HUD, is between 250,000 and 350,000 (Caton, 1990a).

TABLE 13.1 Summary of four approaches to estimating number of homeless persons nationwide (USHUD, 1984).

Approach 1	Extrapolation from highest published estimates	586,000
Approach 2	Extrapolation from estimates in 60 metropolitan areas, obtained in 500+ local interviews	254,000
Approach 3	Extrapolation of estimates from national sample of 125 shelter operators	353,000
Approach 4	Shelter population and local area street count	192,000
	Shelter population and 1980 census street count	267,000
	Most reliable range: 250,000–350,000	

Source: U.S. Department of Housing and Urban Development. *A Report to the Secretary on the Homeless and Emergency Shelters.* Washington, D.C.: U.S. Government Printing Office (1984), Table 1.

There is every indication that the homeless problem worsened over the decade of the 1980s. Since 1985, the U.S. Council of Mayors has conducted its own survey to access the homeless problem. The latest survey results, published in December 1990, are presented in Table 13.2. Mayor Raymond Flynn, acting as spokesperson for the U.S. Council of Mayors, released the figures and announced that the problem had reached crisis proportions. The study of 30 cities reported a 42 percent increase in the number of homeless, a 24 percent increase in the number of families requesting food assistance, and a 24 percent increase in the requests for emergency shelter between 1989 and 1990. At the same time, 57 percent of the cities reported a noticeably negative turn in public attitudes toward the homeless. Nine of the cities had taken action to limit access of the homeless to public facilities. These steps ranged from outlawing panhandling to tearing down makeshift camps to outlawing loitering. In nearly 90 percent of the cities, soup kitchens and other emergency food agencies had turned away hungry people because of a lack of money. In 79 percent of the cities, homeless families were turned away from shelters that were already full. The mayor argued that the problem simply has outstripped cities' ability to cope (Dart, 1990).

The statistics vary, but the message is the same. There is a large and growing number of homeless in the nation. The problem is not isolated in one city or region but is national in scope. Moreover, the problem has become so large that cities do not have the resources to cope.

WHO ARE THE HOMELESS?

Who are the homeless? A variety of people have been identified as homeless: winos, alcoholics, drug users, retired seamen, bag ladies, bottle gangs, vets, displaced families, runaway children, ex-convicts, AIDS victims shunned by their families, immigrants, and mothers with children. The old homeless were mostly vagrants and

TABLE 13.2 Profile of U.S. homeless.

U.S. Conference of Mayors looks at urban homelessness in 1990:

WHO THEY ARE

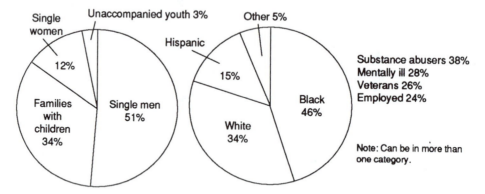

Growing Needs in Selected U.S. Cities
How the cities are faring with the homeless in these categories—percentage increase in demand for emergency food, 1989–90 (and percentage of requests coming from families); percentage increase in requests for emergency shelter (and percentage of requests by families); status of the number of shelter beds; whether families are being turned away:

CITY	FOOD DEMAND (% FAMILIES)	SHELTER REQUESTS (% FAMILIES)	SHELTER BEDS	TURNED AWAY?
Alexandria, VA	17% (NA)	32% (0%)	down	yes
Boston	30% (80%)	18% (NA)	up	no
Charleston, SC	NA% (90%)	142% (0%)	same	no
Charlotte, NC	50% (95%)	50% (20%)	same	yes
Chicago	0% (71%)	7% (25%)	up	yes
Cleveland	20% (70%)	24% (36%)	up	yes
Denver	25% (75%)	15% (23%)	same	yes
Hartford, CT	30% (75%)	0% (NA)	same	yes
Kansas City, MO	7% (80%)	NA (NA)	down	no
Los Angeles	35% (75%)	NA (NA)	up	yes
Louisville, KY	NA (70%)	10% (NA)	up	yes
Minneapolis	12% (56%)	2% (-4%)	up	no
Nashville, TN	5–10% (80%)	0% (20%)	same	yes
New Orleans	27% (78%)	20% (40%)	down	yes
New York	NA (NA)	(b) (c)	down	no
Norfolk, VA	NA (62%)	NA (10%)	same	yes
Philadelphia	NA (80%)	0% (0%)	same	no
Phoenix	15% (60%)	5–10% (60%)	down	yes
Portland, OR	60% (45%)	NA (NA)	down	yes
Providence, RI	30% (50–60%)	35% (30%)	same	yes
St. Paul, MN	10% (68%)	7% (13%)	same	no
Salt Lake City, UT	20–25% (65%)	20% (30%)	up	no
San Antonio	5% (95%)	29% (5%)	same	yes
San Diego	10–15% (75%)	10–15% (same)	up	yes

TABLE 13.2 (*Continued*) Profile of U.S. homeless.

CITY	FOOD DEMAND (% FAMILIES)	SHELTER REQUESTS (% FAMILIES)	SHELTER BEDS	TURNED AWAY?
San Francisco	0% (83%)	10% (-6%)	up	yes
San Juan	1400% (94%)	40% (0%)	same	yes
Santa Monica, CA	20% (25%)	30% (NA)	same	yes
Seattle	(a) (60%)	NA (NA)	down	yes
Trenton, NJ	30% (80%)	33% (33%)	up	yes
Washington, D.C.	NA (NA)	NA (NA)	up	no

NA means not available.

(a) Food bank visits increased by 33%; hot meals provided, by 58%.

(b) Number of men entering shelter system down by 14%; number of women, by 6%.

(c) 934 new homeless in September 1989, 1005 in September 1990.

tramps, usually white, middle-aged, alcoholic men. The new homeless are more diverse; they are younger, often female, sometimes entire families, and more likely members of minority groups.

The results from the most recent U.S. Congress of Mayors survey showed that the homeless population consisted of 51 percent single men, 12 percent single women, 34 percent families with children, and 3 percent youths. On average, just over a fourth were mentally ill, 38 percent were substance abusers, and 6 percent had AIDS (Dart, 1990).

TABLE 13.3 Selected demographic variables (in percent) of the homeless[*].

VARIABLES	PERCENT
Gender	
Male	87
Age	
Mean age	36
Under 40	64
Over 60	5
Ethnicity	
Anglo	65
Black	17
Hispanic	12
Other	6
Marital status	
Unattached	89
Married	11

[*]Mean values for samples from five cities and a statewide study in Ohio.

Source: David A. Snow, Susan G. Baker, and Leon Anderson, "Criminality and Homeless Men: An Empirical Assessment," *Social Problems*, forthcoming, Table 1.

Table 13.3 is a summary of data collected by my colleague, David Snow, one of the major researchers in the field. A general profile of the homeless found in his ethnographic studies of the homeless would be a white male, in his mid-thirties, unmarried, poorly educated, likely to be a veteran, and most often drawn to the community in search of work (Snow, 1991).

Although many descriptions abound, four types of homeless are usually identified in the literature: homeless mentally ill, homeless women, rural homeless, and homeless alcoholics.

HOMELESS MENTALLY ILL[2]

In 1955, there were 560,000 residents of public psychiatric hospitals. In 1981, this number had dropped to around 120,000. Since the 1960s, the catchwords among mental health professionals have been deinstitutionalization and community-based mental health care. The move towards community-based mental health care was motivated by many factors. First, there were the exposés on the horrors of mental hospitals (for example, the movie *Titicot Follies*). Second, there was a revolution in drug therapy, and it was thought that many patients could be safely returned to society. Third, there was the belief there could be less costly, more humane, and less confining treatment at the local community level. There is evidence that community-based programs have not worked. Many people on the street may be there because of deinstitutionalization.

How many of the homeless are mentally ill? Estimates vary. Studies in Boston and Philadelphia report that between 80 and 90 percent of the homeless are mentally impaired. Other studies of sheltered homeless put the figure between 20 and 30 percent. David Snow puts the figure much lower. Professor Snow argues that many of the behaviors labeled as mental impairment may in fact be the result of living on the streets. Severe hypoglycemia (extremely low blood sugar) leads to confusion, tremors, and unfocused staring. A large percentage of those labeled mentally ill may simply be suffering from living on the streets. In his opinion, change the environment, and in many cases the behavior will change. Reliable estimates of the incidence of mental illness among the homeless range from as low as 25 percent to as high as 50 percent (Eagle and Caton, 1990; LaGory et al., 1990a; Snow et al., 1986, 1988).

HOMELESS WOMEN

There is probably no more depressing sight than a bag lady: a homeless women carrying her worldly possession in a grocery cart. There is evidence that the number of homeless women is increasing, and they may now constitute between 15 and 25 percent of the homeless population. Some are married and have left their children with kin; others are victims of marital abuse; still others are victims of economic conditions (Wolf, 1990).

HOMELESS WOMEN AND CHILDREN

Unfortunately, there is still little national data on homeless mothers with children. However, in a Boston study, the researchers found a considerable overlap between these families and multiproblem welfare families. In the Boston study, 80 homeless mothers and 151 children were interviewed. Forty-five percent of the mothers were single, and 45 percent were separated, divorced, or widowed. Their mean age was 27 years. They had an average of 2.4 children living with them in the shelter. Ninety percent were receiving Aid for Dependent Children (AFDC) benefits. The majority of these women were raised in dysfunctional families. Nearly 25 percent of the mothers were under professional care for abuse or neglect of their own children. The majority of these women reported that their move to the shelter was the result of eviction, nonpayment of rent, overcrowding, and housing conversions. Problems with other household members were another major reason for moving to the shelter.

This is a group of homeless that has received much attention in the press. Unfortunately, little is known about them, and this lack of knowledge has hampered attempts to develop programs for them (Sullivan and Damrosch, 1987).

RURAL HOMELESS

In a comprehensive study in Ohio, researchers attempted to measure rural homelessness, a problem that has received scant attention in the literature. The characteristics of the rural homeless population showed that they differed somewhat from their urban counterparts. They often lived in cars or trucks. They tended to live in state parks and roadside picnic areas. They were younger, more often female and married, than the urban homeless. They had been homeless for a relatively short period of time. There was some evidence that over time they drifted to larger cities, where shelters and food aid were more readily available (Caton, 1990b).

HOMELESS ALCOHOLICS

This is the group of men who have been most often studied. They are often hard-core, skid-row alcoholics in the last stages of acute alcoholism. This group of homeless men is generally middle-aged and older, and they are often isolates with little social contact. Studies show that the rate of alcoholism among sheltered men ranges from between 29 to 40 percent. Although widely studied, little is know about their actual drinking habits. Since shelters forbid drinking, much of their drinking is done clandestinely. There is evidence that alcoholism may mask mental health disorders of many of these men. Alcoholism is also a contributing factor to the health problems faced by these men (Caton, 1990b).

THE NEW POOR

Some homeless people are victims of new economic conditions and changes in federal welfare and housing programs; some haven't gotten on their feet since the last recession. Included in this group are homeless youth and homeless families. These are groups that are widely reported in the news, but for which there is still inadequate information in the professional literature (Rossi, 1989; Stefl, 1987).

WHY THE HOMELESS PROBLEM?

What were the causes of homelessness? The most obvious is the economic recession of the early 1980s. The recession was the worst since the Great Depression, and the number of the unemployed swelled. For much of 1982, the unemployment rate was over 10 percent. At the worst point in the recession, the unemployment rate was 10.7 percent, or 12 million people. One-fourth of all those in the work force were affected by the recession at one time or another. More sobering is the fact that these figures reflect only those actively seeking employment. Millions of citizens after exhausting unemployment and other benefits quit looking, and these discouraged workers no longer were counted in official statistics.

The double-digit inflation in the first half of the decade had a devastating affect on people on fixed incomes—social security, pension, and veterans benefit recipients. The economic downturn and inflation led to a 40-year high in farm and home foreclosures. There were other factors at work during the decade that exacerbated this situation (Rossi, 1989).

DECLINE IN HOUSING FOR THE POOR

Affordable housing is considered to be housing that does not exceed one-third of your gross income. For a number of reasons, low-income housing declined dramatically during the 1980s. For renter households with incomes under $3000, the number of available units fell from 5.8 to 2.7 million units between 1970 and 1980. Two factors were at work: First, skyrocketing land values in most U.S. cities removed many of the marginal housing units from the market. Low-cost rooms in residential hotels all but disappeared in large cities as they were converted into luxury apartments and offices. Second, gentrification and urban renewal removed additional units from the low-income housing stock (Carliner, 1987).

REFORMS IN THE SOCIAL SECURITY DISABILITY INSURANCE PROGRAM

Of all the social programs attacked by the Reagan administration, the Social Security Disability Insurance Program received special attention. This is an entitlement program designed for people who have been disabled. By tightening eligibility standards, benefits were cut from anyone capable of performing any type of labor, even if there were no jobs available. The changes were implemented between 1981 and 1984. In 1984, the practice was stopped by the courts. In the interim, between 150,000 and 200,000 people were removed from the rolls, and many probably joined the ranks of the homeless (Koch, 1987; Marcuse, 1990; Phillips, 1990).

DEINSTITUTIONALIZATION OF WARDS OF THE STATE

For almost a century, this society dealt with its most intractable problems by institutionalizing people. The mentally ill, the deviant, and the poor were warehoused in mental hospitals, alms houses, and jails. In the 1960s, community-based mental health care reduced the number of patients in public psychiatric units by 70 percent. Orphanages were replaced by foster care, and the prison population was reduced for a time with halfway houses, work release programs, and community-based parole programs. What works in theory often doesn't translate into reality. Surveys show that a significant percentage of the sheltered homeless are mentally ill, ex-convicts, and runaway youths (Dear and Wolch, 1987).

Other factors contributed to the homeless problem. The first and most important factor is poverty. Poverty not only affects the homeless person, but the person's social network of family and friends. Ultimately, family is the safety net of last resort. If this net has no resources, there is no place else to turn.

Second, the 1980s was a period of economic restructuring. Job opportunities for low-skilled workers vanished as the economy shifted from industry to service and high tech.

Third, there may be changes external to the individual. Figure 13.1 shows the funds expended by the federal government on low-income housing and other social programs. The 1980s was a decade dominated by a conservative ideology and agenda.

FIGURE 13.1 Changing 1980s federal budget priorities.

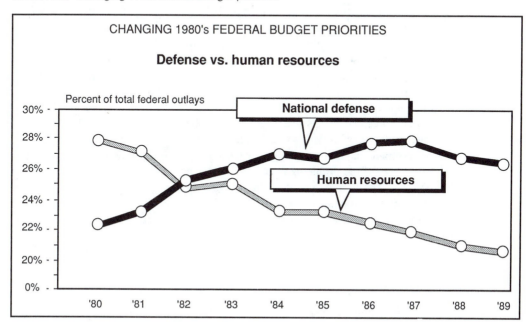

Source: Center on Budget and Policy Priorities.

Funds for most social programs were slashed in the 1980s. Federal money for low-income housing declined by 81 percent between 1981 and 1988. Revelations from the HUD scandal show that much of the money that remained was pilfered by political insiders (Caton, 1990c; Phillips, 1990).

These are structural patterns that transcend the individual. There are important individual patterns as well. Once a person becomes homeless, a vicious cycle begins. Sheer survival—finding shelter, food, and clothing and protecting the few possessions you have—becomes all-consuming, and there is little time for other activities, like job hunting. How do you fill out a job application when you don't have a permanent address or a telephone to list on the form? Is a prospective employer going to hire someone who lives in a shelter? How do you shower and dress appropriately for a job interview? Thus, the labeling and stigmatization of the homeless create barriers to their reentry into society (Eagle and Caton, 1990; LaGory, Ritchey, and Mullins, 1990; LaGory, Ritchey, and Fitzpatrick, 1990).

WHAT CAN BE DONE?

In a perfect world, federal, state, and local governments along with private trusts and agencies would coordinate a comprehensive program for the homeless. The program would have elements of job training, education, substance abuse treatment, affordable shelter, health services, and psychological and family counseling (Caton, 1990c). The question is will or can it be done? I think not. After a decade of excess, the bills have come due in this society. This nation is facing a bewildering set of problems: a declining infrastructure, poor schools, poverty, AIDS, garbage, crime, drug addiction, a lack of competitiveness, a changing political and economic world order, and no money. In a society with all these problems, how are priorities set? Which problems get the resources?

Homelessness, in the final analysis, results from powerlessness and marginality. By definition, these are people detached from the social fabric. They don't vote. They have no money. They are not a constituency. They will not be heard. The pressing problem of the homeless cries for federal intervention. It is a national problem played out in our largest cities. There has been some federal help. A dramatic increase in the funds for low-income housing was voted in the second session of the 101st Congress. There has been stopgap funding for emergency shelters and food, but the appropriations are dwarfed by the size of the problem. What should be done? Much needs to be done, but little will be done. The homeless will haunt our streets, alleys, and shelters into the twenty-first century because homelessness is a part of a much larger issue: the distribution of wealth and social justice. This topic is addressed in the closing chapter.

AIDS

INTRODUCTION[3]

Forty-four thousand cases of AIDS were reported to the Centers for Disease Control (CDC) in 1989. This number jumped to 56,000 cases in 1990, and it is expected to increase to 70,000 in 1991, 87,000 in 1992, and 104,000 in 1993. The cost of treating all the people diagnosed with AIDS during 1989 was $3.3 billion; this figure will jump to $7.8 billion by 1993 (Both figures are in constant 1988 dollars.) (Hellinger, 1990).[4] The number of diagnosed cases is only the tip of the iceberg. A hundred thousand Americans suffer from AIDS Related Complex (ARC), and a million are infected by the human immunodeficiency virus (HIV) but show no symptoms. On the horizon looms one of the most serious public health crises in our history. Just as everyone knows someone who has been called up for the Gulf Crisis, by the middle of this decade everyone will know someone with AIDS (Hellinger, 1990; Jager and Ruitenberg, 1988).

Like many of the social problems facing this society, national problems have a way of becoming urban problems. AIDS is a disease that affects specific groups—homosexuals, IV drug users, babies born to infected mothers, hemophiliacs, and people transfused with infected blood—but these groups are not distributed randomly across our nation; they are concentrated in our cities. Not only are they concentrated in cities, but AIDS cases are clustered in specific neighborhoods in cities (See Figure 13.2.). The elusive nature of the HIV virus stymied medical researchers for years, but a group of researchers known as epidemiologists used this clustering to identify the behaviors that put people at risk. By the early 1980s, epidemiologists were sure that AIDS was a sexually transmitted disease before the HIV virus was discovered (Population Information Program, 1986).

The press also picked up on this concentration early in the epidemic. For example:

> Investigators also believe that AIDS is principally a phenomenon of the raunchy subculture in large cities, where bars and bathhouses are literal hotbeds of sexual promiscuity (*Rolling Stone,* 1983, p. 19).

> But clearly, urban gay lifestyle has put many homosexual males at risk. An infectious agent loose in the hothouse environment of a gay bath, where some men have as many as 10 anonymous sexual contacts in one night.... (*Newsweek,* 1983, p. 80).

These descriptions began in the spring of 1982, during the early years of the epidemic, and peaked in the spring and summer of 1983 (Albert 1990, p. 170). This was followed by sensational portrayals of a reign of terror sweeping gay communities as the death tolls mounted. Examples include:

> Believed to be sexually transmitted, AIDS has thrown homosexual communities into near panic (*People,* 1983, p. 42).

> ...an epidemic of fear is sweeping San Francisco where at least one new case is reported each day (*Macleans,* 1983, p. 6).

> Panic has set in on Greenwich Village streets and in the "the Castro," San Francisco's gay quarter (*Time,* 1982, p. 55).

> ...the specter of AIDS haunts every member of the homosexual community, especially in the cities where it is most prevalent (*New York Times Magazine,* 1983, p. 36).

Other sensationalized reports followed: stories of dying babies, emaciated children, bewildered elderly, and even nuns afflicted by this unknown killer. Scientists

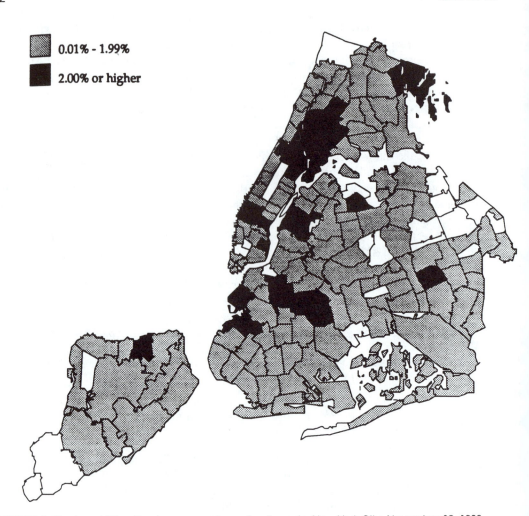

FIGURE 13.2 Newborn HIV antibody seroprevalence by zip code. New York City, November 30, 1988.

Source: New York State Department of Health. *AIDS in New York State.* Albany, NY: New York State Department of Health, 1989.

Note: Approximately 98 percent of newborns are tested. The presence of HIV antibodies in the blood of a newborn infant reflects the infection status of the mother, not of the child. Current studies indicate that 30–50 percent of babies born to infected mothers will be infected.

and the press alike keyed in on the same common denominators—the gay communities in New York, Los Angeles, Houston, and San Francisco, subcultures, and behaviors that put people at risk (Albert, 1986; Baker, 1986).

THE SOCIOLOGY OF THE AIDS EPIDEMIC

It is important to remember that epidemics don't happen by chance. They are biological processes shaped by social and cultural forces. What threw health researchers off for so many years was the fact that such different groups were infected by the disease—gays, IV drug users, heterosexuals in Africa and Haiti, hemophiliacs, and young, middle-aged, and old people who had been transfused at some time in their medical history (Darrow et al., 1986; Des Jarlais et al., 1986). Some examples: The transfusing of blood is quite common today, but only because of technological breakthroughs in the collection, preservation, and distribution of blood and blood products. The practice grew rapidly after World War II. Approximately 2.4 million units were donated to the Red Cross in 1960, 3.2 million units in 1970, and over 6 million units in 1983. The use of blood products has increased faster than the growth of the population for two decades. Until recently, the blood clotting factor, which allows hemophiliacs to live normal lives, was produced from donated plasma. No one thought it would put them at risk for HIV infection. Until 1983, most patients worried about their surgery; few thought twice about the donated blood they would receive in their treatment. Once the virus was identified and tests were developed to screen the blood supply, hemophiliacs and those receiving transfusions were no longer at risk (Callero et al., 1986).

Social and cultural factors also contributed to the spread of AIDS in the other high-risk groups, especially the gay community (Darrow et al., 1986; Bolognone and Johnson, 1986). We have very poor information on the sexual preferences of Americans, but using figures from Kinsey's work in the 1940s and 1950s, the exclusively homosexual male population was estimated to be between 2 and 4 percent. If we assume that the proportion of homosexual men has remained constant (around 2 percent), then the number of men at risk jumped from 3.4 in the 1950s to 4.6 million in 1990 simply by population growth. The true figures are probably much higher.

Other important social and cultural changes have taken place. The gay liberation movement, which began with the Stonewall riot of 1969, brought about important legal, social, and cultural changes. Greater tolerance for people pursuing alternative lifestyles and legal protection from discrimination erased some of the stigma associated with the gay lifestyle. Today, many more Americans now live an open gay lifestyle. One result was a dramatic increase in the number of establishments that catered to the gay community. A publication known as the *Address Book* lists establishments that exclusively serve the nation's gay community. In 1964, there were 690 places; in 1983, the number had grown to more than 5800 (Darrow et al., 1986).

There were other factors involved. The dramatic growth of domestic and international air travel now appears to have been an important factor in the spread of AIDS. Randy Shilts, in *And The Band Played On: Politics, People and the AIDS Epidemic,* identifies one man, Gaetan Dugas, as the carrier who brought AIDS to San Francisco and other cities. Gaetan Dugas was an airline steward, and he regularly traveled to London, Paris, New York, Montreal, Vancouver, San Francisco, and Los Angeles. Figure 13.3 shows the travels of one HIV infected man through a 47-day, 12-city itinerary. Figure 13.4 shows the clustering technique used by medical researchers to trace the sexual contacts that lead to HIV infection. Therefore, the increase in the number of exclusively homosexual men, along with the establishment of

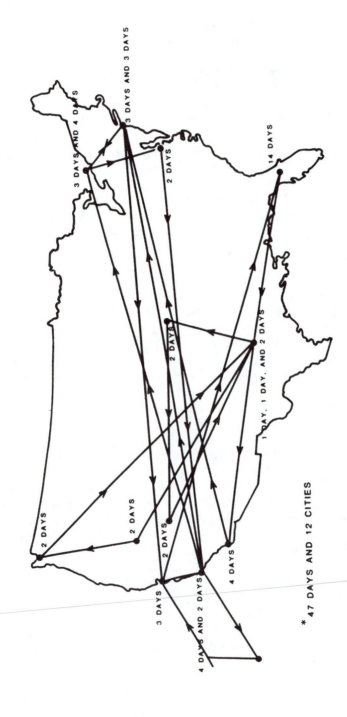

FIGURE 13.3 Travel itinerary (47 days and 12 cities) for a man with AIDS (PCP) from March 1983 to May 1983.

Source: William W. Darrow, Michael Gorman, and Brad P. Glick. The social origins of AIDS: Social change, sexual behavior, and disease trends. In Douglas A. Feldman and Thomas M. Johnson, *The Social Dimensions of AIDS.* New York, NY: Praeger, 1986, Figure 5.4, p. 102. Reprinted by permission of Greenwood Publishing Group, Inc., Westport, CT.

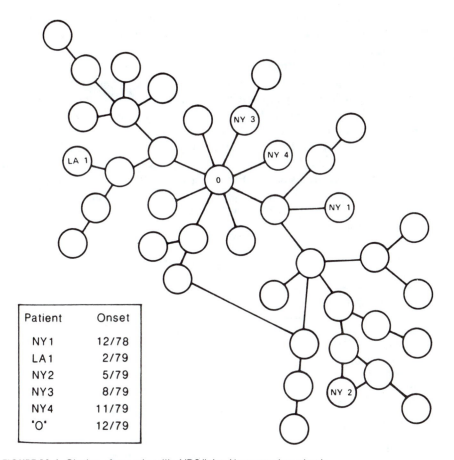

Patient	Onset
NY1	12/78
LA1	2/79
NY2	5/79
NY3	8/79
NY4	11/79
'O'	12/79

FIGURE 13.4 Cluster of people with AIDS linked by sexual contacts.

Source: William W. Darrow, Michael Gorman, and Brad P. Glick. The social origins of AIDS: Social change, sexual behavior, and disease trends. In Douglas A. Feldman and Thomas M. Johnson, *The Social Dimensions of AIDS*. New York, NY: Praeger, 1986, Figure 5.5, p. 103. Reprinted by permission of Greenwood Publishing Group, Inc., Westport, CT.

gay communities in most of our largest cities, combined with cheap air fares, which increased the number of sexual and social contacts between members of the nation's gay communities, represent the convergence of cultural and social factors that led to the growth of the AIDS epidemic (Feldman, 1986).

AIDS AND CITIES

The AIDS epidemic is most closely associated with the city of San Francisco and for good reason. Many of the images Americans have of the gay community are associated with the city's Castro district. San Francisco also has the best organized, wealthy, and politically powerful gay community in the nation. Members of this community provided much of the leadership in the gay liberation movement. The cooperation and participation of San Francisco's gay community in early AIDS research also brought it to the nation's attention.

Table 13.4 shows that San Francisco has the highest rate of AIDS cases, 203.1 per 100,000, but in terms of the sheer number of cases reported, New York City is first. In 1990, New York City alone had one-quarter of all the nation's patients diagnosed with AIDS. For this reason, I've chosen New York to describe the human, social, and economic costs of the epidemic (New York State, 1989).

The U.S. Public Health Service is predicting that by the end of the year 1991, 179,000 Americans will have died of AIDS. Medical experts estimate that more than 2 million Americans are already infected with the virus. In 1990, the federal government spent $970 million dollars on AIDS. But this billion dollars is dwarfed by the problems of New York City alone in trying to come to grips with the AIDS epidemic.

TABLE 13.4 Cumulative AIDS cases by standard metropolitan statistical area (December 26, 1988).

METROPOLITAN AREA[1]	POPULATION[2]	CUMULATIVE TOTAL[3]	RATE/100,000
New York, NY	**9.12**	**18,022**	**197.6**
San Francisco, CA	3.25	6,602	203.1
Los Angeles, CA	7.48	6,010	80.3
Houston, TX	2.91	2,578	88.5
Newark, NJ	1.97	2,460	124.8
Washington, D.C.	3.06	2,382	77.8
Miami, FL	1.63	2,161	132.5
Chicago, IL	7.10	2,128	29.9
Dallas, TX	2.97	1,753	59.0
Philadelphia, PA	4.72	1,639	34.7
Atlanta, GA	2.03	1,393	68.6
Boston, MA	2.76	1,249	45.2
San Diego, CA	1.86	1,132	60.8
Jersey City, NJ	0.56	1,067	190.5
Fort Lauderdale, FL	1.02	1,018	99.8
San Juan, PR	1.09	952	87.3
Nassau–Suffolk, NY	**2.61**	**909**	**34.8**
Seattle, WA	1.61	807	50.1
Baltimore, MD	2.17	762	35.1
Tampa, FL	1.57	740	47.1
Rest of United States	168.62	26,642	15.8
Total	**230.11**	**82,406**	

[1]Data are provided for the 20 SMSAs reporting the highest cumulative number of cases.

[2]Population in millions based on 1980 Census Bureau data.

[3]Cumulative number of cases reported to CDC-AIDS Program as of December 26, 1988.

Source: New York State Department of Health. *AIDS in New York State.* Albany, NY: New York State Department of Health, 1989, p. 41.

THE AIDS EPIDEMIC IN NEW YORK CITY

The problem facing New York and all other large cities is that hospitals have become the care giver of last resort for society's most daunting problems—AIDS, drug abuse, and homelessness. At a time when society is asking more and more from its health-care delivery system, the federal government, facing a $3 trillion deficit, is cutting medical and public health funding. As a result, New York City's hospitals are facing a crisis on a scale unparalleled anywhere else in the country. New York City's hospitals are so overwhelmed that gurneys rolled on top of numbers painted on the floors of hallways become a patient's room. Things have become so bad that poor and rich alike have no assurance of adequate emergency, surgical, or nursing care (Task Force on AIDS, 1987; Task Force on Urgent Fiscal Issues, 1990).

New York is the undisputed center of the country's AIDS epidemic. Approximately 25 percent of the nation's AIDS patients live in New York, and AIDS is now the leading cause of death in the city among women aged 25 to 34, men 25 to 44, and children under 4. In New York City alone, 15,000 have died from AIDS, 10,000 more are dying, and up to 250,000 people are infected with the AIDS virus. This includes up to 60 percent of the city's estimated 200,000 IV drug users, 50,000 men who have had sex with infected men, and thousands of women who have been infected through sex with male IV drug users. About 1800 infants are born to HIV-infected mothers in New York City each year, and about one-third will be diagnosed with AIDS within 15 months. This number is expected to increase tenfold by 1993 (New York State, 1989; Task Force on Urban Fiscal Issues, 1990).

The impact of AIDS on New York City's hospitals is staggering. Currently, AIDS patients fill 10 percent of the city's hospital beds. By 1994, AIDS patients will require an additional 2300 beds, the equivalent of four new medium-sized hospitals, just in this one city. They will require an additional 1100 nursing-home beds, 2600 housing units, and 2000 home-care slots. The annual cost to this one city will be approximately $7.2 billion in 1994: a figure which is larger than the budgets of 13 states (Task Force on Urban Fiscal Issues, 1990).

Where does the money come from? Some comes from private insurance companies, some from Medicare and Medicaid, some from welfare, and some from the hospitals themselves. In 1990, public hospitals in New York City lost, on average, over $600,000 on AIDS care alone. Private hospitals lost, on average, over $200,000 on AIDS care. The impact of the AIDS epidemic on the city's hospitals, even in a city the size of New York, is outstripping their human and financial resources.

There are several trends that will probably make the situation worse. First, the profile of the epidemic is changing. In 1989, IV drug users accounted for 46 percent of new AIDS cases in New York. In the early days of the epidemic, three-quarters of the victims were among homosexual men. Drugs and AIDS are linked. The crack epidemic often associated with sex for drugs is rapidly spreading the disease into the heterosexual population. In one South Bronx drug clinic, among respondents who denied homosexual activity or sex with an IV drug user, 18 percent tested positive for

HIV virus. The problem for health-care providers is that IV drug use is illegal, and this subculture is difficult to reach, educate, and treat.

Second, HIV illness is spreading rapidly into the city's poor and minority communities. Blacks and Hispanics now comprise over 60 percent of AIDS cases reported among all New Yorkers, 84 percent of cases reported among women, and 90 percent among those reported among children. These people have no health insurance, and the city and state will pick up the costs.

Third, the cost of treatment is going up. The drug AZT has been shown to slow the progress of HIV disease in people who are infected but show no symptoms. Estimates are that between 37,000 and 70,000 New Yorkers should be evaluated for possible preventive treatment of low-dose AZT, and between 25,000 to 47,000 New Yorkers should be receiving other medical treatment. The cost of AZT for one patient is over $10,000 per year.

Fourth, the cost of diagnosis, treatment, and drugs are staggering, but patients need more than hospital care. The need for home health care will increase sevenfold between 1989 and 1993. Similar increases are expected for hospice, welfare, counseling, and supportive housing services. Mayor Dinkens has already announced layoffs to reduce the city's ballooning deficit. How can the city cope with an epidemic of this proportion? It can't (Task Force on Urban Fiscal Issues, 1990).

The problems of AIDS in New York are immense, but they are shared by every major city in the nation. It has become apparent that the AIDS epidemic is a national problem being played out on the community level. Moreover, the AIDS epidemic is beyond the ability of cities, and in many cases states, to pay. The federal government in the years to come will be forced into greater involvement. Today, education is the only vaccine to AIDS. We know that AIDS is transmitted primarily through sexual contact and IV drug use, and the federal government is mounting a national campaign to educate all Americans. Former Surgeon General C. Everett Koop spearheaded the educational campaign in 1987 and 1988. The 101st Congress increased funding for the Alcohol, Drug Abuse and Mental Health Block Grant Program to expand AIDS prevention programs (Kotarba, 1986; Lessor, 1986; Valdiserri, 1989). The AIDS Resources Emergency Act of 1990 gives needed money to cities to cope with the staggering costs of AIDS. The Medicaid AIDS and HIV Amendment of 1990 gives states the option to expand Medicaid benefits to HIV-inflected individuals. The critical need for permanent housing for AIDS patients was addressed with the passage of the AIDS Housing Opportunity Act (Task Force on Urban Fiscal Issues, 1990).

The tragedy of the AIDS epidemic is that it could have been prevented. If the AIDS epidemic had first appeared among children or the elderly instead of the gay community, the federal government would have quickly mobilized its resources to identify and address AIDS. It didn't. AIDS was not only a medical problem, it was an issue entwined in the politics of morality. Tragically, mixing the two meant that thousands will die needlessly, billions will be spent on an epidemic that did not have to occur, and other societal and urban problems will fester because of a lack of funds.

CRIME

INTRODUCTION

> They started walking at dusk, two teenagers casually spreading the message that the streets of West Los Angeles were no longer safe. First they stopped Philip Lerner and demanded money. Lerner had no cash, only his infant in a stroller. They let him pass and kept walking. They hailed Akkady and Rachel Muskin at a nearby intersection. The couple quickly handed over $8 and two wristwatches, and gratefully fled. Next the boys intercepted two elderly Chinese women and pulled out a pistol. When one woman tried to push the gun out of her face, ten bullets blazed out, killing both. The boys kept walking. They came upon a trio of friends out for an evening stroll. They took a watch and a few dollars and, without so much as a word, killed one of the three, a Frenchman visiting Los Angeles for the first time. The boys kept walking. At last they reached a drive-in restaurant where they found 76-year-old Leo Ocon walking on the sidewalk. They argued with him for less than a minute and then shot him down. Their evening over, they climbed into an old sedan and then, much as they had started, calmly went off into the night (*Newsweek*, 1981, p. 46).

This excerpt from *Newsweek* has become all too real in most American cities. The media have painted vivid portraits of a 12-year-old boy bleeding to death after a drive-by shooting, a woman jogger beaten and raped by a gang wilding in Central Park, and a man stabbed and robbed after saving an infant from a house fire. Americans fear crime. Urbanites are terrified of being victimized, and many people have changed their behaviors to reduce their risks. Are these fears justified? Is crime, especially urban crime, at epidemic levels? What are the causes of crime, and why is crime so prevalent in urban areas? What can be done? These are the questions addressed in this section.

PERCEIVED AND ACTUAL CRIME RATES

Sociology tells us that if something is defined as real, the social consequences will be real. The fear of crime rose dramatically in the 1960s and has remained high for the past two decades. This public perception is a potent political issue. The law-and-order issue first appeared in the 1968 and 1972 presidential campaigns of Richard Nixon, and has been an element in every campaign since. The release of Willie Horton by the Michael Dukakis administration in Massachusetts, and his subsequent crime spree were a factor in George Bush's victory in the 1988 election. The Gallup organization has been asking Americans a variety of questions on their fear of crime since the mid-1960s. In a 1967 Gallup poll, only 31 percent of Americans were afraid to walk alone at night; throughout most of the 1980s, the percentage was 45 percent. In 1975, Gallup found that 20 percent of Americans felt unsafe in their own homes. Interestingly, this figure dropped to 10 percent in 1989, probably reflecting rapid suburban growth in the 1970s and 1980s (Bureau of Justice Statistics, 1989, Table 2.30, p. 210).

Is this public perception correct? First, a caveat. Official crime statistics are notoriously inaccurate. I'm always chagrined to hear statements on the evening news like, "The crime rate continues to spiral upward, another 3 percent increase this year." This is the official crime rate, the crimes reported to the police. The fact is that much of the crime that occurs in this society is never reported to the police. Murder seldom

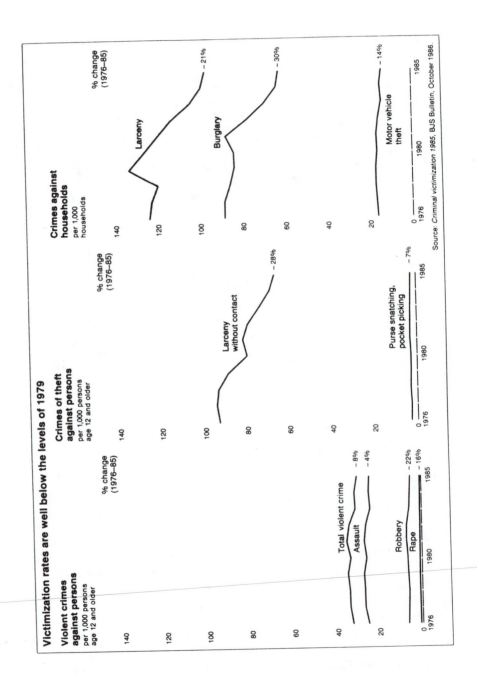

Victimization rates are well below the levels of 1979

Violent crimes against persons
per 1,000 persons age 12 and older

Crimes of theft against persons
per 1,000 persons age 12 and older

Crimes against households
per 1,000 households

% change (1976–85)

Total violent crime
Assault — 8%
— 4%
Robbery — 22%
Rape — 16%

Larceny without contact — 28%

Purse snatching, pocket picking — 7%

Larceny — 21%

Burglary — 30%

Motor vehicle theft — 14%

Source: *Criminal victimization 1985*, BJS Bulletin, October 1986.

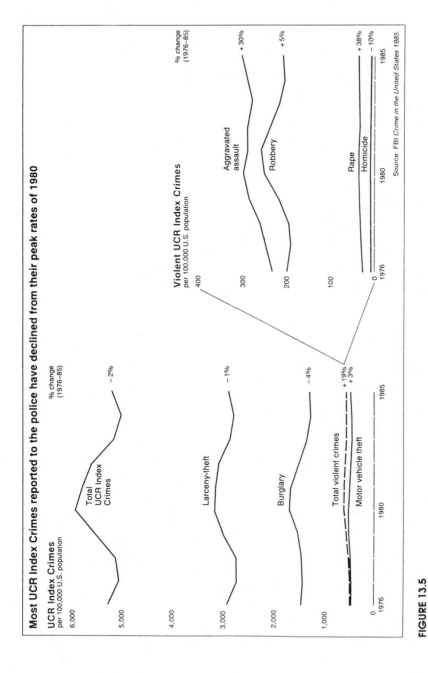

FIGURE 13.5

Source: U.S. Bureau of Justice Statistics. *Report to the Nation on Crime and Justice.* Washington, D.C.: U.S. Government Printing Office, 1988, pp 13-14.

431

goes undetected, but most rapes and assaults never come to the attention of the police. As a result, the Department of Justice collects two types of statistics on crime in this society. The most familiar is the Uniform Crime Report (UCR) collected by the Federal Bureau of Investigation each year. This is a compilation of crimes reported to thousands of local jurisdictions throughout the United States and its territories. These are the figures usually reported in the press. The National Crime Survey (NCS) is a report published by the Bureau of Justice Statistics. The NCS report is a survey of 49,000 households about their experiences as victims of crime during the past year (Bureau of Justice Statistics, 1988). These data include crimes both reported and not reported to the police, and many researchers feel these data more accurately report the level of crime in this society. According to the UCR reports, there were 13,509,000 offenses in 1987; 36 million victimizations occurred according to NCS data (Bureau of the Census, 1990, pp. 168–172).

Watching the news, you come away with the impression that the crime rate is spiraling upward. Figure 13.5 summarizes victimization data from 1976 to 1985, and it suggests that both violent and property crime has declined significantly since their peak in 1979. The bottom panel is data from the UCR. Note that the overall UCR index has declined since 1979, but violent crimes have not. Rape and assault have increased over 30 percent. Murder has increased dramatically. Is there more crime, or are more people reporting crime?

CRIME AND CITIES

Since the beginning of the field of urban sociology, sociologists have known that the larger the city, the higher the crime rate (Federal Bureau of Investigation, 1989, Table 10, pp. 149–150). Sociologists also have known for decades that crime is not evenly distributed across the urban landscape. Many behaviors considered deviant by the larger society—prostitution, juvenile delinquency, and violent and property crime—tend to be concentrated in the older and poorer sections of the city. Some of the earliest studies by human ecologists were on the distribution of deviant behavior in the city. One of the first, by Shaw (1929), showed that the level of juvenile delinquency declined in a regular fashion as one moved from the central business district to the fringe of the city. Shaw found that the same pattern existed for adult crimes (See Figure 13.6.). Schmid (1960a, 1960b) conducted a more detailed analysis of crime in Seattle and found the crime rate highest in the areas near the downtown. Shoplifting, check fraud, burglary, and car theft were the most frequent crimes in the CBD. In the adjacent skid row and slum areas, crimes like assault, robbery, burglary, and disorderly conduct were the most frequent offenses.

Since these pioneering works, a large body of research has been completed on the variation in crime rates in metropolitan areas. The patterns first discovered by Shaw in the 1920s still exist today. Note in Table 13.5 that both violent and property crime rates are considerably lower in the suburbs than the central city. Distance from the CBD, therefore, is an important variable in describing the geographical distribution of crime in metropolitan areas, but it is only a statistical artifact. The urban poor are

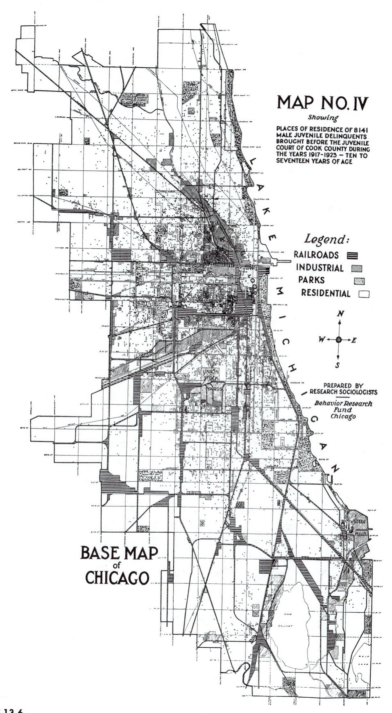

FIGURE 13.6

Source: Shaw, Clifford R., et al. *Delinquency Areas.* Chicago, IL: University of Chicago Press, 1929, p. 74.

TABLE 13.5 Crime rates are highest in major metropolitan areas.

	NUMBER OF UCR INDEX CRIME RATES PER 100,000 POPULATION	
	VIOLENT CRIMES	*PROPERTY CRIMES*
Metropolitan statistical areas (MSAs) Urbanized areas that include at least one city with 50,000 or more inhabitants, or a Census Bureau defined urbanized area of at least 50,000 inhabitants and a total MSA population of at least 100,000	658	5262
Non-MSA cities Cities that do not qualify as MSA central cities and are not otherwise included in an MSA	319	4262
Suburban areas Suburban cities and counties within metropolitan areas	341	3883
Rural Areas	168	1636

Source: U.S. Bureau of Justice Statistics. *Report to the Nation on Crime and Justice.* Washington, D.C.: U.S. Government Printing Office, 1989, p. 19.

overrepresented in national crime statistics both as perpetrators and victims. Since the majority of the poor are concentrated in our central cities, it should come as no surprise that crime rates are higher there.

The UCR and NCS reports provide cold crime statistics, but they are only part of the information we use in assessing our risk of becoming victims. Street crimes—murder, armed robbery, assault, and rape—are the crimes the public fears most, and these are the ones flashed across our TV screens each evening.

Washington, D.C. is now the murder capital of the nation. There were 703 homicides in Washington in 1990. Youth gangs, the drug trade, and the availability of handguns have led to an increase in the number of deadly assaults in this city. These are the events that are dramatized in our media and the ones that tend to exaggerate the amount of street crime in this society. There are 3.7 million people in the Washington, D.C. metropolitan area. Moreover, most of the murders take place in a few central city neighborhoods. Although fewer than two homicides per day in a population of 3.7 million make the odds of becoming a victim remote, this does not allay the fears of many urbanites.

WHY URBAN CRIME?

Over the years, numerous theories have been developed to explain deviance in general and crime in particular. There are, however, two general explanations for the higher incidence of crime in cities—cultural and structural.

CULTURAL EXPLANATIONS[5]

In the opening chapter of this text, Claude Fischer's subcultural theory of urbanism was presented (Fischer, 1975). Fischer's argument is straightforward: The size, density, and heterogeneity of the city provide an environment ripe for the creation of subcultures. Most of these subcultures develop value and normative systems that reinforce the values of the larger society. There are, however, a few subcultures, like street gangs, that lack strong external controls or strong motivations to conform and have the potential for lawlessness and delinquency. Urban gangs are nothing new. Thrasher in the 1920s identified over 1300 gangs in the city of Chicago (Thrasher, 1927). Today, as in the past, high schools in our largest cities bring thousands of students together five days a week. This critical mass of teenagers creates an environment conducive for the creation of groups like the National Honor Society, sports teams, cliques, and gangs. Gangs exist in all of our major cities, and their involvement in the drug trade and their proclivity towards violence are played out in our electronic and print media almost daily.

Another version of the cultural theory is found in the works of Edward Banfield (1970), James Q. Wilson (1983), and William J. Wilson (1987). Edward Banfield argues that crime flourishes in areas of the city where lower-class culture is rooted. Elements of a lower-class culture include a strong present-time rather than future orientation, an inability to defer gratification, low aspirations, and moral irresponsibility. These culture traits, according to Banfield, lead to situations where the poor victimize each other and anyone else who seems an easy mark. The poor are concentrated in the central cities of this society, and these conditions, according to Banfield, create an environment conducive for the creation and perpetuation of the lower-class culture.

James Q. Wilson echoed these same sentiments in his 1983 book, *Thinking About Crime.* According to Wilson, crime does not occur because people are poor, but because many of the poor hold lower-class cultural values. Marginality and a lack of commitment to the goals and values of the larger society are characteristics of this cultural group. These values, according to Wilson, reduce the effectiveness of informal social controls and ultimately destroy the local community. The destruction of the community is crucial to Wilson's argument because our public behavior is regulated by our concern for what our kin, friends, and neighbors think. Informal controls are powerful forces in maintaining conformity and respect for others and their property. Since these controls have broken down in slums, serious crime abounds, especially predatory street crime.

Wilson's interpretation of the link between poverty and crime has been widely criticized. His ideas echo the culture-of-poverty argument widely held in the 1950s and 1960s. The culture of poverty posited that the poor held values that made their participation in the larger society impossible. Social programs from the 1960s, like Head Start, were designed to interrupt the transmission of these cultural values from parents to children. Wilson's solution to crime is more draconian. He argues that since criminal behavior results from a lack of commitment to common principles of decency, then the only remedy is to convince potential criminals there will be consequences for their behavior through swift and certain punishment. According to Wilson, social programs designed to improve the conditions of the poor won't solve the problem because these people are steeped in lower-class culture.

A more benign version of the cultural position is found in the work of the black sociologist William J. Wilson, especially his work, *The Truly Disadvantaged.* In this work, Wilson tries to place the experiences of the ghetto in a larger social context. In the 1960s and 1970s, many black Americans experienced upward social mobility. Black Americans, like all our other ethnic groups, responded to this increase in social status by moving to the suburbs. The problem: People were left behind. In the past, segregation in the central city meant that middle- and lower-class blacks lived in the same communities. Importantly, small businessmen, professionals, and church leaders provided the leadership for these communities. When these leaders left these neighborhoods for the suburbs, the ghetto was deprived of its leadership and role models. Those left, the truly disadvantaged, live in an environment bereft of stable families, appropriate role models, and traditional values. Over time, the cultural values of the truly disadvantaged form barriers to participation in education and job training programs. Moreover, the barriers also limit their contacts with the network of gainfully employed people, a source of role models and leads to employment opportunities.

Crime, according to William J. Wilson, is a predictable outcome of isolating a group from the mainstream of society. Crucial to understanding the problem is the realization that the culture of the truly disadvantaged is like any culture; it reproduces itself from generation to generation through the socialization process. The problem is more serious than in the past because there is no way to break the cycle. William J. Wilson's solution to crime is straightforward: Invest in our human capital, regardless of race and ethnicity. Provide all members of our society with the education and skills necessary for full participation in society.

STRUCTURAL EXPLANATIONS

William J. Wilson's research on the truly disadvantaged is a bridge between the two schools of thought. The structuralists believe that there are important structural problems in our society, which contribute to the problem of crime. The United States is a society with materialism as its core value. Most members of our society hold this value, but not everyone is provided with the means to legitimately reach this goal. Poor schools, a lack of job training programs, and other social factors cut off millions from traditional means of social mobility. Unable to use legitimate means, many resort to illegitimate means. Some structuralists go so far as to argue that crime is a survival strategy for the poor. Many of the poor cannot live on the welfare benefits provided in most cities, so they turn to crime to supplement their incomes.

Marxist theorists, like Manuel Castells (1977), make a similar argument. The city in capitalistic societies reproduces the labor force. It is here where people are born, housed, fed, and schooled to provide the work force necessary to keep the capitalist system working. According to Castells, capitalism benefits relatively few people. Any behavior that interferes with the reproduction of labor threatens the interests of the few. Moreover, those who control the means of production also control the political and police powers of the state, and they erect a legal system to protect their interests. The poor who deviate from laws created by these vested interests are the ones labeled and stigmatized as criminals. White-collar criminals like Michael Milken and Ivan Bosky, who steal hundreds of millions of dollars, usually receive less severe penalties than street criminals. Why? Because white-collar criminals are being judged by a criminal justice system of their social class.

WHAT CAN BE DONE?

Research in the past 20 years has shown that the relationship between poverty and crime is a complex one (Currie, 1985; Duster, 1987; Parker and Horwitz, 1986; Reiss and Tonry, 1986). Poverty alone does not explain crime. Recent research by Blau and Blau (1982) shows this to be the case. The Blaus found income inequality to be a far more sensitive indicator of urban crime than either race or poverty. Cities with the greatest disparity between the rich and poor had the highest crime rates. The notion of relative deprivation—measuring our well-being through comparisons to our neighbors—according to these researchers, is the most important factor in breeding crime. Crime, especially violent crime, is inevitable in a society in which there is such enormous disparity in income. The ecology of inequality—the fact that the poor are concentrated in our central cities—is a major explanatory factor for the higher crime rates in urban areas.

There is no agreement over the relationship between crime and various social and economic factors. As we have seen, some researchers believe that crime results from cultural factors; others hold society at fault. A partial answer may lie in the characteristics of offenders. First, there seems to be a close relationship between crime and family background. Nearly half of those in jail or prison grew up in homes in which there was only one parent, or they were raised by relatives other than their parents. (It is sobering to realize that in 1990 one out of five children under 18 was living with only one parent.) Many of the offenders incarcerated for violent crimes were victims of childhood abuse. Moreover, most offenders have never been married. Thus, the absence of attachments or destructive attachments to the most fundamental of all our social institutions, the family, appear to be a contributing factor to criminal behavior that leads to incarceration (Bureau of Justice Statistics, 1988, pp. 48–50).

Second, economic marginality appears to be a contributing factor to crime. Those in jail or prison have levels of education far below the national average. Most offenders were unemployed at the time of their arrest or lacked steady employment. Those employed were usually in blue-collar occupations, and few were working in their customary occupation. The average inmate was at the poverty level before entering jail, and those with incomes received it from sources other than wages—welfare, disability benefits, and crime (Bureau of Justice Statistics, 1988, pp. 48–50).

Crime can be addressed on two levels—dealing with the symptoms or dealing with the causes. Short-term solutions are defensive in nature. For decades, we have known the principles of defensible space. Designing doorways, windows, halls, and walks in certain ways can dramatically lower the crime rate in high-rise buildings and public housing. Neighborhood watch programs have been found to be an effective deterrent to crime. Today, one out of three Americans lives in a neighborhood with an active watch program. More professional police forces, more effective patrolling, better community–police relations, gang control, and gun control can reduce crime rates. But these solutions are dealing with the symptoms and not the causes.

In my opinion, inequality in this society is responsible for our high crime rate. Since the work of Durkheim we have known that attachments to social groups are the most potent force in bringing about conformity. Full participation in, commitment to, and vested interests in society would probably be the most potent vaccine to the problem of crime in our cities. Lessening inequality in this society through full employment legislation, providing greater access to good jobs through job training programs, and providing greater access to quality education and health and housing services to our citizens would attack the root causes of crime. In short, these solutions get at the heart of the issue of social justice: the social contract between our institutions and our people. The politics of the 1990s will be dominated by the issue of social justice, and domestic issues, like housing, education, and health care, are being debated for the first time in a decade. If the structuralists are correct, investments in our society's most important asset, our human capital, may begin a process that will reduce crime in our cities.

SUMMARY

All cities must maintain their infrastructure, provide services, and maintain social control. This chapter explores three serious problems facing cities in meeting these obligations—homelessness, AIDS, and crime.

This society has always had homeless people, but conditions in the past decade have exacerbated an already bad situation. Throughout our history, the definition of the problem and the solutions that followed have changed. Prior to the Civil War, the homeless were deemed moral failures, and communities solved the problem by placing these people in workhouses. After the Civil War, the rapid industrialization of our society, combined with the rapid settlement of the West, required a large and transient work force. These itinerant workers were known as tramps, and they were defined by society as a dangerous class. By 1900, tramping was illegal in most states. Cities couldn't jail all the homeless, so they depended on municipal shelters and rescue missions for shelter. In the early twentieth century, the growth of populist government and social work professionals redefined the homeless as victims of circumstance, not flawed characters. During the Great Depression, the link between homelessness and economic cycles was firmly established, and all of the major programs in the nation's welfare state were established. In the post-World War II period, an expanding economy meant that the homeless were reduced to a relatively small number of older, single men, surviving on pensions and marginal employment in skid row areas of our cities. In the 1970s and 1980s, conditions changed once again, and homelessness became a national problem.

One of the problems this society faces in dealing with the problem of the homeless is defining who are the homeless. Using conservative definitions, HUD estimates there are between 250,000 and 350,000 homeless in the nation. Other groups put the number much higher. One thing has become apparent: The homeless are not a homogeneous group, but one made up of mentally ill, AIDS victims, alcoholics and drug abusers, women and children, and the new poor. Each group has specific problems and needs, requiring different solutions.

Why is there a homeless problem? A changed economy, a decline in federal funding for low-income housing, reforms in social security, and the deinstitutionalization of the wards of the state are all contributing factors to the problems of the homeless.

What can be done? I feel that little will be done. The homeless by definition are marginal and isolated citizens, and so do not form a constituency. With no one to represent their interests, this society will do little to solve the long-term problem of the homeless.

AIDS is one of the most serious public health problems of the century. In 1990, 56,000 cases were reported to the Centers for Disease Control; that number will increase to 104,000 by 1993. The cost of treating AIDS patients was $3.3 billion in 1989; this figure will more than double by 1993.

Epidemics are complex phenomena that involve biological and social factors. The discovery of the Human Immunodeficiency Virus (HIV) is one of the great scientific discovery stories of the century. But changing values, changing attitudes towards alternative lifestyles, changing transportation technology, and changing economics all contributed to the rapid spread of the disease through the gay community and then to other groups. The disease is no longer the "gay plague," but it is becoming a disease of the poor and minorities.

AIDS victims are concentrated in our largest cities. New York City has the most serious problem, and it was chosen for closer examination. The AIDS epidemic has overwhelmed the city's health care system, making it difficult for the medical establishment to provide quality care for rich and poor alike. As with the other problems discussed in this chapter, massive federal assistance is required to solve the AIDS crisis.

Crime in our cities is perceived as a serious threat to most urbanites. Forty-five percent of Americans are afraid to walk on the streets at night. This fear became a potent political issue in the 1980s. Is this fear justified? Crime is difficult to measure, and two sources of data are used to access the amount of crime in this society. The Uniform Crime Report (UCR) is published annually by the FBI; it is the number of crimes reported each year to the police. These data show that crime declined from a high in 1979 and then began to gradually increase in the late 1980s. The Nation Crime Survey (NCS) is a survey of American households conducted by the Bureau of Justice Statistics. The survey includes reported and unreported crimes, and many researchers feel that it more accurately reflects the level of crime in this society. These data show that crime has declined significantly since 1979.

The larger the city, the higher the crime rate. Sociologists have known for most of this century that crime is not evenly distributed across the city, but concentrated in poorer neighborhoods near the central business district. Two types of explanations have been posited. Cultural explanations argue that the size, density, and heterogeneity of the city create conditions ripe for the emergence of subcultures. Some of these subcultures have value and normative systems that diverge from those of the larger society. Edward Banfield and James Q. Wilson feel that lower-class subcultures are pathological, and the behaviors that result need to be extinguished through the sure, swift retribution of the law. William J. Wilson, in contrast, explores the changes in the larger society that have created the subculture of the truly disadvantaged. He suggests that a massive investment in our people, regardless of race, would be the best solution to the problem of crime in our cities.

Structuralists argue that crime is a result of social structure. Poverty and inequality reduce the commitment of the poor to society. From this perspective, the lack of legitimate means of social mobility, the lack of attachments to social groups, and the lack of commitment to the values of the larger society are the major reasons for crime. Marxists and structural sociologists agree that economic inequality and a lack of social justice are at the root of the problem of crime in our society. I agree with this assessment and point to a changing political climate that may address the issue of social justice in the decade to come.

The three problems are diverse but related in a perverse way to poverty and social inequality. In the final chapter we explore urban policy, or the lack of it, and the prospect for our cities as we enter the twenty-first century.

NOTES

1. The following section on the history of the homeless in the United States is based on two works. The first is Carol L. M. Caton, "Homelessness in Historical Perspective." The second is Charles Hoch, "A Brief History of the Homeless Problem in the United States." A complete citation for each work is found in the bibliography.

2. Much of the following section is based on the book *Landscapes of Despair: From Deinstitutionalization to Homelessness* by Michael J. Dear and Jennifer R. Wolch. A complete citation for the work is in the bibliography.

3. For those interested in the social history of the early phase of the AIDS epidemic, I would strongly recommend the book by Randy Shilts, *And The Band Played On: Politics, People and the AIDS Epidemic*. Randy Shilts was a newspaper reporter in San Francisco in the late 1970s and early 1980s, and he followed the AIDS epidemic during its early stages.

The scientific community has learned more about the HIV virus, which causes AIDS, in a shorter period of time than any organism in history. For those interested in the biology of the virus and the epidemiology of AIDS in the United States, I would recommend the single-topic issue of *Scientific American*, "What Science Knows About AIDS," published in October 1988.

4. The Centers for Disease Control have specific criteria for including persons in the category, "AIDS diagnosed." A person with HIV infection with a relatively high T-helper cell count and an absence of specific opportunistic diseases, like pneumocystis Carinii or Kaposi's sarcoma, are not counted. HIV patients without AIDS, however, require a level of medical care higher than the general public.

5. For those interested in the competing theories on crime and delinquency in urban areas, I would suggest the review article by Robert J. Bursik, Jr., "Social Disorganization and Theories of Crime and Delinquency: Problems and Prospects," in *Criminology*, 26 (4), 1988:519–551.

THE STRUCTURE AND ROLE OF GOVERNMENT IN THE METROPOLIS

INTRODUCTION

In the decade of the 1980s, a series of critical and interrelated problems have struck American cities. Among them are physical blight, a deteriorating infrastructure, an inadequate and poorly conceived transportation system, an increasingly troubled educational system, a rising number of homeless and inadequately housed citizens, an increase in the number of poor and other high-cost citizens, AIDS, and an unacceptable level of violent and property crime. The most intractable problems of society are concentrated in their most visible and pernicious forms in our nation's central cities.

America's cities entered the 1990s in financial peril. They found themselves sandwiched between the need to solve society's problems and decreasing revenues. The continued flight of population from the central city to the suburbs made their financial condition worse. Today, much of the metropolis's wealth is outside the tax jurisdiction of the central city, and the poor and the disadvantaged have few assets to tax. The nation's slow slide into economic recession has made their financial situation worse. In the opening years of the decade, few cities had reserves to fall back on. Cities couldn't turn to state and federal governments for help, because deficits loom in their budgets. The result is that cities from coast to coast are slashing budgets, laying off employees, and reducing city services.

The concentration of the majority of this nation's high-cost citizens—the poor, the homeless, and the aged—in our central cities exacerbates the problem of providing basic services. City governments caught in the middle find themselves on the horns of a dilemma—do they deny the poor food and shelter, or do they reduce fire and police protection? Do they close health clinics and city hospitals, or do they stop repairing streets and bridges? But after a decade of antigovernment rhetoric from Washington, the nation is slowly coming to the realization that all these problems are public in nature, and their solution depends largely on government.

The purpose of this chapter is to examine the role of government in addressing the problems of cities. First, the past and present structure of city government and its position in the nation's federal system are explained. Second, the changing relationships between and within the levels of government are explored, and the changing role of the federal government in urban affairs is surveyed.

Third, the relationship between the structure of metropolitan government and its fiscal affairs is examined with special emphasis on the problems of taxation, spillover of services, and the fragmentation of local government.

Fourth, the consequences of the fragmentation of metropolitan government is presented, and the responses of cities to this fragmentation are discussed.

Fifth, the policy alternatives open to the nation's urban areas are explored. A look at the effects of the Reagan era on the metropolis is presented, followed by a discussion of likely urban policies in the 1990s.

THE STRUCTURE OF CITY GOVERNMENT IN THE UNITED STATES

THE SOURCE OF LOCAL GOVERNMENTAL AUTHORITY

The decision of the founding fathers to create a federal state has had important implications for American governments, particularly in terms of the relations among the levels of government—national, state, and local. According to Webster, a federal system is "formed by a compact between political units that surrender their individual sovereignty to a central authority but retain limited residuary powers of government" (1977, p. 420). In this nation, the document setting forth the distribution of powers in the several levels of government is the United States Constitution. The Tenth Amendment states that all powers not conferred on the federal government are "reserved" to the states. Municipalities and other local governments are not mentioned explicitly in the Constitution, and therefore are assumed to be under the jurisdiction of state governments. A fundamental point that must be kept in mind about cities and other local governments is that they are products of a higher authority. They can exercise only those powers explicitly granted them by the state government. Moreover, whereas the United States Constitution has been interpreted liberally by the Supreme Court, city charters and related documents of incorporation traditionally have been interpreted very narrowly—local government's powers are clearly circumscribed. The classic formulation of the legal position of cities was stated by a famous jurist, Judge John F. Dillon, in a work first published in 1872:

> It is a general and undisputed proposition of law that a municipal corporation possesses and can exercise the following powers, and no others; First, those granted in express words; second, those necessarily or fairly implied in or incident to the power expressly granted; third, those essential to the accomplishment

of the declared objects and purposes of the corporation,—not simply convenient, but indispensable. Any fair, reasonable, substantial doubt concerning the existence of power is resolved by the courts against the corporation, and the power is denied (Dillon, 1911, Vol. 1, Sec. 237).

Dillon's Rule has been tested over the years and has been upheld by state courts and the United States Supreme Court. The doctrine means that cities can be chartered only by the state, which sets forth a city's form of government, rights, and powers. In legal theory, states control cities, but city governments actually exercise considerable autonomy. In fact, over the years, states have granted vast powers to cities. One type of charter, known as a home rule charter, is drafted by a city itself and then is approved by the state legislature. These charters grant the municipal corporation a high degree of independence in making charter changes and revisions. Because state governments seldom take punitive action against cities, the state is supreme in theory, but in reality cities govern themselves (Stedman, 1972, pp. 41–45).

THE UNITED STATES SYSTEM OF LOCAL GOVERNMENT

Counties and municipalities. Since the inception of the federal system more than 200 years ago, local government in the United States has rapidly expanded in terms of the number, size, and scope of governmental units. The expansion is directly attributable to the problems associated with rapid urban growth and to America's conception of the kinds of functions that local governments should perform (Bromley, 1977, p. 470).

Although there are some regional variations, originally the basic forms of local government in this nation were counties and municipalities.[1] Like all forms of government, they came into existence to perform basic functions. Because most states in the United States are too large geographically to carry out services on a statewide basis, states subdivided themselves into conveniently sized administrative units—counties. Counties carry out numerous services to local populations including court services, the registration of vital events (births, deaths, and marriages), the recording of transfers of property, the assessment and collection of taxes, the supervision of state and county elections, and the maintenance of county roads and highways, as well as the preservation of public safety through the sheriff and county health and social service agencies. Similarly, municipalities came into existence to supply local services but to more densely populated places. Though counties together serve an entire state population, municipalities primarily serve residents in urban areas that include only a small portion of the state. In most states, the boundaries of these two basic local governments overlap, although each normally provides a different set of services to the population (Stedman, 1972, pp. 46–58).

Special districts. The explosive growth of the nation's urban places in the nineteenth and twentieth centuries literally overwhelmed local governments. For example, Chicago, which had a population of only 30,000 in 1850, had grown to more than 300,000 by 1870 and to a million by 1890. In the next 40 years, this city absorbed more than a half-million persons per decade, and the service resources of the city were strained to the limit (Bromley, 1977, p. 471). Chicago is not an isolated example. Many American cities had similar rates of growth. It was imperative that these communities find means to preserve the public safety and maintain social control, improve transportation and communication, assimilate and acculturate vast numbers of immigrants, educate the young, and provide for the basic health, safety, and welfare of community members. In response to these problems, a new form of local government was created to fill the needs not being met by counties and municipalities—the special district.

School districts, the earliest special districts, were created "because of the strong conviction that public education was of such importance to the society as to warrant its own local financing and its freedom from the politics of other local governments" (Bollens and Schmandt, 1975, p. 48). Generally, school-district organization is similar to that of a municipality with a city manager–council form of government. A small elected school board appoints a superintendent who runs the school system.

Other types of special districts are water, sewer, fire, transit, park, library, and police districts. They differ considerably in size. Some are so small that they cover only a few city blocks (a city's historic preservation district, for example), whereas others are gigantic. The revenues from the Chicago Sanitary District, for instance, exceeded $365 million in 1987, and, in the same year, the city's transit authority had an income of more than $839 million. One of the largest special districts in United States local government is the New York Port Authority, which has jurisdiction in both New York and New Jersey, and, in 1987, had more than 9000 employees and an annual revenue of about $1.3 billion (U.S. Bureau of the Census, 1987a).

Special districts also differ in terms of organization. Some districts have elected boards that are responsible for their operations. Other districts have appointed boards whose members are selected by local government authorities to serve long, overlapping terms. In this case, local elected officials have little control over the activities of the special district, and the district's board exercises great authority (Stedman, 1972, pp. 55–56).

In the twentieth century, special districts proliferated to meet the needs of a rapidly expanding urban population. As populations grew in and around urban centers, in many cases, it was politically more expedient to set up special districts than to reorganize local government. This trend, combined with legal technicalities in many states that made it easier for a suburb to incorporate than to be annexed to a central city, led to an increase in the number of government units at the local level.

THE FRAGMENTATION OF METROPOLITAN GOVERNMENT

Trends in the number and types of local governmental units are summarized in Table 14.1. On the local level there were 83,136 governmental units in 1987. The 29,532 special districts and 14,721 school districts accounted for a little more than half of this total. The remaining units were 38,933 municipalities, counties, and townships—nearly 20,000 of this number were municipal governments. The average number of government units per state had grown to 1663 by 1987, but Illinois had the most with 6467, and Hawaii the fewest with 18. States with more than 3000 government units were California (4102),

TABLE 14.1 The number of local governments.

GOVERNMENT TYPE	1942	1952	YEAR 1962	1972	1977	1982	1987
School districts	108,579	67,355	34,678	15,781	15,174	14,851	14,721
Special districts	8,299	12,340	18,323	28,855	25,962	28,078	29,532
Municipalities, counties, and townships	38,237	37,111	38,235	38,582	38,731	38,351	38,933
Total number of governmental units	155,115	116,806	91,236	78,218	78,867	81,780	83,136
Average number of governmental units per state	3,231	2,433	1,825	1,565	1,597	1,636	1,663

Source: 1942-1972 data from U.S. Bureau of the Census, *Census of Government, 1977, Government Organization.* Washington, D.C.: U.S. Government Printing Office, 1978, Tables 1–3 and pp. 1–17; 1982-1987 data from U.S. Bureau of the Census. *Statistical Abstract of the United States, 1990.* Washington, DC: U.S. Government Printing Office, 1990.

Illinois (6467), Kansas (3795), Minnesota (3529), Missouri (3117), Nebraska (3324), New York (3249), Ohio (3393), Pennsylvania (5198), and Texas (4180). Together these nine states accounted for nearly half of all government units in the nation (U.S. Bureau of the Census, 1990, p. 291). Although the present number of local governments is enormous, it is substantially smaller than the number 50 years ago. In 1942, there were 155, 115 units. The reduction is due mainly to the consolidation and reorganization of state school systems. In 1942, there were 108,579 school districts, and in 1987 only 14,721. However, during the same period, the number of special districts increased more than threefold to 29,532 in 1987, and the number of counties, townships, and municipalities remained the same.

Reasons for the change in the number of special districts. Why did the number of local governmental units change? School districts were responding to changing transportation technology. In the past, because of transportation, a school could draw its student body only from a relatively small area; thus, school districts were small in size but large in number. In recent years, improved transportation has enabled small districts to be consolidated into larger and more efficient units. The boundaries of these units, however, generally do not coincide with those of other local governments. In municipalities, school districts normally serve not only a city but also its unincorporated fringe areas. Structuring school districts in this way minimizes the risk that they will be taken over by municipal governments. It has also enabled school districts to avoid racial integration.

Though the number of school districts has declined, other types of special districts have become more numerous. One reason for this increase is that special districts have filled the void left by the inaction of municipal and county governments. Special districts have the advantage of being extremely flexible units not tied to the traditional boundaries of county and municipal governments. Water and sewer districts can span two or more counties or municipalities, and special districts can be formed to supply a particular service within a city or county. In addition to its spatial flexibility, the special district has the advantage of having its own budget. Because special districts are normally service providers, they generate their operating revenue through user charges. Consequently, their programs do not compete with other programs when a municipality or county draws up its annual budget.

Negative aspects of fragmentation. Although the structure and flexibility of special districts are advantageous, the fragmentation associated with the proliferation of government jurisdictions may be more negative than positive in its effect.

First, the logistical difficulty of coordinating the activities of dozens of government units makes rational policy planning in an urban area almost impossible. Figure 14.1, a map of St. Louis, shows a typical "governmentally crowded" modern metropolis. Involved in the operation of this single Standard Metropolitan Statistical Area are one federal, two state, and seven county governments, and 197 municipalities (dark-shaded part), plus adjoining unincorporated territory and 657 special districts—275 in Missouri and 382 in Illinois (U.S. Bureau of the Census, 1987c).

A second negative effect of fragmentation is that in large cities governmental authority is so dispersed among federal, state, county, city, and other local governments that no single entity has the power to exercise effective leadership. Big-city mayors have complained for decades that the mayor of a city has no authority over many important city services. The school board is independently elected, the welfare program is county-operated and state-funded, the city housing authority is federally funded, transit system development is usually under state authority, and the health department is part of county government. In most cities authority is dispersed among the mayor, the council, and various independent officials, boards, and commissions that run the myriad of special districts. In addition, a rigid civil service system, with stringent rules covering entrance to positions, promotion, and seniority, further reduces the policy options available to the city's leadership (Palley and Palley, 1977, pp. 62–63). The entrenched civil service combined with the increasing militancy of city police and fire fighters has led one political analyst to comment that local government bureaucracies have led many cities to "become well-run, but ungoverned" (Lowi, 1967, p. 86).

Finally, the fragmentation of government dissipates managerial and leadership ability. In any society, only a limited number of people have the managerial and leadership skills necessary to run a metropolis. Fragmentation of government authority diminishes the effective application of such skills.

INTERGOVERNMENTAL RELATIONSHIPS

In general, the rapid growth of urban population in this century and the decentralization of people and activities outward from central cities to their suburban fringe have brought about a corresponding decentralization and proliferation of local governments. A major

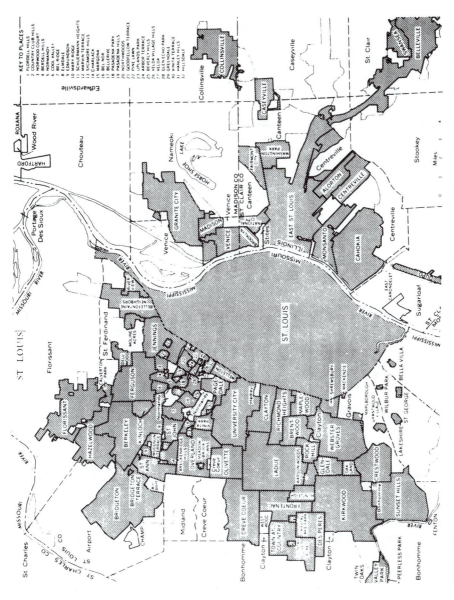

FIGURE 14.1 The St. Louis urbanized area. One example of the "governmentally-crowded" modern metropolis.

Source: Advisory Commission on Intergovernmental Relations. *Urban America and the Federal System: Commission Findings & Proposals.* Washington, D.C.: U.S. Government Printing Office, 1969, Figure 1.

problem of many cities is simply to coordinate the activities of the numerous local government units in order to provide basic services. Interaction between governmental units on the same level (e.g., municipality–municipality or county–county) is called a *horizontal pattern* of intergovernmental relationship. Municipalities and other forms of local government also interact with higher governmental units (for example, with the state or the federal government) in a *vertical pattern* of intergovernmental relationship. Since the Depression years of the 1930s, the vertical relationships between a city and higher levels of government have changed dramatically, especially the link between the national and local governments. This change is interesting because, technically, cities are not recognized in the United States Constitution as part of the federal system. However, cities have had a significant role in the federal system for many years, mainly as a result of the structure of state government.

STATE AND LOCAL GOVERNMENT RELATIONS

State governments are structured by state constitutions, most of which are outmoded and inflexible. Though the federal constitution was written in such a way as to provide wide latitude in its interpretation by the United States Supreme Court, state constitutions are written rigidly and can be changed only by amendment—a time consuming and politically difficult procedure. Whereas the United States Constitution has been amended 26 times, Arkansas's constitution, for example, has been amended 57 times. In addition, the makeup of state legislatures normally does not reflect accurately the distribution of population in the state; state legislatures tend to overrepresent the interests of a rural minority. Ohio, for example, has more cities of 50,000 people or more than any state in the nation, yet rural interests continue to exert an enormous influence in Ohio's legislature. Why? A major reason is that state elections are based on the county system, and urban populations are concentrated in only a few of the state's many counties. Therefore, because of state constitutions and the political realities built into a state's legislative branch, financial resources available to cities are often inadequate by design, and new programs that address urban problems are difficult to implement.

FEDERAL AND LOCAL GOVERNMENT RELATIONS

The United States Senate has traditionally been responsive to urban constituencies because senators are elected on a statewide basis. In the 1960s, the court-ordered reapportionment of United States congressional districts according to the "one man, one vote" principle gave urban populations proportionally greater representation in the United States House of Representatives. At the national level, therefore, government has come to recognize that the major problems facing the nation are basically urban problems and has generated federal policies and programs to address them. The concept of dual federalism (the vertical intergovernmental relationship between the national and state governments) has given way to what might be called cooperative federalism—the sharing of public responsibility by two or more levels of government.

The expanding role of the federal government on the local level. Prior to the 1930s, national–local relations were few. The Depression, however, brought about a dramatic change in the relationships between federal and local governments. Cities, confronted with heavy relief costs and high unemployment, turned to states for help. But the states, which normally operate under a legal debt limit, were hard pressed to meet their own financial obligations. Only the federal government had the flexibility to raise the money needed to cope with the cities' critical problems.

During the Depression, Congress authorized funds to be spent on the local-government level for direct relief purposes. As with many other federal programs, what began as a temporary program eventually was expanded into other areas. By the closing years of the Depression, state and local governments were receiving direct grants and loans for schools, hospitals, highways, and other projects (Stedman, 1972, pp. 58–63).

Federal-local intergovernmental relationships have expanded since the Great Depression. Housing and urban renewal was the focus of federal efforts in the 1950s. It was, however, in the 1960s, during the Johnson administration, when the role of the federal government in urban affairs grew most rapidly. President Johnson's Great Society programs channeled federal money to cities through a variety of grant-in-aid programs. (A grant-in-aid program is a payment of federal funds to a lower level of government for a specified purpose, usually with some supervision.) Two types of grants became common during this decade. Categorical grants were given for specific purposes, like public housing, highway, sewer, and water line construction. A complicated grant writing process had to be followed, and grant funds were carefully monitored by federal agencies. Block grants, in contrast, gave local governments great latitude in program development and budgeting. In the 1970s, the federal government's Community Development Block Grant Program gave cities enormous leeway in assessing needs and developing programs. Monies could be spent on housing assistance, redevelopment, sewers, sidewalks or streets, social services, and many other projects. The only restraint was that these monies had to be spent in low- and moderate-income areas of the city, areas deemed appropriate by the federal government's Department of Housing and Urban Development (Caputo, 1975, pp. 116–188).

Federal urban policy during the 1970s was based on the assumption that cities were especially vulnerable to economic cycles. The largest urban programs during this decade were antirecession programs designed to create temporary jobs and provide cities with a financial cushion during economic downturns. During this decade, a formula system came into wider use to direct aid to those urban areas in the greatest need, usually to those cities with the highest concentration of high-cost citizens (See Chapter 6, "The Classification and Rating of Cities."). The rationale for these programs was that cities were at the core of our national economy. Our population was concentrated in our cities, and so too were the enterprises which created most of our nation's goods and services. It was argued that economic cycles picked up in national statistics mirrored the changes occurring on the metropolitan level. It was thought the nation's oldest and largest cities were particularly vulnerable. Concentrated within their borders were not only large numbers of high-cost citizens—the poor, minorities, and ethnic groups—but also aged infrastructures and large numbers of industries in the final stages of the product cycle. Industries like steel, glass, automobile, and other durable goods manufacturers had enormous fixed capital assets and were thought to be vulnerable to economic downturns. Thus, it was thought the cyclical instability of local economies placed city government in a precarious state during recessions. The near bankruptcies of New York City and Cleveland during the 1970s seemed to bolster policy makers' confidence in their plans.

A fundamental change occurred in federal and local government relations during the 1980s. No other sphere of our society was more profoundly affected by the Reagan revolution than cities and city governments. They bore the brunt of federal budget cuts, and central cities have been especially hard hit. One reason is the backwash from the rapid suburbanization of the nation's population in the postwar period. More people live in suburbs than in central cities. In some cases, individual suburbs have populations that rival the size of the central cities. Central cities, rather than being the major player in regional and national politics, have become just another player. Whereas the concentration of ethnic and racial groups in the central cities of the nation has led to domination of city governments by the Democratic party, the more affluent suburbs are usually Republican. Therefore, the stark reality of national politics is one explanation, but there were deep ideological reasons for a change in federal urban policy.

One reason that Americans elected Ronald Reagan by two of the largest margins in our nation's history was disenchantment with government. The Reagan administration's domestic policy echoed its urban policy. It was based on the notion that cities must be financially self-sufficient. This self-reliance would only come about when the federal government stopped being a financial cushion. Second, it was based on the philosophy that when federal funding is reduced, private charity will step in to replace important public programs, especially for the poor. Third, urban development was based on the assumption that cities should compete with each other for business and industries just like private firms. It was believed it was in the cities' best interests to make their communities as attractive as possible for potential investors, residents, and tourists. Finally, Reagan intended to create a new federalism based on a clean division of authority between levels of government. Drawing on a strict interpretation of the U.S. Constitution, direct federal–local government programs were to be eliminated, and state governments returned to their historical role as mediator between the federal and local governments. This was to occur in both program development and funding (Peterson and Lewis, 1986).

Table 14.2 shows the actual budget cuts in Reagan's 1982 budget. Many domestic cuts were draconian. Programs, like the Comprehensive Employment and Training Act (CETA), for all intents and purposes, were eliminated with a 96.4 percent cut from the previous year's outlays. The cuts were not as deep as the Reagan administration wanted because Congress was able to mediate many of them. But why weren't the cries louder? First, many suburban municipalities weren't adversely affected. They had few CETA workers and didn't compete for mass transit or other

TABLE 14.2 Current policy baseline and actual funding, select urban programs, fiscal 1982 (millions of dollars).

URBAN PROGRAM	ACTUAL FISCAL 1982		PERCENTAGE REDUCTION	
	BUDGET AUTHORITY	OUTLAYS	BUDGET AUTHORITY	OUTLAYS
Community development block grant	3456.0	4127.7	-11.1	-11.3
Urban development action grant	439.7	500.3	-33.6	-31.4
Comprehensive Employment and Training Act, public service employment	0.0	139.0	-100.0	-96.4
Mass transit	3497.7	3868.9	-30.0 ·	-3.5
Wastewater treatment	2400.0	4300.0	-32.3	4.0
Economic development administration	198.5	405.0	-67.5	-24.6
Compensatory education	3033.9	3105.0	-21.9	-8.8
Social services block grant	2580.0	2567.0	-21.3	-21.4
Community services block grant	348.0	376.0	-40.1	-36.5

Source: Adapted from Table 10. *Reagan and the Cities,* edited by George E. Peterson and Carol W. Lewis. (Washington, D.C.: The Urban Institute Press), 1986. Reprinted by permission.

federal grant funds. Second, state governments often filled the gaps in the programs for the poor. Third, Congress reduced the size of many of the proposed cuts. Finally, this was the decade of an unprecedented peacetime expansion of the national economy, and city budgets benefited. The combination of these factors reduced the impact of the change of federal policy on many cities.

In general, the cuts by the Reagan administration affected cities in two ways. In cities like Boston and San Diego, city administrators had reduced their dependence on federal funds years earlier. These cities had segregated federally funded programs from the operational budgets of the city. Police, fire, water, sewerage, and other basic services were funded by local revenues. Federal programs, in contrast, which provided special services to targeted groups, were cut back or eliminated when federal monies dried up. In these cities, federal cuts affected marginal groups and not city service budgets.

Other cities, like Detroit, were hard hit by the federal budget cuts. Over the years, they had integrated federal programs into their service budgets. In Detroit, CETA workers made up a significant part of police, fire, and service departments. Moreover, Detroit and other cities assumed that the federal monies would always be coming. When the ax fell in 1982 and 1983, Detroit was forced to lay off over 10 percent of their city workers, and city services and the quality of life in Detroit declined (Peterson, 1986).

In the short run, many of these changes were probably long overdue. But in the long run, these cuts have meant that the plight of the most disadvantaged citizens of this society worsened. The problem of the homeless in this society is directly attributable to the 81 percent cut in federal housing programs for low-income households in the early 1980s.

THE FISCAL PROBLEMS OF METROPOLITAN GOVERNMENTS

The vertical and horizontal intergovernmental relationships between a single central city and the hundreds of surrounding governments on the local level and the numerous agencies and departments on the state and federal levels form a tangled web of government. Closely tied to the problems created by the fragmentation of governmental jurisdiction are the increasingly serious fiscal problems of many of the nation's largest metropolitan areas. A growing crisis of urban government financing was recognized in 1968, by the presidentially appointed National Commission on Urban Problems. According to the commission, the impending crisis was brought about by (1) an increased demand for urban services, (2) a rapid rise in overall urban expenditures, (3) mounting opposition to urban taxation, and (4) the inability of most cities to tap the economic resources of the entire metropolitan area (1968, p. 355). These financial problems can be divided into two broad categories: problems associated with the costs of providing services and problems in raising revenues to pay for city services.

SERVICES AND THE CITY BUDGET

In the discussion of "The City and Its Fringe" in Chapter 8, the ecological factors responsible for the decentralization of people and industry are examined. Changing transportation technology is identified as a major factor permitting many activities to locate in the urban fringe. Other factors, such as the availability of affordable undeveloped land, a labor force, low taxes, and good schools and other institutions, also are considered in the locational decisions of individuals and business and industry. In many of the largest metropolises in the Northeast, heavy industry and an aged and obsolete housing stock have contributed to the flight of middle-class residents to the suburban rings. Business and industry have followed their markets and labor forces to the urban fringe areas, leaving behind the poor and minority groups in central cities. Because suburbs are outside the taxing jurisdictions of most central cities, the metropolis's central-city government is often faced with both diminishing tax resources and increasing service requirements of low-income residents.

THE PROBLEM OF HIGH-COST CITIZENS

The financial dilemmas of central cities in providing services to their high-cost citizens are exemplified by the situation in Essex County, New Jersey, which serves the city of Newark. In 1987, this city spent 32 percent of its local revenues on public welfare in comparison with the 12 percent of general revenue spent on welfare throughout the state. Moreover, the children of the poor require special education services that further strain the local government's limited financial resources. Newark is not an isolated example. In New York City, general expenditures for education in 1986 and 1987 were more than $5.1 billion, and public welfare expenditures were over $4.4 billion; in Baltimore, public welfare expenditures exceeded $628 million, and education exceeded $395 million during the same period; in Washington, D.C. public welfare expenditures exceeded $558 million, and public education exceeded $567 million (U.S. Bureau of the Census, 1990, Table 483, pp. 296–297). In a few states, where education and welfare are a municipal rather than a state or county function, state intervention has been necessary to avert financial disaster.

LOCAL GOVERNMENTAL EXPENDITURES

Table 14.3 is a summary of the local expenditures of 51 of the nation's largest metropolitan areas and the expenditures of all municipalities for the years 1986 and 1987. Note that services such as sewerage, fire protection, parks and recreation, and sanitation make up a higher percentage of large MSAs than all municipal expenditures. These slight percentage differences, if multiplied into the billions of dollars spent by local governments annually, represent tens of millions of more dollars spent by large metropolitan governments on basic services. These budgetary differences hint at the financial problems created by spillover.

SPILLOVER

Spillover refers to municipal services that are provided directly and indirectly to suburban populations, services for which the central city is never fully reimbursed. Examples are police, fire, sanitation, and sewer services that are provided to

TABLE 14.3 Local expenditures 1986–1987 (percent).

PURPOSE	ALL MUNICIPALITIES	51 LARGEST SMSAs
Education	11.7	13.5
Public welfare	5.0	9.8
Health and hospitals	5.8	7.2
Police protection	11.8	10.2
Transportation	15.0	13.0
Sewerage	7.3	5.5
Fire protection	8.2	5.0
Parks and recreation	4.8	4.0
Sanitation	3.6	3.2
Financial administration	7.2	5.6
Interest on general debt	7.4	6.8
Other	12.2	16.2
Total	100.0	100.0

Source: U.S. Bureau of the Census. *1987 Census of Government: Government Finances.* Washington, D.C.: U.S. Government Printing Office, Table 13.

commuters while they work in central cities. Parks, museums, and libraries are often supported through municipal budgets, though they are facilities that benefit an entire metropolis. Consequently, municipalities have a substantially higher per capita outlay for services than their suburban counterparts. In 1977, for example, the 37 largest central cities had a service outlay (excluding school expenditures) of $408 per person, a figure $100 greater than the service outlays of their neighbors.[2]

This pattern is shown vividly in Chapter 8, in the discussion of Berry and Kasarda's research on the impact of suburban population growth on the costs of central-city services. These investigators clearly demonstrate that suburban populations greatly influence the costs of providing police, fire, highway, sanitation, recreation, and general-administration functions to central cities. The pattern remains strong even when statistical controls are applied for city size, city age, per capita income, and percentage of a city's population that is nonwhite. Although suburban residents do partially reimburse central cities through employment and sales taxes, such revenues do not appear to be adequate to cover costs. The implication to city officials is clear: Attention must be given to trends in population growth in outlying areas when demand for city services is being projected.

FINANCING LOCAL GOVERNMENTS

Between 1945 and 1987, state and local revenue increased by more than 2700 percent, from $30 billion to over $844 billion (U.S. Bureau of the Census, 1987b). Though the amount sounds large, such revenue has not been adequate to meet urban needs. Interestingly, public officials have known for years of impending revenue shortfalls. In the early 1970s, the National Committee for Economic Development projected that between 1965 and 1975 urban revenues would increase by 87 percent and that urban expenditures would increase by 103 percent (Rasmussen, 1973, p. 141). Although this financial dilemma has long been predicted, little or nothing has been done to prevent it from reaching crisis proportions as in Philadelphia, New York, and other cities.

REVENUE SOURCES

Where does the money come from to finance local governments? Much of the money comes from federal and state aid to local governments, but these funds declined substantially in the 1980s. Note in Table 14.4 that in 1976 and 1977 nearly 39.6 percent of municipal revenue came from federal and state sources; by 1986 and 1987, this percentage had dropped ten percentage points to just 29 percent. To make up the revenue shortfalls, municipal governments have relied heavily on special assessments, service fees, and other special taxes. Note that the category, "other revenue" doubled between 1976 and 1977 and 1986 and 1987.

The property tax. Whereas federal revenues are derived largely from individual and corporate income taxes and states have increasingly relied on sales and income taxes,

TABLE 14.4 Sources of municipal revenue (in percent).

	1976–1977	1986–1987
Fiscal aid[a]	39.6	29.0
Property taxes	25.7	20.7
Sales taxes[b]	9.6	12.0
Income taxes[c]	3.1	2.9
Current charges[d]	11.2	16.8
Other revenues[e]	10.8	20.4

[a]Includes both federal and state aid to local governments.
[b]Includes general and specific taxes and gross receipts taxes.
[c]Includes business and personal income taxes.
[d]Includes such charges as those for education, hospitals, and sewerage.
[e]Includes, for example, miscellaneous taxes, special assessments and interest income.
Source: 1976-77 Data adapted from U.S. Bureau of the Census, *1977 Census of Governments: Finances of Municipalities and Township Governments.* Washington, D.C.: U.S. Government Printing Office, 1978, p. 9.

property taxes still are the largest source of locally collected revenues, constituting two-thirds of the total. This tax, however, has always been unpopular, partly because of inequitable tax rules and also because tax payments normally must be made in one lump sum (Stedman, 1972, p. 66). Property taxes apply to real property, such as land and buildings. The tax is based on an assessment, which is an estimate of the cash value of a property. For example, a person's house may be appraised at a cash value of $50,000. The rate of assessment may be 10 percent of the cash value, or $5000. If the rate of taxation is 5 percent of the assessed value ($50,000), then the property tax would be $250. Property taxes, however, usually are erroneously assessed below real property values and are often assessed so as to place the greatest burden on private homeowners, thereby favoring business and industry (Goodall, 1968).

Other tax revenues. Inequities are also built into other taxes used on the local level. A local sales tax not only increases the price of any retail item, but also is regressive in that the poor must pay the same rate as the wealthy. Local income taxes also favor the wealthy if they are based on one's federal income tax. Finally, some cities tax utilities. Large users of these utilities, such as industry, are usually charged at a lower rate than an average citizen (La Greca, 1977, p. 387).

REVENUE LIMITATIONS

The revenues that can be raised by locally-based taxes are limited. In the case of property taxes, certain properties, such as churches, state and federal buildings, universities, and military bases, are exempt from local tax rules. High local income taxes and sales taxes fall most heavily on poor families and may accelerate the movement of the middle class and business to the suburbs, where taxes are lower. However, the greatest financial problem facing central cities is the fiscal fragmentation that typifies most metropolitan areas. Although residents of suburbs utilize the central city for shopping, employment, and recreation, the central city has no effective way of taxing these separately incorporated areas. Clearly, local sources of tax revenues lack the flexibility of state and federal income taxes. The higher levels of government have wider taxing authority, and their ability to tax such intangible assets as savings accounts, bonds, and stocks gives them resources that are simply unavailable to local jurisdictions.

In the 1970s, the federal government taxed this broader base of wealth and returned a portion to state and local governments through the general revenue-sharing program. This program, however, ended in the early 1980s. Today, to raise revenues, local governments must depend on a variety of new taxes and user charges, which often hit the poor the hardest.

THE ROLE OF BIG BUSINESS IN THE FISCAL PROBLEMS OF THE CITY

No analysis of a city's fiscal problems would be complete without recognizing the importance of big business to urban America.[3] For example, it would be impossible to conceive of America's major cities without America's largest business firms. In 1965, Robert Heilbroner (1965) described what would happen to America's cities if this nation's 150 largest firms were suddenly obliterated:

> Not only would the Union and the Southern Pacific, the Pennsylvania, the New York Central, and a half dozen of the other main railroads of the nation vanish [since 1965 they have been part of the federally subsidized Conrail System], leaving the cities to starve, but the possibilities of supplying the urban population by truck would also disappear as the main gasoline companies and the tire companies—not to mention the makers of cars and trucks—would also cease to exist. Meanwhile, within the nine largest concentrations of urban population all activity would have stopped with the termination of light and power, as the utilities in these areas would break down with the disappearance of the telephone company (pp. 11–12).

The above gives a somewhat disturbing picture of the close tie between the large corporations and the well-being of the American city. It gives only a partial picture; it fails to show the pervasive influence of corporations on the entire economy. At present, the corporate sector of the American economy employs nearly half of all those gainfully employed. Moreover, 56 percent of the national income is generated by corporations, and this pattern has remained stable since the 1950s. These figures are for all corporations and do not show the influence of this nation's largest corporations. In 1980, the top 100 industrial firms accounted for half the value added by manufacturing, a third of the manufacturing payroll, a fourth of the manufacturing labor force, about half of all capital expended for new purchases, and over half of the assets of all manufacturers (Feagin and Parker, 1990). Put another way, less than 2 percent of all manufacturing firms in the United States accounted for 88 percent of all net profits in manufacturing. As the Committee for Economic Development states it, "the large corporations are the dominant producers in the industries in which they operate, and their influence is pervasive throughout the business world and much of society" (1971, pp. 18–19).

Since the influence of this nation's largest corporations is so pervasive in the American political economy, it is little wonder that the decisions they make are closely related to the fate of the cities. It appears that corporate decision making influences American cities in at least two major ways: (1) in the redistribution of population and jobs and (2) in the erosion of a city's tax base.

Redistribution of population and jobs. Americans are the most mobile population in the world, with approximately 20 percent of us moving annually. Of these forty million Americans who move to a different home annually, more than half the moves are the result of job changes or corporate transfers. For cities, this movement is a mixed blessing. On the positive side, high rates of residential mobility mean a more open housing market. On the negative side, those leaving a city are usually the most affluent (Nelson, 1988). This loss, of course, can be balanced if there is an equal number of in-migrants with the same or higher economic status, but this is usually not the case in America's older central cities, where large numbers of less affluent minorities, especially blacks,. have been concentrating.

Closely related to this redistribution of population is the redistribution of jobs within and between metropolitan areas. Here corporate decisions directly affect the fiscal well-being of a city. Since World War II, as noted in Chapter 10, corporations have found it in their best interests to locate manufacturing and industry in urban fringe areas. As blue-collar jobs were created in the suburbs, white-collar job opportunities rose in the central cities, since corporations doing business in finance, insurance, real estate, and various services invested in downtown locations. These processes have led to a mismatching of job skills and places of residence. The poor and minorities who live in a central city need suburban blue-collar jobs but often are unable to afford the costs of commuting to the suburban ring.

This is only part of the story. Corporate decision making contributes to the redistribution of population and jobs between metropolitan areas in different regions. The dramatic growth of the Sunbelt cities (See Chapter 7.) is in large part the result of corporate growth in this region. In all employment areas, except service jobs, there have been declines of employment in manufacturing, wholesaling, and retailing in the Northeast, while, in the Sunbelt states, all metropolitan areas have experienced dramatic increases in each category. Since the poor are the least able to migrate from one region to another, these corporate decisions may have contributed to the creation of a permanent unemployed underclass in many of the mature cities of the Northeast.

Decentralization of business and erosion of the tax base. The decentralization of business and industry make it clear that central cities are not in a position to influence large corporations. In the few cases where local officials have formally challenged the policies and actions of businesses, corporations have seldom found it difficult to get higher levels of government or the courts to intervene on their behalf.

To maintain and bolster their economies, local officials have had to make concessions in the form of tax incentives to businesses in order to induce them to remain or relocate within the city's borders. Cleveland, after years of economic stagnation and physical decline in its central business district, instituted a series of tax incentives to attract business to its downtown. The corporations that moved to Cleveland have usually been exempt from property taxation. The result is that other property owners, especially homeowners, must pay a disproportionate share of the costs of running the city. Thus, the ability of corporations to move freely between cities and across state lines makes it impossible to compel large businesses to be more financially responsible to local areas. They are free to exact whatever financial concessions they can from cities and states.

In general, this chapter shows that many metropolitan areas have problems that greatly transcend their financial ability to deal with these problems. A partial solution in recent years has been to increase the role of the federal government in city finances. Revenue sharing is one mechanism whereby the federal government can use its broad taxing authority to lessen central-city financial problems. A second mechanism is to create a national policy compelling large businesses to be more financially responsible to local areas. The federal chartering of corporations and the imposition of tax penalties on corporations that abandon a community are two possible solutions. Thus, the fiscal problems of a city are multifaceted and require not only the cooperation of federal, state, and local governments but also a new relationship with big business, given its influence over our political and social institutions.

THE STRUCTURE OF THE METROPOLIS AND ITS RELATIONSHIP TO FRAGMENTED LOCAL GOVERNMENTS

The chapter to this point has shown that the present fragmented structure of metropolitan government is the end product of a long evolutionary process. That is, the present structure of metropolitan government represents the accumulated effect of decisions made by community leaders in the past in an attempt to solve urban problems. It is important to note that this decision-making process took place within the limits imposed by the organizational structure, technology, and environmental resources of the time. Present metropolitan structure can be understood best by examining the ecological processes that shaped it.

THE CITY IN THE NINETEENTH CENTURY

Through most of the nineteenth century, the fragmentation of local government authority was not a problem because cities were compact, densely settled places, usually no more than three or four miles in diameter. This settlement pattern was dictated by the primitive transportation of the time—horse and foot travel—and groups and institutions were located close to each other out of necessity. Moreover, this was the century in which the nation was transformed from an agrarian-rural to an industrial-urban society. This process drew millions of rural Americans and foreign immigrants to the cities in search of industrial employment, and, by accommodating these masses, cities increased in overall population density. The transportation technology to move people cheaply and efficiently within a city had not yet been invented. As a result, in the second half of the nineteenth century, population densities in cities like Chicago and New York exceeded 100,000 persons per square mile. Not surprisingly, many of this century's most serious urban problems have been related to high population density, and the solution most favored has been to decentralize population.

A breakthrough in transportation technology. The technological breakthrough needed to decongest America's cities came in the last quarter of the nineteenth century with the introduction of the electric trolley. It provided relatively cheap and efficient short-distance travel and enabled large cities to expand from a diameter of three to four miles to a diameter of seven to eight miles. Later in that century, rapid-transit trains extended the distance a person could conveniently commute to the city to between 10 and 20 miles.

The application of rail technology to cities signaled the beginning of the widespread decentralization of urban population and the emergence of the present-day metropolitan structure. Improved transportation meant that people no longer needed to live within walking distance of their place of employment. Places of employment and places of residence became increasingly separated. Similarly, services no longer needed to be distributed across each district of the city, as they had been in the pedestrian city. They could now be concentrated in a specialized subarea—the central business district. The central business district, as a result, became the organizational hub of the city. Rail lines spreading outward from a city's center began to bring outlying small towns and villages under the city's economic and social influence. Although these outlying communities were transformed into suburbs and bedroom communities by the nearby city, they usually retained their political autonomy. They were governmentally independent, but were part of the metropolitan structure. Thus, the seeds of metropolitan government fragmentation were sown.

THE TWENTIETH-CENTURY METROPOLITAN COMMUNITY

As noted in Chapter 9, the intraurban rail system was inflexible and restricted the expansion of a city to those areas near the rail lines. Cities took on a starlike shape with a central core and suburban appendages. The widespread adoption of the motor vehicle in the twentieth century permitted the development of the previously inaccessible fringe areas between the rail lines. The speed and flexibility of the automobile combined with a complex intraurban highway system led to a rapid decentralization of population and the present-day metropolitan structure. The car also expanded the commuting distance to up to fifty miles.

The impact of automobile technology on metropolitan structures. Automobile technology enabled central cities to draw increasing numbers of small towns and villages under their influence, and, as these communities grew, they took on specialized functions.

Some communities that were once low-order central places became bedroom communities. Others were transformed into industrial suburbs. Still others, because of their strategic ecological position, became commercial satellites. All of these communities, however, now have two features in common. First, they are integral parts of a metropolitan community. They are often specialized in a particular function that contributes to the operation of the entire metropolitan system. Second, they are communities with histories and governments of their own. Although under the social and economic influence of a central city, they normally retain their own political identity. Thus, they are economically dependent but politically autonomous.

The process whereby the metropolis expands outward and envelops already existing communities is only one aspect of fringe development. Fringe growth does not always take place around existing towns and villages. Much of it occurs in new suburbs built in unincorporated and undeveloped areas of the fringe. These areas spring up because of nearby employment in a central city (or employing suburb), but the ability of central cities to annex these adjacent areas is severely limited in most states by state constitutions and public laws.

FACTORS CONTRIBUTING TO METROPOLITAN GOVERNMENT FRAGMENTATION

The present fragmented nature of metropolitan government is the result of a number of interrelated factors. One factor is normal ecological processes. Much of the decentralization of population, business, and industry that has occurred in the post-World War II period is the normal response of these activities to changing transportation and industrial technology and to expanding regional and national markets.

A second factor is the decision of this nation's leadership, at all levels of government, to use decentralization as the major solution to urban problems. FHA and VA loans, categorical grants by the federal government for suburban water and sewerage systems, and a high-speed intraurban highway system financed by the Highway Trust Fund are examples of direct subsidies to urban areas that encourage fringe development.

A third factor is recalcitrant and unresponsive state legislatures and rigid and inflexible state constitutions and public laws. Their combined effect has been to make annexation and governmental consolidation impossible.

A fourth factor is the sheer inertia of historical patterns and the unwillingness of small suburban governments to relinquish control to a central authority.

Finally, the social, racial, and ethnic cleavages in American society also contribute to governmental fragmentation of metropolitan areas. Present political structures represent a century of compromises that have formalized the relations between groups and have limited their social interaction.

THE METROPOLIS—AN ECOLOGICAL SYSTEM

A major theme in the second half of the text is the integrated nature of a metropolitan community. Changes in the scale of American society have led to the emergence of specialized subareas of a city—a mosaic of social worlds. Each subarea specializes in a particular function that contributes to the overall functioning of the metropolis. Together they form an ecological system. In this context, the discussion of the suburbanization process in Chapter 10 is particularly relevant. The most recent literature on the suburbs clearly shows that suburbs represent one of the ways cities can grow. Cities can accommodate population growth by maintaining boundaries and increasing population density or by populating fringe areas. In America, the latter process prevails. This process has been viewed as unique because a highly fragmented political structure has been superimposed over the metropolitan community. It is not fringe development that is unusual, but rather the system that has evolved to govern it.

INSTITUTIONAL AND ECOLOGICAL RESPONSES TO GOVERNMENTAL FRAGMENTATION

The hundreds of government units that operate within most large metropolitan areas and the complex intergovernmental relations that have developed among them might appear to be an unworkable system. But this nation's metropolises do work. A number of structures have developed over the years to link political units and aid them in their operation. In the public sphere, the rapid increase in the use of special districts and the expanding role of the federal government in urban affairs are two examples. In the private sphere, managerial and coordinating functions have become more concentrated in the central cities.

Special districts. The use of special districts has increased rapidly in this century because they are flexible governmental units that can effectively span political boundaries. An independent water district is a formal and politically safe way for a central city and suburban government to come together to solve a common problem. Special districts, therefore, provide important linkages between governments on the metropolitan level that permit them to coordinate certain service functions.

The expanding role of the federal government. Since the 1930s, the relationship between the federal and local governments has changed dramatically; it is becoming another institutional response to the fragmentation of metropolitan government. A major problem faced by many central-city governments is the large number of high-service-cost citizens who live in a city that has a shrinking tax base: The financial resources are concentrated in the suburban ring outside the taxing jurisdiction of the central city. In response to this problem, President Nixon signed into law the 1972 State and Local Fiscal Assistance Act, commonly known as general revenue sharing. Under this act, $6 billion a year was to be turned over to state and local governments. One-third of the money was to be given to the states, and two-thirds to local government units. Under the provisions of this legislation, states can spend their funds for any normal and customary purpose, whereas local governments are required to spend their funds for "priority expenditures" and necessary and ordinary capital expenditures (Caputo, 1976, p. 143)—fire and police services, environmental protection, public transportation, health and hospitals, recreation and culture, libraries, financial administration, and social services. Obviously, these categories are so broad that local governments have been able to use considerable discretion in the allocation of funds.

Revenue sharing enables a central city to tap the wealth of its surrounding suburban ring. Ironically, however, these monies that could travel directly only a few miles from suburb to city, instead travel indirectly thousands of miles from the suburban community to the central city via Washington, D.C.

The expanding role of the metropolis's center. A third response to governmental fragmentation often is overlooked by students of a metropolis—the expanding role of the metropolis's center. Berry and Kasarda (1977) found in their study of 157 SMSAs that the expansion of the peripheral areas of metropolitan communities is matched with a parallel development of organizational functions in their centers. Central cities are much more developed in their coordinative and integrative functions than their suburban rings, and the number of these functions increases as the size of the suburban ring expands (p. 209). Thus, changes in both the private and governmental spheres have helped to link and coordinate the operation of the metropolitan community.

POLICY ALTERNATIVES

Public policy does not occur in a vacuum. It is shaped by the political, social, and economic climate of the times. Moreover, past decisions limit the alternatives available to present decision makers in their search for solutions to urban problems. For example, the nation's inability to become less dependent on foreign oil is directly related to past policies that have made the automobile the dominant form of intraurban transportation in the United States. These policies, formulated decades ago, were based on the assumption that energy supplies would always be cheap and plentiful. Therefore, the central issue facing policy makers at all levels of American society is the impact their decisions will have on the quality of life in the future. "This issue is extremely important at the urban level, because policy decisions made by urban leaders inevitably will have a direct and measurable influence on the lifestyles and individual alternatives and destinies of the citizens residing in their particular urban area" (Caputo, 1975, p. 12).

If individuals do exercise some control over their own destiny and the destiny of their society, three broad policy alternatives are available to the leaders who must address the problems of administrative and fiscal fragmentation of the metropolis.

POLICY ALTERNATIVE I—THE STATUS QUO

One alternative is for leaders to do nothing, to accept the status quo and continue to work within the tangle of governmental jurisdictions on the local level. This approach appears to have been chosen in most large metropolitan areas, possibly because it was the only alternative. Even if a city is on the verge of total financial collapse, the structure of local government normally is not changed. Rather, cosmetic changes are made in the existing structure. New York City, for example, in recent years has had difficulty in meeting its payroll and other financial obligations and has been on the verge of bankruptcy.

In 1990, a variety of unpleasant alternatives faced Mayor Dinkens. Since mounting financial problems faced the federal government and the state of New York, Mayor Dinkens had no choice but to slash city programs, lay off city employees, and draw up an austerity budget that put the city on firmer financial ground.

Similarly, Philadelphia, after years of financial mismanagement, is on the verge of bankruptcy. Unable to secure loans from local banks or state and federal sources, Mayor Goode has made cutbacks in public housing, libraries, and food services. In the coming months, the city is planning even deeper staff cuts. Unless the state of Pennsylvania intervenes, the city will be unable to meet its payroll by mid-1991, and it may be the first major metropolitan government to go into bankruptcy since the Great Depression.

New York City and Philadelphia are not alone. The National League of Cities found more than 50 cities in serious financial trouble in a recent survey of city financial officers (Hey, 1991). The financial problems of these cities stem from two sources: The first is the continued decentralization of wealth to the suburbs and the shrinking tax base that results; the second is the nation's economic slowdown of 1990 and 1991, which takes a further bite into city budgets. Complicating matters is the fact that the federal and state governments demand services for the poor, but do not provide funding. Regardless of who is at fault, cities have begun to live within their means. Cuts in services negatively affect the quality of life of all their citizens, but have their greatest impact on minority groups and the economically disadvantaged.

POLICY ALTERNATIVE II—CENTRALIZATION AND CONSOLIDATION

A second policy alternative is to centralize fiscal and governmental jurisdictions in a single governmental unit on the local level and in some cases (for example, transportation, water, and sewer) on the regional level. This alternative was recommended by the Advisory Commission on Intergovernmental Relations. They suggested the following steps (1974, pp. 17–18):

1. The equitable distribution of the costs and benefits of elementary and secondary education and public welfare requires broadening the geographic base of support. State governments should assume the costs of financing education, whereas the federal government should assume the responsibility for public assistance.

2. Because the federal government has the widest tax base and the greatest fiscal power, the commission recommended that intergovernmental fund transfers, in the form of revenue sharing, be increased.

3. A more rational and ordered approach should be taken to both local and state tax efforts, including the rehabilitation of the property tax and an equalization of taxes between local governmental units, such as central cities and their suburbs.

In terms of consolidating governmental jurisdiction, the commission recommended the following (1974, pp. 84–87):

1. In the short run, new regionalized agencies should be superimposed over the existing governmental structures to plan and coordinate transportation and other activities that have a true regional character.

2. All functions and responsibilities should be expanded to the broadest governmental units possible—for example, metropolitan government.

The solutions suggested in the commission's recommendations refer to consolidation, that is, the entire metropolitan area, or the county of which it is a part, should be consolidated under one government. Most consolidations, however, have not been so all-encompassing. In the United States, most consolidations have been designed to cope with a specific problem shared by all communities in a particular metropolis, a problem that requires the coordination of all major governmental units in the metropolitan area. Examples are problems in transportation, pollution, and water and sewer systems.

One example of consolidation has been regional committees. In the 1960s, Washington, D.C. established a regional metropolitan committee on transportation problems composed of delegates from the District of Columbia, Maryland, and Virginia. The committee has had mixed success in alleviating the traffic congestion caused by people commuting into the District. Nationally, such consolidation in transportation and other areas has met with mixed success. Typically, boards have been hampered by organizational problems and limited jurisdiction.

There have been several notable successes in consolidation. In the 1960s and 1970s, Jacksonville, Florida, and the surrounding county and city governments in Duval County and Miami, Florida, and the surrounding governments in Dade County consolidated their operations into a single governmental unit. Nashville, Tennessee, and Oklahoma City, Oklahoma, are additional examples of successful consolidation efforts in the nation. Are these models for the rest of the nation? Probably not. First, most states have stringent laws governing consolidation. Second, it is nearly impossible to persuade suburban voters to approve consolidation. Most communities surrounding central cities either have been there for generations or were developed by people who fled the problems of the central city (La Greca, 1977). These people see little or no advantage in coming under the jurisdiction of one central government.

POLICY ALTERNATIVE III—DECENTRALIZATION

The third possible alternative is to decentralize urban governments. This idea is based on the assumption that when a city grows to more than some critical size, say 100,000 people, the population becomes too large for the city government to be both responsive and representative. Major proponents argue that decentralization would "contribute to improved urban governance by achieving a greater sense of community, redressing an imbalance of power, making public services more effective, promoting the public order, and opening more opportunities for personal development" (Hallman, 1974, p. 12).

There is a long tradition of employing neighborhoods as the geographical basis for city organization. In Chapter 9, the community theory of Robert Park was reviewed. Park analyzed "natural areas" (a term synonymous with neighborhood), seeing them as important spatial units that helped groups of people with similar characteristics to satisfy "fundamental needs and solve fundamental problems." In addition, the functional interdependency that developed among these homogeneous subareas was viewed by Park as the basis for the integration and solidarity of a city.

In the late nineteenth and early twentieth centuries, neighborhoods were the basis for political organization. Urban political machines in New York, Chicago, and elsewhere were built on a foundation of precinct committees. Political reform in this century has stressed nonpartisan elections carried out on a citywide rather than a precinct basis, thus diminishing the political influence of neighborhoods.

Finally, planners, educators, and social welfare workers have long seen neighborhoods as an important social element of a city. Settlement houses, first organized in the United States in the 1880s, served their surrounding neighborhoods. Similarly, community planners and educators have stressed the role of schools as multiple-use centers, drawing residents of a neighborhood together as a community.

Regardless of the historical precedent for using neighborhoods as the basis for city organization, there also appear to be some very pragmatic reasons for considering this use. First, neighborhoods are usually shared by people with similar racial, ethnic, and socioeconomic characteristics. Second, their neighborhood, not their city, is the reference point for most residents. Third, each neighborhood has a unique combination of needs and problems brought on by the characteristics of its people, the age of its housing, and its proximity to the central city. Kotler (1969) and others argue that only neighborhood government can be sensitive to these needs and problems.

In recent years, there have been attempts by many cities to decentralize political and administrative functions. These attempts fall into three broad categories. The first has been the decentralization of administrative and management functions to neighborhoods with retention of political control in central-city government. In the 1970s, New York City began a program of decentralized administration of municipal services. The program included redistricting of police, fire, sanitation, and other service boundaries, formal delegation of increased powers to district personnel, formation of district service cabinets, and appointment of district managers along with small staffs. The district manager served as chairman of the district service cabinet that consisted of field supervisors from city agencies such as city planning, environmental protection, fire, housing, health services, police, and transportation. The rationale for the program was that the district manager and his cabinet were closer to the community that they serve and therefore had a better grasp of the needs of people and were more likely to be responsive to citizen demands. Similar programs have been tried in San Antonio and Washington, D.C. (Hallman, 1974, pp. 88–103).

A second approach has been to decentralize political functions while central-city government retains administrative control over basic city services. A number of cities, most notably Los Angeles, Houston, Boston, and Baltimore, opened neighborhood city halls or multiservice centers. In Boston, for example, little city halls emerged as neighborhood extensions of the mayor's office. Each little city hall was headed by a manager, whose primary role was to serve as the mayor's representative. Although these representatives provided information and referral services, they were not administrators of municipal services carried out on the neighborhood level. The majority of their time was spent in dealing with community issues, meeting with civic groups, conferring with residents, talking with the staff of city agencies, and developing plans for community schools. In general, they emerged as community leaders, acting as spokespeople for city government's interest while also identifying with neighborhood opinion when they communicated with the main city hall. Thus, rather than being neighborhood city managers, they functioned more as neighborhood mayors (Hallman, 1974, pp. 106–17).

A third approach, tried in Columbus, Ohio, Washington, D.C., and many other American cities, has been the formation of nonprofit neighborhood corporations outside of the political and administrative structure of city government. The majority of these organizations were organized to take advantage of federal grants that provided funds to pay the costs of administration and neighborhood service programs.

This third policy alternative, decentralizing city functions, has been tried in a number of American cities with mixed success. This policy alternative looks at problems in relation to the concept of neighborhood. Neighborhoods as conceived by Kotler (1969) and Hallman (1974) simply do not exist in large metropolitan areas. As explained in Chapter 9, social and psychological attachments to local areas are now of a partial and very fragmented character. Second, autonomous neighborhood governments probably could not generate the financial resources necessary to provide basic services. Finally, neighborhood controls could thwart efforts to achieve racial integration and other national goals.

WHICH POLICY ALTERNATIVE?

The question remains of which policy alternative would be most effective. Theoretically, consolidation would be the most judicious. As is stressed throughout the second half of this text, a metropolis is an ecological system. It is impossible to separate the operation of one area of a city from all others. This interdependence among the various elements of a metropolitan system is evident in the daily ebb and flow of people between the central city and its suburban ring. White-collar workers commuting to a central city for work often pass blue-collar workers traveling to their jobs in the factories in the suburban ring. Moreover, the locations of the factories, offices, and businesses are tied to changes in the ecological complex—population, organization, environment, and technology—forces operating across a metropolis as a whole, not just in one area.

Theoretically, it would make sense to remove political boundaries that often impede, if not distort, the rational distribution of people and institutions across the metropolitan landscape. Realistically, consolidation is seldom a feasible policy alternative. First, no two metropolitan governments have exactly the same ecological and political structures, so a structure of government well-suited to the needs of one unit may be unsuited to another. Second, major economic, social, racial, and political cleavages exist in American society that cannot be ignored. The present governmental structure of the metropolis is one means of resolving the conflict among these groups. Third, any system constructed by human beings will be imperfect. Finally, in a democracy, ideally the majority prevails. The present patterns of intergovernmental relationships on the local level, as well as at higher levels, are the result of political compromises made since the conception of the nation more than 200 years ago. Their evolution is a continuing process. Local governmental units will continue to respond to metropolitan needs, modifying their functions and structures, although at a rate slower than many Americans would like.

EPILOGUE

A thread woven through this entire chapter is that cities are part of a complicated web of governmental relationships. Problems on the local level really cannot be addressed without the help of state and federal governments. First, cities do not have the taxing authority they need, and many of the problems are not of their own making: They are national problems played out on the local level. In my opinion, many urban problems result from an absence of a coherent national urban policy.

Since World War II, the focus of the nation's urban policy has changed from housing and urban renewal to employment and job training and enrichment, and from community development and neighborhood revitalization to benign neglect. Through much of this period, federal programs have been designed to prime local economies. They assumed that if developers and employers prospered, then unemployment and poverty would disappear. Massive federal subsidies have reshaped our urban scapes, but who have they benefited? Has the money pumped in at the top of our society trickled down to those in need? Urban renewal in the 1950s and 1960s, model cities and other social action programs in the 1960s, community and neighborhood development programs in the 1970s, and the community empowerment movement in the 1980s have seldom benefited those they were intended to help. If you ask critically, "Who were the programs designed for, and who did they benefit?" the answer is usually the same—those at the top of the power structure.

As noted earlier, the Reagan administration brought a new perspective to social policy in general and urban policy in particular. To quote Ronald Reagan, "Government is not the solution, government is the problem." Swept into office by two of the largest majorities in our electoral history, the Reagan presidency reflected a growing conservatism in the nation. The conservative agenda assumed that government cannot address the problems of our cities or those of the poor. And, if you look at our social history, you find a landscape littered with good intentions. Our past failures seem to say that government cannot solve our urban problems, but maybe the wrong question is being asked. Does federal policy affect the life chances of specific groups in our society? If federal policy improves the material condition of one group, then federal policy can improve conditions in our cities.

Reagan's social policy has four elements: tax bracket reduction, reduction of federal domestic spending, deregulation of business and industry, and tight control of the money supply, which favored lenders over debtors. But the centerpiece of the Reagan era was tax-bracket reduction. Table 14.5 shows the effective shift in federal tax rates and the resulting shift in average family income between 1977 and 1988. Note that benefits were skewed to the top 5 percent of the American population. The top 1 percent of all families experienced a 6.0 drop in their effective federal tax rate and a whopping 50 percent increase in their mean family income. Federal budget policy also dramatically redirected federal policies away from domestic programs towards defense and kept real interest levels at historically high levels, again benefiting those at the top of the income ladder. In the 1980s, federal policies created one of the greatest transfers of wealth in history. Social policy transferred enormous wealth and income from low- and middle-income families to the wealthiest. Governmental policies, therefore, effected social change.

In the area of urban policy, the Reagan administration assumed that cities were part of a national economy. Regional and urban growth and decline, in their view, was the natural result of economic change. To interfere with this natural process was simply delaying the inevitable. The message to cities was pay the painful costs now and benefit later. But did the federal government create a level playing field for this Darwinian

TABLE 14.5 Tax rate of income changes, 1977–1988.

CHANGES IN AVERAGE FAMILY INCOME (1987 DOLLARS)

INCOME DECILE	AVERAGE FAMILY INCOME		PERCENTAGE CHANGE	PERCENTAGE CHANGE IN EFFECTIVE TAX RATE
	1977	*1988*	*1977–88*	*1977–1988*
First	$ 4,113	$ 3,504	-14.8	+1.6
Second	8,334	7,669	-8.0	- .4
Third	13,140	12,327	-6.2	+1.3
Fourth	18,436	17,220	-6.6	+ .6
Fifth	23,896	22,389	-6.3	+ .1
Sixth	29,824	28,205	-5.4	- .1
Seventh	36,405	34,828	-4.3	- .7
Eighth	44,305	43,507	-1.8	0
Ninth	55,487	56,064	1.0	+ .2
Tenth	102,722	119,635	16.5	-1.7
Top 5%	134,543	166,016	23.4	-2.6
Top 1%	270,053	404,566	49.8	-6.0
All Families	33,527	34,274	2.2	

Source: Adapted from Kevin Phillips. *The Politics of Rich and Poor.* New York: Random House, 1990, Tables 1 and 3.

economic competition to take place? The answer is no. The shift of population and economic activity between the Sunbelt and Snowbelt, as we saw in Chapter 7, was due to a massive federal subsidy of Sunbelt development for most of this century. The evidence is clear: Federal policies shape regional and urban growth. The problem is that federal urban policy is often indirect, and the result of programs and policies designed for other problems. All too often, federal agencies are at cross purposes. The nation's transportation policy is not coordinated with our economic policies; our human resource policies are not coordinated with our health policies, and our housing policies are not coordinated with our neighborhood development policies. Since the majority of our people live in urban places and we all live our lives on the local, not the national level, doesn't it make sense that we should have a national urban policy? Doesn't it make sense that our national government, the capstone of our federal system, should coordinate policies that cushion the social costs of economic change on the local level?

Kevin Phillips in his thought-provoking book, *The Politics of Rich and Poor,* argues that our political pendulum is swinging back to a national domestic agenda. National icons like Ivan Boskey and Michael Milkin, have been convicted of felonies; The viewership of shows like *Dallas, Dynasty,* and *Lifestyles of the Rich and Famous* has plummeted, and Americans are now repulsed by the arrogance and avarice of people like Donald Trump. Many of the cuts in federal low-income housing programs have been restored; President Bush has announced that he wants to be known as the education president; national health insurance is being debated. Out of all this debate, it is my hope that policy makers will appreciate the fact that national problems are played out on the local level, and problems like homelessness and AIDS cannot be addressed without federal help. If federal policies in the past decade could bring about one of the greatest redistributions of wealth in our nation's history, then a coherent federal urban policy could begin the long and painful process of reconstituting our urban places.

SUMMARY

This chapter is an overview of government's structure and role in metropolises and government's impact on urban problems. The American governmental structure originally was set forth in the Tenth Amendment to the United States Constitution, which delegates all powers not conferred on the federal government to the states. Municipalities and other local governments are not mentioned in the Constitution, and, therefore, they are under the jurisdiction of the states. Local government units are created by the states through a charter, a document setting forth a city's form of government, powers, and duties to its citizens. Because charters have been strictly interpreted, a city's powers are limited, in some cases to the point of a city's inability to solve its problems.

Originally, the basic units of American government were counties and municipalities, except in the Northeast, where many county functions were carried out by townships. Counties are subdivisions of a state and provide services (such as courts, tax collection, elections, and road maintenance) to a local population. Similarly, municipalities provide essential services, such as water, sewer, sanitation, and police and fire protection, to densely populated areas of a state. Though county and municipal boundaries commonly overlap, the two forms of government usually provide different services to the population.

Special districts are another form of local government. School districts were the first special districts. They were formed in the nineteenth century to provide public education to a state's school-age population. Other types of special districts are water, sewer, fire, park, library, and police districts. They range in size from a few city blocks to several counties and differ considerably in organization. Their boards may be elected or appointed. Their great flexibility is one reason for their appeal, and they have grown rapidly in number in the twentieth century as a means of addressing many urban problems.

The proliferation of special districts and the separate incorporation of suburban communities adjoining a metropolis's central city have led to a fragmentation of local government. The negative aspects of fragmentation include: (1) problems in coordination of the numerous governments in a single metropolis, (2) problems of exercising effective leadership and setting coherent policy, and (3) the underutilization of the nation's limited managerial talent by the dispersal of capable individuals throughout the metropolis.

The relationships among governments on the same local level are called *horizontal intergovernmental relations.* Local governments also have ties to both the state and national governments. These ties, called *vertical intergovernmental relations,* have changed dramatically in the twentieth century.

During the Depression of the 1930s, states and cities turned to the national government for funds. Programs designed to be temporary later became the basis of massive federal programs to the states and cities. These programs involve fund transfers of two major types—categorical grants and block grants. Categorical grants are usually provided for a single specific purpose, such as public housing or urban renewal, and require a detailed grant application, a tedious review process, and federal government audits to ensure compliance with the guidelines set forth in the legislation creating the program. The red tape, high administrative costs on both the local and national levels, and abuses of the guidelines and goals of many programs have led to the creation of block grant programs.

Block grants permit great latitude in local needs assessment, program development, and budgeting. They give local leaders, those closest to the problems of cities, wide discretionary power in how the monies are used and minimize the federal government's role in the program. The Community Development Block Grant Program is one example of this type of fund transfer. Under the Reagan administration, cities were forced to solve their problems on their own.

The fragmentation of local governmental juridications, combined with the decentralization of population, business, and industry to politically autonomous suburbs, has created severe fiscal problems for central cities. In general, the problems of central cities can be divided into two broad categories—providing services and raising revenues.

One of the major problems of central cities is providing services to low-income residents. These people are high-cost citizens, requiring services not demanded by middle- and upper-income groups. Central cities also are forced to provide services to commuters from the suburbs for which they are never fully compensated. The large number of these citizens, combined with the spillover of services, adds to the financial plight of cities.

In terms of revenue, the amount of tax money that can be collected locally is limited. First, a central city has no taxing jurisdiction in areas outside its boundaries. Raising property, sales, and local income taxes only drives more businesses and middle-class persons out to the suburbs and unfairly taxes the poor. For this reason, central cities and other local governments have increasingly turned to the federal government, which has a broader tax base and taxing authority, to generate funds that can be channeled to the local level. General and special revenue sharing are examples of this intergovernmental transfer of funds, but this program ended in the early 1980s.

The rapid expansion of the nation's fringe areas is viewed as a normal response of urban areas to economic and technological change. In the nineteenth century, trolleys and high-speed trains permitted the first decentralization of population. In the twentieth century, this process continued, aided by the flexibility and low cost of the automobile. From this perspective, it is clear that it is not the evolution of the physical form of today's metropolitan community that is unique, but the means that have evolved to govern it.

Three policy alternatives have been applied to solve the problem of metropolitan governmental fragmentation. The first alternative is to maintain the status quo. The second is to consolidate, or centralize, the administration of cities in a metropolitan government. The third is to decentralize, or return control of many urban functions to a local neighborhood unit.

Consolidation appears to be the most reasonable policy alternative. As is stressed throughout the text, the metropolis is an ecological system in which one element or area cannot be separated from another. The boundaries between central city and suburb are artificial and often hinder the orderly and rational structuring of the metropolis. Realistically, however, consolidation is seldom achievable. Politically, suburbs are reluctant to give up power to a central government. The present government structure of metropolitan areas represents decades of compromise among various competing interest groups, and this process continues. The present structure of government in metropolitan areas will continue to change in the future in response to changing problems.

Finally, I reviewed urban policy during the Reagan era and argue that, if federal policies can create one of the most massive transfers of wealth in our nation's history, then urban policy can improve the quality of life in our cities.

NOTES

1.   Townships in New Jersey and Pennsylvania and towns in New England are administratively more important than counties, and records and data are compiled locally for such minor governmental units.

2. Calculations are based on data from the U.S. Bureau of the Census, *Local Government Finances in Selected Metropolitan Areas and Large Counties: 1970–71*. Washington, D.C.: U.S. Government Printing Office, 1972, p. 57.

3. The following is based in part on Chapters 5 and 6 of C. J. Larson and S. R. Nikkel, *Urban Problems: Perspectives on Corporations, Governments, and Cities*. Boston: Allyn and Bacon, Inc.

$\mathcal{B}$IBLIOGRAPHY

CHAPTER ONE

ALIHAN, M. A. (1964). *Social ecology: A critical analysis*. New York: Cooper Square.

ALTHUSSER, L. (1969). *For Marx*. London: Allen Lane.

ALTHUSSER, L. (1971). *Lenin and philosophy and other essays*. London: New Left Books.

ANDERSON, N. (1923). *The hobo*. Chicago, IL: University of Chicago Press.

BARZUM, J. (1958). *Darwin, Marx, Wagner*. New York: Doubleday.

CASTELLS, M. (1983). *The city and the grassroots: A cross-cultural theory of urban social movements*. Berkeley, CA: University of California Press.

CASTELLS, M. (1978). *City, class and power*. New York: St. Martin's Press.

CASTELLS, M. (1977). *The urban question: A Marxist approach*. Cambridge, MA: The MIT Press.

COSER, L. A. (1971). *Masters of sociological thought: Ideas in historical and social context*. New York: Harcourt Brace Jovanovich, Inc.

CRESSEY, P. B. (1932). *The taxi dance hall*. Chicago, IL: University of Chicago Press.

DARWIN, C. (1859). *Origin of species*. London: J. Murray.

DUNCAN, O. D. (1973). From social system to ecosystem. In M. Micklin (editor), *Population, environment, and social organization: Current issues in human ecology*. Hinsdale, IL: Dryden Press, pp. 107–117.

DUNCAN, O., DUNCAN, B., and LIEBERSON S. (1959). Ethnic segregation and assimilation. *American Journal of Sociology* 64: 364–374.

FARIS, R. E. (1967). *Chicago sociology: 1920–1932*. San Francisco, CA: Chandler Publishing Co.

FARIS, R. E.., and DUNHAM, W. (1939). *Mental disorders in urban areas*. Chicago, IL: University of Chicago Press.

FIREY, W. (1947). *Land use in central Boston*. Cambridge, MA: Harvard University Press.

FISCHER, C. (1975). Toward a subcultural theory of urbanism. *American Journal of Sociology* 80(6): 1319–1351.

GANS, H. J. (1962). *The urban villagers: Group and class in the life of Itallian Americans*. New York: Free Press.

GEHLKE, C. E., and BIEL, K. (1934). Certain effects of grouping upon the size of the correlation coefficient in census tract material. *Journal of the American Statistical Association* 24: 169–170.

GETTYS, W. E. (1940). Human ecology and social theory. *Social Forces* 18: 469–476.

HARVEY, D. (1985). *Consciousness and the urban experience*. Baltimore, MD: Johns Hopkins University Press.

HARVEY, D. (1982a). *The limits to capital*. Chicago, IL: University of Chicago Press.

HARVEY, D. (1973). *Social justice and the city*. Baltimore, MD: Johns Hopkins University Press.

HARVEY, D. (1985b). *The urbanization of capital*. Baltimore, MD: Johns Hopkins University Press.

HATT, P. K. (1946). The concept of natural area. *American Sociological Review* 11: 423–428.

HAWLEY, A. H. (1950). *Human ecology: A theory of community structure*. New York: Ronald Press.

HAWLEY, A. H. (1972). Population density and the city. *Demography* 9: 521–529.

HINKLE, G. J., and HINKLE, R. C. (1954). *The development of modern sociology: Its nature and growth in the United States*. New York: Random House.

HOLLINGSHEAD, A. B. (1947). *Elmtown youth*. New York: Random House.

JONASSEN, C. T. (1949). Cultural variables in the ecology of an ethnic group. *American Sociological Review* 14 (5): 32–41.

KUHN, T. (1970). *The structure of scientific revolutions*. Chicago: The University of Chicago Press.

LOGAN, J. R., and MOLTOCH, H. L. (1987). *Urban fortunes: The political economy of place*. Berkeley, CA: University of California Press.

LYON, L. (1987). *The community in urban society*. Chicago, IL: The Dorsey Press.

MARX, K. (1867). *Capital*. New York: International Publishers Edition.

MARX, K., and ENGELS, F. (1967). Manifesto of the Communist Party. In Lewis S. Feuer (editor), *Marx and Engels: Basic writings on politics and philosophy*. Garden City, NY: Doubleday Anchor Books.

NISBET, R. A. (1966). *The sociological tradition*. New York: Basic Books.

PARK, R. E. (1916). The city: Suggestions for the investigation of human behavior in the urban environment. *American Journal of Sociology* 20: 577–612.

PARK, R. E. (1952). *Human communities*. Glencoe, IL: Free Press.

PARK, R. E. (1961). Human ecology. In G. A. Theodorson (editor), *Studies in human ecology*. New York: Harper and Row, Publishers.

QUINN-JUDGE, P. (staff writer) (1989). Rapprochement amid revolt. *Christian Science Monitor* (May 19): 3.

SAUNDERS, P. (1986). *Social theory and the urban question*. New York: Holmes and Meier Publishers, Inc.

SHAW, C. (1929). *Delinquency areas*. Chicago, IL: University of Chicago Press.

SHAW, C. (1930). *The jackroller*. Chicago, IL: University of Chicago Press.

SIMMEL, G. (1950). The metropolis and mental life. In K. H. Wolff (editor), *The sociology of Georg Simmel*. New York: Free Press.

SMITH, M. P. (1979). *The city and social theory*. New York: St. Martin's Press.

TABB, W. K., and SAWERS, L. (1978). *Marxism and the metropolis*. New York: Oxford University Press.

THEODORSON, G. A. (1961). *Studies in human ecology*. New York: Harper and Row Publishers.

THRASHER, F. M. (1927). *The gang*. Chicago, IL: University of Chicago Press.

TIMMS, D. W. G. (1971). *The urban mosaic: Towards a theory of residential differentiation*. Cambridge, England: Cambridge University Press.

WHYTE, W. F. (1955). *Street corner society*. Chicago, IL: University of Chicago Press.

WIRTH, L. (1928). *The ghetto*. Chicago, IL: University of Chicago Press.

WIRTH, L. (1938). Urbanism as a way of life. *American Journal of Sociology* 44: 8–20.

ZORBAUGH, H. (1929). *The Gold Coast and the slum*. Chicago, IL: University of Chicago Press.

CHAPTER TWO

ANDERSON, N. (1959). Urbanism and urbanization. *American Journal of Sociology* 65 (1): 68–73.

ARRIAGE, E. A. (1970). A new approach to the measurement of urbanization. *Economic Development and Cultural Change* 18 (2): 206–218.

BAIROCH, P. (1988). *Cities and economic development: From the dawn of history to the present*. Chicago, IL: The University of Chicago Press.

BLACK, C., et al. (1975). *The modernization of Japan and Russia*. New York: The Free Press.

BRUTKUS, E. (1975). Centralized vs. decentralized pattern of urbanization in developing countries: An attempt to elucidate a guideline principle. *Economic Development and Cultural Change* 23: 633–652.

CARTER, H. (1984). The British settlement system: Development and contemporary characteristics. In L. S. Bourne, R. Sinclair, and K. Dziewonski (editors), *Urbanization and settlement systems: International perspectives*. New York: Oxford University Press, pp. 133–156.

CASETTI, E., and DEMKO, G. J. A. (1975). *A diffusion model of fertility decline: An application of selected Soviet data, 1940–1965*. Columbus, OH: Ohio State University, Department of Geography Working Papers No. 11.

DALMASSO, E. (1984). The French national settlement system. In L. S. Bourne, R. Sinclair, and K. Dziewonski (editors), *Urbanization and Settlement Systems*. New York: Oxford University Press, pp. 157–177.

DAVIDOVICH, F. (1984). Brazilian urban settlement. In L. S. Bourne, R. Sinclair, and K. Dziewonski (editors), *Urbanization and settlement systems: International perspectives*. New York: Oxford University Press, pp. 415–431.

DAVIS, K. (1972b). The urbanization of the human population. In D. Flanagan (editor), *Cities*. New York: Knopf.

DAVIS, K. (1969). *World urbanization 1950–1970, Vol. I: Basic data for cities, countries, and regions*. Berkeley, CA: University of California Press.

DAVIS, K. (1972a). *World urbanization 1950–1970, Vol. II: Analysis of trends, relationships and development*. Berkeley, CA: University of California Press.

DOGAN, M., and KASARDA, J. D. (1988). *The metropolis era, Vol. I: A world of giant cities.* Newbury Park, CA: Sage Publications, Inc.

DOGAN, M., and KASARDA, J. D. (1988). *The metropolis era, Vol. II: Mega-cities.* Newbury Park, CA: Sage Publications, Inc.

DOWNS, A. (1968). Alternative futures for the American ghetto. *Daedalus* (Fall): 1331–1278.

DURKHEIM, E. (1972). (Edited and translated by A. Giddens.) *Emile Durkheim: Selected writings.* Cambridge, England: Cambridge University Press.

DZIEWONSKI, K., JERCZYNSKI, M., and KORCELLI, P. The Polish settlement system. In L. S. Bourne, R. Sinclair, and K. Dziewonski (editors), *Urbanization and settlement systems: International perspectives.* New York: Oxford University Press, pp. 359–376.

ELDRIDGE, H. T. (1956). The process of urbanization. In J. J. Spengler and O. D. Duncan (editors), *Demographic analysis.* Glencoe, IL: The Free Press.

GIBBS, J. P. (1961). *Urban research methods.* New York: Van Nostrand.

GIBBS, J. P., and MARTIN, W. T. (1958). Urbanization and natural resources: A study in organizational ecology. *American Sociological Review* 23: 266–277.

GIBBS, J. P., and MARTIN, W. T. (1962). Urbanization, technology, and the division of labor: International patterns. *American Sociological Review* 27: 667–677.

GREER, S. (1962). *The emerging city: Myth and reality.* New York: The Free Press.

GRIMM, F. (1984). The settlement system of the German Democratic Republic: Its structure and development. In L. S. Bourne, R. Sinclair, and K. Dziewonski (editors), *Urbanization and settlement systems.* New York: Oxford University Press.

HALL, P., and HAY, D. (1980). *Growth centres in the European urban system.* Berkeley, CA: University of California Press.

HAUSER, P. M., GARDNER, R. W., LAQUIAN, A. A., and EL-SHAKHS, S. (1982). *Population and the urban future.* Albany, NY: State University of New York.

IRWIN, P. H. (1975). An operational definition of societal modernization. *Economic Development and Social Change* 23 (4): 595–613.

LANGER, L. N. (1976). The medieval Russian town. In M. F. Hamm (editor), *The city in Russian history.* Lexington, KY: University of Kentucky Press.

LAPPO, G. M., and PIVOVAROV, Y. L. (1984). Settlement in the USSR. In L. S. Bourne, R. Sinclair, and K. Dziewonski (editors), *Urbanization and settlement systems: International perspectives.* New York: Oxford University Press, pp. 335–355.

LERNER, D. (1958). *The passing of traditional society.* New York: Macmillan.

LEVY, M. J. (1967). *Modernization and the structure of societies.* New York: Harcourt, Brace, and World.

MARX, R. W. (1986). The Tiger system: Automating the geographic structure of the United States Census. *Government Publications Review* 13: 181–201.

MAYER, H. M. (1965). A Survey of urban geography. In P. M. Hauser and L. F. Schnore (editors), *The study of urbanization.* New York: John Wiley and Co.

MEADOWS, D. H. (1972). *The limits of growth.* New York: Signet.

MEHTA, S. K. (1963). The correlates of urbanization. *American Sociological Review* 28 (4): 609–616.

MOORE, W. E., and HOSELITZ, B. F. (1963). *Industrialization and society.* New York: UNESCO.

MURVAR, V. (1967). Max Weber's urban typology and Russia. *Sociological Quarterly* 8: 481›494.

POPULATION REFERENCE BUREAU (1989). *1989 World population data sheet*. Washington, DC: Population Reference Bureau, Inc.

ROLAND, R. H. (1976). Urban in-migration in late nineteenth century Russia. In M. F. Hamm (editor), *The city in Russian history*. Lexington, KY: University Press of Kentucky, pp. 115–124.

SCHOLLER, P., BLOTEVOGEL, H. H., BUCHHOLZ, HOMMEL, M., and SCHILLING-KALETSCH, I. (1984). The settlement system of the Federal Republic of Germany. In L. S. Bourne, R. Sinclair, and K. Dziewonski (editors), *Urbanization and settlement systems: International perspectives*. New York: Oxford University Press, 178–199.

SIMMONS, J. S., and BOURNE, L. S. (1984). The Canadian urban system. L. S. Bourne, R. Sinclair, and K. Dziewonski (editors), *Urbanization and settlement systems: International perspectives*. New York: Oxford University Press, pp. 49–70.

SMELSER, N. J. (1963). Essays in sociological explanation. In W. E. Moore and B. F. Hoselitz (editors), *Industrialization and society*. New York: UNESCO.

SUBRAMANIAN, M. (1971). An operational measure of urban concentration. *Economic Development and Cultural Change* 20 (1): 105–115.

U.S. BUREAU OF THE CENSUS (1987). *County and city data book*. Washington, DC: U.S. Government Printing Office.

U.S. BUREAU OF THE CENSUS (1986). *State and metropolitan area date book 1986*. Washington, DC: U.S. Government Printing Office.

U.S. BUREAU OF THE CENSUS (1988). *Statistical abstract of the United States 1988*. Washington, DC: U.S. Government Printing Office.

UN DEPARTMENT OF INTERNATIONAL AND ECONOMIC AND SOCIAL AFFAIRS—Statistical Office (1986). *Demographic yearbook 1983/84*. New York: United Nations Publication.

UN DEPARTMENT OF INTERNATIONAL ECONOMIC AND SOCIAL AFFAIRS (1980). *Patterns of urban and rural population growth*. New York: United Nations Publication.

UN DEPARTMENT OF INTERNATIONAL ECONOMIC AND SOCIAL AFFAIRS—Statistical Office (1988). *World statistics in brief*. New York: United Nations Publication.

WATERBURY, J. (1972). *North for the trade*. Berkeley, CA: University of California Press.

WIRTH, L. (1938). Urbanism as a way of life. *American Journal of Sociology* 44: 1–24.

World Bank (1987). *World development report 1987*. New York: Oxford University Press.

YAMAGUCHI, T. (1984). The Japanese national settlement system. In L. S. Bourne, R. Sinclair, and K. Dziewonski (editors), *Urbanization and settlement systems: international perspectives*. New York: Oxford University Press, pp. 261–279.

CHAPTER THREE

ABRAHAMIAN, E. (1986). Structural causes of the Iranian revolution. In J. A. Goldstone (editor), *Revolutions: Theoretical, comparative, and historical studies*. New York: Harcourt Brace Jovanovich, Publishers.

ABU-LUGHOD, J., and HAY, R. (editors). (1977). *Third world urbanization*. New York: Methuen.

BEIER, G. J. (1984). Can Third World cities cope? In P. K. Ghosh (editor), *Urban development in the Third World*. Westport, CN: Greenwood Press, pp. 57–94.

BENDIX, R. (1964). *Nation-building and citizenship*. Berkeley, CA: University of California Press.

BIRDSALL, N. (1980). Population growth and poverty in the developing world. *Population Bulletin* 35 (5):1–48.

BLAIR, T. L. (editor). (1984). *Urban innovation abroad: Problem cities in search of solutions*. New York: Plenum Press.

BOSERUP, E. (1981). *Population and technological change: A study of long-term trends*. Chicago, IL: The University of Chicago Press.

CHIROT, D. (1976). *Social change in a peripheral society*. New York: Academic Press.

CHIROT, D. (1986). *Social change in the modern era*. New York: Harcourt Brace Javanovich, Publishers.

CHOGUILL, C. L. (1987). *New communities for urban squatters: Lessons from the plan that failed in Dhaka, Bangladesh*. New York: Plenum Press.

DAVIS, K., and GOLDEN, H. H. (1954). Urbanization and the development of pre-industrial areas. *Economic Development and Cultural Change* 3:6–26.

DAVIS, K. (1963). The theory of change and response in modern demographic history. *Population Index* 29 (4):345–366.

DAVIS, K. (1945). The world demographic transition. *The Annals of the American Academy of Political and Social Science* 237:1–11.

FRANK, A. G. (1969). *Latin America: Underdevelopment or revolution*. New York: Monthly Review Press.

GILBERT, A., and GUGLER, J. (1982). *Cities, poverty, and development: Urbanization in the Third World*. New York: Oxford University Press.

GOLDSCHEIDER, C. (1971). *Population, modernization and social structure*. Boston, MA: Little, Brown and Company.

GRAVES, P. E., and SEXTON, R. L. (1979). Overurbanization and its relation to economic growth for less developed countries. *Economic Forum* 8 (1):95–100.

GRIMES JR., O. F. (1976). *Urban land and public policy: Social appropriation of betterment* (World Bank Staff Working Papers 179). Washington, D.C.: World Bank.

GUGLER, J. (1982). The Rural-Urban Interface and Migration. In A. Gilbert and J. Gugler (editors), *Cities, poverty, and development: Urbanization in the Third World*. New York: Oxford University Press, pp. 49–64.

HARVEY, D. (1973). *Social justice and the city*. Baltimore, MD: Johns Hopkins University Press.

HERBERT, J. D. (1979). *Urban development in the Third World: Policy guidelines*. New York: Praeger Publishers.

HERMASSI, E. (1978). Changing patterns in research on the Third World. *Annual Review of Sociology* 4:239–257.

HOROWITZ, I. L. (1977). Review essay: Coming of age of urban Research in Latin America. *American Journal of Sociology* 83 761–765.

JEFFERSON, M. (1939). The law of the primate city. *Geographic Review* 39:226–232.

LINN, J. F. (1983). *Cities in the developing world: Policies for their equitable and efficient growth*. New York: Oxford University Press.

MERRICK, T. W. (1986). World population in transition. *Population Bulletin* 41 (2):1–47.

NOTESTEIN, F. W. (1945). Population—The long view. In T. W. Schultz (editor), *Food for the World*. Chicago, IL: University of Chicago Press.

OGBURN, W. F. (1922). *Social change*. New York: B. W. Huebsch.

POPULATION REFERENCE BUREAU, I. (1989). *1989 world population data sheet*. Washington, D.C.: Population Reference Bureau, Inc.

REPETTO, R. (1987). Population, resources, environment: An uncertain future. *Population Bulletin* 42 (2):1–44.

RONDINELLI, D. A. (1983). *Secondary cities in developing countries*. Beverly Hills, CA: Sage Publications.

SCHWIRIAN, K. P. (1974). *Comparative urban structure*. Lexington, MA: D.C. Heath and Company.

SJOBERG, G. (1960). *The preindustrial city: Past and present*. New York: The Free Press.

SKINNER, R. J., and RODELL, M. J. (editors). (1983). *People, poverty and shelter: Problems of self-help housing in the Third World*. London: Methuen.

SOVANI, N. V. (1964). The analysis of over-urbanization. *Economic Development and Cultural Change* 12:113–122.

STOCKWELL, E. G., and LAIDLAW, K. A. (1981). Population and development. In *Third world development*. Chicago, IL: Nelson-Hall, pp. 65–107.

TAEUBER, I. B. (1962). Asian populations: The critical decade. In *Study of population and immigration problems 1*. Washington, D.C.: U.S. Government Printing Office.

THOMPSON, W. (1929). Population. *American Journal of Sociology* 34 (6):1013–1027.

TILLY, C. (1974). *An urban world*. Boston, MA: Little, Brown and Co.

TODARO, M. P. (1984). Urbanization in developing nations: Trends, prospects, and policies. In P. K. Ghosh (editor), *Urban development in the Third World*. Westport, CN: Greenwood Press, pp. 8–26.

TURNER, J. F. C. (1976). *Housing by people*. London: Marion Boyars.

UN POPULATION DIVISION DEPARTMENT OF ECONOMIC AND SOCIAL AFFAIRS (1982). *Estimates and projections of urban, rural and city populations, 1950–2025: The 1980 Assessment*. New York: United Nations.

UN POPULATION DIVISION DEPARTMENT OF ECONOMIC AND SOCIAL AFFAIRS (1975). *Trends and prospects in the populations of urban agglomerations, 1950–2000*. New York: United Nations.

UNITED NATIONS POPULATION DIVISION DEPARTMENT OF ECONOMIC AND SOCIAL AFFAIRS (1982). *Urban–rural projections from 1950 to 2000*. New York: United Nations.

WALLERSTEIN, I. (1974). *The modern world system*. New York: Academic Press.

CHAPTER FOUR

ABBOTT, C. (1981a). *Boosters and businessmen: Popular economic thought and urban growth in the antebellum Middle West*. Westport, CN: Greenwood Press.

ABBOTT, C. (1981b). *The new urban America: Growth and politics in Sunbelt cities*. Chapel Hill, NC: The University of North Carolina Press.

ADAMS, R. M. (1966). *The evolution of urban society: Early Mesopotamia and pre-Hispanic Mexico*. Chicago: Aldine.

ADAMS, R. M. (1960). The origin of cities. *Scientific American* 203(3): 189–212.

BENDER, B. (1975). *Farming in prehistory: From hunter-gatherer to food producer*. New York: St. Martin's Press.

BRAIDWOOD, R. J. (1960). The agricultural revolution. *Scientific American* 203(3): 131–148.

BRAIDWOOD, R. (1972). From cave to village. In V. V. Lamberg-Karlovsky (Ed.). *Old world archeology*. San Francisco, CA: W. H. Freeman, pp. 67–70.

BRIDENBAUGH, C. (1938). *Cities in the wilderness*. New York: Knopf.

BROWNELL, B. A., and GOLDFIELD, R. (1977). *The city in Southern history: The growth of urban civilization in the South*. Port Washington, NY: Kennikat Press.

CALLOW, A. B. (1969). *American urban history*. New York: Oxford University Press.

CARNEIRO, R. L. (1970). A theory of the origin of the state. *Science* 169: 733–738.

CHANG, K. (1968). *The archaeology of ancient China*. New Haven: Yale University Press.

CHILDE, G. (1950). The urban revolution. *Town Planning Review* 21: 3–17.

CHILDE, V. G. (1957). *New light on the most ancient East*. New York: Grove Press.

CHUDACOFF, H. P., and SMITH, J. E. (1988). *The evolution of American urban society*. Englewood Cliffs, NJ: Prentice Hall.

CLARK, G., and PIGGOTT, S. (1965). *Prehistoric societies*. London: Hutchinson.

CLARK, G. (1977). *World prehistory*. Cambridge: Cambridge University Press.

COHEN, R., and SERVICE, E. R. (1978). *Origins of the state*. Philadelphia: Institute for the Study of Human Issues.

COULBURN, R. (1959). *The origin of civilized societies*. Princeton: Princeton University Press.

DAVIDSON, B. (1966). *African kingdoms*. New York: Time.

DAVIS, K. (1973). The First Cities: How and Why Did They Arise? In K. Davis (Ed.). *Cities: Their origin, growth and human impact*. San Francisco: Freedman Publishing Co.

DEEVEY, E. S. (1960). The human population. *Scientific American* 203(3): 195–205.

DIAMOND, W. (1969). On the dangers of an urban interpretation of history. In A. B. Callow. *American urban history*. New York: Oxford University Press.

DIXON, J. E., CANN, J. R., and RENFREW, C. (1968). Obsidian and the origins of trade. *Scientific American* 218(3): 38–46.

EARLE, C., and HOFFMAN, R. (1977). The urban South: The first two centuries. In B. A. Brownell and D. R. Goldfield (Eds.). *The city in Southern history: The growth of urban civilization in the South*. Port Washington, NY: Kennikat Press, pp. 23–51.

FLANNERY, K. J. (1972). The origins of the village as a settlement type in Mesoamerica and the Near East: A comparative study. In P. J. Ucko et al. (Eds.). *Man, settlement, and urbanism*. London: Duckworth, pp. 23–53.

GOLDFIELD, D. R., and BROWNELL, B. A. (1979). *Urban America: From downtown to no town*. Boston: Houghton Mifflin.

GOLDFIELD, D. R. (1982). *Cotton fields and skyscrapers: Southern city and region, 1607–1980*. Baton Rouge, LA: Louisiana State Press.

GORDON, L. (1978). Social issues in the arid city. In G. Golany (Ed.). *Urban planning for arid zones*. New York: John Wiley and Sons.

HALLOWAY, R. L. (1974). The casts of fossil hominid brains. *Scientific American* 231(7): 106–115.

HAMMOND, N. (1977). The earliest Maya. *Scientific American* 236(3): 116–133.

HARRIS, D. R. (1967). New light on plant domestication and the origins of agriculture: A review. *Geographical Review* 57: 90–107.

HARRISON, H. S. (1954). Discovery, invention and diffusion. In C. Singer, E. J. Holmyard, and A. R. Hall (Eds.). *A history of technology: Volume I*. New York: Oxford.

HASS, E. F. (1977). The Southern metropolis, 1940–1976. In B. A. Brownell and D. R. Goldfield (Eds.). *The city in Southern history: The growth of urban civilization in the South.* Port Washington, NY: Kennikat Press, pp. 159–191.

HAWLEY, A. H. (1971). *Urban society.* New York: Ronald Press.

HOLT, W. S. (1953). Some consequences of the urban movement in American history. *Pacific Historical Review* 22: 337–351.

JACOBSEN, T. W. (1976). 17,000 years of Greek prehistory. *Scientific American* 234(6): 76–87.

KEMP, B. J. (1977). The early development of towns in Egypt. *Antiquity* 5: 185–200.

KIMBER, G., and ATHWAL, R. S. (1972). A reassessment of the course of evolution of wheat. *Proceedings of the National Academy of Sciences* 69(4): 912–915.

LAMBERG-KARLOVSKY, C. C., and LAMBERG-KARLOVSKY, M. (1971). An early city in Iran. *Scientific American* 225(6): 102–111.

LAMPARD, E. E. (1969). American historians and the study of urbanization. In A. B. Callow Jr. (Ed.). *American urban history.* New York: Oxford University Press.

LEAKY, L. S. B. (1967). *Olduvai Gorge 1951–1961, Volume 1: A preliminary report on the geology and fauna.* Cambridge, England: Cambridge University Press.

LOTCHIN, R. W. (1984). *The martial metropolis: U.S. cities in war and peace.* New York: Praeger.

LUBOVE, R. (1965). The urbanization process: An approach to historical research. In A. B. Callow Jr. (Ed.). *American urban history.* New York: Oxford University Press.

LUCKINGHAM, B. (1983). Phoenix: The desert metropolis. In R. M. Bernard and B. R. Rice (Eds.). *Sunbelt cities: Politics and growth since World War II.* Austin, TX: University of Texas Press, pp. 309–327.

MACDONALD, M. C. D. (1984). *American cities: A report on the myth of urban renaissance.* New York: Simon and Schuster.

MAIN, J. T. (1965). *The social structure of revolutionary America.* Princeton, NJ: Princeton University Press.

MANTOUX, P. (1961). T*he Industrial Revolution in the eighteenth century: An outline of the beginnings of the modern factory system in England.* New York: Macmillan Co.

MELLART, J. (1979). Egyptian and Near Eastern chronology: A dilemma? *Antiquity* 53:6–18.

MEYERS, J. T. (1971). The origin of agriculture: An evaluation of three hypotheses. In S. Stoeuver (Ed.). *Prehistoric agriculture.* Garden City, NY: American Museum of Natural History, pp. 101–121.

MUMFORD, L. (1961). *The city in history.* New York: Harcourt, Brace and World.

NASH, G. D. (1973). *The American West in the twentieth century: A short history of an urban oasis.* Englewood Cliffs, NJ: Prentice-Hall.

NASH, G. D. (1985). *The American West transformed: The impact of the Second World War.* Bloomington, IN: Indiana University Press.

PAHL, R. E. (1970). *Patterns of urban life.* New York: Humanities Press.

PERRY, D. C. and WATKINS, A. J. (Eds.). (1977). *The rise of the Sunbelt cities.* Beverly Hills, CA: Sage Publications.

PIGGOTT, S. (1962). *Prehistoric India: To 1000 B.C.* New York: Barnes and Noble.

POLGAR, S. (1975). *Population ecology, and social evolution.* Chicago: Aldine.

RABINOWITZ, H. N. (1977). Continuity and change: Southern urban development, 1860–1900. In B. A. Brownell and D. R. Goldfield (Eds.). *The city in Southern history: The growth of urban civilization in the South.* Port Washington, NY: Kennikat Press, pp. 92–122.

RENFREW, C. (1971). Carbon 14 and the prehistory of Europe. *Scientific American* 225(10): 63–72.

RENFREW, J. M. (1973). *Paleoethnobotany: The prehistoric food plants of the Near East and Europe.* New York: Columbia University Press.

SALE, K. (1975). *Power shift: The rise of the Southern rim and its Challenge to the Eastern establishment.* New York: Random House.

SCHAEDEL, R. P. (1978). The city and the origin of the state in America. In R. Schaedel, J. E. Hardoy, and N. S. Kinzer (Eds.). *Urbanization in the Americas from its beginnings to the present.* The Hague: Mouton. pp. 31–45.

SCHILD, R. (1976). The final Paleolithic settlements of the European plain. *Scientific American* 235(2):88–99.

SCHLESINGER, A. M. (1940). The city in American history. *Mississippi Valley Historical Review* 27; 43–91.

SCHLESINGER, A. M. (1949). *Paths to the present.* New York: Macmillan.

SERVICE, E. R. (1978). Classical and modern theories of the origins of government. In R. Cohen and E. R. Service (Eds.). *Origins of the state.* Philadelphia: Institute for the Study of Human Issues. pp. 21–34.

SJOBERG, G. (1972). The origin and evolution of cities. In D. Flanagan. *Cities.* New York: Alfred A. Knopf.

SJOBERG, G. (1960). *The preindustrial city: Past and present.* New York: Free Press.

SJOBERG, G. (1963). The rise and fall of cities: A theoretical perspective. In G. Breeze (Ed.). *The city in newly developing countries.* Englewood Cliffs, NJ: Prentice Hall.

SMITH, P. E. L. (1976). Stone-age man on the Nile. *Scientific American* 235(8): 30–41.

SOLHEIM, W. G. (1972). An earlier agricultural revolution. *Scientific American* 226(4):34–41.

STILL, B. (1941). Patterns of mid-nineteenth century urbanization. *Mississippi Valley Historical Review* 28: 187–206.

STOEUVER, S. (1971). *Prehistoric agriculture.* Garden City, NY: American Museum of Natural History.

TAYLOR, G. R. (1951). *The transportation revolution, 1815–1860.* New York: Rinehart.

THERNSTROM, S. (1968). Urbanization, migration, and social mobility in late nineteenth-century America. In B. J. Bernstein (Ed.). *Towards a new past: Dissenting essays in American history.* New York: Pantheon.

WADE, R. (1957). *The urban frontier: 1790–1830.* Cambridge, MA: Harvard University Press.

WADE, R. (1969). Urban life in western America, 1790–1830. In A. B. Callow (Ed.). *American urban history.* New York: Oxford University Press.

WADE, R. (1964a). *Slavery in the cities: The South 1820–1860.* New York: Oxford University Press.

WADE, R. (1964b). *The urban frontier: Pioneer life in early Pittsburgh, Cincinnati, Lexington, Louisville, and St. Louis.* Chicago: University of Chicago Press.

WEBER, M. (1958). *The Protestant ethic and the spirit of capitalism* (translated by T. Parsons). New York: Scribner.

CHAPTER FIVE

BERRY, B. J. L., and GARRISON, W. (1958). The functional basis of the central place hierarchy. *Economic Geography* 34: 145–154.

BERRY, B. J. L., and PRED, A. (1965). *Central place studies: A bibliography of theory and applications*. Philadelphia, PA: Regional Science Research Institute.

BERRY, B. J. L. (1967). *Geography of market centers and retail distribution*. Englewood Cliffs, NJ: Prentice-Hall, Inc.

CARTER, H. (1981). *The study of urban geography*. London: Edward Arnold Publishers, Ltd.

CHRISTALLER, W. (1966). Central places in Southern Germany. C. W. Baskin (translator). Englewood Cliffs, NJ: Prentice-Hall.

COOLEY, C. H. (1894). The theory of transportation. *American Economic Association* 9: 312–322.

COTTRELL, W. F. (1951). Death by dieselization: A case study in the reaction to technological change. *American Sociological Review* 16: 358–365.

DUNCAN, O. D., SCOTT, W. R., LIEBERSON, S., DUNCAN, B., and WINSBOROUGH, H. H. (1960). *Metropolis and region*. Baltimore, MD: Johns Hopkins Press.

DUNN JR., E. S. (1980). *The development of the U.S. urban system: Volume 1 Concepts, structures, regional shifts*. Baltimore, MD: The Johns Hopkins University Press.

FARMER, F., and SCHWAB, W. A. (1989). Economic recession and community change: An analysis of an agricultural region's central place hierarchy. *Forthcoming*.

GREEN, H. L. (1955). Hinterland boundaries of New York City and Boston in southern New England. *Economic Geography* 31: 300–328.

LOSCH, A. (1958). The nature of economic regions. *Journal of Sociology* 5: 71–78.

MARK, H., and SCHWIRIAN, K. P. (1969). Ecological position, urban central place function, and community population growth. *The American Journal of Sociology* 73: 30–41.

PFOUTS, R. W. (1962). Patterns of economic interaction in the Crescent. In F. S. Chapin, and S. R. Weiss (editors), *Urban growth dynamics*. New York: John Wiley and Sons.

RUBIN, J. (1961). Canal or railroad? Imitation and innovation in the response to the Erie Canal in Philadelphia, Baltimore, and Boston. *Transactions of the American Philosophical Society* 51 (7): 1–178.

SWEDNER, H. (1960). *Ecological differentiation of habits and attitudes*. Lund, Sweden: CWK Cleerup.

THOMLINSON, R. (1969). Urban structure: *The social and spatial character of cities*. New York: Random House.

THOMPSON, W. R. (1965). *A preface to urban economics*. Baltimore, MD: Johns Hopkins Press.

ULLMAN, E. (1941). A theory of location for cities. *American Journal of Sociology* 46: 853–864.

VON THUNEN, J. H. (1826). *De isolierte staat in beziehung auf landwirschaft and nationalokonomie*. Hamburg, Germany.

WADE, R. (1964). *The urban frontier: Pioneer life in early Pittsburgh, Cincinnati, Lexington, Louisville, and St. Louis*. Chicago, IL: University of Chicago Press.

ZIPF, G. K. (1949). *Human behavior and the principle of least effort: An introduction to human ecology*. Reading, MA: Addison-Wesley.

CHAPTER SIX

Advisory Commission on Intergovernmental Relations (1973). *City financial emergencies: The intergovernmental dimension*. Washington, DC: Advisory Commission on Intergovernmental Relations.

ALFORD, R. R. (1972). Critical evaluation of the principles of city classification. In B. J. L. Berry (editor), *The city classification handbook: Methods and applications*. New York: Wiley-Interscience.

ANGOFF, C., and MENKEN, H. L. (1931). The worst American state: Parts I, II, III. *American Mercury* 24 (93–95): 1–16, 175–188, 355–370.

BAER-SINNOTT, S. (1987). Hot spots: INC.'s list of the 50 fastest-growing U.S. cities. *INC.* (April): 50–52.

BAYLESS, M., and BAYLESS, S. (1982). Current quality of life indicators: Some theoretical and methodological concerns. *American Journal of Economics and Sociology* 41 (4): 421–437.

BERRY, B. J. L. (1972). *City classification handbook: Methods and applications*. New York: Wiley-Interscience.

BICKFORD, D. J. (1980). *A multidimensional approach to city classification and need.* Unpublished doctoral dissertation, University of Massachusetts, Amherst, MA.

BOWMAN, T. F., GIULANI, G. A., and MINGE, M. R. (1981). *Finding your best place to live in America.* New York: Warner Books.

BOYER, R., and SAVAGEAU, D. (1981). *Places rated almanac.* Chicago, IL.: Rand McNally.

BOYER, R., and SAVAGEAU D. (1983). *Places rated retirement guide.* Chicago, IL.: Rand McNally.

BOYER, R., and SAVAGEAU, D. (1985). *Places rated almanac*, revised edition. Chicago, IL.: Rand McNally.

CAMPBELL, A., CONVERSE, P. E., and RODGERS, W. L. (1976). *The quality of American life: Perceptions, evaluations and satisfactions.* New York: Russell Sage.

CAMPBELL, A. (1981). *The sense of well-being in America, recent patterns and trends.* New York: McGraw-Hill (Source: Wish 1986).

CARTER, H. (1981). *The study of urban geography.* London: Edward Arnold.

CATSAMBAS, T. (1978). *Regional impacts of federal fiscal policy: Theory and estimation of economic incidence.* Lexington, MA: Lexington Books.

CLARK, T. (1977a). Fiscal management of American cities: Function and flow indicators. *Journal of Accounting Research*, Supplement 15.

CLARK, T. (1976b). How many more New Yorks? *New York Affairs* 3 (4): 18–27.

CLARK, T., and FERGUSON, L. (1977b). *Fiscal strain and fiscal health in American cities: Six basic processes.* Chicago, IL: University of Chicago Press and National Research Center.

CLARK, T., and RUBIN, I. S. (1977a). *Fiscal Strain in American Cities: Where and Why?* (Comparative Study of Community Decision-Making). Chicago, IL: University of Chicago.

Committee on the Health of Towns (1840). *Report of the Select Committee on the Health of Towns.* London: Committee on Towns.

CONWAY, H., and LISTON, L. L. (1981). *The good life index: How to compare quality of life throughout the U.S. and around the world.* Atlanta, GA.: Conway Publications.

CUTTER, S. (1985). *Rating places: A geographer's view on quality of life.* Washington, DC: Association of American Geographers.

DAHMANN, D. C. (1981). Subjective indicators of neighborhood quality. In D. F. Johnston (editor), *Measurement of subjective phenomena*. Washington, DC: U.S. Department of Commerce, Bureau of the Census.

DUNCAN, O. D. (1984). *Notes on social measurement, historical and critical.* Beverly Hills, CA.: Sage Publications.

DUNCAN, O. D. (1969). *Towards social reporting: New steps.* New York: Russell Sage Foundation.

DUNCAN, O. D., and REISS, A. J., JR. (1956). *Social characteristics of urban and rural communities.* New York: John Wiley and Sons.

EISENBERG, R., and ENGLANDER, D. W. (1987). The best places to live in America. *Money* (August): 34–44.

EISENBERG, R., and ENGLANDER, D. W. (1988). The best places to live in America. *Money* (August): 76–84.

ELGIN, D., LOGOTHETTI, T. I., and COX, S. (1974). *City size and the quality of life.* Washington, DC: National Science Foundation (Source: Wish, 1986).

FISCHER, C. S. (1982). *To dwell among friends: Personal networks in town and city.* Chicago, IL: University of Chicago Press.

FLAX, M. J. (1971). *A study in comparative indicators: Conditions in 18 large metropolitan areas.* Washington, DC: Urban Institute.

FORSTALL, R. L. (1967). Economic classification of places over 10,000, 1960–1963. In *The municipal year book, 1967.* Chicago, IL: International City Managers Association.

FORSTALL, R. L. (1970). A new social and economic grouping of cities. In T*he municipal year book, 1970.* Washington, DC: International City Managers Association.

GARN, H. et al. (1977a). *A framework for national urban policy: Urban distress, decline, and growth.* Washington, DC: The Urban Institute.

GARN, H., et al. (1977b). *Urban economic development strategies: Improving economic and fiscal performance.* Washington, DC: The Urban Institute.

GARWOOD, A. N. (editor) (1984). *199 American cities compared.* Burlington, VT.: Information Publications.

HADDEN, J. K., and BORGATTA, E. F. (1965). *American cities: Their social characteristics.* Chicago, IL: Rand McNally.

HARRIS, C. D. (1945). A functional classification of cities in the United States. *The Annals of the American Academy of Political Science* 242: 7–17.

HART, J. F. (1955). Functional and occupational structures of cities of the American South. *Annals of the Association of American Geographers* 45 (3): 269–286.

JONASSEN, C. T. (1961). Functional unities in eighty-eight community systems. *American Sociological Review* 26: 398–407.

JONASSEN, C. T. (1959). *The measures of community dimensions and elements.* Columbus, OH: Ohio State University.

JONES, V. (1953). Economic classification of cities and metropolitan areas. In *Municipal year book, 1953.* Chicago, IL: International City Managers Association.

JONES V., and COLLVER, A. (1960). Economic classification of cities and metropolitan areas. In *Municipal year book, 1960.* Chicago, IL: International City Managers Association.

JONES, V., and FORSTALL, R. L. (1963). Economic and social classification of metropolitan areas. In *Municipal year book, 1963.* Chicago, IL: International City Managers Association.

JONES, V., FORSTALL, R. L., and COLLVER, A. (1963). Economic and social characteristics of urban places. In *Municipal year book, 1963.* Chicago, IL: International City Managers Association.

KEELER, E., and ROGERS, W. (1973). *A classification of large American urban areas.* Santa Monica, CA: Rand Corporation.

KNEEDLER, G. (1945). Economic classification of cities. In *Municipal year book, 1945.* Chicago, IL: International City Managers Association.

486

LEVINE, R. (1988). City stress index: 25 best, 25 worst. *Psychology Today* (November): 53–58.

LIU, B. (1975). *Quality of life indicators in U.S. metropolitan areas, 1970: A comprehensive assessment.* Washington, DC: U.S. Environmental Protection Agency.

LIU, B. (1976). *Quality of life indicators in U.S. Metropolitan areas: A statistical analysis.* New York: Praeger Publishers.

MACDONALD, M. C. D. (1984). *American cities: A report on the myth of urban renaissance.* New York: Simon and Schuster.

MARLIN, J. T., and AVERY, J. S. (1983). *The book of American city rankings.* New York: Facts on File.

MARLIN, J. T. (1974). Jobs and well-being: Which cities perform the best? *Business and Society Review/Innovation* 10: 43–54.

MULLER, T. (1976). Paper presented to the Subcommittee on Urban Affairs of the Joint Economic Committee, U.S. Congress. *Statement on the fiscal outlook for state and local governments.* Washington, DC.

MYERS, D. (1987). Community-relevant measurement of quality of life: A focus on local trends. *Urban Affairs Quarterly* 23 (1): 108–125.

NELSON, H. J. (1955). A service classification of American cities. *Economic Geography* 31: 189–210.

NELSON, K. P. (1988). *Gentrification and distressed cities.* Madison, WI: The University of Wisconsin Press.

NOYELLE, T. J., and STANBACK, J. T. M. (1983). *The economic transformation of American cities.* Totowa, NJ: Rowman and Allanheld.

OGBURN, W. F. (1937). *Social characteristics of cities.* Chicago, IL: International City Managers Association.

PACIONE, M. (1982). The use of objective and subjective measures of life quality in human geography. *Progress in Human Geography* 6: 495–514.

PERLE, S. (1964). *Factor analysis of American cities: A comparative analysis.* Unpublished doctoral dissertation, University of Chicago, Chicago.

PIERCE, R. M. (1985). Rating America's metropolitan areas. *American Demographics* 7 (7): 20–25.

POWNALL, L. L. (1953). The functions of New Zealand towns. *Annals of the Association of American Geographers* 45 (4): 332–350.

President Hoover's Research Committee on Social Trends (1933). *Recent social trends in the United States.* New York: McGraw Hill (Source: Wish, 1986).

PRICE, D. O. (1942). Factor analysis in the study of metropolitan centers. *Social Forces* 20 (4): 449–455.

SAWERS, L., and TABB, W. K. (1984). *Sunbelt, Snowbelt: Urban development and regional restructuring.* New York: Oxford University Press.

STANLEY, D. (1976). *Cities in trouble.* Columbus, OH: Academy for Contemporary Problems.

Temporary Commission on City Finance, City of New York (1977c). The city in transition: Prospects and policies for New York. In T. Clark and E. Fuchs (editors), *New York City in comparative perspective.* New York: City of New York, pp. 295–311.

THORNDIKE, E. L. (1939). *Your city.* New York: Harcourt, Brace and Co.

U.S. Department of Housing and Urban Development (1978). *The 1978 HUD survey on the quality of community life: A data book.* Washington, DC: U.S. Government Printing Office.

VAUGHAN, R. J. (1977). *The urban impacts of federal policies*, 2 vols. Santa Monica, CA: Rand Corporation.

WISH, N. B. (1986). Are we really measuring the quality of life?: Well-being has subjective dimensions, as well as objective ones. *American Journal of Economics and Sociology* 45 (1): 93–99.

WISH, N. B. (1986). Some issues about the quality of Sunbelt/Frostbelt life: Factor analysis of the better data demonstrates that this dichotomy is hopelessly biased. *American Journal of Economics and Sociology* 45 (3): 343–357.

CHAPTER SEVEN

Advisory Commission on Intergovernmental Relations (1989). *The fiscal relationship between federal, state, and local governments: Intergovernmental transfers.* Washington, DC: American Council on Intergovernmental Relations.

BLUMFIELD, H. (1970). The economic base of the metropolis. In R. B. Putnam, F. J. Taylor, and P. G. Kettle (editors), *Geography of urban places.* Toronto, Canada: Methuen.

BORCHERT, J. R. (1967). American metropolitan evolution. *Geographical Review* 57: 301–323.

DUNN, E. S., JR. (1983). *The development of the U.S. urban system: Volume II—Industrial shifts and implications.* Baltimore, MD: Johns Hopkins Press.

DUNN, EDGAR S., JR. (1980). *The development of the U.S. urban system: Volume I—Concepts, structures, regional shifts.* Baltimore, MD: The Johns Hopkins University Press.

MACDONALD, M. C. D. (1984). *America's cities: A report on the myth of urban renaissance.* New York: Simon and Schuster.

NELSON, K. P. (1988). *Gentrification and distressed cities: An assessment of trends in intrametropolitan migration.* Madison, WI: The University of Wisconsin Press, Ltd.

NORTON, R. D. (1979). *City life-cycles and American urban policy.* New York: Academic Press.

NOYELLE, T. J., and STANBACK, T. M., JR. (1983). *The economic transformation of American cities.* Totowa, NJ: Rowman and Allanheld.

PRED, A. R. (1966). *The spatial dynamics of U.S. urban-industrial growth, 1800–1914: Interpretive and theoretical essays.* Cambridge, MA: The M.I.T. Press.

RUBEN, J. (1961). Canal or railroad?: Imitation and innovation in the response to the Erie Canal in Philadelphia, Baltimore, and Boston. *Transactions of the American Philosophical Society* 51 (7): Part 7.

SALE, P. K. (1975). *Power shift: The rise of the Southern rim and its challenge to the Eastern establishment.* New York: Random House.

SAWERS, L., and TABB, W. K. (editors). (1984). Sunbelt/Snowbelt: Urban development and regional restructuring. New York: Oxford University Press.

SCHUMPETER, J. A. (1947). *Capitalism, socialism, and democracy.* New York: Harper.

STANBACK T. M., JR. and NOYELLE, T. J. (1982). *Cities in transition: Changing job structures in Atlanta, Denver, Buffalo, Phoenix, Columbus (Ohio), Nashville, Charlotte.* Totowa, NJ: Allanheld, Osmun and Co. Publishers, Inc.

WALKER, R. A. (1978). Two sources of uneven development under advanced capitalism: Spatial differentiation and capital mobility. *The Review of Radical Political Economics* 10 (3): 28–38.

WATKINS, A. J., and PERRY, D. C. (1977). Regional change and the impact of uneven urban development. In D. C. Perry and A. J. Watkins (editors), *The rise of the Sunbelt cities*. Beverly Hills, CA: Sage Publications.

CHAPTER EIGHT

ABBOTT, W. F. (1978). Social area analysis in comparative perspective: Moscow in 1897 as a preindustrial city. *The Sociological Quarterly* 19 (Winter): 24–36.

ABU-LUGHOD, J. L. (1971). *Cairo: 1001 years of the city victorious*. Princeton, NJ: Princeton University Press.

ABU-LUGHOD, J. L. (1969). Testing the theory of social area analysis: The ecology of Cairo, Egypt. *American Sociological Review* 34 (1): 189–212.

ALIHAN, M. A. (1964). *Social ecology: A critical analysis*. New York: Cooper Square.

ANDERSON, T. R., and BEAN, L. (1961). The Shevky–Bell social areas: Confirmation of results and a reinterpretation. *Social Forces* 40: 119–124.

ANDERSON, T. R., and EGELAND, J. A. (1961). Spatial aspects of social area analysis. *American Sociological Review* 26: 392–399.

BELL, R. (1982). Personal crime and delinquency rates in Los Angeles—A social area analysis. *Mid-American Review of Sociology* 7 (2): 87–104.

BELL, W. (1955a). Comment on Duncan's review of social area analysis. *American Journal of Sociology* 61: 260–261.

BELL, W. (1955b). Economic, family and ethnic status: An empirical test. *American Sociological Review* 20: 45–52.

BELL, W. (1953). The social areas of the San Francisco Bay region. *American Sociological Review* 18: 29–47.

BELL, W. (1959). Social areas: Typology of urban neighborhoods. In M. Sussman (editor), *Community structure and analysis*. New York: Thomas Crowell.

BELL, W. (1965). Urban neighborhoods and individual behavior. In M. Sherif and C. W. Sherif (editors), *Problems of youth*. Chicago, IL: University of Chicago Press.

BELL, W. (1961). The utility of the Shevky typology for the design of urban subarea field studies. In G. A. Theodorson (editor) *Studies in Human Ecology*. New York: Harper and Row.

BELL, W., and BOAT, M. (1957). Urban neighborhoods and informal social relations. *American Journal of Sociology* 62: 391–393.

BELL, W., and FORCE, M. (1956b). Social structure and participation in different types of formal associations. *Social Forces* 34: 345–350.

BELL, W., and FORCE, M. (1956a). Urban neighborhood types and participation in formal associations. *American Sociological Review* 21: 25–34.

BELL W., and GREER, S. (1962). Social area analysis and its critics. *Pacific Sociological Review* 5: 79–86.

BERRY, B. J. L., and MURDIE, R. A. (1969). *Socioeconomic correlates of housing condition*. Toronto, Canada: Metropolitan Planning Board.

BERRY, B. J. L., and REES, P. H. (1969). The factorial ecology of Calcutta. *American Journal of Sociology* 74: 447–491.

BERRY, B. J. L., and SPODEK, H. (1971). Comparative ecologies of large Indian cities. *Economic Geography* 47: 266–275.

BRADY, J., and PARKER, A. J. (1975). Factorial ecology of Dublin—A preliminary investigation. *Economic and Social Review* 7 (1): 35–54.

BRINDLEY, T. S., and RAINE, J. W. (1979). Social area analysis and planning research. *Urban Studies* 16: 273–289.

BURGESS, E. W., and BOGUE, D. J. (editors) (1964). *Contributions to urban sociology.* Chicago, IL: University of Chicago Press.

CLIGNET, R., and SWEEN, J. (1969). Accra and Abidjan: A comparative examination of the theory of increasing scale. *Urban Affaris Quarterly* 4: 297–324.

CROTHERS, C. (1984). Social area indicators of educational need. *New Zealand Journal of Educational Studies* 19 (1): 87–89.

CULLINGFORD, D., and OPENSHAW, S. (1982). Identifying areas of rural deprivation using social area analysis. *Regional Studies* 16 (6): 409–417.

DAVIE, M. R. (1938). The pattern of urban growth. In G. D. Murdock (editor), *Studies in the science of society.* New Haven, CN: Yale University Press.

DUNCAN, O. D. (1955). Review of social area analysis. *American Journal of Sociology* 61: 84–85.

FORM, W. H., SMITH, J., STONE, G. P., and COWHIG, J. (1954). The compatibility of alternative approaches to the delimitation of urban subareas. *American Sociological Review* 19: 176–187.

FULCOMER, M. C., PELLEGRINI, S. G., and LEFEBVRE, L. C., JR. (1981). Demographic and health-related predictors of the incidence of sudden infant death. *Evaluation and Program Planning* 4 (1): 43–56.

GOODMAN, A. B., RAHAV, M., and POPPER, M. M. (1982). A social area analysis of Jerusalem—Implications for mental health planning and epidemiologic studies. *Israel Journal of Psychiatry and Related Sciences* 19 (3): 185–197.

GREEN, H. W. (1931). *Characteristics of Cleveland's social planning areas.* Cleveland, OH: Welfare Federation of Cleveland.

GREER, S. (1956). Urbanism reconsidered: A comparative study of local areas in a metropolis. *American Sociological Review* 21: 19–25.

GREER, S., and KUBE, E. (1959). Urbanism and social structure: A Los Angeles study. In M. Sussman (editor), *Community structure and analysis.* New York: Thomas Crowell.

HATT, P. K. (1946). The concept of natural area. *American Sociological Review* 11: 423–428.

HAWLEY, A. H., and DUNCAN, O. T. (1957). Social area analysis: A critical appraisal. *Land Economics* 33: 337–345.

HERBERT, D. T. (1967). Social area analysis: A British study. *Urban Studies* 4: 41–60.

JACKSON, D. J., BORGATTA, E. F., and GOLDSMITH, H. F. (1979). Data analysis in factorial ecology. *Sociological Methods and Research* 7 (3): 356–368.

LATIF, A. H. (1972). *Residential segregation and location of status and religious groups in Alexandria, Egypt.* Columbus, OH: Ohio State University, Department of Sociology.

MCELRATH, D. (1962). The social areas of Rome. *American Sociological Review* 27: 376–391.

MCKENZIE, R. D. (1923). *Neighborhood.* Chicago, IL: University of Chicago Press.

MILCAREK, B. I., and LINK, B. G. (1981). Handling problems of ecological fallacy in program planning and evaluation. *Evaluation and Program Planning* 4 (1): 23–28.

MURDIE, R. (1969). *Factorial ecology of metropolitan Toronto, 1951–1961* (Research Paper 116, Department of Geography). Chicago, IL: University of Chicago Press.

PETERSON, P. O. (1967). An empirical model of urban population structure in Copenhagen. In *Proceedings of the First Scandinavian-Polish Regional Science Seminar*. Warsaw: Polish Scientific Publishers.

PLASECKI, J. R., and KAMIS-GOULD, E. (1981). Social area analysis in program evaluation and planning. *Evaluation and Program Planning* 4 (1): 3–14.

PITTMAN, J., and ANDREWS, H. (1986). The use of zip coded population data in social area studies of service utilization. *Evaluation and Program Planning* 9 (2): 309–317.

REES, P. H. (1970). The factorial ecology of metropolitan Chicago. In B. J. L. Berry and F. E. Horton (editors), *Geographical perspectives on urban systems*. Englewood Cliffs, NJ: Prentice-Hall.

ROBSON, B. T. (1969). *Urban analysis: A study of a city structure with special reference to Sunderland*. Cambridge, England: Cambridge University Press.

ROSEN, B. M., and GOLDSMITH, H. F. (1981). The health demographic profile system: Current and longitudinal data base for social area analysis. *Evaluation and Program Planning* 4 (1): 57–73.

SCHWIRIAN, K. P., and MATRE, M. (1974). The ecological structure of Canadian cities. In K. P. Schwirian (editor), *Comparative urban structure: Studies in the ecology of cities*. Lexington, MA: D. C. Heath.

SCHWIRIAN, K. P., and SMITH, R. K. (1974). Primacy, modernization and urban structure: The ecology of Puerto Rican cities. In K. P. Schwirian (editor), *Comparative urban structure: Studies in the ecology of cities*. Lexington, MA: D. C. Heath.

SCOTTSAMUEL, A. (1977). Social area analysis in community-medicine. *British Journal of Preventive and Social Medicine* 31 (3): 199–294.

SHEVKY, E., and BELL W. (1955). *Social area analysis: Theory, illustrative application and Computational Procedures*. Stanford, CA: Stanford University Press.

SHEVKY, E., and WILLIAMS, M. (1949). *The social areas of Los Angeles: Analysis and typology*. Berkeley, CA: University of California Press.

STAHURA, J. M. (1979). A factorial ecology of suburban America: 1960–1970. *Sociological Focus* 12 (1): 9–19.

STROBION, D. M., CHASE, G. A., SALIM, J. H., and CORNELY, D. A. (1982). Evaluation of perinatal services: An application of social area analysis. *Evaluation Review* 6 (1): 127–139.

STRUENTIN, E. L. (1974). Approaches to evaluation—Social area analysis. *International Journal of Health Services* 4 (3): 503–514.

SWEETSER, F. L. (1965a). Factor structure as ecological structure in Helsinki and Boston. *Acta Sociologica* 8: 205–225.

SWEETSER, F. L. (1965). Factorial ecology, Helsinki, 1960. *Demography* 2: 372–385.

THEODORSON, G. A. (editor) (1961). *Studies in human ecology*. New York: Harper and Row, Publishers.

TIMMS, D. W. G. (1971). *The urban mosaic: Towards a theory of residential differentiation*. Cambridge, England: Cambridge University Press.

TRLIN, A. D. (1977). Somoan immigrants in Auckland—Factorial ecology. *Australian and New Zealand Journal of Sociology* 13 (2): 152–160.

VAN ARSDON, M. D., CAMILLERI, S. F., and SCHMID, C. F. (1958). The generality of urban social area indexes. *American Sociological Review* 23: 277–284.

WHITE, M. J. (1987). *American neighborhoods and residential diffeentiation.* New York: Russell Sage Foundation.

WIRTH, L. (1928). *The ghetto.* Chicago, IL: University of Chicago Press.

WIRTH, L. (1938). Urbanism as a way of life. *American Journal of Sociology* 44: 1–24.

ZORBAUGH, H. (1929). *The Gold Coast and the slum.* Chicago, IL: University of Chicago Press.

ZORBAUGH, H. (1961). The natural areas of the city. In G. A. Theodorson (editor), *Studies in human ecology.* New York: Harper and Row, Publishers.

CHAPTER NINE

ALONSO, W. (1965). *Location and land use: Toward a general theory of land rent.* Cambridge, MA: Harvard University Press.

ALONSO, W. (1960). A theory of the urban land market. *Paper and Proceedings of the Regional Science Association* 6 (1): 147–158.

BACH, R. L., and SMITH, J. (1977). Community satisfaction: Expectations of moving and migration. *Demography* 14: 147–167.

BROWNING, C. E. (1964). Selected aspects of land use and distance from the city center: The case of Chicago. *Southeastern Geographer* 4 (1): 29–40.

BURGESS, E. W. (1925). The growth of the city: An introduction to a research project. In R. Park, E. W. Burgess, and R. D. McKenzie (editors), *The city.* Chicago, IL: The University of Chicago Press, pp. 47–62.

BUTLER, E. W., SABAGH, G., and VAN ARSDOL, D. (1964). Demographic and social psychological factors in residential mobility. *Sociology and Social Research* 46 (1): 139–154.

FOOTE, N., et al. (1960). *Housing choices and housing constraints.* New York: McGraw-Hill.

GANS, H. J. (1962a). *The urban villagers: Group and class in the life of Italian Americans.* New York: Free Press.

GANS, H. J. (1962b). Urbanism and suburbanism as ways of life: A re-evaluation of definitions. In A. Rose (editor), *Human behavior and social processes.* Boston, MA: Houghton Mifflin.

GUEST, A. M., and LEE, B. A. (1985). Consensus on locality names within the metropolis. *Sociology and Social Research* 67 (4): 374–391.

HARRIS, C. D., and ULLMAN, E. L. (1945). The nature of cities. *The Annals of the American Academy of Political Science* 242 (1): 7–17.

HARVEY, D. (1985). *The urbanization of capital: Studies in the history and theory of capitalist urbanization.* Baltimore, MD: The Johns Hopkins University Press.

HOOVER, E. M., and VERNON, R. (1959). *Anatomy of a metropolis.* Cambridge, MA: Harvard University Press.

HOYT, H. (1939). *The structure and growth of residential neighborhoods in American cities.* Washington, DC: Federal Housing Administration.

HUNTER, A. (1974). *Symbolic communities: The persistence and change of Chicago's local communities.* Chicago, IL: University of Chicago Press.

LAND, K. C. (1969). Duration of residence and prospective migration: Further evidence. *Demography* 6: 133–140.

LESLIE, B. R., and RICHARDSON, A. H. (1961). Life cycle, career patterns, and decision to move. *American Sociological Review* 26 (4): 894–902.

LIPSET, S. M., and BENDIX, R. (1959). *Social mobility in industrial society*. Berkeley, CA: University of California Press.

LOGAN, J. R., and COLLVER, O. A. (1983). Residents' perceptions of suburban community differences. *American Sociological Review* 48 (2): 428–433.

MICHELSON, W. (1977). *Environmental choice, human behavior, and residential satisfaction*. New York: Oxford University Press.

MICHELSON, W. (1970). *Man and his urban environment*. Reading, MA: Addison-Wesley.

MORRISON, P. A. (1967). Duration of residence and prospective migration: The evaluation of a stochastic model. *Demography* 4: 4.

NIEDERCORN, J. H., and HEARLE, E. F. (1964). Recent land use trends in 48 large American cities. *Land Economics* 40 (1): 105–110.

PARK, R. E. (1952). *Human communities*. Glencoe, IL: Free Press.

REES, P. H. (1970). Concepts of social space: Toward an urban social geography. In B. J. L. Berry and F. E. Horton (editors), *Geographical perspectives in urban systems*. Englewood Cliffs, NJ: Prentice-Hall.

ROSS, H. L. (1962). The local community: A survey approach. *American Sociological Review* 27 (1): 75–84.

ROSSI, P. H. (1955). *Why families move: A study in the social psychology of urban residential mobility*. New York: Free Press.

SABAGH, G., VAN ARSDOL, M. D., and BUTLER, E. W. (1969). Some determinants of intermetropolitan residential mobility: Conceptual considerations. *Social Forces* 48 (1): 88–98.

SELL, R. R., and DEJONG, G. F. (1985). Deciding whether to move: Mobility, wishful thinking and adjustment. *Sociology and Social Research* 67 (2): 146–165.

SEMYONOV, M., and KRAUS, V. (1982). The social hierarchies of communities and neighborhoods. *Social Science Quarterly* 63 (4): 780–789.

SHEVKY, E., and BELL, W. (1955). *Social area analysis: Theory, illustrative application and computational procedures*. Stanford, CA: Stanford University Press.

SHEVKY, E., and WILLIAMS, M. (1949). *The social areas of Los Angeles: Analysis and typology*. Berkeley, CA: University of California Press.

SIMMONS, J. (1968). Changing residence in the city: A review of intra-urban mobility. *Geographical Review* 58 (4): 622–651.

SPEARE, A. (1970). Home ownership, life cycle stage, and residential mobility. *Demography* 7 (4): 449–458.

SPEARE, A. (1974). Residential satisfaction as an intervening variable in residential mobility. *Demography* 11 (2): 173–188.

TOBIN, G. A., and JUDD, D. R. (1982). Moving the suburbs to the city: Neighborhood revitalization and the "amenities bundle". *Social Science Quarterly* 63 (4): 771–779.

VARADY, D. P. (1989). The impact of city/suburban location on moving plans: A Cincinnati study. *Growth and Change* 20 (2): 35–49.

WHITE, M. J. (1987). *American neighborhoods and residential differentiation*. New York: Russell Sage Foundation.

WOLPERT, J. (1965). Behavioral aspects of the decision to migrate. *Papers of the Regional Science Association* 15: 159–169.

CHAPTER TEN

ABBOTT, C. (1981). *The new urban America: Growth and politics in Sunbelt cities*. Chapel Hill, NC: University of North Carolina Press.

ABBOTT, C. (1987). The suburban Sunbelt. *Journal of Urban History* 13 (3):275–301.

BALDASSARE, M. (1986). *Trouble in paradise: The suburban transformation in America*. New York: Columbia University Press.

BAUMGARTNER, M. P. (1988). *The moral order of a suburb*. New York: Oxford University Press.

BELL, W. (1958). Social choice, life styles, and suburban residence. In R. Dobriner (editor), *The suburban community*. New York: G. P. Putnam's Sons.

BERGER, B. M. (1960). *The working-class suburb: A study of auto workers in suburbia*. Berkeley, CA: University of California Press.

BERRY, B. J. L., and KASARDA, J. D. (1977). *Contemporary urban ecology*. New York: Macmillan.

BINFORD, H. C. (1985). *The first suburbs: Residential communities on the Boston periphery, 1815–1860*. Chicago, IL: The University of Chicago Press.

BOOTH, A., and CHOLDIN, H. (1985). Housing type and the residential experiences of middle-class mothers. *Sociological Focus* 18 (2):97–107.

BOSKOFF, A. (1970). *The sociology of urban regions*. New York: Appleton-Century-Crofts.

CLARK, T. A. (1979). *Blacks in suburbs: A national perspective*. New Brunswick, NJ: Rutgers University, Center for Urban Policy Research.

COOK, C. C. (1988). Components of neighborhood satisfaction: Responses from urban and suburban single-parent women. *Environment and Behavior* 20 (21):115–149.

DANIELSON, M. N. (1976). *The politics of exclusion*. New York: Columbia University Press.

DENOWITZ, R. M. (1984). "Where have all the people gone?" Recent inconsistencies between population growth and housing development in suburban Chicago. *Urban Affairs Quarterly* 20 (2):255–264.

DOUGLAS, P. H. (1925). *The suburban trend*. New York: Century.

EBNER, M. H. (1988). *Creating Chicago's North Shore: A suburban history*. Chicago, IL: The University of Chicago Press.

EDMONSTON, B., and GUTERBOCK, T. M. (1984). Is suburbanization slowing down? Recent trends in population deconcentration in U.S. metropolitan areas. *Social Forces* 62 (4):905–925.

FARLEY, J. E. (1987). Suburbanization and central-city crime rates: New evidence and a reinterpretation. *American Journal of Sociology* 93 (3):688–700.

FARLEY, R. (1976). Components of suburban population growth. In B. Schwartz (editor), *The changing face of the suburbs*. Chicago, IL: University of Chicago Press.

FARLEY, R. (1974). Suburban persistence. In K. P. Schwirian (editor), *Comparative urban structure*. Lexington, MA: D.C. Heath Co.

FAVA, S. F. (1958). Contrasts in neighboring: New York City and a suburban community. In W. M. Dobriner (editor), *The suburban community*. New York: G. P. Putnam's Sons.

FAVA, S. F. (1985). Residential preferences in the suburban era: A new look? *Sociological Focus* 18 (2):109–117.

FISCHER, C. S. (1982). *To dwell among friends: Personal networks in town and city*. Chicago, IL: University of Chicago Press.

FISCHER, C. S., and JACKSON, M. (1976). Suburbs, networks, and attitudes. In B. Schwartz (editor), *The changing face of the suburbs*. Chicago, IL: University of Chicago Press.

FITZPATRICK, K. M., and LOGAN, J. R. (1985). The aging of the suburbs, 1960–1980. *American Sociological Review* 50 (February):106–117.

FOGLESONG, R. E. (1986). *Planning the capitalist city: The colonial era to the 1920s*. Princeton, NJ: Princeton University Press.

GANS, H. J. (1962). *The urban villagers: Group and class in the life of Italian Americans*. New York: The Free Press.

GREER, S. (1962). *The emerging city: Myth and reality*. New York: The Free Press.

GUEST, A. M. (1978). Suburban social status: Persistence or evolution. *American Sociological Review* 43 (2):251–263.

GUTOWSKI, M., and FIELD, T. (1979). *The graying of suburbia*. Washington, DC: The Urban Institute.

HAMILTON, F. E. I. (1967). Models of industrial location. In R. Charley and P. Haggett (editors), *Models in geography*. London: Methuen.

HAMILTON, F. E. I. (1974). *Spatial perspectives on industrial organization and decision making*. London: John Wiley and Sons.

JACKSON, K. T. (1985). *Crabgrass frontier: The suburbanization of the United States*. New York: Oxford University Press.

KRIVO, L. J., and FRISBIE, P. W. (1982). Measuring change: The case of suburban status. *Urban Affairs Quarterly* 17 (4):419–444.

LAKE, R. W. (1981). *The new suburbanites: Race and housing in the suburbs*. New Brunswick, NJ: Center for Urban Policy Research, Rutgers University.

LAM, F. (1986). Suburban residential segregation of Chinese and Japanese Americans: 1960, 1970, and 1980. *Sociology and Social Research* 70 (4):263–265.

LEES, A. (1985). *Cities perceived: Urban society in European and American thought, 1820–1940*. New York: Columbia University Press.

LOGAN, J. R., and GOLDEN, R. M. (1986). Suburbs and satellites: Two decades of change. *American Sociological Review* 51 (3):430–437.

LOGAN, J. R., and SCHNEIDER, M. (1982). Governmental organization and city/suburb income inequality, 1960–1970. *Urban Affairs Quarterly* 17 (3):303–318.

LOGAN, J. R., and SCHNEIDER, M. (1984). Racial segregation and racial change in American suburbs, 1970–1980. *American Journal of Sociology* 89 (4):874–888.

LOGAN, J. R., and SCHNEIDER, M. (1981). The stratification of metropolitan suburbs, 1960–1970. *American Sociological Review* 46 (April):175–186.

LOPATA, H. Z. (1980). The Chicago woman: A study of patterns of mobility and transportation. *Signs: Journal of Women in Culture and Society* 5 (3):161–169.

MARSHALL, H., and STAHURA, J. M. (1986). The theory of ecological expansion: The relation between dominance and suburban differentiation. *Social Forces* 65 (2):352–369.

MARTIN, W. T. (1958). The structuring of social relationships engendered by suburban residence. In W. M. Dobriner (editor), *The suburban community*. New York: G. P. Putnam's and Sons.

MASETTI, L. H., and HADDEN, J. K. (1973). *The urbanization of the suburbs*. Beverly Hills, CA: Sage Publications.

MASSEY, D., and DENTON, N. A. (1988). Suburbanization and segregation in U.S. metropolitan areas. *American Journal of Sociology* 94 (3):592–626.

MCKELVEY, B. (1963). *The urbanization of America, 1860–1915*. New Brunswick, NJ: Rutgers University Press.

MICHELSON, W. (1976). *Man and his urban environment: A sociological approach.* Reading, MA: Addison-Wesley.

MICHELSON, W. (1977). *Environmental choice, human behavior, and residential satisfaction.* New York: Oxford University Press.

MILLER, Z. L. (1981). *Suburb: Neighborhood and community in Forest Park, Ohio, 1935–1976.* Knoxville, TN: The University of Tennessee Press.

MOWRER, E. R. (1958). The family in suburbia. In W. M. Dobriner (editor), *The suburban community.* New York: G.P. Putnam's Sons.

MULLER, P. O. (1981). *Contemporary suburban America.* Englewood Cliffs, NJ: Prentice-Hall, Inc.

PETERSON, G. E., and LEWIS, C. W. (1986). *Reagan and the cities.* Washington, DC: The Urban Institute.

REISMAN, D. (1958). The suburban sadness. In W. M. Dobriner (editor), *The suburban community.* New York: G.P. Putnam's Sons.

ROSENBERG, C. E. (1962). *The cholera years: The disease in America, 1832, 1846, 1867.* Chicago, IL: University of Chicago Press.

ROTHBLATT, D. N., GARR, D. J., and SPRAGUE, J. (1979). *The suburban environment and women.* New York: Praeger Publishers.

SCHNEIDER, M. (1980). *Suburban growth: Policy and process.* Brunswick, OH: King's Court Communications, Inc.

SCHNEIDER, M., and LOGAN, J. (1985). Suburban municipalities: The changing system of intergovernmental relations in the mid-1970s. *Urban Affairs Quarterly* 21 (1):87–105.

SCHNORE, L. F. (1957). Satellites and suburbs. *Social Forces* 36 (1):122–127.

SCHNORE, L. F. (1965). *The urban scene.* New York: The Free Press.

SCHWARTZ, B. (1976). *The changing face of the suburbs.* Chicago, IL: University of Chicago Press.

SCHWIRIAN, K. P. (1977). *Contemporary topics in urban sociology.* Morristown, NJ: General Learning Press.

SEELEY, J. F., SIM, R. A., and LOOSLEY, E. W. (1956). *Crestwood Heights.* New York: Basic Books.

SLOVAK, J. (1985). City spending, suburban demands, and fiscal exploitation: A replication and extension. *Social Forces* 64 (1):168–190.

SPAIN, D. (1988). An examination of residential preferences in the suburban era. *Sociological Focus* 21 (1):1–8.

SPECTORSKY, A. C. (1955). *The exurbanites.* New York: Berkeley Publishers.

STAHURA, J. M. (1988b). Black and white population change in small American suburbs since World War II: Regional differences. *Sociological Focus* 21 (4):317–329.

STAHURA, J. M. (1988a). Changing patterns of suburban racial composition, 1970–1980. *Urban Affairs Quarterly* 23 (3):448–460.

STAHURA, J. M. (1987b). Characteristics of black suburbs, 1950–1980. *Sociology and Social Research* 71 (2):135–138.

STAHURA, J. M. (1982). Determinants of suburban job change in retailing, wholesaling, service and manufacturing industries, 1960–1972. *Sociological Focus* 15 (4):347–357.

STAHURA, J. M. (1984). A research note on the metropolitan determinants of suburban persistence. *Social Forces* 62 (3):767–774.

STAHURA, J. M. (1986). Suburban development, black suburbanization and the civil rights movement since World War II. *American Sociological Review* 51 (February):131–144.

STAHURA, J. M. (1987b). Suburban socioeconomic status change: A comparison of models, 1950–1980. *American Sociological Review* 52 (2):268–277.

STAHURA, J. M., and MARSHALL, H. H. (1982). The role of annexation in the growth of American suburbs. *Sociological Focus* 15 (1):15–24.

STANBACK, T. M., JR., and KNIGHT, R. V. (1976). *Suburbanization and the city*. Montclair, NJ: Allanheld, Osmun and Co. Publishers, Inc.

TEAFORD, J. C. (1979). *City and suburb: The political fragmentation of metropolitan America, 1850–1970*. Baltimore, MD: Johns Hopkins University Press.

TOBIN, G. A. (1976). Suburbanization and the development of motor transportation: Transportation technology and the suburbanization process. In B. Schwartz (editor), *The changing face of the suburbs*. Chicago, IL: University of Chicago Press.

U.S. BUREAU OF LABOR STATISTICS (1989). *Geographic profile of employment and unemployment 1988*. Washington, DC: U.S. Government Printing Office.

U.S. BUREAU OF THE CENSUS (1983). *State and metropolitan Area data book*. Washington, DC: U.S. Government Printing Office.

U.S. BUREAU OF THE CENSUS (1987). *State and metropolitan area data book 1986*. Washington, DC: U.S. Government Printing Office.

U.S. BUREAU OF THE CENSUS (1984). *Statistical abstract of the United States 1983*. Washington, DC: U.S. Government Printing Office.

U.S. BUREAU OF THE CENSUS (1989). *Statistical abstract of the United States 1989*. Washington, DC: U.S. Government Printing Office.

WARD, D. (1964). A comparative historical geography of streetcar suburbs in Boston, Massachusetts and Leeds, England: 1850–1920. *Annals of the Association of American Geographers* 54:1477–1489.

WARNER, S. B. (1962). *Streetcar suburbs: The process of growth in Boston*. Cambridge, MA: Harvard University Press.

WEBER, A. F. (1963). *The growth of cities in the nineteenth century: A study of statistics*. Ithaca, NY: Cornell University Press.

WEBER, A. (1929). *Theory of the location of industries*. Chicago, IL: University of Chicago Press.

WEKERLE, G. R. (1980). Women in the urban environment. *Signs: Journal of women in culture and society* 5 (3):188–214.

WELFELD, I. H. (1986). Our graying suburbs: Solving an unusual housing problem. *The public interest* 85 (Fall):50–57.

WHYTE, W. F. (1956). *The organization man*. Garden City, NJ: Doubleday.

CHAPTER ELEVEN

AXELROD, M. (1955). Urban structure and participation. In P. K. Hatt and A. J. Reiss (editors), *Cities and society*. Glencoe, IL: Free Press.

BELL, C., and NEWBY, H. (1972). *Community studies: An introduction to the sociology of local community*. New York: Praeger Publishers.

BERKOWITZ, S. D. (1982). *An introduction to structural analysis: The network approach to social research*. Toronto, Canada: Butterworths.

COSER, L. A. (1971). *Masters of sociological thought*. New York: Harcourt Brace Jovanovich, Inc.

DAVIE, M. R. (1938). The pattern of urban growth. In G. D. Murdock (editor), *Studies in the science of society*. New Haven, CN: Yale University Press.

FISCHER, C. S. (1982). *To dwell among friends: Personal networks in town and city*. Chicago, IL: University of Chicago Press.

FISCHER, C. S. (1976). *The urban experience*. New York: Harcourt Brace Jovanovich.

FISCHER, C. S., JACKSON, R. M., STUEVE, C. A., GERSON, K., JONES, L. M., and BALDASSARE, M. (1977). *Networks and places: Social relations in the urban setting*. New York: The Free Press.

FORM, W. H., SMITH, J., STONE, G. P., and COWHIG, J. (1954). The compatibility of alternative approaches to the delimitation of urban subareas. *American Sociological Review* 19 (2): 176–187.

GANS, H. J. (1962). *The urban villagers: Group and class in the life of Italian Americans*. New York: The Free Press.

GIDDENS, A. (1972). *Emile Durkheim: Selected writings*. Cambridge, England: Cambridge University Press.

GREER, S. (1962). *The emerging city: Myth and reality*. New York: The Free Press.

GREER, S. O. P. (1962). The mass society and the parapolitical structure. *American Sociological Review* 27 (4): 634–646.

GREER, S. (1970). The social structure of the political process of suburbia. In R. Gutman and D. Popenoe (editors), *Neighborhood, city, and metropolis: An integrated reader in urban sociology*. New York: Random House.

HATT, P. K. (1946). The concept of natural area. *American Sociological Review* 11: 423–428.

HAWLEY, A. H. (1950). *Human ecology: A theory of community structure*. New York: Ronald Press.

HAWLEY, A. H., and ZIMMER, B. (1970). *The metropolitan community*. Beverly Hills, CA: Sage Publications.

HUNTER, A. (1974). *Symbolic communities: The persistence and change of Chicago's local communities*. Chicago, IL: University of Chicago Press.

JANOWITZ, M. (1961). *The community press in an urban setting: The social elements of urbanism*. Chicago, IL: University of Chicago Press.

KARP, D. A., STONE, G. P., and YOELS, W. C. (1977). *Being urban: A social psychological view of city life*. Lexington, MA: D. C. Heath and Co.

KASARDA, J. D., and JANOWITZ, M. (1974). Community attachments in mass society. *American Sociological Review* 39: 328–339.

KELLER, S. (1968). *The urban neighborhood: A sociological perspective*. New York: Random House.

LIEBOW, E. (1967). *Tally's corner*. Boston, MA: Little, Brown and Co.

LYON, L. (1987). *The community in urban society*. Chicago, IL: The Dorsey Press.

MICHELSON, W. (1970). *Man and his urban environment*. Reading, MA: Addison-Wesley.

MORRIS, R. N., and MOGEY, J. (1965). *The sociology of housing*. London: Cambridge University Press.

NISBET, R. A. (1966). *The sociological tradition*. New York: Basic Books, Inc.

PARK, R. E. (1952). *Human communities*. Glencoe, IL: The Free Press.

PARK, R. E., and MILLER, H. A. (1921). *Old World traits transplanted*. New York: Harper and Bros.

SIMMEL, G. (1955). The web of group-affiliations. In K. Wolff and R. Bendix (translators and editors), *Conflict and the web of group affiliations*. Glencoe, IL: The Free Press.

STEIN, M. (1972). *The eclipse of community: An interpretation of American studies*. Princeton, NJ: Princeton University Press.

SUTTLES, G. (1968). *The social orders of the slums*. Chicago, IL: University of Chicago Press.

SUTTLES, G. (1972). *The social construction of communities*. Chicago, IL: University of Chicago Press.

THRASHER, F. (1926). *The gang*. Chicago, IL: University of Chicago Press.

WARREN, R. L. (1978). *The community in America*. Chicago, IL: Rand McNally.

WELLMAN, B. (1979). The community question: The intimate networks of East Yorkers. *American Journal of Sociology* 84: 1201–1231.

WHYTE, W. F. (1943). Social organization in the slums. *American Sociological Review* 8 (1): 34–39.

WHYTE, W. F. (1955). *Street corner society*. Chicago, IL: University of Chicago Press.

WIRTH, L. (1928). *The ghetto*. Chicago, IL: University of Chicago Press.

ZORBAUGH, H. (1929). *The Gold Coast and the slum*. Chicago, IL: University of Chicago Press.

CHAPTER TWELVE

AGOCS, C. (1981). Ethnic settlement in a metropolitan area: A typology of communities. *Ethnicity* 8: 127–148.

ALBA, R. D., and CHAMLIN, M. B. (1983). A preliminary examination of ethnic identification among whites. *American Sociological Review* 48 (April): 240–247.

ALDRICH, H. (1975). Ecological succession in racially changing neighborhoods: A review of the literature. *Urban Affairs Quarterly* 10: 327–348.

ALDRICH, H., and REISS, A. J., JR. (1977). Continuities in the Study of ecological succession: Changes in the race composition of neighborhoods and their businesses. *American Journal of Sociology* 81: 846–866.

ARMOR, D. J. (1972). The evidence of busing. *The Public Interest* 20: 90–126.

BIERSTEDT, R. (1974). *The social order*. New York: McGraw-Hill.

BLEDEA, S. E. (1978). Intergenerational differences in patterns and bases of ethnic residential dissimilarity. *Ethnicity* 5: 91–107.

BLEDEA, S. E. (1979). Socioeconomic, demographic, and cultural bases of ethnic residential segregation. *Ethnicity* 6: 147–167.

BOAL, F. W. (1981). Ethnic residential segregation. In H. Johnston (editor), *The geography of housing*. London: Aldein, pp. 41–77.

BRUECKNER, J. (1977). The determinants of residential succession. *Journal of Urban Economics* 4: 45–59.

BURGESS, E. W. (1925). The growth of the city: An introduction to a research project. In R. E. Park, E. K. Burgess, and R. D. McKenzie (editors), *The city*. Chicago: University of Chicago Press.

BURGESS, E. W. (1928). Residential segregation in American cities. *Annals of the American Academy of Political and Social Sciences* 140 (November): 105–115.

CHRISMAN, N. J. (1981). Ethnic persistence in an urban setting. *Ethnicity* 8: 256–292.

CLARK, W. A. V. (1986). Residential segregation in American cities: A review and interpretation. *Population Research and Policy Review* 5: 95–127.

COLEMAN, J. (1966). *Equality of educational opportunity.* Washington, D.C.: U.S. Government Printing Office.

COWGILL, D. (1978). Residential segregation by age in American metropolitan areas. *Journal of Gerontology* 33: 446–453.

DUNCAN, O. D., and DUNCAN, B. (1957). *The Negro population of Chicago.* Chicago: University of Chicago Press.

EDWARDS, O. (1972). Family composition as a variable in residential succession. *American Journal of Sociology* 77: 731–741.

ERBE, B. M. (1975). Race and socioeconomic segregation within a metropolitan ghetto. *American Sociological Review* 40: 801–812.

FARLEY, J. E. (1987). Disproportionate black and Hispanic unemployment in U.S. metropolitan areas: The roles of racial inequality, segregation and discrimination in male joblessness. *The American Journal of Economics and Sociology,* 46 (2): 129–150.

FARLEY, J. E. (1984). P* segregation indices: What can they tell us about housing segregation in 1980. *Urban Studies* 21: 331–336.

FARLEY, R., and WILGER, R. (1987). *Recent changes in the residential segregation of blacks from whites: An analysis of 203 metropolises* (Report 15). Ann Arbor, MI: Population Studies Center.

FITZPATRICK, K. M., and LOGAN, J. R. (1985). The aging of the suburbs, 1960–1980. *American Sociological Review* 50 (February): 106–117.

FOSSETT, M., GALLE, O. R., and KELLY, W. R. (1986). Racial occupational inequality, 1940–1980: National and regional trends. *American Sociological Review* 51 (June): 421–429.

FOSSETT, M., and SWICEGOOD, G. (1982). Rediscovering city differences in racial occupational inequality. *American Sociological Review* 47 (October): 681–689.

GALSTER, G. C. (1987). The ecology of racial discrimination in housing: An exploratory model. *Urban Affairs Quarterly* 23 (1): 84–107.

GLAZER, N., and MOYNIHAN, D. (1963). *Beyond the melting pot: The Negroes, Puerto Ricans, Jews, Italians, and Irish of New York City.* Cambridge, MA: M.I.T. Press.

GOLANT, S. M., and JACOBSEN, C. W. (1978). Factors underlying the decentralized residential locations of Chicago's ethnic population. *Ethnicity* 5: 379–397.

GORDON, M. M. (1964). *Assimilation in American life.* New York: Oxford University Press.

GRODZINS, M. (1957). Metropolitan segregation. *Scientific American* 197: 33–41.

HANLIN, O. (1969). *Boston's immigrants: 1790–1880.* New York: Atheneum.

HERSHBERG, T., BURSTEIN, A. N., ERICKSEN E. P., GREENBERG, S., and YANCEY, W. L. (1979). A tale of three cities: Blacks and immigrants in Philadelphia: 1850–1880, 1930, and 1970. *The Annals of the American Academy of Political and Social Science* 441 (January): 55–81.

HERSHBERG, T., COX, H., LIGHT, D., and GREENFIELD, R. R. (1981). The journey to work: An empirical investigation of work, residence and transportation in Philadelphia, 1850–1880. In T. Hershgerg (editor), *Work, space, family and group experience in the nineteenth century.* New York: Oxford University Press, pp. 392–434.

KAIN, J. F., and QUIGLEY, F. (1972). Housing market discrimination, home ownership and savings behavior. *American Economic Review* 62: 263–277.

KANTROWITZ, N. (1973). *Ethnic and racial segregation in the New York metropolis.* New York: Praeger.

KATZMAN, D. (1973). *Before the ghetto: Black Detroit in the nineteenth century.* Urbana, IL: University of Illinois Press.

KENNEDY, J. M., and DE JONG, G. F. (1977). Aged in cities: Residential segregation in 10 USA central cities. *Journal of Gerontology* 32: 97–102.

KLAFF, V. Z. (1980). Pluralism as an alternative model for the human ecologist. *Ethnicity* 7: 102–118.

KLAFF, V. Z. (1977). Residence and integration in Israel: A mosaic of segregated people. *Ethnicity* 4: 102–121.

KOLKO, G. (1972). *Wealth and power in America: An analysis of social class and income distribution.* New York: Praeger.

LAGORY, M., WARD, R., and JURAVICH, T. (1980). The age segregation process: Explanation for American cities. *Urban Affairs Quarterly* 16: 59–80.

LEWIN-EPSTEIN, N. (1986). Effects of residential segregation and neighborhood opportunity structure on the employment of black and white youth. *The Sociological Quarterly* 27 (4): 559–570.

LIEBERSON, S., and CARTER, D. K. (1982). A model for inferring the voluntary and involuntary causes of residential segregation. *Demography* 19 (4): 511–526.

LOGAN, J. R., and SCHNEIDER, M. (1984). Racial segregation and racial change in American suburbs, 1970–1980. *American Journal of Sociology* 89 (4): 874–888.

MASSEY, D. S. (1981a). Dimensions of the new immigration to the United States and the prospects for assimilation. *Annual Review of Sociology* 7: 57–87.

MASSEY, D. S. (1979). Effects of socioeconomic factors on the residential segregation of blacks and Spanish Americans in U.S. urbanized areas. *American Sociological Review* 44 (December): 1015–1022.

MASSEY, D. S. (1985). Ethnic residential segregation: A theoretical synthesis and empirical review. *Sociology and Social Research* 69 (3): 315–350.

MASSEY, D. S. (1981c). Hispanic Residential Segregation: A Comparison of Mexicans, Curbas, and Puerto Ricans. *Sociology and Social Research*, 65(3), 311–322.

MASSEY, D. S. (1986). The settlement process among Mexican migrants to the United States. *American Sociological Review* 51 (October): 670–684.

MASSEY, D. S. (1981b). Social class and ethnic segregation: A reconsideration of methods and conclusions. *American Sociological Review* 46 (October): 641–650.

MASSEY, D. S. (1987). Understanding Mexican migration to the United States. *American Journal of Sociology* 92(6): 1372–1403.

MASSEY, D. S., and DENTON, N. A. (1987). Trends in the residential segregation of blacks, Hispanics, and Asians: 1970–1980. *American Sociological Review*, 52 (December): 802–825.

MASSEY, D. S., and SCHNABEL, K. M. (1983). Recent trends in Hispanic immigration to the United States. *International Migration Review* 17 (2): 212–244.

MOLTOCH, H. (1969). Racial change in a stable community. *American Journal of Sociology* 75: 226–238.

NEIDERT, L. J., and FARLEY, R. (1985). Assimilation in the United States: An analysis of ethnic and generation differences in status and achievement. *American Sociological Review* 50 (December): 840–850.

NOVAK, M. (1971). *The rise of the unmeltable ethnics*. New York: Macmillan.

PARK, R. E. (1926). The urban community as a spatial pattern and a moral order. In Ernest W. Burgess (editor), *The urban community*. Chicago, IL: University of Chicago Press.

PRANDY, K. (1980). Residential segregation and ethnic distance in English cities. *Ethnicity* 7: 367–389.

PRYOR, F. L. (1971). An empirical note on the tipping point. *Land Economics* 47: 413–417.

SCHNELLING, T. C. (1972). A process of residential segregation: neighborhood tipping. In A. H. Pascal (editor), *Racial discrimination in economic life*. Lexington, MA: D. C. Heath.

SCHWAB, W. A. (1988). The predictive value of three ecological models. *Urban Affairs Quarterly* 23 (2): 295–308.

SCHWAB, W. A. (1980). The tipping point model: Prediction of change in the racial composition of Cleveland, Ohio's neighborhoods, 1940–1970. *Environment and Change* 11 (March): 121–128.

SCHWAB, W. A. (1982). *Urban sociology: A human ecological perspective*. Reading, MA: Addison-Wesley Publishing Company.

SCHWIRIAN, K. P., and RICO-VELASCO, J. (1971). The residential distribution of status groups in Puerto Rico's metropolitan areas. *Demography* 8: 81–90.

SIMKUS, A. A. (1978). Residential segregation by occupation and race in ten urbanized areas, 1950–1970. *American Sociological Review* 48: 81–93.

SMITH, T. L., and ZOPF, P. E. (1976). *Demography: Principles and methods*. Port Washington, NY: Alfred.

SORENSON, A., TAEUBER, K. E., and HOLLINGSWORTH, L. J. (1975). Indexes of racial residential segregation for 109 cities in the United States, 1940–1970. *Sociological Focus* 8: 125–142.

STAHURA, J. M. (1988). Changing patterns of suburban racial composition, 1970–1980. *Urban Affairs Quarterly* 23 (3): 448–460.

STAHURA, J. M. (1986). Suburban development, black suburbanization and the civil rights movement since World War II. *American Sociological Review* 51 (February): 131–144.

STEARNS, L. B., and LOGAN, J. R. (1986). Measuring trends in segregation: Three dimensions, three measures. *Urban Affairs Quarterly* 22 (1): 124–150.

STEARNS, L. B., and LOGAN, J. R. (1986). The racial structuring of the housing market and segregation in suburban areas. *Social Forces* 65 (1): 28–42.

STEINNES, D. N. (1977). Alternative models of neighborhood change. *Social Forces* 55: 1043–1057.

TAEUBER, K. E. (1968). The effect of income redistribution on racial residential segregation. *Urban Affairs Quarterly* 4: 4–14.

TAEUBER, K. E., and TAEUBER, A. R. (1965). *Negroes in cities*. Chicago: Aldine.

TAYLOR, H. L. (1986). Spatial organization and the residential experience: Black Cincinnati in 1850. *Social Science History* 10 (1): 45–69.

TECHATRAISAK, B. (1978). *The changes in residential patterns of an ethno-religious group: The case of Greeks in Cincinnati, Ohio*. Unpublished doctoral dissertation, University of Cincinnati, Cincinnati, OH.

TIMMS, D. W. G. (1971). *The urban mosaic: Towards a theory of residential differrentiation*. Cambridge, England: Cambridge University Press.

U.S. BUREAU OF THE CENSUS (1982). *Census of the population. 1980: Characteristics of the population: Number of inhabitants*. Washington, DC: U.S. Government Printing Office.

U.S. BUREAU OF THE CENSUS (1982). *Statistical abstract of the United States, 1986*. Washington, DC: U.S. Government Printing Office.

U.S. COMMISSION ON CIVIL RIGHTS (1975). *Twenty years after Brown: Equal opportunity in housing*. Washington, DC: U.S. Govermental Printing Office.

WHITE, M. J. (1984). Racial and ethnic succession in four cities. *Urban Affairs Quarterly* 20 (2): 165–183.

WIENK, R. E., et al. (1979). *Measuring racial discrimination in American housing markets: The housing market practices survey*. Washington, DC: The U.S. Department of Housing and Urban Development, Office of Policy Development and Research.

WILSON, W. J. (1987). *The truly disadvantaged: The inner city, the underclass, and public policy*. Chicago: The University of Chicago Press.

WOLF, E. T. (1965). The tipping-point in racially changing neighborhoods. *Papers of the Regional Science Association* 15: 159–169.

CHAPTER THIRTEEN

AD HOC TASK FORCE ON AIDS. (1987). Committee on the Budget of the House of Representatives of the 100th Congress, *AIDS crisis as related to the federal budget*. Washington, DC: U.S. Government Printing Office.

ALBERT, E. (1986). Illness and deviance: The response of the press to AIDS. In D. A. Feldman and T. Johnson (editors), *The social dimensions of AIDS*. New York, NY: Praeger, pp. 163–178.

BAKER, A. J. (1986). The portrayal of AIDS in the media: An analysis of articles in the New York Times. In D. A. Feldman and T. Johnson (editors), *The social dimensions of AIDS*. New York: Praeger, pp. 179–196.

BANFIELD, E. C. (1970). *The unheavenly city*. Boston, MA: Little, Brown and Co.

BERRY, B. J., et al. (1974). *Land use, urban form and environmental quality*. Chicago, IL: University of Chicago Press.

BLAU, J. R., and BLAU, P. M. (1982). Metropolitan structure and violent crime. *American Sociological Review* 47: 114–128.

BOLOGNONE, D., and JOHNSON, T. M. (1986). Explanatory models for AIDS. In D. A. Feldman and T. Johnson (editors), *The social dimensions of AIDS*. New York, NY: Praeger, pp. 211–226.

BURSIK, R. J., JR. (1988). Social disorganization and theories of crime and delinquency: Problems and prospects. *Criminology* 26 (4): 519–551.

CALLERO, P. L., et al. (1986). Fear of AIDS and its effects on the nation's blood supply. In D. A. Feldman and T. Johnson (editors), *The social dimensions of AIDS*. New York: Praeger, pp. 227–234.

CARLINER, M. S. (1987). Homelessness: A housing problem? In R. D. Bingham, R. E. Green, and S. B. White (editors), *The homeless in contemporary society*. Newbury Park, CA: Sage Publications, pp. 119–129.

CASTELLS, M. (1977). *The urban question*. London: Edward Arnold.

CATON, C. L. (1990b). The epidemiology of homelessness. In C. L. Caton (editor), *Homeless in America*. New York: Oxford University Press.

CATON, C. L. (1990a). Homelessness in historical perspective. In C. L. Caton (editor), *Homeless in America*. New York: Oxford University Press, pp. 1–18.

CATON, C. L. (1990c). Solutions to the homeless problem. In C. L. Caton (editor), *Homeless in America*. New York: Oxford University Press, pp. 174–190.

CURRIE, E. (1985). *Confronting crime: An American challenge*. New York: Pantheon Books.

DARROW, W. W., et al. (1986). The social origins of AIDS: social change, sexual behavior, and disease trends. In D. A. Feldman and T. Johnson (editors), *The social dimensions of AIDS*. New York: Praeger, pp. 95–110.

DART, B. (December 19, 1990). Americans turning away the homeless: Mayors' survey finds public tolerance waning. *The Arkansas Gazette*, p. 21.

DEAR, M. J., and WOLCH, J. R. (1987). *Landscapes of despair*. Princeton, NJ: Princeton University Press.

DES JARLAIS, D. C., et al. (1986). AIDS and needle sharing within the IV-drug use subculture. In D. A. Feldman and T. Johnson (editors), *The social dimensions of AIDS*. New York: Praeger, pp. 111–126.

DUSTER, T. (1987). Crime, youth unemployment, and the black urban underclass. *Crime and Delinquency*, 33 300–316.

EAGLE, P. F., and CATON, C. L. (1990). Homelessness and mental illness. In C. L. Caton (editor), *Homeless in America*. New York: Oxford University Press, pp. 59–75.

FELDMAN, D. A. (1986). AIDS health promotion and clinically applied anthropology. In D. A. Feldman and T. Johnson (editors), *The social dimensions of AIDS*. New York: Praeger, pp. 145–162.

FISCHER, C. S. (1975). Toward a subcultural theory of urbanism. *American Journal of Sociology* 80: 1319–1341.

HELLINGER, F. J. (1990). *Updated forecasts of the cots of medical care for persons with AIDS, 1989–93*. Washington, DC: U.S. Agency for Health Care Policy and Research.

HOCH, C. (1987). A brief history of the homeless problem in the United States. In R. D. Bingham, R. E. Green, and S. B. White (editors), *The homeless in contemporary society*. Newbury Park, CA: Sage Publications, pp. 8–16.

JAGER, J. C., and RUITENBERG, E. J. (1988). *Statistical analysis and mathematical modelling of AIDS*. New York: Oxford University Press.

JAHIEL, R. I. (1987). The situation of homelessness. In R. D. Bingham, R. E. Green, and S. B. White (editors), *The homeless in contemporary society*. Newbury Park, CA: Sage Publications, pp. 99–118.

KOCH, J. Q. (1987). The federal role in aiding the homeless. In R. D. Bingham, R. E. Gree, and S. B. White (editors), *The homeless in contemporary society*. Newbury Park, CA: Sage Publications, pp. 216–230.

KOTARBA, J. A., and LANG, N. G. (1986). Gay lifestyle change and AIDS: Preventive health care. In D. A. Feldman and T. Johnson (editors), *The social dimensions of AIDS*. New York: Praeger, pp. 127–144.

LAGORY, M., RITCHEY, F. J., and MULLIS, J. (1990). Depression among the homeless. *Journal of Health and Social Behavior*, forthcoming.

LAGORY, M., RITCHEY, F. J., O'DONOGHUE, T., and MULLINS, J. (1989). Homelessness in Alabama: A variety of people and experiences. In J. A. Momeni (editor), *Homelessness in the United States*. New York: Greenwoood Press, pp. 1–20.

LAGORY, M., RITCHEY, F., and FITZPATRICK, K. (1990). *Homelessness and affiliation*. Birmingham, AL: University of Alabama, Department of Sociology.

LESSOR, R., and JURICH, K. (1986). Ideology and politics in the control of contagion: The social organization of AIDS care. In D. A. Feldman and T. Johnson (editors), *The social dimensions of AIDS*. New York: Praeger, pp. 245–260.

MARCUSE, P. (1990). Homelessness and housing policy. In C. L. Caton (editor), *Homeless in America*. New York: Oxford University Press, pp. 138–159.

MELOSI, M. V. (1981). *Garbage in the cities: Refuse, reform, and the environment, 1880–1980*. College Station, TX: Texas A & M University Press.

NEAL, H. A., and SCHUBEL, J. R. (1987). *Solid waste management and the environment: The mounting garbage and trash crisis*. Englewood Cliffs, NJ: Prentice-Hall, Inc.

NEW YORK STATE (1989). *AIDS in New York State*. Albany, NY: New York State Department of Health.

PARKER, R. N., and HORWITZ, A. V. (1986). Unemployment, crime, and imprisonment: A panel approach. *Criminology* 24: 251–273.

PHILLIPS, K. (1990). *The politics of rich and poor: Wealth and the American electorate in the Reagan aftermath*. New York: Random House.

POPULATION INFORMATION PROGRAM (1986). *AIDS—A public health crisis*. Baltimore, MD: The Johns Hopkins University.

REISS, A. J., and TONRY, M. (editors) (1986). *Communities and crime*. Chicago, IL: University of Chicago Press.

ROSSI, P. H. (1989). *Down and out in America: The origins of homelessness*. Chicago, IL: University of Chicago Press.

SCHMID, C. F. (1960a). Urban areas, Part I. *American Sociological Review* 25:527–542.

SCHMID, C. F. (1960b). Urban areas: Part II. *American Sociological Review* 25: 655–678.

SHAW, C., ZORBAUGH, H., McKAY, H. D., and COTTRELL, L. S. (1929). *Delinquency areas*. Chicago, IL: University of Chicago Press.

SHILTS, R. (1987). *And the band played on: Politics, people and the AIDS epidemic*. New York: St. Martin's Press.

SNOW, D. A., BAKER, S. G., and ANDERSON, L. (1991). Criminality and homeless men: An empirical assessment. *Social Problems*, forthcoming.

SNOW, D. A., BAKER, S. G., and ANDERSON, L. (1986). The myth of pervasive mental illness among the homeless. *Social Problems* 33 (5): 407–423.

SNOW, D. A., BAKER, S. G., and ANDERSON, L. (1988). On the precariousness of measuring insanity in insane contexts. *Social Problems* 35 (2): 192–196.

STEFL, M. E. (1987). The homeless: A national perspective. In R. D. Bingham, R. E. Green, and S. B. White (editors), *The homeless in contemporary society*. Newbury Park, CA: Sage Publications, pp. 46–63.

SULLIVAN, P. A., and DAMROSCH, S. P. (1987). Homeless women and children. In R. D. Bingham, R. E. Green, and S. B. White (editors), *The homeless in contemporary society*. Newbury Park, CA: Sage Publications, pp. 82–98.

TASK FORCE ON URGENT FISCAL ISSUES. (1990). Committee on the Budget of the House of Representatives of the 101st Congress, *Hospitals in crisis: Financial impact of AIDS on New York City's hospitals*. Washington, DC: U.S. Government Printing Office.

THRASHER, F. M. (1927). *The gang*. Chicago, IL: University of Chicago Press.

U.S. FEDERAL BUREAU OF INVESTIGATION (1989). *Crime in the United States: Uniform crime reports*. Washington, DC: U.S. Government Printing Office.

U.S. BUREAU OF JUSTICE STATISTICS (1988). *Report to the nation on crime and justice.* Washington, DC: U.S. Government Printing Office.

U.S. BUREAU OF JUSTICE STATISTICS. (1989). Sourcebook of criminal justice statistics—1988. K. M. Jamieson and T. J. Flanagan (editors) Washington, DC: U.S. Government Printing Office.

U.S. BUREAU OF THE CENSUS (1990). *Statistical abstract of the United States*, 1990. Washington, DC: U.S. Government Printing Office.

VALDISERRI, R. O. (1989). *Preventing AIDS: The design of effective programs.* New Brunswick, NJ: Rutgers University Press.

WILSON, J. Q. (1983). *Thinking about crime.* New York: Vintage Books.

WILSON, W. J. (1987). *The truly disadvantaged: The inner city, the underclass, and public policy.* Chicago, IL: University of Chicago Press.

WOLF, L. C. (1990). Homeless women. In C. L. Caton (editor), *Homeless in America.* New York: Oxford University Press, pp. 46–55.

CHAPTER FOURTEEN

ADVISORY COMMISSION OF INTERGOVERNMENTAL RELATIONS (1969). *Urban America and the federal system: Commission findings and proposals.* Washington, DC: U.S. Government Printing Office.

BERMAN, D. R. (1975). *State and local politics.* Boston, MA: Holbrook Press.

BERRY, B. J., and KASARDA, J. D. (1977). *Contemporary urban ecology.* New York: Macmillan and Co.

BOLLENS, J. C., and SCHMANDT, H. J. (1975). *The metropolis.* New York: Harper and Row.

BROMLEY, D. G. (1977). Power, politics and decision making. In K. P. Schwirian (editor), *Contemporary topics in urban sociology.* Morristown, NJ: General Learning Press.

CAPUTO, D. A. (1976). *Urban America: The policy alternatives.* San Francisco, CA: W. H. Freeman.

COMMITTEE FOR ECONOMIC DEVELOPMENT (1971). *Social responsibilities of business corporations.* New York: Committee for Economic Development.

DILLON, J. F. (1911). *Commentaries on the law of municipal corporations.* Boston, MA: Little Brown and Co.

FEAGIN, J. R., and PARKER, R. (1990). *Building American cities: The urban real estate game.* Englewood Cliffs, NJ: Prentice Hall.

FLINN, T. A. (1970). *Local government and politics.* Glenview, IL: Scott, Foresman.

GOODALL, L. (1968). *The American metropolis.* Columbus, OH: Charles E. Merrill.

LA GRECA, A. J. (1977). Critical urban problems. In K. P. Schwirian (editor), *Contemporary topics in urban sociology.* Morristown, N.J.: General Learning Press.

GREINER, J. M., and PETERSON, G. E. (1986). Do budget reductions stimulate public sector efficiency? Evidence from Proposition 2 1/2 in Massachusetts. In G. E. Peterson and C. W. Lewis (editors), *Reagan and the cities.* Washington, DC: The Urban Institute Press.

HALLMAN, H. W. (1974). *Neighborhood government in a metropolitan setting.* Beverly Hills, CA: Sage Publications.

HEILBRONER, R. L. (1965). *The limits of American capitalism.* New York: Harper and Row.

HEY, R. P. (January 3, 1991). As economy slides, local governments feel the squeeze. *The Christian Science Monitor*, pp. 1–2.

KOTLER, M. (1969). *Neighborhood government*. Indianapolis, IN: Bobbs-Merrill.

LARSON, C. J., and NIKKEL, S. R. (1979). *Urban problems: Perspectives on corporations, governments, and cities*. Boston, MA: Allyn and Bacon, Inc.

LOWI, T. J. (1967). Machine politics—Old and new. *The Public Interest* 9:84–98.

MARTIN, R. C. (1970). *The cities and the federal system*. New York: Atherton Press.

NELSON, K. P. (1988). *Gentrification and distressed cities: An assessment of trends in intrametropolitan migration*. Madison, WI: The University of Wisconsin Press.

NORTON, R. D. (1979). *City life-cycle and American urban policy*. New York: Academic Press.

PALLEY, M. L., and PALLEY, H. A. (1977). *Urban America and public policies*. Lexington, MA: D. C. Heath and Co.

PETERSON, G. E. (1986). Urban policy and the cyclical behavior of cities. In G. E. Peterson and C. W. Lewis (editors), *Reagan and the cities*. Washington, DC: The Urban Institute Press.

PETERSON, G. E., and LEWIS, C. W. (1986). *Reagan and the cities*. Washington, DC: The Urban Institute Press.

PHILLIPS, K. (1990). *The politics of rich and poor: Wealth and the American electorate in the Reagan aftermath*. New York: Random House.

RASMUSSEN, D. W. (1973). *Urban economics*. New York: Harper and Row.

STEDMAN, M. S. (1972). *Urban politics*. Cambridge, MA: Winthrop.

U.S. BUREAU OF THE CENSUS (1978b). *1977 census of governments: Finances of municipalities and township governments*. Washington, DC: U.S. Government Printing Office.

U.S. BUREAU OF THE CENSUS (1987a). *1987 census of governments: Finances of special districts*. Washington, DC: U.S. Government Printing Office.

U.S. BUREAU OF THE CENSUS (1987b). *1987 census of governments: Government finances*. Washington, DC: U.S. Government Printing Office.

U.S. BUREAU OF THE CENSUS (1987c). *1987 census of governments: Government organization*. Washington, D.C.: U.S. Government Printing Office.

U.S. BUREAU OF THE CENSUS (1978a). *Census of government, 1977, government organization*. Washington, DC: U.S. Government Printing Office.

U.S. BUREAU OF THE CENSUS (1990). *Statistical abstract of the United States 1990*. Washington, DC: U.S. Government Printing Office.

Webster's New Collegiate Dictionary. (1977). Springfield, Ma: G. and C. Merriam Co.

*I*NDEX

507

SUBJECT INDEX